Third Edition

Effective Reading in a Changing World

Rose Wassman and Lee Ann Rinsky

De Anza College

PRENTICE HALL
Upper Saddle River, New Jersey 07458

Library of Congress Cataloging-in-Publication Data

Wassman, Rose.
   Effective reading in a changing world/Rose Wassman and Lee Ann Rinsky.—3rd ed.
      p. cm.
   Includes bibliographical references and index.
   ISBN 0–13–011579–7
   1. Reading (Higher education)   2. Reading comprehension.
3. Study skills.   I. Rinsky, Lee Ann, II. Title.
LB2395.3.W374   2000
428.4′071′1—dc21   99–41128
                                                                             CIP

Editorial Director: Charlyce Jones Owen
Editor-in-Chief: Leah Jewell
Acquisitions Editor: Craig Campanella
Editorial Assistant: Joan Polk
Director of Production and Manufacturing: Barbara Kittle
Senior Managing Editor: Bonnie Biller
Senior Project Manager: Shelly Kupperman
Manufacturing Manager: Nick Sklitsis

Prepress and Manufacturing Buyer: Mary Ann Gloriande
Art Director: Anne Bonanno Nieglos
Interior Designer: Anne Bonanno Nieglos
Cover Designer: Joe Sengotta
Photo Researcher: Beaura Ringrose
Electronic Art Creation: Maria Piper
Marketing Manager: Gina Sluss

Cover Art: Peter Maltz, "Hands Holding Book," Stock Illustration Source, Inc.

Credits and acknowledgments appear on pages 650–652, which constitute a continuation of this copyright page.

This book was set in 10/12 New Baskerville by Typographics and printed by R. R. Donnelley-Harrisonburg. The cover was printed by Phoenix Color Corporation.

Printed in the United States of America
10   9   8   7   6   5   4   3   2   1

ISBN 0-13-011579-7

Prentice-Hall International (UK) Limited, *London*
Prentice-Hall of Australia Pty. Limited, *Sydney*
Prentice-Hall Canada Inc., *Toronto*
Prentice-Hall Hispanoamericana, S.A., *Mexico*
Prentice-Hall of India Private Limited, *New Delhi*
Prentice-Hall of Japan, Inc., *Tokyo*
Pearson Asia Pte. Ltd., *Singapore*
Editora Prentice-Hall do Brasil, Ltda., *Rio de Janeiro*

Contents

iii

2 Building Vocabulary Through Context and Structure 31

5 Learning Paragraph Patterns   232

PART TWO: THE READER AS CRITIC: REFINING CRITICAL COMPREHENSION

WORKING WITH THE WORLD WIDE WEB   424

8 Understanding the Power of Persuasive Language   425

The Two Dimensions of Word Meanings: Denotation and Connotation   426

Denotation   426
Connotation   426

The Persuasive Power of Words   427
Connotative Language   430
Figurative Language   443
Figuring Out Figures of Speech   443

Similes and Metaphors   443
Personification   444
Euphemisms   455

Summary   460

9 Recognizing Tone, Purpose, and Point of View: Aids to Critical Thinking   485

Tuning in to Tone   486
Major Tones in Writing   487

Words Used to Describe Tone   490
Examples of Various Tones   491

WORKING WITH THE WORLD WIDE WEB   494

Understanding the Author's Purpose   509
Assessing the Author's Reliability   518
Evaluating the Reliability of Internet Information   522
Looking at the Author's Point of View   524
Summary   546

10 Reading Visual Information 579

This edition is dedicated in loving memory to
Lee Ann Rinsky,
an outstanding scholar, energetic and devoted teacher, wonderful colleague,
and dear friend,

Taken too soon to her eternal rest on March 3, 1999.

Preface

The third edition of *Effective Reading in a Changing World* has undergone considerable changes to strengthen and improve its content. Incisive suggestions of instructors and reviewers as well as the helpful comments of the many students who have used this text have guided us in our revisions. *Effective Reading* has been expanded with new pedagogy, reading selections, and practice activities, but its primary purpose remains the same: to help students view reading as a positive experience and to help them develop the essential strategies needed for successful college and life-long reading. These strategies address literal and inferential comprehension, critical thinking, study techniques, and vocabulary development.

Goals and Purpose of the Text

Designed for adult readers with varying backgrounds, *Effective Reading in a Changing World* again strives to help students develop a positive attitude toward learning and a love of reading, strengthen their cognitive abilities, and expose them to reading and thinking critically about controversial issues. It successfully integrates the concept of reading and writing, provides a broad mix of reading selections that are current and highly engaging to students' interests, encourages vocabulary development throughout the text, and is thorough in both explanatory prose and mastery learning activities. The mature and high-interest reading selections focus on many of the issues students face today in our rapidly changing, technologically oriented world.

Using an eclectic approach, *Effective Reading in a Changing World* is an extremely comprehensive and educationally sound text. The activities allow the professor to use a scope and sequence approach to teach specific reading skills at the college level, while simultaneously using three reading selections found at the end of most chapters to teach holistically. Activities cover the information thoroughly but are not excessive, nor are they repetitive, workbook-style exercises. Holistic reading activities provide students with a broad, realistic reading experience. They also make clear, particularly in the critical reading unit, the close relationship between reader as audience and reader as critic. We have designed in-depth practice activities, together with a broad spectrum of reading comprehension questions, as well as suggested discussion questions and journal-writing assignments, thereby integrating reading and writing. Chapters 2 through 5 and 7 through 9 each include a topical essay, a textbook excerpt, and a literary selection, since these reading genres have unique styles and structures. Our aim is to help students read effectively in all their college studies and to become informed, literate citizens and lifelong learners.

Features New to the Third Edition

A number of new features and significant changes have been made to augment the effectiveness of *Effective Reading in a Changing World.*

New Features

- **World Wide Web:** Students are introduced to working effectively on the Internet and given optional exercises and Web site addresses. A section in Chapter 9 addresses **evaluating the reliability of information on the Internet.**
- **Acronyms:** Acronyms are shown to be a useful mnemonic tool as well as another aid to vocabulary development.
- **Marginal notations of an essay:** A model essay, with notation markings, has been developed to help students follow writers' organizational patterns and uncover implied main ideas and theses.
- **Annotated Suggested Reading List:** An annotated list of fourteen best-selling novels by a diverse group of award-winning authors has been added to encourage students to discover the pleasures of reading as a lifelong activity.
- **Sixty new readings:** At least sixty of the paragraph, essay, and textbook excerpts are new. Of these, **thirty** are essays that vary in length from 500 to 900 words. These readings cover a broad range of timely social, political, and philosophical issues adult learners can often relate to, such as homelessness, impeachment, abortion, spousal abuse and murder, AIDS, date rape, the glass ceiling, cloning, and advertising tobacco and alcohol. **Six** of the end-of-chapter textbook readings have been updated or replaced to keep the information as current as possible; **two** of the end-of-chapter essay readings have also been changed for the same reason.
- **Photographs:** Numerous photographs that complement essay and textbook readings have been included.

Expanded Areas

- **Explanatory prose:** More than thirty percent of the explanatory prose has been expanded or rewritten for greater clarification and elaboration of concepts.
- **Word Analogy:** Practice has been expanded and the concept of **cause and effect word relationships** is taught in Chapter 9.

- **Visual and graphic information:** How to read and understand **flowcharts** and **pictograms** has been added to Chapter 10 as well as a section on recognizing the **reliability of statistical information.**

Reorganization

- **Chapter 1: Test taking** has been placed at the end of the first chapter since students need to know how to handle test taking at the outset of a course.
- **Chapter 2:** The **difference between literal and figurative language** has been placed toward the end of this chapter rather than being introduced in Chapter 8 since students need to recognize this difference in analyzing essays and fiction.
- **Chapters 3 and 4:** The order of these chapters has been reversed. Understanding a topic, main idea, and supporting details is now introduced in Chapter 3, and summary charts in both chapters have been reordered for easy reference. The introductory information in Chapter 4 on the **difference between essay, textbook, and fiction reading** has been compressed, with more emphasis on practice and examples rather than explanation.
- **Chapter 5:** The order of **organizational patterns** has been altered so that the last pattern taught is **example,** since exemplification is a chief means of developing all the other patterns and a natural lead-in to teaching patterns in combination.
- **Chapter 7:** The **Fact/Opinion** section has been reorganized, and essay readings replace sentence practice.
- **Chapter 9:** The activities on recognizing **tone** have been reordered and updated. Additionally, more activities are included to help students recognize **differing points of view.**
- **Chapter 10:** The explanatory prose on **how to interpret visual information** and on **integrating text with graphics** are presented together at the beginning of the chapter.
- **Several readings on the same topic** within most chapters have been included to help develop a frame of reference for students.

Continuing Features in the Third Edition

Many features, successful in both the first and second editions of this text, continue to be stressed in the new edition:

- Skills are presented in a hierarchy of learning, but *each chapter is self-contained* to provide flexibility and individualization in teaching.
- Each chapter provides the broadest approach possible to reading: a major *topic-related selection* in most chapters includes an *essay,* a *textbook excerpt,* and *short story* or an excerpt from a *novel.*

- The text offers *versatile content reading* from recently published textbooks, including sources in anatomy and physiology, astronomy, biology, business essentials, computer science, criminal justice, geography, history, intercultural communication, philosophy, political science, psychology, sociology, and Western civilization.
- Each chapter focuses on *critical reading* and *thinking* and includes numerous essay questions that demand analysis and synthesis.
- *Vocabulary* words in each chapter include phonetic pronunciations and definitions.
- The reading activities give practice and understanding of the major types of complex sentences that often cause reading difficulty.
- Each chapter ends with *journal-writing* suggestions that connect concepts.

Structure and Organization

By leading students through a sequential development of skills and strategies that promote critical reading and thinking, while providing varied reading selections, we combine the best methodologies for teaching adult learners. Additionally, we present critical reading skills holistically, and we ensure that strategies learned in one chapter are expanded, reinforced, and incorporated in subsequent chapters. This structure, in addition to a detailed chapter on study techniques, gives our text its unique format.

As in the previous edition, we have incorporated recent research in the development of questions. In addition to answering comprehension questions, students must *always apply* the author's thesis or main ideas to their own lives and experiences. In so doing, they become truly active readers. The questions can be used in writing and discussion and for evaluative purposes.

Vocabulary

An in-depth chapter on vocabulary development and extended practices reinforce the vocabulary in the reading selections. To make the readings more meaningful and to help students increase their vocabulary knowledge, definitions have also been provided.

Critical Thinking

All of the twenty-four reading selections in Chapters 2 through 10 include questions that focus on inferential and critical thinking. Additionally, more than fifty activities in the text, using both short and longer passages, help guide students to develop inferential and critical thinking. Chapters 7 through 9 specifically emphasize inference, fact and opinion, bias, connotation, persuasive language, author's tone and purpose, author's reliability, assessing Internet information, and point of view.

Adapting the Text

Chapters 4, 6, and 10 can be presented in any sequence. Chapter 4, "Reading and Organizing for More Effective Study," and/or Chapter 6, "Refining Reading Style and Improving Rate," can be presented at either the beginning or the end of a semester, depending on instructor preference. All selections of more than 250 words are identified and can be used for reading rate practice.

⤳ Instructor's Manual with Tests

The comprehensive Instructor's Manual with Tests has been reorganized by chapters. It includes a reading comprehension pretest, quizzes for each chapter, sample midterm and final exams, suggestions for each teaching unit, readability information, and suggested answers for all activities and practices. Additionally, sample summary maps are provided for some of the chapters.

⤳ Companion Website: www.prenhall.com/wassman

Written specifically for *Effective Reading in a Changing World,* third edition, this website parallels the text's organization and offers a wealth of additional exercises for students. The **Companion Website**™ makes integrating the Internet into your course exciting and easy. Features of this site include:

- Four readings per chapter with self-grading vocabulary and comprehension quizzes.
- Journal essay exercises that help strengthen critical thinking skills.
- A built-in e-mail routing option which allows students to forward essay responses and graded quizzes to their instructors.
- An easy-to-follow **Syllabus Manager**™ tool that allows instructors to post an online syllabus for their course.

⤳ Acknowledgments

A number of people have provided invaluable assistance, giving generously of their time, talent, and expertise in the preparation of the third edition. We are very grateful for the helpful suggestions and ideas of our reviewers: Suzanne G. Weisar, San Jacinto College South; Barbara Brennan Culhane, Nassau Community College; Edith Alderson, Joliet Junior College; Nora Davenport Lawson, Alabama State University; Carlotta W. Hill, Oklahoma City Community College; Suzette Cohen, Cleveland State University.

At Prentice Hall, we are indeed indebted to Maggie Barbieri, former Senior Editor of Developmental English, who always "went the extra mile" in her editorial assistance and support throughout the project. Our special thanks and gratitude also go to Joan Polk, editorial assistant, whose patience, efficiency, and coopera-tion have helped us immeasurably; to Diane Nesin for her detailed manuscript copyediting; and to Shelly Kupperman, Senior Project Manager, for her astute sug-gestions, creative energy, and impeccable judgment in the book's design and production.

We are also most grateful to the many students whose comments and suggestions as they used the text helped shape the direction of the new edition, and to one instruc-tor at DeAnza College, Natalie Panfili, who helped field-test the new materials and gave unstintingly of her time and talent. Last, and of special note, we wish to thank Bob Wassman for his loving support and patience and many hours of proofreading.

As noted on the dedication page, Lee Ann Rinsky never lived to see this edition to its completion, but her contributions to its original development will remain omnipresent throughout any edition of the text. Even during her final days, she was enthusiastic about the revised edition and eager for its success. She is truly missed, but having known Lee so well, I feel she would be happy to know that her desire to help students continues with the teaching and writing she accomplished in her lifetime.

Rose Wassman

1

You Make the Difference

This chapter will help you

* Review your present reading habits.
* Determine your reading needs.
* Learn how to become an effective reader.
* Become a successful test taker.

Before you begin to read

* Think about the chapter's title and above-stated objectives and try to predict what its contents might include.
* Ask yourself some questions based on the title, objectives, and your predictions; questioning helps you focus your reading.

Think about these questions.

* How do you feel about reading?
* How often do you read newspapers, magazines, books, or search the World Wide Web for information?
* What do you think your major field of study in college will be?

Jot down your responses to the above questions in the space provided.

_____

_____

_____

As the twenty-first century begins, we are faced with an explosion of technological and general knowledge that is accelerating at an **unprecedented*** rate in this, the so-called Information Age. Much of the information on the ever-expanding road, the "information superhighway," is recorded and communicated through the printed word. In the United States alone, approximately 62,000 books were published annually in the late 1990s, an increase from the 46,000 the previous decade. This print explosion also applies to newspapers and **periodicals** (over 10,000 of each are published annually), paperbacks, pamphlets, brochures, "junk mail,"† and the 20 to 50 million estimated pages of data made available by Internet service providers such as America Online, Microsoft Network, and EarthLink as well as search engines such as Yahoo, AltaVista, and Lycos.‡ It takes an effective reader to make sense out of the print with which we are bombarded daily; therefore, the primary purpose of this text is to help you become an effective reader for this Information Age.

As a college student, you will encounter in your introductory courses some of the heaviest reading loads of your academic career. For example, textbook chapters for such courses as Introduction to Psychology, Accounting, and American Government average thirty-five pages, and often, students are required to read more than one chapter per week in each course. The effective reader knows how to read, how to understand, and how to organize this **prodigious** amount of information for a successful college experience.

ꙅ The Effective Reader

You do not have to be a genius or have an exceptionally high intelligence quotient (IQ) to read well. Rather, you need an understanding of the reading process and an understanding of how to go about reading different types of printed information. In this way, you can practice techniques that will help you succeed in becoming an effective reader. Two main ingredients are needed: the willingness to change those reading habits that interfere with or limit your reading ability, and the willingness to practice, practice, practice.

---

unprecedented (un pres´ ə dent´ əd) unheard of; never happened before
periodicals (pir ē od´ i kəlz) publications issued on a regular basis, such as magazines
prodigious (prə dij´ əs) impressively great in size or intent

* All boldfaced words are defined at the bottom of the page to assist you with comprehension and vocabulary growth. Chapter 2 focuses on specific strategies for improving vocabulary and using context clues.
† *Statistical Abstract of the United States,* Bureau of the Census (Washington, DC: GPO, 1997) 573–74.
‡ Cynthia B. Leshin, *Dictionary of the World Wide Web* (Upper Saddle River, NJ: Prentice Hall, 1998).

Practice

Think back to when you first learned to play a particular sport or when you learned to play a musical instrument. Think what your ability was as a beginner and then think of your skill as you became more **proficient.** You probably practiced almost daily, and the more you practiced, the more confident you became. To become a skillful reader takes the same kind of effort and practice. The fact that you are reading this textbook shows you have taken the first step toward wanting to become that effective reader.

Organize Yourself for Reading and Study

One of the first requirements for effective reading and study is to understand the importance of *disciplined* study. You must plan undisturbed blocks of time to devote to reading and study. At the same time, after arranging such a schedule, realize the need to be flexible when something unforeseen occurs. Essentially, however, consistency in maintaining a schedule as much as possible is invaluable to success. After reading the brief instructions for a weekly schedule, complete your plan for developing a realistic schedule.

Generally, a forty- to fifty-minute reading-study session is recommended. A good idea that adds to reading efficiency is to take a short break of five to ten minutes after a reading-study period. Have all needed supplies, such as marking pens and paper for notes, close by so it will be unnecessary to break your concentration.

Weekly Schedule

1. Block out your school/work schedule as well as any other of your scheduled responsibilities.
2. For each unit of class time, try to block out one to two hours of study. For a three-hour class, plan on about five to six hours of study per week—depending on how familiar you are with the subject.
3. Be specific. Do not write "study," for example, but write "study American History." Use colored ink or pencil to highlight study hours.

---

proficient (prə fish´ənt) expert in an art or skill

	Sun.	Mon.	Tues.	Wed.	Thurs.	Fri.	Sat.
7:00 A.M.							
8:00							
9:00							
10:00							
11:00							
12:00 P.M.							
1:00							
2:00							
3:00							
4:00							
5:00							
6:00							
7:00							
8:00							
9:00							
10:00							

Improve Your Concentration and Develop a Positive Attitude

The inability to concentrate while reading is experienced by many students. The difficulty, however, rarely has a **neurological** basis. The mind is not faulty; rather, the inability to concentrate is generally a problem of attitude toward a reading assignment. A selection may be extremely challenging or one in which you have no immediate interest. However, having a positive attitude and a commitment to learning can go a long way toward improving your ability to concentrate. Commitment and attitude can also lead to success when students regard the task as a rewarding learning experience.

Concentration is actually a skill that can be developed through careful planning, self-control, and practice. Things that might interfere with concentration, such as thirst or hunger, should be taken care of prior to any reading-study session. Try to resolve or put aside temporarily any personal or emotional problems you may have. Make your family members or roommates aware that you need *mental space* to study by removing as many distractions, such as the telephone or television or loud

---

neurological (no͞o rō lăj´ i kəl) related to the nervous system and its diseases and disorders

music, that may interfere with comprehension. Give your undivided attention to reading and study; psychologists claim that two things that require mental activity when done at the same time are rarely successful!

Maintain Confidence

Confidence in reading is chiefly the result of preparedness. If you take good lecture notes, complete assignments on time, and maintain your reading-study schedule, you will set in motion a pattern that builds your confidence.

When personal and career goals are established, confidence also develops. Check with your counselor or find out about taking an interest inventory if you are undecided about a career goal. Most counseling centers have an excellent book called the *Occupational Outlook Handbook* with information on careers and the future of specific fields. Having a career goal can be a great motivator for a positive outlook on the future and the desire to excel in school.

Maintain Curiosity

There are a number of factors to consider regarding your attitude toward reading. Some students ignore reading assignments because they consider the subject boring. The boredom, you should realize, may stem from the person doing the reading, not in the assignment to be read. Right now, you are probably interested in some things that do not appeal to some of your friends. On the other hand, you probably have lost interest in some subjects that once absorbed you or have acquired an interest in areas that formerly did not appeal to you at all. Try to maintain a curiosity about the exciting, **dynamic** world around us, developing interest in many subjects. The prodigious amount of reading materials will not only help you learn about these subjects but can also help you experience a wealth of satisfaction and pleasure.

Acquire a Framework of Knowledge

Reading is always easier, always faster, and comprehension is always higher when you have some familiarity with the subject. Writers of articles often make reference to people, events, and ideas unfamiliar to you. This, at times, may be why you find a reading assignment uninteresting. But the very same people, events, or ideas may appear repeatedly in print. Learning about them helps familiarize you with their

---

dynamic (dī nam´ ik) marked by energy and vigor

particular contributions or importance. With broad reading, you begin to acquire a framework of knowledge into which you can fit additional information as you read. As one authority has explained it by the use of a **metaphor,** "The head is not really like a pot—the more empty it is of ideas, the more difficult it is to put anything in it! . . . [but]The fuller it is with a wealth of background information, the more you can add to it, retain, and remember." As you can see from the illustration that follows, the more you acquire a network of information and encode or store it, the more readily it can be retrieved.

CONNECTIONS MATTER

Our brains aren't designed to retain random bits of information. We remember things by linking them to what we already know. The process is called "elaborative encoding."

Why We Forget   **How We Remember**

I'm Carol   I'm Joanne

❶ A name is easy to forget when its only point of reference is a face. Lacking links to other memories, it fades within seconds.

CAROL

JOE – FRIEND
JOANNE – COFFEE
FRASIER – SEATTLE
PSYCHOLOGIST

❷ As you learn facts about a person, such as her profession, her name gets embedded in a web of thoughts and impressions. If you don't know her, random associations have a similar effect.

Norma? Doris? Lisa? Karen?   Joanne!

❸ As the web of associations grows, so does the number of paths leading back to the name. Well-encoded memories last a lifetime.

"How Memory Works," *Newsweek* 15 June 1998.

---

metaphor (met´ ə fôr) speech in which a term that ordinarily describes an object or idea is used to describe a dissimilar object or idea, in order to make a clearer comparison

Be an Active Reader

To be an effective reader, be an *active* reader—one who mentally engages in a dialogue with the writer. While reading, active readers agree and disagree, applaud and criticize, weigh and reconsider what the writer is saying. They involve themselves with the ideas, responding intellectually and/or emotionally to what they read. In other words, they interpret what they read. Also, they constantly ask questions, interacting with the writer's written statements. Active reading, then, involves *thinking* seriously in order to understand the author's ideas. One prominent writer has stated that what he puts on paper is "a transaction" between himself and the reader, sharing who he is. Active readers involve themselves in that transaction, which in turn becomes a valuable aid to both improved concentration and comprehension. While active reading may take more time than passive reading, comprehension and retention of information are generally vastly improved.

Develop a Flexible Reading Rate*

Perhaps the most serious misconception about reading is that everything should be read at the same rate: cartoons, an editorial, and a legal contract! Certain types of reading demand a slower, more careful approach, with every piece of information critical to comprehension. The key is to be a flexible reader, varying your rate according to the *difficulty* of the material and your *purpose* for reading. Also, your prior knowledge should help you determine how quickly you can acquire what you do not know from the information you are reading in print. To become aware of the wide range in reading rates, study the suggested rates for various types or **modes** of reading material in the table on the next page.

The average person reads the newspaper, magazines like the *Reader's Digest,* and popular novels at a rate of about 250 words per minute with about 75 percent comprehension. The more complex, abstract, and challenging the material, the slower a person should read, covering the material at less than 200 words per minute. However, the same peson should be able to skim quickly to get the gist of some material at rates well over 500 words per minute. As the chart demonstrates, being an efficient reader entails knowing how to be a flexible one.

---

modes (mōdz) forms or variety of things

* Reading rate will be dealt with in more detail in Chapter 6.

Mode, Examples, and Purpose

Reading Rate Means Reading Flexibility

	Mode	Purpose	Rate	Recommended Rate Range
Decrease (BASE RATE)	1. Analytical reading (legal documents, persuasive essays)	To analyze information for **inference,** language, tone, bias; to evaluate logic and writer's craft.	Usually the *slowest* rate. Varies with complexity of material. May require more than one reading.	150–250 wpm
	2. Study reading (textbooks)	To learn, **synthesize,** and retain information; gaining complete understanding of text material.	Rate varies with amount to be learned and type of material.	150–300 wpm
	3. General reading (newspapers, magazines, novels)	To read as a leisure-time activity for pleasure and general information.	Rate varies with material, purpose, and familiarity.	250–500 wpm
	4. Skimming (initial research)	To get a general idea of the material and some details; to get a mental outline of material's organization.	Can be twice as fast as general reading rate.	500–1000 wpm
Increase	5. Scanning (phone numbers, airline schedules)	To locate specific information and answer questions as quickly as possible.	*Fastest* rate with no specific wpm determined.	1000+ range

⤸ Other Factors

After examining the various rates, you should also be aware that your rate is always affected by

Your familiarity with the topic.
Your interest.
The difficulty of the vocabulary and sentence structure.

---

inference (in´ fər əns) to conclude by reasoning from what is known or assumed
synthesize (sin´ thə sīz) to combine parts to form a whole idea

Consider how the factors in the following table may affect your rate.

Gauging Reading Difficulty

Selection/Purpose	Topic Familiarity	Interest	Difficulty
1. A quick look at an essay in *Sports Illustrated* (recreational reading)	I'm very comfortable with this topic.	High	I recognize all the vocabulary. Sentence length average. Frequent paragraphs.
2. A contemporary novel (an English assignment)	I have read another novel by this author.	Neutral	Some difficult words. Sentences are somewhat long.
3. A textbook with technical material, needing 100% comprehension (will be tested)	I know nothing about this subject.	I have some interest.	Vocabulary is quite difficult. Sentences are average.

Obviously, you could read an essay in *Sports Illustrated* much more rapidly than the others. To understand a technical book, you would certainly have to modify your reading rate.

Examine the following list of selections and purposes for reading. Fill in the blanks, determining the rate at which you would read each: rapidly, at an average rate, or more slowly.

Selection/Purpose	Topic Familiarity	Interest	Difficulty	Selected Rate
1. "Capital Punishment: Does It Work?" (class assignment)	_____	_____	Easy words, short sentences	_____
2. *Domina,* a novel about one of the first woman doctors (recreational reading)	_____	_____	Difficult words, long sentences	_____
3. "States of Consciousness," a psychology chapter (study purposes—will be tested)	_____	_____	Very difficult vocabulary, long sentences	_____

ᕲ A New Commitment

> ✓ Check those areas in which you need to work. Write in your journal (page 30) explaining how you plan to carry out your goals.

Practice Needs

_____ **1.** I need to read meaningful selections from a variety of materials.
_____ **2.** I need to read on a daily basis.

Organize for Study

_____ **1.** I need to establish a weekly schedule.
_____ **2.** I need to establish self-discipline and maintain a reading-study schedule.
_____ **3.** I need to improve my concentration by increasing my attention span.

Maintain Confidence and Develop a Positive Attitude

1. I need to develop a positive outlook by
_____ Taking good lecture notes.
_____ Completing assignments on time.
_____ Being prepared for class.
2. I need to set some personal or career goals by
_____ Seeing a career counselor.
_____ Checking the *Occupational Outlook Handbook*.

Develop a Flexible Reading Rate

_____ **1.** I need to be aware of the difficulty of the reading material.
_____ **2.** I need to determine my purpose when reading.

✓ Maintain Curiosity: Acquire a Framework of Knowledge

Following are titles of some recently published articles and essays. Place a check mark next to those topics with which you are unfamiliar or about which you would like more information. Read some articles in these areas.

Working with the WORLD WIDE WEB

An easy way to find information on these topics is to use a search engine on the Internet. Simply type the *topic* once you're online.

_____ 1. Winning the Drug War: The Marijuana Path

_____ 2. New Views on Why We Sleep

_____ 3. Scientists Argue Pros-Cons of Cloning Humans

_____ 4. Law Enforcement Under Attack

_____ 5. Music Videos Reinforce Stereotypes

_____ 6. New Careers for the Twenty-first Century

_____ 7. How to Build Your Own Web Page

_____ 8. The Space Program's Expanding Horizons

_____ 9. Chemicals in Your Food

_____10. Violence in U.S. Cities

Write a *summary paragraph* of one of the most interesting articles you read. A *summary* is generally a brief paragraph of about five to seven sentences; it is a shortened version of the text material written in your own words. In writing a summary, state the most significant point the author has made as well as the major details; you do not need to include examples or minor points. Before you begin writing a summary, you can mark or outline the text material. See page 24 for a chapter summary to use as a model.

The Importance of Previewing Before Reading

The importance of previewing cannot be overstated: It

1. Leads to better comprehension and gives you a quick picture of the overall idea and some supporting points.
2. Helps you determine the topic and the organization of the passage.
3. Helps you note what parts of the material justify a more careful reading.
4. Is like consulting a map before leaving on a trip; you develop confidence and interest because you know where you are going.

Previewing Procedures

When previewing, you will note that the organization of many articles and essays usually follow this sequence: the topic may be suggested in the title; the main idea may appear somewhere at the beginning of the passage in the first, second, or third paragraph; the remaining paragraphs support the main idea; and the conclusion often summarizes or restates the main idea. Therefore, in previewing the essay, you should read

1. The title (see if it gives you a clue to the topic; then turn it into a question and read to answer it).
2. Any introductory information—usually the first paragraph or two.
3. The first sentence or part of the first sentence of the remaining paragraphs.
4. The last paragraph or two.

With any preview, it is likely you will have to modify our suggested procedure to accommodate the writer's style. For example, if there are many one-line paragraphs, you do not have to read each of them. Also, sometimes the first sentence of a paragraph is simply a transition or "attention-getter"; so you need to read the second or third sentence too.

After you have previewed, and before you begin a close reading, think about what you have previewed to try to predict what the author's message or viewpoint will be and to sort out what you already know and think about the issue at hand.

What follows is a demonstration of how you might preview an article written on the subject of *previewing*.

Read the title and turn it into a question, such as "How do you learn to preview?" Then read to find the answer.

Learning How to Preview

Rose Wassman and Lee Ann Rinsky

Read the entire first paragraph at your normal speed. It may contain a statement of the main idea. The first paragraph, however, can be merely an introduction with the author trying to get your attention.

Sometimes you may have to read the second paragraph. Here, the main idea may be expressed or important clues presented.

Start reading the first sentence or two of each paragraph. _____
_____
_____
_____
_____

The writing patterns of most reading selections, whether articles, textbooks, or essays, follow a sequence of stating the main idea of each paragraph first around sixty percent of the time _____

_____

_____

_____

_____

_____

Sometimes the first sentence of a paragraph is just a transition or introductory sentence. You have to read the second sentence. _____

_____

_____

_____

_____

_____

Look for key ideas as you preview. _____

_____

_____

_____

_____

_____

_____read only what's important.

Sometimes the main idea of the paragraph is implied. You have to read _____

_____

_____

_____

_____

much of it to make sense_____

On the other hand, you may have to skip some paragraphs _____

_____

They are simply transitions _____

_____

_____

_____

_____ or one-line paragraphs.

Previewing enables you to decide _____ the

material justifies more careful reading _____

_____

_____

You can cover a lot of material to find what you wish to use _____

_____

Previewing is like consulting a map before leaving on a trip. _____

_____

_____

_____

Speed up as you read, but _____

_____

_____

_____ slow down if the information is puzzling or needs more careful

_____

_____

Expect lower comprehension _____

_____

_____

_____ fifty percent is about right _____

_____

_____

Practice is essential. As you practice previewing, you learn to preview. Remember, your purpose is *to get the main ideas as quickly as possible* so you have some familiarity with the material when you give it a more thorough reading.

Practice previewing now with an article that focuses on a major cause of the explosion of information—the World Wide Web—which has made it all the more important for you to be an efficient, effective reader.

If you have never tried previewing before, *underline* the appropriate sections of the article to preview. Next, follow the suggested previewing procedures by first changing the title into a question and then searching to answer your question. By previewing, you should be able to answer the first question that follows the article. Then, read the full selection and answer the remainder of the questions.

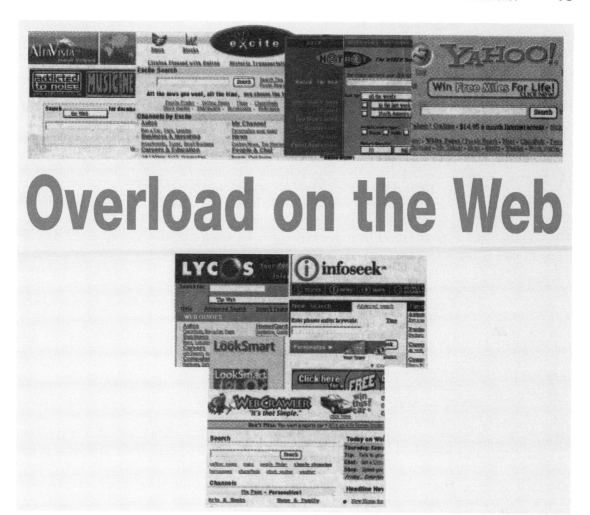

With more than 320 million Web pages out there, searchers can be swamped with data, yet still hungry for information.

Overload on the Web

Paul Recer

Cyberdata pile up, and search engines can't keep pace, new study says

Washington—A computer search for a needle in the cyberstack now involves sorting through about 320 million Web pages and even the best search agents index no more than 40 percent of them.

And things are unlikely to get easier on the Internet because the number of Web pages is expected to grow 1,000 percent in the next few years, according to Steve Lawrence of the NEC Research Institute, co-author of a study to be published in the journal *Science*.

"Hundreds of pages are being added constantly," said Lawrence. "There is no simple way to index it all. There could be any percentages of pages out there that nobody has actually accessed yet."

Lawrence and C. Lee Giles, also of NEC, analyzed how well scientists are able to find specific information on the Web using index services—which are kind of like electronic librarians that sort and index millions of pages of data by subject or phrase. These services are commonly called "search engines."

What they found, said Lawrence, is that the amount of information on the Web overwhelms even the most sophisticated efforts to sort it all out and there may be huge numbers of pages existing in an electronic shadowland never seen by humans. . . .

The researchers analyzed the responses to 575 scientific search questions from the five largest search engines. . . .

Based on the study, Lawrence said, he estimates the Web has about 320 million pages that are accessible to casual browsers. . . .

Hyman Hirsh, a computer science professor at Rutgers University, said that knowing the size of the problem could help people find ways to control the explosion of information.

"Everybody knows the Web is enormous and that finding things on it is very difficult," he said. "It is an unorganized, uncoordinated collection of information sources that is totally overwhelming."

A search engine called HotBot had the most comprehensive index of the Web, the researchers said, but still only covers about 34 percent of the indexable pages. At the bottom of the search engine list was Lycos, with 3 percent coverage.

The study said that of the other three engines, AltaVista had 28 percent coverage; Northern Light about 20 percent and Excite about 14 percent.

Graham Spencer, chief technical officer of Excite, said it would be impractical for a search engine to attempt to index the entire Web because people already are complaining about being flooded with information.

A single inquiry can produce a response involving millions of pages, leaving people drowning in data while still thirsting for information.

Spencer said that instead of trying to swallow the whole Web, Excite and other search engines gobble up only what they consider the best of the data.

"We try to focus on relevance, the information our customers will actually use," he said. . . .

People searching the Web, [Lawrence] said, could increase their chances of success by using two or more of the search engines. When all five engines were turned loose on one query . . . up to three times more of the Web was scanned than if only one engine was used.

Lawrence said the Web's data explosion may be better controlled by the "meta-search engines," such as Meta-Crawler and Ahoy, which have developed "thinking techniques" that sense what readers are looking for and seek out pages not found on most indexes. . . .

approximately 535 words

Paul Recer, "Overload on the Web," *San Francisco Examiner* 3 Apr. 1998

Answer this question once you complete your preview.

1. Eventually, will it become easier or more complicated to search for information on the Web? Support your answer with an example.

_____

_____

_____

Answer questions 2 and 3 after reading the entire article.

2. Generally, how much pertinent information do people receive quickly when exploring on the Web?

_____

_____

_____

3. (a) What specific reading skills might a person need to make maximum use of information the Web can provide?   (b) What kind(s) of information would you find most useful or interesting to access quickly?

_____

_____

_____

_____

⤳ Become a Successful Test Taker

Success or failure in college is determined in large part by your ability to perform well on tests and examinations. *Effective* test taking can be accomplished by applying the following rules.

Rule 1:   Come to the test with a positive attitude that you will be successful and *be on time*.

Rule 2:   Always preview and skim a test so as to plan the time you will need to answer certain sections. Don't plunge in and start answering the first question immediately. Determine how many questions there are and note the point value of each question. Plan to spend the most time answering the questions worth the most points. Often, instructors give more points or credit for answers to essay questions. Planning ahead will help you make the maximum use of your time.

     Tests sometimes include choices, asking students to answer *some* of the questions. If you do not preview the test first, it is easy to overlook this kind of important information.

Rule 3:   Read the directions slowly and carefully. Directions can sometimes be different from what you expect. For example, in some multiple-choice tests, an instructor might want you to mark two correct answers instead of only one, the way most tests are designed.

Rule 4:   Answer the easiest questions first. Some of the answers you failed to remember will become obvious through reading other test questions, which may jog your memory. Also, answering the easiest questions first helps build your confidence.

Rule 5:   Make an educated guess where necessary. Don't leave questions blank, even if you are not totally sure of an answer. Write *something*. It may help trigger your memory and earn you some needed points.

Rule 6:   *Proofread* what you've written. Always allow a few minutes at the end of the test session to check over what you've written.

Answering Multiple-Choice Questions

1. Multiple-choice questions usually ask you to select the best single answer out of several choices. Read carefully to be sure the directions do not ask for the *worse* answer, to make *more than one choice,* or to select *none* or *all of the above.*

2. Multiple-choice questions may include three or four choices.

Example: The decade of the 1990s has been called the Information Age because
     a. the twenty-first century is here.
     b. we are bombarded with information from many different sources.
     c. information is important to know.
     d. our technology has improved tremendously.

Often, you will note immediately that two choices are incorrect, so you can disregard them. See choices *a* and *c*. In most multiple-choice questions, it comes down to one of the two remaining answers. Cross out the incorrect answers *a* and *c* now. Concentrate on the two you must decide between. Before you read either of the remaining choices again, think about what the stem, the statement part you need to answer, is asking and how you would have completed it were it a fill-in-the-blank statement.

Read the stem, "The decade of the 1990s has been called the Information Age because," and one of the choices, *b*.

Read the stem and the second choice, *d*. This makes it much easier to decide on one of the two. Choice *b* is the correct one.

3. Often, a word or term you have never heard of may be incorrect; it may have been included simply to distract you.

Example: A substance found in the red blood cells which binds and transports oxygen and carbon dioxide is
    a. hemoglobin. (the correct answer)
    b. tripepglobin. (made-up word to distract you)

4. In the stem (the statement part you need to answer), watch for words like *not, except, incorrect,* or other *negatives*. These words make a tremendous difference in what answer you should select.

Example: Which name was *not* mentioned as being an Internet provider?

5. The phrase *all of the above* is used frequently by instructors and often, but not always, is the correct answer.

Example: The author believes that most women in the marketplace
    a. do not earn as much as men.
    b. are held back on the corporate ladder more than men.
    c. must still juggle housework and their job.
    d. all of the above.

In this case, *d* is the correct answer.

6. The most complete and longest statement is sometimes the correct one.

Example: The introduction of New Math in the 1960s
    a. led to an end of the "back to basics" movement.
    b. was meant to improve reasoning and problem-solving skills.
    c. was embraced by math teachers.
    d. was welcomed by parents.

Choice *b*, of course, is the correct answer.

Answering True-False Statements

You will not encounter this form of questioning in this text, but many instructors, especially in the sciences, frequently use the true-false format.

1. *For statements to be true, all parts must be true.* Therefore, if any part is not true, the statement is false.

   Example: Hemoglobin is found in the white blood cells and transports both oxygen and carbon dioxide. (Hemoglobin is found in the red blood cells—therefore, you must choose *false* as the answer even though part of the answer is correct.)

2. As with multiple choice, if you have never heard a word mentioned in class or seen it in your text, the statement is probably false. Similarly, absolute statements with words like *always, all, none,* and *never* are often false because they do not allow for exceptions.

3. Words such as *frequently, probably, some,* and *generally* are different from words such as *always* and *never.* These words signal that the statement may be true.

Answering Matching Questions

Although either column may be used to match a statement and matching term, it is best to begin with the column having the longer statements because this eliminates a lot of rereading. Also, match everything you are certain is correct first, because making one error generally means you are going to make another. Complete the following example now.

Example: _____ antonym   a. a word very similar in meaning to another word
            _____ glossary   b. a word opposite in meaning to another word
            _____ synonym   c. a list of specialized words with their definitions

Answering Essay Questions

1. Before you begin to write your answers, take a few minutes to analyze what type of information is being asked. Concentrate on the topic (the specific subject) and what point about it is being questioned. The point of the question is generally found in the *key terms* used in the test question. Know the meaning of the terms used by instructors who test with essay questions.

Three types of questions are generally asked by instructors: literal, interpretive, and application questions. Literal questions are the easiest to answer because the expected answer is expressed directly. Interpretive questions ask you to analyze and synthesize information you have read. Application questions ask you to go a step further, applying the information to another situation.

Chapter 1
Vocabulary Review

A. Select the appropriate word for each of the sentences in the paragraph from the boldfaced words below and write it in the space provided. Use the sentence context* to help you determine the word's meaning.

inference   dynamic   prodigious   periodicals   synthesize

For some time, we have needed a/an (1) _____ leadership in Washington to bring about some needed reforms in our court system. Recently, our government held hearings on the need to change some court procedures reported as particularly unfair. Essay writers in newspapers and other

(2) _____, in response to citizen dissatisfaction, have been criticizing many court practices. It will require a/an (3) _____

effort to (4) _____ and put together the best ideas for court reform into a final plan. But based on what has happened, we can make the

(5) _____ that some reforms in our court system will take place.

B. Write the correct word in the space provided.

neurological   unprecedented   metaphor   proficient   mode

1. Related to the nervous system   —————————————

2. A form or variety of something   —————————————

3. Words used figuratively to compare things   —————————————

4. Having expertise at doing things   —————————————

5. Never happened before   —————————————

* Context is discussed in detail in Chapter 2.

Preparation for Reading

The next selection, "Illiteracy in the Information Age," is followed by a set of questions typical of those found with longer selections at the conclusion of each chapter. **Preview** the selection first, then read it and answer the questions. Note the following defined words before reading the essay. They are underlined in the text.

to the **viability**	capable of living or surviving
maneuvering through . . . a service	using skill to arrive at a goal
writes **eloquently**	movingly expressive
deleterious effect	injurious; hurtful
pundits have even coined	learned or authoritative persons
becoming a quaint **anachronism**	something out of its proper time
revert to a pre-**Renaissance** model	the great revival of art and learning in Europe from the fourteenth to the seventeenth century
cognitive skills	involving learning through mental processes
is **ineluctably** linked	inevitably; unavoidably

Illiteracy in the Information Age

Marcia Kaplan

Since I write about and work with the computer industry, people frequently ask me if I think that electronic distribution of newspapers, magazines, articles, and books will mean the death of the publishing industry as we know it. 1

I tell them that they have little to fear from electronic distribution. The biggest threat to the <u>viability</u> of the publishing industry—and our society—is illiteracy, something that is increasing at an alarming rate in our country. 2

Each year, 700,000 people who graduate from high school can't read their diplomas, U.S. education officials say, while one in five American adults is functionally illiterate. Educators sensibly no longer measure literacy by the simple ability to read and write. Rather, they view literacy as a continuum of skills integral to functioning in society—certainly a more useful assessment. 3

While functional illiterates can read words, they cannot comprehend their meanings, synthesize information, or make decisions based on what they read. Few of them own computers, and they are as unlikely to go searching for reading materials on-line as they are to sit down with a newspaper or novel. <u>Maneuvering</u> through a commercial on-line service, a BBS, or the Internet requires an intellectual dexterity that poorly educated people lack. Marginally literate people feel most comfortable receiving information in a visual format, relying more on television than print media for information. 4

At the same time that Americans' skills are declining, entertainment, computer, and telecommunications companies are creating new, technologically advanced methods to amuse and educate us. In the excitement about the information superhighway and new com- 5 munications gadgets, businesses are ignoring a troubling fact—a substantial number of Americans are not intellectually capable of using their technologies.

Peter Drucker, a noted management 6 expert, writes eloquently about the advent of the knowledge society and the knowledge worker—the individual who relies on technology and intellect rather than brawn to accomplish work.

Perhaps Drucker has not visited a typical 7 workplace recently. "Workplace literacy" projects have sprung up across the United States. To obtain a skilled work force, businesses have to devote substantial resources to duplicate the efforts of our school systems. In many cases they are teaching basic reading, writing and arithmetic. If our future need for knowledge workers is to match Drucker's expectations, our country will have to rely on immigration or robots.

Technology actually may be contributing to 8 our declining capabilities because it has made us intellectually lazy. Our collective attention span gets shorter all the time. We "channel surf" and "Net surf," looking for content that will hold our interest for more than a few minutes. Only short sound bites or brief written summaries appeal to us. We seem to want to run our lives by remote control, fast-forwarding through the dreary parts, and replaying the brief moments that engage us.

The educational system has arguably suf- 9 fered the most deleterious effects of technology. Children no longer use pencil and paper to learn math; they use machines. But when they rely on calculators and computers for mathematical outcomes, children memorize a series of keystrokes instead of learning a deductive process. Similarly, instead of learning to write well, children with computers depend on software programs to check their spelling and correct their grammar. Some parents and educators have endorsed the philosophy that

unless learning is fun, children are within their rights to decline to participate. Only a multimedia extravaganza of audio, video, and graphics is worthy of children's attention.

Pundits have even coined a fashionable 10 term for this trend. They glorify our "post-literate" society, as if the inability to comprehend the written word is a great accomplishment. Important skills are the ability to manipulate a joystick, a mouse, or a remote control. It should be deeply disturbing to anyone who cares about the future of our society that literacy is becoming a quaint anachronism.

In the 21st century we may very well revert 11 to a pre-Renaissance model which only an elite class—the clergy in that era, the technical specialist in ours—will know how to read and write. Rather than having a multitude of knowledge workers, we will have a narrow knowledge elite that others will seek out for assistance.

Already, across industries, writing is consid- 12 ered a specialized task. Marketing communications, or "marcom" is a recently created sub-specialty of marketing that focuses on the dissemination of written information such as press releases and product descriptions. Apparently, a marketing generalist cannot be entrusted with the important task of writing. Some companies have turned this task over to public relations firms. Technology businesses entrust technical writers with the task of writing manuals to explain how their products function. Although this specialization creates more jobs, it also relieves others of the responsibility of communicating in a written form that people can understand.

Publishing is not the only industry that will 13 suffer if literacy is relegated to a narrow segment of the populace. Any business that sells products or services that require a user's ability to exercise cognitive skills will face a shrinking market. As for electronic distribution, my own experience has been that people who read avidly are the most intense users of commercial on-line services and the Internet. They use electronic media as a supplement, not as a replacement for hard copy materials.

No other industrialized country treats literacy with such contempt as the United States. We **14** haven't grasped that our society's future is <u>ineluctably</u> linked to the preservation of the written word. We will suffer for our disregard.

approximately 1100 words

Marcia Kaplan, "Illiteracy: A Looming Crisis in the Information Age," *San Francisco Sunday Examiner* 7 May 1995: B5–7. Reprinted by permission of the author.

COMPREHENSION CHECK

Part I
General Comprehension Questions: Literal and Interpretive

Write the correct letter in the space provided.

_____1. The author's experience is chiefly with
- a. newspapers.
- b. schools.
- c. the computer industry.
- d. the publishing business.

_____2. As defined by U.S. education officials, functional illiteracy is based on
- a. alarming illiteracy.
- b. a particular assessment.
- c. the ability to read and write.
- d. skills necessary to function in society.

_____3. According to the author, people who are only marginally literate would prefer getting the news from
- a. radio.
- b. television.
- c. magazines and newspapers.
- d. friends and family.

_____4. The writer and Peter Drucker are
- a. writing together.
- b. in agreement.
- c. in disagreement.
- d. none of the above.

_____5. The writer believes that what causes Americans to be "technologically lazy" is
- a. a need to watch only what engages them.
- b. a shortened attention span.
- c. their stressful lifestyle.
- d. both a and b.

_____6. A "marcom's" major task is to
- a. find a good public relations firm.
- b. engage in handling written communication.
- c. entrust technical writers.
- d. create more jobs.

7. Would the writer be in favor of software programs in schools that check spelling and correct grammar?

_____

Why or why not? _____

_____

_____

8. Why does the writer suggest we may need increased immigration and the use of robots?

_____

_____

_____

Part II
Application Questions for Writing and Discussion

9. Imagine that you are an advisor to our government in Washington. What are some suggestions you might make about the effects of a decline in literacy, and how might these problems be remedied?

_____

_____

_____

10. What are some of the writer's predictions regarding literacy and social class in the twenty-first century?

_____

_____

_____

JOURNAL ENTRY

This is your first journal entry. Write how you plan to carry out your goals and become a more effective reader. You may wish to refer to page 10 to note the areas you checked. In your writing, describe your career goals and how you plan to pursue them.

2

Building Vocabulary Through Context and Structure

This chapter will help you

* Recognize the importance of vocabulary to improve reading comprehension.
* Use the context effectively to determine the meaning of unknown words.
* Learn the meanings of the most common word parts: prefixes, roots, and suffixes.
* Transfer knowledge of word parts to unknown words.
* Develop a personal word collection.
* Use mnemonics (memory devices) to retain word meanings.
* Strengthen your use of the dictionary, thesaurus, and World Wide Web.

Before reading, think about these questions.

* What can you do to improve your vocabulary?
* Why does a strong vocabulary improve reading comprehension?
* Why is vocabulary important today?

Jot down your thoughts in the space provided.

_____

_____

Chapter 1 indicated that *the more you read, the better you read.* Reading more is also the best way to increase your vocabulary. It gives you a background of knowledge and helps you experience life through others, or **vicariously.** In turn, this background and these experiences give you the ideas and concepts associated with words. This helps you understand words better, remember them longer, and use them correctly. The more words you know, the better and faster you can understand what you read.

You will recall that definitions of challenging words were included at the bottom of the same page in the previous chapter. This same format continues here. You should look over these words before reading, but study those unfamiliar to you after you have finished reading a section.

Students are often surprised to learn how many English words there actually are. At present, in our **burgeoning** technological age, English can boast a total of over a million words. A paperback dictionary generally includes about 100,000 entries, representing, perhaps, only about ten percent of all the words in the English language! Look through an **abridged** dictionary such as *Webster's New Collegiate* or the *American Heritage* to see how many words even a shortened version contains.

Several Types of Vocabulary

All of us have several kinds of vocabulary: one each for speaking, writing, reading, and listening. Your speaking vocabulary tends to be the most limited since you have to feel very comfortable with a word to say it. Your writing vocabulary is somewhat larger because here you have time to think and select words. Still greater is your reading vocabulary. Finally, your broadest vocabulary includes the words you understand when listening, since a speaker often clarifies a word by **inflections,** physical gestures, or facial expressions.

Conversational versus Formal Vocabulary

We also have a conversational vocabulary and a more formal one. The first consists of those words we use every day in speaking and listening. They **emanate** from words with roots in our Anglo-Saxon heritage, those early English words such as *childish, break,* and *frighten.* The second kind includes **erudite** words used in more formal reading, writing, and speaking. These words are less familiar and often have their roots in Greek and Latin.

---

vicariously (vī kâr e əs lē) experience through participation in the feelings of another
burgeoning (bûr′jən ng) developing rapidly
abridged (a brijd′) shortened
inflections (in flek′ shənz) alterations in tone or pitch of the voice
emanate (em′ ə nāt′) originate or come forth
erudite (er′ yo͞o dī t′) very learned; scholarly

The following two lists of words with similar meanings, called **synonyms,** show the difference in difficulty between "everyday" or conversational words and more formal words. Knowing a substantial number of the latter makes the difference between a marginal vocabulary and a superior one.

Conversational Words	Formal Words
begin	commence
free	emancipate
name	appellation
fire	conflagration
large	gargantuan

ACTIVITY 2.1

How many of the two sets of synonyms can you match correctly?

Conversational Words	Formal Words
———— 1. end	a. covenant
———— 2. speed	b. nuptials
———— 3. fat	c. avarice
———— 4. greed	d. terminate
———— 5. wedding	e. velocity
———— 6. promise	f. corpulent
———— 7. shorten	g. assuage
———— 8. funny	h. abridge
———— 9. soothe	i. minuscule
————10. tiny	j. jocular

Stages in Learning Vocabulary

Is there such a thing as "Ten, twenty, or thirty days to a more powerful vocabulary"? Not really. We learn words best through a series of stages, often over a period of time. The following **paradigm** suggests the varying stages of word recognition.

---

synonyms (sin′ ə nimz′) words similar in meaning to other words
paradigm (par′ ə dīm′) example or model

1. I never saw this word before.	← →	*The <u>ablation</u> has been scheduled for tomorrow.*
2. I've heard or read this word, but I don't know what it means.	← →	*His comments are too <u>sanctimonious</u>*
3. In this sentence, I think I recognize the word.	← →	*His actions were quite <u>uncouth</u> and his manners disgusting.*
4. I recognize and know the meaning of this word when I read or hear it.	← →	*They argued there had been no <u>mandate</u> from the people for the president's actions.*
5. I recognize this word when I read or hear it; I can use this word in my speaking and writing.	← →	*It can only be described as a <u>courageous</u> act.*

ACTIVITY 2.2

Classify your knowledge of each of the following words according to the stages of vocabulary development. Do not use a dictionary, and rate your own knowledge by placing a check mark in the appropriate space.

Word	STAGE 1 I never saw this word.	STAGE 2 I've heard or read this word but don't know it.	STAGE 3 I think I recognize this word.	STAGE 4 I know this word.	STAGE 5 I can use this word in speaking and writing.
1. adversity					
2. candid					
3. demise					
4. efficacious					
5. graphite					
6. insousiant					
7. omniscient					
8. tantalize					
9. theology					
10. valid					

Now that you have completed this activity, you can see that as you improve and increase your vocabulary, you will be at different stages of development.

How many words do you think you know and can define? Recent surveys of vocabulary knowledge indicate that the average high school graduate can recognize anywhere from 30,000 to 45,000 words, or fewer than 5 percent of all the words in the English language! However, because researchers define words and word knowledge differently, statistics about word knowledge can vary. Steven Pinker, a language researcher, claims that between the ages of one and eighteen, high school graduates must have been learning a new word about every ninety waking minutes.* But unless we continue to make a **conscientious** effort to learn new words, our command of language remains limited.

Developing a Superior Vocabulary

Just as there are mistaken notions about the reading process, there are also mistaken ideas about how to develop a strong vocabulary. Looking up words in the dictionary is not necessarily the best way to learn the meaning of unfamiliar words. While the dictionary is an important tool for vocabulary growth, it is not the only, or even the first, approach to finding word meanings. Why? When you stop to look up a word's meaning, you disrupt the flow of ideas and interrupt your comprehension of the reading. You can't read and look up words in the dictionary **simultaneously!**

Memorizing lists of words also does not necessarily increase your vocabulary. *Rote* learning of words—memorizing by repetition *without understanding*—makes it difficult to remember their meaning. It is the concept or idea of the word that must be understood. Equally important is an understanding of the word's general context (*where* it is used). For example, *murky* means "dark and gloomy" and is often used to describe water, as in the phrase "The water looks *murky.*" However, we would never

---

conscientious (kon′ she ən′shəs) careful to do what is right; thorough and painstaking
simultaneously (sī′ məl tā nē əs lé) existing or done at the same time

* Steven Pinker, *The Language Institute: How the Mind Creates Language* (New York: Morrow, 1994) 150.

say "The *costume* looks *murky*." The word is not used in the context of describing a costume.

While there is not an instantaneous way to acquire a superior vocabulary, certain strategies can help you to improve it. Remember, however, that prodigious *reading remains the best way to expand word knowledge.*

⤳ Strategies to Increase Your Vocabulary

There are at least six ways you can increase your vocabulary.

1. Learn to use the context efficiently.
2. Use the word parts (prefixes, suffixes, and roots) you already know and apply them to unknown words. Learn additional common word parts.
3. Develop a *systematic* way of your own to collect words you read and hear but whose meaning is unclear.
4. Use mnemonics with visualization and association.
5. Use the dictionary routinely to help you pronounce words and understand their meanings.
6. Use the thesaurus to find synonyms and **antonyms.**

⤳ Using the Context – A Powerful Strategy

What is context? To be more specific, what is the context of a word? Context is often confused with the word *contents*. The contents of a book are the pages within that book. Context, however, refers to the writing—a word or group of words—surrounding a word. This writing can be a phrase, a sentence, or sometimes even a paragraph. Context may help you determine the meaning of an unknown word *if you take advantage of all available clues.* Moreover, it is the context that gives a word its exact meaning. For example, what is your understanding of the word *bank?*

Bank means _____.

Its actual meaning is determined only by its use.

She placed all her money in the *bank*. (a place to deposit money)
The river*bank* overflowed from the storm. (the earthen sides of a river)
A plane appeared out of the fog, *banked,* and stopped. (tilted and caused to turn)

---

antonyms (an′ tə nims′) words opposite in meaning to other words

Remember, it is the context surrounding the word *bank* that gives this word in each sentence its **unique** meaning. A word's meaning then is clearly dependent on *how it is used in a sentence*. Using the sentence context is, in part, *guessing intelligently* about a word's meaning. Your guess cannot be a wild one, but rather an educated guess, based on clear and serious thinking and on the information the writer has provided.

How Well Do You Use the Context?

How well do you use context? To find out, follow a two-step procedure. First, complete Activity 2.3A without any context to assist you. Write your answers in the A column. Then, do Activity 2.3B, in which the same words are used in a sentence. Write your answers in the B column. You should have more correct answers in the B column because the sentence context helped you with the unfamiliar word.

ACTIVITY 2.3A

Choose the correct definition and place its letter in column A.

		A	B
1. inadvertently	a. deviously b. approvingly c. indeed d. accidentally	————	————
2. endemic	a. mysterious b. in a particular area c. unknown d. peculiar	————	————
3. impede	a. spoil b. anticipate c. set apart d. hinder	————	————
4. halcyon	a. cool b. stormy c. calm, peaceful d. rainy	————	————
5. indolence	a. revision b. lacks dignity c. clumsiness d. laziness	————	————

———————

unique (yōo nēk′) the only one of its kind

6. abrogated a. removed by authority ———— ————
b. amended
c. strengthened
d. ignored

7. sanctioned a. disliked ———— ————
b. approved
c. amended
d. repealed

8. vacillate a. waver ———— ————
b. agree
c. try
d. prove

9. officious a. official ———— ————
b. good-natured
c. cheerful
d. meddlesome

10. facile a. creative ———— ————
b. long
c. easy
d. boring

ACTIVITY 2.3B

Using context, now choose the correct definition from the list in Activity 2.3A. Place your answers in column B.

1. In the course of regulating business, the Congress, perhaps **inadvertently,** caused delays in setting up small businesses.

2. The disease seems **endemic** to that section of the country.

3. Officials believe the committee is using delay tactics to **impede** progress.

4. The resort, which is known for its **halcyon** climate, pleasant all year long, attracts visitors from around the world.

5. The sudden warm weather increased our **indolence;** we failed to complete the job.

6. When the rebels took control, they ruled by their own laws and **abrogated** the constitution.

7. They have **sanctioned** the proposed law because they know it will benefit the environment.

8. Each day she **vacillated** about whether to take the job; she could not make a decision.

9. The **officious** clerk interfered in things that were not his concern and often annoyed his co-workers.

10. A **facile** assignment is completed easily and quickly.

⤳ Types of Context Clues

Two types of context clues are useful in understanding unknown words.

1. A **semantic** clue provides "meaning" information about the unknown word.
2. A **syntactic** clue provides grammatical information about the unknown word, indicating whether it is a noun, a verb, an adjective, or an adverb.

Although context clues are not always obvious and may require detective-like thinking, their use constitutes an important strategy in vocabulary development. The two types of clues are interdependent, and together they can help you in anticipating and confirming the meaning of a word. For example,

The flood was a **calamitous** event and resulted in the loss of many lives.

Recognizing the syntactic or grammar clue, you can see that the word *calamitous* is an adjective—calamitous event. By noting the semantic clue, "resulted in the loss of many lives," you can judge that the phrase *calamitous event* has something to do with a major misfortune.

Although context clues do have limitations and do not always clarify the word's **precise** meaning, their usefulness in helping to determine the general meaning of a word cannot be overemphasized.

Here are five major kinds of context clues to look for when you are puzzled by an unfamiliar word in print.

---

semantic (sə man′ tic) relating to meaning in language
syntactic (sin tak′ tik) referring to the way in which words are put together grammatically
calamitous (kə lam′ i təs) disastrous
precise (pri sīs′) clearly expressed; exact

Kinds of Context Clues

Definition: Direct Explanation

The direct explanation, or definition clue, is the easiest clue to spot, and the one most commonly used in textbooks. Some writers explain words directly by giving synonyms—other words with similar meaning; others simply tell you what a word means, using signal words such as *that is, is, is defined as, for example, namely, in other words,* or *for instance.*

> In the skeletal system, a *foramen,* that is, an opening through a bone, serves as a passageway for blood vessels, nerves or ligaments.
>
> John W. Hole, Jr., *Human Anatomy and Physiology*

> *Cyberphobia* is the irrational fear of, and aversion to, computers.
>
> Larry Long, *Introduction to Computers and Information*

Sometimes, the writer uses punctuation marks to provide a signal to the reader that a word is being defined. The most common marks used today are commas and dashes. Parentheses are occasionally used.

> A *numismatist*—a collector of gold medals—needs considerable capital to get started in business.

> Famous as a writer and lecturer, he popularized *transcendentalism,* a romantic philosophical theory claiming that there was an ideal, intuitive reality transcending ordinary life.
>
> John Mack Faragher et al., *Out of Many, A History of the American People*

> Aristotle said that *rhetoric* (argumentation) involves using all the available means of persuasion, and he defined the means of persuasion as *ethos* (personal credibility), *logos* (logical organization and reasoning) and *pathos* (emotional appeal).
>
> Sherry Diestler, *Becoming a Critical Thinker*

Contrast

Often, words such as *but, however, yet,* or *in contrast* signal an opposite meaning.

> Her sister was always at ease with everyone she met; Minette, *however,* was quite gauche in social situations.

The word *however* indicates that a contrast will follow the first statement; therefore, *gauche* must mean the opposite of having the right manners. The dictionary definition is "lacking social grace."

Past Experience—Making an Educated Guess

You can use your own familiarity with situations to help understand or explain a word or predict its meaning.

> Scrooge was such a *skinflint* that he wouldn't give any of his employees a Christmas gift or even the day off from work.

Even if you did not recognize the character Scrooge from Dickens's *A Christmas Carol*, your own experience could suggest that anyone unwilling to give employees time off during Christmas is miserly or stingy, a skinflint.

Summary

Sometimes, an unfamiliar word is explained in summary form.

> There was bitterness in her voice, a scowl on her face, and then an angry reply—as usual, she was in a *captious* mood as she spoke to the children.

The meaning of *captious*—quick to find fault—can be deduced from the summary preceding it.

Examples

Often, the author will give examples that relate to a word in order to **clarify** it. Noting these examples can help you determine the word's meaning. Examples are sometimes used to point out instances, characteristics, or incidents that illustrate the meaning of a word. Signal words such as *like* and *for instance* are sometimes used.

> *Dieseling* happens when you shut off the engine and it keeps running. It will chug, jump, smoke and cough, and, if you turn the key back on, the engine will just keep running.
> Dorothy Jackson, *What Every Woman Should Know About Her Car*

---

clarify (klar′ ə fī) make or become clear

ACTIVITY 2.4 **Practice with Context Clues**

Read each of the following sentences, underline the context clues for the boldfaced words, and then write a definition for the word.

Example: Default, or failure to pay the interest or principal amount of the promissory note on its due date, can result in bankruptcy.

Walter Meigs et al., *Accounting: The Basis for Business Decisions*

Definition: failure to pay the interest or principal amount of a promissory note on its due date.

1. But it is a long leap from a matrilocal home where the father is absent, to a **matri-archal** one, in which the females take total charge from the males.

Gloria Naylor, "The Myth of the Matriarch"

Definition: _____

2. **Ethics**—the standards of conduct and moral judgment accepted by society—has a strong influence on business communication.

David Popenoe, *Sociology*

Definition: _____

3. **Interdiction** involves efforts aimed at stopping drugs from entering the United States. The Coast Guard, Border Patrol and Customs agents have played the most visible roles in interdiction efforts over the last few decades.

Frank Schmalleger, *Criminal Justice Today*

Definition: _____

4. The debate revolves around a computer programmer and author of "Pretty Good Privacy," a program that lets computer users **encrypt** or "scramble" their files.

"Subpoena Follows Articles on Encryption," *San Francisco Examiner*

Definition: _____

5. The most ignored fact of all about pain is that the best way to eliminate it is to eliminate the abuse. Instead, many people reach almost instinctively for the painkillers—aspirins, barbiturates, codeine, tranquilizers, sleeping pills, and dozens of other **analgesics** or desensitizing drugs.

Norman Cousins, "Pain Is Not the Ultimate Enemy"

Definition: _____

ACTIVITY 2.5

Look at these sentences with context clues taken from several sources: essays and articles, literature, and a textbook. After you complete the exercises, decide which area may present the most difficulty for you in using context clues. In the space provided after the exercise, explain why you think this is so.

ESSAYS AND ARTICLES

Determine the meaning of the boldfaced word from the choices. Underline the clues in the sentence and write the correct letter in the space provided.

_____ 1. Radon gas is a **carcinogen** which the EPA and others consider to be, next to cigarette smoking, the most widespread cause of lung cancer. (*Hint:* What suggestion is made about cigarette smoking and lung cancer?)
(a) medicine   (b) test   (c) cancer-causing agent   (d) painkiller

_____ 2. The car bomb was the start of **carnage** in the holy city, and among the many killed were women and children.
(a) massive killings   (b) understanding   (c) renewal   (d) plans

_____ 3. A **dilemma** faces battered wives: reporting a beating might stop their mates from repeating the offense, but it might also cause them to become violent.
(a) physical exam   (b) choice between   (c) dangerous trip   (d) debt

_____ 4. The parents of an embassy guard found shot in a bar in El Salvador have had his body **exhumed** twice in an attempt to prove he was murdered.

Newsweek

(a) blessed   (b) moved   (c) dug out   (d) hidden

_____ 5. The horror movie **titillated** the audience and kept them on the edge of their seats throughout the showing.

San Francisco Chronicle

(a) excited   (b) bored   (c) confused   (d) annoyed

_____ 6. There are many ways to **disseminate** information. One of the most effective means of getting a message across involves an easy trick, known to schoolteachers for years and years: Make learning fun.

Television Producing and Directing

(a) contradict   (b) assemble   (c) distort   (d) spread widely

THE TEXTBOOK

Determine the meaning of the boldfaced word from the choices that follow, and write the letter of the correct word in the space provided.

_____ 1. The most effective approaches so far have been group-oriented programs like Alcoholics Anonymous, which focus on the individual's recognition of their problem, total **abstinence,** and the emotional support of fellow alcoholics.

Psychology

(*Hint:* What does an alcoholic need to do to help solve his or her problem?)
(a) argument   (b) refraining from drinking   (c) overindulgence
(d) compromise

_____ 2. Doctors often prescribe them [drugs] for hyperactive children to lengthen attention span and control restlessness, to **narcoleptics** to keep them awake, to sufferers of short-term depression.

Psychology

(a) salesclerks   (b) people who sleep excessively
(c) excessive eaters   (d) rock stars

_____ 3. Under that doctrine, wives were **chattels** of their husbands; they could not legally control their own earnings, property, or children unless they had drawn up a specific contract before marriage.

America, Past and Present

(a) partners   (b) slaves   (c) novices   (d) friends

_____ 4. Susan B. Anthony, a veteran of many reform campaigns, tried to vote in the 1872 presidential election and was fined $100 which she refused to pay. In 1890, she helped form the National American Woman Suffrage Association to work for the **enfranchisement** of women.

America, Past and Present

(a) right to vote   (b) job opportunities   c) right to compete
(d) persuasion

_____ 5. Students for a Democratic Society (SDS) **epitomized** the early new left.

David Goldfield et al., *The American Journey*

(a) protested   (b) rejected   (c) represented   (d) questioned

_____ 6. Most current researchers adopt an **eclectic** approach in studying species, employing the theories and techniques of morphology, ecology, biochemistry, behavior, growth, and genetics.

Oceanography: An Introduction

(a) from one source   (b) from many sources   (c) frequently changing
(d) patterned

CONTEXT CLUES FROM LITERATURE

Read the following sentences from literary novels and short stories. Again determine the meaning of the boldfaced word from the choices provided. Underline the clues in the sentence and write the correct letter in the space provided.

_____ 1. They had come to believe he was **invincible,** a strong muscular man with a drill sergeant's booming voice and a bricklayer's hands. . . .

Isabel Allende, "A Discreet Miracle"

(*Hint:* Look at all the descriptive words that help explain his personality.)
(a) hard to see   (b) hard to resist   (c) impossible to overcome
(d) easy to change

_____ 2. James went out into the snowy night and his thoughts were **inchoate,** unclear, but still miserable; they had nothing to tell him except rain. . . .

Taylor Caldwell, *Bright Flows the River*

(a) generous   (b) interesting   (c) undeveloped   (d) surprising

_____ 3. I felt that she was not bored, but her **reticence** puzzled me, and I wished to make her speak.

Henry James, "Four Meetings"

(a) unwillingness to speak   (b) abuse   (c) costume   (d) talkativeness

_____ 4. Yet Samantha remained **dauntless.** With each rejection her determination grew.

Barbara Wood, *Domina*

(a) agreeable   (b) prosperous   (c) fearless   (d) worn out

_____ 5. He lived **parsimoniously,** was frugal in food and drink, his clothes were beyond description; he looked like a beggar, but kept on saving and putting money in the bank.

Anton Chekhov, "Gooseberries"

(a) extravagantly   (b) far away   (c) stingily   (d) alone

_____ 6. The real truth was that I was not . . . a sissy and there had never been anything **effeminate** about me.

Anne Rivers Siddons, *Peachtree Road*

(a) careful   (b) distant and cool   (c) mistaken   d) like a female

In using context clues, which of the three areas—essays and articles, literature, or the textbook—proved most difficult for you, and why?

_____

_____

ACTIVITY 2.6 Context Clues in Short Reading Selections

As you read each of the following selections, underline the context clues that assist in explaining the meaning of each of the boldfaced words. Generally, context clues are given within the context of paragraphs rather than isolated sentences. Sometimes, it is necessary to read several sentences, or the entire paragraph, before a word's meaning becomes clear.

Write your definitions in the spaces provided. Your definitions do not have to be worded exactly like those in a dictionary.

PASSAGE 1

Most of the world's 6,000 languages will be either extinct or on the road to **extinction** by the end of the next century, **linguistic** experts say.

The loss is especially acute in California, which has been called the world's third most linguistically diverse region, after New Guinea and the Caucasus.

"There are still 50 native American languages being spoken in California but not a single one of them is spoken by children. The vast majority are spoken by less than 10 individuals over 70 years old," . . . said a U.C. Berkeley linguist at the University of California, who also said native American languages were **suppressed** until the 1960s. Indian children sent to boarding schools were punished for speaking their parents' language. Now, a movement exists among California Indians to learn the elders' tongue before it's too late.

Michael Krauss, a language researcher at the University of Alaska, warned that the rate at which native tongues were dying would cause **irreparable** damage to human civilization. "I call this a catastrophe—the rate of loss of mankind's linguistic diversity," he said.

Between 20 and 50 percent of the world's languages are no longer being learned by children, he said. "For the next century, something up to 95 percent of mankind's languages will either become extinct or become **moribund** and headed toward extinction."

"World's Languages Dying at Alarming Rate," *San Francisco Examiner*

1. extinction _____

2. linguistic _____

3. suppressed _____

4. irreparable _____

5. moribund _____

PASSAGE 2

In the spring of 1938, on the eve of his greatest triumphs, Adolf Hitler entered his fiftieth year. His physical appearance was unimpressive, his bearing still awkward. The falling lock of hair and the smudge of his moustache added nothing to a coarse and curiously undistinguished face, in which the eyes alone attracted attention. In appearance at least Hitler could claim to be a man of the people, a **plebeian** through and through, with none of the physical characteristics of the racial superiority he was always **invoking.** The quality which his face possessed was that of **mobility,** an ability to express the most rapidly changing moods, at one moment smiling and charming, at another cold and imperious, cynical and sarcastic, or swollen and **livid** with rage.

Speech was the essential medium of his power, not only over his audiences but over his own temperament. Hitler talked **incessantly,** often using words less to communicate his thoughts than to release the hidden spring of his own and others' emotions, whipping himself and his audience into anger or exaltation by the sound of his voice.

Allan Bullock, "The Dictator," *Hitler: A Study in Tyranny*

1. plebeian _____

2. invoking _____

3. mobility _____

4. livid _____

5. incessantly _____

PASSAGE 3

Belisa Crepusculario had been born into a family so poor they did not even have names to give their children. She came into the world and grew up in an **inhospitable** land where some years the rains became **avalanches** of water that bore everything away before them and others when not a drop fell from the sky and the sun swelled to fill the horizon and the world became a desert. Until she was twelve, Belisa had no occupation or virtue other than having withstood hunger and the exhaustion of centuries. During one **interminable** drought, it fell to her to bury four younger brothers and sisters; when she realized that her turn was next, she decided to set out across the plains in the direction of the sea, in hopes that she might trick death along the way. The land was **eroded,** split with deep cracks, strewn with rocks, fossils of trees and thorny bushes, and skeletons of animals bleached by the sun. From time to time, she ran into families who, like her, were heading south, following the **mirage** of water. Some had begun the march carrying their belongings on their backs or in small carts, but they could barely move their own bones, and after a while they had to abandon their possessions.

Isabel Allende, *The Stories of Eva Luna*

1. inhospitable _____

2. avalanches _____

3. interminable _____

4. eroded _____

5. mirage _____

ACTIVITY 2.7 Context Clues in a Longer Passage

Read the following selection, noting the boldfaced words, all of which have context clues. The main clues have been underlined. After you complete the reading, answer the questions that follow.

Sydney Harris was a well-known syndicated columnist. His essays are collected in two books, *Best of Sydney J. Harris* and *Pieces of Eight* and frequently deal with that branch of semantics concerned with how the meaning of words affects our communication with one another. This essay examines one such word, *love,* how it was used by the ancient Greeks and how we use it today.

Using Love in Whatever Way We Like

Sydney J. Harris

1 The word that has been most cheapened and **devalued** in our language is "love." We use it for everything—we "love" our mothers, we "love" our new car, we "love" ice cream and Mozart and picnics and being left alone.

2 Most people suppose that first we think, and then we find words to express our thoughts. Actually, we think in and with words, and the words we have at our command shape our thoughts, rather than the other way around.

3 Although the ancients had fewer words (because there were fewer things in the world), they discriminated more than we do among the ones they had.

4 They had at least three different words to express what we call "love"—there was **philia,** for love of family and friends and countrymen; there was **eros,** for love between the sexes; and there was **agape,** for love of God.

5 They did not apply the word "love" to objects such as chariots and clothing and food and drink and worldly pleasures, for love is not a univocal word. A **univocal** word is one that has only a single specific meaning, and cannot be attached loosely to a wide variety of objects.

6 Obviously, we do not love our children in the same way we love our wives or sweethearts.

We do not love our country in any sense that we love the color blue or the taste of peppermint or the smell of roses. We do not love God in the way we love our pet cockatoo.

7 Our failure to make these verbal distinctions is more than "a manner of speaking"; it is a manner of **conceptualizing,** of defining and distinguishing. The words we use control and direct and limit the thoughts they express. We are spurred to action by slogans and catchwords rather than by the concrete realities they embody.

8 If we "love" the things that give us pleasure, because they give us pleasure, we will stop loving them when they give us pain. But Job's "love" of God had nothing to do with pleasure or pain, happiness or unhappiness; it was wholly on another level of trust and **fealty.**

9 Because we use words so loosely and **indiscriminately,** we are able to justify almost anything we want to do. People who are willful call themselves "independent" and take their defect for a virtue; people who are **predatory** call their greed "enterprise" and are proud of what should shame them.

10 If so distinctive a word as "love" is invariably misused and abused and flattened and coarsened, imagine what we do with language gen-

erally, every day in every way. Like Humpty Dumpty, when we use a word, it means just what we choose to make it mean, because the "mean-ings" are not in the words themselves, but in the people who use them.

approximately 475 words

Sydney J. Harris, excerpt from "Using Love in Whatever We Like" in *The Best of Sydney J. Harris* (New York: Houghton Mifflin). Originally appeared in the *Chicago Sun-Times.* Copyright 1986 by Sydney J. Harris. Reprinted with the permission of the *Chicago Sun-Times.*

Vocabulary Review

Write your answers in the spaces provided.

———— 1. A **univocal** word
(a) has two meanings.   (c) has one meaning.
(b) has three meanings.   (d) lacks meaning.

———— 2. The meaning of the sentence "We are spurred to action by slogans and catchwords rather than by . . . realities" means
(a) we act too slowly and this causes problems.
(b) we act without really understanding a situation.
(c) we act by shouting slogans and catchwords.
(d) both a and c.

———— 3. According to Harris, we react more to which kind of words?
(a) catchwords   (c) slogans and catchwords
(b) newly coined words   (d) loving words

———— 4. Something that is **devalued** is
(a) praised.   (c) given less worth.
(b) ignored.   (d) given more worth.

———— 5. When we **conceptualize** an idea, we
(a) blame.   (c) predict.
(b) confuse.   (d) think.

———— 6. Someone who is **indiscriminate** is
(a) not careful.   (c) too careful.
(b) an alarmist.   (d) a racist.

7. To show **fealty** to someone means to _____

_____

8. Based in Greek, the difference in meaning between the words **philia** and **eros** is

_____

_____

Questions for Writing and Discussion

9. Explain the meaning of this sentence: "People who are willful call themselves 'independent' and take their defect for a virtue; people who are predatory call their greed 'enterprise' and are proud of what should shame them."

_____

_____

_____

10. In what ways do you generally use the word *love?* Give three examples of things you believe you love. Show how your idea of love varies in each case. Then try to think of other words in our vocabulary that are used loosely.

_____

_____

_____

_____

_____

_____

⤳ Using Word Structure

Another way to develop a superior vocabulary is to acquire a general knowledge of how words are structured—to learn to use these word parts: prefixes, roots, and suffixes. Some linguists claim that language contributions from Latin and Greek word parts outweigh all others and give meaning to over 50 percent of our words. Using word parts goes hand in hand with using context clues. However, word part meanings usually give you a *general* sense of a word's meaning, while context makes the meaning more *specific*.

Let's look at how *benediction* differs from *malediction*, how *prediction* differs from *contradiction*. All four words share the Latin root *dic/t,* meaning "to speak or say," and a suffix ending *-ion,* which has the general meaning "the condition or state of." The difference in meaning lies in the first syllable that gives each word its distinct meaning.

Word	Prefix + Root + Suffix	Word Meaning
benediction	**bene** ("good") + dict + ion	"speaking good"; a blessing
malediction	**mal** ("bad") + dict + ion	"speaking bad"; a curse; speaking evil
prediction	**pre** ("before") + dict + ion	"speaking before"; saying something before it happens; foretelling
contradiction	**contra** ("against") + dict + ion	"speaking against"; saying the opposite of something

For some words, the literal meaning and the definition are pretty much the same, as in *prediction* and *contradiction,* but this is not always the case. Even though the literal meaning may not always give you a word's *exact* meaning, it will help suggest its general sense.

You will come across unfamiliar words, not in isolation as in these words, but when you are reading; that is, words will be used in the context of sentences and paragraphs. Use of context clues *together with* knowledge of word parts can give you a good idea of the word's meaning. Be aware too that words do not *always* have a prefix and/or suffix and also that a root may vary in spelling when combined with certain prefixes.

Let's examine how each word part functions. We will use a variety of words.

Prefix: *Pre-* means "before." The prefix (a group of letters) always comes *before* the main part of the word and changes the word's meaning.

use **re**use   place **mis**place   sure **un**sure

Root: All words must have a root or stem. It is the main part of the word and carries the basic meaning of the word.

vitamin   **vita**lity   re**vita**lize   (vita = life)

Suffix: The suffix (a group of letters) comes *after* the main part of a word. Often, the suffix indicates what part of speech the word is, that is, whether it is a noun, verb, adjective, or adverb. The suffix carries only limited word meaning.

amaze amaze**ment** (n.)   nation nation**al** (adj.)   special special**ize** (v.)

Suffixes may sometimes modify a root word's meaning, as in *shape* and *shape* less (without shape). Many suffixes have a rather "generic" meaning, such as "related to." Unlike prefixes, suffixes rarely change the basic meaning of the word but rather alter the word's part of speech; this is the *major role of the suffix.*

Prefix	Root Word	New Word	Suffix	New Word
mis- ("wrong")	judge	misjudge (v.)	-ment (n.)	misjudgment (n.)
dis- ("not")	obedient	disobedient (adj.)	-ly (adv.)	disobediently (adv.)
re- ("again")	place	replace (v.)	-able (adj.)	replaceable (adj.)

The term *affix* is sometimes used to refer to either a prefix or suffix since it means "to add" or fix to something.

Commonly Used Word Parts

The following charts list some of the most commonly used word parts. Becoming aware of their meanings will enable you to determine the definitions of many seemingly difficult words. You do not have to memorize these lists but rather try to get the essence of the meanings for commonly used word parts through the categories in which they are grouped.

Write one example of your own in the Your Example column for each word part listed. You may choose to work with a group.

ACTIVITY 2.8

PREFIXES

WORD PART	MEANING	EXAMPLE	YOUR EXAMPLE
Learn the prefixes that suggest something *negative* or that can mean "not."			
a-, an-	not; without	atheist; anonymous	_____
anti-	against; opposite	antifreeze	_____
dis-	not; opposite	disown; disconnect	_____
in- (im- *before* b, m, p;	not	inactive; immature	_____
il- *before* l; ir- *before* r)*		illegal; irresponsible	_____
mis-	wrong	misnomer	_____
non-	not	nonessential	_____
un-	not	unavailable	_____
Learn the prefixes that change time.			
ante-	before	antedate	_____
post-	after	postgraduate	_____
pre-	before	precondition	_____
re-	again; back	reactivate	_____
retro-	backward	retrogress	_____

* Sound/spelling changes make the pronunciation of words easier.

| re- ("again") | rejoin | **Reconstruction** of the eroded highway, littered with potholes, began in January. | _____ |
| sub- ("under") | subway | Because of the ice storm, the frozen **subterranean** soil could not be penetrated. | _____ |

Complete this table in the same way as the previous one. Again, transfer your working knowledge of the roots to new words. The first one has been done for you.

Root and Meaning	Familiar Word	New Word in Context	Your Definition of the Word
dict ("speak")	dictator	The woman whispered **maledictions** at the accused kidnapper.	_saying bad things: curses_
fid ("faith")	confide	Her **infidelity** and recklessness led to a divorce.	_____
tort ("twist")	distort	The CEO's **extortion** of funds caused the company to collapse.	_____
vers ("turn")	invert	Don't travel by plane if you have an **aversion** to flying.	_____
vid ("see")	video	Can you **envision** the beautifully decorated tree in your mind?	_____
mitt/miss ("send")	dismiss	We canceled the game because of **intermittent** rain.	_____
chron ("time")	chronic	Mainframe computers are an **anachronism** today.	_____
dem ("people")	democracy	**Demographic** studies give us an insight into people's lifestyles.	_____
graph ("write")	graffiti	According to the **seismographic** reading, it was a 6.6 earthquake.	_____

More About the Suffix

Recall that the major role of the suffix is to derive a new word that is usually a different part of speech from the root word.

ACTIVITY 2.11

Write the derived or suffixed word and the new part of speech. You may have to adjust the spelling of words marked with an asterisk. The first one is done for you.

Suffix and Part of Speech	Root Word	Suffixed Word	Part of Speech
		accessible	adj.
-ible (adj.)	access (v.)	_____	_____
-ance (n.)	repent (v.)	_____	_____
-ate (v.)	active* (v.)	_____	_____
-ity (n.)	vulgar (adj.)	_____	_____
-ion (n.)	rebel* (v.)	_____	_____
-ize (v.)	immortal (adj.)	_____	_____
-ly (adv.)	adept (adj.)	_____	_____
-ment (n.)	denounce (v.)	_____	_____
-ous (adj.)	harmony* (n.)	_____	_____

Strategies for Remembering Vocabulary

Having determined the meanings of unfamiliar words as you read does not necessarily mean you will remember them. There is a difference between figuring out the meanings of words as you read and *learning* them.

How can you remember the meanings of new words? Which words should you remember? You need to be selective in your choices and concentrate on those words that appear repeatedly in your reading, words you see frequently but the meaning of which is unclear.

Often, textbook terms will be given in a **glossary** or printed in boldface type to signal their importance. Instructors frequently point out words that commit to memory. Learning just 10 to 20 new words a week increases your vocabulary by 500 to 1000 words a year.

To learn words, you can draw upon several options to help you master their meanings, including a personal word bank, a computerized glossary, and memory devices incorporating visualization and association techniques.

A Personal Word Bank

Many students create their own personal vocabulary system for mastering new words by using index cards. Such a system is likely to be best suited for your needs because

1. *You* decide which words you want and need to add to your vocabulary.
2. *You* collect them from your reading or listening.

Just selecting words **randomly** from the dictionary and noting their definitions is not productive, as the definitions are unrelated to a context. Again, when you read, find words that appear frequently but whose meaning is unclear. Have a stack of 3-by-5-inch index cards handy for your word notations. Also, carry a few extra cards with you to class to jot down important lecture terms you hear.

In building your own word bank, follow these steps.

1. On the front side of the card, neatly write or print in large letters the word you want to remember and the part of speech.
2. Beneath it, write the **phonetic** spelling to help you with pronunciation.
3. Beneath that, copy the context phrase or sentence in which the word appeared. This phrase/sentence will help jog your memory and help you to retain the meaning of the word.
4. On the back of the card, write a short definition of the word, the definition that applies to the phrase or sentence context.
5. Beneath the definition, write a sentence of your own, using the word.

Students generally like the personal vocabulary card system because they can study only the words they need to learn and do it any time, anywhere. Since the cards are small and portable, you can carry them around with you whether on campus, at home, or even running errands. Also, you can reorder them by category or subject.

When you have accumulated your first five to ten cards, begin practicing with them every day, pronouncing and defining the words. To practice, start by looking at

---

glossary (glos′ ə rē) list of specialized words with their definitions
randomly (ran′ dəm lē) having no particular pattern or purpose
phonetic (fə net′ ik) the way it actually sounds

Front Side

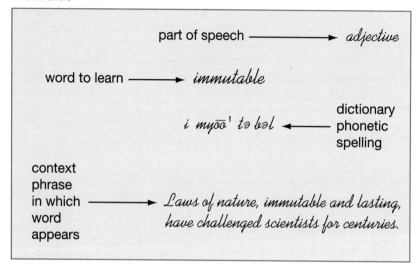

Back Side

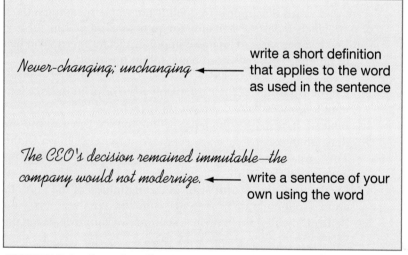

FIGURE 2.1   Sample—Front and Back Sides of a Vocabulary Card

the word, saying it aloud, and trying to tell yourself the definition. The act of recitation begins to lock the word's meaning in your memory bank, activating your thinking process. As you check your memory, by looking at the back of the card, make two groups: place the cards for the words you know immediately and feel confident about in one group and place those you need more practice with in the other group. Continue studying the difficult ones until all the cards are in the "I Know It" group. Then, shuffle the cards and do a final practice to prevent rote learning.

Choosing Your Words to Begin

Construct your first vocabulary card by choosing a word from the following remarks by the late Howard Cosell, a well-known sports broadcaster.

HOWARD COSELL SPEAKS

- "Arrogant, pompous, obnoxious, vain, cruel, verbose, a showoff. I have been called all of these. Of course, I am."
- "There's one thing about [broadcasting]: There is no place for talent. That's why I don't belong. I lack mediocrity."
- "Boxing is the only sport in the world where the clear intention is for one person to inflict bodily harm upon the other person, mainly to the head where brain damage must ensue . . . I don't think improvements or controls are the answer. I think the answer is abolition."
- "If ever there was a trailblazer, a broadcaster [who] sought to bring sports out of the juvenile, out of the banal—this, you see, is my mission. I have been an electronic first, and I don't mean that egotistically."

San Jose Mercury News

Can you define *arrogant, pompous, obnoxious, verbose, mediocrity, abolition, trailblazer, banal,* and *egotistically*? If not, select some of these words and begin your vocabulary card collection now.

Vocabulary Sheet

Copy your words on the Vocabulary Collection sheet on page 62 for practice. Each time you define a word correctly, record a plus (+). Each time you cannot recall its meaning, record a minus (−). Three successive pluses for each word indicate you probably know that word. You may want to photocopy the sheet.

⤺ A Personalized Computer Glossary

 Just as you can create vocabulary *cards,* you might want to consider using your computer to develop a master list of words, particularly for textbook study, by subject. The computer permits greater flexibility, allowing you to move words and categories around on a screen; you can add, delete, or rearrange words at will. You can also use boldface, italics, or underline to highlight ideas. To create your own glossary of computerized words, simply alphabetize your list. You should make a print copy of your words and keep it with lecture and textbook notes to review before taking quizzes and exams.

VOCABULARY COLLECTION

Name_____

Word	Practice Dates										
1											
2											
3											
4											
5											
6											
7											
8											
9											
10											
11											
12											
13											
14											
15											
16											
17											
18											
19											
20											
21											
22											
23											
24											
25											
26											
27											
28											
29											
30											

Plus (+) = Correct   Minus (−) = Incorrect — Study Again

Experiment with making several vocabulary cards and a computerized glossary to see which method best suits your learning style. Once this is determined, use either method; it's not necessary to do both!

Using Mnemonics, or Memory Devices

Visualization and Association

One way to remember new words is to repeat a word and its definition while studying your vocabulary master list, computer glossary, or card collection. Another effective memory technique is to make vivid associations or to visualize information. Two principles of memory training apply in learning unfamiliar words.

1. It is always easier to remember things that have meaning than to remember things that do not.
2. The mind can think in pictures.

When you come across a new word you want to remember, associate or relate it to a word or idea you already know. For example, suppose you wanted to learn the word *arduous* from the sentence "Learning vocabulary words need not be an arduous task." Here is how you might use association: *arduous* sounds like *harduous*. Even though there is no such word as *harduous,* you can use this made-up term as a **mnemonic** to help you associate the new word, *arduous,* with one you already know, *hard.* Once you have made an association, try to create a visual image. If you exaggerate the image somewhat, you will recall it more easily. Picture yourself, perhaps, with stacks of vocabulary cards and several dictionaries, trying to learn a new word: *arduous.*

Study the following table to see how this technique works.

Word You Want to Remember	Definition		Association
callow (kal´ ō)	inexperienced; immature	sounds like	*shallow.* If something is shallow, it's not very deep.
jounce (jouns)	the compression of a suspension spring (auto-tech term)	sounds like	*bounce.* When something bounces, it springs.
eschew (es chōo´)	to shun, evade, or avoid	sounds like	*shoo.* If you shoo something away, you want to avoid it.
libelous (lī´ bel əs)	an act that can injure a person's reputation unjustly	sounds like	*lie.* When you lie, someone can get hurt.

---

mnemonic (ni män´ ik) of or helping the memory

Practice with Visualization and Association

Examine the definitions for the following words and then make up some associations and visualization clues. Compare your responses with those of your classmates.

1. **hirsute** (hur′ sōōt) hairy
2. **impale** (im pāl′) to pierce with something pointed; to torture or kill by fixing on a sharp stake
3. **stupefaction** (stōō pə fak′ shən) the act of being amazed or astounded
4. **myopic** (mī ăp′ ik) lacking insight; nearsighted
5. **insipid** (in sip′ id) tasteless, flat, bland

Sketching the Meaning on a Card

Another way to use visualization and associations in trying to remember words is to sketch out ideas on your vocabulary cards to help illustrate a word's meaning. Examine the sample illustrating this procedure on this page and then make a sketch for one of the words you have chosen to learn with your own vocabulary cards.

FIGURE 2.2   Sample Vocabulary Card with Sketch

☜ Etymology

Studying a word's etymology, that is, its origin or history, is another method to aid recall. Once you associate the word with a story or visualize an interesting situation related to a word's history, you make it easy to learn the word permanently. The word *bowdlerize,* for example, means "to expurgate, or to leave out or change offensive words in a passage." *Bowdlerize* derives its meaning from a person. Dr. Thomas Bowdler was an English editor who in 1818 published an edition of Shakespeare's works in which he left out words or phrases he found personally offensive. To remember the meaning of *bowdlerize,* you might picture someone cutting out the words in a book with a huge pair of scissors and you should easily recall the word's meaning.

Investigate any of the following words, each derived from a person's name. You may consult an **unabridged** dictionary or a book such as Nancy Sorel's *Word People.**

boycott	malapropism	narcissism
chauvinism	mausoleum	nicotine
guillotine	mesmerize	sadism
machiavellian		

Working with the WORLD WIDE WEB

Countless new words, *neologisms,* have been created during the past decade because of our increased use of computer technology. Their history is interesting and fascinating! One such word is *spam,* the meaning of which has been lately in daily newspaper articles because of its recent coinage as a computer term: "Bright Light Technologies . . . has only one mission: to kill "spam"—the nickname for unsolicited bulk messages glutting digital mailboxes worldwide."[†] Why "spam" to describe this phenomena? It is named after a Monty Python skit involving a diner menu of "Spam, Spam, Spam."

To learn the history of some other terms used by the **digerati** of the computer world, consult the *Dictionary of the World Wide Web* by Cynthia B. Leshin.[‡] How many of the following terms can you define or explain etymologically?

Boolean operators	cracker	cyberspace
easter eggs	emoticon	e-zine
Gutenberg	mozilla	wired

---

unabridged (un′ ə brijd′) not shortened

digerati (dij ə ra′ te) a community of computer professionals who are becoming increasingly wealthy through their creative and innovative use of digital technology.

* Nancy Caldwell Sorel, *Word People* (New York: American Heritage Press, 1970).

[†] Matt Beer, "South of Market's Bright Light Technologies Develops Ammo Against Unwanted E-Mail," *San Francisco Examiner* 20 July 1998.

[‡] Cynthia B. Leshin, *Dictionary of the World Wide Web* (Upper Saddle River, NJ: Prentice Hall, 1998).

⤳ Acronyms

An *acronym* is a word formed from the first letter or letters of other words. It is a kind of "verbal shorthand," a way to describe something quickly in an abbreviated manner. A number of everyday words have been created this way: scuba (*s*elf-*c*ontained *u*nderwater *b*reathing *a*pparatus) and zip, as in zip code, (*z*one *i*mprovement *p*lan) are but two examples. A number of acronyms are the names of organizations, such as CORE (*C*ongress *o*f *R*acial *E*quality) and SWAT (*S*pecial *W*eapons *a*nd *T*actics). Acronyms can be a useful mnemonic device; students often use them to help them quickly remember important information.

Perhaps nothing has generated the explosion of acronyms as have the specialized worlds of business (CPA, CEO, IBM, for example), medicine (HMO, AIDS, HIV, for instance), and technology, in which the computer industry's pioneer programming language generated the acronym BASIC (*B*eginner's *A*ll-purpose *S*ymbolic *I*nstruction *C*ode). Abbreviated forms describing video technology are constantly evolving; we've gone from TV to VCR to CD-ROM to the digital world of DVD and DIVX. With the advent of the Internet, "AOL" became an overnight household word. To become aware of some of the acronyms frequently used by World Wide Web users, complete the following practice.

 ## Working with the WORLD WIDE WEB

Match each acronym with the words from which it was derived.

Column I	Column II
_____ 1. GIF	a. Frequently Asked Questions
_____ 2. PPP	b. Multi-User Domain
_____ 3. FAQ	c. What You See Is What You Get
_____ 4. HTML	d. Uniform Resource Locator
_____ 5. MUD	e. Very Easy Rodent-Oriented Net-Wide Index
_____ 6. RAM	f. Wide Area Network
_____ 7. WYSIWYG*	g. Graphic Interchange Format
_____ 8. URL	h. Random Access Memory
_____ 9. VERONICA	i. Hypertext Mark Up Language
_____ 10. WAN	j. Point-to-Point Protocol

* Pronounced "wizzy-wig"

To learn more about memory techniques, try the following site by Mind Tools, which gives articles on various mnemonics for remembering names, dates, foreign language words, and so on.

http://www.gasou.edu/psychweb/mtsite/memory.html

The Dictionary

You will not always be able to figure out a word's meaning from the context or the word parts and may need to use the dictionary. The key to using a dictionary successfully is to be aware of the basic aids it provides a reader and to learn and understand its organization.

GUIDE WORDS: Two words, generally printed at the top pages of the dictionary, indicate alphabetically what words are included on a page; the left word signals the *first* word and the right one the *last* word on a page.

Assume the following guide words are at the top of a dictionary page.

flood   flounce

Place a check mark next to each word that would be listed on the page.

———— 1. florid

———— 2. flotilla

———— 3. flourish

———— 4. flout

———— 5. fluent

PRONUNCIATION KEY: Helps you to say the word correctly. For a word to actually be "yours," not only should you know its meaning, but you should feel comfortable using it in writing and speaking. The dictionary gives you the phonetic spelling immediately following the listing of the word, either in parenthesis or between slanted lines. The pronunciation key may be found at the front of the dictionary and, sometimes, at the bottom of pages. If you consult more than one dictionary, you may find a slight variation in pronunciation.

Three special markings **facilitate** pronunciation.

1. *Long and short vowels:* Long vowels are marked with a line (¯) called a *macron,* for example, aimless (ām lis). Short vowels have a curved mark (˘) called a *breve,* for example, ăgony (ăg ə nē). Some dictionaries do not place any mark

———————

facilitate (fə′ sil′ ə tāt) make easier; aid

over short vowels; therefore, in these dictionaries all unmarked vowels are short. A long vowel (so called because it takes longer to say) is simply the name of the vowel: *a, e, i, o, u.* The short vowel takes less time to say, hence its name.

2. *Stressed and unstressed syllables:* Stress means the degree of loudness or harshness with which a syllable is spoken. Stress is indicated in one of three ways.

  a. An unmarked syllable indicates the weakest stress.

  b. A bold mark (′) indicates the strongest stress.

  c. A lighter mark (′) indicates a light stress.

  Which pronunciation is correct, moth ER′ or MOTH′ er? With any word, if you cannot decide what syllable to stress, try using the word in a sentence.

3. *Schwa:* This mark is written like an upside-down *e* (ə). Its sound, "uh," often replaces the sound of the short vowels *a, e, i, o,* and *u* in unstressed syllables. The sound is "shorter" and less definite than even that of short vowels. Try pronouncing each of the following words, listening for the "uh" sound:

astonish   unravel   quality   pardon   success

ACTIVITY 2.12

Practice with a dictionary entry. To strengthen your ability to use the dictionary, study Figure 2.3 below and answer the questions that follow on page 69 about the word *carnivorous.*

car·ni·val (kär′nə-vəl) *n.* 1. The season just before Lent, marked by merrymaking and feasting. 2. A traveling amusement show. [Ital. *carnevale.*]
car·ni·vore (kär′nə-vor′, -vōr′) *n.* A flesh-eating mammal, esp. one of a group including dogs, cats, and bears.
car·niv·o·rous (kär-niv′ər-əs) *adj.* 1. Belonging or pertaining to the carnivores. 2. Flesh-eating or predatory. [Lat. *carnivorus.*] —**car·niv′o·rous·ly** *adv.* —**car·niv′o·rous·ness** *n.*
car·ny (kär′nē) *n., pl.* **-nies.** Also **car·ney** *pl.*
-neys. *Slang.* 1. A carnival. 2. One who works with a carnival.
car·ol (kär′əl) *n.* A song of praise or joy, esp. for Christmas. —*v.* **-oled** or **-olled, -ol·ing** or **·ol·ling.** 1. To celebrate in song. 2. To sing joyously. [< OFr. carole.] —**car′ol·er** *n.*
car·om (kär′əm) *n.* 1. A billiards shot in which the cue ball successively strikes two other balls. 2. A collision followed by a rebound. —*v.* 1. To collide with and rebound.

FIGURE 2.3

Source: Entries in *The American Heritage Dictionary of the English Language,* ed. Peter Davies. Copyright © Houghton Mifflin Company. Reproduced by permission of publisher.

1. List what the guide words might be.   _____

2. How many syllables does the word have?   _____

3. Does *sit* or *hive* rhyme with the second
   syllable of *carnivorous?*   _____

4. What part of speech is it?   _____

5. What language does the word come from?   _____

6. What is the difference between *carnivorous*
   and the word that precedes it?   _____

Finding the Exact Meaning

To use the dictionary to improve your vocabulary, you need to find the exact meaning of the word as it is used in context. The *first* given definition is not necessarily
the one you are seeking. Many words have *more* than one meaning; therefore, dictionary writers try to include all the possible definitions of a word. One language
expert says the 500 conversational words most people use routinely have *14,000 different dictionary* definitions!* It is important to THINK about how the word was used
when you came across it in your reading and to select the appropriate meaning from
the choices given. For example, three of the seven definitions of the word *sanctions*
would appear this way in the dictionary:

> 1. authoritative *permission* or *approval . . .* 5. the *penalty* for noncompliance . . .
>   7. a *coercive measure . . . against a nation.*

Obviously, selecting the definition of *permission* or *approval* rather than *penalty* or
coercive measure against a nation would lead to a totally different understanding of a
writer's ideas.

Sometimes a word is explained with another word, a synonym, the meaning
of which is also unclear. You should not memorize a word's meaning without
understanding it fully. For example, the dictionary's first definition of the word
garrulous is

> 1. given to prosy, rambling, or tedious loquacity

but the second definition (2. wordy, talkative) is much clearer, so that the word *garrulous* is readily understood.

* L. M. Boyd, "The Grab Bag," *San Francisco Examiner* 25 July 1998.

As you can see, one word can have several different meanings, while several can sometimes mean the same thing, such as *car* and *automobile*.

Review the following list of 100 ways to express the word *said,* each with a slightly different meaning. Were you to make a point about something in a gentle way, you might choose the word *suggested* rather than *said*. If you wanted to indicate anger, you might use *warned* rather than *said*.

One Hundred Ways of Saying *Said*

1. acknowledged	26. confessed	51. expressed	76. recited
2. admitted	27. confided	52. foretold	77. recounted
3. advised	28. confirmed	53. growled	78. reiterated
4. affirmed	29. consented	54. hinted	79. related
5. alleged	30. considered	55. imparted	80. remarked
6. announced	31. consoled	56. implied	81. repeated
7. answered	32. contended	57. indicated	82. replied
8. argued	33. countered	58. informed	83. reported
9. asked	34. crowed	59. inquired	84. requested
10. asserted	35. cursed	60. insinuated	85. responded
11. avowed	36. declaimed	61. insisted	86. retorted
12. bellowed	37. declared	62. intimated	87. revealed
13. blasted	38. denied	63. jabbered	88. specified
14. blurted	39. described	64. maintained	89. spoke
15. boasted	40. dictated	65. mentioned	90. stated
16. cautioned	41. disclosed	66. mumbled	91. stressed
17. charged	42. discussed	67. murmured	92. submitted
18. chattered	43. divulged	68. muttered	93. suggested
19. chuckled	44. emphasized	69. noted	94. told
20. cited	45. encouraged	70. notified	95. urged
21. claimed	46. exaggerated	71. pleaded	96. uttered
22. commended	47. exclaimed	72. predicated	97. verbalized
23. commented	48. explained	73. proclaimed	98. viewed
24. conceded	49. expostulated	74. pronounced	99. voiced
25. concluded	50. expounded	75. reasoned	100. warned

Suffixed Forms in the Dictionary

One difficulty with using the dictionary is that you often are searching for a word with a suffixed form, words such as cruel*ty,* astonish*ment,* or obedient*ly.* The paper-back dictionary, usually an abridged or shortened form, does not always have the suffixed form as an entry word but instead places it at the very end of the definitions. Therefore you may have difficulty finding it as an entry word.

---

as · ton · ish (ə stăn′ish) *pf.* [<L. exintens. + *tonare,* to thunder] to fill with sudden surprise; amaze —**as-ton′ish · ing** *adj.* —**as · ton′ ish · ing · ly** *adv.* —**as · ton′ ish · ment** *n.*
o · be · di · ent (ō bē′dē ənt) *adj.* obeying or willing to obey —**o · be′ · di · ence** *n.* —**o · be′ · di · ent· ly** *adv.*
cru · el (kro͞o′əl) *adj.* [see prec.] causing pain and suffering; pitiless —**cru′el · ly** *adv.* —**cru′el · ty** *n., pl. -ties*

A change in the pronunciation of the word can occur when a suffix is added since the stress on particular syllables changes. Three common pronunciation changes are with the suffixes *-ic, -ity,* and *-ion.* Adding these suffix endings to words places the stress on the syllable *before* each of these suffixes. Abridged dictionaries do not usually show these stress changes.

Examples: ANgel   anGELic   FEASible   feasiBILity   DOMinate   dominAtion

ACTIVITY 2.13 Issues Facing Dictionary Compilers

Read the following article, which discusses the issue of whether some words should be excluded from the dictionary. Can you think of any words that should be labeled "taboo" and be forbidden from usage? As you read, pay particular attention to the italicized words and use your knowledge of context clues to help you determine the meanings of unknown words.

Defining Power of Words—The Taboo Ones

Joanna Connors

When you open the "F" file drawer at the 1 Webster's New World Dictionaries offices, a loud buzzer goes off.

That's what Webster's chief editor Mike 2 Agnes tells *gullible* visitors, anyway.

Dictionary-office humor. The "F" drawer is 3 not, in fact, *wired.*

The odd thing is, when you open it, you 4 do expect some kind of alarm to go off. Because there, underlined and cited and neatly organized on hundreds of index cards, is the word.

Go ahead. You are old enough. Open the "F" drawer. 5

In the beginning is the word—cards and cards of examples of the word—followed by its many and *inventive* elaborations. . . . 6

You know which word. The word that you patiently explain to your own kids is not *acceptable* in society, even though they hear it on CDs and in movies and sometimes, by mistake, on TV, and see it *emblazoned* on T-shirts and bumper stickers. The word Webster's declined to include in its pages until 1988. 7

Webster's was the last of the Big Four American dictionaries to take the *plunge;* the American Heritage Dictionary jumped first, in 1969. . . . 8

Agnes shrugs: Dictionaries merely record how we use language; they do not guard and protect language. . . . 9

If these are *linguistic* crimes, some would say we are in the middle of a massive crime wave. In the past couple of decades, the word—and its brothers and sisters in four-letter *larceny*—have stolen not just into the dictionary but into common usage. 10

Some people see this change and call for a return to linguistic law and order. Others, though, shrug and say: "It's just a word. What's the big deal?" 11

It's a very big deal. Linguists say words are *totems* that reveal a culture's values, fears and *taboos.* The way we use words reveals who we are, as individuals and as a society. Words can identify us by class, by *ethnicity,* by age, by gender. In fact, they carry such enormous cultural power 12

that if we thought about them, we would be left tongue-tied.

Skeptical? Consider the O.J. Simpson trial. It could be argued that a single word—the n-word—decided the outcome. 13

So if words are so powerful, why is it that *profanities* have become so casually used? 14

Robin Lakoff, professor of linguistics at the University of California-Berkeley, views it as a natural progression from the sexual *revolution* of the '60s. 15

"As usual," she says, "language is following society. We're much freer generally in sex and religion than we were 20 or 30 years ago. So it makes sense that sexual and religious references don't have the same level of terror that they once did." 16

As it becomes more and more common in conversation and the media, the word loses its punch, too, Lakoff says. Are there any words left that strike terror in American culture? Or does a modern, hip society even need taboo words? . . . 17

And Lakoff, for one, sees this as positive, a reflection of the *democratization* of American society. "All those people who used to be referred to that way are now taken as full members of the conversation, *symbolically* speaking." 18

Groups might still call each other those names, within the group. Some blacks, for instance, use the n-word affectionately and jokingly. But the word is fast becoming taboo for everyone. . . . 19

Let's test the theory. Ask yourself: Which would shock you more, to hear your sweet 8-year-old child say the f-word or the n-word? 20

Case closed. 21

approximately 475 words

Joanna Connors, "Defining Power of Words—The Taboo Ones," *San Jose Mercury News* 22 November 1997

Dictionary Review

A. Each of the following words, italicized in the text, has more than one meaning. Use a dictionary to first select and then write the one that best suits the context in which each word has been used. The paragraph in which the word was used is given for easy reference.

1. wired (para. 3) _____

2. emblazoned (para. 7) _____

3. plunge (para. 8) _____

4. taboos (para. 12) _____

5. revolution (para. 15) _____

B.   Write the part of speech for each of the following words. Use your knowledge of words parts (the suffixed forms) to assist you before consulting a dictionary.

Word   **Part of Speech**

1. gull*ible* (para. 2) _____

2. invent*ive* (para. 6) _____

3. accept*able* (para. 7) _____

4. linguis*tic* (para. 10) _____

5. ethni*city* (para. 12) _____

6. skepti*cal* (para. 13) _____

7. democratiz*ation* (para. 18) _____

8. symbolical*ly* (para. 18) _____

Context Clue Review

Write a definition for each of the following words based on the clues provided by the author.

1. gullible (para. 2) _____

2. linguistic (para. 10) _____

3. larceny (para. 10) _____

4. totems (para. 12) _____

5. profanities (para. l4) _____

Questions for Writing and Discussion

1. Do "bad words"—taboo words—reflect an uncivilized society?

   _____

   _____

2. How would you respond to the questions posed by the writer at the end of paragraph 17? At the end of paragraph 20?

   _____

   _____

3. Are there any words that should be excluded from the dictionary? From common usage? Why, or why not?

   _____

   _____

The Thesaurus

Unlike the dictionary, which gives the definitions of words, the thesaurus lists synonyms, words meaning almost the same thing, and antonyms, words opposite in meaning. Probably the best known and most frequently used thesaurus is the one first developed by Peter Roget, known as *Roget's Thesaurus*, which is available in paperback form. If you have access to the Internet, you can also access Roget's work at *<http://www.refdesk.com>*.

Before you view a sample entry from both the book form thesaurus and the Internet's version that lists words related to *language,* write as many synonyms as you can for this word.

Words Similar in Meaning to *LANGUAGE*

_____   _____

_____   _____

_____   _____

_____   _____

Compare your listing now with the one from the book form of *Roget's Thesaurus.*

LANGUAGE.—**I.** *Nouns.* **language,** speech, parlance, tongue, mother tongue, native tongue, prose, parent language, *Ursprache* (*Ger.*); king's English; secret language, cryptology; flowery language, sillabub, rhetoric, poetry; confusion of languages, babel, polyglot.

vernacular, dialect, cant, argot, idiom, jargon, lingo, patois, patter, slang, jive (*slang*), vulgate; commercialism, lingua franca, basic English, journalese, legalese, telegraphese, gobbledygook (*colloq.*), technology.

universal language, pasigraphy, international language; Volapük, Esperanto, Ido, Mondolingue, Kosmos, Myrana, Spelin, Universala, Idiom Neutral, Ro.

linguistics, glossology, glottology, philology, comparative philology, lexicology, morphology, etymology; grammar, rhetoric, syntax, accidence; Anglistics.

II. *Adjectives.* **linguistic,** glottic, glossological, philological, etymological, grammatical, syntactical, rhetorical.

vernacular, colloquial, dialectal, idiomatic, slangy, vulgar.

multilingual, polylingual, polyglot, bilingual, diglot, trilingual, quadrilingual.

See also EXPRESSION, STATEMENT, TALK, WORD. *Antonyms*—See SILENCE.

How many synonyms listed in the thesaurus for *language* do you recognize? Do you know, for example, words such as *vernacular, parlance,* and *rhetoric?* These words are synonymous with *language,* but each word has its own shade of meaning. The dictionary, then, is the source to use when you want the meaning of a word clarified, while the thesaurus is the source to use for finding substitute terms for a particular word.

Now, examine the way the information about the word *language* appears on the Internet.

Roget's Thesaurus Az ≔ ⌖ ? **of English Words and Phrases**
Index Outline Links Help

Find: [   ] NOW

IV. WORDS RELATING TO THE INTELLECTUAL FACULTIES; COMMUNICATION OF IDEAS

III. MEANS OF COMMUNICATING IDEAS

2. Conventional Means; Language Generally

Language. —**N.** language; phraseology &c. [*more*]; speech &c. [*more*]; tongue, lingo, vernacular; mother tongue, vulgar tongu, native tongue; household words; King's or Queen's English; dialect &c. [*more*].

confusion of tongues, Babel, pasigraphie; pantomime &c. (signs) [*more*]; onomatopoeia; betacism, mimmitation, myatism, nunnation; pasigraphy.

lexicology, philology, glossology, glottology; linguistics, chrestomathy; paleology, paleography; comparative grammar.

literature, letters, polite literature, belles lettres, muses, humanities, literate humaniores, republic of letters, dead languages, classics; genius of language; scholarship &c. (scholar) [*more*].

V. express by words &c. [*more*].

Adj. lingual, linguistic; dialectic; vernacular, current; bilingual; diglot, hexaglot, polyglot; literary.

Is the Internet version an exact duplicate of the book form? _____

Which resource would you most likely use when you want to find a precise word or a synonym, the Internet or the book form? Why?

_____

_____

Figurative Language

While reading, you may encounter words that instructors refer to as "figurative language." The term is sometimes confusing because it has nothing to do with figures or numbers. Rather, in figurative language a particular word or phrase is not used literally but is used in a different way. Figurative language, then, consists of words or phrases departing from their usual meaning.

Expressions that use figurative language are generally referred to as *figures of speech*. They are short, vivid comparisons that are either stated or implied; they mean something other than what is actually stated. Remember, they are not meant to be interpreted literally. Figurative language gives stronger impact to ideas and opinions, often using comparisons to clarify or enrich abstract ideas, create emotional responses, or make ideas more interesting and colorful. We use figures of speech so much we often take their implied meaning for granted. If someone says, "This assignment is driving me up a wall," the exaggerated expression is not taken literally—the person is not sitting in a car being driven vertically up a wall! The expression means the assignment is creating some kind of anxiety or frustration. Whether in speaking or writing, when figurative expressions are used, they say one thing but mean another.

The following examples illustrate the difference between figurative and literal language:

Figurative: I *bombed* on the physics test.
Literal: The terrorists *bombed* the bank building.
Figurative: I'll see to it that you *eat* those words.
Literal: They will *eat* their meals in the new facility.

ACTIVITY 2.14 Distinguishing Literal and Figurative Expressions

In the following exercise, decide whether the statement can be read literally (L), meaning precisely what it states, or figuratively (F). If you decide the statement is figurative, ask yourself

What two things are being compared?

What is the connection between them?

Write L or F in the space provided. For those you mark F, write out the implied meaning. Study the example first.

Example:

___F___ The blue eyes are frosted, looking inward like the windows of a snowbound cottage.

Richard Selzer, "The Discus Thrower"

Meaning: *Someone's eyes are clouded, and the person is unable to see clearly*

in the same way that one cannot see clearly out of an icy window.

_____ 1. Human beings are restless and dissatisfied, always in search of new experiences, seldom content with the familiar.

L. Rust Hills, "How to Eat an Ice Cream Cone"

Meaning: _____

_____

_____ 2. Before the girls got to the porch, I heard their laughter crackling and popping like pine logs in a cooking stove.

Maya Angelou, "Grandmother's Victory"

Meaning: _____

_____

_____ 3. He looked at her. He took off the sunglasses and she saw how pale the skin around his eyes was, like holes that were not in shadow but instead in light. His eyes were like chips of broken glass that catch the light in an amiable way.

Joyce Carol Oates, "Where Are You Going, Where Have You Been"

Meaning: _____

_____

_____ 4. The tiny foreigner tensed like a viper at the first provocation, ready to lash out at anyone who stood in his way.

Isabel Allende, *The Stories of Eva Luna*

Meaning: _____

_____

_____ 5. Waves, tired and angry and carrying their own weight over so many unin-terrupted miles of water, unburden themselves in a tantrum of surf on the tiny cove.

Susan Hand Schetterly, *Pitcairn Island*

Meaning: _____

_____

Figures of speech include *similes* and *metaphors,* which compare dissimilar things, making statements more vivid and thereby capturing the reader's attention. Sometimes another form of figurative language called *hyperbole,* which is deliberate exaggeration, is used for emphasis. Figurative language is dealt with in more detail in Chapter 8, along with the denotation and connotation of words.

For now, these brief definitions and examples are given to help you recognize figurative language as you read.

ACTIVITY 2.15

The figurative language is underlined.

Simile: a comparison between otherwise dissimilar things using the words *like* or as.

" 'You aren't happy.' A woman tries that idea out on you <u>like ice on a pond . . . trying to see where she will fall through into your secret self</u>. <u>But here you're not on very thin ice</u>, Teddy, for I am happy."

Diane Johnson, Lying Low

Explain what this means._____

_____

Metaphor: a comparison between otherwise dissimilar things without using the words *like* or as.

" . . . <u>Stock your mind</u>. <u>It is your house of treasure</u> and no one in the world can interfere with it. If you won the Irish Sweepstakes and bought a house that needed furniture, would you fill it with bits and pieces of rubbish? <u>Your mind is your house and if you fill it with rubbish from the cinemas, it will rot in your head</u>. You might be poor, your shoes might be broken, but <u>your mind is a palace</u>."

Frank McCourt, Angela's Ashes

Explain what this means. _____

_____

Hyperbole: a deliberate exaggeration for emphasis.

"<u>Only a polar bear could live in that house</u>; everyone walked about with heavy sweaters, scarves, and gloves."

Explain what this means. _____

_____

✎ Summary

English has over a million words, but most of us use only a fraction of that number. Words consist of two types: informal words used in everyday conversation and formal words used in both reading and writing in more academic settings. Formal words often have their roots in Latin and Greek; knowing how to use them leads to a superior vocabulary.

Words are learned in stages; therefore, in order to improve your vocabulary, you must make a conscientious effort to add new words to your existing vocabulary. Wide and varied reading continues to be the best approach, but additional strategies are important.

Using the context while reading is one of the best methods, as writers provide several kinds of context clues that can help unlock the meaning of unknown words. Learning the meanings of the most widely used word parts—prefixes, roots, and suffixes—can also boost vocabulary. Other aids include developing a personal word bank, visualizing and associating words through the use of mnemonics, and finding out the etymology or history of particular words. Acronyms are also useful to know and use, particularly if you want to be computer literate. The dictionary helps you focus on the exact meaning of a word, while the thesaurus aids you in finding synonyms or antonyms for particular words.

While reading, you will encounter figurative language—words and phrases that depart from their usual meaning—used to enhance language and capture your interest.

Chapter 2
Vocabulary Review

Using the Context: Select the appropriate word from the words given below and write it in the space provided. Use the context to help determine the word's meaning. You will not use all the words.

abridged	conscientious	inflections	precise
antonyms	erudite	mnemonics	synonyms
clarify	glossary	phonetic	unabridged

The instructor was determined to help make her students more knowledgeable or

(1) _____ through vocabulary study. First, she suggested that every-

one buy an inexpensive, portable (2) _____ dictionary for everyday

use. It would be more practical than an (3) _____ one, which would have more words than could be learned in a brief school term. She said students would find a portable dictionary useful whenever they needed to

(4) _____ or understand the meaning of unfamiliar words. Then, she suggested that everyone also buy a thesaurus, which is a book mainly of

(5) _____ so that the students could substitute new words for those they already know and may overuse. With a thesaurus, students are often able to

find the (6) _____ or exact word they need. Both the dictionary and

the thesaurus often list word opposites, called (7) _____. The teacher

taught them how to use memory aids called (8) _____. She

emphasized that they needed to make a (9) _____ effort not only to learn the meanings but also to learn how to pronounce these words. She discouraged rote learning, or memorizing without understanding. Now, all she had to do

was sit back and enjoy the sophisticated tones, or (10) _____, emanating from her students as they spoke.

Selection 1: **ESSAY**

 Preparation for Reading

William Lutz

The following essay, "Double-Talk," was written by William Lutz, a professor of English at Rutgers University and the author of *Doublespeak,* a classic text concerned with the misuse of language in both business and government in order to conceal the truth.

Note the meaning of these boldfaced words before reading. They are underlined in the text.

euphemistic language	substituting inoffensive words for offensive or harsh ones
visual **acuity**	sharpness or keenness of vision
aggregate living community	entire amount; sum total
consensus among all users	general agreement; collective opinion
camouflage our problems	conceal or disguise
outright **bigotry**	attitude of intolerance or prejudice
prove to be **irreparable**	incapable of being repaired or mended

Preview, then read the selection.

Double-Talk

William Lutz

Lately I have become fascinated with the growth of a new kind of <u>euphemistic</u> language called "politically correct," or P.C. Since the words we use reveal how we see the world—and how we want others to see it—people who use P.C. language want us to see the world their way—and act accordingly. Just for instance: In everyday usage fat people may be called *stout, stocky, overweight, heavy* or even *fat.* But in P.C. language they are *calorically disadvantaged, differently sized,* or are *size-acceptance advocates.* Going even further, P.C. language has created new oppressions: *sizeism,* the bias against the *differently sized* that is practiced by *sizists;* and *lookism,* the belief that some people are easier on the eyes than others. (I guess I'm guilty of *lookism;* I do indeed find some people easier on the eyes than others—my wife, for example.)

I call my two cats pets, but in P.C. language **2** they're *animal companions, friends* or *protectors*. Well, in some ways, cats *are* friends and companions, but they're still pets, and I don't treat them the same way I treat my friends (nor do my friends treat me the way my cats do). Thanks anyway, but I'd like to reserve "friend" and "companion" for the important human relationships in my life.

In my youth I spent some time at a Shriners **3** Hospital for Crippled Children in Chicago. Most of us in that hospital had had the same bad experience with polio. Sure, we were crippled in one way or another, and we knew we were, but the word *crippled* never bothered us. What bothered us were the people who treated us as if we were untouchables. It was the *actions* of others, not their words, that hurt. Now, of course, thanks to P.C., we would be described as *physically challenged, uniquely abled, differently abled, orthopedically impaired,* or as having *differing abilities.* Just as blind people have become *differently sighted, visually impaired, print handicapped,* or have *reduced visual acuity,* and people who stutter are *speech impaired.* (What's next: Will someone who's dead be called *differently alive?*)

I have never been fond of the term *senior* **4** *citizen,* but its meaning is certainly clearer than *chronologically gifted.* And I have no problem with *retirement community;* what is gained by calling it a *senior aggregate living community?* In my language, kids misbehave sometimes, but in P.C. they *engage in negative attention-getting;* and they don't just learn to read any more but to *interact with print.*

Racial and ethnic groups have always been **5** sensitive to the terms applied to them, and surely we should call them what they want to be called. But to avoid chaos they need to agree among themselves; and we need a consensus among all users of the language as to what words mean. In P.C., for instance, *Indian* and *Native American* have been replaced by *Indigenous People, Amerind* or *Abo-American,* short for *Aboriginal-American.* How many people really know what these terms mean? And are they really an improvement over the terms they are supposed to replace?

To their credit, many people who insist on **6** P.C. usage believe that changing our language can eventually change our thinking and thus our behavior—thereby eliminating racism, sexism and all the other isms we deplore. I disagree. We can camouflage our problems, ranging from thoughtlessness to outright bigotry, with fancy "correct" words, but we can't cure them. Instead, we lull ourselves into the false sense that, in calling a rose by another name, we've changed it.

I find much of P.C. language absurd and **7** funny—so why do I care? I am concerned, as I said, that its users want to force their view of the world, its people and its problems, on the rest of us. But I have another concern as well: P.C. language attempts to gloss over and distort truth—to prettify it. As George Orwell warned us, "If thought corrupts language, language can also corrupt thought." Compassion must temper truth and reality at times, as when we call mentally retarded children *exceptional* children; but compassion and sensitivity must never be the reason for compromising truth and reality as we experience it. The damage we do to our words, to our minds and to our society may prove to be irreparable.

approximately 600 words

William Lutz, "Double-Talk," *Family Circle* 26 Nov. 1991: 168. Reprinted by permission.

COMPREHENSION CHECK

Part I
General Comprehension Questions: Literal and Interpretive

Write the correct letter in the space provided.

_____ 1. *P.C.* stands for
a. perfectly correct.
b. politically correct.
c. practically correct.
d. precisely correct.

_____ 2. According to the essay, *lookism* actually refers to
a. using foul language.
b. stockiness or stoutness.
c. attractiveness or unattractiveness.
d. women and not men.

_____ 3. Insofar as the words *friend* and *companion* are used, the author wishes people would
a. use more appropriate words for them.
b. refer to their pets by these terms.
c. treat one another more civilly.
d. use them only to refer to human relationships.

_____ 4. In his youth, Lutz evidently had become crippled because he had
a. an accident.
b. been engaged in street fights.
c. a diving accident.
d. polio.

_____ 5. The writer believes that P.C. can help eliminate
a. sexism.
b. racism.
c. both a and b.
d. none of the above.

_____ 6. The P.C. phrase "engage in negative attention-getting" refers to
a. misbehaving children.
b. cranky adults.
c. stubborn pets.
d. angry ethnic groups.

7. What is meant by this statement: "If thought corrupts language, language can also corrupt thought"?

_____

_____

_____

8. P.C. terms are used to describe people who are (a) overweight, (b) impaired in some way, (c) older, and (d) racially or ethnically varied. Which category of P.C. terms used to characterize groups do you find most inappropriate, and why?

Are there any which you believe are appropriate? _____

_____

Part II
Application Questions for Writing and Discussion

9. Lutz states that some advocates of P.C. believe that changing our language can eventually change our thinking and behavior. Do you agree with this statement? Why, or why not?

_____

_____

10. Former Family Court judge Judy Sheindlin, now star of the television show *Judge Judy,* said in an interview in *New York* magazine, "You have to use language that people understand . . . I know lawyers who practice their *Webster's* skills on **litigants.** There was a judge who was sentencing a 14-year-old child of poverty, putting him in jail, and he said, 'This will have a **prophylactic** effect.' So that entire message got lost on the kid. *Good, bad, normal, right, wrong*—these are words people understand. P.C. doesn't cut it."* Do you agree with Judge Judy? Why, or why not?

_____

_____

---

litigants (lit′ i gǝnts) parties to a lawsuit
prophylactic (pro fǝ lak′ tik) preventive or protective
* Barbara Lippert, "Punchin' Judy," *New York* 15 June 1998: 85.

Part III
Extend Your Vocabulary

Use the context of the sentences to help you supply the correct word from those listed below. You will not use all the words.

euphemistic   acuity   camouflage   irreparable   consensus   aggregate

1. Humans cannot begin to match the hearing _____ of most animals.

2. Soldiers daub paint on their faces, wear uniforms that resemble forests, and

   place small twigs and branches in their helmets, all in order to _____ their positions.

3. With no _____ on how to proceed, the two attorneys continued bickering with one another.

4. Politicians are masters in the use of _____ language because they wish to convince us of their views.

5. The Oklahoma City bombing resulted in _____ damage to the Federal building.

Selection 2: **TEXTBOOK**

 Preparation for Reading

In this excerpted textbook selection, you will learn the relationship between thought and language and be given new insights into whether language, as suggested by William Lutz in "Double-Talk," can eventually *change* our thinking. You will also learn why language is uniquely human and how it helps shape our thoughts.

In reading this selection, you will meet some terms used by linguists and psychologists that pertain to language. As in most textbook writing, the author has carefully defined many important terms within their context, such as *concepts, prototype, anomia, aphasias, semanticity, morphemes, phonemes, generativity, iteration, recursion, syntax, displacement,* and *pragmatics.*

Before reading, note the meaning of the boldfaced words. They are underlined in the text. Note also the author's use of boldface and italics as signals to introduce important terms in the text and the actual definitions he has provided within the margins of the text.

humans use for **articulating** concepts	expressing oneself clearly or distinctly
beings are **physiologically** capable	relating to normal functions of living things
arcane knowledge of the rules of grammar	known or understood only by a few; secret
the linguistic-relativity **hypothesis**	an assumption or concession made for the sake of argument
celebrated its **bicentennial**	a 200th anniversary or celebration

Preview, then read the selection.

Thought and Language

Saul Kassin

Using Words to Shape Thoughts

More and more, psychologists who study the way people think and those interested 1 in the way people communicate have come to realize that thought and language are seamlessly interconnected. In this chapter, we'll see that language is a tool we humans use for underlined articulating concepts, solutions to problems, and other thoughts. . . . [T]he words we use to describe events can, to some extent, shape the way we think.

We humans are a funny species. As a civilization, we have invented the wheel, **2** kept historical records to guide present and future generations, landed space ships on the moon, unlocked the atom, cracked the genetic code, and revolutionized the face of all we do with the development of the computer. . . . Yet at the same time, we massacre each other in war, wreak havoc on the environment, discriminate against other racial and ethnic groups, mistreat our partners in marriage, [and] take drugs that make us sick. . . .

What is it about the way we humans think that leads us to be both rational and **3** irrational? How do we solve difficult problems and then evaluate the solutions, and what kinds of errors are we prone to make along the way? . . . And what role does language have to play in the way we think? What is language, and is it this capacity that most clearly separates humans from other animal species? In the coming pages, we will examine some of the basic processes of thought and language, then address the question of how they are related. But first, let's examine *concepts*—the basic building blocks of abstract thought and language.

Concepts

What are concepts, and how are they stored in memory? What is a prototype, and how does it explain why a robin is considered "birdier" than a chicken?

concept A mental grouping of persons, ideas, events, or objects that share common properties.

Freedom. Sports. Cancer. Animals. Education. Furniture. Sex. Peace. Music. . . . Each of **4** these words represents a distinct **concept**—a mental grouping of persons, places, ideas, events, or objects that share common properties. . . . [W]e saw that our long-term store of knowledge can be pictured as a complex but orderly network of semantic concepts. So when one concept in the network is activated, other closely related concepts pop to mind, or are *primed*. Look at the semantic network depicted in Figure 2.4. Note that the fact that a robin is a type of bird is illustrated by its linkage, and this linkage in itself is a concept that is stored in memory. What's interesting about semantic networks is that one concept can be used to bring others to mind. Thus, hearing the word *bird* makes it easier to pull *robin, chicken,* and *animal* from memory. . . .

prototype A "typi-cal" member of a category, one that has most of the defining features of that category

Some members of a category are perceived to be more typical than others. Thus, **5** to most people, a robin is a "birdier" bird than a chicken, an ostrich, or a penguin— which all have wings and feathers and hatch from eggs but do not fly. What makes a category member more or less typical? Look again at Figure 2.4 and notice the partial list of characteristics that are linked to the concepts *bird, robin,* and *chicken.* When people are asked to list properties of different concepts, the most typical members, called **prototypes,** have more of these properties. Consider the categories listed in Table 2.1. The more prototypical an item is, the more easily we recognize that it is a member of the group and use it to make judgments about the group as a whole.

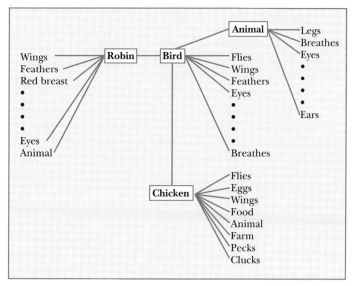

FIGURE 2.4   A Semantic Network
Long-term memory can be pictured as a complex web of concepts, some of which are cognitively closer than others. When
one concept is "activated," others nearby in the network are
primed.

Language

> With 4,000 to 6,000 languages spoken, why is it often said that all humans speak in
> the same tongue? What are the universal properties of all languages, and why don't
> even the most elaborate animal communication systems qualify? . . .

A colleague's friend, who is a psychology professor, had a frightening experience a **6**
few years ago. While in his office talking to a graduate student, he found himself
suddenly unable to recall words that are basic to his work, like *data* and *experiment*.
These words were not on the tip of his tongue, waiting to be retrieved. Instead, he
was suffering from anomia, an inability to recall familiar words. While in this state,

TABLE 2.1
Typicality of Members in Three Categories

Category	Typicality		
	High	*Moderate*	*Low*
Furniture	Chair	Lamp	Vase
Fruit	Apple	Lemon	Coconut
Vehicle	Car	Boat	Blimp

he knew what concepts he wanted to express but could not come up with the right labels. Fortunately, the experience lasted for only forty-five minutes. It was caused by a temporary reduction of blood flow to part of the left hemisphere. With surgery, doctors were able to prevent a relapse. If the anomia had resulted from brain damage—due to a stroke, for example—the effects would have been more lasting.

Two lessons relevant to the study of language can be drawn from this episode   7
(Ashcraft, 1993). First, anomia suggests that there is an important distinction between concepts and the words used to represent them. Even when our semantic networks are intact, we can lose the connections between concepts and their verbal representations. The implication is that thought and language are separate. The second lesson is that in trying to understand the psychology of language, it helps to study people with language disturbances, or **aphasias** (Caplan, 1992). Anomia is one type of aphasia. . . .

aphasias The loss or impairment of language abilities following brain damage, often to the left hemisphere.

People who lose part of the capacity for language find the experience devastat-   8
ing. This is not terribly surprising. Language is essential to social living and is the defining milestone in human evolution. . . . Cognitive scientist Steven Pinker (1994) argues that the ability to learn, speak, and understand language is thus a powerful human instinct—"so tightly woven into the human experience that it is scarcely possible to imagine life without it" (p. 17).

Arguing that the capacity for language is innate, Steven Pinker (1994) states, "Language is no more a cultural invention than is upright posture" (p. 18).

Communication in the Animal World

Among humans, language is a primary means of communication. Other animal   9
species have complex forms of communication as well. Ants send chemical signals secreted from glands in order to share information about food and enemies with other members of the colony. When honeybees discover a source of nectar, they return to the hive and communicate its location to the other worker bees through an intricate dance that signals both direction and distance. Male songbirds of various species sing in the spring to attract female mates and also to warn other males to stay away from their territory to avoid a fight. Dolphins talk to each other at great depths of the ocean by making a combination of clicking, whistling, and barking sounds. . . .

Characteristics of Human Language

According to *The Universal Almanac* of 1997, there are between 4,000 and 6,000 lan-   10
guages worldwide, to say nothing of the different dialects within each language. When all the dialects are taken into account, tens of thousands of variations can be distinguished. It's amazing how different the many languages seem on the surface. To appreciate this point, consider the principal languages, ranked in order of usage in the world's population: Chinese, English, Hindi, Spanish, Russian, Arabic, Malay, Bengali, Portuguese, French, German, Japanese, Urdu, and Javanese. Despite the differences, however, linguists are quick to note that from a Martian's perspective, all humans speak a single tongue. The reason is that all languages share three universal properties: semanticity, generativity, and displacement.

semanticity The property of language that accounts for the communication of meaning.

morphemes In language, the smallest units that carry meaning (e.g., prefixes, root words, suffixes).

phonemes The basic, distinct sounds of a spoken language.

generativity The property of language that accounts for the capacity to use a limited number of words to produce an infinite variety of expressions.

Most English sentences contain twenty words or fewer. According to the Guinness Book of World Records, *however, the longest sentence ever printed contains 1,300 words.*

Semanticity   **Semanticity** refers to the fact that there are separate units in a **11** language and that these units have *meaning*. The smallest unit that carries meaning is called a **morpheme.** Every word has one or more morphemes. Simple words like *dog, run,* and *think* contain one. The word *unthinkable* has three morphemes—the prefix *un-,* the root word *think,* and the suffix *-able*—and each adds to the total meaning of the word.

In all spoken languages, morphemes are composed of **phonemes,** the basic **12** *sounds* of a language. Each separate sound you hear when you pronounce the word *unthinkable* is one phoneme. English has twenty-six letters, but forty to forty-five phonemes. The word *tip* has three phonemes: *t, i,* and *p.* So do the words *ship* (*sh, i,* and *p*) and *chip* (*ch, i,* and *p*). Linguists estimate that human beings are <u>physiologically</u> capable of producing one hundred basic sounds. No one language uses all of them, however. Most contain between twenty and eighty phonemes. English speakers say *s* and *z* differently. In Spanish, they're one and the same. As a result of such differences in vocal experience, people sometimes struggle to pronounce the phonemes of other languages. For example, many Americans struggle to roll the German *r* or cough up the guttural *ch* sound of Arabic.

The average American high-school graduate knows about 45,000 different **13** words, and the average college graduate has a vocabulary that is nearly twice that size (Miller, 1991). It is really quite remarkable that human beings are able to master a full language vocabulary so well, and so quickly, given that most word sounds are unrelated to meaning. There is no reason why a cat is called a *c-a-t* as opposed to a *d-o-g.* It just happens to be that way. . . .

Generativity   A second property of language is **generativity,** the capacity to use a **14** finite number of words and rules for combining words to produce an infinite variety of novel expressions. Think about it. When I listened to the news one recent night, I heard the network commentator say, "Well, Tom, it's been quite a night, with both the President's State of the Union and the verdict in the O.J. Simpson trial." It was a pretty mundane sentence. But I'll bet no one in history had ever uttered it before.

Generativity gives language virtually unlimited flexibility as a communication **15** system. There are two features of human language that enable this flexibility: iteration and recursion. *Iteration* means that a phrase can always be added to the end of a sentence in order to form an entirely new sentence. Through iteration, you could go from the sentence "I like psychology" to "I like psychology this semester" to "I like psychology this semester, thanks to the professor," and so on. *Recursion* refers to a related fact of language: One expression can always be inserted inside another. This makes possible the construction of long, embedded sentences. . . .

If language is so generative that we can produce limitless numbers of novel sen- **16** tences, how are we able to comprehend each other as competently as we do? The key to managing generativity is **syntax,** rules of grammar that govern how words can be arranged in a sentence. Expressions are not random strings of unrelated sounds but rather words that are combined in familiar and orderly ways. Every language has a unique syntax. For example, adjectives usually come *before* the noun in English (*white wine*) but *after* the noun in Spanish (*vino blanca*). . . . [C]hildren learn to speak correctly by the age of five, and they do so without explicit instruction. . . .

This brings us to another point about the generativity of language: Any one 17 thought can be expressed in different ways. Regardless of whether I say, "The Bulls won the championship," "The championship was won by the Bulls," or "What the Bulls won was the championship," you grasp the underlying meaning. Linguist Noam Chomsky . . . explained this phenomenon by making a distinction between the deep structure and surface structure of language. The *deep structure* refers to the underlying meaning of a statement, apart from the particular way that it is expressed. The *surface structure* consists of the words that are actually used to communicate that meaning. According to Chomsky, syntax provides us with a set of "transformational" rules for how to (1) put meaning into words when we speak and (2) derive meaning from words when we are spoken to. . . .

Displacement A third property of language is displacement. **Displacement** 18 refers to the fact that language can be used to communicate about things that are not in our immediate surroundings, matters that extend beyond the limits of the here-and-now. Thus, we reminisce about the good old days, we talk about our hopes and dreams for the future, we gossip about others behind their backs, and we discuss abstract ideas concerning God, politics, social justice, and love.

As a means of communication, language is a social activity—and displacement 19 enables us to tell others what we're thinking, how we're feeling, or what we plan to do next. These are complex messages, however, and social interaction is just that, a two-way interaction. To converse with others effectively, therefore, we need more tools than just an extensive vocabulary and an <u>arcane</u> knowledge of the rules of grammar. We must also have a sense of the *pragmatics,* or social context, of language and an understanding of how to use it (Hilton, 1995; Kumon-Nakamura et al., 1995). In the words of Herbert Clark (1985), "Language is a social instrument. When we talk, we direct our words not to the air but to other people." Accordingly, says Clark, intricate rules guide the way speakers and listeners position themselves physically from each other, take turns in conversation, and communicate through the face, voice, body, and other nonverbal channels. We also tailor what we say to suit our audience and the situation we're in. People tend to take language pragmatics for granted. But tension frequently arises when these pragmatics break down—as when natives of very different cultures neglect to realize that the person they're trying to communicate with does not know their local expressions, jargon, and buzzwords. In *You Just Don't Understand,* sociolinguist Deborah Tannen (1990) claims that conflicts between men and women often arise because of gender differences in their communication style, or pragmatics.

To illustrate the importance of pragmatics, consider the story of an early 20 attempt to use computers to translate text from one language to another. After programming a computer to convert material from English to Russian, researchers gave

---

According to the Arts and Humanities Citation Index, *Noam Chomsky is the eighth most cited writer in all the humanities—behind only Marx, Lenin, Shakespeare, the Bible, Aristotle, Plato, and Freud. (He's the only living member of this group.)*

syntax Rules of grammar that govern the arrangement of words in a sentence.

the computer the task of decoding "The spirit is willing, but the flesh is weak." As the story goes, the Russian translation came out "The vodka is fine, but the meat is tasteless." So much for machines. Without pragmatic knowledge, ironic or metaphoric expressions are likely to be interpreted in rather bizarre ways.

The Relationship between Thought and Language

> Everyone assumes that thought gives rise to language, but is the reverse sequence also true? Do words we speak determine, constrain, or shape the way we conceptualize the world? In this regard, what is the impact of using sexist language? . . .

This chapter has shown that thought and language are separate but interrelated **21** cognitive activities. Having now examined them separately, we are faced with the question "What is the nature of their interrelationship?"

The Linguistic-Relativity Hypothesis

The mystery of language was revealed to me. . . . Everything had a name, and each name gave birth to a new thought."

—HELEN KELLER

The traditional, intuitive position is that language is a tool for expressing thought, **22** that thought → language. Consistent with this view, child-development researchers often find that young children understand concepts before they have the words to explain them. . . . But what about the reverse sequence, that language → thought? Does language have the power to shape thought? . . . Inspired by anthropologist Edward Sapir, Benjamin Lee Whorf (1956), a self-educated linguist, theorized that the language we speak—the words, syntax, and so on—shapes the way we conceptualize the world. This notion, that our thoughts are "relative" to our linguistic heritage, is known as the **linguistic-relativity hypothesis.** . . .

Today, . . . most psychologists . . . agree . . . that language *influences* the way **23** we think (Hardin & Banaji, 1993; Lucy, 1992). . . . In one study, researchers showed subjects line drawings and varied the label that accompanied each one (see Figure 2.5). Afterward, subjects redrew these figures from memory in ways that were distorted by the labels. In a second study, subjects were presented with pictures of faces or color chips, and half were asked to describe them. Those who had put what they saw into words later had more difficulty recognizing the original faces and colors. Did language in this case disrupt thought? Yes, according to the investigators, "some things are better left unsaid" (Schooler & Engstler-Schooler, 1990). . . .

If language can influence thought, then words are tools that can be used to **24** socialize our children, sell products, mold public opinion, and stir the masses. People in power are aware of this connection, so they choose their words carefully. As colorfully documented by William Lutz (1989), the result is "doublespeak"—language that is designed to mislead, conceal, inflate, confuse, and distort meaning. Thus, we are told that the new tax is just a "user's fee," that acid rain is "poorly buffered precipitation," that a recession is "negative economic growth," . . . and that plastic handbags are made of "genuine imitation leather."

Original figures	Labels	Sample drawings
	Curtains in a window	
	Diamond in a rectangle	
	Crescent moon	
	Letter "C"	
	Eyeglasses	
	Dumbbell	
	Ship's wheel	
	Sun	
	Kidney bean	
	Canoe	

FIGURE 2.5   Words That Distort Memory for Images
Subjects who saw figures like those shown (*left*) later redrew these figures from memory in ways that fit the different labels they had been given (*right*).

Psychological Impact of Sexist Language

During the 1993–1994 academic year, Williams College celebrated its bicentennial **25** and rewrote its catalog. Despite 200 years of tradition, the term *freshman* was replaced by *first-year student*. In that same year, controversy erupted at the University of Massachusetts over whether to keep or change the name of its sports teams, called the Minutemen (they kept it). In both cases, the existing terms were labeled sexist for using the generic masculine form.

Whatever the political arguments, the psychological question is: "Does sexist **26** language influence the way we think about men and women?" What do you think? Is the term *mail carrier* rather than *mailman* silly and awkward, or does the change help break down gender stereotypes? Does it seem harmless or sexist to talk about "the evolution of *man*," our "fore*fathers*," "*brother*hood," and the "chair*man* of the board"? And what about the generic use of the masculine pronoun *he* to refer to all human beings? Is it okay to say that "a doctor must be trained if *he* is to be competent?" Drawing on the linguistic-relativity hypothesis, many people feel strongly about this issue.

TABLE 2.2
Guidelines for Nonsexist Language

Common Sexist Terms	Nonsexist Alternatives
Man, mankind	People, humanity, human beings
Manpower	Work force, personnel
Freshman	First-year student
Chairman	Head, chair, chairperson
Foreman	Supervisor
Policeman	Police officer
He, his, him	He or she, his or her, him or her, *or* they, their, them
Mothering	Parenting, nurturing, caregiving
Female doctor	Doctor
Male nurse	Nurse

For psychologists, the task is to determine whether the use of generic masculine **27** nouns and pronouns triggers images of men to the exclusion of women. Consistently, the results of this research support the hypothesis that *man, he,* and other masculine words, even when used generically, lead people to think of men. In one study, for example, male and female college students were asked to make up stories based on a topic sentence: "In a large co-ed institution, the average student will feel isolated in courses." Into the blank, the researchers inserted the pronoun *his, his or her,* or *their*. Did the pronoun in the topic sentence make a difference? Yes, when *his* rather than a neutral term was used, 65 percent of the stories written were about men. Similar results have been found in both adults and school-age children. . . .

Whorf's original hypothesis—that we can think only in terms provided for in **28** language—was undoubtedly overstated. But this should not blind us to the fact that language does make it easier to conceptualize the world in some ways rather than others. The use of sexist words is one practical implication of linguistic relativity, but there are other implications, too. In the global village, translating ideas from one language to another is tricky and sometimes results in misunderstanding. We need to recognize that the people of the world do not just speak differenty but also interpret events through different lenses. Certainly more research is needed to explore this link between language and thought and what it means for intercultural relations.

approximately 3000 words

From Saul Kassin, "Thought and Language," *Psychology* (Upper Saddle River, NJ: Prentice Hall, 1998) 256–58; 274–79; 284–87. Reprinted by permission.

COMPREHENSION CHECK

Part I
General Comprehension Questions: Literal and Interpretive

Write the correct letter in the space provided.

——— 1. Psychologists currently believe that thought and language are
    a. completely separate issues.
    b. easily understood.
    c. quite interrelated.
    d. rarely discussed.

——— 2. Which word is *not* representative of a distinct concept?
    a. freedom
    b. love
    c. happiness
    d. feathers

——— 3. The psychology professor's anomia, his inability to recall simple words temporarily, illustrates
    a. the important distinction between concepts and words used to represent them.
    b. that everyone forgets words sometimes.
    c. that studying language disturbances helps us to understand how language works.
    d. both a and c.

——— 4. The universal properties of language do not include
    a. semanticity.
    b. ethnicity.
    c. generativity.
    d. displacement.

——— 5. A morpheme may be defined as the
    a. lexicon of English.
    b. smallest language unit possessing meaning.
    c. unit of sound.
    d. both b and c.

——— 6. According to the author, the use of masculine nouns and pronouns
    a. does not affect gender image.
    b. influences a small number of people's images.
    c. is not politically correct.
    d. causes people to exclude women from their images.

7. Give an example from the textbook excerpt of how the words we use to describe events can shape the way we think.

_____

_____

_____

_____

8. (a) Although other animal species have complex forms of communication, why do some scientists claim that "language" is a uniquely human capacity? (b) Do you agree or disagree? Why, or why not?

_____

_____

_____

_____

Part II
Application Questions for Writing and Discussion

9. As you saw in the section on sexist language, a host of terms such as *chairperson, supervisor,* and *police officer* have changed from words formerly ending in *man.* Do you believe this has brought about any improvement in women's status, roles, and careers?

_____

_____

_____

_____

10. We assume that our thoughts help shape the language we use. Do you believe, for example, that people from different cultures think differently because of the language they use?

_____

_____

_____

_____

Part III
Extend Your Vocabulary

Study the boldfaced words below. Using the context, write the correct word in the blank provided.

articulated   semantics   arcane   cognitive   hypothesis

1. Having little computer experience, Tim could not follow the _____ directions for loading the software.

2. Doctors are not in complete agreement with the _____ that second-hand smoke is as harmful as the act of smoking itself.

3. We debated the _____ of whether to title the selection, "A Study of Mankind" or "A Study of Humankind."

4. Through our _____ ability, we are able to recall *robin* or *chicken* from memory when we hear the word *bird*.

5. Monica Lewinsky _____ some of her innermost thoughts about Kenneth Starr's investigation in her 1999 autobiography.

Selection 3: **LITERATURE**

 ## Preparation for Reading

Evan Hunter

Evan Hunter is one of today's most prolific and versatile writers, having authored more than eighty novels as well as numerous short stories, plays, and film scripts. He writes under several pseudonyms, using names such as Ed McBain, which currently he uses most frequently. Under this name, he began his famous 87th Precinct series of detective novels. In 1986, he won the Grand Master Award for mystery writers. Hunter is perhaps best known for his work *The Blackboard Jungle,* a semi-autobiographical work about an idealistic young man who confronts the often violent realities of trying to teach delinquent teenagers in a big city vocational school. That experience, teaching in New York City, may have also helped give him the background for the short story included here.

Gang culture reflects to some extent the complexity of our society. We have become accustomed to newspaper accounts that report on the violence that accompanies many gang encounters. The effect of violence on the life of just one gang member is the focus of the short story that follows. To create the mood of the story, the author uses many explicit details and sets it on a late rainy night outside a dance.

Note these boldfaced words and their meanings. They are underlined in the text.

excruciating pain	intensely painful
a fierce **rumble**	a gang fight; this slang term was popular in the 1950s
lurched away	made a sudden swaying, tipping movement
relentless tattoo	unyielding; persistent
searching and **foraging**	looking for food
an enormous **loathing**	detestation; very strong dislike
ran **hysterically**	with excessive or uncontrollable fear or emotions

As you read, note the author's use of the term *The Royals.* Why might he have chosen this particular term, and what effect did it have on Andy's fate?

On the Sidewalk, Bleeding

Evan Hunter

The boy lay bleeding in the rain. He was sixteen years old, and he wore a bright pur- 1
ple silk jacket, and the lettering across the back of the jacket read THE ROYALS. The
boy's name was Andy, and the name was delicately scripted in black thread on the
front of the jacket, just over the heart. *Andy.*

He had been stabbed ten minutes ago. The knife had entered just below his rib
cage and had been drawn across his body violently, tearing a wide gap in his flesh.
He lay on the sidewalk with the March rain drilling his jacket and drilling his body
and washing away the blood that poured from his open wound. He had known
excruciating pain when the knife had torn across his body, and then sudden comparative relief when the blade was pulled away. He had heard the voice saying,
"That's for you, Royal!" and then the sound of footsteps hurrying into the rain, and
then he had fallen to the sidewalk, clutching his stomach, trying to stop the flow of
blood.

He tried to yell for help, but he had no voice. He did not know why his voice had
deserted him, or why the rain had become so suddenly fierce, or why there was an
open hole in his body from which his life ran redly, steadily. It was 11:30 p.m., but
he did not know the time.

There was another thing he did not know.

He did not know he was dying. He lay on the sidewalk, bleeding and he 5
thought only: *That was a fierce rumble. They got me good that time,* but he did not know
he was dying. He would have been frightened had he known. In his ignorance, he
lay bleeding and wishing he could cry out for help, but there was no voice in his
throat. There was only the bubbling of blood from between his lips whenever he
opened his mouth to speak. He lay silent in his pain, waiting, waiting for someone
to find him.

He could hear the sound of automobile tires hushed on the muzzle of rainswept
streets, far away at the other end of the long alley. He lay with his face pressed to the
sidewalk, and he could see the splash of neon far away at the other end of the alley,
tinting the pavement red and green, slickly brilliant in the rain.

He wondered if Laura would be angry.

He had left the jump to get a package of cigarettes. He had told her he would
be back in a few minutes, and then he had gone downstairs and found the candy
store closed. He knew that Alfredo's on the next block would be open until at least
two, and he had started through the alley, and that was when he'd been ambushed.
He could hear the faint sound of music now, coming from a long, long way off, and
he wondered if Laura was dancing, wondered if she had missed him yet. Maybe she
thought he wasn't coming back. Maybe she thought he'd cut out for good. Maybe
she'd already left the jump and gone home. He thought of her face, the brown eyes
and the jet-black hair, and thinking of her he forgot his pain a little, forgot that

blood was rushing from his body. Someday he would marry Laura. Someday he would marry her, and they would have a lot of kids, and then they would get out of the neighborhood. They would move to a clean project in the Bronx, or maybe they would move to Staten Island. When they were married, when they had kids. . . .

He heard footsteps at the other end of the alley, and he lifted his cheek from the sidewalk and looked into the darkness and tried to cry out, but again there was only a soft hissing bubble of blood on his mouth.

The man came down the alley. He had not seen Andy yet. He walked, and then 10 stopped to lean against the brick of the building, and then walked again. He saw Andy then and came toward him, and he stood over him for a long time, the minutes ticking, ticking, watching him and not speaking.

Then he said, "What's a matter, buddy?"

Andy could not speak, and he could barely move. He lifted his face slightly and looked up at the man, and in the rainswept alley he smelled the sickening odor of alcohol and realized the man was drunk. He did not feel any particular panic. He did not know he was dying, and so he felt only mild disappointment that the man who had found him was drunk.

The man was smiling.

"Did you fall down, buddy?" he asked. "You mus' be as drunk as I am." He grinned, seemed to remember why he had entered the alley in the first place, and said, "Don' go way. I'll be ri' back."

The man <u>lurched</u> away. Andy heard his footsteps, and then the sound of the 15 man colliding with a garbage can, and some mild swearing, and then the sound of the man urinating, lost in the steady wash of the rain. He waited for the man to come back.

It was 11:39.

When the man returned, he squatted alongside Andy. He studied him with drunken dignity.

"You gonna catch cold here," he said. "What's a matter? You like layin' in the wet?"

Andy could not answer. The man tried to focus his eyes on Andy's face. The rain spattered around them.

"You like a drink?"   **20**

Andy shook his head.

"I gotta bottle. Here," the man said. He pulled a pint bottle from his inside jacket pocket. He uncapped it and extended it to Andy. Andy tried to move, but pain wrenched him back flat against the sidewalk.

"Take it," the man said. He kept watching Andy. "Take it." When Andy did not move, he said, "Nev' mind, I'll have one m'self." He tilted the bottle to his lips, and then wiped the back of his hand across his mouth. "You too young to be drinkin', anyway. Should be 'shamed of yourself, drunk an' layin' in a alley, all wet. Shame on you. I gotta good minda calla cop."

Andy nodded. Yes, he tried to say. Yes, call a cop. Please. Call one.

"Oh, you don' like that, huh?" the drunk said. "You don' wanna cop to fin' you   **25**
all drunk an' wet in a alley, huh? Okay, buddy. This time you get off easy." He got to
his feet. "This time you lucky," he said. He waved broadly at Andy, and then almost
lost his footing. "S'long, buddy," he said.

Wait, Andy thought. *Wait, please, I'm bleeding.*

"S'long," the drunk said again. "I see you aroun'," and then he staggered off up
the alley.

Andy lay and thought: *Laura, Laura. Are you dancing?*

The couple came into the alley suddenly. They ran into the alley together, running from the rain, the boy holding the girl's elbow, the girl spreading a newspaper
over her head to protect her hair. Andy lay crumpled against the pavement, and he
watched them run into the alley laughing, and then duck into the doorway not ten
feet from him.

"Man, what rain!" the boy said. "You could drown out there."   **30**

"I have to get home," the girl said. "It's late, Freddie. I have to get home."

"We got time," Freddie said. "Your people won't raise a fuss if you're a little late.
Not with this kind of weather."

"It's dark," the girl said, and she giggled.

"Yeah," the boy answered, his voice very low.

"Freddie . . . ?"   **35**

"Um?"

"You're . . . you're standing very close to me."

"Um."

There was a long silence. Then the girl said, "Oh," only that single word, and
Andy knew she'd been kissed, and he suddenly hungered for Laura's mouth. It was
then that he wondered if he would ever kiss Laura again. It was then that he wondered if he was dying.

No, he thought, *I can't be dying, not from a little street rumble, not from just getting cut.*   **40**
Guys get cut all the time in rumbles. I can't be dying. No, that's stupid. That don't make any
sense at all.

"You shouldn't," the girl said.

"Why not?"

"I don't know."

"Do you like it?"

"Yes."   **45**

"So?"

"I don't know."

"I love you, Angela," the boy said.

"I love you, too, Freddie," the girl said, and Andy listened and thought: *I love you,*
Laura. Laura, I think maybe I'm dying. Laura, this is stupid but I think maybe I'm dying.
Laura, I think I'm dying!

He tried to speak. He tried to move. He tried to crawl toward the doorway where   **50**
he could see the two figures in embrace. He tried to make a noise, a sound, and a
grunt came from his lips, and then he tried again, and another grunt came, a low
animal grunt of pain.

"What was that?" the girl said, suddenly alarmed, breaking away from the boy.

"I don't know," he answered.

"Go look, Freddie."

"No. Wait."

Andy moved his lips again. Again the sound came from him.   55

"Freddie!"

"What?"

"I'm scared."

"I'll go see," the boy said.

He stepped into the alley. He walked over to where Andy lay on the ground. He   60
stood over him, watching him.

"You all right?" he asked.

"What is it?" Angela said from the doorway.

"Somebody's hurt," Freddie said.

"Let's get out of here," Angela said.

"No. Wait a minute." He knelt down beside Andy. "You cut?" he asked.   65

Andy nodded. The boy kept looking at him. He saw the lettering on the jacket
then. THE ROYALS. He turned to Angela.

"He's a Royal," he said.

"Let's . . . what . . . what do you want to do, Freddie?"

"I don't know. I don't want to get mixed up in this. He's a Royal. We help him,
and the Guardians'll be down on our necks. I don't want to get mixed up in this,
Angela."

"Is he . . . is he hurt bad?"   70

"Yeah, it looks that way."

"What shall we do?"

"I don't know."

"We can't leave him here in the rain." Angela hesitated. "Can we?"

"If we get a cop, the Guardians'll find out who," Freddie said. "I don't know,   75
Angela. I don't know."

Angela hesitated a long time before answering. Then she said, "I have to get
home, Freddie. My people will begin to worry."

"Yeah," Freddie said. He looked at Andy again. "You all right?" he asked. Andy
lifted his face from the sidewalk, and his eyes said: *Please, please help me,* and maybe
Freddie read what his eyes were saying, and maybe he didn't.

Behind him, Angela said, "Freddie, let's get out of here! Please!" There
was urgency in her voice, urgency bordering on the edge of panic. Freddie stood
up. He looked at Andy again, and then mumbled, "I'm sorry," and then he took
Angela's arm and together they ran toward the neon splash at the other end of the alley.

Why, they're afraid of the Guardians, Andy thought in amazement. *But why should
they be? I wasn't afraid of the Guardians. I never turkeyed out of a rumble with the Guardians.
I got heart. But I'm bleeding.*

The rain was soothing somehow. It was a cold rain, but his body was hot all over,   80
and the rain helped to cool him. He had always liked rain. He could remember

sitting in Laura's house one time, the rain running down the windows, and just look-ing out over the street, watching the people running from the rain. That was when he'd first joined the Royals. He could remember how happy he was the Royals had taken him. The Royals and the Guardians, two of the biggest. He was a Royal. There had been meaning to the title.

Now, in the alley, with the cold rain washing his hot body, he wondered about the meaning. If he died, he was Andy. He was not a Royal. He was simply Andy, and he was dead. And he wondered suddenly if the Guardians who had ambushed him and knifed him had ever once realized he was Andy? Had they known that he was Andy, or had they simply known that he was a Royal wearing a purple silk jacket? Had they stabbed *him*, Andy, or had they only stabbed the jacket and the title, and what good was the title if you were dying?

I'm Andy, he screamed wordlessly. *For Christ's sake, I'm Andy!*

An old lady stopped at the other end of the alley. The garbage cans were stacked there, beating noisily in the rain. The old lady carried an umbrella with broken ribs, carried it with all the dignity of a queen. She stepped into the mouth of the alley, a shopping bag over one arm. She lifted the lids of the garbage cans delicately, and she did not hear Andy grunt because she was a little deaf and because the rain was beating a steady <u>relentless</u> tattoo on the cans. She had been searching and <u>foraging</u> for the better part of the night. She collected her string and her newspapers, and an old hat with a feather on it from one of the garbage cans, and a broken footstool from another of the cans. And then she delicately replaced the lids and lifted her umbrella high and walked out of the alley mouth with queenly dignity. She had worked swiftly and soundlessly, and now she was gone.

The alley looked very long now. He could see people passing at the other end of it, and he wondered who the people were, and he wondered if he would ever get to know them, wondered who it was on the Guardians who had stabbed him, who had plunged the knife into his body.

"That's for you, Royal!" the voice had said, and then the footsteps, his arms 85 being released by the others, the fall to the pavement. "That's for you, Royal!" Even in his pain, even as he collapsed, there had been some sort of pride in knowing he was a Royal. Now there was no pride at all. With the rain beginning to chill him, with the blood pouring steadily between his fingers, he knew only a sort of dizziness, and within the giddy dizziness, he could only think: *I want to be Andy.*

It was not very much to ask of the world.

He watched the world passing at the other end of the alley. The world didn't know he was Andy. The world didn't know he was alive. He wanted to say, "Hey, I'm alive! Hey, look at me! I'm alive! Don't you know I'm alive? Don't you know I exist?"

He felt weak and very tired. He felt alone and wet and feverish and chilled, and he knew he was going to die now, and the knowledge made him suddenly sad. He was not frightened. For some reason, he was not frightened. He was only filled with an overwhelming sadness that his life would be over at sixteen. He felt all at once as if he had never done anything, never seen anything, never been anywhere. There were so many things to do, and he wondered why he'd never thought of them before, wondered why the rumbles and the jumps and the purple jacket had always seemed so important to him before, and now they seemed like such small things in a world he was missing, a world that was rushing past at the other end of the alley.

I don't want to die, he thought. *I haven't lived yet.*

It seemed very important to him that he take off the purple jacket. He was very **90** close to dying, and when they found him, he did not want them to say, "Oh, it's a Royal." With great effort, he rolled over onto his back. He felt the pain tearing at his stomach when he moved, a pain he did not think was possible. But he wanted to take off the jacket. If he never did another thing, he wanted to take off the jacket. The jacket had only one meaning now, and that was a very simple meaning.

If he had not been wearing the jacket, he would not have been stabbed. The knife had not been plunged in hatred of Andy. The knife hated only the purple jacket. The jacket was a stupid meaningless thing that was robbing him of his life. He wanted the jacket off his back. With an enormous <u>loathing</u>, he wanted the jacket off his back.

He lay struggling with the shiny wet material. His arms were heavy, and pain ripped fire across his body whenever he moved. But he squirmed and fought and twisted until one arm was free and then the other, and then he rolled away from the jacket and lay quite still, breathing heavily, listening to the sound of his breathing and the sound of the rain and thinking: *Rain is sweet, I'm Andy.*

She found him in the alleyway a minute past midnight. She left the dance to look for him, and when she found him she knelt beside him and said, "Andy, it's me, Laura."

He did not answer her. She backed away from him, tears springing into her eyes, and then she ran from the alley <u>hysterically</u> and did not stop running until she found the cop.

And now, standing with the cop, she looked down at him, and the cop rose and **95** said, "He's dead," and all the crying was out of her now. She stood in the rain and said nothing, looking at the dead boy on the pavement, and looking at the purple jacket that rested a foot away from his body.

The cop picked up the jacket and turned it over in his hands.

"A Royal, huh?" he said.

The rain seemed to beat more steadily now, more fiercely.

She looked at the cop and, very quietly, she said, "His name is Andy."

The cop slung the jacket over his arm. He took out his black pad, and he flipped **100** it open to a blank page.

"A Royal," he said.

Then he began writing.

approximately 3000 words

Questions for Writing and Discussion

1. Why do you think the author chose the word *Royals?* When does Andy begin to rebel against his association with it?
2. What is the meaning of the sentence "I never turkeyed out of a rumble with the Guardians" (paragraph 79)? Why is there a reference to a turkey and not another type of bird? What can you tell about Andy on the basis of this particular thought of his?
3. Three people could have helped Andy but failed to do so. Who were they? Why did they not help Andy? How does the young couple's attitude toward Andy contrast with Laura's attitude?
4. Why was Andy anxious to get the jacket off his back (paragraphs 90–92)?
5. Do you think Freddie's refusal to help Andy (paragraph 78) is a typical human response? Why or why not?

JOURNAL ENTRY

In the essay by William Lutz, you learned that language is sometimes misused in both business and government to conceal the truth. In the textbook selection, you read about the interrelatedness of thought and language. In the short story "On the Sidewalk, Bleeding," you saw that the gang's name *The Royals* was significant in developing the plot and theme; wearing the name embroidered on his purple jacket led to Andy's death.

Write a journal entry reflecting on how your *awareness* of the significance of the words we use and their impact on our lives may have been increased by these readings. Then, describe a situation in which language has played a role in shaping some important event in your life. Also, write about some specific word(s) you use or hear that impact your life in a special way.

3

From Sentence to Paragraph to the Main Idea: Steps to Eliminate Problems in Comprehension

This chapter will help you

* Understand the meaning of complicated sentences.
* Know the difference between a paragraph topic and a main idea.
* Recognize both stated and unstated (implied) main ideas in paragraphs.
* Separate major details from minor details.

Before reading, think about this question.

* What is particularly troublesome for you in recognizing and restating the main idea?

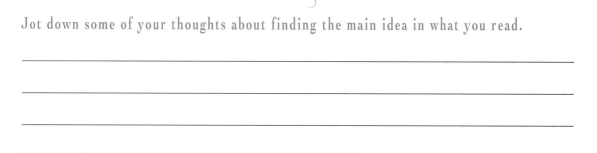

Jot down some of your thoughts about finding the main idea in what you read.

_____

_____

_____

_____

In this chapter, we will examine why particular sentences and paragraphs may cause difficulty in determining the main points in reading, and we offer suggestions to make the task simpler. Additionally, we will show you the importance of making notations by marking important points in paragraphs; ultimately, any organizational method starts with good notes. The difference in recognizing the main point of sentences, paragraphs, articles, and essays is essentially one of *degree;* the paragraph generally contains more information about an idea than a sentence, while an essay or article elaborates even further on an idea than does a paragraph.

Sentences and Their Relationships

While the basic structure of sentences usually consists of three parts—subject, verb, object—most sentences have at least one key idea that can generally be found within the subject and verb. The *subject,* usually a noun or noun phrase, identifies the main person or thing in the sentence. The *verb* or *verb phrase** indicates what the person or thing is doing, has done, or may be thinking or feeling. Additional information about the subject and verb may also be included.

> **Example:**   The <u>American economy</u>, *though weakened, still* <u>grew significantly</u> *in the past few years.*

The key idea of this sentence is the *American economy grew significantly.*

The subject, *American economy,* tells what the sentence is about. The words *though weakened* add more information about the economy.

The verb phrase, *still grew significantly,* explains what the subject is doing. The words *in the past few years* simply add more information.

In longer sentences with combined ideas, the key idea is not always obvious.

> Extensive information networks continue to grow both inside and outside business organizations and require better writing skills from a growing number of American workers.

Two key questions help determine the key idea.

1. Who or what is the sentence chiefly about? *identifies the <u>subject</u>*
2. What is/was happening to the subject? *identifies <u>the verb or verb phrase/s</u>*

---

* Also referred to as the *predicate.*

In the preceding sentence, the answer to the first question, "What is the sentence about?," is *extensive information networks*. The verb is more complex because it includes two ideas, *continues to grow* and *requires greater writing skills*. The key idea, then, is that *extensive information networks continue to grow and require better writing skills*. Longer sentences frequently have more than one main subject and more than one main verb.

What Types of Sentences May Cause Difficulty?

In many sentences, particularly short ones, the key parts (the subject and verb) express a complete thought that is easily understood. In some sentences, however, intervening information separates the key parts. When the subject and the verb are split, you must find and recall the subject while reading the additional information so you can connect it to the verb. Some common types of sentences can interfere with comprehension.

1. Sentences with long introductions.
2. Sentences that are interrupted with paired dashes.
3. Sentences composed of many smaller sentences joined together.
4. Sentences with weak pronoun referents.

Sentences with Long Introductions

Some sentences contain much introductory information in phrases or clauses, modifying the key idea, which appears later. In the following examples, the introductory phrase is underlined; the key idea is in italics.

> <u>Less than a year after announcing they had found evidence of the missing piece of matter essential to understanding the universe,</u> *scientists* this week *are expected to proclaim the discovery of the* elusive subatomic particle, the "*quark.*"
>
> Associated Press 1 Mar. 1995

> <u>If you search for an understanding of problems related to depletion of the ozone layer, or crystalline structures in rocks, or materials for superconductors, or metabolism and respiration, or the effects of medications on the body,</u> *chemistry is there.*
>
> Ralph A. Burns, Essentials of Chemistry

Sentences That Use Paired Dashes

To make longer sentences somewhat easier to read, writers often use dashes to break up the information. The sentence part enclosed with dashes *is never the key idea;* it simply provides related information. In the following example, the key idea is in italics.

> *Reports about the production of atomic fission from uranium* written by famed mathematician Albert Einstein—who regarded the development of atomic warfare as a perversion of his life's efforts—*alerted the U.S. government* to potential military uses.
>
> John Mack Faragher et al., *Out of Many*

Sentences Composed of Many Short Sentences Joined Together

Another difficulty with reading some sentences is that short sentences are joined together through clauses and connecting words. In the following sentence from a sociology textbook, the key idea is italicized.

> Currently, *a heated debate is under way* between advocates of retaining our drug laws and their opponents, who believe that criminalization has failed and encourage adoption of a policy of decriminalization combined with an intensified emphasis on education and therapy.
>
> David Popenoe, *Sociology*

The sentence includes the following ideas:

> Currently, a heated debate is under way; the debate is between advocates of retaining our drug laws and their opponents.
> Opponents believe that criminalization has failed.
> They encourage adoption of a policy of decriminalization.
> They want this policy combined with an intensified emphasis on education and therapy.

Here is another example of ideas joined together in a sentence. Try to underline the key idea.

> Other researchers have found that disapproval of the marriage by friends and family is an important indicator of instability ahead, since this disapproval represents not only a prediction by people who know the couple but also a vote of non-confidence from those who could have helped bind the couple together.
>
> David Popenoe, *Sociology*

Did you underline "Other researchers . . . of instability ahead" as the key idea? How many ideas do you think have been combined?

Paraphrasing is one of the best things to do when sentences are particularly troublesome. To paraphrase this sentence, we might say, "Researchers have found that a marriage is unstable when those who know the couple disapprove of the union."

Pronoun Substitution in Sentences

Pronouns—words that take the place of nouns, such as *he, she, it, they,* and *them*—may serve as substitutions for other words and can be confusing. In the following sentence, note that the key idea includes the pronoun *they.*

Example: More materialistic than the boomers but less so than the generation of the Reagan era, *they* see a real need for social reform but worry that the escalation of the national debt may make it impossible to implement needed changes.

David Popenoe, *Sociology*

The key idea is _____.

In this sentence the *they* actually refers to America's adolescent and college-age peer group that appeared in the previous two paragraphs of the text!

Examine the following sentence, noting the pronouns in italics.

Although the law is often slow to catch up with changing mores (customs), *it* usually does catch up with *them* in democratic societies because the legislators . . . change the laws to suit the voters' new goals and desires.

Michael G. Roskin et al., *Political Science*

Here you must determine what the pronouns stand for. Does *it* refer to mores (customs) or to the law? Does *them* refer to customs or to the law?

It refers to _____ . *Them* refers to _____ .

Careful reading reveals that *it* refers to the law while *them* refers to customs. In paraphrasing this sentence, the key idea is that *the law usually does catch up with changing customs.*

Reading Sentences That May Present Difficulty

Writers frequently combine related ideas into one sentence to clarify the key idea. To understand these sentences, you should

1. Identify the key idea.
2. Recognize how additional information relates to or modifies the meaning of the key idea.
3. Paraphrase the sentence, splitting it into several sentences if necessary.

With sentences that are particularly troubling, refer to the glossary or to a dictionary if the vocabulary is confusing.

ACTIVITY 3.1

Underline the key idea in the following sentences. Place one line under the subject (who or what the sentence is about) and two lines under the verb (what is happening to the subject). Look at the example first.

> **Example:** In a study published Tuesday in Proceedings of the National Academy of Sciences, <u>researchers</u> at Duke University <u>report</u> that the skulls of Neanderthals and of some other early higher primates show they may have had the nerve complex needed to control the subtle and varied movement of the tongue required for speech.
>
> *San Francisco Examiner* 28 Apr. 1998

1. The simple, often gruntlike puffs of air which we call words may be used by the writer with such skill that they can bring to a reader, who cannot even hear whatever tone of voice the writer would give them, a form and sense that will move him.

   Paul Engle, *Salt Crystals, Spider Webs, and Words*

2. A short, gaunt figure, with a smooth, tight, black-as-coal skin, large prominent jaws, thin, uneven lips whose sole function seemed to be the production of sneers, a broad nose with slightly flaring nostrils, small, bloodshot eyes which never cried, small, close-set ears, and a wide, prominent forehead—such were my father's features.

   Mark Mathabane, *My Father's Tribal Rule*

3. But if literature can strip other cultures of their strangeness, unveiling what we have in common, it also has the important function of preserving the cultures.

   Carlos Fuentes, interview, *San Francisco Chronicle* 14 May 1994

4. Having but limited success with the crude contraceptive techniques that were available to them, the ancients were much more likely to resort to abortion and **infanticide** in an effort to keep their population within the bounds of the existing food supply.

   Jedlicka Kephart and William M. Kephart, *The Family, Society, and the Individual*

5. Long accustomed to the assumption that each generation would be able to maintain a higher standard of living than its parents, children of the middle and working class are today facing the bleak reality that they may have to be fortunate as well as hardworking in order to do even as well as their parents did.

   David Popenoe, *Sociology*

6. The need for physical contact is so great that when monkeys were placed in a cage with two substitute "mothers"—one made of wire and the other covered by soft cloth—the monkeys spent most of their time clinging to the soft-cloth mother.

   David Popenoe, *Sociology*

---

infanticide (in fan′ tə sīd) murder of a baby

7.   The war that had begun at Pearl Harbor escalated into battles and strategic standoffs across a region of the world far larger than all of Europe, stretching from Southeast Asia to the Aleutian Islands.

John Mack Faragher, *Out of Many*

8.   One of the largest studies of air quality and health ever conducted shows that fine particles emitted by automobile engines, power plants and other sources can increase the risk of death 15 percent in the cities with the dirtiest air compared with the cleanest cities.

New York Times

⁀ Punctuation: An Aid to Understanding Sentences

Punctuation can be a guide to sentence comprehension. To demonstrate how important punctuation is, try to read the following paragraph, from which all punctuation has been deleted.

> Marriage both illustrates and reinforces the importance of thinking of others for as long as there has been human society men and women have recognized their need to mate to establish a lifelong bond that provides the essence of the support that each human being needs as he/she struggles to face the challenges of life throughout history it has been this union in which each partner is concerned with the good of the other which above all other forces has made it possible for men and women to experience their greatest joy it is this built in support system that enables them to be the best that that they can be sharing life's best and worst times increasing their ability to find meaning in life a sunset watched in solitude on a foreign shore only increases loneliness the same sight shared with a loved one is a special moment

Now, read the same material with punctuation and note the difference.

> Marriage both illustrates and reinforces the importance of thinking of others. For as long as there has been human society, men and women have recognized their need to mate— to establish a lifelong bond that provides the essence of the support that each human being needs as he/she struggles to face the challenges of life. Throughout history, it has been this union—in which each partner is concerned with the good of the other—which above all other forces has made it possible for men and women to experience their greatest joy. It is this built-in support system that enables them to be the best that that they can be, sharing life's best and worst times, increasing their ability to find meaning in life. A sunset watched in solitude on a foreign shore only increases loneliness; the same sight shared with a loved one is a special moment.

McFarlane, "Meaning of Marriage"

Reading these two versions of the same paragraph illustrates that an awareness of punctuation while reading makes a real difference in understanding what is being stated. In addition to marking the end of sentences and separating them from each other, punctuation also separates other parts of a sentence. It indicates relationships, showing the relative importance of the various parts.

ACTIVITY 3.2

Read the following paragraph quickly, noting how you hesitate and are unsure where meaningful phrases begin and end because the paragraph lacks punctuation.

> I was in the middle row of the formation slingshot in hand I had been grazed several times by rocks and bottles but fought on mothers called their sons home but we paid no heed amidst whistling yelling and cursing something whizzed past me barely missing my head but struck a barrel-chested thirteen-year-old boy to my left he clutched his face and shrieked the bastards theyve hurt my eye a couple of us rushed to his side someone said let go of your face and lets see he removed his bloodied hand from his face his right eye had been completely gouged out by a stone from a slingshot blood spurted out from the socket down his cheeks like giant teardrops there were no cars nearby no phones no means of getting him to the clinic he might bleed to death and he would be one-eyed for the rest of his life those thoughts numbed me then and there i decided to quit the gang permanently
>
> Mark Mathabane, *Kaffir Boy*

Now, add the correct punctuation to see how much easier it is to understand the paragraph's meaning.

What is the main idea? _____

_____

_____

_____

⤳ Distinguishing the Topic from the Main Idea

A paragraph is a group of related sentences that explains or develops a particular topic. Identifying the topic can generally help the reader understand the main idea or point of a selection. It is important, however, for readers to distinguish the topic from the main idea. The *topic* is the subject of a paragraph or passage and is most general in nature. On the other hand, the main idea makes a particular statement or emphasizes a special aspect of the topic. The topic may be stated in a word or short phrase and may often be mentioned or repeated over and over again, whereas the main idea is usually expressed as a complete thought. Some topic examples include the following:

1. Affirmative Action
2. Child Abuse
3. Global Warming
4. Surfing the Web for Sperm Donors
5. Advances in Technology
6. Terrorism in the United States
7. Sports in Schools

Notice that none of the topics is a complete idea or sentence but rather just the focus of some area, such as sports, drugs, child abuse, or terrorism. Any particular point developed from these topics could become a main idea. If you wanted to focus on the topic "sports in schools," for example, you could emphasize any of the following aspects:

1. Sports in schools create **elitist** groups among students.
2. Sports in schools build character among participants.
3. Sports in schools develop morale throughout the student body.
4. Sports in schools waste the taxpayers' money.
5. Sports in schools interfere with the learning process.

Simply asking one of the same questions that helps unlock sentence meaning—"What is it about?"—can help you determine the topic. For example, with each of the above titles to a selection, the answer to "What is it about?" would be "sports in school." That would be the topic but *not* the main idea.

Read the following beginning paragraphs from "A Historical Legend Worth Its Salt," and circle the topic each time it appears. Notice how many times the topic is repeated and explained.

Salt has been an important commodity throughout time:

"With all thine offerings thou shalt offer salt," Moses commanded of the Jews in the Book of Leviticus, and the ancient Greeks **consecrated** salt to the gods.

Jesus called his disciples "the salt of the earth," a statement commemorated during Roman Catholic baptismal ceremonies by placing a few grains of salt on the child's tongue. Those in mourning or crisis might abstain from eating salt.

Salt was once so precious in China that little cakes of salt impressed with the emperor's likeness were used as money, and salt from Ethiopia's Plains of Danakil is still

---

elitist (a lēt′ ist) a person who considers himself or herself part of the best group
consecrated (′kän-sə krāt id) dedicated to a sacred purpose

used as money by the nomads who cut salt bricks for trade. Roman soldiers were some-times paid in salt, bringing us our word "salary," which comes from "sal," the Latin word for salt.

John Evans and Lynette Evans, "A Historical Legend Worth Its Salt," San Francisco Examiner

You should have circled the word *salt* at least a dozen times. While most authors do not repeat their topic this excessively, they do use words to help the reader focus on the topic.

How Supporting Details Help Reveal the Topic

Many of the passage's specific supporting details should also help you form an impression that will reveal the topic. The support can take the form of examples, reasons, statistics, explanation, or simply relevant information. To see how this works, study the following example of a topic, its main idea, and specific support.

Topic: Development of English words

Main idea: Foreign languages are constantly acquiring English words and reworking them into their own language systems.

Support: A. The Germans, for example, have words such as *Power stimmung,* meaning "great mood," and *relaxter,* meaning "more relaxed than their neighbors."

B. The Japanese have imported the term *word processor* and changed it to *wa-pro,* adding another meaning later, "worst proportions," to describe a person with an unflattering figure.

C. In the Philippines, an exciting close game is said to have a **cardiac** finish.

ACTIVITY 3.3

In the space provided, label each of the three items as the topic (T), the main idea (M), or the supporting statement (S). Look at the example first.

Example: a. __T__ Business competition.

b. __S__ For example, if you decide to buy a pair of athletic shoes, you have a choice of several different stores in which to shop.

c. __M__ If profits motivate individuals to start businesses, competition moti-vates them to operate the businesses efficiently.

---

cardiac (kär′ dē ak′) of, near, or affecting the heart

From Sentence to Paragraph to the Main Idea: Steps to Eliminate Problems in Comprehension

1. a. _____ The teaching of calculus—when to do it and even why to do it—has become a major issue in mathematics, inspiring a growing reform movement.
   b _____ The necessity for calculus reform.
   c. _____ Calculus reform is considered urgent because of the course's demanding position in the early undergraduate experience of students hoping to go on to science, engineering, business, and other fields.

2. a. _____ One of the biggest shortcomings of IQ tests is how deficient they are in probing the link between intelligence and everyday activity.
   b. _____ Recent IQ tests.
   c. _____ One study showed that homemakers who performed dismally in conventional mathematics tests were quite adept at doing comparison shopping.

3. a. _____ Witnessing a hanging.
   b. _____ When I saw the prisoner step aside to avoid the puddle, I saw the mystery, the unspeakable wrongness, of cutting a life short when it is in full tide.
   c. _____ His nails would still be growing when he stood on the drop, when he was falling through the air with a tenth of a second to live.

4. a. _____ People kiss **icons,** dice, and other objects, of course, in prayer, for luck, or as part of a ritual.
   b. _____ Among cultures of the West, the number of nonsexual uses of the kiss is staggering.
   c. _____ Kissing as a learned response.

5. a. _____ Native American culture has maintained a remarkable **resiliency,** continuity, and **mystical** determination to survive despite Westerners' attempts to eradicate it.
   b. _____ Native American culture.
   c. _____ For example, of the estimated 300 different languages spoken at the time of discovery by tribes in that portion of the New World that became the United States, at least half survive and are in current use.

_____

icons (ī' kans) religious images
resiliency (ri zil' yən sē) ability to bounce or spring back
mystical (mis' ti kəl) relating to something mysterious; of a spiritual nature

ACTIVITY 3.4

Read the following paragraphs, and then, in the space provided, write the topic and the main idea and copy one supporting statement.

PASSAGE 1

Lack of self-esteem is a basic cause of failure. To be committed—indeed, to be successful at anything—you have to believe you can do it. Employers search for this as much as any other job qualification. People who lack self-esteem, although they may say all the right things, often say them with a question mark in their voices. You can get better at projecting a sense of self-esteem—even if you don't really feel it. Like an actor in a play, monitor your voice and actions to be sure you sound self-confident. Tape-record an imaginary interview and listen to yourself.

Carole Hyatt and Linda Gottlieb, *When Smart People Fail*

Topic: _____

Main idea: _____

Supporting statement: _____

PASSAGE 2

In much of the world male dominance has both existed and been reinforced by the writings of male philosophers and religious leaders. Sexist **ideology** is promoted in the sacred books of the world's three major religions, evoking supernatural justification for male supremacy. Islam's Koran states, "Men are superior to women on account of qualities in which God has given them pre-eminence." In the New Testament Saint Paul proclaims, "Let the woman learn in silence with all subjection. But I suffer not a woman to teach, nor to **usurp** authority over the man, but to be in silence . . . she shall be saved in childbearing, if they continue in faith and charity and holiness with sobriety." Finally, the morning prayer of the Orthodox Jews includes the line, "Blessed art Thou, oh Lord our God, King of the Universe, that I was not born a woman."

Vincent N. Parrillo, *Strangers to These Shores: Race and Ethnic Relations in the U.S.*

Topic: _____

Main idea: _____

Supporting statement: _____

---

ideology (ī dē al′ ə jē) way of thinking of an individual, class, etc.
usurp (yo͞o sərp′) to take or assume power or position

PASSAGE 3

Another promising approach to calculus reform is the introduction of writing as part of the mathematics curriculum. **Proponents** such as David Smith of Duke University stress the relationship between writing and reasoning. According to Smith, "Failure to read and analyze instructions prevents students from getting started on a problem, and their ability to understand a solution process is related to their ability to explain in English what they have done." Robert Webber of Longwood College, for instance, requires students to write documentation of computer programs: explanations of what their programs are meant to do and how they work. He requires revision of any project that has inadequate documentation. Webber notes that about one quarter of the students receive a lower letter grade because of their writing. He tells them that "If they don't write good documentation as professionals, they'll lose more than just a letter grade."

Barry A. Cipra, "Calculus: Crisis Looms in Mathematics' Future"

Topic: _____

Main idea: _____

Supporting statement: _____

PASSAGE 4

Despite the **universality** of parenthood, many mothers and fathers experience problems in these seemingly natural roles. Many of the difficulties stem from our unrealistic and one-sided expectations of parenting roles. To begin with, unlike other jobs, parenthood has no margin for error. Just as students accept the fact that some professors are better than others, most of us accept occasional mistakes from lawyers, ministers, social workers, and other professionals. Not every case can be won, not every parishioner will accept religious teachings, and not every child who is mistreated will be detected and moved to a safe environment. Parents, however, are expected to succeed with every child. Furthermore, because families today typically are smaller, parents feel especially guilty if each child does not turn out "as expected."

Nijole V. Benokraitis, *Marriages and Families*

Topic: _____

Main idea: _____

Supporting statement: _____

---

proponents (prō pō′ nənts) people who support a cause
universality (yo͞o nə vər′ sa lə tē) present or occurring everywhere

PASSAGE 5

The Internet emerged from a government-sponsored project to promote the inter-change of scientific information. This spirit of sharing continues as the overriding theme over the Internet. For example, aspiring writers having difficulty getting read or pub-lished can make their writing available to thousands of readers, including agents and publishers, in a matter of minutes. Unknown musicians also use the Internet to gain recognition. *Surfers* on the Internet (Internet users) desiring to read a story or listen to a song, download the text or a digitized version of a song (like those on an audio CD) to their personal computer, then read it or play it through their personal computer. Downloading is simply transmitting information from a remote computer (in this case, an Internet-based computer) to a local computer (in most cases, a PC). Information (perhaps a story or a song) transmitted from a local computer to a remote computer is said to be *uploaded*. Some writers and musicians have not only won the acclaim of fellow surfers, but have gone on to commercial success as well.

Larry Long and Nancy Long, *Introduction to Computers and Information Systems: The Internet Edition*

Topic: _____

Main idea: _____

Supporting statement: _____

⤢ Finding the Main Idea in a Paragraph

A paragraph is a group of related sentences that develops the same general topic. All the information regarding the topic, when summarized, helps to reinforce the writer's main point, generally referred to as the *main idea*. The main idea usually indicates the author's reason or purpose for writing and the message he or she wants to share with the reader.

A paragraph may contain anywhere from five to twelve sentences, but it is also possible for one sentence to stand alone as a paragraph. Within most paragraphs, there is often one sentence that specifically states the main idea. It can appear any-where in the paragraph or can be implied, that is, suggested, rather than stated directly. The other sentences are the details or points that the author makes to sup-port, reinforce, or add interest to the main idea.

Strategies to Use in Finding the Main Idea

Several strategies can be used to find and understand the main idea, the chief ones being

1. Asking key questions about the paragraph's content.
2. Locating a general statement within the paragraph that expresses the author's message.
3. Noting how the sum of the details emphasizes a main point.

We can begin finding the main idea by making use of what we have learned about the topic, and then asking, "What important thing is being said about the topic?" or "What is happening to the topic?" Words, phrases, or ideas that are repeated are *clues* to answering this question. Underlining these clues can sometimes help you see a main idea almost immediately.

Next, ask yourself, "How much support does the writer give for this idea?" The amount of detail and support mentioned by the writer will give you a general impression of his or her overall point. Remember, the writer can use examples, reasons, and situations to help develop or support the main point.

Let's examine how these questions can be applied to finding the main idea in the following paragraph.

Excess fat puts increased strain on the heart and circulatory system in two direct ways. First, the muscles of the body must work harder to carry the extra weight; the circulatory system, in turn, must work harder to meet the increased oxygen and nutritional demands of these muscles. Second, the extra fat cells themselves require oxygen and nutrients. It has been estimated that each pound of excess fat requires an extra mile of capillaries to nourish it. Thus, the heart must work harder to pump blood through an increased number of blood vessels.

John LaPlace, *Health*

Answer the following questions in the space provided.

1. Who or what is the paragraph about? What is the topic?

    The topic is _____

2. What is stated about the topic? What is the topic's specific focus?

    The topic's specific focus is _____

    _____

The combined answers to these questions give you the author's main point: There are two ways in which excess fat adds an extra strain on the heart and circulatory system.

Although the author stated the main idea precisely in the first sentence, we have paraphrased it—changed several of the words and the word order. All the remaining sentences of this paragraph that deal with excess fat support the first sentence and answer a third key question.

3. With what specific details does the author support his point?
Copy two supporting statements.

a. _____

b. _____

Did you include "The circulatory system must work harder" and "The extra fat cells themselves require oxygen and nutrients"? To help the reader follow the flow of ideas, the writer used (1) signal words, such as *first* and *second,* and (2) repetition of words like *extra* and *fat* to connect ideas.

Locating Stated Main Idea Sentences

The position of the stated main idea sentences in paragraphs can vary. They can and often do appear anywhere in the paragraph—at the beginning, middle, or end.

First and Last Sentence Main Idea

An important clue in locating the main idea is the position of the sentence. About fifty percent of the time, the first sentence of the paragraph contains the main idea. Actually, this makes reading easier; therefore, many essay and textbook paragraphs are written this way. Study the following paragraph for an illustration of a first sentence main idea. The *topic* is circled, the *main idea* sentence is underlined, and the *supporting statements* are italicized to help you recognize all three facets of the paragraph.

> Researchers now believe that the most important influence on the (emotional health of) (children) is the quality of their relationships within their family, however that family might be structured, according to Robert Emery, a psychologist at the University of Virginia. For example, psychologists used to think that boys needed their father within the home until at least age 7 or 8. Now, they have discovered that the *physical presence of a father in the family is less important to boys than are warm and supporting adults. . . .* But the focus on relationships also means that *if divorced parents are angry and bitter, children will suffer and they will suffer more if they are exposed more to conflict through joint custody.*
>
> Gina Kolata, "Child Splitting"

Rather than state the main idea at the beginning of a paragraph, some writers conclude a paragraph with the main idea sentence to create suspense or to challenge you to reason **inductively.** A concluding sentence often emphasizes how

---

inductively (in duc′ tiv 1ē) reasoning from a particular to the general

strongly the writer feels about an idea. Thus, the author presents supporting information at the beginning of the paragraph, leading you to the main idea in the final sentence. Although you may not ordinarily read the last sentence of a paragraph first, do so now. Then, read the entire paragraph. The paragraph has been marked to point out the topic, support, and main idea.

> Our species evolved on the move. Recent research on the (effects of exercise) and the consequences of sedentary living has shown that physical activity is crucial to the proper processing of foods that we eat. In fact, most of the chronic and often life-threatening ailments that **besiege** Americans in epidemic proportions could be tempered by regular exercise. Among them are heart disease, diabetes, high blood pressure, arthritis, and **osteoporosis.** But let's face it: most people are not motivated to exercise by what it may do for them 20 years down the pike. *What gets people like me out moving every day is what exercise does for me right now, especially how it allows me to enjoy eating without gaining.* I, along with millions of Americans, have discovered that exercise is the key to permanent and painless weight control.
>
> Jane Brody, "Exercise: A New Dietary Requirement"

Restated Main Idea in First and Last Sentence

Sometimes, writers help their readers grasp the main point by restating it at the end of a paragraph even though it was stated in the beginning. Read the following paragraph and then answer the questions.

> Today *American Gothic* pervades our popular culture. Caricatures of the plain and nameless couple wish us well on anniversary cards or sell us cereal and cars on television. On dental hygiene posters the man holds a toothbrush instead of his pitchfork, urging us to brush our teeth; when the woman holds the pitchfork, she speaks for women's liberation. In political cartoons the rural couple becomes the nation's first family, posed in front of the White House rather than a tiny farmhouse. On homemade cards, husbands with wives, boyfriends with girlfriends, fathers with daughters, stand holding pitchforks, babies or drinks, against bungalows, ranch houses or churches. In short, *American Gothic* has become an infinitely variable mirror in which Americans can see themselves. It has become a kind of collective self-portrait, one which haunts and entertains us.
>
> Wanda Corn, "The Painting That Became a Symbol of a Nation's Spirit," *Smithsonian*

1. What is the topic? _____

2. What main point is made about the topic? _____

---

besiege (bē sēj′) to overwhelm; to crowd around
osteoporosis (äs′ tē ō pə′ rō′ sis) a bone disorder

Original Portrait of *American Gothic* by Grant Wood

Grant Wood *American Gothic.* Courtesy of the Art Institute of Chicago.

Modern Day Versions of the Original Art

3. What information is given in support of the main idea? _____

_____

Main Idea in the Middle

Sometimes, the writer first makes a broad statement or begins with a quotation or question, particularly when the main idea is stated in the second or third sentence, as illustrated below. Note the italicized main idea sentence.

> Was the collapse of the constitutional monarchy inevitable? If so, why? *Critics have pointed to some shortcomings in the design of the 1791 constitution that helped hasten its **demise**.* The logic of national **sovereignty** may have favored the idea of a one-house legislature, but practical experience in France and elsewhere has suggested that a **bicameral** system provides for more thorough airing of controversies and more careful legislation. Giving the king the power to delay legislation with the suspensive veto but not to reject it altogether made him the target of protests if he opposed popular proposals, but it didn't give him real authority to defend his point of view. Even so, the internal flaws of the constitution were not so obvious as to make it unworkable. Experience in a number of European countries during the nineteenth century demonstrated that constitutional monarchy could be a successful form of government, capable of evolving in the direction of fuller democracy.
>
> Jeremy Popkin, *A Short History of the French Revolution*

Also, some authors begin with a statement to help create interest and get the reader involved before making the main point. At other times, the beginning sentences may be a transition from the ideas in the previous paragraph.

As you read the following paragraphs, circle the words that are clues to the topic and underline some of the supporting details to help you find the precise main idea statement.

PASSAGE 1

[1]Not so long ago, the foods that people ate, the kind of exercise they got, the way they raised their children, and the quality of their sex lives were seen by most people as personal issues. [2]Today, to varying degrees, all these spheres of life, and many others as well, have come under medical jurisdiction. [3]That is, medical scientists have researched diet, exercise, child rearing, and sex, and have given physicians a store of knowledge on which to draw in recommending certain courses of action over others and in treating "problems" in these areas. [4]This expansion of medical jurisdiction to include problems that once were not regarded as medical has been termed the *medicalization of life*.

David Popenoe, *Sociology*

_____

demise (di ´mīz) death
sovereignty (sov´ ər ən tē) a supreme power; royal rank or authority
bicameral (bī´ kam rəl) based on two legislative chambers

Which sentence contains the main idea statement? _____

_____

PASSAGE 2

[1]"We are Mexican," my mother and father would say. . . . [2]Yet regarding my family, I see faces that do not closely resemble my own. [3]Like some other Mexican families, my family suggests Mexico's confused colonial past. [4]My father's face recalls faces I have seen in France. [5]His complexion is white—he does not tan; he does not burn. [6]My mother . . . has an olive complexion; people have frequently wondered if, perhaps, she is Italian or Portuguese. [7]My older brother would come home from high school with girl-friends who seemed to me glamorous (because they were blonde); and during those years I envied him his skin that burned red and peeled like the skin of the **gringos.** [8]My youngest sister is **exotically** pale, almost ashen. [9]She is delicately featured, Near Eastern, people have said. [10]Only my older sister has a complexion as dark as mine, though her facial features are much less harshly defined than my own. [11]To many people meeting her, she seems (they say) Polynesian.

Richard Rodriguez, Hunger of Memory: The Education of Richard Rodriguez

Which is the main idea sentence? _____

_____

What sentences support it? _____

_____

Understanding the Unstated Main Idea

In some paragraphs, especially in essay reading, you may have to supply the main idea if the author does not state it directly in any one sentence. Ideas from several sentences may have to be pieced together and summarized. This requires that you draw a conclusion based on the supporting statements that have been made. Usually, the writer gives you numerous clues that, "added together," help you form your own main idea statement. Start by identifying the topic; then, look at all the supporting details and ask: "What is the writer telling me about the topic," or "What does the writer want me to know?" In answering these questions, summarize the details of the paragraph to create your own main idea statement. Try to draw a conclusion about the main point the writer makes about his alcoholic father in the following paragraph.

_____

gringos (grē ng′ gōs) a slang term, often considered offensive, for foreigners—especially for Americans

exotically (ig zät′ ik lē) fascinating or interesting because strange or different

My father drank. He drank as a gut-punched boxer gasps for breath, as a starving dog gobbles food—compulsively, secretly, in pain and trembling. I use the past tense not because he ever quit drinking but because he quit living. That is how the story ends for my father, age sixty-four, heart bursting, body cooling, slumped and forsaken on the linoleum of my brother's trailer. The story continues for my brother, my sister, my mother, and me, and will continue as long as memory holds.

Scott Russell Sanders, "Under the Influence: Paying the Price"

In the above paragraph, there is no directly stated main idea, but the **implied** main idea is that *addictive drinking can have lifelong effects on the families of alcoholics*. Reread the last sentence to see how the main point has been suggested but not stated directly by the writer. Whenever you find a passage with no directly stated main idea, use your knowledge of finding the topic and support to form or phrase the main idea.

The following paragraph also has an implied main idea. As you read it, think about the topic and what the author is saying about it; then, write the implied main idea in the space provided.

Alexander Graham Bell thought the telephone should properly be answered by saying, "Hoy! Hoy!"—an odd term from the Middle English that became the sailor's "ahoy!" and reflected Bell's sense that those speaking on early telephones were meeting like ships on a lonely and vast electronic sea. The world has now grown electronically dense, densest of all perhaps among the Japanese, who answer the telephone with a crowded, tender, almost cuddling quick-whispered *mushi-mushi*. The Russians say *slushaiyu* (I'm listening). The hipper Russians say *allo*, Italians say *pronto* (ready). The Chinese say *wei, wei* (with a pause between the words, unlike the Japanese *mushi-mushi*).

Lance Morrow, *Time*

Main idea: _____

_____

ACTIVITY 3.5 Practice Identifying the Main Idea

Read the paragraphs that follow to identify the topic, main idea, and important supporting points. Remember that the main idea may appear at the beginning, middle, or end of a paragraph. It may be scattered throughout the passage or stated in more than one sentence. In the case of an unstated main idea, the main point must be supplied by you, the reader.

In the space provided, write the topic, main idea, and at least one supporting statement for each passage. If the main idea appears in more than one sentence, write out a main idea summary statement. If the main idea is unstated, formulate it in your own words.

---

implied (im plīd) suggested but not stated directly

PASSAGE 1

With more than 300,000 Hispanic immigrants a year pouring into Florida and the Southwest, the extensive use of Spanish has alarmed some nativists, who have spearheaded efforts to make English the official language for all public business. The largest national lobbying group, U.S. English, was co-founded by Japanese immigrant S. I. Hayakawa, a former U.S. senator from California and former president of and linguistics professor at San Francisco State University. By 1995, the group claimed 600,000 contributors, and its success prompted attacks on it as being anti-immigrant, racist, **divisive,** and dangerous. The group's goals are to eliminate or at least reduce bilingual education, to abolish multilingual ballots, and to prevent state and local expenditures on translating road signs and government documents and translating to assist non-English-speaking patients at public hospitals.

Vincent Parrillo, Strangers to These Shores

Topic: _____

Main idea: _____

Supporting statement: _____

PASSAGE 2

One reason kids might be extra-vulnerable to pesticides is that they weigh less; a little bit of poison to an adult is more to a child. Also, kids are weird eaters. A toddler might eat nothing but applesauce this week; as a result she will also swallow more of whatever pesticides remain on apples than does an adult who eats just an apple a day. Over 1 million children consume more than the "safe" adult dose of organophosphates (insecticides that work by poisoning the nervous system) daily, concluded the private Environmental Working Group in a 1998 analysis of government data. And physiologically, kids are not mini-adults. Their cells divide more (that's how they grow); during division cells are vulnerable to chemicals that trigger cancer. And children's nervous systems keep developing after birth. "Exposure to neurotoxic compounds at levels believed to be safe for adults," concluded the NRC, "could result in permanent loss of brain function if it occurred [prenatally or in early childhood]."

Sharon Begley and Mary Hager, "Pesticides and Kids' Risks," Newsweek

Topic: _____

Main idea: _____

Supporting statement: _____

---

divisive (də′ vī siv) creating disunity or discord

PASSAGE 3

Good fathering is not an issue for teenage boys who avoid making babies in the first place. That is why many pregnancy prevention efforts are now targeting boys as well as girls. Planned Parenthood and other family planning clinics that were once considered "female" facilities are now reaching out more strongly to males. The most common advice given to boys is, in a word, condoms—the most effective preventative measure they can use, next to abstinence. Communities have also put pressure on school systems to balance their sex education curricula, which tend to focus on the female side of the issues. Boys are therefore less likely to sign up for the courses. But knowing the details about making babies is not enough. Boys as well as girls need to clearly understand that becoming parents too soon is not in their best interest.

Shelley Moore, "Father and Child"

Topic: _____

Main idea: _____

Supporting statement: _____

PASSAGE 4

American men don't cry because it is considered unmasculine to do so. Only sissies cry. Crying is a "weakness" characteristic of the female, and no American male wants to be identified with anything in the least weak or feminine. Crying, in our culture, is identified with childishness, with weakness and dependence. No one likes a crybaby, and we disapprove of crying even in children, discouraging it in them as early as possible. In a land so devoted to the pursuit of happiness as ours, crying really is rather un-American. Adults must learn not to cry in situations in which it is permissible for a child to cry. Women being the "weaker" and "dependent" sex, it is only natural that they should cry in certain emotional situations. In women, crying is excusable. But in men, crying is a mark of weakness. So goes the American **credo** with regard to crying.

Ashley Montagu, "Don't Cry."

Topic: _____

Main idea: _____

Supporting statement: _____

---

credo (krē′dō) a statement of belief

PASSAGE 5

"I am about to be heartless," a columnist wrote in *Newsweek* in December of 1986. "There are people living on the streets of most American cities, turning sidewalks into dormitories. They are called the homeless, street people, vagrants, beggars, vent men, bag ladies, bums. Often they are called worse. They are America's living nightmare—tattered human bundles. They have got to go." The writer noted that it was his taxes that paid for the paving and the cleaning of the streets where some of the homeless lived. "That makes me their landlord," he wrote. "I want to evict them."

Jonathan Kozol, Rachel and Her Children: Homeless Families in America

Topic: _____

Main idea: _____

Supporting statement: _____

ACTIVITY 3.6 Practice Understanding the Main Idea

As you read the following paragraphs, make mental or written notes to help you to identify the topic, main idea, and important supporting details. Then answer the questions that follow in the space provided.

PASSAGE 1

The crowds and speed of California life were only one of the many culture shocks Deborah had experienced since fleeing Kenya and seeking refuge here. There was so much that she didn't understand, and feared she never would—inside jokes and references which evoked responses from everyone else but which only left her baffled. She had once asked where the Twilight Zone* was, and everyone had laughed. She didn't ask questions after that. Eventually she had discovered that much of the California way was derived from television, something which, in all her life, Deborah had never seen. She felt as if she had missed out on a wedge of history, as if she were some sort of Rip Van Winkle† who had slept through a revolution. So much of what she observed and overheard seemed to be connected in some way to television or derived from it—language, mannerisms, jingles, even fashion and food. But more perplexing to her was that she had found, directly alongside this deep-rooted cultural anchor to television, a sweeping denial, by those same people, of ever watching it!

Barbara Wood, Green City in the Sun

1.   Why is neither the first nor the last sentence the precise main idea statement?

_____

_____

---

* *Twilight Zone* was a TV series in which people found themselves in strange places and on other planets.

† Rip Van Winkle is the main character in a book by Washington Irving. He sleeps for several hundred years and awakens to find himself in a modern world.

2. Which supporting details help you understand the writer's implied main idea—that Deborah's previous life experiences (she is from another country) had not prepared her to adjust easily to California living?

_____

_____

PASSAGE 2

The Internet (the Net) connects more than 40,000 networks, millions of large multiuser computers, and tens of millions of users in almost every country. The Internet can be accessed by people in organizations with established links to the Internet and by individuals with PCs. Most colleges are on the Net; that is, they have an Internet account. A growing number of corporations are also becoming authorized Internet users. If you have access to a computer at work or go to college, you're probably "on the Net." If not, you can link your PC to a computer at an organization with an Internet account. As an alternative, you can subscribe to a commercial information service, such as America Online, CompuServe, or Prodigy. These and other commercial information services have one or several large computer systems that offer a wide range of information services, including up-to-the-minute news and weather, electronic shopping, e-mail, and much, much more. The services provided by information services are online; that is, once the user has established a communications link via his or her PC, the user becomes part of the information network. When online, the user interacts directly with the computers in the information network to obtain desired services. When the user terminates the link, the user goes offline.

Larry Long, *Introduction to Computers and Information Systems: The Internet Edition*

1. Summarize the main idea. _____

_____

2. What is the difference between the terms *online* and *offline?* _____

_____

PASSAGE 3

Some people take abortion very lightly and measure its discomfort in physical or economic terms. For others, however, it involves a severe emotional trauma. People who long to be parents may make the extremely difficult decision to abort the fetus and may be surprised at their own anguish. As the offspring of efficient reproducers, we can expect that abortion would go against the grain to some degree, but for some, it can produce real agony. The agony of the woman has often been mentioned, but we may neglect the emotional upset of the man. No one is very happy about it, to say the least.

"Reproduction"

1. Summarize the main idea. _____

    _____

2. List two supporting statements that reinforce your main idea statement.

    a. _____

    b. _____

PASSAGE 4

The Chinese were neither the first nor the last immigrants in America to **tote** their culture in their baggage. What set them apart—and this is true of other, more recent Asian immigrants to the United States as well—was the extent of their mutual support systems. They established their own schools taught in their own language, read their own newspapers and attended their own operas. Wherever possible they made a living working with, and selling to, one another. Groups of merchants organized **de facto** banks by putting money into a pool from which anybody in the group could borrow. They banded together in associations based on their home districts in China.

Donald Dale Jackson, "Sojourners Who Came to Stay"

1. Circle the correct letter for the topic for this paragraph.

    a. Mutual support systems of immigrants
    b. Recent Asian immigrants to the United States
    c. Chinese industries in the United States

2. Paraphrase the main idea. _____

    _____

3. List two supporting statements.

    a. _____

    b. _____

PASSAGE 5

[1]As previously mentioned, citizens watching out for each other is nothing new. [2]Back in the early 1800s, before the emergence of a police force, major cities like New York employed "citizen watches," consisting of citizens who strolled around all night and kept an eye out for fires or burglars or vandals. [3]They would sound an alarm or ring a bell to warn their sleeping neighbors of trouble. [4]Just keep in mind that there is a big difference

---

tote (tōt) to carry
de facto (de fak′ tō) existing or being so in actual fact

between being vigilant and being a vigilante. [5]Both words are based upon the root word *vigil*, taken from the Latin, meaning to be awake. [6]A vigil is also a watch kept during night hours, or a surveillance. [7]Each of us should be *vigilant* in our homes and communities, in that we should keep watch against crime and help each other avoid becoming a victim. [8]The word *vigilante* means one who is a member of a vigilance committee—an organization that takes upon itself the power of pursuing and punishing criminals. [9]We, citizens, are not and should not be in the business of dealing out punishment, but we had better be in the business of watching out for criminals and alerting the authorities of their activities.

James D. Brewer, *The Danger from Strangers*

1. What is the topic? _____

   _____

2. Two sentences in the paragraph must be combined in order to state the main idea. Write the numbers of these sentences.

   _____

   _____

3. Explain the difference between a *vigil* and a *vigilante,* according to the author.

   _____

4. Do you agree with the author that citizens should be *vigilant* but not *vigilantes?* Why, or why not?

   _____

   _____

PASSAGE 6

Black social scientists have been studying aspects of black nonverbal communication, which have been often misunderstood by people in positions of authority. Psychologist Richard Majors at the University of Wisconsin has termed a certain stance and posturing as the "cool pose," which is demonstrated by many young black men from the inner city. "While the cool pose is often misread by teachers, principals and police officers as an attitude of defiance, psychologists who have studied it say it is a way for black youths to maintain a sense of integrity and suppress rage at being blocked from usual routes to esteem and success" (Goleman, 1992).

Majors explains that while the "cool pose" is not found among the majority of black men, it is commonly seen among inner city youth as a "tactic for . . . survival to cope with such rejections as storekeepers who refuse to buzz them into a locked shop." The goal of the pose is to give the appearance of being in control. However, a storekeeper, a passerby, or a police officer may perceive this stance as threatening, so a negative dynamic enters the interaction (e.g., the officer seeing the "cool pose" feels threatened, and so becomes more authoritarian in response). This form of nonverbal communication may include certain movements and postures designed to emphasize the youth's masculinity. The pose involves a certain way of walking, standing, talking, and remaining aloof facially. It can include cultivating a certain style in appearance (e.g., an unbuckled belt and thick gold chains). The pose, writes Majors, is a way of saying, "[I'm] strong and proud, despite [my] status in American society" (Goleman, 1992).

approximately 265 words
Robert Shursta, *Multicultural Law Enforcement*

1. Copy a sentence that best expresses the main idea of the passage.

   _____

   _____

2. Explain what is meant by the "cool pose" and discuss whether you believe it is actually "cool" to be able to use such a pose.

   _____

   _____

   _____

PASSAGE 7

On June 28, 1993 Kirk Bloodsworth walked out of a Jessup, Maryland, prison a free man—after serving nine years for a murder he did not commit. Standing before media cameras, Bloodsworth sobbed for his mother, who had died before seeing him cleared. Bloodsworth had been convicted in 1984 of the rape-murder of 9-year-old Dawn Hamilton and sentenced to die. He had consistently claimed he'd never met the girl. Recently, an FBI DNA test of semen found on the girl's underwear showed that Bloodsworth could not have been the killer. Were it not for modern technology, Bloodsworth would doubtlessly have remained imprisoned.

Modern technology will change many of the practical aspects of the criminal justice system of the twenty-first century—from the way in which evidence is gathered to the development of innovative forms of sentencing. Even so, the criminal justice system of the next century will look much like the system we know today. It will rest upon constitutional **mandates** and will be responsive to court **precedent.** The system itself will remain recognizable through its backbone of subsystems: the police, courts, and corrections. Deterrence, apprehension, and reformation will continue to serve as the philosophical trilogy guiding the day-to-day operations of criminal justice agencies. New issues will arise, but most of them will be resolved within the context of the question which has guided American criminal justice since its inception: how to ensure public safety while guaranteeing justice in a free society.

Frank Schmalleger, *Criminal Justice Today*

---

mandates (man′ dāts) commands by authorities
precedent (pres′ i dint) a judicial decision that may be used as a standard in subsequent similar cases; custom

1. Will the criminal justice system change much in the twenty-first century? Support your answer.

   _____

   _____

2. What will be the guiding principles of the criminal justice system in the twenty-first century?

   _____

   _____

PASSAGE 8

The past two decades have witnessed a remarkable political **phenomenon** throughout the world. On one continent after another there has been a movement toward the expansion of democratic political rights. Authoritarian political regimes of both the left and the right have undergone internal reform or have collapsed. Dictatorships, military governments, one-party communist states, and governments based on legalized racial discrimination have fallen, to be replaced in an unprecedented manner by more nearly democratic governments. This process of political change, usually termed *democratization,* involves the expansion of the numbers of people who participate in the selection of executive leaders and legislative representatives, the orderly change in or confirmation of leadership through elections, the participation of a wider spectrum of citizens in the political processes, and a lessening of the extent of governmental control over the daily lives of citizens. The movement has also tended to involve a shift from regulated to free market economies. In some nations the process has gone further than in others, but at no time in history have so many nations around the world seen such an extension of democratic government.

Donald Kagan et al., *The Western Heritage*

1. The main idea is that the political phenomenon *democratization* has resulted in

   _____

2. Name at least two specific ways democracy has been extended in countries previously led by dictatorships or military governments.

   a. _____

   b. _____

_____

phenomenon (fi ′nom ə non) an unusual, significant or unaccountable fact; a rare fact or event

⤳ Major Details/Minor Details

How Do You Recognize the Difference?

In order to know what is important to remember when you study and to readily understand what you read, you need to identify the important *details*. *Details are those statements that are used to explain, expand, and support a writer's ideas.* However, all details are not necessarily of equal importance. For example, look at the following "to do" list:

> Keep doctor's appointment
> Wash car
> Study for quiz
> Attend final lab class
> Check with Bill about Saturday night
> Pick up dry cleaning

Which of the items are essential, and which are less important? Circle those of major importance and draw a line through the others.

Did you circle "Keep doctor's appointment," "Study for quiz," and "Attend final lab class"? Similarly, all the facts, reasons, illustrations, and examples a writer includes in a passage may relate to the main idea but may not have the same significance. They can be ranked by their level of importance. It is the reader's task to decide which details are important. The most important ones are called *major details,* and they directly and specifically explain, develop, or reinforce the main idea. *Minor details,* on the other hand, are statements that very specifically explain, develop, or reinforce the major details. In other words, a minor detail is less important than a major one. Whether a particular detail is a major one depends on

a. The main point the writer is making, and
b. Whether the detail is essential in supporting, explaining, or changing the main idea in a significant way.

The chart on the next page contrasts important differences between major and minor details. When in doubt about whether a detail is major, first determine the main idea and then ask yourself these key questions:

> *Does the detail explain, support, or prove the main idea?*
> *Does the detail add essential information or change the main idea in a major way?*

Major Details	Minor Details
Directly support or explain the main idea	Often add information to a major detail
Are essential to the basic understanding of the paragraph or selection	Are not essential in developing a main idea—they simply help hold our attention and interest

To determine if the detail is minor, ask:

Which statements are added simply to make the reading more interesting but could be easily left out?

Which statements give more information than is essential?

As you read the following paragraph, notice how the underlined major details directly explain and give concrete examples of the main idea, which has been italicized.

Much concern has been expressed about tropical deforestation, and some concrete steps have been taken. The development of agro-forestry (planting crops with trees, rather than cutting down the trees and replacing them with crops) is being fostered in many areas. In Brazil, which has by far the largest expanse of rainforest, some 46,000 square miles (119,000 km²) of reserves have been set aside, and Brazilian law requires that any development in the Amazon region leave half the land in its natural state. In 1985 a comprehensive world plan, sponsored by the World Bank, the World Resources Institute, and the United Nations Development Programme, was introduced. It proposes concrete, country-by-country strategies to combat tropical deforestation. It is an $8 billion, five-year project, dealing with everything from fuel-wood scarcity to training extension foresters. Its price tag makes its implementation unlikely.

Tom L. McKnight, *Essentials of Physical Geography*

The writer supports the main idea by giving specific examples of the concrete steps taken in Brazil to remedy the problem of tropical deforestation. The fact that it costs $8 billion or is a five-year project is not essential to learning the actual concrete steps, nor is it necessary to know the names of the three organizations that have sponsored the plan; these are *minor* points but do give interesting support to the major details. Remember that the difference between a major detail and minor one is the relative degree of its significance.

ACTIVITY 3.7

For each of the following paragraphs, determine the main idea and the major details. There may be more than one major detail.

PASSAGE 1

Sesame Street is expensive in every respect. Estimates have put the cost of producing each viewing hour anywhere from ninety-two thousand to one million dollars. No one questions that this monumental product reflects good and earnest intentions on the part of its generators and producers, Children's Television Workshop. Yet when we encourage preschoolers to watch *Sesame Street,* we are programming them to "enjoy"—and perhaps even need—overstimulation, manipulation, and neural habits that are **antagonistic** to academic learning. In my opinion, it is a serious **travesty** of the educational enterprise particularly because it has assumed the mission and garnered parents' trust.

Jane M. Healy, *Endangered Minds: Why Our Children Don't Think*

1. Circle the letter of the main idea.

   a. *Sesame Street* is worth the money it costs to produce.
   b. The programmers of *Sesame Street* have good intentions and should be praised.
   c. The writer believes programs like *Sesame Street* are antagonistic to academic learning.

2. Circle the letters of the major detail/s.

   a. Each hour of producing *Sesame Street* costs close to a million dollars.
   b. *Sesame Street* is a serious travesty of its educational endeavors.
   c. *Sesame Street* is produced by the Children's Television Workshop.

PASSAGE 2

Pleading the Fifth Amendment

The Fifth Amendment to the U.S. Constitution is one of the best known entries in the Bill of Rights. Television shows and crime novels have popularized phrases such as "pleading the Fifth," or "taking the Fifth." As these media recognize, the Fifth Amendment is a powerful ally of any criminal defendant. When the accused, generally upon the advice of counsel, decides to invoke the Fifth Amendment right against self-incrimination, the state cannot require the defendant to testify. In the past, defendants who refused to take the stand were often **denigrated** by comments the prosecution made to the jury. In 1965 the U.S. Supreme Court, in the case of *Griffin* v. *California,* ruled that the defendant's unwillingness to testify could not be interpreted as a sign of guilt. The Court reasoned that such interpretations forced the defendant to testify and effectively negated Fifth Amendment guarantees. Defendants who choose to testify, however, but who fail to adequately answer the questions put to them, may lawfully find themselves the target of a **prosecutorial** attack.

Frank Schmalleger, *Criminal Justice Today*

---

antagonistic (an tag ō ′nis tik) openly expressed opposition or hostility
travesty (trav′ is tē) a distorted or grossly inferior imitation
denigrated (den′ i grāt əd) to be belittled; defamed
prosecutorial (pros i kyōō tor′ i əl) by legal action

1. Circle the letter of the main idea.
    a. The rights of those who plead the Fifth Amendment have been upheld by the Supreme Court.
    b. Defendants who choose to testify in court can face hard questions by the prosecutors.
    c. The accused take the advice of their counsel as to whether they will testify.

2. Circle the major detail/s.
    a. TV shows and crime novels have created phrases such as "taking the Fifth" popular.
    b. The Fifth Amendment is a powerful ally of the criminal defendant.
    c. In the past, defendants who refused to testify were often criticized by the prosecutors.

PASSAGE 3

Stalin of Russia; Truman of the United States

These two men, one the veteran revolutionary who had been in power for two decades, the other an untested leader in office for barely three months, symbolized the enormous differences that now separated the wartime allies. Stalin was above all, the realist. Brutal in securing total control at home, he was more flexible in his foreign policy, bent on exploiting Russia's victory in World War II rather than aiming at world domination. Cunning and caution were the **hallmarks** of his diplomatic style. Small in stature, ungainly in build, he radiated a catlike quality as he waited behind his unassuming facade, ready to dazzle an opponent with his "Brilliant, terrifying tactical mastery." Truman, in contrast, personified traditional Wilsonian idealism. Lacking Roosevelt's **guile,** the new President placed his faith in international cooperation. Like many Americans, he believed implicitly in his country's **innate** goodness. Self-assured to the point of cockiness, he came to Potsdam clothed in the armor of self-righteousness.

Robert A. Divine, *America, Past and Present*

1. Circle the letter of the main idea.
    a. Stalin was a veteran revolutionary, whereas Truman was an untested leader in office.
    b. The two leaders symbolized the enormous difference between Russia and the United States.
    c. Truman was self-assured to the point of cockiness when he came to meet Stalin.

2. Circle the major detail/s.
    a. Stalin, brutal in securing total control at home, was bent on exploiting Russia's victory in World War II.

---

hallmarks (hôl′ marks) qualities or marks of excellence
guile (gīl) craftiness; cunning
innate (i nāt′) inborn

b. Truman placed his faith in international cooperation and believed in his country's goodness.

c. Stalin was small in stature and ungainly in build.

Jules Verne Predicted the Future in 1863 Novel

Jules Verne

An 1863 novel by science-fiction writer Jules Verne, containing prophetic descriptions of modern technology that a contemporary publisher rejected as far-fetched, has been published for the first time. In the novel, Verne predicted mass-transit trains, faxes, cars, and the electric chair.

Verne's great-grandson found the manuscript of *Paris in the 20th Century* in the family house in Toulon five years ago. It was published this week. It is believed to be the only novel by Verne—author of *Around the World in 80 Days* and *20,000 Leagues Under the Sea*—not published previously. Verne died in 1905.

Verne's publisher rejected the manuscript, writing in the margin, "My dear Verne, had you been a prophet, no one today would believe your prophecy." But the novel's hero, Michel, sees sights in the future Paris not so different from the reality today—cars running through the city, automated mass-transit trains suspended in the air, electric lights everywhere.

Money and technology are the guiding forces in Verne's bleak city, run by an all-powerful state seeking to erase the memory of classic culture.

Verne's book predicted the emergence of automobiles driven by the combustion engine, invented four years earlier. He also forecast the electric chair, which was invented in the United States in 1888, as a replacement for the guillotine.

Imagining the fax and the telephone, Verne wrote: "Photo-telegraphy allowed any writing, signature or illustration to be sent far away, and any contract to be signed at a distance of (12,400 miles) . . . Every house was wired."

San Jose Mercury News

1. Write the main idea of this short article.

_____

_____

2. Which details are major (MJ) and which are minor (MN)?

_____ a. Jules Verne's great-grandson found the manuscript five years ago.

_____ b. The manuscript was originally rejected as being too unrealistic.

_____ c. The importance of money and technology are themes in the novel.

_____ d. The electric chair has replaced the guillotine.

_____ e. The manuscript was published this week.

_____ f. Verne's book predicted the coming of the automobile with a combustion engine, the telephone, and the fax machine.

PASSAGE 5

Read the following textbook excerpt in which the main idea is italicized for each of the paragraphs. Underline the major details in each paragraph, and then answer the question that follows.

Child Care and Parental Leave

Very few U.S. families, and especially those on welfare, can afford quality child-care services (Offner, 1994). Moreover, because mothers are much more likely than fathers to take time off from work to care for their children, women workers, as a group, fall permanently behind male workers in terms of pay, benefits, and seniority. *Women who are heads of households are even worse off.* One national study found that nearly 23 percent of mothers between 21 and 29 years of age are out of the labor force because of child-care problems. Because many of these mothers lack high school diplomas, they have difficulty competing in the labor market (Cattan, 1991). And even for two employed parents, paying an average of $8540 per year per child for high-quality child care is more than most working-class or middle-class parents can afford (Gardner, 1995).

Middle-class families also have child-care problems, especially if the parents are divorced and the mother is working long hours. Recently, for example, Marcia Clark, the high-profile prosecutor in the O. J. Simpson case, filed for a divorce from her husband, Gordon Clark, before the Simpson murder trial began and has primary physical custody of their two boys, 3 and 5. The boys' father has frequent and regular visitation rights. Six months into the trial, Marcia Clark, who earns $97,000 a year (twice the salary of her computer engineer husband) and employs a housekeeper, asked the court to allot her more financial support because her 16-hour per day, 7-day workweeks had increased her child-care costs to more than $1000 a month. Her husband then petitioned for temporary custody, claiming that because he worked regular hours there was "absolutely no reason why the children shouldn't be with me instead of continually being with babysitters" (Hancock et al., 1995: 55).

The case generated angry reactions from other educated, hardworking, divorced mothers who claimed that they must often choose between a good job and living with their children. According to some mothers, judges still see "good mothers" as those who are home full time and may "punish" them if they are "career-oriented" (Holcomb, 1995). Divorced fathers, on the other hand, argue that courts often take fatherhood less seriously than motherhood by assuming that mothers are "naturally" better parents. According to a study in Massachusetts, however, when men sued for custody, they won sole or joint custody about 70 percent of the time (reported in Holcomb, 1995).

Some observers note that such battles would be unnecessary if we had high-quality day-care centers at workplaces and more reasonable work schedules for both mothers and fathers. Compared to those of other industrialized countries, *the United States record of child-care provisions has been **abysmal.*** Congresswoman Pat Schroeder of Colorado once remarked, "Under our tax laws, a businesswoman can deduct a new Persian rug for her

---

abysmal (ò biz′ mòl) immeasurably bad

office but can't deduct most of her costs for child care. The deduction for a thorough-bred horse is greater than that for children."

approximately 525 words
Nijole V. Benokraitis, *Marriages and Families*

According to the author, are middle-class working families in a better position to pay for child care than those on welfare? Why, or why not?

_____

_____

_____

ACTIVITY 3.8

Read the following paragraph and write the main idea on the line provided *before* answering the questions that follow.

The Reagan Revolution

Political change began in 1980, when Ronald Reagan rode the tide of American discontent to a narrow but decisively important victory in the presidential election. Building on a conservative critique of American policies and on issues that Jimmy Carter had placed on the national agenda, he presided over revolutionary changes in American government and policies. Reagan was a "Teflon president" who managed to take credit for successes but avoid blame for problems and rolled to a landslide reelection in 1984. The consequences of his two terms were startling. They included an altered role for government, powerful but selective economic growth, and a shift of domestic politics away from bread-and-butter issues toward moral or lifestyle concerns.

David Goldfield et al., *The American Journey*

Main idea: _____

_____

_____

_____

Which of the following details support the author's main idea? Write major (MJ) or minor (MN) in the space provided.

_____ 1. Jimmy Carter's political philosophy influenced Reagan.

_____ 2. Reagan was a "Teflon" president.

_____ 3. Political change began in 1980.

_____ 4. Reagan won a landslide victory in 1984.

_____ 5. Domestic politics moved from bread-and-butter issues to moral concerns.

⤳ A Note About the Main Idea in Reading Fiction

You may have noticed that many of the paragraphs you have read are taken from essays, articles, and textbooks—information-based reading rather than fiction. Literary fiction seldom includes topic or main idea sentences because the story or narrative usually moves in a time-order sequence. Sometimes the writing is simply broken up into large and small paragraph chunks and conversation with implied main ideas. Some paragraphs simply elaborate on what has already been presented. The following is an excerpt from a classic novel, *An American Tragedy*. In this story set in the early 1900s, Clyde, the main character, has decided to "do away" with Roberta, a former girlfriend who is pregnant and stands in the way of a new love, a new career, and a better social position. The main idea in these paragraphs is simply to evoke a general feeling, to create a mood and tone as the reader senses Clyde's desperation in carrying out his plan to drown Roberta in the lake.

The stillness of these pines lining this damp yellow road along which they were traveling; the cool and the silence; the dark shadows and purple and gray depths and nooks in them, even at high noon. If one were slipping away at night or by day, who would encounter one here? A blue-jay far in the depths somewhere uttered its metallic shriek; a field sparrow, tremulous upon some distant twig, filled the silver shadows with its perfect song. And Roberta, as this heavy, covered bus crossed rill and thin stream, and then rough wooden bridges here and there, commented on the clarity and sparkle of the water: "Isn't that wonderful in there? Do you hear the tinkling of that water, Clyde? Oh, the freshness of this air!"

And yet she was going to die so soon!

God!

But supposing now, at Big Bittern—the lodge and boathouse there—there were many people. Or that the lake, peradventure, was literally dotted with those that were there—all fishermen and all fishing here and there, each one separate and alone—no privacy or a deserted spot anywhere. And how strange he had not thought of that. This lake was probably not nearly as deserted as he had imagined, or would not be today, any more than Grass Lake had proved. And then what?

Well, flight then—flight—and let it go at that. This strain was too much—hell—he would die, thinking thoughts like these. How could he have dreamed to better his fortunes by any so wild and brutal a scheme as this anyhow—to kill and then run away—or rather to kill and pretend that he and she had drowned—while he—the real murderer—slipped away to life and happiness. What a horrible plan! And yet how else? How? Had he not come all this way to do this? And was he going to turn back now?

approximately 375 words

Theodore Dreiser, *An American Tragedy*

ACTIVITY 3.9

We have stated that literature, with its narrative writing, often consists of paragraphs without stated main ideas. Instead, the central thought is implied through the details provided by the writer.

Read the following passage that introduces the short story "The First Seven Years," and note how the details add up to the central thought the writer wishes to convey. Then answer the questions.

Feld, the shoemaker, was annoyed that his helper, Sobel, was so insensitive to his reverie that he wouldn't for a minute cease his fanatic pounding at the other bench. He gave him a look, but Sobel's bald head was bent over the last as he worked, and he didn't notice. The shoemaker shrugged and continued to peer through the partly frosted window at the nearsighted haze of falling February snow. Neither the shifting white blur outside, nor the sudden deep remembrance of the snowy Polish village where he had wasted his youth, could turn his thoughts from Max the college boy (a constant visitor in the mind since early that morning when Feld saw him trudging through the snowdrifts on his way to school), whom he so much respected because of the sacrifices he had made throughout the years—in winter or direst heat—to further his education. An old wish returned to haunt the shoemaker: that he had had a son instead of a daughter, but this blew away in the snow, for Feld, if anything, was a practical man. Yet he could not help but contrast the diligence of the boy, who was a peddler's son, with Miriam's unconcern for an education. True, she was always with a book in her hand, yet when the opportunity arose for a college education, she had said no she would rather find a job. He had begged her to go, pointing out how many fathers could not afford to send their children to college, but she said she wanted to be independent. As for education, what was it, she asked, but books, which Sobel, who diligently read the classics, would as usual advise her on. Her answer greatly grieved her father.

A figure emerged from the snow and the door opened. At the counter the man withdrew from a wet paper bag a pair of battered shoes for repair. Who he was the shoemaker for a moment had no idea, then his heart trembled as he realized, before he had thoroughly discerned the face, that Max himself was standing there, embarrassedly explaining what he wanted done to his old shoes. Though Feld listened eagerly, he couldn't hear a word, for the opportunity that had burst upon him was deafening.

He couldn't exactly recall when the thought had occurred to him, because it was clear he had more than once considered suggesting to the boy that he go out with Miriam. But he had not dared speak, for if Max said no, how would he face him again? Or suppose Miriam, who harped so often on independence, blew up in anger and shouted at him for his meddling? Still, the chance was too good to let by: all it meant was an introduction. They might long ago have become friends had they happened to meet somewhere, therefore was it not his duty—an obligation—to bring them together, nothing more, a harmless connivance to replace an accidental encounter in the subway, let's say, or a mutual friend's introduction in the street? Just let him once see and talk to her and he would for sure be interested. As for Miriam, what possible harm for a working girl in an office, who met only loudmouthed salesmen and illiterate shipping clerks, to make the acquaintance of a fine scholarly boy? Maybe he would awaken in her a desire to go to college; if not—the shoemaker's mind at last came to grips with the truth—let her marry an educated man and live a better life.

approximately 600 words

Bernard Malamud, "The First Seven Years," *The Stories of Bernard Malamud*

1. Circle the letter of the main idea.
   a. Feld is anxious about repairing Max's shoes because they are too worn.
   b. Feld is an impossible dreamer with fanciful thoughts.
   c. Feld wants his daughter to improve her chances in life.

2. Write three major details that support the main idea you have chosen.

   _____

   _____

   _____

⌒ Summary

It is necessary to make sense out of sentences and paragraphs in order to locate the main idea in extended readings. This chapter has shown that when the subject and verb of long sentences are separated, or when extensive introductory material precedes the subject and verb, the key idea may not be readily apparent. By asking key questions such as "Who or what is the sentence about?" (the *subject*) and "What is being said about the subject?" (the *verb*), you can make the meaning of that sentence become clearer.

In finding the main idea of paragraphs, it is important to distinguish the topic, which is general in nature, from the main idea, which makes a particular statement. Strategies useful in finding the paragraph main idea include (1) asking key questions about the paragraph content, (2) locating a general statement within the paragraph that expresses the author's message, and (3) noting how a summary of the details can pinpoint the main idea of a paragraph.

The main idea may be found in different places in a paragraph. It is usually found in the first sentence in most informational paragraphs. Sometimes, however, it may be found in the last sentence. Main ideas are sometimes restated and found in both the first and last sentences, where they complement each other.

When writers use introductory information in paragraphs, the main idea is usually in the second or third sentence. Last, the writer may not state a main idea directly, but may instead require you to draw a conclusion on the basis of other statements.

Major and minor details differ. Major details directly support or explain the main idea, while minor details are not essential to the main idea and simply help hold our attention and interest.

Novels and literary fiction sometimes use a different writing style, thereby limiting the use of sentence clues in finding the main idea.

Chapter 3
Vocabulary Review

A. Using the Context: Select the appropriate word from the words given below and write it in the space provided. Use the context to help determine the word's meaning.

proponents   ideology   antagonistic   besieged   inductively   usurp

As the congresswoman arrived to speak about gun control at the rally, she was

suddenly (1) _____ by an angry and extremely

(2) _____ group of citizens. These opponents of gun control

shouted that she, as a member of the government, could not

(3) _____ their *right* to have all the guns and assault weapons

they wished. Meanwhile, the (4) _____ of stricter gun control

laws were peacefully waving white flags. What a difference in

(5) _____ the two sides represented!

B. Answer *yes* or *no* to the following statements.

_____ 1. Are popular class members more likely to be members of an **elitist** group?

_____ 2. If a person is identified as being in **cardiac** arrest, is he or she going to prison?

_____ 3. Are **icons** likely to be found in churches?

_____ 4. Is **resiliency** important in running a marathon race?

_____ 5. Do the major religions employ **mystical** symbols?

Selection 4: **ESSAY**

 # Preparation for Reading

Russell Baker, who wrote "Hooked on Anger," has received many awards as both columnist and journalist, and in addition, he has written many books. He received two Pulitzer Prizes, one for a column he wrote in *The Observer* and a second one in 1982 for *Growing Up,* an autobiography of his bittersweet early years. For the past several seasons, he has replaced Alistair Cooke as the host of *Masterpiece Theater,* a PBS television program that performs English classics.

Before reading, note these boldfaced words and their meanings. The words are underlined in the text.

vile speech	hateful; disgusting
rustic America	typical of country life; uncomplicated
inevitable **vagaries** of national life	odd, erratic, or freakish happenings
scowling models	looking angry or showing strong disapproval
obdurate government	unyielding; stubborn; obstinate
pursue war **ad infinitum**	without end; limitless
habituated to crying rage	accustomed by repetition
amenable to solution	responsive; open to suggestion

Preview, then read the selection.

Hooked on Anger

Russell Baker

Russell Baker

Anger has become the national habit. You see it on the sullen faces of fashion models who have obviously been told that anger sells. It pours out of the radio all day. Washington journalism hams snarl and shout at each other on television. Generations exchange sneers on TV and printed page. Ordinary people abuse congressmen and president with shockingly personal insults. Rudeness is a justifiable way of showing you can no longer control the fury within. Vile speech, justified on the same ground, is inescapable. 1

America is angry at Washington, angry at the press, angry at immigrants, angry at television, angry at traffic, angry at people who are well off and angry at people who are poor, angry at blacks and angry at whites. 2

The old are angry at the young, the young angry at the old. Suburbs are angry at cities, cities are angry at suburbs, and rustic America is angry at both whenever urban and suburban intruders threaten the peaceful rustic sense of having escaped from God's Angry Land. 3

Enough: A complete catalog of the varieties of bile spoiling the American day would fill a library. The question is why. Why has anger become a reflexive response to the inevitable vagaries of national life?

Living perpetually at the boiling point seems to leave the country depressed and pessimistic. Study those scowling models wearing the latest clothes in the Sunday papers and magazines. Those are faces that expect only the worst. What a pity to waste such lovely new clothes on people so incapable of happiness.

The popularity of anger is doubly puzzling, not only because the American habit even in the worst of times has traditionally been mindless optimism, but also because there is relatively little nowadays for the nation to be angry about.

The country happily re-elected President Eisenhower in 1956 because it believed his campaign boast about giving it peace and prosperity. The "peace," of course, was life under the endless threat of nuclear devastation.

By contrast the country now, at last, really does enjoy peace, and if the prosperity is not so solid as it was in the 1950s, American wealth is still the world's vastest. So, with real peace and prosperity, what's to be furious about?

The explanation, I suspect, is that the country got itself addicted to anger and can't shake the habit. It was hooked long ago when there was very good reason for anger.

Massive, irritating and even scary expressions of it were vital in shaking an obdurate government, contemptuous of public opinion, ~m its determination to pursue war ad infini-
ᵻ   in Vietnam.

Massive, irritating and even scary expression of anger—from Americans both black and ᵻite—were needed for the triumph of

4   Martin Luther King and the civil rights movement.

These were monumental victories. If the 12 nation had been unwilling to get mad—to shout, "We're not going to take it anymore!"—
5   they might not have been won.

But what monumental struggle confronts us 13 now? Giving young black people a stake in America is our most pressing problem, but nobody shouts much about that. Most other problems are so unmonumental that we might think the times ripe for greatness: an era of civil-
6   ity conducive to good feeling among neighbors of all races and persuasions, a golden age of progress in learning and the arts and science.

Is this making you angry? It's easy to imag- 14 ine the cries of rage from a people habituated to crying rage: Are women not still oppressed by glass ceilings? Do black Americans no longer
7   have to suffer the disrespect of a racist world? Who dares talk of prosperity when the wealth is distributed so unfairly?

True, all true. There is far too much poverty, 15 racism remains an affliction, women still don't
8   have economic equality with men. These present economists, philosophers and statesmen with exceedingly complex problems not amenable to solution by red-hot anger.

Politically minded people concerned with 16 these issues have always known that low-grade
9   anger must be maintained, that political feet must be kept to the fire, that the squeaky wheel gets the grease, and so on. The high-intensity fury now seething through the land on these and a hundred other issues, however, doesn't seem focused on any social or economic goal.
10 It's as though the nation got mad as hell a long time ago, got good results, and now can't shake the anger habit.

approximately 800 words

Russell Baker, "Hooked on Anger," *San Jose Mercury News* 8 Feb. 1995: 7B. Reprinted by permission.

COMPREHENSION CHECK

Part I
General Comprehension Questions: Literal and Interpretive

Write the correct letter in the space provided.

_____ 1. Baker is puzzled by so many expressions of anger because

    a. of traditional mindlessness.
    b. the United States enjoys relative peace and prosperity.
    c. there is little for the nation to be angry about.
    d. both b and c.

_____ 2. Baker points out that the United States under President Eisenhower had

    a. a fear of nuclear devastation.
    b. people angry at Congress and Washington.
    c. considerable racial tension.
    d. both a and b.

_____ 3. Baker believes that anger helped bring about

    a. the end of the Vietnam War.
    b. the election of Dwight D. Eisenhower.
    c. the triumph of the civil rights movement.
    d. both a and c.

_____ 4. He believes our most pressing problem today is

    a. depression and pessimism.
    b. our economy.
    c. improving opportunity for young black people.
    d. peaceful coexistence with other nations.

_____ 5. The author is surprised that

    a. today is not a time of greatness.
    b. we do not show great civility to one another.
    c. this is not a golden age of progress.
    d. all of the above.

_____ 6. The main idea of paragraph 15 is that

    a. serious problems are not solved by anger alone.
    b. racism is still a problem.
    c. women are still held back by the glass ceiling.
    d. we need better economists, statesmen, and philosophers.

7. State the main idea of paragraph 16. _____

_____

_____

8. Indicate whether the following details are major (MJ) or minor (MN).

_____ a. Fashion models have sullen faces.

_____ b. Anger is puzzling today because there is really little to be angry about.

_____ c. The nation re-elected President Eisenhower in 1956.

_____ d. Anger, by itself, will not solve our complex problems.

_____ e. We do not seem focused on any social or economic goals.

Part II
Application Questions for Writing and Discussion

9. Do you believe talk-show hosts are responsible for much of the hostility and anger prevalent in our country? _____ Support your answer.

_____

_____

10. Which group in the United States do you feel has the most justification to feel angry today?

_____

_____

Support your answer. _____

_____

_____

_____

_____

Part III
Extend Your Vocabulary

Choose the correct word for the following sentences and write it in the space provided. You will not use all the words.

amenable   vile   vagaries   obdurate   rustic   ad infinitum

1. What a _____ speech! We were shocked to hear such language in a public place.

2. It reminded me of our farm in a nearby state—the scene was so _____.

3. We left the meeting in a happy mood because the change in plans had proved

   _____ to all parties.

4. The governor's _____ position on the budget angered the groups who had lobbied against the proposed cuts.

5. With the speaker rambling on _____, we left hurriedly, anxious to be spared any more of his repetitive remarks.

Selection 5: **TEXTBOOK**

 # Preparation for Reading

While we have seen a decrease in the total number of crimes committed in the United States, the number of terrorist groups and terrorist crimes has been escalating. Terrorist killings shock the general public and receive intense media coverage. According to sociologist John J. Macionis, citizens of the United States have been the targets of about one in four terrorist incidents worldwide. Read what challenges the American criminal justice system faces and why twenty-first century technology is increasing rather than lessening the problem.

Note the meaning of the boldfaced terms before reading. They are underlined in the text.

coerce a government	force to act or think in a given manner
buffeted by the expanding power	blown around or hit by
endemic groups	prevalent to a particular locality or people
ideological component	relating to the beliefs or opinion of a group
under the **tutelage**	being under a guardian or tutor
rabid antigovernment groups	violent; fanatical
disaffected domestic groups	no longer loyal; alienated
covert paramilitary organizations	concealed; hidden; secret

Preview, then read the selection.

Terrorism

Frank Schmalleger

terrorism A violent act or an act dangerous to human life in violation of the criminal laws of the United States or of any state to intimidate or coerce a government, the civilian population, or any segment

The American criminal justice system of the twenty-first century will be buffeted by 1 the expanding power of politically oriented endemic groups with radical agendas. Throughout the 1960s and 1970s, domestic terrorism in the United States required the expenditure of considerable criminal justice resources. The Weathermen, Students for a Democratic Society, the Symbionese Liberation Army, the Black Panthers, and other radical groups challenged the authority of federal and local governments. Bombings, kidnappings, and shootouts peppered the national scene. As overt acts of domestic terrorism declined in frequency in the 1980s international terrorism took their place. The war in Lebanon, terrorism in Israel, bombings in France, Italy, and Germany, and the many violent offshoots of the Iran-Iraq war occupied the attention of the media and of much of the rest of the world. Vigilance

thereof, in furtherance of political or social objectives. While we usually think of terrorism as involving bombings, kidnappings, and hijackings, other forms of terrorism might include attacks on the information systems of financial institutions and threats to reveal trade or industry secrets. Crimes which lack the ideological component necessary to qualify as terrorism can be described simply as murder, vandalism, blackmail, and so on.

by the FBI, CIA, and other agencies largely prevented the spread of terrorism to the United States.

After incidents such as the terrorist attacks on Rome's Leonardo da Vinci airport in 1987 and the 1988 bombing of Pan American's London–to–New York flight, Americans began to realize that international terrorism was knocking on the domestic door. Pan American flight number 103 was destroyed over Scotland by a powerful two-stage bomb as it reached its cruising altitude of 30,000 feet, killing all the 259 passengers and crew aboard. Another 11 people on the ground were killed, and many others injured as flaming debris from the airplane crashed down on the Scottish town of Lockerbie. **2**

The 1993 bombing of the World Trade Center in New York City, and the 1995 conviction of Sheik Oma Abdel-Rahman and eight other Muslim fundamentalists on charges of plotting to start a holy war and conspiring to commit assassinations and bomb the United Nations, indicate to many observers that the quietude of the last decade has ended. Senator Alfonse D'Amato (R., N.Y.), a staunch supporter of Israel and advocate of the death penalty for terrorists, and other lawmakers were apparently targeted by the same fundamentalist group for assassination. Many of those arrested in the plot were Sudanese nationals who had gained U.S. residency in the late 1980s by marrying U.S. citizens. Sudan is a well-known breeding ground for Islamic holy warriors, often trained there under the tutelage of Iranian Revolutionary Guards. Many now suspect that sleeper agents, planted by nations as diverse as Libya, Syria, North Korea, Cuba, Iran, and Iraq, have taken up residence throughout the United States and are awaiting the appropriate signal to attack. **3**

According to some terrorism experts, the bombing of the World Trade Center ushered in an era of serious domestic terrorism. Robert Kupperman, of the Center for Strategic and International Studies, says, "We're in for very deep trouble. The terrorism infrastructure operating in the United States is altogether deeper than what we've thought so far." Confirming Kupperman's observations, Siddig Ibrahim Siddig Ali, one of the eight accused terrorists said, following his arrest, "We can get you anytime." The United States has lax security according to Philip Jenkins, a counterterrorism expert. "In Europe," says Jenkins, "if you leave a bag at a railroad station, it will be blown up when you come back 30 minutes later. Here, it will be taken to lost and found." **4**

In 1994 321 terrorist attacks were reported internationally, of which 66 were anti-American. A total of 314 deaths resulted from attacks in 1994, and 663 people were wounded. **5**

The technological sophistication of state-sponsored terrorist organizations is rapidly increasing. Handguns and even larger weapons are now being manufactured out of plastic polymers and ceramics. Capable of firing Teflon-coated armor-piercing bullets, such weapons are extremely powerful and impossible to uncover with metal detectors. Evidence points to the black market availability of other sinister devices, including liquid metal embrittlement (LME). LME is a chemical which slowly weakens any metal it contacts. It could be applied easily with a Magic Marker® to fuselage components in domestic aircraft, causing delayed structural failure. **6**

Backpack-type electromagnetic pulse generators may soon be available to terrorists. Such devices could be carried into major cities, set up next to important computer installations, and activated to wipe out billions of items of financial, military, or other information now stored on magnetic media. International terrorists, along with the general public, have easy access to maps and other information which could be easily used to cripple the nation. The approximately 500 extremely high-voltage (EHV) transformers on which the nation's electronic grid depends are entirely undefended, but specified with extreme accuracy on easily available power network maps.

Equally worrisome are endemic underground survivalist groups and potentially **7** violent special interest groups with their own vision of a future America, such as David Koresh's Branch Davidians whose fiery end under federal siege in 1993 captured the nation's attention. Supremacist groups are already committing acts of terrorism. . . . A few years ago, for example, members of the Order were convicted in the machine gun slaying of Denver radio talk show host Allen Berg who they claimed was a puppet of ZOG, the "Zionist Occupational Government." Later testimony revealed that many others were targeted for murder, including Henry Kissinger, Norman Lear, David Rockefeller, and Morris Dees, director of the Southern Poverty Law Center. Other Order members have been found guilty of the murder of highway patrol troopers, while one of the group's leaders was killed in a shootout with the FBI.

Special interests gained violent notoriety with the 1993 murder of a well-known **8** Florida abortion clinic doctor, David Gunn, 47, was shot three times in the back with a .38-caliber pistol as he walked from his car to the Pensacola Women's Medical Services building. Harassment and arson have also characterized antiabortion groups. Besides antiabortionists, many other special interest groups with the potential for violence exist throughout the United States. Some are <u>rabid</u> antigovernment groups with a survivalist bent, such as those involved in the 1995 bombing of the Alfred P. Murrah federal building in Oklahoma City, which killed 168 people and wounded many more, causing millions of dollars worth of property damage.

Also in 1995 a terrorist bomber code named the Unabomber by the FBI (so **9** called because the bomber's original targets were universities and airlines) began a letter-writing campaign—sending quasi-political tracts to magazines and newspapers across the country. The Unabomber was suspected in an 18-year-long series of incidents which involved as many as 6 bombings, resulting in 3 deaths and 23 injuries. . . . In April 1996, 52-year-old Theodore Kaczynski, a Lincoln, Montana recluse was arrested and charged in the bombing. . . .

As most experts would readily agree, the American justice system of today is ill **10** prepared to deal with the threat represented by supremacist and radical groups. Intelligence gathering efforts focused on such groups have largely failed, and military-style organization and training are characteristic of a number of the groups that are known—especially those with a survivalist bent. The armaments of some domestic groups include weapons of mass destruction which the firepower and tactical mobility of law enforcement agencies could not hope to match.

Devastation in downtown Oklahoma City—the result of a massive terrorist truck bomb detonated in front of the Alfred P. Murrah federal building in 1995.

Even more frightening is the prospect of cooperation between international ter- **11** rorist organizations and <u>disaffected</u> domestic groups. Such joint activities have already occurred. In 1986, for example, around the time of the Libyan crisis which led to the American bombing of Tripoli, the FBI intercepted communications between a Chicago-based drug gang and the Libyan government. The gang, seeing the opportunity for fast profit, proposed to engage in acts of domestic terrorism for the Libyans. Gang leaders were sentenced to prison for the scheme.

Rules of Terrorism

According to criminologist Gwynn Nettler, any terrorism, domestic or international, **12** has six characteristics. They are

- *No rules.* There are no moral limitations upon the type or degree of violence which terrorists can use.

- *No innocents.* No distinctions are made between soldiers and civilians. Children can be killed as easily as adults.
- *Economy.* Kill 1, frighten 10,000.
- *Publicity.* Terrorists seek publicity, and publicity encourages terrorism.
- *Meaning.* Terrorist acts give meaning and significance to the lives of terrorists.
- *No clarity.* Beyond the immediate aim of destructive acts, the long-term goals of terrorists are likely to be poorly conceived or impossible to implement.

Controlling Terrorism

Terrorism represents a difficult challenge to all societies. The open societies of the   13
Western world, however, are potentially more vulnerable than are totalitarian regimes such as dictatorships. Democratic ideals in the West restrict police surveillance of likely terrorist groups and curtail luggage, vehicle, and airport searches. Press coverage of acts of terrorism encourage copycat activities by other fringe groups or communicate information on workable techniques. Laws designed to limit terrorist access to technology, information, and physical locations are stop-gap measures at best. The federal Terrorist Firearms Detection Act of 1988 is an example. Designed to prevent the development of plastic firearms by requiring handguns to contain at least 3.7 ounces of detectable metal, it applies only to weapons manufactured within U.S. borders.

There are no signs that international terrorism will abate anytime soon. If diplo-   14
matic and other efforts fail to keep terrorism at bay, the criminal justice system may soon find itself embroiled in an undeclared war waged on American soil. The system, whose original purpose was to resolve disputes and to keep order among the citizenry, cannot be expected to adequately counter well-planned, heavily financed, covert paramilitary operations. As long as terrorists can find safe haven in countries antagonistic to the rule of international law their activities will continue. Until all nations of the world are willing to work together to ensure the safety of people everywhere, there can be little hope that the problem of terrorism will be solved. As Nettler has observed, "[t]errorism that succeeds escalates."

approximately 1500 words

Frank Schmalleger, *Criminal Justice Today* 662–66. Copyright © Prentice Hall, 1997.

COMPREHENSION CHECK

Part I
General Comprehension Questions: Literal and Interpretive

Write the correct letter in the space provided.

_____ 1. In the twenty-first century, the power of radical groups will
    a. decrease.
    b. increase.
    c. be commonplace.
    d. none of the above.

_____ 2. Which terrorist group was not mentioned in the selection?
    a. The Weathermen.
    b. The White Patriot Party.
    c. The Black Panthers.
    d. Students for a Democratic Society.

_____ 3. International terrorism first became obvious in the United States in the
    a. 1960s.
    b. 1970s
    c. 1980s.
    d. 1990s.

_____ 4. What event ushered in an era of serious domestic terrorism?
    a. the bombing of the World Trade Center.
    b. the Branch Davidian siege.
    c. the bombing of Pan American's London–New York flight.
    d. the murder of a well-known Florida abortion clinic doctor.

_____ 5. The main idea of paragraph 6 is that
    a. Terrorists have more guns than law enforcement officers.
    b. The criminal justice system needs to make more technological advances.
    c. Technology is aiding state-sponsored terrorist groups to expand their activities.
    d. both a and b.

_____ 6. The main point in the last paragraph is that
    a. The criminal justice system's purpose is to keep order among its citizens.
    b. All nations must be willing to combat terrorism.
    c. Terrorism that succeeds escalates.
    d. The criminal justice system may soon be combating an undeclared war on American soil.

7. What is the meaning of the following sentence? "Laws designed to limit terrorist access to technology, information, and physical locations are stopgap measures at best." (para. 13)

_____

_____

8. Is the American justice system adequately prepared to deal with terrorism? Why, or why not?

_____

_____

Part II
Application Questions for Writing and Discussion

9. Should membership in terrorists groups in the United States be allowed? Why, or why not?

_____

_____

10. We mentioned at the beginning of this selection that terrorist acts are given intense media coverage. Read the excerpt that follows, taken from a letter written by the Unabomber and mailed to the *New York Times* to help you decide whether it should have been published.

> . . . freedom of the press is of very little use to the average citizen as an individual. The mass media are mostly under the control of large organizations that are integrated into the system. Anyone who has a little money can have something printed, or can distribute it on the Internet or in some such way, but what he has to say will be swamped by the vast volume of material put out by the media, hence it will have no practical effect. To make an impression on society with words is therefore almost impossible for most individuals and small groups. Take us (FC) for example. If we had never done anything violent and had submitted the present writings to a publisher, they probably would not have been accepted. If they had been accepted and published, they probably would not have attracted many readers, because it's more fun to watch the entertainment put out by the media than to read a sober essay. Even if these writings had had many readers, most of those readers would soon have forgotten what they had read as their minds were flooded by the mass of material to which the media expose them. In order to get our message before the public with some chance of making a lasting impression, we've had to kill people. . . .

(a) Should the *New York Times* have published the Unabomber's letter? Why, or why not? (b) Should the media's recognition and coverage of terrorist activities be restricted? If so, to what extent? If not, why not?

_____

_____

Part III
Extend Your Vocabulary

Use the context of the selection to define the following words.

1.   vigilance (para. 1) _____

2.   terrorism (see inset on pp. 152–53) _____

3.   armaments (para. 10) _____

4.   totalitarian (para. 13) _____

5.   antagonistic (para. 14) _____

Selection 6: **LITERATURE**

 # Preparation for Reading

One reason we enjoy literature is that we meet characters who, though imaginary, seem real. In the short story "El Patrón" that follows, the character development relates to generational differences between parents and children. "El Patrón" is from a collection of short stories, *Imagining America,* that reflects the diversity in American life.

The author of the story is a descendant of families who founded Albuquerque, New Mexico. He has been published in *Cuentos Chicanos* and has published a trilogy of New Mexican novels: *Memories of the Alhambra, Not by the Sword,* and *Inheritance of Strangers.*

Note the meaning of the boldfaced words before reading. They are underlined in the text.

talking **banalities**	of little interest; commonplace
belligerently received	in an aggressively hostile manner
impassioned call	filled with passion
perverse gourmet	away from what is right or good
summit meeting	the highest point
an **inanimate** warning	without spirit

El Patrón

Nash Candelaria

My father-in-law's hierarchy is, in descending order: Dios, El Papa, y el patrón. It is   1
to these that mere mortals bow, as in turn el patrón bows to El Papa, and El Papa bows to Dios.

God and the Pope are understandable enough. It's this el patrón, the boss, who causes most of our trouble. Whether it's the one who gives you work and for it pay, the lifeblood of hardworking little people, or others: our parents (fathers affectionately known as "jefe," mothers known merely as "Mamá"), military commanders ("el capitán"), or any of the big shots in the government ("el alcalde," "el gobernador," "el presidente," and never forget "la policia"). It was about some such el patrón trouble that Señor Martínez boarded the bus in San Diego and headed north toward L.A.—and us.

Since I was lecturing to a midafternoon summer school class at Southwestern U, my wife Lola picked up her father at the station. When I arrived home, they were sitting politely in the living room talking <u>banalities</u>: "Yes, it does look like rain. But if it doesn't rain, it might be sunny. If only the clouds would blow away."

Lola had that dangerous look on her face that made me start talking too fast and too long in hope of shifting her focus. It never worked. She'd sit there with a face like a brown-skinned kewpie doll whose expression was slowly turning into that of an angry maniac. When she could no longer stand it, she'd give her father a blast: "You never talk to me about anything important, you macho, chauvinist jumping bean!" Then it would escalate to nastiness from there.

But tonight it didn't get that far. As I entered, Señor Martínez rose, dressed in   5 his one suit as for a wedding or a funeral, and politely shook my hand. Without so much as a glance at Lola he said, "Why don't you go to the kitchen with the other women."

"There are no other women," Lola said coldly. She stood and <u>belligerently</u> received my kiss on the check before leaving.

Señor Martínez was oblivious to her reaction, sensing only the absence of "woman," at which he visibly relaxed.

"Rosca," he said, referring to me as he always did by my last name. "Tito is in trouble with the law."

His face struggled between anger and sadness, tinged with a crosscurrent of confusion. Tito was his pride and joy. His only son after four daughters. A twilight gift born to his wife at a time when he despaired of ever having a son, when their youngest daughter Lola was already ten years old and their oldest daughter twenty.

"He just finished his examinations at the state university. He was working this   10 summer to save money for his second year when this terrible thing happened."

I could not in my wildest fantasies imagine young Vicente getting into trouble. He impressed me as a bright, polite young man who would inspire pride in any father. Even when he and old Vicente had quarreled about Tito going to college instead of working full time, the old man had grudgingly come around to seeing the wisdom of it. But now. The law! I was stunned.

"Where is he?" I asked, imagining the nineteen-year-old in some filthy cell in the San Diego jail.

"I don't know." Then he looked over his shoulder toward the kitchen as if to be certain no one was eavesdropping. "I think he went underground."

Underground! I had visions of drug crazed revolutionary zealots. Bombs exploding in Federal Buildings. God knows what kind of madness.

"They're probably after him," he went on. Then he paused and stared at me as   15 if trying to understand. "Tito always looked up to you and Lola. Of all the family it would be you he would try to contact. I want you to help me." Not help Tito, I thought, but help *me*.

I went to the cabinet and poured from the bottle that I keep for emergencies. I took a swallow to give me courage to ask the question. "What . . . did . . . he do?"

Señor Martínez stared limply at the glass in his hand. "You know," he said, "my father fought with Pancho Villa."

Jesus! I thought. If everyone who told me his father had fought with Pancho Villa was telling the truth, that army would have been big enough to conquer the world. Besides—what did this have to do with Tito?

"When my turn came," he continued. "I enlisted in the Marines at Camp Pendleton. Fought los japoneses in the Pacific." Finally he took a sip of his drink and sat stiffly as if at attention. "The men in our family have never shirked their duty!" He barked like the Marine corporal he had once been.

It slowly dawned on me what this was all about. It had been *the* topic during sum-   **20**
mer school at Southwestern U. Registration for the draft. "No blood for mideast oil!" the picket signs around the campus post office had shouted. "Boycott the Exxon army!"

"I should never have let him go to college," Señor Martínez said. "That's where he gets such crazy radical ideas. From those rich college boys whose parents can buy them out of all kinds of trouble."

"So he didn't register," I said.

"The FBI is probably after him right now. It's a Federal crime, you know. And the Canadians don't want draft dodgers either."

He took a deep swallow, polishing off the rest of his drink, and put the empty glass on the coffee table. There, his gesture seemed to say, now you know the worst.

Calmer now, he went on to tell me more. About the American Civil War: a   **25**
greater percentage of Spanish-speaking men of New Mexico had joined the Union Army than the men from any other group in any other state. About the Rough Riders, including young Mexican-Americans, born on horseback, riding roughest of all over the Spanish in Cuba. About the War-to-End-All-Wars, where tough, skinny, brown-faced doughboys from farms in Texas, New Mexico, Arizona, Colorado, and California gave their all "Over There." About World War II, from the New Mexico National Guard captured at Bataan to the tough little Marines whom he was proud to fight alongside; man for man there were more decorations for bravery among Mexican-Americans than among any other group. Then Korea, where his younger brother toughed it out in the infantry. Finally Vietnam, where kids like his nephew, Pablo, got it in some silent, dark jungle trying to save a small country from the Communists.

By now he had lost his calm. There were tears in his eyes, partly from the pride he felt in this tradition of valor. But partly for something else, I thought. I could almost hear his son's reply to his <u>impassioned</u> call to duty: "Yes, Papá. So we could come back, if we survive, to our jobs as busboys and ditch diggers; that's why I have to go to college. I don't want to go to the Middle East and fight and die for some oil company when you can't even afford to own a car. If the Russians invaded our country, I would defend it. If a robber broke into our house, I would fight him. If someone attacked you, I would save you. But this? No, Papá."

But now Tito was gone. God knows where. None of his three sisters in San Diego had seen him. Nor any of his friends in the neighborhood or school or work.

I could hear preparations for dinner from the kitchen. Señor Martínez and I had another traguito while Lolita and Junior ate their dinner early, the sounds of their childish voices piercing through the banging of pots and pans.

When Lola called me Emiliano instead of by my nickname, Pata, I knew we were in for a lousy meal. Everything her father disliked must have been served. It had taken a <u>perverse</u> gourmet expending a tremendous amount of energy to fix such rotten food. There was that nothing white bread that presses together into a doughy flat mess instead of the tortillas Papá thrived on. There was a funny little salad with chopped garbage in it covered by a blob of imitation goo. There was no meat. *No meat!* Just all those sliced vegetables in a big bowl. Not ordinary vegetables like beans and potatoes and carrots, but funny, wiggly long things like wild grass—or worms. And quivering cubes of what must have been whale blubber. But enough. You get the idea.

Halfway through the meal, as Señor Martínez shuffled the food around on his   30 plate like one of our kids resisting what was good for them, the doorbell rang.

"You'd better get that, Emiliano," Lola said, daring me to refuse by her tone of voice and dagger-throwing glance.

Who needs a fight? In a sense I was lucky because I could leave the table and that pot of mess-age. When I opened the door, a scraggly young man beamed at me. "I hitchhiked from San Diego," Tito said.

Before I could move onto the steps and close the door behind me, he stumbled past into the house. Tired as he was, he reacted instantly to seeing his father at the table. "You!" he shouted, then turned and bolted out the door.

Even tired he could run faster than me, so I hopped into the car and drove after him while Lola and Señor Martínez stood on the steps shouting words I couldn't hear.

Two blocks later Tito climbed into the car when I bribed him with a promise of   35 dinner at McDonald's. While his mouth was full I tried to talk some sense into him, but to no avail. He was just as stubborn as his father and sister. Finally, I drove him to the International House on campus where the housing manager, who owed me a favor, found him an empty bed.

"You should have made him come back with you," Lola nagged at me that night.

"He doesn't want to be under the same roof with his father." From her thoughtful silence I knew that she understood and felt the same way. When I explained to her what it was all about—her father had said nothing to her—it looked for a moment as if she would get out of bed, stomp to the guest room, and heave Señor Martínez out into the street.

The next day was an endless two-way shuttle between our house and the I House. First me. Then Lola. If Señor Martínez had had a car and could drive, he would have followed each of us.

Our shuttle diplomacy finally wore them down. At last there were cracks in father's and son's immovable positions.

"Yes. Yes. I love my son."   40

"I love my father."

"I know. I know. Adults should be able to sit down and talk about their differences, no matter how wrong he is."

"Maybe tomorrow. Give me a break. But definitely not at mealtime. I can't eat while my stomach is churning."

The difficulty for me, as always, was in keeping my opinions to myself. Lola didn't have that problem. After all, they were her brother and father, so she felt free to say whatever she pleased.

"The plan is to get them to talk," I said to her. "If they can talk, they can reach some kind of understanding."   45

"Papá has to be set straight," she said. "As usual, he's wrong, but he always insists it's someone else who messed things up."

"He doesn't want Tito to go to jail."

"That's Tito's choice!" Of course she was right; they were both right.

The <u>summit</u> meeting was set for the next afternoon. Since I had only one late morning lecture, I would pick up Tito, feed him a Big Mac or two, then bring him to the house. Lola would fix Señor Martínez some nice tortillas and chili, making up for that abominable dinner of the night before last. Well fed, with two chaperones mediating, we thought they could work something out.

When Tito and I walked into the house, hope started to tremble and develop goose bumps. It was deathly silent and formal. Lola had that dangerous look on her face again. The macho, chauvinist jumping bean sat stiffly in his suit that looked like it had just been pressed—all shiny and sharply creased, unapproachable and potentially cutting, an <u>inanimate</u> warning of what lay behind Señor Martínez's stone face.   50

Tito and I sat across from the sofa and faced them. Or rather I faced them. Both Tito and Señor Martínez were looking off at an angle from each other, not daring to touch glances. I smiled, but no one acknowledged it so I gave it up. Then Lola broke the silence.

"What this needs is a woman's point-of-view," she began.

That's all Señor Martínez needed. The blast his eyes shot at her left her open-mouthed and silent as he interrupted. "I don't want you to go to jail!" He was looking at Lola, but he meant Tito.

Tito's response was barely audible, and I detected a trembling in his voice. "You'd rather I got killed on some Arabian desert."

The stone face cracked. For a moment it looked as if Señor Martínez would burst into tears. He turned his puzzled face from Lola toward his son. "No," he said. "Is that what you think?" Then, when Tito did not answer, he said, "You're my only son. Damn it! Sons are supposed to obey their fathers!"   55

"El patrón, El Papa, and Dios," Tito said with a trace of bitterness.

But Lola could be denied no longer. "Papá, how old were you when you left Mexico for the U.S.?" She didn't expect an answer, so didn't give him time to reply. "Sixteen, wasn't it? And what did your father say?"

Thank God that smart-ass smile of hers was turned away from her father. She knew she had him, and he knew it too, but he didn't need her smirk to remind him.

He sighed. The look on his face showed that sometimes memories were best forgotten. He shook his head but did not speak. Lola had seen her father's reaction, and her voice lost its hard edge and became more sympathetic.

"He disowned you, didn't he? Grandpa disowned you. Called you a traitor to   60
your own country. A deserter when things got tough."

"I did not intend to stay in Mexico and starve," he said. He looked around at us one by one as if he had to justify himself. "He eventually came to Los Estados Unidos himself. He and Mamá died in that house in San Diego."

"What did you think when Grandpa did that to you?"

No answer was necessary. "Can't you see, Papá?" Lola pleaded.

Meanwhile Tito had been watching his father as if he had never seen him before. Only the older children had heard Papá's story of how he left Mexico.

"I don't intend to go to jail, Papá," Tito said. "I just have to take a stand along   65
with thousands of others. In the past old men started wars in which young men died in order to preserve old men's comforts. It just has to stop."

"There's never been a war without a draft. Never a draft without registration. And this one is nothing but craziness by el patrón in Washington, D.C. If enough of us protest, maybe he'll get the message."

"They almost declared it unconstitutional," I said. "They may yet."

"Because they aren't signing women," Papá said in disgust. But from the look on Lola's face, I'd pick her over him in any war.

"If they come after me, I'll register," Tito said. "But in the meantime I have to take this stand."

There. It was out. They had had their talk in spite of their disagreements.   70

"He's nineteen," Lola said. "Old enough to run his own life."

Señor Martínez was all talked out. He slumped against the back of the sofa. Even the creases in his trousers sagged. Tito looked at his sister, and his face brightened.

"Papá," Tito said. "I—I'd like to go home if you want me to."

On Papá's puzzled face I imagined I could see the words: "My father fought with Pancho Villa." But it was no longer an accusation, only a simple statement of fact. Who knows what takes more courage: to fight or not to fight?

"There's a bus at four o'clock," Señor Martínez said.   75

Later I drove them in silence to the station. Though it was awkward, it wasn't a bad silence. There are more important ways to speak than with words, and I could feel that sitting shoulder to shoulder, father and son had reached some accord.

Papá still believed in el patrón, El Papa, and Dios. What I hoped they now saw was that Tito did too. Only in his case, conscience overrode el patrón, maybe even El Papa. In times past, Popes too declared holy wars that violated conscience. For Tito, conscience was the same as Dios. And I saw, in their uneasy truce, that love overrode their differences.

I shook their hands as they boarded the bus, and watched the two similar faces, one old, one young, smile sadly at me through the window as the Greyhound pulled away.

When I got back home, Junior and Lolita were squabbling over what channel to watch on TV. I rolled my eyes in exasperation, ready to holler, but Lola spoke first.

"I'm glad Papá got straightened out. The hardest thing for parents is to let go of their children." 80

Yeah, I started to say, but she stuck her head into the den and shouted at Junior and Lolita to stop quarreling or they were going to get it.

approximately 1850 words

Nash Candelaria, "El Patrón," from *The Day the Cisco Kid Shot John Wayne* (Bilingual Press Editorial Bilingüe, Arizona State University, 1988) 23–30. Copyright © 1988 by Bilingual Press. Reprinted by permission.

Questions for Writing and Discussion

1. What can you deduce about Señor Martínez from his remark to Rosca in paragraph 16, "I want you to help me"? Remember, Señor Martínez did not mention Tito.

2. What is the main idea of paragraphs 25 and 26? Why did the author go to such great lengths with the details in paragraph 25?

3. Did Rosca, the storyteller, handle the situation between the father and son well? What would you have done?

4. How did Lola's remark to her father in paragraph 57 — "How old were you when you left Mexico?" — help to bridge the difference between father and son?

5. Have you experienced a similar difficulty with your parents when your values were in disagreement? Explain.

 *J*OURNAL *ENTRY*

The three selections at the end of this chapter emphasize the themes of anger and violence: the anger of citizens, the anger and hatred that cause people to commit violent acts of terrorism, and the anger that often erupts when there are generational differences. Do you agree with Russell Baker ("Hooked on Anger") that people today really have little to be angry about and, in actuality, there is *less* reason to be angry now than at any other time in history? What specifically angers you the most about our society today? About those close to you? How do you transcend your own anger when it surfaces? Write also about how you react to acts of terrorism and what you believe can be done to lessen the hatred that leads some people to such acts of violence.

Reading and Organizing for More Effective Study

This chapter will

 ✳ Explain the differences in the organization of essays, textbooks, and novels.

 ✳ Discuss differences in purpose in reading essays, textbooks, and novels.

 ✳ Suggest different organizational approaches for study that complement your unique learning style.

Before reading, think about these questions.

 ✳ What steps do you now take when reading an essay or studying textbook material?

 ✳ What are your study habits when you want to retain and recall information for quizzes and exams?

 ✳ What do you look for in reading a novel?

Jot down your thoughts after considering your own study habits and reading techniques.

_____

_____

At the end of Chapters 2 and 3, you read an essay, a textbook excerpt, and a literature selection. This chapter will focus on how to organize these three reading **genres** for study and learning, for questions, and for test taking.

How an Essay, a Textbook, and a Work of Literature Require Different Reading Strategies

Carefully look over the following chart before you begin to study the contents of this chapter. It outlines how essays, textbook materials, and literature selections are organized, how their purposes differ, and what study strategies to apply to each type of reading.

How to Study an Essay, a Textbook, and a Work of Literature

	Essay	Textbook	Literature
Organization	A series of literary paragraphs on a single subject; usually presents the author's viewpoint.	Uses boldfaced headings and subheadings; divides and subdivides a lot of detailed information; major and minor topics.	A narrative that depends on the plot and consists of a conflict, a climax, and a resolution.
Purpose	To see whether you agree with the author's thesis; to note whether the thesis is supported; to be aware of language that strengthens or diminishes it; to develop social awareness.	To understand and retain information so it can be used for discussion purposes and for further written evaluation, such as quizzes, tests, and exams.	For pleasure and to learn the elements of character, conflict, plot, setting, and theme; to determine how good storytellers are at their craft; to raise social consciousness.
Study Methods	Preview, and then read. Write in the margins the main idea of each important paragraph. Note how all these add up to the thesis. Find support for the thesis. Note the language,	Survey the chapter. Read and mark each section, using coded notations in the margin. Highlight only what is important. Organize and restate, using any of these methods: summary,	Ask what will happen to the characters and how they develop as you follow the plot. Look for metaphorical language, often a part of good fiction. Ask yourself if the author has a higher

(continued)

---

genres (zhan′ rəz) kinds or types

Essay	Textbook	Literature
subtle expressions. Evaluate what you read. Does the writer have a point?	answering questions, outline, note cards, a divided page, or map. Include summaries with each method. Evaluate what you read to determine its reliability and usefulness.	purpose th: entertain. V theme? What does it say about life? Evaluate and form a critical opinion of the novel.

⤳ The Essay

Differences Between the Essay and the Article

Some people use the terms *essay* and *article* **interchangeably.** An essay, however, differs somewhat from an article. An article is simply a nonfictional composition, but the essay is generally considered a **literary** composition on a single topic, usually presenting the *opinion* of the author. An essay is composed of several paragraphs that all support a central idea called the *thesis.* The traditional essay has three parts.

1. The beginning paragraphs of an essay are called its *introduction.* In the introduction, the writer states the subject or topic, tries to engage the reader's interest, and often states the thesis.

2. All the paragraphs between the beginning and ending of an essay are called the *body.* These paragraphs develop the writer's thesis with supporting details and explanations.

3. The ending paragraphs are called either the *conclusion* or *summary.* There are several ways a writer can end an essay: restate the key ideas and make a final comment; summarize the main point; give a related point so the reader can think further about the thesis; or suggest how the thesis could affect the reader's thinking or life.

Essays are often found in magazines and editorial sections of newspapers, whereas articles are usually newspaper presentations of current events. Articles are generally informational in nature, while essays are essentially opinionated

---

interchangeably (in tər chan′ jə blē) capable of changing places
literary (lit′ ər er ē) writing with permanent value and excellence of form (Do not confuse with *literal,* meaning "based on the actual words in their ordinary meaning.")

arguments on **topical** issues. Additionally, in some essays, the author may evaluate a problem and, perhaps, offer a solution. Since the writer gives his or her personal viewpoint on the topic, you must decide whether or not the viewpoint is logical, well presented, and believable.

The Thesis Statement

All the paragraphs within an essay should support a unifying thought or central viewpoint, the *thesis*. Sometimes, the thesis is suggested in the title or is stated plainly in one sentence of the essay's introductory paragraphs. However, often the thesis is not stated directly but rather is implied, that is, it is not clearly stated anywhere in the passage. In such cases, the reader has to determine the thesis from the supporting details or evidence given, noting the main idea of each paragraph. One way to do this is to jot down in the margins of the essay various points from important paragraphs to see how they develop into one major point, then mentally compose a thesis sentence that encompasses those ideas. In effect, you need to come up with your own sentence that summarizes the overall idea or point of the entire selection.

The thesis statement of an essay is similar to the main idea of a paragraph. Recall in Chapter 3, you learned that a paragraph focuses on a particular subject or topic and develops some point or main idea; in an essay, the thesis is the point or main idea of *all* the paragraphs. Whether the thesis is stated or unstated, the key to finding it is the same as with a single paragraph: identify the topic (who or what is it about?) and what the writer feels, thinks, or wants you to know about the topic (what point is the writer making?). After you have made marginal notes on the essay, tie them together to see what specific examples the author provides and ask: *What do these examples and details tell me the author is saying?* Then, decide whether you agree or disagree with the author's viewpoint. Since the essay is a *literary* composition, you must also note how the author's language strengthens or **diminishes** the thesis statement.

Identifying the Thesis and Supporting Statements in Essays

There are specific steps you can take to help you read an essay effectively. Sometimes the essay's title is simply one word, such as "Beauty," and is quite general. In other cases the title may be in the form of a phrase, such as "The Meaning of Marriage," offering clues to the topic and thesis statement. With this title, the writer may try to prove what marriage should be like. Sometimes the title is in the form of a question, such as "Anglo versus Chicano: Why?" Here, the writer may suggest *how* he or she

---

topical (tăp i kəl) current or local
diminishes (di min′ ish iz) becomes smaller or less important

feels the conflict between the Anglos (Anglo Americans) and the Chicanos (Hispanic Americans) came about and why. Thinking about the essay's title prior to reading may help you predict the thesis.

In order to identify the thesis and supporting statements in college essays, you may often need to take additional steps after considering the title, previewing, and careful reading. These steps include

1. Identifying the main ideas of important paragraphs.
2. Writing brief marginal notes for these paragraphs.
3. Examining how the notes relate to a single point.

After you have identified the author's main point, you will find it much easier to understand the supporting information.

How to Mark an Essay with Marginal Notations

The best way to achieve good comprehension of an author's ideas, particularly in an essay that may cause difficulty in your initial reading, is to read the essay a *second* time and mark or notate it to discover its message. Many students develop a coding system of their own when analyzing an essay; if you have not ever tried marking an essay, use the ten suggestions listed below. You can modify this list in any way you choose to accommodate your own personal learning style. You may not always use

---

Ten Kinds of Notations for Marking an Essay

1. Ask *questions* about the title.
2. *Circle words* if their meanings are unclear. Try to figure out each meaning through the context or look up the meaning later in the dictionary.
3. Next to sentences in which different types of *support* appear for the thesis, write **SUPPORT.**
4. Mark *examples*. Write **EX.** and number each example.
5. Mark *definitions* given by the writer. Write **DEF.**
6. Use an asterisk (*) to mark important *quotations* the writer may use.
7. Put a question mark (?) next to *confusing sentences* or *passages*. Ask about them in class.
8. Write comments if you can make *associations* or *connections* with ideas you already have; also, write your reaction if something really makes you think or surprises you.
9. Mark **THESIS** and **SUMMARY** statements, if given.
10. Draw a line where the *introduction ends* and another where the *summary or conclusion begins*. This is particularly helpful if the thesis has been implied.

all ten of the suggested markings, depending on how the writer has developed his or her essay. Marking an essay is particularly useful if the thesis has not been stated directly or if an instructor wants you to summarize its contents.

ACTIVITY 4.1   Identifying the Thesis and Supporting Statements in Essays

Preview, then read to find the author's thesis in the essay that follows, which deals with parents doing their children's homework. Then, examine how the markings help you identify the thesis. We have keyed the ten suggestions for marking by number with square brackets [ ] next to each notation.

[1] Look what up?   # You Could Look it Up—But Don't   [1] Don't—Why not?

Donna Cole

Well, it happened again today. In fact, it happened **1** three times—which made this a slow day as these things go. "It" is a fairly common occurrence, one that makes public librarians like me (go absolutely ballistic.) No, I'm not (peeved) about people ripping pages out of magazines or putting Super Bubble on chairs. I'm not complaining about last-minute photocopy hogs who justify their demands by saying they pay my salary. I'm not even griping about screaming babies or about patrons who insist upon eating their finger-lickin'-good lunches at the reference tables.

[2] Slang—get really angry
[2] Upset

[8] Ha, ha, she's joking

I'm talking about those earnest, (conscientious) **2** parents who do their kids' homework. You know, the ones who are so ambitious for their precious (progeny) [2]   that they end up (stunting) the kids' learning processes.

[2]

[2]

What's the point, (people?) Just what is your child **3** learning from your labors? And how about you—do you really want to spend your valuable time photocopying pictures of fossils or making a chart of how a bill becomes a law?

[7] Who?

[8] Author's credibility   (I've been a librarian for more than 10 years,) and **4** I've heard all of the excuses. "My son has football practice." "Brittany has a gymnastics class." "It seems like an awful lot of work for a sixth grader." (Imagine a Japanese parent saying this.) Parents who offer these exemplary explanations seem to have an [2]   (inkling) that something is not quite kosher here, but they are still doing their kids' work. Some are pretty unhappy about it, too, and often vent their wrath on

[4] Ex. #1

[7] ? Ask classmate

[2]   the (hapless) library staff. They can even become vile when the needed materials have been checked out by other students (one hopes that's who did it, anyway). Maybe they should just let their children take the F's for putting off the assignment until the last minute. Now, that would be a *real* learning experience.

[10] Introduction ends here

Then there are the ones who just do the work **5** without complaint, apparently thinking it's part of their job. Hey, it's not up to me to make judgment calls, or to hint that I tend to think kids get more out of homework when they do it themselves. I'm just an underpaid public servant. But do I ever grit my teeth in frustration when an adult comes up to me and says, "My daughter has to do a paper on . . . "

[4] Ex. #2

Many of these parents don't even have a clear **6** idea of what the assignment involves. Librarians are presented with hastily scrawled class notes, or "reading lists" that often lack basic information like the author or an accurate title. Sometimes teachers assign topics so obscure that little information exists, never bothering to check in advance to see what resources are available (but that's another story).

[4] Ex. #3   Equally annoying are the (ventriloquists)—those **7** parents who accompany their children but refuse to allow the kids to do their own talking.

[8] Metaphor learned in Chap. 2 (parent = ventriloquist, kid = puppet) I like this!

PARENT: He has to write something on a scientist.

LIBRARIAN (attempting to address the child): Can you tell me a little about your assignment? Which scientist interests you, and how much do you have to write? When is it due? Are you limited to certain kinds of sources?

PARENT: Oh, it isn't a long assignment—just four pages. You know, written out, not typed or anything. And it's supposed to be about an American scientist, maybe someone who lived a long time ago. I can't remember his name.

LIBRARIAN (still trying to talk to the child): Why don't we go over to that section . . .

PARENT (walking up the librarian's heels): And he needs at least five sources, and he's not supposed to use encyclopedias.

See what I mean? This poor kid is probably too **8** insecure to open his mouth, let alone discuss his project. Maybe someday he will venture into a library on his own, and then he might be <u>as confused</u> <u>as the 17-year-old girl</u> who complained to me that she couldn't find anything about Joseph Stalin in the encyclopedia. It turned out she was looking in the "J" volume.

[4] Ex. #4

[2]   I've seen the end results of this parental (overzealousness) at the college level, too. Students walk into a large university library, and they're overwhelmed by the vast array of resources. Academic librarians just don't have time to spoon-feed all of [2] the (baffled) freshmen who line up at the reference desk. Some of these students have no idea how to use a traditional card catalog, let alone the sophisticated computerized information tools available to them. One wonders how they ever got to college without learning to use a library. And I wonder, sadly, if igno-[2] rance and (intimidation) will lead to avoidance. Will these students turn to the library for their future information needs? Will they ever know the thrill and satisfaction of "looking it up"—and finding it?

9

[3] Support: results at college level

I recently attended a program at a professional conference that sought new ways for librarians to work with teachers. Some good ideas came out of the session. But although everyone expressed frustration (teachers even more than librarians) at parents doing school assignments for their children, nobody had any solutions to the problem.

10

[10] Body ends; summary begins

Remember the (Information Age?) It's one of the many labels slapped onto our era. Samuel Johnson must <u>have foreseen the current information culture</u> <u>when he talked about the two kinds of knowledge:</u> "We know a subject ourselves, or we know where we can find information upon it." That's as true today— even more so—as it was in 1775. Since none of us knows everything, we need to know how to find it. Teaching people—like your kids—how to do that is a librarian's job.

11

[5] DEF. used in Chap. 1
[3] Support

[6]*

[6]*

[9]

[2]   So let us do it. The information explosion continues (unabated.) There are cultural treasures and vital information and just fun reading experiences on library shelves. The need to know will never die. And the future will belong to the <u>information literate</u>.

12

[9] Solution/Summary

[8] Mentioned in Chap. 1 "Illiteracy in Info. Age"

approximately 850 words

Donna Cole is the Director of the Leeds Public Library. Donna Cole, *Newsweek* 4 Oct. 1993

What is the author's thesis? Remember that a thesis or thesis statement is the *unifying thought* or *central viewpoint*. What examples does the author present to support the thesis? Write your responses on the lines below, and then compare them with those of a classmate. Are you in agreement?

Thesis: _____

_____

_____

Support: _____

_____

_____

_____

Now compare your answers with the suggested ones at the bottom of this page.

Your answers do not have to be worded exactly like these but should include the general idea.

Thesis: Parents must encourage their youngsters to do their own homework so that "kids" learn how to learn.

Support: Maybe they should just let their children take the F's. . . . Now, that would be a *real* experience.

[parents] thinking it's part of their job.

. . . someday he will venture into a library on his own, and then he might be as confused as . . .

. . . we need to know how to find it.

The need to know will never die. And the future will belong to the information literate.

ACTIVITY 4.2 Practice Writing Marginal Notes

How well do you take notes? Test yourself by writing marginal notes on the short essay in the following activity. Using your notes, write a summary of the essay. Compare your summary with the work of a classmate, then with the original essay. Did your notes explain the thesis? Did you include sufficient support? Think about how you might improve your note-taking ability.

Reversal of Fortune: Attitude Can Reroute Adversity

Alice Steinbach

1 It was a few minutes before air time and the talk-show host was about to begin his daily radio program. He poured himself a cup of coffee and then, turning to me, said something surprising:

2 "You know, this job never gets any easier," said this erudite man who for years has presided over an extremely popular call-in show. "Every time I go on the air, I have to overcome a fear that I'll fail; that the show won't be any good."

3 He paused. "But I've found out something interesting about failing. And that is, you can build on success but you really learn only from failure."

4 A few days later, a letter arrived that seemed, in a way, to continue this line of thought. Written by a young man I know quite well, the letter concerned itself with the idea that adversity might offer, in the long run, more rewards than getting what you thought you wanted. My correspondent wrote:

5 "What I guess I'm learning from my difficult situation is a deeper sense of who I am. And what I'm capable of when it comes to handling disappointment. I think—at least I hope—I'll come out of this a stronger person."

6 Then last week, in what seemed a curious completion of the philosophy lurking beneath both these remarks, I came across this unattrib-

uted quotation in a book on mountain climbing:

   "Today is a new day; you'll get out of it just   7
what you put into it. If you have made mistakes,
even serious mistakes, you can make a new start
whenever you choose. For the thing we call failure is not the falling down but the staying
down."

   Few among us can claim the distinction of   8
not knowing the sting of falling down, of "failure": the promotion not gotten; the honor not
won; the job lost; the praise denied, we've all
known the loss of self-esteem that comes with
such moments. And because the wound of failure is a deep one, we seldom risk sharing our
feelings about such moments.

   "Success does not necessarily build charac-   9
ter—sometimes it doesn't even build self-
confidence," says a friend, one judged by the
world to be successful. "But most people I
know—including myself—can point to a disappointment or a failure that resulted in what J
would call a quantum leap of self-knowledg
and self-confidence. The confidence con
from knowing that you can get through 'fai'
and come out stronger on the other side

   Still, she admits that it is a "painful   ess 10
to go through."

   Some successful people find   they 11
become "addicted" to honors and   colades.
And when they don't get them—v   n they're
just doing well at their job—not   nsationally
well—they feel depressed.

   "It's taken me a long time   ) understand 12
that prizes and honors, while wonderful to
receive, have a short shelf life," says one successful journalist. "I have found that the sense
of achievement you get from 'winning' needs to
be constantly renewed. It's easy to feel good
about yourself when you're winning. It's not
winning that's hard. But that's when you learn
to dig deeper and do your best work. Not for
the rewards of success but for the rewards of
self-respect."

A few years back, I found myself needing to 13 dig down deep (and not for the first time in my life) to find a firmer foundation upon which to build my understanding of what success is and what failure is. And my friend was right: It is quite a painful experience to confront the loss of some trapping or another that seems bound up with success.

But eventually what emerged from the dig- 14 ging was a sense of something akin to freedom. A realization that there's a feeling of accomplishment and success that comes from mastering the pain of failure. And then getting on with the job.

Honors and accolades are wonderful. 15 Promotions are wonderful. Success—however you define it—is wonderful. But none of them, in my experience, really teaches you anything of lasting value about yourself.

Adversity, on the other hand, can be an 16 inspirational teacher.

It is written somewhere that you stand on 17 the summit for only a few moments, then the wind blows your footprints away.

Life's like that, too. 18

Harvard Business School probably doesn't 19 teach that to its MBA's. But you know what? Maybe it should.

approximately 850 words

Thesis: _____

_____

Support: _____

_____

⌒ The Textbook

Differences Between Reading the Textbook and the Essay

When reading textbooks, we are sometimes asked to evaluate the information presented. This evaluation generally differs from analyzing ideas developed in essays because textbook writers usually present *both sides* of an issue and tend to be **objective,** whereas essayists usually present their own view and are **subjective.**

Another difference is in the organization of material. The textbook chapter is usually arranged for ease of study with headings and subheadings, but essays usually omit this organizational aid. Additionally, the writing style of a textbook is generally straightforward—facts and events are presented clearly and directly. Essay writing, on the other hand, being more literary, may use **nuance** and **metaphorical** language that is not as easy to understand.

A textbook chapter, however, is much longer than most essays and contains much detailed information as well as specialized vocabulary particular to that discipline. Moreover, college textbook reading assignments are followed by quizzes, midterms, and final exams, to test whether the information has not only been understood but *retained.* So, an important part of textbook reading is the more detailed study you must do, which enables you to remember extensive amounts of information over extended periods of time.

Table of Contents

The importance of a textbook's table of contents cannot be minimized. It can quickly provide you with

An *outline* of the book's contents.

An *overview* of the book's contents and organization of major topics.

Chapter-by-chapter *headings,* breaking the chapter into smaller units, revealing the main ideas and important points of each chapter.

---

objective (əb jek′ tiv) not influenced by personal bias; impersonal
subjective (sub jek′ tiv) personal; resulting from feelings of self
nuance (n$\overline{oo}$′ äns) a slight degree of difference in meaning, color, or tone
metaphorical (met′ ə for′ ə kəl) using a figure of speech in which dissimilar things are compared, or in which a word may depart from its usual meaning, for example, "the *evening* of life"

Surveying the Entire Textbook

ACTIVITY 4.3 Surveying a Textbook

Use a textbook you are currently reading in another class, or use this textbook to answer the following questions and complete a textbook survey.

1. Think about the title to determine what it suggests about the book's contents. Think about what you already know about the subject matter. This will tell you a great deal about how you must plan for study.

   I know _____

2. Look at the table of contents to note the major divisions. Most undergraduate courses are survey courses, so authors select the areas to emphasize. The table of contents will give you a clue as to where the author is taking you.

   Areas emphasized: _____

3. Skim the preface, wherein you will find the author's philosophy—why he or she wrote the book, and what the author hopes the book can accomplish for you. If there is a section called "To the Student," read it.

   Comments: _____

4. Note how the chapters are "introduced." Is there a preview? Are objectives or quotes given? Is there a chapter outline of headings and subheadings?

   Comments: _____

5. Glance through the index, then the glossary. What kinds of terms will you be learning? Is the vocabulary difficult or easy? Does the glossary help you with key vocabulary and specialized terms, or will you frequently have to refer to the dictionary?

   Index: _____

   Glossary: _____

6. Check the appendix—what supplementary material or information is given? Often this information is extremely helpful.

   Supplementary material: _____

7. Find the answer key—if the text provides one. Where is it? At the end of the chapter or in an appendix?

   The answer key is found _____

8. Skim to see whether the author uses many graphs, charts, and tables th; need to integrate as you read. What does the inclusion of these visuals mean for your study?

   Comments: _____

9. Read a few pages of text at the beginning, in the middle, and at the end of the text. What is the author's writing style? Is it straightforward with explanations or detailed and complex?

   The style is _____

10. What other helpful study aids are provided for you? Are there summaries that restate the main points or review questions at the end of each chapter? How will you use these?

    Comments: _____

Reading and Study of the Textbook: SQ3R*

A common misconception is that reading and study are identical processes. Reading—in preparation for study—is the process we use to understand the main ideas of the textbook assignment. On the other hand, studying is the process we use to interpret, retain, and recall more detailed information, in order to answer questions, participate in class discussions, and succeed in tests or examinations.

A second misconception is the idea of how much time is needed to study a textbook. Many students underestimate what *real* study involves. *Study steps are essential* in order to transfer what you have read and learned to your long-term memory. Using a study system enables you to study "smarter" and with greater efficiency.

Is there a best reading-study system? Research has not identified any one of the following study systems as superior to any other. We do know that using any one of them is far superior to *merely reading and rereading, which is not a study system at all!*

Note the variety of study systems and what their acronyms stand for.

SQ4R: Survey, Question, Read, Recite, Review, Reflect
Survey to get an overview; raise questions as a result of the survey; read with understanding; recite by restating in some way; review the information; and reflect on what you have read.

POINT: Purpose, Overview, Interpret, Note, Test
Have a purpose for reading; get an overview; interpret what you read; take notes; test yourself.

OK5R: Overview, Key ideas, Read, Reword, Recite, Review, Reflect
Get an overview and look for key ideas; read with understanding; reword important ideas; recite as you study; review important ideas; reflect on them.

* Most study systems are based on the initial work of Francis Robinson, a psychologist who developed SQ3R: Survey, Question, Read, Recite, Review.

Reading and Study of the Textbook: A Simplified System

The study steps we suggest in this text—*survey* (or preview), *read, restate,* and *organize*—incorporate the essential features of the best study systems and are easy to use.

1. *Survey* to get an overview of the chapter and raise questions as you do.
2. *Read* to understand and select what needs to be remembered.
3. *Restate* and *organize,* then study the information to retain it.

These steps will be described in detail in the following section.

Step 1: Survey a Textbook Chapter to Focus Your Reading-Study Time

You will be able to concentrate better, and to understand and remember more, if you have a general idea of the contents of the textbook chapters. The key to efficient reading-study and to gaining the needed background information is to survey (or "preview") a chapter. *Surveying makes you think in advance* about the subject, associating what you read with the world you live in. As you survey, think of some questions you might have in order to interact with the printed information and to set your "thinking gear" in motion.

The benefits of surveying cannot be overestimated. Surveying

1. Leads to better comprehension and gives you a quick picture of the overall idea and some details.
2. Helps you determine the organization of the chapter.
3. Helps you note what parts of the material require a more careful reading.
4. Is similar to consulting a map before leaving on a trip; you develop confidence because you know where you are going.

Surveying a textbook chapter is simply an extension of previewing a smaller piece and well worth the five to fifteen minutes it takes. It enables you immediately to see the chapter as a whole and how the various parts relate to its central idea. When surveying a textbook chapter, apply the ten-step procedure that follows.

Surveying Procedure

1. Check the **OUTLINE** of the chapter in the table of contents. This gives you a quick overview of the subject matter.
2. Return to the chapter and really **THINK ABOUT THE TITLE,** turning it into a question. For example, the title "Political Behavior: The American Voter" suggests the chapter will examine the American people's voting patterns, not the behavior of politicians. Raise some additional questions about the chapter, if you can. This helps you focus on the main points immediately, setting a purpose for the reading.   *(continued)*

---

3. Look over the chapter's **OBJECTIVES.** This will give you a general idea of the key concepts.

4. Read the **INTRODUCTION,** if there is one. In addition to needed background information, it can introduce you to the most important points.

5. Read any **BOLDFACED HEADINGS** and **SUBHEADINGS** for each section you plan to study. Headings organize the information for you, outlining what is important.

6. Notice carefully the chapter's **GRAPHIC AIDS:** graphs, charts, diagrams, maps, tables, photographs, cartoons, and illustrations. These often clarify concepts of a text **concisely.***

7. Note placement of the **DEFINITION OF IMPORTANT WORDS**—at the chapter's beginning or end. Usually, there is also a **GLOSSARY** of important terms. Familiarize yourself with the meanings of the important words/terms *before* you begin your actual reading.

8. Dip into the text here and there, **SKIMMING** the chapter. *Skimming* involves quickly glancing over a chapter to determine structure, length, and format. Read some of the first and last paragraph's sentences, familiarizing yourself with the concepts the author will emphasize.

9. Read the **SUMMARY** or **CONCLUDING PARAGRAPHS;** these often restate the most important points covered in the chapter.

10. Read any **QUESTIONS** provided at the end of the chapter *before* reading the chapter, preparing you for what the author thinks is important and will stress.

An abbreviated example of steps 5 and 8 of how to survey a textbook chapter follows.

Running the Small Business in the U.S. Economy

The Importance of Small Business in the U.S. Economy

. . . 99 percent of the nation's 16 million businesses employ fewer than 100 people. . . .

_____

_____

     Economists and politicians alike extol the virtues of small businesses as generators of jobs.

_____

_____

---

concisely (kən sīs′ lē) expressing much in a few words

* Chapter 10 will give you further assistance with this important reading skill.

Popularity Types of Small Business Enterprise

. . . more common in some industries . . . more resources needed . . . the less likely to be dominated by small firms.

_____

_____

   Service Businesses   . . . because they require a relatively low level of resources, services are the largest and the fastest-growing segment of small business . . .

   Modifying your survey   Once you have completed your survey but before you begin your actual reading, ask yourself some general questions, such as

1.   How familiar am I with this subject?
2.   What is important to know?
3.   How should I divide up the sections, and how much time do I need to read a section? The chapter?
4.   Are there key terms and words I need to master?

With any survey, it is likely you will have to modify our suggested procedure to accommodate the writer's style. Not all reading assignments have headings, visual aids, summaries, or questions. Once you have completed your survey, you will be well prepared for the second step, reading to understand.

Step 2: Read to Understand and Select What Needs to Be Remembered

   The survey familiarizes you with some of the main points of the chapter, its specific purpose, and its organization. After you complete the survey, apply the following procedure to the first section, remembering to search for major concepts.

1.   Read the entire section to get an overall view, actively searching for answers to questions you read or raised before reading, based on the title and survey.
2.   Think about what is really important. Do not dwell on trivial details.
3.   Selectively mark your textbook as you read. Have a pen or pencil in hand, placing marginal symbols next to key lines. Develop a simple coding system for these marks, like some of the ones we suggested for essay notation, such as

= (main idea)	– – – (important support)	* (important)	1, 2, 3 (specific points to recall)
K (key term)	ex. (example)	? (difficult, unclear)	def (definition)

Read the entire section before underlining, highlighting, or making extensive marginal notes. After you make your original brief marginal markings, you will have a better idea as to what is important. Initially, everything may seem important, but after reading the entire section, you should realize this is untrue. Do not underline or highlight too much—you might as well not underline at all! Be selective and underline in thought units, using key words and phrases.

Try to say aloud in your own words what you understand to be the answers to questions you have posed and also what you have gained from the reading. Connect the key points that have been stressed. Remember, the most important question to keep asking is

What does the author want me to know, that is, what is important here?

Step 3: Restate and Organize the Information to Retain It

Most students wish they could read their textbook assignments once, highlight or underline while reading, and remember everything they read. Although this is not possible, following Step 3 will enable you to retain much more of what you read. When you find a logical or natural break, after you have read several pages, take time for this **critical** step. Paraphrase, or restate the ideas in your own words, so as to **heighten** your concentration. This shows what you remember, a sure way to test what you have understood and learned.

The form of organization you choose depends on your familiarity with the reading material, your learning style, and the type of textbook you are reading. You may choose to take notes, write an abbreviated outline, answer some key questions, write key notes on index cards, create a divided page, or map **salient** features.

Remember, you must restate the material in your own words and "make" the knowledge yours by paraphrasing in order to retain it. Be certain, also, that in organizing your information, you have included some of the important supporting details. Realize that instructors can compose dozens of questions from just one section of a textbook chapter. Plan additional study time for reviews of the information you have organized instead of cramming before a textbook test.

ACTIVITY 4.4

Practice Step 3, the restatement step, now with this textbook passage. Read and make marginal symbols of the information you will need to restate later. Then, go back and paraphrase in the margins or on your own paper.

---

critical (krit′ i kəl) of major importance
heighten (hīt′ ən) make stronger or greater; intensify
salient (sāl′ yənt) prominent; standing out

The Expansion and Limits of Suffrage

Westward expansion changed the nature of American politics. **Mobility** itself promoted   1
change by undermining the traditional authority structures in the older states. "Old
America seems to be breaking up and moving westward," an observer commented in
1817. Rapid westward expansion encouraged the national pride that Americans felt in
their successful republican revolution and fostered a spirit of self-reliance. As Andrew
Jackson, recruiting troops for the War of 1812, boasted, "We are the free born sons of
America; the citizens of the only republic now existing in the world; and the only people
on earth who possess rights, liberties, and property which they dare call their own."

The new western states extended the right to vote to all white males over the age of   2
twenty-one. . . . By 1820, most of the older states had followed suit. Some states liberal-
ized voting in the hopes of **dissuading** disgruntled nonvoters from moving west or
because it seemed unfair to recruit men to fight in the War of 1812 but not allow them
to vote. . . .

In Connecticut, the Democratic Republicans, appealing to young, democratically   3
minded but propertyless young men, first challenged the state's controlling Federalists
in 1802 and finally in 1817 achieved suffrage for all men who paid taxes or served in the
militia (that is, nearly everyone). In South Carolina, the rivalry was geographical, pitting
the more numerous up-country residents who supported Jefferson's Democratic
Republicans against the wealthy Federalist slave-owning political elite of the low country
who controlled the state legislature. . . . [R]edistribution of power led directly to a
demand for universal white manhood suffrage, which became law (with a 2-year residency requirement) in South Carolina in 1810. There were laggards—Rhode Island,
Virginia, and Louisiana did not liberalize their voting qualifications until later—but by
1840, more than 90 percent of adult white males in the nation could vote. . . .

The right to vote, however, was by no means universal; it was limited to adult white   4
males, and neither free black men nor women of any race could vote. Many white
Americans associated African Americans exclusively with slavery and thus ignored the
civil rights of the nation's 500,000 free African Americans. Only in five New England
states (Maine, New Hampshire, Vermont, Massachusetts, and Rhode Island) could free
black men vote before 1865. In most of the other northern states the right of free African
American men to vote was limited, first by custom and later by law. . . .

In the new western states, the civil rights of free African Americans were even more   5
restricted. The Ohio constitution of 1802 denied African Americans the rights to vote, to
hold public office, and to testify against white men in court cases. Later restrictions
barred black men from serving in the state militia and on juries. The constitutions of
other western states—Illinois, Indiana, Michigan, Iowa, Wisconsin, and, later, Oregon—
attempted to solve the "problem" of free African Americans by simply denying them
entry into the state at all.

The denial of suffrage to white women stemmed from **patriarchal** beliefs that men   6
were always heads of their households and represented the interests of all of its members.

---

suffrage (suf′ rij) the right to vote
mobility (mō bil′ ə tē) ability or readiness to move or be moved
dissuading (di swād′ ing) discouraging a course of action by persuasion or advice
patriarchal (pā′ trē är′ kŏl) characteristic of the paternal leader, or father, of a family or tribe

Women were always subordinate, therefore even wealthy single women who lived alone were denied the vote, except in New Jersey, where some women voted until 1807.

approximately 525 words

John Mack Faragher et. al. *Out of Many: A History of the American People* 276–78.
Copyright © 1997 by Prentice Hall. Reprinted by permission.

Check your notes with your instructor. Do you know the meanings of *laggard* and *suffrage?*

Laggard means _____ . *Suffrage* means _____ .

Ways to Organize and Restate Information

Besides marginal notations, there are at least *five* other ways to restate information: outlining, using cards, dividing the page, mapping, and summarizing. An example of each of these methods follows based on a chapter excerpt from a history text. Read the chapter excerpt first, noting the many points to be remembered. Then, study the sample notes for the first five paragraphs. Space has been left after each example for you to practice each method with the last two paragraphs of the chapter later on. Without good notes, the information would be difficult to remember.

Epidemics: Drugs, AIDS, Homelessness

The **scourge** of drug addiction and drug trafficking took on frightening new dimensions in the early 1980s. The arrival of crack, a cheap, smokable, and highly addictive form of cocaine, made that drug affordable to the urban poor. As crack addiction spread, the drug trade assumed alarming new proportions both domestically and internationally. Crack ruined hundreds of thousands of lives and led to a dramatic increase in crime rates. Studies showed that over half the men arrested in the nation's largest cities tested positive for cocaine. The crack trade spawned a new generation of young drug dealers who were willing to risk jail and death for enormous profits. In city after city, drug wars over turf took the lives of dealers and innocents. . . .

1   = Drug addiction & traffic greatly increased early 1980s

– – –Crack cocaine, very addictive, now available to working poor U.S. & Intl.

– – –Ruined thousands of lives; higher crime rates; 50% males arrested used crack cocaine

– – –Young dealers in urban areas felt only way open to them; turf wars—much violence

scourge (skûrj) cause of widespread affliction and severe suffering

Well-financed and carefully organized groups like the Medellin **cartel** in Colombia linked coca plant farmers in Boliva, money launderers in Panama, and smugglers in Mexico and the United States. Drug money corrupted large numbers of public officials in all of these countries. By the end of the 1980s, opinion polls revealed that Americans identified drugs as the nation's number one problem. The Reagan administration declared a highly publicized "war on drugs" to bring the traffic under control. This multi-billion-dollar campaign focused on stopping the flow of illegal drugs into the United States, destroying cocaine-producing labs in Bolivia, and stiffening the penalties for those convicted of violating federal drug statutes. Critics charged that the war on drugs placed undue emphasis on the supply of drugs from abroad when it needed to look more closely at the demand for them at home. They urged more federal money for drug education, treatment, and rehabilitation. Drug addiction and drug use, they argued, were primarily health problems, not law enforcement issues.

In 1981 doctors in Los Angeles, San Francisco, and New York began encountering a puzzling new medical phenomenon. Young homosexual men were dying suddenly from rare types of pneumonia and cancer. Researchers at the U.S. Public Health Service's Centers for Disease Control (CDC) in Atlanta named the mysterious disease acquired immune deficiency **syndrome** (AIDS). AIDS destroyed the body's natural defenses against illness, making its victims susceptible to a host of opportunistic infections. The virus was transmitted through semen or blood, but full-blown AIDS might not appear for years after initial exposure to the virus. . . . Although tests could

2 = Well-financed cartels

Ex. Colombia, Bolivia, Panama, Mexico, U.S.

– – –Much corruption

– – –In 1980s, #1 problem = drug use

—K
= Reagan mounts multi-billion-$ campaign against cartels.

– – –People argue problem one of use & health, not crime issue. Education needed

3 = 1981, AIDS identified

– – –Associated with homosexual men
　　No cure

– – –CDC center for disease control

—K

– – –Transferred through semen or blood

---

cartel (kär tel′) organization formed to regulate production, pricing and marketing of goods
syndrome (sin′ drōm) group of signs and symptoms indicating disease

determine whether one carried the AIDS virus, there was no cure. Because the preponderance of early AIDS victims were homosexual men who had been infected through sexual contact, many Americans thus perceived AIDS as a disease of homosexuals.

– – –Amer. associated with gay men

As more and more gay men fell victim to 4 the disease, AIDS aroused fear, anguish, and anger. It also brought an upsurge of organization and political involvement. The Gay Men's Health Crisis, formed in New York in 1981, drew thousands of volunteers to care for the sick, raised millions of dollars for education and research, and lobbied vigorously for federal funding of research toward finding a cure. In city after city, gay communities responded to the AIDS crisis with energy and determination. Most gay men changed their sexual habits, practicing "safe sex" to reduce the chances of infection. The Reagan administration, playing to antihomosexual prejudices, largely ignored the epidemic. One important exception was Surgeon General C. Everett Koop, who urged a comprehensive sex education program in the nation's schools, including information about condoms. . . .

= Fear of AIDS

– – –form organizations

– – –Gay men health crisis

– – –Ignored by Reagan admin.

– – –Only Surg. Gen. Koop said—need educ. program in schools & knowledge of condoms

By the 1990s the AIDS epidemic had spread 5 far beyond gay men. The fastest-growing group of AIDS victims were intravenous drug users, their sex partners, and their babies. The AIDS epidemic spread rapidly among African Americans and Latinos as well. By the end of 1995 the CDC had confirmed nearly 320,000 deaths from the disease. As many as 1.5 million Americans could be infected with the HIV virus. Revelations that well-known public figures such as actor Rock Hudson and athletes Magic Johnson and Arthur Ashe were infected helped remove some of the **stigma** and increased AIDS awareness in the public. More important were the continuing political and

= 1990s, epidemic spread to women & babies

Ex. —Latinos & Africa. Amer. quickly infected. Most intravenous drug users.
– – –1995—320,000 deaths already.
– – –1.5 million Amer. could be infected

– – –Celebrities infected
Ex. Rock Hudson, Magic Johnson, Arthur Ashe
Reduced stigma somewhat

---

stigma (stig′ mò) a mark of disgrace

educational efforts mounted by groups like the . . . AIDS Quilt Project, which stitched together a moving tribute to AIDS victims out of thousands of individual memorial quilts.

Another chronic social problem plagued **6** America during the 1980s. In cities throughout the country citizens could not help noticing the disturbing presence of homeless people. Often disoriented, shoeless, and forlorn, growing numbers of "street people" slept over heating grates, on subways, and in parks. Homeless people wandered city sidewalks **panhandling** and struggling to find scraps of food. Winters proved especially difficult. In the early 1980s, the Department of Housing and Urban Development placed the number of the nation's homeless at between 250,000 and 350,000. But advocates for the homeless estimated that the number was as high as 3 million.

Who were the homeless? Analysts agreed **7** that at least a third were mental patients who had been discharged from hospitals during the large-scale deinstitutionalization that took place in the 1970s. Many more were alcoholics and drug addicts unable to hold jobs. But the ranks of the homeless also included female-headed families, battered women, Vietnam veterans, AIDS victims, and elderly people with no place to go. Some communities made strong efforts to place their homeless residents in city-run shelters. But the shelters themselves scared away many homeless people, who often encountered violence and theft there. Some cities pointed to the decline in decent housing for poor people and the deterioration of the nation's health care system. No matter how large and what its components, the permanent class of American homeless reflected the desperate situation of America's poor.

– – –Political, educ. efforts mounted

– – –Gigantic quilt in DC memory of those who died of AIDS

approximately 900 words

John Mack Faragher et al., *Out of Many: A History of the American People* 1018–020. Copyright © 1997 by Prentice Hall. Reprinted by permission.

panhandling (pan′ han′ dling) begging, especially on the streets

The AIDS Quilt in Washington, D.C., October 1992. The quilt project united thousands of individual memorials to AIDS victims into one powerful statement expressing the national sense of loss from the disease.

Study each of the following examples of note making based on five different methods to organize and restate information.

Informal Outlining

One way to determine whether you have understood and can recall what you have read is to outline it. Outlining is an organized form of note making in which you try to see quickly how key ideas are related to each other and to supporting details. It is important that you not simply *recopy* what you have read. Instead, think about the information, organize it mentally, sort out ideas, see connections by making associations, and write down what is important to help you remember it. The very act of writing the information helps you learn it and confirm what part of it you have understood. As you begin to outline,

- List in order only main ideas or major topics, relating them to the subheadings and major details.
- Indent to separate important points.
- Use phrases, omit unnecessary words, and abbreviate whenever possible. Be brief.
- Use your own words as much as possible.

Example of an Informal Outline

Epidemics: Drugs, AIDS, Homelessness

Drug addiction & traffic greatly increased early 1980s
    Crack cocaine, very addictive, now available to working poor
    Ruined thousands of lives; higher crime rates;
        50% males arrested used crack cocaine
    Young dealers in urban areas felt only way open to them;
        Turf wars led to much violence

Well-financed cartels
    Operated in Colombia, Bolivia, Panama, Mexico, U.S.
    In 1980s, No. 1 problem = drug use
    Reagan mounts multi-billion-dollar campaign against cartels.
    Problem, not crime issue; education needed

1981, AIDS identified
    Transferred through semen or blood
    Associated with homosexual men
    No cure
    CDC center for disease control

Fear of AIDS
    Form organizations
    Gay men health crisis
    Ignored by Reagan admin.
    Only Surg. Gen. Koop said—need educ. program in schools and knowledge of condoms

1990s, epidemic spread to women & babies
    Ex. —Latinos & Africa. Amer. quickly infected. Most intravenous drug users.
    1995—320,000 deaths already.
    1.5 million Amer. could be infected
    Celebrities infected
        Rock Hudson, Magic Johnson, Arthur Ashe
    Reduced stigma somewhat
    Political, educ. efforts mounted
    Gigantic quilt in DC memory of those who died of AIDS
Homelessness

_____

_____

_____

Using Cards

Although it is easier to underline and write notes in the margin of your text, sometimes you are unable to do so. There are other alternatives for study. You can use index cards and write your restatement notes after reading each section. Use the lined side, and, on the blank side, write the chapter heading or subheading. Number the cards so they are organized and write a summary card.

Index cards have certain advantages.

1. You can integrate class notes with them.
2. They are convenient for study purposes.
3. It is easy to separate cards to determine what information is known from what information is not known

Epidemics: *Drugs, AIDS, Homelessness*
Drugs: '80s   *Drug addiction and traffic greatly increased*
          Crack cocaine, addictive, available to working poor
          Ruined thousands of lives; higher crime rates
          50% males arrested used crack cocaine
          Young dealers in urban areas
          Turf wars led to much violence

Cartels   *Operated in Colombia, Bolivia, Panama, Mexico, U.S.*
          Reagan mounts multi-billion-dollar campaign
              against cartels

AIDS '81   *AIDS identified*
          Transferred through semen or blood
          Associated with homosexual men
          No cure

Homeless '80s

FIGURE 4.1   Example of a Study Card

The Divided Page

The divided page, or Cornell method, is still another way to organize for study. Begin by drawing a line down your paper about two inches from the left edge to create a margin and a wide area in which to take notes. After reading a text section, write the key points to be remembered on the right-hand side of your paper. Then, write either the key words or questions based on your notes in the left-hand column to test yourself later and to help you recall the information. The dividing line makes it possible to fold your answers underneath or cover them completely as you study. This method is often used together with other methods, such as mapping, an explanation of which follows.

Example of a Divided Page

early 1980s	drug addiction, trafficking increases crack cocaine — highly addictive available to urban poor led to higher crime rates 50% men arrested used crack cocaine
epidemic rises	urban youth leads to turf wars — much violence cartels operate in Col., Bolivia, Pan., Mex. & U.S.
Reagan	U.S. considers #1 problem = drugs Reagan mts. multi-billion-$ campaign against cartels People say drugs = health problem
1981	AIDS identified Associated with gay men No cure
AIDS Fear	Organizations formed Problem ignored = Reagan Surg. Gen. Koop concerned; wants education; condoms
1990s	Epidemic spreads — women/babies
1995	320,000 deaths 1.5 million maybe infected Political, educ. efforts
homelessness	

Mapping

Mapping is the creation of a graphic chart or word picture so that all pertinent information is visible at one time. "Mind" or "concept" maps (sometimes also referred to as "think links") should be constructed so as to visually represent relationships among concepts. Major and minor supporting information to remember is placed in a form that resembles a map or chart, hence the term *mapping* is used. For some students, this visualization enables them to recall the textual information much more readily, and it stimulates "creative thinking." Maps are not as rigidly organized as outlines, allowing greater flexibility in note making: You can incorporate information more easily and move items around on a page.

Most chapters divide into three or four major sections. You can map each section separately, or if there are many small headings, you can sometimes combine them into one map. When mapping a textbook chapter, you can proceed initially by

1. Surveying the chapter, then previewing each section.
2. Reading, marking, and organizing the important parts.
3. Producing the map, as explained below.

Guidelines for Mapping

1. Write the main chapter section or title (or the thesis if you are reading an essay) in the center of the paper and build the rest of the information around it. Turn your paper sideways so you can use the width of the paper for your major headings.
2. To highlight the main chapter section or thesis, draw a square or circle or any other shape around it.
3. Add key words that express the major points. Write these points as branches off the central hub and box or circle them. If the selection is already divided into labeled sections, your task is easy. If there are no divisions, you must group and label the information.
4. Complete the map by adding minor important details off the branches. Try to do some of this from memory.
5. Use larger print for major or important ideas, decreasing size with items of lesser importance.

The survey and markings or underlining should be done before the mapping so that you reduce the information placed on the map to key ideas. You are creating a study guide so that, before a quiz, you need only spend a brief amount of review time. Moreover, while you are creating the map, you are actually doing further organizing, consolidating the information, and reconstructing for yourself what needs to be remembered into a **hierarchy.**

---

hierarchy (hī ə rär′ kē) arrangement in a graded series of importance

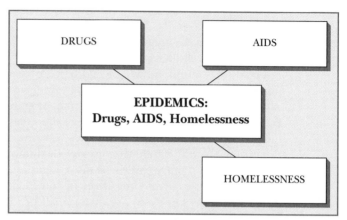

FIGURE 4.2   Example of the Main Idea and Major Headings

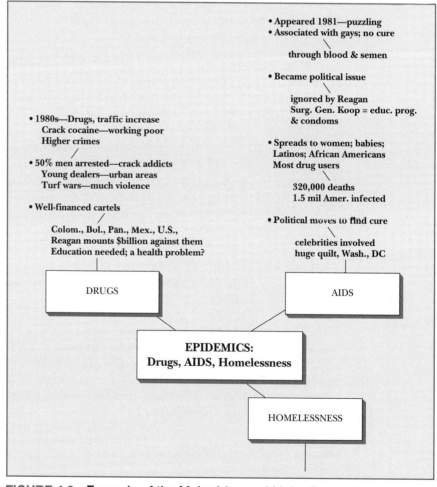

FIGURE 4.3   Example of the Major Idea and Major Support

Frequently, students use mapping in conjunction with the divided page. They place the vocabulary they need to remember, or particular details, on the divided page. This prevents the map from becoming too cluttered. With mapping, you want to show the relationships so details can be more easily visualized and recalled.

An additional mapping technique that aids retention is to use color, separating or relating important ideas and details as the case may be. You can color-code any map rather than simply write in black or blue pen. Color is a powerful linking device that can help you remember related information. When you add color, the map, rather than being simply a graphic representation of printed information, actually becomes a picture of ideas—something your mind can see rather than merely read—and *this is at the heart of mapping*. If you wish, you can also draw or paste a picture in the center of the page to represent the topic or thesis of the selection.

Study the maps in Figures 4.4 ad 4.5, noting how the key ideas about mapping have been organized.

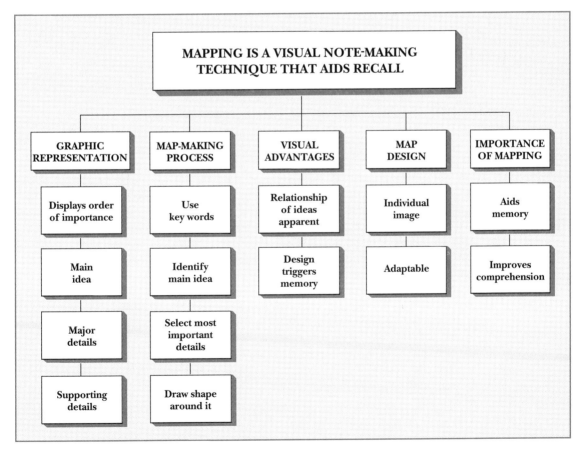

FIGURE 4.4   Example of Mapping Format

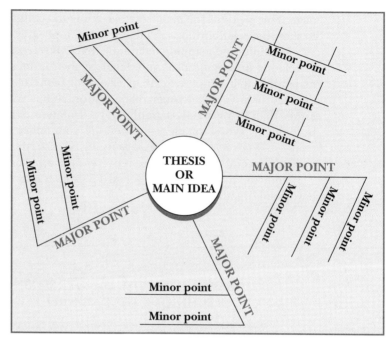

FIGURE 4.5   **Example of a Mapping Format**

A Summary: The Final Step with All Study Systems

The final step with all study systems—and the fifth example of ways to restate information—is to write a good summary of the chapter. You learned in Chapter 1 that an essay's summary is a brief paragraph that condenses information and shows the *connection* between the main idea and the support. It includes only the most significant details. On the other hand, a textbook's summary may require more than one paragraph, depending on the amount of information to be learned. Write your summary in an organized way *in your own words* as you would when doing an outline or mapping. If necessary, use some connecting words, such as *first, second,* or *additionally.* Writing summaries is an excellent study technique to help you think actively about the information and determine whether you have understood it.

To summarize difficult text material, first mark your text and

1.   Circle the topic or subject.

2.   Highlight or underline key ideas; combine these as you write.

3. Cross out unimportant or **redundant** information.

4. Develop a topic sentence that explains the overall key idea.

Here is an example that summarizes the main points of "Epidemics: Drugs, AIDS, Homelessness."

> Three epidemics faced Americans in the 1980s. The first was drugs; crack cocaine, a highly addictive substance, became accessible to everyone, including the poor. It helped create many young drug dealers who engaged in turf wars that led to an increase in crime. Cartels were formed from Latin America to the United States, increasing government corruption. By the end of the 1980s, Reagan mounted a multi-billion-dollar campaign, a "war on drugs," to control its traffic. Officials said drugs were a health, not a crime, issue.
>
> A second epidemic, AIDS, was identified in 1981. It is a disease that destroys the body's natural defenses against illness. At first, it was thought to be a gay men's disease and created great fear. The Reagan administration ignored the problem. It spread to heterosexuals by the 1990s, particularly to drug users and also African Americans and Latinos. Public figures who got AIDS, such as Rock Hudson and Magic Johnson, helped increase public awareness and sympathy. Groups formed to address the problem and give it political clout.
>
> The third major problem in the 1980s was that of homeless people.

_____

_____

_____

ACTIVITY 4.5 **The Five Methods of Note Making**

Practice the five methods for restating textbook information with paragraphs 6 and 7 of the textbook excerpt, "Epidemics: Drugs, AIDS, and the Homeless. Reread them, making marginal notes, and then copy your notes in the spaces provided at the end of each of the note-making examples. Afterward, decide which note-making methods best suit your learning style. Use one or more methods whenever you have textbook material to learn.

_____

redundant (ri dun' dònt) exceeding what is necessary; more than enough

◈ Works of Literature

What is literature and why do we read and study it? Literature usually refers to fictional writing: short stories, novels, poetry, and plays. Reading literature differs from reading essays and textbooks, which deal primarily with information. We read literature for pleasure and, in part, we study it to learn the elements of character, conflict, plot, setting, point of view, and theme that determine how good the storyteller is at his or her craft. Perhaps more important than the study of the structure of literature, however, are the reasons described in the following paragraph.

> Literature with a social consciousness speaks out against social, economic and political injustice; it exposes the many faces of racism, sexism, militarism, and elitism; literature extends our capacity for compassion . . . its social conscience reminds us of our commitment to the real democratic covenant—the real meaning of the 4th of July and the flag—that what unites people is not color or gender or religion but moral conscience. . . . Literature therefore becomes crucial in the struggle to activate people.*

In studying literature we learn to mentally interact with characters so as to understand human experiences or what is often called "the human condition"—what it is that makes people, including ourselves, behave in certain ways. We understand ourselves better when we become aware of and analyze the motives, **aspirations,** successes, and failures of others. Through identification with particular characters, we can learn values.

What happens—the plot or the narration—while important, is usually secondary to the development of character through which we better understand the writer's theme. Our focus with literature, therefore, is not the same as with essays or textbooks; your reading strategies should be modified to reflect that difference.

Some Literary Elements Defined

It is important to be aware of the terms frequently used in discussing literature. These include

> *Character:* Three techniques are usually used by writers to create a character. A writer may describe a character's physical appearance and situation, reveal a character's words and thoughts, or show the reaction of other characters toward him or her. The main character is often referred to as the *protagonist*. Get to know the characters and think of them as human beings. Try to picture them in your mind and imagine that you know

---

aspirations (as pə rā′ shənz) desires for high achievement
* Arthur I. Blaustein, "A Novel Idea to Keep America Afloat," Perspective, *San Jose Mercury News* 1 July 1990: 4–6.

them as well as your own actual friends. Listen to them speaking and hear their voices when reading **dialogue.**

Conflict: If there is no conflict or problem, there is no story! The conflict is the main problem that must be resolved. It may be an internal conflict of the protagonist or a conflict between people, nature, society, or the unknown. There may be more than one conflict. Think how you would resolve the conflict; try to predict the outcome of the **dilemma.**

Plot: The plot consists of a series of related events and their purpose. A problem or conflict is presented; events take place leading to a **climax** and eventually to a resolution. The plot involves *what* happens and *why* it happens. Look for any hints or clues the writer may give and try to guess what will happen next. Imagine yourself to be a character and how you might behave in similar situations.

Setting: The setting consists of the time and place in which the action occurs. At times, the setting directly controls the plot's development, and, sometimes, helps give the reader better understanding of the characters. Picture the setting; imagine yourself in the place and time of the action.

Point of View: The point of view is the angle from which the story is told and gives you the writer's relationship to the characters. The writer might use "I" or "we," in which case, it is known as the *first person point of view* and may present a rather biased perspective. One of the characters tells the story. If the writer uses "he, she, they," it is called the *third person* or *objective point of view;* the writer distances himself or herself from the story. Finally, the point of view may be called *omniscient,* or "all-knowing"; here, the narrator, rather than a character, tells the story. The narrator knows everything that is happening in the story, but the characters may not. Understanding the point of view helps you think with the narrator and main characters.

Theme: A theme is the underlying, universal message of a literary work. It involves a statement or opinion about the subject and is often implied. Its message is developed through the plot and characters. Mysteries or adventure stories, often written entirely for a reader's entertainment, do not always have a theme.

Difference Between a Short Story and a Novel

The scope and size of a short story is often what distinguishes it most from a novel. The short story may have all the components of a novel—plot, character, setting, and so on—but rather than focusing on many complicated plots and dozens of characters, it generally has a few characters, a limited setting, and one main, tightly knit plot. In a short story, the writer has to concentrate on developing a single theme or impression, has limited space and, therefore, must be brief. Usually, a short story can be read in a single sitting.

---

dialogue (dī′ ò lôg′) a conversation between two or more people
dilemma (di lem′ ò) undesirable or unpleasant choice
climax (klī′ maks) the part in a series of events marked by the greatest intensity

ACTIVITY 4.6 **Recognizing the Literary Elements in a Short Story**

Alice Walker

Read the following short story to see how all the elements you just learned are skillfully developed by Alice Walker in her brief but touching story, "Am I Blue?" Then, answer the questions that follow; you may wish to refer to pages 200–01 to clarify the terms in the questions.

Alice Walker is a Pulitzer Prize–winning African-American writer who was born in 1944, the eighth child of sharecropper parents. She has written sixteen books, including five novels, several collections of essays, short stories, children's books, and poems. In her writings she addresses such topics as spousal abuse, fear of death, female sexuality, and incest. She is, perhaps, best known for her third novel, *The Color Purple,* which has been translated into twenty-two languages.

 # Working with the WORLD WIDE WEB

You can learn more about Alice Walker's life and accomplishments by typing her name into a search engine and finding an appropriate Web site.

Am I Blue?

Alice Walker

"Ain't these tears in these eyes tellin' you?"

For about three years my companion and I rented **1** a small house in the country that stood on the edge of a large meadow that appeared to run from the end of our deck straight into the mountains. The mountains, however, were quite far away, and between us and them there was, in fact, a town. It was one of the many pleasant aspects of the house that you never really were aware of this.

It was a house of many windows, low, wide, **2** nearly floor to ceiling in the living room, which faced the meadow, and it was from one of these that I first saw our closest neighbor, a large white horse, cropping grass, flipping its mane, and ambling about—not over the entire meadow, which stretched well out of sight of the house, but over the five or so fenced-in acres that were next to the twenty-odd that we had rented. I soon learned that the horse, whose name was Blue, belonged to a man who lived in another town, but was boarded by our neighbors next door. Occasionally, one of the children, usually a stocky teen-ager, but sometimes a much younger girl or boy, could be seen riding Blue. They would appear in the meadow, climb up on his back, ride furiously for ten or fifteen minutes, then get off, slap Blue on the flanks, and not be seen again for a month or more.

There were many apple trees in our yard, and one by the fence that Blue could   **3** almost reach. We were soon in the habit of feeding him apples, which he relished, especially because by the middle of summer the meadow grasses—so green and **succulent** since January—had dried out from lack of rain, and Blue stumbled about munching the dried stalks half-heartedly. Sometimes he would stand very still just by the apple tree, and when one of us came out he would whinny, snort loudly, or stamp the ground. This meant, of course: I want an apple.

It was quite wonderful to pick a few apples, or collect those that had fallen to the   **4** ground overnight, and patiently hold them, one by one, up to his large, toothy mouth. I remained as thrilled as a child by his flexible dark lips, huge, cubelike teeth that crunched the apples, core and all, with such finality, and his high, broad-breasted *enormity;* beside which, I felt small indeed. When I was a child, I used to ride horses, and was especially friendly with one named Nan until the day I was riding and my brother deliberately spooked her and I was thrown, head first, against the trunk of a tree. When I came to, I was in bed and my mother was bending worriedly over me; we silently agreed that perhaps horseback riding was not the safest sport for me. Since then I have walked, and prefer walking to horseback riding—but I had forgotten the depth of feeling one could see in horses' eyes.

I was therefore unprepared for the expression in Blue's eyes. Blue was lonely. Blue   **5** was horribly lonely and bored. I was not shocked that this should be the case; five acres to tramp by yourself, endlessly, even in the most beautiful of meadows—and his was—cannot provide many interesting events, and once rainy season turned to dry that was about it. No, I was shocked that I had forgotten that human animals and nonhuman animals can communicate quite well; if we are brought up around animals as children we take this for granted. By the time we are adults we no longer remember. However, the animals have not changed. They are in fact *completed* creations (at least they seem to be, so much more than we) who are not likely to change, it is their nature to express themselves. What else are they going to express? And they do. And, generally speaking, they are ignored.

After giving Blue the apples, I would wander back to the house, aware that he was   **6** observing me. Were more apples not forthcoming then? Was that to be his sole entertainment for the day? My partner's small son had decided he wanted to learn how to piece a quilt; we worked in silence on our respective squares as I thought . . .

Well, about slavery: about white children, who were raised by black people, who   **7** knew their first all-accepting love from black women, and then they must "forget" the deep levels of communication between themselves and "mammy" that they knew. Later

---

succulent (suk′ yōō lònt) full of juice; juicy

they would be able to relate quite calmly, "My old mammy was sold to another good family." "My old mammy was _____." Fill in the blank. Many more years later a white woman would say: "I can't understand these Negroes, these blacks. What do they want? They're so different from us."

And about the Indians, considered to be "like animals" by the "settlers" (a very **8**
benign euphemism for what they actually were), who did not understand their description as a compliment.

And about the thousands of American men who marry Japanese, Korean, Filipina, **9**
and other non-English-speaking women and of how happy they report they are *"blissfully,"* until their brides learn to speak English, at which point the marriages tend to fall apart. What then did the men see, when they looked into the eyes of the women they married, before they could speak English? Apparently only their own reflections.

I thought of society's impatience with the young. "Why are they playing the music so **10**
loud?" Perhaps the children have listened to much of the music of oppressed people their parents danced to before they were born, with its passionate but soft cries for acceptance and love, and they have wondered why their parents failed to hear.

I do not know how long Blue had inhabited his five beautiful, boring acres before **11**
we moved into our house; a year after we had arrived—and had also traveled to other valleys, other cities, other worlds—he was still there.

But then, in our second year at the house, something happened in Blue's life. One **12**
morning, looking out the window at the fog that lay like a ribbon over the meadow, I saw another horse, a brown one, at the other end of Blue's field. Blue appeared to be afraid of it, and for several days made no attempt to go near. We went away for a week. When we returned, Blue had decided to make friends and the two horses ambled or galloped along together, and Blue did not come nearly as often to the fence underneath the apple tree.

When he did, bringing his new friend with him, there was a different look in his eyes. **13**
A look of independence, of self-possession, of **inalienable** *horse*ness. His friend eventually became pregnant. For months and months there was, it seemed to me, a mutual feeling between me and the horses of justice, of peace. I fed apples to them both. The look in Blue's eyes was one of unabashed "this is *it*ness."

It did not, however, last forever. One day, after a visit to the city, I went out to **14**
give Blue some apples. He stood waiting, or so I thought, though not beneath the tree. When I shook the tree and jumped back from the shower of apples, he made no move. I carried some over to him. He managed to half-crunch one. The rest he let fall to the ground. I dreaded looking into his eyes—because I had of course noticed that Brown, his partner, had gone—but I did look. If I had been born into slavery, and my partner had been sold or killed, my eyes would have looked like that. The children next door explained that Blue's partner had been "put with him" (the same expression that old people used, I had noticed, when speaking of an ancestor during slavery who had been impregnated by her owner) so that they could mate and she conceive.

---

benign (bi nīn′) harmless; having no significant effect; doing little or no harm
inalienable (in āl′ yòn ò bòl) that cannot be taken away or transferred

Since that was accomplished, she had been taken back by her owner, who lived some-where else.

Will she be back? I asked.   15

They didn't know.   16

Blue was like a crazed person. Blue *was,* to me, a crazed person. He galloped   17 furiously, as if he were being ridden, around and around his five beautiful acres. He whin-nied until he couldn't. He tore at the ground with his hooves. He butted himself against his single shade tree. He looked always and always toward the road down which his partner had gone. And then, occasionally, when he came up for apples, or I took apples to him, he looked at me. It was a look so piercing, so full of grief, a look so *human,* I almost laughed (I felt too sad to cry) to think there are people who do not know that animals suffer. People like me who have forgotten, and daily forget, all that animals try to tell us. "Everything you do to us will happen to you; we are your teachers, as you are ours." We are one lesson is essentially it, I think. There are those who never once have even considered animals' rights, those who have been taught that animals actually want to be used and abused by us, as small children "love" to be frightened, or women "love" to be mutilated and raped . . . They are the great-grandchildren of those who honestly thought, because someone taught them this: "Women can't think," and "niggers can't faint." But most disturbing of all, in Blue's large brown eyes was a new look, more painful than the look of despair: the look of disgust with human beings, with life; the look of hatred. And it was odd what the look of hatred did. It gave him, for the first time, the look of a beast. And what that meant was that he had put up a barrier within to protect himself from further violence; all the apples in the world wouldn't change that fact.

And so Blue remained, a beautiful part of our landscape, very peaceful to look at   18 from the window, white against the grass. Once a friend came to visit and said, looking out on the soothing view: "And it *would* have to be a *white* horse; the very image of free-dom." And I thought, yes, the animals are forced to become for us merely "images" of what they once so beautifully expressed. And we are used to drinking milk from con-tainers showing "contented" cows, whose real lives we want to hear nothing about, eating eggs and drumsticks from "happy" hens, and munching hamburgers advertised by bulls of integrity who seem to command their fate.

As we talked of freedom and justice one day for all, we sat down to steaks. I am eat-   19 ing misery, I thought, as I took the first bite. And spit it out.

approximately 1850 words

"Am I Blue?" from *Living by the Word: Selected Writings 1973–1987.* Copyright 1986 by Alice Walker. Harcourt Brace & Company. Reprinted by permission.

Questions for Writing and Discussion

Character

1. What techniques does Alice Walker use to create the character of Blue?

_____

_____

Conflict

2. Both Blue and the narrator must deal with an internal conflict. Describe both conflicts.

_____

_____

Plot

3. At what point in the story is the climax of the plot revealed? How is this tension resolved?

_____

_____

Setting

4. Describe the story's setting. How does this setting help us better understand the narrator's feelings?

_____

_____

Point of View

5. Why do you believe the author chose to tell the story from the first person point of view?

_____

_____

Theme

6. In your own words, state the author's message. Then, describe how you reacted to this message.

_____

_____

_____

ACTIVITY 4.7 **Create Your Own Story with Danielle Steel's Help**

Danielle Steel is one of the world's most popular novelists, having written more than sixty-eight novels that have been translated into twenty-eight languages; she has appeared on the best-seller list for a record 390 weeks! Some critics believe that Steel uses a formula and that her stories are predictable. To see how all the elements of a novel are used by Danielle Steel, complete the story printed below as it appeared in *People* magazine.

Danielle Steel

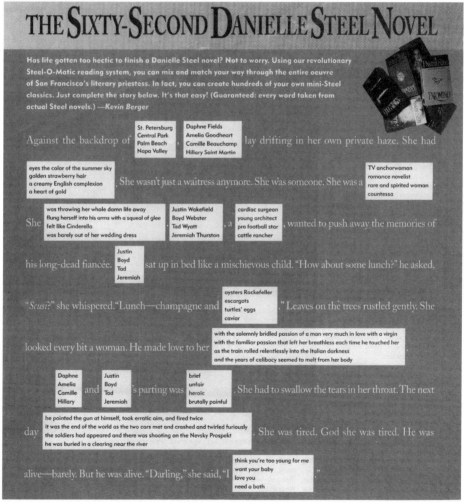

Suggested Reading List

Most of the literary selections that appear in *Effective Reading* are short stories. What follows is a list of suggested novels for you to consider reading for pleasure and to discover the wonderful world of imaginative writing.

Allende, Isabel. *The House of Spirits.*
  Born in Peru, Isabel Allende was a journalist in Chile before moving to America. *The House of Spirits,* her first novel, was an international best-seller. Her writing has a South American flavor, with some mysticism and a deep understanding of important issues for different generations of women. Also try *The Stories of Eva Luna* and *Paula* by the same author.

Bellow, Saul. *Henderson the Rain King.*
  Bellow is a post–World War II American Nobel Prize–winner. In this novel, a rich but unfocused American finds purpose and meaning in his life by trying to save an African village from a natural disaster. The book is both hilarious and serious.

Berg, Elizabeth. *Talk Before Sleep.*
  This is a short, modern novel about a diverse group of women brought together as they care for a mutual friend who has cancer. Berg handles the themes of friendship and mortality with a poignant sense of humor and a keen eye for descriptive detail. Other books by the same author include *Range of Motion,* about a marriage in the midst of a medical crisis, and *Durable Goods,* about a young girl growing up with an overbearing, military father and no mother to protect her.

Grisham, John. *The Client.*
  Grisham, a former lawyer, is now one of America's "hottest" contemporary authors. He writes gripping novels dealing realistically with a frustrating judicial system he obviously knows in great detail. The client of this book's title is a ten-year-old boy who stumbles on a secret that makes him a threat to not just one but two terrifying foes. His dilemma will bring back memories of what you felt like as a helpless, confused child in a scary, grown-up world. Other best-sellers by Grisham include *The Firm, The Chamber,* and *The Street Lawyer.*

Irving, John. *A Prayer for Owen Meany.*
  This novel, set in New England in the tumultuous 1960s and 1970s, is the story of two boyhood friends and a cast of memorable characters from their

small town. The misadventures of the narrator and his friend will remind you of some of your own childhood experiences and give you a good understanding of the conflicting emotions generated by the Vietnam War. Owen Meany is a character you will *never* forget! Other titles by this popular author include *The Hotel New Hampshire, The World According to Garp, The Cider House Rules,* and his 1998 best-seller, *A Widow for a Year.*

Kozinski, Jerzy. *Being There.*

Kozinski, born in Poland in the 1930s, was caught in the horrors of World War II as a child, which may explain his rather dark view of humanity. He arrived in the United States in 1957 and has written most of his books in English, although it is not his native language. *Being There* is a novel that operates on two levels. On the surface, it is the tale of a simple man named Chance who makes his meager living as a gardener on a fancy estate. When Chance is suddenly mistaken for the wealthy owner of the estate, the results are comical until he starts to symbolize the question of what gives any one of us our true identity and the novel reveals its deeper structure. The film version stars Peter Sellers and Shirley MacLaine. It is very funny yet disturbing at the same time.

Lamb, Wally. *She's Come Undone.*

Written in 1992, this best-seller describes the life of Dolores Price from her childhood to her thirties, and what a wild ride it is! At first, the novel is a touchingly funny childhood reminiscence, but soon you are aware that this young girl's life is headed nowhere but down—and fast! In spite of yourself, you will be turning the pages as quickly as you can, watching in horror as Dolores self-destructs. Hang on for the end of the ride; it's worth it. That a male writer could capture a female protagonist in such intimate detail is astonishing. Mr. Lamb's second novel, *I Know This Much Is True,* has also received rave reviews.

Lee, Harper. *To Kill a Mockingbird.*

Harper Lee is a southern American writer whose only novel deals with many great American themes: racial prejudice, class differences, justice, inhumanity, and the nature of heroism. The story is told as a flashback from the point of view of a spunky young girl named Scout. Her innocent point of view adds a touch of humor and mystery to an otherwise serious book. The movie, starring Gregory Peck, is fabulous. Just wait until you meet Boo Radley.

Lodge, David. *Changing Places.*

   This contemporary British author and academic is one of the funniest men around. In *Changing Places,* he deals with the experience of culture shock when a professor from a small city in England exchanges his job, and his house, with a professor from Berkeley, California, for a year. The novel is hilarious yet thought-provoking. Among other titles, Lodge has also written *Small World* and *The British Museum Is Falling Down* about life in academia.

Morrison, Toni. *Song of Solomon.*

   Awarded the Nobel Prize for her contributions to literature, this author's style is stunningly poetic, emotional, almost mythic. In this novel, characters are so detailed you will feel as if you know them personally. Readers have found the book spellbinding, describing it as so hypnotic that you feel caught in an embrace of words which will not let you go until the ending. Other works by Morrison, an African American, include *Sula, Beloved,* and *Paradise.*

Quindlen, Anna. *One True Thing.*

   A former award-winning columnist, Ms. Quindlen gave up the newsroom to become a novelist. Although this book is fiction, it feels real in its depiction of an adult daughter caring for her ailing mother. The book ends with an amazing turn of events, believable yet totally unanticipated! Also try one of this writer's earlier books, *Object Lessons,* or her 1998 story about spousal abuse, *Black and Blue.*

Remarque, Erich Maria. *All Quiet on the Western Front.*

   This is a poetically written, powerful antiwar novel, told from the point of view of a young soldier named Paul, as he and his buddies suffer through unthinkable brutalities of trench warfare during World War I. Some of the images will stay with you long after you've finished the book.

Steinbeck, John. *Of Mice and Men.*

   An American classic, this book takes place in the 1930s in rural America. It tells the story of two poor laborers who move from ranch to ranch with only the bundles on their backs, their deep need for each other, and their impossible dream of some day owning their own farm. In fact, every character in this short novel has his or her own version of the American dream. Be sure to keep some Kleenex nearby as you read the ending. *Tortilla Flat* and *The Grapes of Wrath* are two other much-beloved Steinbeck works.

Yoshimoto, Banana. *Kitchen.*

   The publication of this short work by a young woman in Tokyo started a craze called "Bananamania." Using amazingly simple yet poetic language, Yoshimoto tells the touching story of how a young woman, quite alone in a crowded world, triumphs over grief. Her second novel, *np,* also features a young female heroine, this time a translator working on a mysterious manuscript. Reading Yoshimoto is not just a literary experience but also a cultural one, giving you a good feeling for the details of everyday life in urban Japan.

A Last Note on Literature

Look over the following cartoon, drawn by the same artist who gave us the one on page 76 in Chapter 2 when we were discussing double-talk and euphemisms, and see if you are familiar with the actual book titles of these famous literary works.

Copyright © by T. O. Sylvester. Reprinted by permission.

The actual book titles are: _____

_____

_____

_____

⪍ Summary

This chapter has focused on reading and organizing for more effective study and learning. Three genres of reading—essays, textbooks, and literature—have unique structures and, therefore, particular study strategies can help in organizing their contents for discussion purposes, for answering questions, and for test taking.

An essay's thesis must be identified and evaluated together with its supporting information. Its more literary style differentiates it from the textbook, and it usually does not include the helpful graphic organizers and headings found in a textbook.

The textbook, on the other hand, usually has a unique vocabulary peculiar to its discipline that sometimes may be equated to learning a second language. Textbook chapters, moreover, are long, with many concepts to retain and remember, and quizzes and tests that usually follow, necessitating a more detailed kind of study and organization to memorize the information. Study strategies suggested included note taking, simplified outlining, using index cards, using a divided page, and mapping.

Literature study focuses on certain elements of a narrative: character, plot, setting, style, point of view, and theme. A short story is generally brief, has a single plot, fewer characters, and a concise theme compared to a novel. A study of literature raises our social consciousness in a unique way, as we identify with particular characters and situations.

Chapter 4
Vocabulary Review

Write the correct answer in the space provided. The first one is done for you.

1. If an item is **topical,** is it dated or current? _current_

2. When something **diminishes,** does it grow smaller or larger? _____

3. Is a **syndrome** a kind of place like the astrodome? _____

4. Who would most likely use **nuance,** a classroom instructor or a writer? _____

5. Does one who speaks **concisely** usually use many or few words? _____

6. Are **salient** features important or unimportant in note taking? _____

7. Is a boss at the top or the bottom of a **hierarchy?** _____

8. Is a **panhandler** someone who washes pots and pans for a living or who relies

    on others for a livelihood? _____

9. Is a **dialogue** a discussion with others or simply talking to one's

    self? _____

10. Should college students have low or high **aspirations?** _____

Selection 7: **ESSAY**

 ## Preparation for Reading

The following essay, "Stop Blaming Working Moms," is based on the studies of the sociologist and historian Stephanie Coontz, who feels that people in some segments of American society are blaming working mothers for many of society's current problems, particularly the breakdown of the family as it was traditionally conceived.

Before reading the essay, note these words and their meaning. The words are underlined in the text.

were **naive** to think	lacking worldly wisdom or informed judgment
pervasive discrimination	that which tends to spread everywhere
with its **portents** of doom	foreshadowing a coming event
correlation between families	relationship between things
does not prove **causation**	an act that produces an effect

After reading the essay, make some marginal notes to help you understand the essay's implied thesis.

Preview, then read the essay.

Stop Blaming Working Moms

Joy Rothke

Sociologist-historian Stephanie Coontz has a message for the stressed-out working 1 mothers of America: This is not just *your* problem.

"We remain with a system in total denial," she says. "It's not an individual prob- 2 lem, it's a social problem. And until employers, government, as well as our personal attitudes change, it's going to be a continuous struggle."

In her new book "The Way We Really Are: Coming to Terms with America's 3 Changing Families," Coontz squarely challenges the prevailing wisdom about the "breakdown" of the family and nostalgia for another time.

A professor at Evergreen State College in Olympia, Wash., and the mother of a 4 son in high school, Coontz, 52, is blunt when she confronts the problems '90s families have. "We (baby boomer females) were <u>naive</u> to think we could "have it all" without changing the social/economic/value systems. We go through cycles—that's a major thesis in my book. And until we admit we can't solve this at the individual level, we're going to keep going through cycles. We're acting as if only women can solve this problem—by quitting (work). We have all this research showing that fathers want to be involved with their kids. Just as the woman who quits for two or three years reinforces her secondary position in the labor market, she reinforces her husband's secondary position as a nurturer. Just as she never catches up economically, he never catches up emotionally. The more involved fathers are from day one, the better fathers they become."

Coontz accuses politicians and right-wing leaders who glorify or look back nostalgically at the '50s family of engaging in a "tricky chronological shell game," saying they are selective in their memories, and forget the vast number of government programs and family subsidies available in that era (G.I. Bill, FHA home loans, etc.). And she also urges us to remember the <u>pervasive</u> discrimination against non-traditional, non-white and non-Christian families.   **5**

Nor is the outcry against the "breakdown of the family" new with its <u>portents</u> of doom for the next generation. But do untraditional upbringing, divorce, working mothers, etc. have a permanent negative effect on the children? As sociologists Arlene Skolnick and Stacey Rosencrantz said in a recent article in the *American Prospect,* "Family restorationists seem to misunderstand the social science enterprise in ways that seriously undermine their conclusions. For example, they trumpet findings about correlation between family structure and poverty, or lower academic achievement, or behavior problems, as proof of their arguments. Doing so, however, ignores the principle taught in elementary statistics that <u>correlation</u> does not prove <u>causation</u>."   **6**

Coontz urges flexibility on the part of employers. "We need to start discussing this, and stop asking individual families, or all too often, individual women, to shoulder the burden. We have to up the pressure on our institutions to change."   **7**

"There's also some encouraging research being done on working mothers," says Coontz. "A study out in April 1997 shows that when a woman has a high degree of control at work and supportive partners, she is happier than childless or single women. Many women get a great deal of satisfaction with their multiple roles. The ones whose kids might be hurting because their mothers work are the ones with low-status jobs, with very little control and such low pay they can't afford good child care. We say poor women have to work, but we guilt-bait middle-class women when it turns out not to be the very best idea for the wife to solve this problem."   **8**

"Yes, there are individual cases when it makes sense for the wife to quit work," says Coontz. "But I don't have a one-size-fits-all answer. It's not always the right decision, and as a society and as a group, working mothers have to keep fighting for their right to combine work and family, and not have to shoulder all of it."   **9**

"As a mother and a researcher, I've found that it's the parents of teenagers who need the most flexibility. If you quit for three or four years, you have to come back and start a new career, and you're a lot less likely to get that flexibility. And people talk about 'making a sacrifice for your kids.' But sacrificing your career for kids isn't always in their best interests either. Research clearly shows that if a woman is satisfied in her role, even if there is stress involved, she's going to be a better mother."   **10**

"Reglorifying motherhood doesn't really help the kids and doesn't solve long-term problems," says Coontz. "That puts women at a real disadvantage and loses the advantage of having fathers involved. If you can afford to quit work completely, you'd probably be better off in cutting back your work hours, or taking turns with your husband or partner, and investing in higher quality child care. That's better   **11** than this 'all or nothing' rigidity. Again, this is something we have to fight for from employers. In Sweden, working parents can cut back . . . without losing benefits or seniority. Our society makes it all or nothing. People become afraid to cut back at all, afraid to refuse overtime, because they may lose their jobs entirely."

Coontz says she writes books directed at a general audience because of her impatience with academics who only talk to each other. "I'm passionate about the opportunity to talk to ordinary people," she says. She appears regularly on TV, and in community and PTA forums across the country.   **12**

"My job is to make this work accessible. Though I'm very discouraged about our political leaders, I'm extremely encouraged by my meetings with citizens, and talking *with* them, not at them."   **13**

approximately 800 words

Joy Rothke, "Stop Blaming Working Moms," *San Francisco Examiner* 26 May 1997: C1–7. Reprinted by permission.

COMPREHENSION CHECK

Part I
General Comprehension Questions: Literal and Interpretive

Write the correct letter in the space provided.

_____ 1. Stephanie Coontz believes that the problem working mothers face is

    a. an individual problem.
    b. the children's problem.
    c. an employer's problem.
    d. a social problem.

_____ 2. According to Coontz, the problems families face today reflect a

    a. crisis.
    b. cycle.
    c. normal occurrence.
    d. sexist attitude.

_____ 3. Coontz says leaders who glorify the family structure of the '50s

    a. are right to do so.
    b. do not have valid arguments.
    c. like the past better than the present.
    d. have selective memories.

_____ 4. Some sociologists contend that untraditional upbringing, divorce, and working mothers are responsible for

    a. a permanent negative effect on kids.
    b. the breakdown of the family.
    c. society's major problems.
    d. none of the above.

_____ 5. The author's thesis is that because of the increasing number of women in the workforce

    a. family values have changed.
    b. children's needs are ignored.
    c. their role in society is evolving and changing constantly.
    d. men no longer hold their traditional

dominant status.

_____ 6. A study on working mothers
done in April 1997 showed
that they are

a. overburdened and overwhelmed.
b. happier than single or childless
women.
c. quicker to divorce.
d. earning more than their spouses.

7. It is stated at the end of paragraph 6 that " . . . correlation does not prove causation." Explain the meaning of this statement, and discuss how it applies to the
"breakdown of the family."

_____

_____

8. What does Coontz mean in paragraph 9 when she says, " . . . there are individual
cases when it makes sense for the wife to quit work. . . . But I don't have a one-
size-fits-all answer"?

_____

_____

Part II
Application Questions for Writing and Discussion

9. Do you agree with Coontz in paragraph 11 that "Reglorifying motherhood doesn't
really help the kids and doesn't solve long-term problems"? Why, or why not?

_____

_____

10. What do you believe should be women's role in society today?

_____

Part III
Vocabulary

These words were included in the essay. Use the sentence context to place the appropriate word in the blank provided.

nurturer   chronologically   nostalgically   restorationists   flexibility

1. To have a full-time job and to go to school full time requires one to have

   _____ should an emergency arise.

2. Because Jan was a _____, kind and compassionte, she attended to the wounded bird's every need.

3. We tried to list the events _____ in order to give the reporter accurate details of the accident.

4. The storyteller described the scene _____, recalling pleasant memories of his childhood.

5. The city's _____ have worked diligently to bring the Frank Lloyd Wright building back to its former majesty.

Selection 8: **TEXTBOOK**

 # Preparation for Reading

Read the following textbook chapter excerpt that deals with sexual harassment, particularly as it affects women in the workplace. Before reading, look over Table 4.1 and take the Ask Yourself quiz; also, note the boldfaced words, underlined in the text.

perpetrated by a boss	committed; carried out
derogatory terms	detracting from one's character
leering, or **ogling**	making eyes at, usually feeling desirous
few **reprisals**	injury done to repay injury; retaliation
prestigious law firms	high reputation or influence; honored

Preview and then read-study the selection, marking important and key ideas. Organize the information in writing, choosing any one of the study methods presented in this chapter before answering the questions that follow.

Sexual Harassment

Nijole V. Benokraitis

In [an earlier chapter] we defined *sexual harassment* as any unwelcome sexual 1 advance, request for sexual favors, or other conduct of a sexual nature that makes a person uncomfortable and interferes with her or his work. Sexual harassment is not only behavior that is unwelcome to its target. As we pointed out, it was held illegal by the Supreme Court in 1986 (*Meritor Savings Bank* v. *Vinson*). It was designated an illegal form of sex discrimination as early as 1964, in Title VII of the Civil Rights Act of 1964, and in the 1980 EEOC guidelines.

Sexual harassment behavior can take verbal, nonverbal, or physical forms (see 2 Table [4.1]), and it may occur in almost any situation, although it is generally documented in workplace or educational settings. Because harassing someone in the workplace, whether sexually or nonsexually, is a display of power, sexual harassment is usually <u>perpetrated</u> by a boss on a subordinate. Because men dominate positions of power in business and industry, it is far more likely that a harasser will be a man than a woman. The superior-subordinate relationship of perpetrator and victim also accounts for the fact that women often fail to report incidents of harassment. One study found, for example, that 60 percent of the women who experienced sexual harassment never reported it because they felt nothing would be done and they feared they would lose their jobs if they complained (Pollack, 1990).

TABLE 4.1
Sexual Harassment Can Take Many Forms

> **VERBAL SEXUAL HARASSMENT**
>
> Sexually offensive or suggestive comments, jokes, or teasing
>
> Whistles or catcalls
>
> Sexual remarks about a person's body or clothing
>
> Use of crude or offensive language or of <u>derogatory</u> terms for the opposite sex
>
> Pressure for dates even after the victim has said no
>
> Demands for sexual favors in return for hiring, promotion, or tenure
>
> Sexually oriented verbal abuse
>
> Threats or insults
>
> **NONVERBAL SEXUAL HARASSMENT**
>
> Staring, leering, or <u>ogling</u>
>
> Using indecent gestures such as winks or licking one's lips
>
> Displaying posters, photos, or drawings of a sexual nature
>
> Sabotaging the victim's work
>
> **PHYSICAL SEXUAL HARASSMENT**
>
> Patting, pinching, or grabbing
>
> Brushing up against the victim's body
>
> Touching, hugging, or kissing
>
> Cornering or trapping
>
> Physical assault or threat of physical assault
>
> Threat of rape, attempted rape, or rape

Sources: Paludi and Barickman, 1991; Shoop, 1992.

Some people argue that there is a fine line between sexual harassment and flirt- **3**
ing or simply giving a compliment. Wrong. If someone says "stop it" and the perpetrator does not stop, it is sexual harassment. Most people know—instinctively and
because of the other person's reaction—when sexual attentions are unwelcome or
threatening. Take the quiz in the box "Do You Recognize Sexual Harassment?" It
may help you discover how attuned you are to what sexual harassment really is.

The Prevalence of Sexual Harassment

In the film *Disclosure,* a male executive is the target of sexual harassment by a woman **4**
who is his former lover and new boss. As one commentator observed, "Too bad it's
based on a scenario that hardly reflects reality" (Schuyler, 1995: 12).

Although men can be targets of sexual harassment, the overwhelming number **5**
of victims are women. According to the EEOC, only about 9 percent of the almost
12,000 sexual harassment cases in 1994 were filed by men (Schuyler, 1995). Men are

---

ASK YOURSELF

Do You Recognize Sexual Harassment?

Indicate for each statement whether you think the behavior it describes is acceptable or unacceptable. The answers are at the end of the box.

BEHAVIOR	ACCEPTABLE	UNACCEPTABLE
1. "Hey, great legs!"	☐	☐
2. Buying and enjoying pornographic books, tapes, etc., at home.	☐	☐
3. Making eye contact while speaking; giving someone a friendly pat on the shoulder.	☐	☐
4. Continuing to ask someone for dates despite the person's repeated refusals.	☐	☐
5. Telling bawdy jokes to friends who enjoy them in social, nonworkplace settings.	☐	☐
6. Asking a colleague with whom you're on good terms to accompany you to a company-sponsored social event.	☐	☐
7. Telling off-color or sexual jokes that you know will make some people uncomfortable.	☐	☐
8. Staring up and down someone's body.	☐	☐
9. Putting pornographic material on company bulletin boards or in lockers; accompanying such displays with sexual comments about coworkers.	☐	☐
10. "You look very nice today."	☐	☐
11. Patting a person on the behind.	☐	☐
12. Making frequent comments to coworkers on sexually oriented material in the media (films, television, magazines).	☐	☐

Answers: 2, 3, 5, 6, and 10 are acceptable; 1, 4, 7, 8, 9, 11, and 12 are sexual harassment.

Sources: Based on Bravo and Cassedy, 1992: Langelan, 1993.

---

probably more likely to be harassed when they are young, and especially if they are gay. In a survey of students in grades 8 through 11, 76 percent of boys and 85 percent of girls said they had experienced sexual harassment by being targets of obscene jokes, the subjects of graffiti on rest-room walls, or by being openly called gay (*U.S. News & World Report,* 1993). Yet only 7 percent of these students reported the incidents. Most victims don't report them because they fear <u>reprisals</u>, feel that no one will believe them, or expect ridicule from their peers.

One researcher has claimed that as many as half of all women will be harassed **6** at some point during their academic or working lives (Fitzgerald, 1993). Other studies have reported claims of harassment ranging from 21 to 42 percent of women and 14 percent of men. In one study 42 percent of women said they knew someone who had been harassed (Kantrowitz et al., 1991). On an annual basis, 15 percent of women in Fortune 500 companies experienced sexual harassment, and according to a 1993 survey, as many as 59 percent of women executives may have been harassed at some time in their careers (Walsh, 1995). In the highest estimate of the incidence of sexual harassment, the Government Accounting Office, the investigative arm of Congress, found that *97 percent* of the female students at the nation's military academies have experienced sexual harassment (*Baltimore Sun,* 1994f).

Among the perpetrators of sexual harassment who escape prosecution are some of our best known public servants. For example, although Republican Senator Robert Packwood of Oregon has been accused of sexual harassment by more than two dozen women, as yet there have been no political or legal sanctions for his actions. In fact, corporate officials, prominent politicians, and labor groups have contributed generously to a fund to hire the most <u>prestigious</u> law firms in Washington, D.C., to defend Packwood (St. George, 1993). **7**

Sexual harassment takes place throughout the world. Studying 23 industrialized countries, Husbands (1992) found that sexual harassment in the workplace was widespread, although the perception of what constitutes sexual harassment varied greatly. In one survey by a French magazine, for example, 48 percent of women respondents said they did not consider it sexual harassment if a woman seeking a promotion was asked by her supervisor to go away with him for the weekend. **8**

Sexual harassment can be very costly, both emotionally and financially, to victims, perpetrators, employers, corporations, and indeed, to all of us. As the box "Who Pays for Sexual Harassment? *You* Do!" shows, in the long run it's the taxpayer who pays for sexual harassment. **9**

Dealing with Sexual Harassment

Many companies have instituted grievance procedures for victims of sexual harassment. Victims can also file civil or criminal charges against an offender. One of the most important ways to prepare a case is to keep a "paper trail" that documents the offenses. Here are some suggestions for preparing such evidence: **10**

Document each incident of harassment. Include memos that record the dates, times, and specific details of offensive actions. Note the names of any witnesses. **11**

Confront the harasser. There are several ways to do this. You can **12**

- Write a letter to the harasser (a) describing the offensive behavior and when and where it occurred, (b) explaining why you object to the behavior, and (c) stating what you want to happen next; for example, "I am willing to forget what happened if our relationship is a purely professional one from this point on."
- Confront the person who is harassing you either in person or by telephone. Neither of these approaches provides you with written documentation, however. Both are more likely to elicit an emotional response than other tactics.
- Have an attorney write the harasser for you, telling him or her immediately to stop such behavior or to run the risk of a lawsuit. Such a letter lets a harasser know you mean business.

File a grievance. File a formal complaint with the appropriate person, such as a union officer, an affirmative action officer, a personnel director, or an academic dean. **13**

In what is probably the most widely reported case of sexual harassment, members of the Tailhook Association were accused by women midshipmen of both verbal and physical sexual assault during a drunken convention. In the wake of the negative publicity and lawsuits that followed this event, Admiral Frank Kelso resigned his post as Chief of Naval Operations a few months earlier than scheduled.

Seek help from sympathetic coworkers. If confronting the offender and filing a griev- **14** ance do not work, check with coworkers. You may discover that others have been victims of the same harasser. Consider forming a group to discuss and deal with this issue.

File a formal complaint. If the forgoing steps do not get results, you can file a com- **15** plaint with the Equal Employment Opportunity Commission or take the offender to court.

CRITICAL ISSUES

Who Pays for Sexual Harassment? *You* Do!

Sexual harassment is costly for victims and their families, organizations, and society at large. On the *individual level,* victims of sexual harassment experience many emotional and behavioral problems, including depression; dissatisfaction with work or study; a sense of powerlessness, helplessness, and vulnerability; changes in attitude toward sexual relationships or in sexual behaviors; irritability with family, friends, or coworkers; a general sense of anger, fear, or anxiety; and/or alcohol and drug dependency (Koss, 1990; Rabinowitz, 1990).   **16**

Many problems also manifest themselves at the *organizational level.* For example, sexual harassment victims may have high absenteeism, low productivity, and high turnover rates. One study found that sexual harassment had cost 160 major U.S. companies almost $7 million per year in such expenses (Husbands, 1992). Another study found that harassment of women in government jobs led to workplace problems that cost the government approximately $100 million per year in productivity costs (Fitzgerald, 1993).   **17**

Employers incur another cost for sexual harassment in terms of the management time that must be devoted to investigating and defending claims of harassment, to say nothing of the legal expenses and settlements associated with such cases. In one case a San Francisco jury awarded a secretary $7.1 million in punitive damages after finding that her former employer, Baker & McKenzie, one of the nation's biggest law firms, failed to stop a partner from harassing her (Solomon and Miller, 1994).   **18**

On the *societal level,* all of us pay for sexual harassment both directly and indirectly. As taxpayers, we all paid for the female employee who was awarded more than $210,000 in a lawsuit against the United Nations' Undersecretary-General Luis Maria Gomez, an Argentine diplomat, who harassed the employee and tried to fire her after she rejected his advances. We also paid for the $25.2 million that the EEOC paid out in 1993 in sexual harassment claims (Nayyar and Miller, 1994). And, of course, we all pay for the costs of maintaining the EEOC and other similar watchdog agencies throughout the United States.   **19**

Perhaps the most significant costs we pay are the nonmonetary ones: the loss of creative people and their valuable talents. Sexual harassment produces insecurity and destroys self-confidence. These reactions discourage the creative thinking that can produce scientific breakthroughs, entrepreneurial innovations, and artistic contributions.   **20**

approximately 1425 words

COMPREHENSION CHECK

Part I
General Comprehension Questions: Literal and Interpretive

Write the correct letter in the space provided.

_____ 1. Sexual harassment is defined as

    a. any unwelcome sexual advance.
    b. making eye contact when speaking.
    c. sexual conduct that interferes with a person's work.
    d. both a and c.

_____ 2. The author says the percentage of women who never report sexual harassment may be as high as

    a. 75%.
    b. 60%.
    c. 90%.
    d. 83%.

_____ 3. One form of sexual harassment *not* mentioned was

    a. intellectual.
    b. verbal.
    c. nonverbal.
    d. physical.

_____ 4. One reason *not* given for women's failure to report sexual harassment is

    a. they feel nothing will come of it.
    b. they fear they'll lose their jobs.
    c. they think no one will believe them.
    d. they don't like to attract attention.

"WATCH IT.. I HEAR HE JUST TOOK OUT SEXUAL HARASSMENT INSURANCE !"

_____ 5. The highest estimates of sexual harassment incidents have been found in

      a. colleges.
      b. military academies.
      c. the workplace.
      d. homes.

_____ 6. The main idea of the first paragraph is

      a. it is important to define sexual harassment.
      b. sexual harassment is an illegal form of sex discrimination.
      c. sexual harassment first became prominent in 1964.
      d. everyone experiences some form of sexual harassment.

7. Explain what the author means in paragraph 10 by keeping a "paper trail" for victims of sexual harassment.

_____

_____

8. In answering the question "Who pays for sexual harassment?" (paragraphs 16–20), the author replies "You do!" In what ways do we all "pay," and what is the most significant cost we pay?

_____

_____

Part II
Application Questions for Writing and Discussion

9. a. Look again at Table 4.1. Is there anything listed that you would not classify as a form of harassment? Why, or why not?

_____

_____

   b. What would you add to the list that might be considered harassment?

_____

10. a. Beginning with paragraph 10, the author gives a series of procedures for dealing with sexual harassment. Explain how helpful you believe her suggestions are.

_____

_____

   b. What advice would you give a friend—or what steps did you personally take—experiencing harassment?

_____

_____

Part III
Extend Your Vocabulary

Underline the prefixes and suffixes in these boldfaced words. Look at the root. Can you tell the meaning of the word in the phrase? Write the meaning and the part of speech of the boldfaced word.

	Meaning	Part of Speech
1. it was held **illegal** (para. 1)	_____	_____
2. The superior **subordinate** (para.2)	_____	_____
3. the **investigative** arm of Congress (para. 6)	_____	_____
4. may have high **absenteeism** (para. 17)	_____	_____
5. in **punitive** damages (para. 18)	_____	_____

Selection 9: **LITERATURE**

 # Preparation for Reading

Bharati Mukherjee was hailed as "a writer of grace and powerful imagination" when she was inducted into the American Academy of Arts and Sciences in 1993. She left her wealthy existence and sheltered home in India to attend the University of Iowa writing program in 1982, thereafter earning a Ph.D., marrying the writer Clark Blaise, and raising two sons. She has taught at many universities in the United States and Canada and published several novels, books of nonfiction, and collections of short stories. In 1988, she won the National Book Critics Circle Award for her collection *The Middleman and Other Stories.* The basis for her fiction has been the immigrant experience in America. In her writings, she explores how immigrants and their adopted country change one another. Their transformations are often very painful, but with sympathy and insight, Mukherjee creates a vision of hope. The writer Ishmael Reed has said that her point of view has given a new dimension to American literature and that she is the best argument for immigration. Mukherjee herself has been transformed from an obscure writer into one of America's most respected novelists. She currently resides in California and is a professor at the University of California, Berkeley. *Jasmine,* her third novel, was published in 1989 and continues to receive accolades from both critics and readers.

In this excerpt, Jasmine finds herself in an unknown area of Florida. At eighteen, she has left India, her birthplace, after her husband, Prakash, whom she loved passionately, was savagely murdered by a gang of hoodlums. Jasmine unknowingly puts her trust in an evil sea captain, Half-Face, who promises to bring her to America after she pays him all the money she has. He subsequently rapes her, and filled with hatred for both him and herself, she kills him, then flees from the motel where she had been violated.

You will meet some terms used in Indian culture, defined below. As you read the selection, think about the kind of person Jasmine is becoming.

From **Jasmine**

    Bharati Mukherjee

Bharati
Mukherjee

I found Taylor and Wylie Hayes through Lillian Gordon, a kind 1
Quaker lady who rescued me from a dirt trail about three miles east
of Fowlers Key, Florida. In my fake American jacket, *salwar-kameez,*
and rhinestoned *Jullundhari sandals,* with only a purse, Ganpati and
forged documents, I had walked out of an overpopulated, deserted

---

salwar-kameez clothing
Jullundhari sandals name-brand sandals

motel and followed a highway headed north; that's all I knew. In India, I would have come upon at least a village or two, but in Florida there was only the occasional country store or trailer park. I hadn't a penny.

Honoring all prescriptions for a purified body, anticipating only release from this world, I had not eaten in two days. I had taken no water, especially not in the glass that Half-Face offered.   2

Around noon, I could go no farther. My swollen festering tongue was an agony, nearly choking me. A sandy trail tunneled through a distant row of mossy trees. Battered trucks full of produce kept pulling out. More trucks, filled with laborers, turned in. It was as though I'd never left India. After a few minutes, a station wagon driven by a lone woman followed. Fields on either side of the highway were dense with tomatoes, eggplants, and okra (still aubergines and ladies' finger in Masterji's English). I had traveled the world without ever leaving the familiar crops of Punjab. Thinking I was among farmers, that I might find food, water, and work, I decided to follow the trail.   3

Trash cans lined one edge of the clearing. So much trash in America! Bony dogs leaped and snarled at the end of short chains. Mangy hens scuttled in and out of dried-out tire ruts. Short, thick, dark-skinned men with vaguely Asian features—Nepalese, I thought at the time, *Gurkhas;* can this torture all be a dream? where have I come to?—shadowed the windows and doorways of an old barracks, and a wingless parrot hopped on a rusty bar.   4

A boy whistled at me from behind a tree. I couldn't tell his age. He had a child's body: fat stomach and thin legs with crusting sores, but a wrinkled, cynical face. I had been in America nearly a day and had yet to see an "American" face. He carried a plastic Uzi, not that different from the hardware of the Khalsa Lions, and he had the Uzi pointed at me. He did impressive sound effects, too. Kssss! Kssss!   5

"Water," I tried to say. "Pump." Blood still drained from my mouth.   6

The boy dropped down into a sniper's crouch and sprayed me one more time.   7

I made a pumping, drinking gesture.   8

At the far end of the clearing, by the trash cans, a man was teaching two others to drive a low-sprung old sedan. I waved my hands over my head, then pointed to my mouth. "Wah-huh!" I shouted at them. The man behind the steering wheel got out of the sedan. He mimicked the way I talked and walked. The boy and all three men laughed.   9

The driver of the sedan kicked a cola can and sent it clanking toward me. "No work!" he snapped. "This Kanjobal crew. Vamoose! Fuck off! Get lost!"   10

At that moment, an old white lady came out of the barracks. She wore a wide-brimmed straw hat, dark glasses, a T-shirt, and black pants. She must have been seventy. From the doorway she called, "Carlos! How dare you speak to a young lady in such a despicable fashion. She asked for water—well, get her water, man!"   11

She came to me and put her hands on my shoulders. "Child! What is it? You're trembling." She led me to the stairs and sat me down on the middle one. "What in   12

Gurkhas warlike people of Nepal, near India

God's name is this country coming to!" She stood and clapped her hands and shouted out a series of names or commands in a rapid language. Soon, a woman appeared with food on a paper plate and a plastic fork. It was the first hot, prepared food I'd had in over a month. But when I laid a forkful of it on my tongue, I nearly passed out with pain. The woman walked me to her car.

"My name is Lillian Gordon," she said. "I won't ask yours because it's probably a   **13** fake. *This* I take it—she was feeling my kameez—isn't Guatemalan, is it? Are we talking India here? Punjab? Are you Sikh?"

I managed only to shake my head vigorously, no. "Hin—du," I finally said.   **14**

"Lord. Well, there's nothing we can do here, is there? And I suppose those chap-   **15** pies from the INS would leap at the sight of you in those sandals." She motioned me to get in the station wagon.

Lillian Gordon took me home with her. Home was a wooden house on stilts on   **16** blackish swampy ground. But over there, she said, over the black muck and just beyond a fringe of bent Sabal palms, was the Gulf. I got her older daughter's bedroom. Framed, amateurish photos lined the walls. "Kate took those in high school," Lillian said. Sunsets on the beach, a dog. Pretty, but not special. In college she'd come back one summer and shot* in a migrant-worker camp. Five years later she'd done work with the Kanjobals in Florida, the basis of a book that had won a prize. Lillian showed me the book. The pictures brought back such memories of Hasnapur, I wept. That daughter now lived in New York and was a professional photographer. Another daughter was in Guatemala working with Kanjobal Indians. Three Kanjobal women slept in bunk beds in that daughter's room.

I didn't tell Mrs. Gordon what she'd rescued me from. In some fundamental   **17** way, she didn't care. I was no threat, and I was in need. The world's misery was a challenge to her ingenuity. She brought a doctor in to sew my tongue. The Kanjobal women in her house had all lost their husbands and children to an army massacre. She forbade all discussion of it. She had a low tolerance for reminiscence, bitterness or nostalgia. Let the past make you wary, by all means. But do not let it deform you. Had I said, "I murdered a man last night," she might have said, "I'm sure you had an excellent reason. Next time, please, less salt in the eggplant." If I had said, "He raped me," she certainly would have squinted sympathetically, then said, "You're not the first and you won't be the last. Will you be needing an abortion?" She wasn't a missionary dispensing new visions and stamping out the old; she was a facilitator who made possible the lives of absolute *ordinariness* that we ached for.

I was lucky, she said, that India had once been a British colony. Can you imag-   **18** ine being stuck with a language like Dutch or Portuguese? "Look at these poor Kanjobal—they barely speak Spanish!" Lillian, of course, had taught herself Kanjobal. She felt it was the least she could do.

She gave me her daughter's high-school clothes: blouses with Peter Pan collars,   **19** maxi shirts, T-shirts with washed-out pictures, sweaters, cords, and loafers. But beware the shoes, she said, shoes are the biggest giveaway. Undocumented aliens

---

* A term used in photography meaning to take a picture or a series of pictures.

wear boxy shoes with ambitious heels. She opened her thumb and index finger a good six inches like a crocodile's mouth.

Suddenly it all came back: Jullundhar, Prakash, a day just before the end, at Bata 20 Shoes. An image triggered the tears, the screams. The Kanjobal women left the room; Lillian stayed with me, brewing tea.

Prakash in his peach-colored bell-bottomed slacks, kicking off his chappals and 21 asking to see their best "Western" burra sahib leather shoes. Oh, he looked so tall, so proud, lifted in those shoes that gleamed like oiled hair in their boxy brilliance.

"See how tall I am, Jasmine?"   22

"Put these things away," he said to me back in the apartment. "No more chap- 23 pals for me." I felt love like a razor slash across my eyes and tongue, and now with a touch of shame.

"My daughter calls them Third World heels," Lillian said, laughed, after the tea 24 had calmed me down. Walk American, she exhorted me, and she showed me how. I worked hard on the walk and deportment. Within a week she said I'd lost my shy sidle. She said I walked like one of those Trinidad Indian girls, all thrust and cheekiness. She meant it as a compliment.

"Tone it down, girl!" She clapped as I took a turn between the kitchen and bath. 25 I checked myself in the mirror, shocked at the transformation. Jazzy in a T-shirt, tight cords, and running shoes. I couldn't tell if with the Hasnapuri sidle I'd also abandoned my Hasnapuri modesty.

We drove into a mall in Clearwater for the test. Time to try out my American talk 26 and walk. Lillian called me "Jazzy." In one of the department stores I saw my first revolving door. How could something be always open and at the same time always closed? She had me try out my first escalator. How could something be always moving and always still?

At the bottom of the escalator she said, "They pick up dark people like you 27 who're afraid to get on or off." I shut my eyes and stepped forward and kept my eyes closed all the way to the top. I waited for the hairy arm of the law to haul me in. Instead, Lillian said, "You pass, Jazzy." She gave me two dollars. "Now, how about buying me a Dairy Queen?"

I remember Dairy Queen as my first true American food. How it soothed my 28 still-raw tongue. I thought of it as healing food.

approximately 1600 words

Excerpted from Bharati Mukherjee, *Jasmine* (New York: Globe Weidenfeld, 1989) 127–33. Copyright © by Bharati Mukherjee. Reprinted with permission of Grove/Atlantic, Inc. and Penguin Books Canada.

Questions for Writing and Discussion

1. The skill of a writer is often evident by how she or he creates minor characters. How would you describe Lillian Gordon? What kind of a person is she? Why do you suppose she befriends Jasmine and others?

2. Why were the shoes and the walk an important part of Jasmine's transformation? How does Jasmine now see herself?

3. Why does Jasmine refer to a Dairy Queen as "healing food"? There is more than a simple explanation.

4. Part of a writer's skill is setting up conflict in a story. At this point in the novel, what is the major conflict in *Jasmine?*

 Working with the WORLD WIDE WEB

If you would like more information about Bharati Mukherjee, the following Web address will give you a short biography, photos, and links:

http://www.eng.fju.edu.tw/worldlit/india/mukherjee.html

Here is what the top of the Web page looks like:

Bharati Mukherjee

biography and   Relevant links: Further Studies
background   General

For Course Discussion:

    World Literature in English
    (undergraduate course) (syllabus)
    Postconial Literature and Theory
    (graduate course)
• **General issues:**

from "American Dreamer"

(from SAWN)

JOURNAL ENTRY

The essay in this chapter, "Stop Blaming Working Moms," focuses on the blame placed on working mothers for many of society's problems. The textbook selection focuses on sexual harassment in the workplace and educational circles. Also included is an excerpt from the novel *Jasmine,* a story about a young Hindu woman who comes to America. How do you see Jasmine's prospects in this country in the future? What are the opportunities that may or may not be available to her? Write a journal entry that expresses your feelings about these opportunities. Add a statement about how you view *your own* future opportunities and what societal problems you think you may have to face. Does the essay or textbook excerpt give you clues to your answer?

5

Learning Paragraph Patterns

This chapter will help you

❋ recognize patterns used by writers to organize their ideas.

❋ understand how signal words are used to help connect ideas.

❋ identify the relationship between the topic, the main idea, and the writer's patterns of organization.

❋ practice note taking for understanding and remembering information.

Before reading, think about these questions.

❋ What do you imagine a writing pattern might be?

❋ What clues do authors use to show how their writing is organized?

❋ How might writing patterns be similar to speaking patterns?

Jot down your thoughts about the above ideas in the space provided.

_____

_____

◈ Types of Writing

The *type* of writing found in essays, textbooks, and literature is generally classified into four broad categories.

1. *Narration:*   The writer relates, or "narrates," events in some kind of sequence or order. In literature, this means the writer tells a story.
2. *Exposition:*   The word *exposition* means "explanation." In expository writing, the author *exposes* information or ideas. The primary purpose of exposition is *not* to tell a story, as in narration, but rather to explain or inform—for example, to describe how a computer works.
3. *Persuasion:*   In persuasive writing, the author attempts to convince or persuade you of something, to think as he or she does, often trying to change your mind. The topics chosen frequently lend themselves well to argumentation and may be quite controversial in nature. Persuasive writing, which is most often found in essays and editorials, requires critical thinking, a skill emphasized in Part Two of *Effective Reading.*
4. *Description:*   Description is generally used as a supporting device for any of the other three types of writing. Description is most helpful in creating a word picture of something concrete, such as a scene, a person, or a new technology. The writing often gives details that rely on a person's sense to make the reader see how things look or to experience how they may feel, taste, or smell. In textbooks, writers can describe abstract concepts, such as truth or justice.

◈ Understanding the Basic Patterns for Organizing Information

To understand a paragraph, you have to see how the arrangement of the sentence parts fit together to shape the meaning. This arrangement is often referred to as an "organizational pattern." Authors *want* readers to understand the information presented, so they organize it in ways that make learning easier. For this reason, they use thinking and speech patterns with which we are all familiar. How do you normally go about explaining your ideas to someone? Most of us do pretty much the same thing; we use certain patterns.

Patterns of Speech/Thinking	An Example of the Pattern
Classifying and *enumerating* information or *dividing* it into parts	List class assignments
Explaining the order in which something happened	Give directions

Patterns of Speech/Thinking	An Example of the Pattern
Listing the steps in a process	Access computer information
Giving *examples*	Discuss the kinds of exercises you do
Comparing and *contrasting*	Decide whether to buy an American car or a foreign car
Discussing a *cause* and its *effect*	Pass a course, because of diligent study
Defining ideas or concepts	Explain your feelings about a career

Although there are many ways to express ideas, writers rely on these seven basic patterns, generally mixing, overlapping, or combining them in paragraphs and passages. Therefore, the patterns can vary from page to page. Like computer programmers, writers create *programs* or *patterns* to communicate information to their readers. When readers recognize the patterns, they are better able to process the information and think with the author. Further, these patterns help predict and anticipate information, clarify topics or key ideas, and show the relationship of supporting statements.

The writer's purpose and the topic help determine the pattern or patterns to be used. Terms that signal to the reader which pattern is being utilized should be familiar to you, since these are often the very words instructors use in exams and quizzes—for example, *define, compare, contrast, explain, list, describe, analyze*. You have probably encountered these words many times. Understanding writing patterns not only assists you in your reading-study tasks but also better prepares you to take examinations. These patterns can also serve as models or examples for your own writing assignments.

Pattern 1: Classification

Information is often **categorized** or classified into data groups on the basis of similarities and differences. The classification pattern is used extensively by textbook authors, especially in the sciences. Its purpose is to divide a broad topic into categories and analyze the information by breaking it into parts or to explain a series of things by discussing the individual **components.** The reader needs to determine the kinds of categories and how they have been organized. By means of this pattern, lengthy subject matter can be divided into many parts or "chunks," making it easier for the reader to understand and remember.

The process used in classification often takes the form of an outline. The topic or main idea sentence usually helps identify the type of category. Writers often use

---

categorized (kat′ ə gə rīzd′) put into a specifically defined division
components (kəm pó nənts) part of a system or element

numbers to signal a class or division, for example, *two classes,* or *three categories,* or *four divisions,* or *five groups.*

Signal or guide words are an obvious clue for this pattern. Guide words, also sometimes called "transition words," help connect ideas together in a paragraph. Study those listed here so you will recognize them when you are reading and use them when you write answers on examinations and in your general writing.

Signals for Classification				
categories	classification	groups	parts	types
characteristics	elements	kinds	sorts	ways
classes	features	numbers		

Generally, a writer classifies information in a series of statements giving supporting facts or details. The order in which the information is presented is usually not significant and can be switched around without changing the meaning. Read the following paragraph to see whether the meaning would change if the second and third sentences were switched. The signal words are circled.

The Chinese responded to prejudice and persecution in (two ways.) (First,) they created an insulated society-within-a-society that needed little from the dominant culture. (Second,) they displayed a **stoic** willingness to persevere, and to take without complaint or resistance whatever America dished out.

Donald Dale Jackson, "Sojourners Who Came to Stay," *Smithsonian*

When studying textbook material, you may find it helpful to make some notations of the signal or guide words to assist you in understanding information. Circling, highlighting, or underlining after an initial reading can help you recognize the parts of the classification. Then, outlining or mapping by creating a chart or diagram will simplify remembering the information when you study.

Read the following passage, marking the signal words as you do, and then study how it has been outlined on a chart.

Many people have to communicate and work with members of other cultures, and social skills training is now being given to some of these who are about to work abroad. Intercultural communication is necessary for several kinds of people:

1. Tourists are probably the largest category, though they stay for the shortest periods and need to master only a few simple situations—meals, travel, shopping, taxis, etc. To a large extent they are shielded from the local culture by the international hotel culture.

---

stoic (stō′ ik) displaying little emotion

2. Business, governmental, and university visitors, on short business trips, have to cope with a wider range of problems, but are often accommodated in hotels or somewhere similar, and looked after by other expatriates. They, too, are somewhat shielded from the local culture; they rarely learn the language and are given a great deal of help.

3. Businessmen, or others on longer visits of up to five years, students who stay from one to three years, and members of the Peace Corps and Voluntary Service Overseas who stay for two years. This is much more demanding, involving living in a house or apartment, coping with many aspects of the local culture and learning at least some of the language.

Larry A. Samovar and Richard E. Porter, eds., *Intercultural Communication:
A Reader,* 6th ed. (Wadsworth)

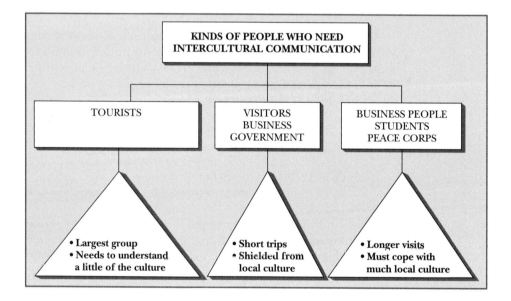

ACTIVITY 5.1

After reading the passages that follow, make notes in the text itself on the main ideas and signal words. The first passage divides phobias (fears people experience) into three general categories. Which one of the fears do you believe would cause people the most anxiety? After reading the passage, without looking back, fill in the map to see what you can remember.

PASSAGE 1

Basically phobias fall into three broad categories. Firstly, a fear of a specific object, such as a cat or spider. Secondly, a fear of a specific situation, such as being in a place, restaurant, school, or outside the home. Thirdly, and more abstract, a fear of a specific illness, or death.

Phobias in the first category—of a specific *object*—are often related to a previous, frightening incident. For example, a child who is already nervous of dogs could be knocked down or bitten by one, causing the fear to develop into a phobia. Or a child of a parent with a snake phobia may have modelled herself on the parent and "caught" it. Sometimes a child under stress at home or school may have an unpleasant experience with an insect or animal, and transfer its anxiety to the creature concerned. The insect or animal may then arouse the anxiety and fear. Fears of animals, birds, insects and so on are almost entirely confined to women—possibly because upbringing still dictates that boys should not show fear of such objects.

Phobias in the second category—of a specific *situation*—can also relate to a frightening incident. For example, a fear of being in a **lift** could be due to having been trapped in one once, or having been locked in a room. But social phobics—with their fear of social situations—and agoraphobics, with their fear of going out into the street, have more complex reasons connected with anxiety behind the onset of their phobia. Indeed, agoraphobia is known as the "calamity syndrome" because it is so often a reaction—sometimes delayed—to the shock of the death of a parent or an operation, or a change of life-style. Sometimes these events are the triggering point of the underlying stress, or depression.

The third category—fear of illness and death—often starts by a friend or relative contracting a particular illness, like cancer or heart trouble. Sometimes the phobic has nursed a dying parent and then becomes **morbidly** convinced he or she will now get the same illness. A specific fear of death—not necessarily tied up with illness—can be a continuation of a childhood fear.

approximately 400 words

Joy Melville, *Phobias and Obsessions*

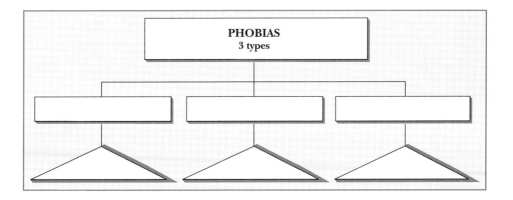

---

lift (lift) British term for elevator

morbidly (mor′ bid lē) preoccupied with unwholesome thoughts or matters

Three major types of computer crimes are explained in the following textbook excerpt.

    a.   Mark the signal words and main idea sentences in the passage.

    b.   After you complete the reading, answer the questions that follow.

PASSAGE 2

Computer Crime

What exactly is computer crime? A computer crime involves the use of a computer to commit a broad range of offenses, including fraud, theft, vandalism, sabotage, embezzlement, tax evasion, treason, and espionage. Computer crimes fall into one of three categories. *Hacking* is unauthorized access to a computer system. Some hackers simply want to enter well-protected, high-security systems because they represent a challenge. Others seek to steal or destroy data stored in the computer system. Where the average low-tech bank robber steals $5000, the average hacker nets $500,000. One quarter of American businesses report losses due to hacking totaling over $700 million annually. Many more companies do not report such losses, fearing embarrassment and loss of customers. The FBI has authority to investigate such crimes under the Computer Fraud and Abuse Act of 1986. The National Security Agency is responsible for protecting government computers.

A second type of computer crime involves the duplication of copyrighted software without the permission of the copyright owner. This is the most commonly committed computer crime, depriving publishers of profits and authors of royalties. A third type of computer crime, called *phreaking* by those in the industry, involves the use of calling cards. Phreakers use computers to randomly dial eleven-digit phone numbers until they find an account's access code. The account is then used to charge long-distance phone calls anywhere in the country—or the world. These numbers may be posted on one or more of the 1000 bulletin boards around the world.

Other games and crimes committed by hackers include *time bombs,* programs inserted in a system and left hidden until triggered to perform some task; the *Trojan horse,* a seemingly useful program but one that can destroy a database; and *superzapping,* bypassing all system controls. Computer crimes are very difficult to detect, and criminals know how to erase the evidence of their illegal activity, which may have lasted only milliseconds. Victims often refuse to report or prosecute and may take weeks to discover a crime has been committed against them.

approximately 300 words

Robert G. Thobaben et al., *Issues in American Political Life*

Remember now to mark the signal words and main idea sentences, and then try to answer these questions without looking back at the passage.

1.   List and briefly explain the three major types of computer crimes.

_____

_____

2. Which type of computer crime do you think deserves the greatest punishment? Explain why.

_____

_____

3. What, if anything, do you believe can be done to deter the spread of computer crimes?

_____

_____

☜ Pattern 2: Sequence or Process

Study the chart that follows, which outlines the various ways writers make use of the sequence pattern.

Type of Sequence	Means	Example
Chronology	Order in which things happen	Trace events that led to Clinton's political problems
Spatial	Where things are located; physical location	Location of position of stars in the galaxy
Order of importance	Most or least important	Factors to consider in leasing a car
Process	Methods or stages in something; "how to"	Steps to follow in a chemical experiment

Writers of history textbooks rely heavily on the sequence pattern to write about events that need to be presented in the order in which they happened, that is, in a chronological or time order. On the other hand, a sequence pattern using **spatial** order emphasizes the size, the place, or location of things, that is, the details

_____

spatial (spā′ shəl) happening or existing in space

are organized by their relative position. A novelist can use spatial order, for example, to describe an indoor or outdoor setting—a room, a building, a forest. Spatial order can also be used to describe a geographical location; thus, the pattern is often used by writers of science textbooks. With order of importance, the writer may detail information from the most important to the least important events or do the opposite, giving the least important first. Finally, in process analysis, a procedure or way of doing something is presented; the writer may present a series of steps in a procedure or the stages in which things develop. This type of sequence frequently appears in science, business, and math textbooks.

The order in sequence is significant and cannot be **transposed.** This is the major important difference between classification and sequence. For example, a history book can use time order to explain a series of events in a war, while a biology text can use a time sequence to show the evolutionary stages of animals. A manual on automotive transmissions can explain repairs in their order of importance, in a sequence of steps.

Generally, signal words help the reader see which important details will be developed in a sequential pattern. As with the classification pattern, numbers may be used, but for the purpose of showing time order or steps in a process, not for the purpose of merely listing at random. Dates are also often a clue to time order. The major signal words to help you recognize the sequence pattern follow.

Signals for Sequence		
first	now	later
second	after	stages
third	before	steps
next	finally	then
most important	furthermore	when
last		

Read the following paragraphs and note the circled signal words, which help the reader follow Hemingway's step-by-step analysis of what makes some Spaniards declare a bullfighter's work to be "vulgar." Then, complete the outline of ideas.

The (three absolute) acts of the tragedy are (first) the entry of the bull when the **picadors** receive the shock of his attacks and attempt to protect their horses with their lances. (Then) the horses go out and the (second act) is the planting of the banderillas. This is one of the most interesting and difficult parts but among the easiest for a new bull fight fan

---

transposed (trans pōzd′) reversed

picadors (pik′ ə dôrs) horsemen who jab the bull with a lance to weaken its neck and shoulder muscles

to appreciate in technique. The banderillas are three-foot, gaily colored darts with a small fish hook prong in the end. The man who is going to plant them walks out into the arena alone with the bull. He lifts the banderillas at arm's length and points them toward the bull. (Then) he calls "Toro! Toro!" The bull charges and the **banderillero** rises to his toes, bends in a curve forward and (just) as the bull is about to hit him drops the darts into the bull's hump just back of his horns.

They must go in evenly, one on each side. They must not be shoved, or thrown or stuck in from the side. This is (the first time) the bull has been completely baffled, there is the prick of the darts that he cannot escape and there are no horses for him to charge into. But he charges the man again and again and each time he gets a pair of the long banderillas that hang from his hump by their tiny barbs and flop like porcupine quills.

(Last) is the death of the bull, which is in the hands of the **matador** who has had charge of the bull since his first attack. Each matador has two bulls in the afternoon. The death of the bull is most formal and can only be brought about in one way, directly from the front by the matador who must receive the bull in full charge and kill him with a sword thrust between the shoulders just back of the neck and between the horns. (Before) killing the bull he must (first) do a series of passes with the muleta, a piece of red cloth he carries about the size of a large napkin. With the muleta the torero must show his complete mastery of the bull, must make the bull miss him again and again by inches, before he is allowed to kill him. It is in (this phase) that most of the fatal accidents occur.

approximately 400 words

Mary Hemingway, *By-Line: Ernest Hemingway*

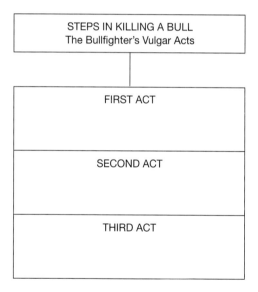

STEPS IN KILLING A BULL
The Bullfighter's Vulgar Acts

FIRST ACT

SECOND ACT

THIRD ACT

---

banderillero (ban′ də rel yar′ ō) man who thrusts in the banderillas in a bullfight
matador (mat′ ə dôr) bullfighter who has the principal role in the fight

Questions for Discussion and Writing

1. Is bullfighting more barbaric than any sports followed in the United States? If so, which sports? Why do you think so?

    _____

    _____

2. Why do people attend events like the bullfight?_____

    _____

    _____

3. Would you like to see a bullfight? Why, or why not?_____

    _____

    _____

ACTIVITY 5.2

PASSAGE 1

In the passage that follows, the history of white-collar crime is traced.

    a. Circle the key dates as you read.
    b. List the significance of major dates in the space provided.
    c. Answer the questions that follow.

White-collar crime, an umbrella term coined in 1949 by Edwin Sutherland, implies a violation of the law by an individual who uses his or her position or influence for the purpose of illegal gain. In the 1950s and 1960s, criminologists specializing in this new field usually studied **antitrust** offenses. During the 1970s the emphasis shifted to illegal corporate activity, such as harming workers in nuclear facilities, causing injury to consumers,

_____

antitrust (an′ ti trust′) designed to prevent restraints on trade as by business monopolies or damaging the environment. In the late 1980s the focus shifted to the **deviant** behavior of individuals in the white-collar workplace, with emphases on the stock market and computers. White-collar crime costs U.S. businesses between $40 and $200 billion annually, and the FBI's white-collar crime section is devoting more resources to this problem than ever before, having declared it in 1988 to be one of the top national investigative priorities, along with organized crime, terrorism, and **espionage.**

In 1986, two well-known figures on Wall Street, Dennis Levine and Ivan Boesky, pleaded guilty to charges of insider trading. Levine paid an $11 million fine, and Boesky agreed to a plea-bargained arrangement in which he paid $100 million in penalties and was sentenced to three years in a minimum-security prison. The Securities and Exchange Commission (SEC) and FBI continued the investigations, bringing charges against Drexel Burnham Lambert and Michael Milken, the junk bond czar. . . . The firm pleaded guilty to six federal felony charges and paid $650 million to close the largest securities fraud case in history, a fine four times larger than the SEC's annual budget. Federal investigations expanded in 1989 to examine possible trading practice violations on Chicago's two commodity exchanges and four New York futures exchanges. What exactly is insider trading and why has it assumed such a high profile for law enforcement in the 1990s?

The Securities Exchange Act of 1934 prohibits fraud in connection with the sale of any securities, and Rule 14e-3 specifically makes it illegal for anyone with inside information regarding a pending takeover to trade the targeted company's stock. The exotic world of speculating on stock became a major enterprise in the 1980s when American businesses conducted a record number of corporate takeovers and mergers.

approximately 270 words

Robert G. Thobaben et al., *Issues in American Political Life*

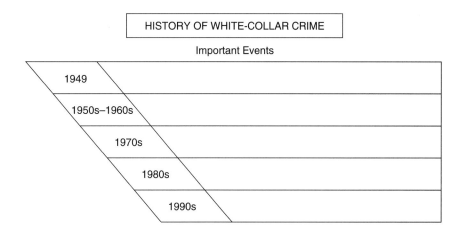

deviant (dē' vē ənt) turn away from what is considered normal in a group or society

espionage (es' pē ə näzh') spying; the use of spies by a government to learn the military secrets of other nations

1. How has the meaning of "white-collar crime" changed during the past half century?

   _____

2. Do you think that white-collar crimes are as serious a threat to society as organized crime, terrorism, or espionage? Why, or why not?

   _____

   _____

PASSAGE 2

Choosing a mate or partner involves three stages, according to one textbook author.

a. As you read the following passage, mark the signal word clues and main idea sentences.

b. On the basis of your own experiences in selecting a mate, decide whether the order given is logical.

c. List the three stages, and indicate which you believe is the most important one.

Several researchers have studied the mate-selection process, and according to a synthesis of their findings, choosing a mate occurs in three stages: the **stimulus** stage, the values stage, the roles stage.

In the first stage, one or more initiating stimuli—appearance, intellect, popularity, social status—make two parties notice each other. Physical attractiveness, of course, is a powerful stimulus, especially for men. Women look for attractiveness, too, but they are also drawn by status, preferring a leader over a follower, or a slightly older man over a slightly younger one, or a man with more education, or a better job. . . .

In the second stage, the couple compares their values. They discuss their attitudes toward work, marriage, religion, culture, and society. The more similar their views are, the more likely it is that the attraction will deepen, since such **concurrence** enhances each party's self-image. Similar values and interests also lead to shared activities through which the couple may further confirm their suitability.

Finally, as the couple interacts more frequently and becomes more intimate, they begin to develop their roles with each other. Role development is far deeper than the comparison of general values in the previous stage: it is a testing of the relationship in which each partner discovers how the other copes with the situations of daily life—finding out whether the other person shoulders or shirks responsibility, is honest or deceitful, is basically happy and stable or moody and unpredictable. . . .

Kathleen Berger, *The Developing Person Through the Life Span*

---

stimulus (stim′ yə ləs) action that causes an activity
concurrence (kən kûr′ əns) agreement

1. The three stages in choosing a mate are as follows: _____

_____

_____

2. The most important stage is _____

3. Do you think the order is logical? _____

As you read the following descriptive paragraph, use the marked phrases to help you follow the author's details. Try to visualize the kitchen, and then, make a simple sketch that shows you have pictured the spatial order that Kazin has presented.

PASSAGE 3

The kitchen held our lives together. My mother worked in it all day long, we ate in it almost all meals except the Passover **seder,** I did my homework and first writing at the kitchen table, and in winter I often had a bed made up for me on three kitchen chairs near the stove. On the wall just over the table hung a long horizontal mirror that sloped to a ship's prow at each end and was lined in cherry wood. It took up the whole wall, and drew every object in the kitchen to itself. The walls were a fiercely **stippled** whitewash, so often rewhitened by my father in slack seasons that the paint looked as if it had been squeezed and cracked into the walls. A large electric bulb hung down the center of the kitchen at the end of a chain that had been hooked into the ceiling; the old gas ring and key still jutted out of the wall like antlers. In the corner next to the toilet was the sink at which we washed, and the square tub in which my mother did our clothes. Above it, tacked to the shelf on which were pleasantly ranged square, blue-bordered white sugar and spice jars, hung calendars from the Public National Bank on Pitkin Avenue and the Minsker Progressive Branch of the Workman's Circle; receipts for the payment of insurance premiums, and household bills on a spindle; two little boxes engraved with Hebrew letters. One of these was for the poor, the other to buy back the Land of Israel. Each spring a bearded little man would suddenly appear in our kitchen, salute us with a hurried Hebrew blessing, empty the boxes (sometimes with a sidelong look of **disdain** if they were not full), hurriedly bless us again for remembering our less fortunate Jewish brothers and sisters, and so take his departure until the next spring, after vainly trying to persuade my mother to take still another box.

approximately 325 words

Alfred Kazin, *A Walker in the City*

_____

seder (sā′ dər) the feast commemorating the exodus of the Israelites from Egypt
stippled (stip′ əld) painted in dots or short touches
disdain (dis dān′) to despise or treat with contempt

Sketch of the Kitchen

Question for Writing and Discussion

Is there a room or place that is special in your life? Using signal words that help show spatial order, write a paragraph describing your special place.

_____

_____

_____

_____

_____

_____

_____

Read the following short textbook excerpt to decide which type of sequence the writer has used.

PASSAGE 4

To compare decimal numbers:

1. Compare whole-number parts.
2. If whole-number parts are equal, compare digits place by place, starting at the tenths place and moving to the right.
3. Stop when two digits in the same place are different.
4. The digit that is larger determines the larger decimal number.

Cheryl Cleaves et al., *College Mathematics for Technology*

Circle the letter of the sequence type used:

a. chronology   b. order of importance   c. spatial   d. process

◈ Pattern 3: Simple Listing

There is a significant difference between using the patterns of classification and sequence and simply listing details.

- In the classification pattern, numbers are used to designate various components—*two ways, three kinds,* and so on. The components are presented in random order. In the sequence pattern, numbers are used to indicate a *particular* order and are not random: *the first step, the second step,* and so on.
- In the simple listing pattern, writers develop their ideas by *listing* their supporting statements. They simply list or enumerate a series of ideas, facts, statistics, or other details that support a point. The details may be examples, reasons, or types of things, and they are often, *but not always,* numbered. This pattern is used frequently by textbook authors, as it is a clear, easy way to organize information, particularly when an author wants to present several important points.

    Remember, the order in which the listing is done is not important; it can be changed without changing the meaning. The reader must try to make a connection between items to see how they are related to each other to help remember them. For example, an author might list the four main functions of e-mail but not necessarily develop or expand them.

Signals for Simple Listing	
1, 2, 3, 4	another
a, b, c, d	moreover
first, second	next
also	then

Notice the random order of the following list of views of God from a philosophy textbook.

> But God is also pictured more widely in terms of men's work and crafts and professions. . . .
>
> 1. *The shepherd.* God is a shepherd whose sheep are men: 'Ye are my sheep, the sheep of my pasture are many . . . saith the Lord God' (Ezek. 34.31).
> 2. *The farmer.* 'I will sift the house of Israel . . . like as corn is sifted into a sieve; yet shall not the least grain fall on the earth' (Amos 9.9).
> 3. *The dairymaid.* Job speaks of God as one who has 'poured me out as milk, and curdled my like cheese' (Job 10.10).
> 4. *The fuller—the laundress.* In Mal. 3.2 God is said to be 'like fuller's soap,' a theme further developed in Isa. 4.4 which speaks of a time when God will have 'washed away the filth of the daughters of Zion.'
> 5. *The builder.* In Amos 7.7 we read that 'the Lord stood beside (or upon) a wall made by a plumbline, with a plumbline in his hand.'
> 6. *The potter.* 'Behold, as the clay in the potter's hand, so are you in mine hand O house of Isreal' (Jer. 18.6)—and the verse has echoes in Isaiah where as the 'father and friend' of Jeremiah, we now have God as 'father and potter': 'O Lord, thou are our father: we are the clay, and thou art our potter' (Isa 64.8).
>
> David Stewart, *Exploring the Philosophy of Religion*

ACTIVITY 5.3

Read the following textbook excerpts on the topic of listening to determine which pattern is being used in the section "Forms of Listening" and which in "Becoming an Effective Listener." Then answer the questions that follow.

PASSAGE 1

Forms of Listening

Many types of listening behavior are as common in business as they are in personal communication.

- *Cynical listening* is a type of defensive listening that occurs when people fear that a message is intended to take advantage of them. . . .
- *Offensive listening* is listening that attempts to catch the speaker in a mistake or contradiction, much as a lawyer does when cross-examining a witness. . . .
- *Polite listening* is a kind of mechanical listening characterized by inattention. The listener really wants the speaker to stop talking so that he or she can begin. Because polite listeners often rehearse their own lines instead of paying attention, polite

TABLE 4

Percentage of Population in Metropolitan Areas in Different
Size Groups, by Continents, 1960

	ONE MILLION AND OVER	100,000 AND OVER
North America	27.2	49.7
Latin America	14.7	27.4
Europe *	12.5	29.6
Asia	6.2	12.3
Africa	2.6	8.1
Oceania	23.6	43.3
World Total	9.6	19.9

* Including all of the USSR.
SOURCE: Adapted from Homer Hoyt, *World Urbanization,* Technical Bulletin #43
(Washington, D. C.: Urban Land Institute, 1962), Table II, p. 26.

Africa).[17] One authority predicts that by the year 2000 over 42 per cent
of the world's population will live in metropolitan areas of at least 100,000
inhabitants, in contrast to the 19.9 per cent of the world's population
living in such areas in 1960.[18]

CAUSES OF WORLD METROPOLITAN GROWTH

Among the obvious reasons for growth of metropolitan agglomerations
are population increase and industrial advances. The birth rate throughout the world is much higher than the death rate. Therefore, even if there
were no migration to metropolitan areas, the population in these areas
would increase substantially. But heavy migration to cities is also taking
place. In the industrialized countries the exodus from farms and villages
is spurred by agricultural mechanization which reduces the need for farm
labor. Metropolitan growth has been spurred in the already industrialized
countries, because as their industries become increasingly large-scale,
bureaucratic, and specialized, they require larger and more interlocking
labor forces. Other technological advances that have promoted metropolitan development in the industrialized countries include fast, flexible
transportation such as the auto, which enables the metropolis to expand
territorially without losing its unity.

The metropolitan areas of England and western Europe are among
the largest in highly industrial countries. The London "conurbation," as
metropolitan areas are called in Great Britain, contains over 10 million
people and covers more than 700 square miles. The second largest con-

[17] Gibbs, *op. cit.,* p. 384.   [18] Hoyt, *op. cit.,* Table XVII, p. 50.

and Calcutta, in countries with little urban or industrial development.

In general, as Table 4 shows, metropolitan development is concentrated in the most industrialized regions of the world. Asia and Africa, the least developed regions, are conspicuously below the world average in proportion of population living in metropolitan areas. It should be noted, however, that Asia and Africa do have significant metropolitan populations.

THE METROPOLITAN FUTURE

Metropolitan areas are a major component of the urban population now and will become even more so in the future. Computation of growth rates for the metropolitan areas delineated by the IUR indicates that virtually all of them are growing rapidly. An outstanding finding was that the highest growth rates are those of metropolitan areas in the less industrialized regions (southern Asia, the Middle East, and southern

large country town of 34,000 in 1930, but in 20 years it had 208,000 residents, a seven-fold increase; and by 1959 it had a population of 402,000. Abidjan, Ivory Coast, had only 22,000 inhabitants in 1930 but was more than seven times as large in 1960. Nairobi, Kenya, doubled in size during the 1940–50 decade and then doubled again in the 1950–60 decade.[10]

Accra, capital of Ghana, had only 40,000 inhabitants in 1930, had doubled in population by 1950, and had a population of almost a half-million by 1960. In Nigeria, Lagos had a population of 126,000 in 1930 and had more than doubled to 364,000 by 1960. Dar-es-Salaam, capital of Tanganyika, almost doubled its population of 69,000 in less than 10 years; by 1957 it had 129,000 inhabitants.

Urban growth in Latin America is also at very high levels. Venezuela has the highest rate, with an annual increase of 7 per cent in urban population. At that rate Venezuela's urban population will double in less than 10 years. In seven additional Latin American countries, out of the 15 for which data are available, urban population will double in less than 18 years. Individual cities have even more striking rates. Lima had roughly a half-million inhabitants in 1940 and by 1957 had 1.3 million, thus tripling its population in just 17 years.[11]

São Paulo added a million and a half inhabitants during the 1950–60 period, and had a population of 3.6 million in 1960. The new capital of Brazil, Brasilia, had only 12,000 people in 1957 but 131,000 only four years later. Guatemala City grew from 284,000 in 1950 to 382,000 in 1960, a 35 per cent increase. Equally spectacular has been the growth of Mexico City, which has mushroomed into a gigantic metropolis of five million, one of the largest in the Western Hemisphere.

Elsewhere in the underdeveloped countries, large cities have also grown rapidly. Not all cities in underdeveloped countries are growing this fast, but these are perhaps fairly representative of a widespread trend toward urbanism. Many of the cities of great size in underdeveloped areas are commercial-administrative centers, and some are seaports through which may be transported raw products from the hinterlands.

The world's future is clearly urban. The industrialized Western nations are already highly urbanized, and the underdeveloped non-Western nations are on an upswing of urban growth. The completion of this process may mark the end of what Davis and Golden have called a "gigantic cycle"—the urbanization of the world.

WORLD METROPOLITAN DEVELOPMENT

Not only is the world becoming more urban; it is also becoming more metropolitan. A metropolitan community is an extensive geographic unit

---

[10] *Ibid.*, and *Demographic Yearbook, op. cit.*, Table 7.
[11] Philip Hauser (ed.), *Urbanization in Latin America* (1961), pp. 76, 178.

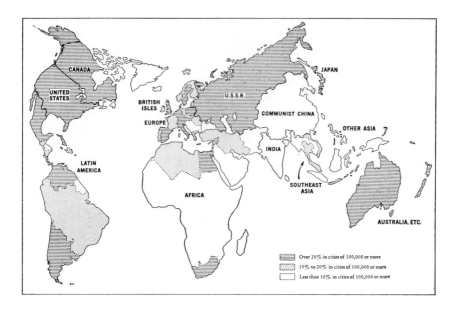

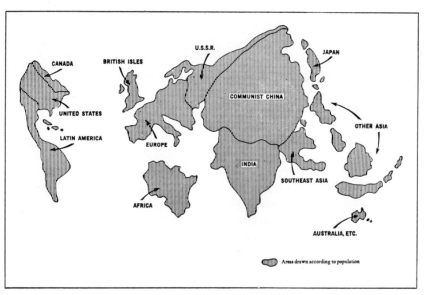

Figure 7. Upper map, showing degrees of urbanization in major world regions, indicates that highly urbanized countries are concentrated in North America and Europe. Lower map, showing areas of the world drawn to scale according to total population in 1960, indicates why the study of cities must include those in non-Western, less-urbanized areas. Many of the least urbanized countries have enormous populations and hence already contain large numbers of urban dwellers. SOURCE: Lower map is adapted from *The New York Times*, June 3, 1962, p. E11. © 1962 by the New York Times Company.

whose social and economic activities form a more or less integrated system centering around a large city. Although metropolitan development has gained most headway in the United States and in other highly industrialized countries, metropolitan areas are now found in every part of the world.

Delineation of World Metropolitan Areas

Comparison of metropolitan development among the various countries of the world runs headlong into the problem of scarcity of basic data and of widely varying definitions used by the countries that do gather such statistics. The International Urban Research staff at the University of California has greatly remedied this situation by developing a set of criteria suitable for international comparisons.[12] Applying them on a worldwide basis resulted in the delineation of approximate boundaries for 720 metropolitan areas out of a probable total of 1,046 such areas in the world in 1954. By 1959 there were 1,064 metropolitan areas.[13] Of the 202 countries and territories investigated, 105 proved to have at least one metropolitan area. The IUR applied the same definition in each country, and hence the resulting metropolitan areas are comparable units.

Comparison of metropolitan areas of the United States with those of the United Kingdom and Canada, when all these metropolitan areas have their boundaries defined by IUR criteria, shows a common tendency for the outer rings of the metropolitan area to expand more rapidly than the central cities. This tendency had already been noted in the United States. Now it is established that it also occurs in other highly urban-industrial countries. For example, the IUR criteria yield 58 metropolitan areas in the United Kingdom (52 in England and Wales, 5 in Scotland, and 1 in Northern Ireland); in 47 of them the outlying part of the metropolitan area grew faster than the central city.[14] Many of the United Kingdom's central cities, in fact, showed a tendency for actual declines in population, comparable to trends observed in the United States. In Canada, where the metropolitanization process began later than in the United States and the United Kingdom, the outer metropolitan rings

[12] International Urban Research, *The World's Metropolitan Areas* (1959). The criteria are a modification of those used by the United States census in delineating Standard Metropolitan Areas. The IUR definition of metropolitan area is "An area with 100,000 or more inhabitants, containing at least one city (or continuous urban area) with 50,000 or more inhabitants, and those administrative divisions contiguous to the city (or to the continuous urban area) which meet certain requirements as to metropolitan character." The "requirements as to metropolitan character" for the adjacent territory include at least 65 per cent of the labor force working at occupations other than agriculture.

[13] Jack Gibbs, "The Growth of Individual Metropolitan Areas: A Global View," *Annals of the Association of American Geographers* (December, 1961), p. 381.

[14] Leo Schnore, "Metropolitan Development in the United Kingdom," *Economic Geography* (July, 1962), 215–33.

Rapidly growing cities in non-Western nations. India and Jordan are among the many as yet little-urbanized countries beginning an upswing of urban expansion. Above: A street scene in Amman, capital of Jordan. Amman's population rose from 25,000 in 1950 to 300,000 in 1960. Facing page: A busy intersection in Calcutta, India. The Calcutta metropolitan area grew by 52 per cent between 1941–51 and by another 33 per cent between 1951–61, reaching a population of 5.5 million in 1961. (Courtesy United Nations.)

are growing faster than the central cities, but the central cities are not generally declining in population.[15]

DISTRIBUTION OF THE WORLD'S METROPOLITAN AREAS

Applying the IUR criteria, the New York-Northeastern New Jersey metropolitan area, with a population of over 14.5 million in 1960, is the largest in the world. Tokyo-Yokohama ranks second with a population of about 11.5 million and London's 10.5 million places it third. Moscow ranks fourth with a metropolitan population of almost 7.5 million. Other very large metropolitan areas are Paris, Osaka-Kobe, Shanghai, Chicago–Northwestern Indiana, Buenos Aires, Calcutta, and Los Angeles.[16] Significantly, the list includes several metropolitan areas, such as Shanghai

[15] Leo Schnore and Gene Petersen, "Urban and Metropolitan Development in the United States and Canada," *The Annals of the American Academy of Political and Social Science,* 316 (March, 1958), 60–68.

[16] "The World's Great Cities," *Population Bulletin,* 16 (September, 1960), Table 3.

listening usually accomplishes very little. Many job applicants are guilty of polite listening. Instead of actively listening to what the job recruiter is saying, they are planning what to say next. . . .

- *Active listening*, on the other hand, is a form of listening that requires both sincere involvement with the information and **empathy** with the speaker's situation. . . . In business, active listening is the basis for effective communication.

Becoming an Effective Listener

You can improve your listening skills in both formal and informal business situations by applying the following principles. Many of the same principles can also be used to improve reading.

Learn the Art—and Wisdom—of Silence Silence not only gives someone else the opportunity to speak but gives you the opportunity to learn from another person's perspective. . . .

Be Aware of "Emotional Filters" Ask yourself whether you have strong opinions about the subject of the message or about the person to whom you are listening. Emotional reactions to words, people, or situations can cloud your thinking.

Be Slow to Judge If your natural tendency is to interrupt and argue when you disagree with what you hear, you may lose the opportunity to learn and, perhaps, to change your opinions for the better. Realizing that we all come to listening situations with preconceived viewpoints will help you avoid judging alternative ideas too quickly. Keeping an open mind often means being aware of your prejudices and seeking out evidence to disprove your own point of view.

Ask Questions to Focus Your Listening "The only dumb question is the question not asked." This **maxim** is as true in business as it is in personal communication. When you do not understand a concept, word, or phrase, be direct and ask, "What does that mean?" In the end, these interruptions are time savers, not time wasters. Listening patiently without understanding accomplishes little.

When you are finished asking questions, use clarifying statements to make sure that you have understood the message correctly. . . .

Focus on What Is Important It is estimated that only one in four people listening to a formal speech actually grasps the speaker's main idea. In normal business conversation as in public speaking, when poorly organized speakers intermingle unrelated facts with key points, it may be difficult to focus on critical issues. You can make listening easier by asking pointed questions, taking clear notes, being sensitive to repetition, and recognizing language transitions that focus attention on key concepts.

Be an Active Listener To avoid becoming an inattentive listener, focus your "extra" listening time—the time available to you because listening is faster than speaking—on the speaker's message: Try to anticipate what will be said next, review and summarize the points already

---

empathy (em′ pə thē) deep understanding of the feelings, thoughts, and motives of one person by another

maxim (mak′ sim) a short rule or principle of conduct

made, evaluate and question the presentation, and listen between the lines (remember that changes in volume, tone, and body language can be more important than words). *Active concentration* is the key to effective listening.

approximately 600 words

Louis E. Boone and David L. Kurtz, *Contemporary Business Communication*
Copyright © 1994, Prentice Hall. Reprinted by permission.

1. The pattern used for "Forms of Listening" is _____.

    Reason for choice: _____

2. The pattern used for "Becoming an Effective Listener" is _____.

    Reason for choice: _____

3. Which principle of listening do you think most people find difficult to practice?

    _____

4. In what ways are the principles of listening related to reading improvement?

    _____

PASSAGE 2

Read the following article on how to find something you've misplaced. Notice the signal word *steps* as well as the numerical listing of the points. After reading the article, decide

a. Must the steps be followed in sequence?
b. Has the author used one particular pattern or a combination of several patterns?
c. Has the writer of this article overlooked any steps that you would find helpful in locating a misplaced item?

Lose your car keys? Can't find your wallet? Have no clue what you did with that last Visa bill?

When in doubt, call on St. Anthony—patron saint of lost things. If you'd rather search in a more conventional fashion, call on Professor Solomon. Solomon—a sometimes bookstore clerk, substitute teacher, magician and actor—is the author of the newly published "How to Find Lost Objects."

Calling on his experience maintaining the lost-and-found box at a public high school, Solomon developed a method for finding lost stuff. Here are the steps:

1. Don't look for it. Though your first inclination might be to ransack your home, don't start searching until you have an idea where to look.
2. It's not lost—you are. There are no missing objects. Only unsystematic searchers.
3. Remember the three C's. Search with comfort, calmness and confidence.
4. It's where it's supposed to be. Or at least it might be. So look there first.
5. Domestic drift. Objects are often left where last used, instead of where they are normally kept.
6. You're looking right at it. An agitated mind would allow you to look right at an object and not see it.
7. The camouflage effect. Be sure to check under anything that might be camouflaging your object.
8. Think back. You were there when your object was misplaced, so you have to have some faint memory of what happened.
9. Look once. Look well. Check every place thoroughly once.
10. The Eureka Zone. Objects tend to travel no more than 18 inches from their original location.
11. Tail thyself. Recreate the scene of the crime.
12. It wasn't you. When all else fails, explore the possibility that your item was misappropriated, not misplaced.

approximately 280 words

Mary Jo Dilonardo, "Just Don't Misplace This Book," *San Francisco Examiner.*
Reprinted by permission of Scripps Howard News Service.

Answer these questions.

1. Must the steps be followed in sequence? _____

2. The pattern the writer used is _____.

3. Are there any steps the writer overlooked that you use in finding lost or misplaced items? _____

_____

_____

⥽ Pattern 4: Comparison and Contrast

In *comparing* ideas or items, writers explain similarities between them; in *contrasting* ideas or items, writers show differences. Writers often use the comparison and contrast method to show the positive and negative sides, or advantages and disadvantages, of an issue or event; the material can be organized to either emphasize likenesses, differences, or both. Frequently, writers may make comparisons and contrasts within the same paragraph.

Often, the writer uses something people are familiar with or know well to help the reader understand something unknown or different. When you encounter this writing pattern, asking the following questions can help you understand the writer's organization. Ask:

What subject or subjects are being compared or contrasted?

In what ways are these things similar? Different?

What is the main idea that is being explained?

Making a list of similarities or differences in a column format is a good note-taking device because it helps you sort out and remember points readily.

The comparison and contrast pattern is a useful one for you to learn to use when writing, whether your goal is to provide information or to emphasize, evaluate, or persuade. Readers should be able to spot this pattern because of the terms used to signal likenesses and differences.

Signals for Comparison		
compare	like/alike	resembles
in comparison	likewise	similar
in the same way/manner	parallels	similarly
Signals for Contrast		
although	however	on the other hand
as opposed to	in contrast to	rather than
but	instead	unlike
conversely	nevertheless	whereas
difference	on the contrary	yet
different		

Below are *the first two sentences* of the paragraph that follows on page 253. Read them, noting the word *resemble*, which signals comparison.

Elephants are the biggest land creatures on Earth, and among the smartest and most endearing. In their lives and social dynamics they resemble humans in many ways.

a. Try to predict what similarities might be discussed.

b. List a few details you might expect to find in the paragraph on the following chart.

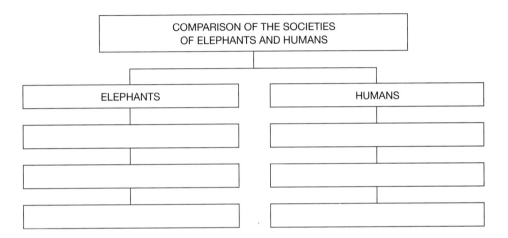

Now, read the rest of the paragraph to see how well you anticipated the details.

> They live in **matriarchal** societies—groups of sisters, aunts, nieces and nephews, often headed by a wise old grandmother. The bonds formed within an elephant family can last a lifetime that may span 60 or more years. Scientists who have studied elephants in the wild have noted in them such human-like characteristics as joy, grief, anger, loyalty, patience, playfulness, and sibling rivalry. To the 17th century poet John Donne, the elephant was "Nature's great masterpiece . . . the only harmless great thing."
>
> Jim Merritt, "Requiem for a Heavyweight," *Modern Maturity*

List three ways in which the author compared elephants and people.

1. _____

2. _____

3. _____

---

matriarchal (mā trē är′ kəl) ruled by the female

ACTIVITY 5.4

PASSAGE 1

Richard Cohen, a columnist for the *Washington Post,* analyzes some of the accomplishments of two former presidents, Kennedy and Reagan, in the following editorial. Circle the signal words to help you decide whether the writing pattern is comparison, contrast, or both.

Leaders' Private Lives May Be Irrelevant

. . . In some ways, John Kennedy is the functional equivalent of Ronald Reagan. Just as some people cannot deal with the fact that Kennedy might have been a pretty lousy husband but a pretty good president, others—and I was once one—could not accept the fact that Reagan could be a pretty good president while being intellectually lazy. In other words, it was hard to accept that he might have been right on a few big things—the state of the Soviet Union, the **perniciousness** of the welfare state—while being so wrong about so many other ones.

In Kennedy's case, his personal morality seems not to have affected his presidency at all (although he took some frightful chances). His approval ratings were astronomical—his 78 percent was higher than Ike ever reached and only George Bush's post–Gulf War 83 percent exceeded it—and he did **imbue** the nation with the now-odd notion that government service was both wonderful and noble. He had, in other words, innate leadership qualities. Women loved him—but so, in their own way, did men.

Reagan, too, had innate leadership abilities. Like Kennedy's, they were rooted in a personal **charisma** that was part physical and part ideological. Reagan was a famously passive person who had no fire wall at all between what he had seen in the movies and real life. Thus, he was capable of telling Israeli Prime Minister Yitzhak Shamir that he had been present at the liberation of a German death camp when, really, he had only seen the films. . . .

At the same time, though, Reagan knew—or maybe just sensed—that the Soviet Union was not a lean, mean totalitarian machine, but a crumpling, sagging empire. He was going to give it the push needed to topple it—and he did. . . . Reagan was right about the state of the Soviet Union and many others—and here my hand is raised—were not. In Isaiah Berlin's famous formulation, Reagan was a **hedgehog.** He knew one big thing.

Kennedy, of course, was a fox. He knew many things. But whatever they were, both Reagan's and Kennedy's careers suggest that we make too much of both intellectual brilliance and private morality. . . . What matters most is leadership ability—that certain something, learned or innate, that silences a room when that person enters.

approximately 390 words

Richard Cohen, "Leaders' Private Lives May Be Irrelevant," *San Jose Mercury News* 11 Nov. 1997: B7

---

perniciousness (pòr nish′ ŏs nes) the act of causing great injury; destruction or ruin
imbue (im byo͞o′) to fill the mind or to inspire
charisma (kò riz′ mò) a special quality of leadership that captures the imagination, that inspires allegiance and devotion

1. The writing pattern used is _____.

2. The writer's thesis is _____

    _____.

3. State the author's supporting details that illustrate why he compared Reagan to a "hedgehog" and Kennedy to a "fox."

    _____

    _____

4. Explain whether or not Richard Cohen has convinced you that a leader's private life and deeds should not diminish his or her political accomplishments. You may also wish to consider Bill Clinton's place in history in answering the question.

    _____

    _____

PASSAGE 2

Let's examine how writers can use both comparison and contrast within the same passage.

> The sex of the instructor affected the extent of active student participation. In classes taught by men with roughly equal proportions of male and female students, male students were responsible for about 75 percent of all class discussion; with women as instructors, female student participation rose from 25 percent to 42 percent, while male participation slipped from 75 percent to 58 percent. Many female students are apparently more comfortable in a class taught by a female instructor. Why? Perhaps because female instructors were as likely to direct specific questions to female students as to male students, while male teachers were more than twice as likely to direct questions to male students. Gender is, therefore, part of the interpersonal dynamics of the class.
>
> David Popenoe, *Sociology*

1. In your own experience, have you found any difference in the way you respond to male and female instructors?

    _____

    _____

---

hedgehog (hej′ hôg′) a mammal that rolls into a ball to defend itself; a military defensive obstacle

2. Does this paragraph seem to indicate that instructors prefer students of one sex over the other? Which one?

_____

_____

PASSAGE 3

Read the following passage, which contrasts envy and jealousy, and circle the signal words. Underline the important point that shows the difference between the two, and note whether there are any similarities. Then, explain in a sentence whether envy or jealousy is the least desirable trait to possess.

Long lumped together by ordinary folks and scholars alike, envy and jealousy are not a single, formless "super emotion." On the contrary, they are distinct, with different components, and are in fact elicited by completely different situations and in completely different settings.

According to a Georgetown University psychologist . . . envy occurs when a person lacks another person's superior quality, achievement, or possession, and desires it—or wishes that the other person lacked it.

Jealousy, by contrast, occurs in the context of a close relationship when a person fears losing an important other to a rival—in particular, losing a relationship that is important to one's sense of self.

For all their distinctiveness, envy and jealousy sometimes occur together. For instance, when a romantic partner gives attention to an attractive rival, a person may feel both jealous of that attention and envious of the rival for being so attractive. And since jealousy involves the loss of a personal relationship, it's usually more intense than envy.

"A Devastating Difference," *Psychology Today* Jan.–Feb. 1994

1. Which is the least desirable trait, envy or jealousy? Explain. _____

_____

_____

2. In what significant ways do envy and jealousy differ? _____

_____

_____

3. Is there any way in which envy and jealousy are similar? _____

_____

_____

Look at the following chart.

Envy	Jealousy
• Feelings of inferiority • Longing • Resentment of circumstance • Ill will toward envied person, often accompanied by guilt about these feelings • Motivation to improve • Desire to possess the attractive rival's qualities • Disapproval of feelings	• Fear of loss • Anxiety • Suspicion or anger about betrayal • Low self-esteem and sadness over loss • Uncertainty and loneliness • Fear of losing an important person to an attractive other • Distrust

4. Which is more destructive to one's personality—envy or jealousy? Discuss the reasons.

_____

_____

_____

⤳ Pattern 5: Cause and Effect Relationship

When writers present arguments or describe events, one of their most frequently used organizing patterns is cause and effect. Using this pattern, writers explain *why* or *how things happen* and *what the result is* or might be. The cause is the *reason* or *motive;* the effect is the *result, consequence,* or *outcome.*

This pattern is used extensively in scientific and technical textbooks as well as in the social sciences. In math or computer science texts, for example, the pattern helps a student understand the reason for or the functioning of things, to go beyond mere rote memorization of the "how to" steps to do things such as equations or programming. Since this pattern is one of the chief techniques of reasoning, it is commonly used in persuasive and argumentative essays. Cause and effect can be employed in various combinations to express a paragraph's main idea.

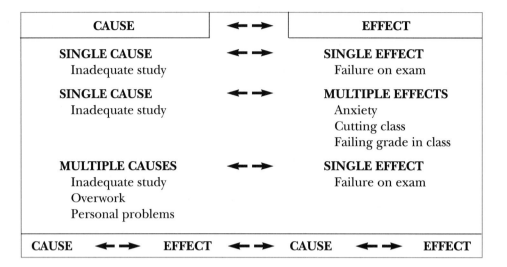

The cause-and-effect pattern can sometimes be recognized by signal words.

Signals for Cause		
because	for this reason	since
cause	on account of	why
due to		
Signals for Effect		
as a result	in effect	therefore
consequently	results in	thus
hence	the outcome is	

Notice the various key words that signal a series of cause-and-effect relationships in the following paragraph. The notations in the margin will make these relationships clear to you.

Atherosclerosis is the result of the buildup of fat, fibrin (formed in clots), parts of dead cells and calcium on the inside of arteries. These substances reduce the elasticity of the vessel, and by decreasing the diameter of the vessel, they raise blood pressure, just as you would raise the pressure in a garden hose by holding your thumb over the end. If the artery is in

results { elasticity of
blood vessels
decreases

result { blood pressure
rises

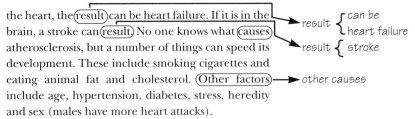

the heart, the result can be heart failure. If it is in the brain, a stroke can result. No one knows what causes atherosclerosis, but a number of things can speed its development. These include smoking cigarettes and eating animal fat and cholesterol. Other factors include age, hypertension, diabetes, stress, heredity and sex (males have more heart attacks).

Robert A. Wallace, *Biology: The World of Life*

While textbook writers often use signal words to alert the reader to the cause-and-effect pattern, writers of articles and essayists do not always provide such signals; then you must analyze what is being said to recognize the pattern. If the writer explains *what* happened and *why* it happened, then the writing approach is usually cause and effect. Read the following passage and look for the main idea, based on the arguments the writer gives. Then, fill in the cause-and-effect chart that follows.

> For years, trainers and coaches have wondered why certain athletes are able to shut out the noise, bright lights and frenzy that go along with competition, while their teammates are unnerved by such distractions. The answer, as it turns out, may have to do with psychological training. Some researchers believe that the ability to cope with stress makes the difference between giving a mediocre performance and a dazzler.
>
> "It's the ability to take control of yourself—not to give in to the emotional factor in competition," says Dr. Thomas Tutko, a psychology professor at San Jose State University, co-author of *Sports Psyching: Playing Your Best Game All of the Time* and a firm believer in psychological conditioning in athletes. "After talking to literally thousands of athletes, we found that people who were successful practiced a certain kind of self–mind control, using any one of a series of techniques that got them to relax, concentrate or change their attitudes. These people were doing it automatically. They thought everybody did."
>
> Nancy Josephson, "Why Some Athletes Excel," *Family Weekly* 20 Dec. 1981

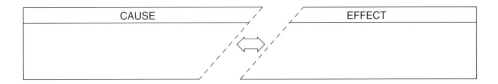

Do you agree with this author's thesis: "Some athletes excel because of their ability to handle stress"? List some causes and effects you feel were not included.

_____

_____

ACTIVITY 5.5

PASSAGE 1

As you read the following excerpt, mark any signal words that develop the cause-and-effect pattern. Then answer the questions that follow.

Cutting back on sleep to make more time for work and play may not be as harmless as once thought. Scientists are finding that skimping on slumber—which most Americans do—plays havoc with important hormones, possibly harming brain cells, depleting the immune system and promoting the growth of fat instead of muscle.

There is even concern that sleep **deprivation** may accelerate the aging process.

"There is a new message coming out of this research," said Eve Van Cauter, a University of Chicago sleep researcher who discovered that cheating on sleep for only a few nights increases brain levels of cortisol, a potentially dangerous stress hormone. . . .

In their quest to understand the mystery of why people sleep, scientists have discovered the first evidence of a biological feedback loop between the body's use of energy, its need to resupply energy and the brain's mechanism for maintaining the proper energy balance.

Their findings are helping to explain why lack of sleep dulls the brain, saps energy, increases irritability and depression and makes people more accident-prone.

"People who are sleep-deprived are operating their brain on a **metabolically** depleted level," said Dr. Robert Greene, a Harvard Medical School neuroscientist who is tracking the brain's chemical sleep signals. "You may think you're doing OK, but you still have to pay the piper," he added. "If sleep is needed for brain metabolism to be working in an optimal way, you're losing that." . . .

A National Sleep Foundation survey found that nearly two out of three Americans did not get the recommended eight hours of sleep a night. A third of those get less than six hours of sleep. For most people, eight hours of sleep is about right, although some can function well on six hours, while others need 10.

Two-thirds of those in the survey said they had sleep-related problems such as insomnia, snoring or restless legs. More than one out of three said sleepiness interfered with their daily activities, and one of four reported falling asleep at the wheel in the last year. . . .

Effects on Hormones

To find out what lack of sleep does to the body's hormones, Van Cauter takes round-the-clock blood samples of volunteers when they are awake and asleep. A plastic tube attached to a needle in a vein allows the researchers to take the samples from another room without disturbing a subject's sleep.

---

deprivation (dep′ rò vā shòn) a loss; act of taking away
metabolically (mòt′ ò bãl′ ò kòl lē) functioning of any specific substance within the living body

She has found that lack of sleep causes blood levels of the stress hormone cortisol to go up, while two other important hormones—muscle-building human growth hormone and prolactin, which oversees the immune defense system—go down. These reactions are just the opposite of what they should be. Cortisol levels are supposed to decline before sleep, and human growth hormone and prolactin are supposed to increase during sleep.

In other words, the body does not like to be deprived of sleep. Staying awake longer than normal may be at the cost of stress-related memory impairment, increased risk of infection and more flab. . . .

Why People Sleep

A good night's sleep rests and refreshes people, but what is going on biologically that makes sleep necessary has long puzzled scientists.

Researchers have found two sleep clocks. One is the circadian rhythm system that regulates the 24-hour sleep-wake cycle. However, when the tiny brain center governing the circadian system is removed, animals still fall asleep, although not on a 24-hour schedule.

Harvard's Greene believes the second sleep clock is based on energy depletion. The body, and especially the brain, use sleep to make more energy molecules called adenosine triphosphate to replace those used up during daily activities.

ATP is made inside cells by mitochondria from the food we eat and the oxygen we breathe. ATP is in effect tiny packets of energy used by cells to carry out all their activities, from moving muscles to forming thoughts. But when ATP is burned as fuel, one of the byproducts it creates is adenosine, which Harvard researchers identified as the body's fatigue factor.

As adenosine builds up, it tells the brain it is running low on ATP and it needs to curtail its activities while mitochondria make more ATP energy packets.

"This provides a reasonable link between metabolism and sleep that wasn't there before," Greene said. "This may be a major reason why we sleep: The brain needs to replenish its energy supplies."

Sleep deprivation forces the brain to struggle along on dwindling energy stores. "Your judgment goes way down when this happens," Greene explained. "You're not as aroused, your alertness suffers, and your reaction time decreases. With increasing sleep deprivation, people can't avoid becoming drowsy and dropping off when they don't want to."

approximately 700 words

Ronald Kotulak (*Chicago Tribune*), "New Views on Why We Sleep,"
San Francisco Examiner and Chronicle 7 June 1998: A3

1. List three results of sleep deprivation on the body.

_____

_____

_____

2. Explain what researchers have discovered that makes it necessary biologically for humans to sleep.

_____

_____

3. Study the following results of a survey on the sleeping habits of American adults.

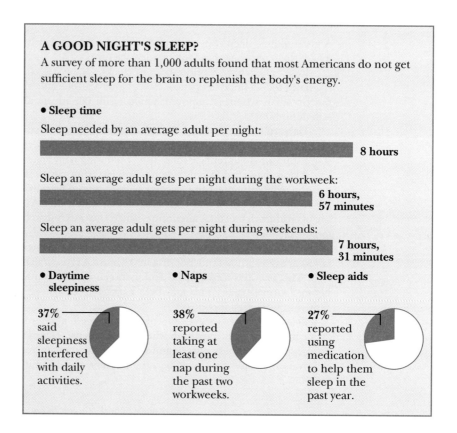

A GOOD NIGHT'S SLEEP?
A survey of more than 1,000 adults found that most Americans do not get sufficient sleep for the brain to replenish the body's energy.

• **Sleep time**
Sleep needed by an average adult per night:

8 hours

Sleep an average adult gets per night during the workweek:

6 hours, 57 minutes

Sleep an average adult gets per night during weekends:

7 hours, 31 minutes

• **Daytime sleepiness**

37% said sleepiness interfered with daily activities.

• **Naps**

38% reported taking at least one nap during the past two workweeks.

• **Sleep aids**

27% reported using medication to help them sleep in the past year.

How much sleep do you get compared to the people in the survey? Discuss how important you believe sleep is to your own personal well-being.

_____

_____

PASSAGE 2

Read to find out why poor economic conditions result in hate violence.

Poor economic times contribute greatly to hate violence. In many areas of the country, when major industries such as steel and auto manufacturing have had downturns, go out of business, or relocate, the likelihood of economic distress among the low and unskilled increases. **Scapegoating** and blaming often results when blue-collar jobs are unavailable. The distress that accompanies unemployment and rising prices is often directed toward immigrants and minorities and manifests itself in harassment and violence. There seems to be a childlike tendency that exists within some people wherein they must blame others for their own misfortune or society's failings. New York City experienced an increase of 19 percent in reported hate crimes in 1988 after a recession hit the region following the stock market crash of 1987. In 1990, the Massachusetts unemployment rate had risen to a level of 8.6 percent, one of the highest rates in the nation. For the same year, the Boston police reported 273 bias crimes, which was up from 202 the previous year. . . . Los Angeles County reported an increase of 45 percent in bias crimes in 1990 after a nationwide recession caused unemployment in the state to jump up to 7 percent, from under 6 percent one year earlier. Thus the frequency and intensity of such acts are shown to increase when the economy deteriorates.

Sociologists indicate that hate frequently stems from being deprived or having one's needs unsatisfied—so the poor can despise the rich, the uneducated ridicule the intellectual, the poor envy the **affluent,** and the established ghetto inhabitant can hate the new immigrant/refugee who moves into the area. Social scientists argue that the government definition of poverty does not measure the real depths or the changes taking place in inner cities (i.e., that, not only have the number of ghetto poor increased but the severity of economic deprivation among them has risen as well). Ghetto poverty and concentrations of large numbers of a diverse population in one area often lead to conflict in those neighborhoods. The stresses of urban life, especially in inner cities, give rise to increased incidents of violence, especially in depressed conditions and reduced space.

approximately 350 words

Robert M. Shusta et al., *Multicultural Law Enforcement*

1. Restate the main idea. _____

   _____

2. List two supporting details that help develop the main idea. _____

   _____

   _____

---

scapegoating (skāp′ gō ting) blaming a person or thing for the mistakes of others
affluent (af′ lо̄о̄ ənt) having an abundance of money or property; wealthy; rich

3. What can be done to help reduce the number of bias-related crimes nationwide? In your neighborhood?

_____

_____

_____

_____

➣ Pattern 6: Definition

In the definition pattern, the author's purpose is to explain the meaning of an important term or concept; it can take an entire paragraph to do so. In all academic subjects, some key terms and concepts are crucial to understanding the text or subject matter. Sometimes, a title, a subtitle, or the first sentence of a paragraph, appearing in question form, indicates that the definition pattern will be used. Often, other writing patterns are incorporated into a passage in which a definition is being presented, particularly by *example,* the final writing pattern that will be discussed in this chapter.

In textbook writing, definitions tend to be **straightforward,** as in scientific textbooks. In other situations, authors use the definition pattern to explain technical language, important terminology, and concepts. **Abstract** terms, such as those used in sociology and philosophy, are less precise in meaning, however, and may require more lengthy explanations. The following paragraph demonstrates how even a simple term like *self-esteem* has its own special meaning in a contemporary textbook.

> By self-esteem, we refer to the evaluation which the individual makes and customarily maintains with regard to himself (or herself); it expresses an attitude of approval or disapproval, and indicates the extent to which an individual believes himself to be capable, significant, successful and worthy. In short, self-esteem is a personal judgment of worthiness and is expressed in the attitudes that the individual holds towards himself. It is a subjective experience which the individual conveys to others by verbal reports and other overt expressive behavior.
>
> H. Douglas Brown, *Principles of Language Learning and Teaching*

---

straightforward (strāt fôr′ ward) direct; proceeding in a straight course
abstract (ab′ stract) not easily understood; not concrete

This definition can be mapped as follows.

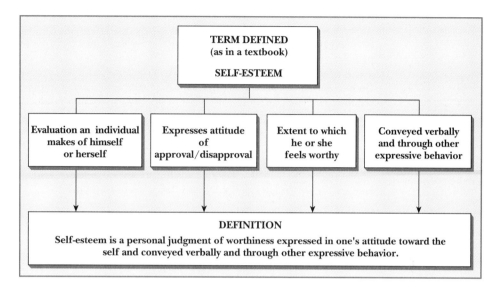

One way to recognize the writer's pattern is through signal or clue words. Signal words most commonly used to indicate the definition pattern include those in the following list.

Signals for Definition		
define	known as	we mean
is	that is (i.e.)	we can state
is defined as	the term means	

ACTIVITY 5.6

PASSAGE 1

The question of doctor-assisted suicide is hotly debated. Read to determine the difference in meaning between *active* and *passive* euthanasia. Circle the signal words as you read.

> The most important individual in matters of life and death is you. Modern society gives you many options not only for life, but also for death. Euthanasia is the practice of

ending a life for reasons of mercy. The word is derived from a Greek word meaning "good death." There are two kinds, active and passive. Active euthanasia involves an act that deliberately ends a life. One example would be purposely administering a lethal dose of medication. Passive euthanasia involves withholding a treatment that would probably prolong life. An example would be withholding chemotherapy from a cancer patient.

A controversial form of active euthanasia is assisting in someone's suicide. The Dutch Supreme Court allows physicians to perform such active euthanasia if five criteria are met: (1) The patient has no hope of improving from an intolerable condition; (2) there is no way to relieve the condition; (3) the patient is capable of making rational decisions; (4) the patient over time repeatedly requests assistance with ending his or her life; (5) two physicians agree with the patient's request. In contrast, the United States prosecutes physicians (and anyone else) for assisting in suicide. Dr. Jack Kevorkian, a Michigan physician, challenged this law by assisting in several suicides (*New York Times,* 1994). Neither the Dutch law nor the U.S. law has universal support.

Stephen Worchel and Wayne Shebilske, *Principles and Applications: Psychology*

1. Explain what is meant by *active* euthanasia. _____

   _____

   _____

2. Do the Dutch Supreme Court's five criteria for assisting in someone's suicide help to explain why this act is considered active euthanasia? Why, or why not?

   _____

   _____

3. Since this psychology textbook was published, Dr. Kevorkian has assisted in countless suicides, taping one that was aired on a national television station, daring prosecution and life in prison. Discuss whether physicians should be prosecuted for assisting in someone's suicide.

   _____

   _____

PASSAGE 2

Is causing harm to the environment a *crime*? See how the author's concept of crime has been applied to environmental harm, and decide whether you agree with his thesis. Circle the signal words as you read.

Crime can be defined best as a violation of the criminal law. Looking behind most criminal **statutes,** however, we can generally catch a glimpse of the concept of harm. Criminal activity, such as theft and assault, most of us would agree, is harmful to others. Some crimes, however, such as drug abuse, prostitution, gambling, and pornography, are sometimes referred to as "victimless crimes" (or social order offenses) because the harm they cause is not readily identifiable at the individual level. Statutes outlawing social order offenses are rooted in the notion of social harm—that is, although no who participates in prostitution, say, runs to the police to file a complaint (unless they are robbed, or in some other way directly victimized) lawmakers recognize that the act somehow lessens the quality of social life. Prostitution, many lawmakers argue, is harmful to the family and (in the case of heterosexual prostitution) **demeans** the status of women in society.

Today, a whole new class of criminal offenses is emerging based upon the notion of environmental damage. In what may be the best-known environmental catastrophe to date, the Exxon *Valdez*, a 1,000-foot supertanker, ran aground in Alaska in 1989 and spilled 11 million gallons of crude oil over 1,700 miles of **pristine** coastline. Animal life in the area was devastated. The U.S. Fish and Wildlife Service reported **decimation** to salmon spawning grounds, the death of 580,000 birds (including 144 bald eagles), and the demise of an unknown, but presumably vast amount of sea life. . . . The initial cleanup involved over 10,000 people and cost more than $1 billion. Damages were estimated as high as $5 billion. . . .

The *Valdez* incident, while prosecuted under both civil and criminal laws, was clearly not intended. No one (including the ship's captain, who was later prosecuted on charges akin to "drunk driving") wanted the *Valdez* to run aground. Other environmental crimes, however, some of which occur on an everyday basis, are quite intentional. Such crimes range from **ecological** terrorism, like that waged against Kuwait during the Gulf War by retreating Iraqi troops who set oil fields on fire throughout the country, to littering and small-scale recycling offenses, which are frequently committed by individual citizens.

As ecological awareness continues to expand, new prohibitions are legislated and previously unheard-of offenses created. Today, a highly concerned society stands increasingly ready to define abuse of the environment in criminal terms. As a consequence, words like "curbside criminals," "recycling police," and "garbage crime" are becoming commonplace. The state of Pennsylvania, for example, recently enacted a recycling law which mandates stiff sanctions, including fines and jail sentences for violators. Under the law, what had formerly been routine daily activities (throwing out the trash) become criminal offenses unless properly conducted (plastics and glass separated from paper products, and lawn clippings and yard trash appropriately bagged).

---

statutes (stach′ o͞ots) laws enacted by the legislative branch of a government; a formally established rule

demeans (di mēnz′) lowers character, status, or reputation; humbles; degrades

pristine (pris′ tēn) remaining in a pure state; uncorrupted

decimation (des i mā′ shun) destruction of a large quantity of something

ecological (ēk′ ə loj′ i kəl) having to do with relationships between organisms and their environment

While human beings have insulted the environment since before the dawn of history, it has only been in this century, as our dependence on the planet has become progressively obvious, that such activities have been ascribed criminal status. Hence, the question: What taken-for-granted aspects of our contemporary everyday lives will become subject to criminal sanctions in the twenty-first century?

approximately 550 words

Frank Schmalleger, "What Is Crime: The Example of Crimes Against the Environment," *Criminal Justice Today*

1. Is harming the environment a "victimless crime"? Why, or why not?

_____

_____

2. What do terms such as *curbside criminal, recycling police,* and *garbage crimes* reveal about society's attitude toward protecting the environment?

_____

_____

_____

3. Reread the last sentence of the passage. How would you answer the question posed by the author?

_____

_____

⁀ Pattern 7: Example

Example, in which illustrations are used to support a thesis or main idea, is one of the most frequently used writing patterns and quite easy to recognize. Often, one or more specific examples, illustrations, or instances will be given to support and develop a thesis or main idea, to clarify a concept through concrete details, or to prove the **validity** of an argument. Good examples help make general ideas more

---

validity (və lid′ ə tē) sound reasoning

specific and also aid in holding the reader's interest. The following signal words often help the reader to identify this pattern.

Signals for Example		
for example	for instance	to illustrate
specifically	such as	

Reread the passages dealing with phobias (Activity 5.1, pp. 236–37) and euthanasia (Activity 5.6, pp. 265–66) to see how the authors gave numerous examples to develop their main points. If you first determine the main idea, you will readily see how examples are used to illustrate or clarify the important information.

In textbook writing, examples are rarely the main point or only pattern used; rather, they support the major ideas and are used in *combination* with other patterns. For instance, in the following passage, the first two paragraphs use the contrast pattern to reveal the main idea, whereas the third paragraph, in support of this idea, is developed entirely by the example pattern.

California lawmakers are congratulating themselves for toughening up the state's drunken driving laws by increasing the penalties.

But they may be shocked to find out that in other countries, if a drunk is caught behind the wheel for the first time the penalty could be anything from throwing his wife in jail to an execution.

In Malaysia, for example, the drunk driver is jailed and if he or she is married, the spouse also goes to jail on the first offense, according to research published by the National Traffic Safety Institute. In Finland, England and Sweden, drunken drivers are sentenced to one year in jail on their first conviction. In Germany, driving with a blood alcohol level of .08 percent requires that you lose your license for a year. (In California, the legal presumption for driving under the influence is .08 percent.) You would also receive a one-year minimum jail sentence if you are caught in Germany driving without a license. . . . South Africa is even tougher, with a 10-year prison term and a fine of $10,000 or both upon the first conviction. In Bulgaria, your second conviction will be your last because the penalty is execution. In San Salvador, you may not get a second chance. There, drunken drivers can be executed immediately by a firing squad.

> Ellen Norman, "Other Nations Are Tougher on Drunk Drivers," *The Peninsula Times Tribune*. Reprinted by permission of *The Peninsula Times Tribune*.

As you can see, the numerous examples reinforce the writer's main point that other nations have tougher drunken driving laws than those in the United States.

Read the following selection, noting the important examples, and then answer the questions that follow.

Most cultures have a number of forms of polite usage which may be misleading. These may take the form of exaggeration or modesty. Americans ask questions which are really orders or requests ("Would you like to . . . ?"). In every culture, in many situations, there are special forms of words, or types of conversation, which are thought to be appropriate—to ask a girl for a date, to disagree with someone at a committee, to introduce people to each other, and so on. Americans prefer directness, but Mexicans regard openness as a form of weakness or treachery, and think one should not allow the outside world to penetrate their thoughts. Frankness by Peace Corps volunteers in the Philippines . . . led to disruption of smooth social relationships.

Larry A. Samovar and Richard E. Porter, eds., *Intercultural Communication: A Reader,* 6th ed. (Wadsworth)

1. What is the main idea? _____

   _____

2. List at least two examples that support the main idea. _____

   _____

ACTIVITY 5.7

PASSAGE 1

While the writer of the following selection defines the term "snap judgments," examine how the example makes it easier to understand the term.

snap judgments
instant evaluation
without the benefit
of fact or experience

Do you know someone who exclaims proudly, "I can size up a person right away"? Most of us from time to time are guilty of making **snap judgments** before we have gathered enough facts to come to valid conclusions. Here's an example of a supervisor named Carla who made a snap judgment at work. An employee, Anne, received a telephone call an hour before quitting time from a doctor saying that her son had just been hit by an automobile and was badly injured. The doctor requested that Anne come to the hospital immediately to be with her son. Anne looked for her boss, Carla, to ask permission to leave, but Anne could not find her. Anxious to see her son, Anne wrote a note informing Carla of the situation and suggesting that an hour's pay be deducted from her wages if necessary. Anne placed the note in Carla's incoming basket.

About 15 minutes later, as Carla was returning from a meeting upstairs, she was stopped by Harry, one of Anne's coworkers, who told Carla that Anne had left work early. Carla was furious. "Why didn't she check with me before she left. I had something important I wanted her to do this afternoon. For that behavior, she is going to be suspended for one week without pay."

Michael W. Drafke and Stan Kossen, *The Human Side of Organizations*

1. Restate the writer's main idea in your own words.

    _____

2. Using the example pattern, write about an incident in which you made a snap judgment and explain its consequences.

    _____

    _____

    _____

PASSAGE 2

Writers sometime use very specific examples to give concrete form to their implied or abstract ideas. Use the specific examples given in the opening chapter of the book *The Peter Principle* to discover what the authors have to say about incompetence in our society, based on their experiences in Canada.

> When I was a boy I was taught that the men upstairs knew what they were doing. I was told, "Peter, the more you know, the further you go." So I stayed in school until I graduated from college and then went forth into the world clutching firmly these ideas and my new teaching certificate. During the first year of teaching I was upset to find that a number of teachers, school principals, supervisors and superintendents appeared to be unaware of their professional responsibilities and incompetent in executing their duties. For example my principal's main concerns were that all window shades be at the same level, that classrooms should be quiet and that no one step on or near the rose beds. The superintendent's main concerns were that no minority group, no matter how fanatical, should ever be offended and that all official forms be submitted on time. The children's education appeared farthest from the administrator mind.
>
> At first I thought this was a special weakness of the school system in which I taught so I applied for certification in another province. I filled out the special forms, enclosed the required documents and complied willingly with all the red tape. Several weeks later, back came my application and all the documents!
>
> No, there was nothing wrong with my credentials; the forms were correctly filled out; an official departmental stamp showed that they had been received in good order. But an accompanying letter said, "The new regulations require that such forms cannot be accepted by the Department of Education unless they have been registered at the Post Office to ensure safe delivery. Will you please remail the forms to the Department, making sure to register them this time?"
>
> I began to suspect that the local school system did not have a monopoly on incompetence.

As I looked further afield, I saw that every organization contained a number of persons who could not do their jobs.

approximately 400 words

Laurence J. Peter and Raymond Hull, *The Peter Principle*

1. What is the authors' main point about the subject of incompetence?

    _____

    _____

2. Were the authors justified in being upset about how teachers and administrators handled their professional responsibilities? Explain your answer.

    _____

    _____

3. How effective is the second example regarding one of the author's application for certification?

    _____

    _____

    _____

4. Discuss an example of "incompetence" you have experienced in school or in your daily activities at home, at work, or in your community.

    _____

    _____

    _____

ACTIVITY 5.8 Practice Recognizing Organizational Patterns

As you read each of the following passages, mark the signal words that help identify the writer's predominant writing pattern, noting how the pattern helps develop or clarify the main idea. Then, answer the questions that follow.

PASSAGE 1

The word *corruption* has a variety of meanings, the most common of which includes immorality or dishonesty. In a broader sense, corruption refers to a process that destroys or **subverts** honesty or **integrity.** Analyses of political corruption use the term in both its narrow and broader meanings. Defined narrowly, political corruption refers to acts by public officials that are dishonest and illegal. Taking a bribe is an obvious example. Viewed more broadly, corruption may encompass actions by public officials that are not illegal but are questionable in terms of the integrity of a system of democratic governments. For example, consider the decision by an elected official to accept a large campaign contribution from a wealthy individual or to accept a $10,000 lecture fee for giving a campaign speech to an interest group. Even though campaign contributions and lecture honoraria are legal, the ability of a public official to make an independent decision in the public interest may be compromised by their acceptance. It is, in fact, sometimes difficult to distinguish clearly among bribes, gifts, favors, honoraria, and campaign contributions.

Robert G. Thobaben et.al., *Issues in American Political Life*

1. The predominant writing pattern is _____. A second writing pattern

    used by the author is _____.

2. The author's main idea is _____.

3. Explain the difference in the meaning of *corruption* in its broadest and in its narrowest sense.

    _____

    _____

PASSAGE 2

Here's a short, sweet and undoubtedly incomplete history of the bed and its room:

The ancient Greeks devised a couch-style bed called a kline, which was used for resting during the day and sleeping at night.

The Romans took the lounge act one further, creating single, double and even triple beds upon which they ate, drank, were merry and, sometimes, even slept. . . .

Beds—and many other furnishings—fell out of fashion after the fall of Rome in the 5th century and people (even the wealthy) fell back to sleeping on pallets or stuffed sacks.

---

subverts (sòb vurts′) undermines or corrupts, as in morals; overthrows or destroys something established

integrity (in teg′ rò tē) quality or state of being of sound moral principle; honesty; sincerity

In the Middle Ages, furniture was rare, simple and, of necessity, mobile. But beds—most often roughly constructed wooden boxes with straw-filled mattress sacks—staged a steady comeback. Bedding, rather than the beds themselves, became a status symbol. Because textiles were extremely expensive, the wealthy not only bedded down with the finest fabrics, they took their bedding (mattress, sheets, pillows and canopies) and sometimes even their beds along with them when they traveled.

Communal beds were common through the 11th century. In homes, entire families bedded down together. In inns, travelers slept with strangers—perhaps as many as a dozen.

Early in the Renaissance, beds were little more than sacks stuffed with straw or pea shucks dressed up in rich velvets or brocades. Later, beds became more permanent and were built on platforms or into alcoves.

During the 16th and early 17th centuries, separate rooms for sleeping became more common and beds became status symbols. . . .

By the 18th century, bedrooms were growing in size and number, and well-designed and well-crafted beds became available to the growing middle class. . . .

After the turn of the century, beds were downsized and bedding was simplified. Brass beds (which were considered sanitary) were mass-produced and Shaker and other ultra-simple styles reigned supreme. . . .

Beds haven't changed much in the 20th century, but here are some of the improvements that have made for sounder sleep: the introduction of the inner spring mattress (1920s), the invention of the box spring (late 1930s) and the use of foam in bedding (1950s). This century has also seen the introduction of "alternative sleep systems," such as water beds and adjustable beds (1960s) and air beds (1980s).

approximately 500 words

Connie Nelson *(Minneapolis-St.Paul Tribune)*, "Beds: From Ancient Days Through Tomorrow," *San Francisco Examiner* 27 Sept. 1998

1. The predominant writing pattern is _____.

2. How have the design of beds changed from ancient days to the present?

   _____

   _____

3. In the history of beds, which time period did you find most interesting? Why?

   _____

   _____

PASSAGE 3

The following excerpt is from the writings of Tracey Wilen, an expert on international business travel for women. Her fourth book on the subject is *Europe for Women in Business.*

If your job leads you to do business with Europeans, keep in mind that the American view of time, relationships, competition and business can be overwhelming for them.

American culture is open, and Americans seek to develop relationships quickly so they can move into business discussions straightaway. . . .

Americans tend to use first names, be informal and try to establish a quick **rapport.** Europeans tend be more formal or reserved during initial meetings and perhaps for some time, until a comfort zone is established. . . .

Americans and Europeans also differ on their view of leisure activities. When Americans engage in social activities, they often combine it with business and discuss deals over lunch, drinks or dinner. Many Americans work weekends and are on call for their firms with pagers and cell phones.

Most Europeans view the time after work and on weekends as personal time with their families. Europeans view the United States as a competitive culture. For the most part, our capitalistic society fosters competitive behaviors. Many European firms are more socially oriented, and competition is not fostered. . . .

Change, competition, getting ahead and the **entrepreneurial** spirit are acceptable attributes in the U.S. **Longevity,** sociability and stability are frequently cited as more acceptable attributes in Europe.

Tracey Wilen, "Work As the Romans Do," *San Francisco Examiner* 27 Sept. 1998

1. Which signal word helped you decide the main organizational pattern?

   _____

2. Name two ways (the major support for the selection) in which Americans' views of time, relationships, or competition are not the same as that of Europeans.

   _____

   _____

3. Which workplace attitude do you find more agreeable: American or European? Explain your answer.

   _____

   _____

PASSAGE 4

"To cross that glass ceiling barrier to success (in their own businesses), women need to   1 adopt a more aggressive, open-minded attitude," says Cathleen Faerber of the Wellesley Group in Lake Zurich, Ill., an executive search firm.

---

rapport (ra pôr′) a relationship, especially a close or sympathetic relationship; agreement; harmony

entrepreneurial (än trò prò nur′ ē òl) act of organizing, managing, and assuming the risk for a business venture

longevity (lä jev′ ò tē) long life

. . . It's not a glass ceiling that keeps women-owned businesses down, it's a glass atti- **2**
tude. Here are some tips that might help:

Find a mentor. Find someone you admire with the aggressive traits you need, male or **3**
female. Join the organizations they join, support the activities they support, and get to
know that person on a first-name basis. Ask their advice. Examine the traits your **mentor**
displays, then work on developing a similar style.

Promote high visibility. Join professional organizations and become active as quickly **4**
as possible. Rotary, Entrepreneur and Kiwanis are **viable** opportunities for you as they are
hands-on organizations. Stay away from organizations, including your local Chamber of
Commerce, where you're not likely to find like-minded people. . . .

Develop a plan. Winging it just won't work. If you want to achieve success in business, **5**
you need a plan. And then you need to work your plan. I know you've heard this before,
so why haven't you done it? A plan is a tool for success. Ignoring this will mean either failure or a relegation to second status, neither of which should be acceptable.

Decide where you want your business to be in six months, one year, two years and **6**
five years. Spend the time it takes to make these pictures complete. Next make a list of
the things that must happen to make your goals come true. Again, do it right. List the
number of new customers or clients, the increased cash flow and all the other factors that
must occur in order for your goal or dream to happen.

Finally, make a list of exactly what you must do on a daily basis to make the things **7**
happen. How many new contacts must you make? How many widgets must you produce?
What should be the value of each client you add? Put your list on the wall, and look at it
every day.

approximately 300 words

Paul Tulenko (Scripps Howard News Service), "Some Aggressiveness Is Needed for
Shattering the Glass Ceiling," *San Francisco Examiner* 29 Oct. 1997

1. The writer shifts his writing technique beginning with paragraph 6. He uses the

   _____ organizational pattern in paragraphs 2 through 5 but changes

   to the _____ pattern in paragraphs 6 and 7.

2. In what specific ways does a "glass attitude," not the "glass ceiling," keep
   women-owned businesses from thriving?

   _____

   _____

PASSAGE 5

. . . Zell Miller of Georgia came up with a novel proposal as part of his state budget: to **1**
make $105,000 available so that each newborn child in the state—approximately 100,000
children a year—would be sent home from the hospital with a CD or tape of classical music.

---

mentor (men′ tòr) a wise, loyal advisor; a teacher or coach
viable (ví ò bòl) workable; that can work or be put to use

"No one doubts that listening to music, especially at a very early age, affects the rea- **2**
soning that underlies math and engineering and chess," the governor told law-makers.
"I believe it can help Georgia children to excel."

Governor Miller may be on to something. New scientific studies have shown that **3**
early musical training shapes children's growing brains and boosts their learning power,
aiding in the development of logic, abstract thinking, memory and creativity.

The Mozart effect. In 1993, two researchers reported that college students who lis- **4**
tened to 10 minutes of Mozart's Sonata in D Major for Two Pianos scored 8 or 9 points
higher on a spatial-temporal test than when they had 10 minutes of silence or relaxation
tapes. (Spatial-temporal reasoning is the ability not only to recognize objects as the same
or different but also to be able to form the mental images of physical objects. It is a key
to the higher brain function required in mathematics, physics and engineering.)

The researchers—Dr. Gordon Shaw, a physicist at the University of California at **5**
Irvine, and Dr. Frances Rauscher, a psychologist now at the University of Wisconsin
at Oshkosh—called their findings the "Mozart effect." Actually, the Mozart experiment began in 1990, when researchers discovered that the brain in a sense made its own
music. . . .

Drs. Rauscher and Shaw began working with inner-city preschoolers to see how **6**
musical training might affect their brain development. They had four groups: One was
given keyboard lessons; the second, computer lessons; the third, singing sessions; and the
fourth, no lessons, only the standard curriculum. Six months later, the keyboard students
performed 34 percent better on spatial-temporal ability tests than any other group,
including the computer students.

. . .

Teach music first? More than 2300 years ago, Plato said: "Music is a more potent **7**
instrument than any other for education, and children should be taught music before
anything else." Some educators have taken that position as a guiding principle: . . .

• When people ask what is the most important subject that we teach, I say it's music," says **8**
   Miriam Kronish, a principal at John Eliot Elementary School in Needham, Mass.,
   where students are engaged daily in music and other arts classes.

The academic achievements resulting from this approach can be impressive. For **9**
years the students at John Eliot—one of the least-affluent schools in Needham—have
scored among the highest in Massachusetts on the basic skills test. When the school's
fourth-graders recently were tested by the state, they got 1600 out of 1600 in math (the
state average is 1330), 1580 in reading, 1570 in science and 1560 in social studies.

The gains appear to be social as well. **10**

"With music the children interact better," says Diane Fraggos, a fifth-grade teacher **11**
at John Eliot. "They stay more focused on the task and listen better to directions."

approximately 525 words
Vadim Prokhorov, "Will Piano Lessons Make My Child Smarter?"
Parade 14 June 1998

1. Which signal word in the second paragraph enables you to recognize this selection's main organizational pattern?

_____

_____

2. According to researchers, what is the influence of classical music on spatial-temporal reasoning?

    _____

    _____

3. Do you agree with Plato's statement in paragraph 7 that " . . . children should be taught music before anything else"? Why, or why not?

    _____

    _____

⤳ Patterns in Combination

As you have seen in some of the passages we have been studying, although writers generally use a particular overall or dominant organizational pattern, they often mix or combine patterns to suit their writing purpose. Therefore, whether in a paragraph or passage, you should expect to find a good deal of overlap of patterns. Being aware that writers do this should prevent you from being confused when more than one pattern is present. *Learning these patterns makes you aware of the general organizing principles of writing.* This can aid your comprehension, your retention of information, and your own writing.

The following passage has been marked to show you the extent to which a writer can provide clues when a number of patterns are used. After reading the selection and studying the notations, you should understand the role of sports in society.

A hundred years ago, when sport was confined largely to games played in the backyard or on the farm, one could hardly have imagined the attention that it has come to receive (in the twentieth century.) (Today,) the importance of sport in society is clearly demonstrated by the fact that even the CBS Evening News can be preempted for the finals of a tennis match or the airing of the Super Bowl. A survey conducted in the (late 1980s) revealed that fully 81 percent of all adults follow some organized sport, mostly on television. And the phenomenon of weekend "sports widows"—women abandoned by their husbands for weekend sports on television—is entering its (third generation.)

time order

The Functions of Sport

Sport is (defined) sociologically as competitive physical activity that is performed under established rules. Like all social institutions, sport serves (numerous) (functions.) (First,) it provides society with a vast array of leisure-time activities for all segments of the population. Although it is an overstatement to say that modern society is a leisure society, there has been a significant increase in the amount of nonwork time that most people have available. (Furthermore,) recreational activity has become increasingly necessary in a society in which the vast majority of jobs provide little or no physical activity.

(Second,) sport provides an outlet for energies that, if not diverted, could (cause) serious strain on the social order. For both fan and participant, sport permits the expression of emotions (such as anger and frustration) in ways that are acceptable to, even encouraged by, society.

(Finally,) sport provides society with role models. Athletes at all levels, but especially famous athletes, provide (examples) of conduct and employment of skills that others can **emulate.** (For example,) many children's heroes today are professional football and baseball players.

definition

simple listing

cause/effect

example

The Conflict Perspective

(Although) sports promote many positive aspects of a society, conflict theorists are quick to point out that they also reflect society's inequalities. Like most other social institutions, sports are characterized by inequalities of class, race, and gender.

(For example,) certain sports—such as polo, tennis, and skiing—have traditionally appealed to the wealthy. People with lower incomes often simply cannot afford to purchase and maintain horses or expensive tennis and ski equipment. Other sports—such as boxing, which is often associated with urban poverty—are distinctly lower class in origin and participation. In general, members of the lower and working classes have tended to participate in sports

contrast

example

---

emulate (em′ yə lāt′) to try to equal or surpass another, especially through imitation

(like) baseball and basketball: games that require little more than a field, a ball, and some players.

(Although) sport is sometimes considered exempt from racial inequality, sociological evidence has shown this not to be the case. (Although) it is true that *contrast* nonwhites in American society have enjoyed greater opportunities for high incomes in professional sports than in other occupations, it is also true that virtually all managers and owners of sports teams are white. There are very few nonwhite sportscasters, administrators, umpires, or referees. Furthermore, nonwhites are all but absent (even as players) from all professional sports except baseball, basketball, boxing, and football.

The history of women in traditionally male-oriented sports is also one of discrimination and inequality. When the first modern Olympic Games were held in 1896, women were virtually excluded from all forms of competition. Until fairly recently, girls were not even allowed to play Little League baseball. But the position of women in sports is currently changing (as a result) of the women's move- *cause/effect* ment, court decisions, and governmental policies. Today many women excel not only in such traditional "female" sports as gymnastics and figure skating but also in more aggressively "male" sports (like) *example* race car driving and basketball.

approximately 625 words

David Popenoe, "Sports and Society: Using the Theoretical Perspectives," *Sociology*. Copyright © 1995 by Prentice Hall. Reprinted by permission.

1. Which writing pattern has the author used most extensively? _____

   _____

2. List three supporting details the writer provides to make the reader understand the important functions of sports in society.

   _____

   _____

   _____

3. In your own experience, have you found inequalities in sports because of your class, race, or gender? How do you react to such inequalities?

_____

_____

_____

ACTIVITY 5.9

The writer of the following textbook selection uses several writing patterns to develop his main point. Circle any signal words you may find; after you have completed the reading, make marginal notations to indicate the patterns. Then, answer the questions that follow. For easy reference, the paragraph patterns and their signal word clues are listed in the chart on page 283.

Mixed Signals

Although the world may seem to be getting smaller every day, and its people becoming   1
more **homogeneous** through a gradual merging of cultures, sociologists recognize the
need to be aware of the differences among cultural groups and the misunderstandings
these differences can cause.

One way to explore group differences is to study the various meanings of _gestures,_   2
bodily signals that communicate information to onlookers. An analysis of gestures whose
meanings differ from country to country, and sometimes from region to region within a
country, points out how a common gesture can convey quite different meanings.

For example, in England, tapping the side of the nose with a forefinger indicates   3
secrecy or conspiracy: "This is between us; don't spread it around." In Italy, the nose-tap
gesture is a helpful warning: "Take care—they're tricky." Both gestures encourage caution, but the emphasis changes from the personal _us_ to the **adversarial** _them._

Another gesture whose meaning changes from culture to culture is the "chin flick"   4
(back of fingers swept up and forward against the underside of the chin). In France and
northern Italy, this conveys an insult: "Get lost; you're annoying me." In southern Italy, it
loses its insulting character and becomes simply a negative message: "No" or "I don't
know why" or "There is nothing." . . .

Multimessage gestures (gestures that have many, often contradictory meanings) can   5
be the stuff of U.N. nightmares. Making a circle with the thumb and forefinger is the
"O.K." sign in America, but means money in Japan, zero or worthless in France, a male
homosexual in Malta, and an obscene comment in Greece.

Even a simple gesture meant to signify "yes" or "no" may not always be under-   6
stood in another culture. The head-nod gesture (moving the head up and down) for

_____

homogeneous (hō′ mō jē′ nē òs) the same in structure or quality; uniform; similar or
identical

adversarial (ad′ vòr ser′ ē òl) expressing opposition or hostility

affirmation is widespread and has been observed among Australian aborigines, Europeans, African tribes, Chinese, and Japanese. But the degree of agreement varies. The gesture can mean full agreement ("Yes, I will"), acknowledgment ("Yes, I'm listening"), encouragement ("Yes, go on"), understanding ("Yes, I see what you mean"), or accuracy ("Yes, that's correct"). The head shake (moving the head from side to side) as a negative gesture also has degrees of meaning varying from "I can't" or "I won't" to "I don't know" or "I disagree." To complicate the matter even further, the head sway (tilting the head from side to side) means "Maybe yes, maybe no" to most Europeans, but "Yes" to people from Turkey and parts of Iran. . . .

How can such culturally based misunderstandings be avoided? Clearly, there is no   7 substitute for familiarity with the foreign culture, since many potentially misunderstood customs and values are often deeply ingrained in a culture and taken for granted by its members. As many businesspeople have discovered, an awareness and understanding of the culture and customs of a foreign country can be as important a business tool as a calculator or computer.

approximately 525 words

David Popenoe, "Mixed Signals," *Sociology*

1. The primary organizational pattern in paragraph 1 is _____,

   while the pattern in paragraph 2 is _____.

2. In how many paragraphs does the writer use the organizational pattern of example?

   _____

   _____

3. Explain how the writer's use of numerous examples helps you understand that multimessage gestures often cause misunderstanding.

   _____

   _____

---

affirmation (af′ ȯr mā shòn) positive declaration; assertion

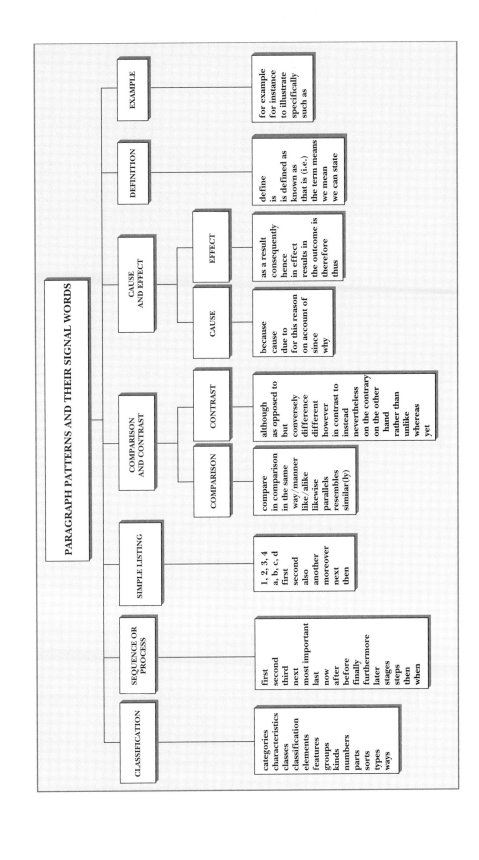

PARAGRAPH PATTERNS AND THEIR SIGNAL WORDS

EXAMPLE

for example
for instance
to illustrate
specifically
such as

DEFINITION

define
is
is defined as
known as
that is (i.e.)
the term means
we mean
we can state

CAUSE AND EFFECT

CAUSE

because
cause
due to
for this reason
on account of
since
why

EFFECT

as a result
consequently
hence
in effect
results in
the outcome is
therefore
thus

COMPARISON AND CONTRAST

COMPARISON

compare
in comparison
in the same
way / manner
like / alike
likewise
parallels
resembles
similar(ly)

CONTRAST

although
as opposed to
but
conversely
difference
different
however
in contrast to
instead
nevertheless
on the contrary
on the other
hand
rather than
unlike
whereas
yet

SIMPLE LISTING

1, 2, 3, 4
a, b, c, d
first
second
also
another
moreover
next
then

SEQUENCE OR PROCESS

first
second
third
next
most important
last
now
after
before
finally
furthermore
later
stages
steps
then
when

CLASSIFICATION

categories
characteristics
classes
classification
elements
features
groups
kinds
numbers
parts
sorts
types
ways

ᔕ Summary

Although there are many ways to express ideas, writers usually use the basic methods we have discussed, often mixing or combining them in paragraphs and passages. Recognizing the writer's pattern for developing ideas and being aware of signal words can help you follow the flow of ideas, understand the main idea better, and recognize the author's purpose. There are seven major writing patterns.

> Classification
> Sequence or process
> Simple listing
> Comparison and contrast
> Cause and effect
> Definition
> Example

Writers can employ the seven organizational patterns separately or in combination. Be aware of the signal words so you can recognize them both in reading and in examinations. You need to realize, however, that signal words, like the patterns themselves, can overlap. This is the case with classification and sequence, which both use numbers (1, 2, 3; first, second, third). Also, numbers are used frequently when a writer wants to present a *list* of items. The different patterns that writers use are good models when you are composing your own essays.

Chapter 5
Vocabulary Review

A. Cross out the word that does not belong in defining the boldfaced words.

1. **disdain**	ridicule	scorn	regain	reject
2. **affluent**	wealthy	rich	influence	prosperous
3. **concur**	agree	consent	assent	deny
4. **integrity**	numerical	honesty	sincerity	uprightness
5. **morbidly**	gruesomely	hideously	frightfully	truthfully

B. Answer *yes* or *no* to the following statements.

_____ 1. Would an **abstract** idea be one that is easily understood?

_____ 2. If you **demean** someone, would that person's feelings be hurt?

_____ 3. Is a person who has **charisma** the same as someone who is a deviant?

_____ 4. Does **longevity** mean the same thing as long life?

_____ 5. Do we usually try to **emulate** people we admire?

Selection 10: **ESSAY**

 Preparation for Reading

The following excerpt is from an essay about compulsive behavior. Much of the essay *defines* compulsiveness by the use of many *examples*. The essay further *compares* and *contrasts* destructive compulsiveness with a type that is "normal." It describes the *cause* of much compulsiveness and the *effect* that may follow.

While reading the essay, consider whether there are areas in your life that are controlled by compulsiveness. Is compulsiveness a positive or negative trait to possess?

The author uses the dash liberally, even though this is not considered a good writing style. After reading the selection, decide why she did so.

Note the meaning of the boldfaced words before reading. They are underlined in the text.

compulsive **chic**	smart elegance; stylish
the **mantra** of a whole generation	a hymn or portion of a text chanted as a prayer
to the **bizarre**	odd; strange
slightly obsessive, **meticulous**	extremely careful about details
ritualistic pattern	done like a solemn act
ironically, the more compulsive	opposite to what might be expected
frenetically neat people	frantically

Preview, then read the essay.

Control Freaks

Amanda Lovell

If it's possible for entire personality types to go in and out of fashion (remember when laid-back was in and uptight was out?) then the Nineties may well go down as the decade of Compulsive Chic. 1

People who used to go around saying, "I'm so disorganized" (code, as everyone knew, for "I'm so zany and creative and warm and wonderful") are piping down. The trendy plaint—if you haven't noticed—is "I'm so compulsive" (meaning: "I get things done"). At a time when being in control has become the mantra of a 2

whole generation, being compulsive is seen as the only way to achieve all one's goals.

In fact, "compulsive" means a lot of things, 3 ranging from the benign to the bizarre, from garden variety ashtray-emptying to nonstop shopping to the marathon hand washing of full-blown obsessive-compulsive disorder. All of these, oddly, appear to be either more in evidence or more talked about these days. Which raises a number of interesting questions.

When are compulsions—the hyper-neat 4 house, the never-missing-an-exercise-class, the need to shopshopshop—helpful and when are they over the top? Sometimes this is so obvious; sometimes it's a fine line. What might a bout of compulsive behavior symbolize—about an individual's emotional state? About our society? And what can be done about compulsiveness when it starts running amok?

Most experts agree that ordinary, everyday, 5 half-of-us-have-it compulsiveness is a nonproblem. "What we call the compulsive character style—the perfectly normal but slightly obsessive, <u>meticulous</u>, perfectionistic approach to things—is often quite helpful and productive. Occasional checking, wondering if one has forgotten something—that's normal," says Dr. Joseph DeVeugh Geiss, a director of clinical research from Summit, New Jersey.

Maybe a little better than normal. 6 "Compulsiveness correlates with intelligence and perfectionism," says New York psychologist Loretta Walder, Ph.D. "It's well-represented in the professions—in surgeons, lawyers, accountants, entrepreneurs, chefs." The word is that 70 percent of medical students have this character style—which may help to explain its good press among those who succeed in becoming doctors.

Walder claims, "What compulsive behavior 7 does *for* a person is to organize chaos and reduce anxiety. If a woman has six thousand things to do, it helps to make lists, stick to schedules, prioritize; it's okay to be a little rigid. When someone's feeling overwhelmed, the routines of doing things in a set, <u>ritualistic</u> pattern can prevent confusion and scatteredness. In general, any high level achievement that requires a person to be compulsive in professional life has a carryover into one's personal life."

"Compulsive behavior is about control," 8 asserts Sharon Hymer, an associate professor of psychology at New York University. "<u>Ironically</u>, the more compulsive the behavior, the more out of control the person probably feels deep

down. . . . However, one doesn't have to be a compulsive type to act compulsively. Just as even the most <u>frenetically</u> neat people often have little pockets of chaos in their lives—overflowing closets or handbags . . . so the generally laid-back have areas of drivenness. There's compulsive shopping, compulsive talking, compulsive eating, dieting, exercising, party going—you name it and someone has probably worked up a compulsion around it."

Strictly speaking, most of these urges aren't 9 compulsions in the textbook sense. There's a distinct difference involved: True compulsions usually involve some form of counting, checking or cleaning—and no fun, only a grim sense of "gotta do it." But some of the features are similar: low self-esteem, a consequent need to assert control over some facet of one's life, stress acting as a trigger—and constant uncertainty, so that whatever one has, does or says never quite suffices. . . .

"Narrowing it down, the symbolism of one's 10 unconscious choice is almost embarrassingly obvious," says Dr. Hymer. "The compulsive eater is trying to fill up a void in her life; . . . the compulsive talker is saying, "I don't think anyone will listen to me, so I have to control the situation by going on and on. The compulsive cleaner or exerciser is seeking self-esteem through a perfect body or pristine house. But it doesn't work, because too lean or too clean is never enough."

Still, one might not be a compulsive shop- 11 per, talker, party goer. One might merely be a passionate collector, a brilliant storyteller, a bon vivant . . . might one not? Georgia Witkin, Ph.D., assistant clinical professor of psychiatry at Mount Sinai School of Medicine in NYC and author of *Quick Fixes & Small Comforts,* suggests asking these questions: Is the behavior realistic? How does it leave you feeling afterward? What are the consequences? Is it possible to stop? And—since compulsions often start as anxiety reducers—is the hobby/passion/compulsion covering up an underlying problem? If a person gets the feeling, he or she is winning the game but losing at real life, it's time to rethink.

When compulsiveness goes from being a **12** coping style—for good or ill—and takes over the entire persona, it becomes what psychiatrists call a compulsive personality. "It's the classic condition of someone who is cold, unemotional, rigid, moralistic and an unbearable perfectionist," so says Michael Liebowitz, MD., director of the Columbia-Presbyterian Medical Center Anxiety Disorders Clinic.

"It's rampant right now," says Jay Lefer, **13** MD., associate professor of psychiatry at New York Medical College. "It's really a consequence of how people adapt to society. The hysteric was nineteenth-century Vienna: the obsessive-compulsive is late-twentieth-century America. People feel helpless in urban society—and helplessness leads to a necessity to control oneself and others. The compulsive personality develops in an attempt to protect self-esteem."

approximately 800 words

Excerpted and adapted from Amanda Lovell, "Control Freaks," *Self* Jan. 1989: 81–84. Reprinted by permission.

COMPREHENSION CHECK

Part I
General Comprehension Questions: Literal and Interpretive

Write the correct letter in the space provided.

_____ 1. "... The Nineties may well go down as the Decade of the Compulsive Chic." This means

    a. it's not good to be compulsive.
    b. it's a drug society.
    c. it's better to be organized.
    d. compulsiveness has become a way of life.

_____ 2. Ordinary compulsiveness

    a. is still considered a problem by psychologists.
    b. is not considered a problem by psychologists.
    c. leads to more serious dangerous behavior.
    d. can lead to drug abuse.

_____ 3. According to psychologists, there is a relationship between compulsiveness and

    a. intelligence.
    b. perfectionism.
    c. the professions.
    d. all of the above.

_____ 4. Professionals, according to the author, are well represented among the compulsives. Professionals who were not mentioned were

    a. doctors.
    b. lawyers.
    c. engineers.
    d. accountants.

———— 5. According to one psychologist, the more compulsive the behavior,

    a. the more control one has over his or her actions.
    b. the less control one has over his or her actions.
    c. the more sleep is needed.
    d. the more often eating disorders appear.

———— 6. Acting compulsively can be described as

    a. ritualistic behavior.
    b. a medical problem.
    c. animal-like behavior.
    d. both b and c.

7. What is the meaning of this sentence: "But it doesn't work, because too lean or too clean is never enough"? _____

_____

_____

8. What is the main organizational writing pattern in each of the paragraphs listed below?
(Choose from: simple listing; cause and effect; compare and contrast; definition; classification)

a.   paragraph 3 _____

b.   paragraph 7 _____

c.   paragraph 9 _____

Part II
Application Questions for Writing and Discussion

9. Define *compulsiveness.* What does compulsive behavior say about an individual's emotional state?

_____

_____

_____

_____

_____

10. Why do you believe our present society produces so much more compulsive behavior? According to this article, are men or women more compulsive? Why do you think so?

_____

_____

_____

_____

_____

_____

Part III
Extend Your Vocabulary

In these excerpts from the selection, use the context of the article and of the sentence to determine the meaning of the boldfaced word. Write the correct letter in the space provided.

_____ 1. What can be done about compulsiveness when it starts running **amok?**
   a. backward   b. wild   c. in a straight line   d. and stops

_____ 2. The compulsive cleaner . . . is seeking self-esteem through . . . a **pristine** house.
   a. neat   b. perfectly clean   c. soiled   d. prim

_____ 3. It's well represented in the professions—in surgeons, lawyers, accountants, **entrepreneurs.** . . .
   a. blue-collar workers   b. sanitary engineers   c. secretaries
   d. business organizers

_____ 4. One might merely be a passionate collector, a brilliant storyteller, or a **bon vivant.**
   a. one who lives cautiously   b. one who lives fearfully
   c. one who lives life fully   d. one who lives miserly

_____ 5. When compulsiveness goes from being a **coping** style—for good or evil—and takes over. . . .
   a. uplifting   b. successful handling   c. stylish trend   d. harmful look

Selection 11: **TEXTBOOK**

 # Preparation for Reading

Learn some of the ways researchers suggest that stress can best be handled, and evaluate the suggestions given for college students.

Before reading, note the meaning of the boldfaced words. They are underlined in the text.

finding is **correlational**	having a mutual relationship; parallel
an **aversive** event	causing strong dislike or unwillingness
level of **arousal**	stirred to action; excitement
increased **vulnerability**	sensitive to criticism; easy to attack or hurt
psychological effects of stress	derived from the mind or emotions

Preview the chapter excerpt before you begin reading it.

The Nature of Stress

John G. Seamon and Douglas T. Kendrick

Some researchers have studied the range of potentially stressful events, from losing a loved one to dropping the bag of garbage. . . .

Life Changes

In an effort to find out how stressful events are 1 linked to illness, Thomas Holmes and Richard Rahe asked tuberculosis patients about their lives just before they became ill. The researchers expected that unpleasant events would be linked with the onset of illness. Consistent with this expectation, many patients reported such things as the death of a spouse and the loss of a job. Unexpectedly, the patients also reported many seemingly neutral changes in recreational activities, sleep patterns, or domestic arrangements. Most unexpectedly, many of them reported seemingly positive events, including taking a vacation or getting married. From this information, the researchers developed the hypothesis that any disruption of our daily routine can be a stressor.

Following this hunch, Holmes and Rahe developed the Social Readjustment Rating Scale. The scale assigns readjustment values (or LCUs, "life change units") to 43 common life events. (See Table 5.1.)

In later studies, researchers found that 2 higher scores on the readjustment scale were associated with more illness. For instance, 79 percent of those who scored over 300 LCUs (and had therefore undergone major life stress) had had a serious illness during the year following the events. Fifty-one percent of those with moderate amounts of change (between 200 and 299 LCUs) had fallen ill, as had 37 percent of those with mild change (between 150 and 200 LCUs). Note that this finding is <u>correlational</u>, and does not prove that the stress led to illness. Perhaps the life changes were caused by other factors that also led to illness, or perhaps people recall more negative changes after they have fallen ill. There is some evidence that people with different dispositions bring different levels of stressful events on themselves.

TABLE 5.1
The Holmes and Rahe Social Readjustment Scale

Life Event	Mean Value
Death of spouse	100
Divorce	73
Marital separation	65
Jail term	63
Death of close family member	63
Personal injury or illness	53
Marriage	50
Fired at work	47
Marital reconciliation	45
Retirement	45
Change in health of family member	44
Pregnancy	40
Sex difficulties	39
Gain of new family member	39
Business readjustment	39
Change in financial state	38
Death of close friend	37
Change to different line of work	36
Change in number of arguments with spouse	35
Mortgage over $10,000*	31
Foreclosure of mortgage or loan	30
Change in responsibilities at work	29
Son or daughter leaving home	29
Trouble with in-laws	29
Outstanding personal achievement	28
Wife beginning or stopping work	26
Beginning or ending school	26
Change in living conditions	25
Revision of personal habits	24
Trouble with boss	23
Change in work hours or conditions	20
Change in residence	20
Change in schools	20
Change in recreation	19
Change in church activities	19
Change in social activities	18
Mortgage or loan less than $10,000*	17
Change in sleeping habits	16
Change in number of family get-togethers	15
Change in eating habits	15
Vacation	13
Christmas	12
Minor violations of the law	11

* Note: $10,000 was a figure based on the economy in the mid-1960s. An equivalent figure today would be $50,000.

Minor Everyday Problems

Instead of focusing on monumental stressors, **3** some psychologists believe that we can learn more about the effects of stress by studying what are sometimes called "daily hassles." These are the undramatic inconveniences of everyday life—returning to the car to find a parking ticket, arguing with your roommate about the dishes, or discovering that the cat has made a mess on the rug.

Researchers have asked subjects to record **4** these daily hassles, and found that, compared with major life changes, the minor inconveniences are actually better predictors of mental and physical distress. Obviously, some daily inconveniences are more relevant than others. Spilling the garbage is probably less upsetting than being stuck in traffic for an hour when you are already late for work. Psychologists Lee Anna Clark and David Watson found that arguments were the daily events most related to negative emotion. Having health problems, perhaps a cold or a flu, was also related to negative moods. Table 5.2 lists some common daily hassles found in a study of middle-aged adults, along with the things that were most likely to give them an "uplift."

Positive and negative daily events, and even **5** positive and negative daily moods, can occur at the same time. Good and bad things sometimes happen on the same day, and you can feel partly good and partly bad at the same moment. If you have an argument on Thursday, you are likely to rate yourself high on unpleasant moods, such as anger and depression. However, if you also get a good grade on the same day, you will rate your positive mood high as well. Research on college students' life events indicates that positive moods are related to such reinforcing events as getting a good grade or an unexpected gift, while negative moods are independently affected by painful events, including arguments with friends or parents. Positive events seem to raise our positive feelings but do not generally do much to erase the effects of painful experiences.

TABLE 5.2
A List of the Ten Most Frequent Daily Hassles and "Uplifts" Reported by Middle-Aged Adults over a Nine-Month Period

Hassles		Uplifts	
Item	% of Times Checked*	Item	% of Times Checked*
1. Concerns about weight	52.4	1. Relating well with your spouse or lover	76.3
2. Health of a family member	48.1	2. Relating well with friends	74.4
3. Rising prices of common goods	43.7	3. Completing a task	73.3
4. Home maintenance	42.8	4. Feeling healthy	72.7
5. Too many things to do	38.6	5. Getting enough sleep	69.7
6. Misplacing or losing things	38.1	6. Eating out	68.4
7. Yard work or outside home maintenance	38.1	7. Meeting your responsibilities	68.1
8. Property, investment, or taxes	37.6	8. Visiting, phoning, or writing someone	67.7
9. Crime	37.1	9. Spending time with family	66.7
10. Physical appearance	35.9	10. Home (inside) pleasing to you	65.5

* Note: The "% of times checked" figures represented the mean percentage of people checking the item each month averaged over the nine monthly administrations.

Features of Stressful Events: Uncertainty and Lack of Control

We are often confronted with stressors that are **6** outside of our control, from rare natural disasters to everyday traffic jams. There is a good deal of evidence that *uncontrollable events* are particularly stressful. The importance of controllability has been shown in studies of "executive rats," in which two rats receive exactly the same electric shock, but one is given a lever that could be used to turn the shock off after it occurs. Over a long series of such trials, the partner rat, helpless to do anything about its plight, is more likely to develop ulcers than is the "executive." In studies with humans, subjects are also more upset by electric shock if they have no means to control or prevent the shocks. In fact, subjects who simply *believe* that they can control the stressful events in their lives are less upset by unpleasant but naturally occurring life events. This research is closely related to the phenomenon of "learned helplessness," in which people give up in the face of stressors that seem to be uncontrollable.

An important aspect of having control over **7** the day-to-day inconveniences in your life, such as dental appointments, is that you know when they are going to occur. Animal studies indicate that *uncertainty* about an <u>aversive</u> event makes it much more disrupting. Human studies also show that uncertainty is aversive. One study found that subjects who were told that they had a 5 percent chance of receiving an electric shock were actually more aroused than those who were told that they had a 50 percent chance. Based on their discussions with the participants, the researchers concluded that those in the 50 percent group were resigned to receiving a shock, and could brace themselves. Those in the 5 percent group, on the other hand, were uncertain about how to prepare themselves.

In sum, then, there is evidence that certain **8** types of events are more stressful than others.

Major life changes, including divorce and the death of a spouse, are particularly stressful. Daily hassles, especially arguments, can also be quite stressful. Any given event is more stressful when it is novel, when it is uncertain, or when it cannot be controlled.

Stressful categories of events often involve **9** many of these stress-inducing features. For instance, the death of a spouse leaves the widowed person helpless to do anything about it and with a high degree of uncertainty about the future. It is important to keep in mind that the same event that is stressful to one person at one time may be exhilarating to that same person at another. . . . Totally familiar situations may be boring, while a certain amount of novelty causes a pleasant level of <u>arousal</u>. It is only when the arousal gets out of control that it is aversive. Recall also that some sensation-seeking individuals repeatedly seek out high levels of novelty and challenge in their lives.

Think About It . . .

If you fail an exam and call a friend for social support, is that an example of what Lazarus would call a "problem-focused" or an "emotion-focused" coping strategy? How would Lazarus categorize the use of a cognitive defense mechanism, such as rationalization?

Coping with Stress

When grouchy bosses or difficult examinations **10** start to get on your nerves, you need not just sit passively as the fatty acids and catecholamines course through your arteries. If you are like the hardy executives in Suzanne Kobasa's research, you can try to take control and do something about it. Removing the cause of stress is probably the most effective coping strategy, but sometimes, . . . it is not possible. Barring an immediate solution to our problems, we may try a number of other strategies to make them less aversive—we may seek the support of friends, we may reinterpret our situation to make it seem less unpleasant, we may laugh or cry, go for a drink, and so on. These attempts to control stress are called *coping mechanisms.*

Richard Lazarus and his colleagues have 11 made a useful distinction between problem-focused and emotion-focused coping strategies. Problem-focused strategies are those aimed at doing something to change the problem causing the distress (perhaps talking to the boss about what he or she expects of you). Problem-focused strategies tend to be used in situations that we regard as changeable. Emotion-focused strategies, used more in situations that are appraised as unchangeable, are aimed at regulating our distressing emotional responses. Compared with women, men are less likely to use emotion-focused strategies, such as seeking support from a friend.

Psychologists Susan Folkman and Richard 12 Lazarus examined undergraduate students' coping strategies at three time periods—two days before a midterm examination; a week later, two days before the grades were announced; and five days after the grades were posted. Before the exam, students tended to use such problem-focused strategies as studying—a guaranteed way to reduce the potential problems caused by an upcoming exam. If they sought out others, it was more likely to be for information than for emotional support. After the exam, when their fates were sealed, they tended to use the emotion-focused cognitive strategy of "distancing" (measured by such phrases as "Try to forget the whole thing"). If they sought out others afterwards, it was for emotional support rather than for information. Our discussion will focus on these two related lines of defense in coping with stress: seeking social support from others and reinterpreting the meaning of a stressful situation to ourselves.

Social Support

Like other animals, humans have always 13 been safer in groups. However, there is increasing evidence that people provide more than physical protection for one another. They provide *emotional support* and reassurance that can reduce the psychological and physiological symptoms of stress. A lack of support can increase our susceptibility to illness. For instance, short-term loneliness is associated with a decrease in immune response. This increased vulnerability can take a toll over time. Students who described themselves as "loners" in medical school had, compared with other medical students, the highest rates of cancer at a follow-up several decades later.

In contrast, people who get a lot of social 14 support from their friends and co-workers are less upset by life changes and daily hassles. In the long run, those who have strong social ties are likely to be more resistant to disease and to live longer. For instance, after being diagnosed as having a life-threatening disease, married people are likely to survive longer than unmarried people with the same disease. One team of researchers found that those who lived alone after a heart attack had a 16 percent likelihood of a relapse, whereas those who lived with someone else had only a 9 percent relapse rate.

In addition to providing protection and 15 emotional support, people give other types of support to one another. Several types of social support are listed in Table 5.3. For instance, other people may provide *appraisal support,* helping to evaluate and clarify how serious a problem is. If a professor tells you that he had also failed his first college algebra exam, the consequences of your failure will seem less devastating. Others can also provide *informational support,* giving advice about how to deal with the problem. In the search for solutions to problems at school or on the job, two heads are likely to be better than one.

TABLE 5.3
Different Types of Social Support

Type of Support	Example
1. Emotional	A sympathetic hug
2. Appraisal	A story about someone who did much worse than you did on the first math exam, and went on to get an A
3. Informational	A suggestion about where to get tutoring to help you pass a difficult course
4. Instrumental	A loan to help you pay for a tutor

Based on House (1981).

16   Finally, friends and relatives may give us *instrumental support,* providing material goods or services to overcome the stress. If your father lends you some money when your car breaks down, you can stop tearing your hair out and just fix it. One way that relatives and friends may provide support is by facilitating laughter and tears. There is emerging evidence that both may reduce the physiological and psychological effects of distress.

17   Do we need another person to provide us with social support? Interestingly, recent research suggests that a pet dog may provide the same benefit, and sometimes the dog might be even better. Participants in one study were exposed to a stressful task either alone, in the presence of a friend, or with their pet dog around. The presence of a friend did not improve performance on a stressful task at all; it seemed to make matters worse. On the other hand, a pet dog seemed to have a significant calming effect. Over a period of years, elderly people with dogs make fewer contacts with doctors, and those who have a pet at home are more likely to survive a heart attack. From a social support perspective, then, a dog may serve at least as well as a best friend.

approximately 2700 words

Excerpted from John G. Seamon and Douglas T. Kenrick, "Stress, Coping, Health," *Psychology:* 459–78. Copyright © by Prentice Hall, 1994. Reprinted by permission.

COMPREHENSION CHECK

Part I
General Comprehension Questions: Literal and Interpretive

Write the correct letter in the space provided.

_____ 1. Researchers have reported that

    a. unpleasant events can trigger stress.
    b. neutral changes can trigger stress.
    c. positive events can trigger stress.
    d. all of the above.

_____ 2. People who score very high on the Social Readjustment Scale would most likely have

    a. less illness the following year.
    b. more illness the following year.
    c. several nervous breakdowns.
    d. family adjustments.

_____ 3. The daily events most related to negative emotions are

    a. inconveniences.
    b. arguments.
    c. misplaced things.
    d. relocations.

_____ 4. More stress is associated with events that

    a. are uncertain.
    b. cannot be controlled.
    c. both a and b.
    d. are significant.

_____ 5. Of major life changes, the most stressful is a

    a. first child.
    b. business readjustment.
    c. new marriage.
    d. spouse's death.

_____ 6. The most effective coping strategy for stress is to

    a. get enough rest and relaxation.
    b. develop better eating habits.
    c. remove its cause.
    d. both a and b.

7. What is the relationship between stress and strong social ties? _____

    _____

8. What basic organizational pattern do the writers use in discussing the nature of

    stress and its consequences? _____

    _____

Part II
Application Questions for Writing and Discussion

9. Describe a real or imaginary situation in which you used either problem-focused coping strategies or emotion-focused coping strategies. Indicate which type you described.

_____

_____

_____

10. Which strategies are most effective in coping with stress?

_____

_____

Part III
Extend Your Vocabulary

Change the part of speech of each italicized word to complete the phrases.

1. Change *aversive,* an adjective, to a noun.

   her _____ to taking an exam

2. Change *arousal,* a noun, to a verb.

   had been _____ by a prowler

3. Change *cognitive,* an adjective, to a noun.

   when _____ is lacking

4. Change *psychological,* an adjective, to a noun.

   studying the _____ of stress

5. Change *correlational,* an adjective, to a noun.

   a direct _____ between cause and effect

Selection 12: **LITERATURE**

 Preparation for Reading

The following short story was written by Tobias Wolff, who received the PEN-Faulkner award for another story, "The Barracks Thief."

"The Rich Brother" first appeared in *Vanity Fair* and is part of a collection of short stories, *Back in the World*. Tobias Wolff teaches English at Syracuse University in upstate New York.

As you read, be aware of Wolff's major organizational writing pattern: comparison and contrast. Think about the description of the two brothers, Pete and Donald, to see in what ways their personalities are similar and how they differ. It is their differences that create the major conflict in the story. The setting of the story is northern California.

Note the meaning of the boldfaced words before reading. They are underlined in the text.

an **ashram** in Berkeley	a communal retreat, often a secluded place
innuendo, looks of mild despair	indirect hint or suggestion, often meant to discredit someone
look of an **inquisitor**	official investigator
aware of Donald's **scrutiny**	close examination; careful inspection
"**Stygian,**" the man said.	dark; gloomy; of the lower world
tone was **sepulchral**	suggesting a tomb; dismal or gloomy
land and rights in **perpetuity**	existence forever

The Rich Brother

Tobias Wolff

There were two brothers, Pete and Donald.

Pete, the older brother, was in real estate. He and his wife had a Century 21 franchise in Santa Cruz. Pete worked hard and made a lot of money, but not any more than he thought he deserved. He had two daughters, a sailboat, a house from which he could see a thin slice of the ocean, and friends doing well enough in their own lives not to wish bad luck on him. Donald, the younger brother, was still single. He lived alone, painted houses when he found the work, and got deeper in debt to Pete when he didn't.

No one would have taken them for brothers. Where Pete was stout and hearty and at home in the world, Donald was bony, grave, and obsessed with the fate of his soul. Over the years Donald had worn the images of two different Perfect Masters around his neck. Out of devotion to the second of these he entered an <u>ashram</u> in

1

Berkeley, where he nearly died of undiagnosed hepatitis. By the time Pete finished paying the medical bills Donald had become a Christian. He drifted from church to church, then joined a pentecostal community that met somewhere in the Mission District to sing in tongues and swap prophecies.

Pete couldn't make sense of it. Their parents were both dead, but while they were alive neither of them had found it necessary to believe in anything. They managed to be decent people without making fools of themselves, and Pete had the same ambition. He thought that the whole thing was an excuse for Donald to take himself seriously.

The trouble was that Donald couldn't content himself with worrying about his   5 own soul. He had to worry about everyone else's, and especially Pete's. He handed down his judgments in ways that he seemed to consider subtle: through significant silence, innuendo, looks of mild despair that said, *Brother, what have you come to?* What Pete had come to, as far as he could tell, was prosperity. That was the real issue between them. Pete prospered and Donald did not prosper.

At the age of forty Pete took up sky diving. He made his first jump with two friends who'd started only a few months earlier and were already doing stunts. They were both coked to the gills when they jumped but Pete wanted to do it straight, at least the first time, and he was glad that he did. He would never have used the word "mystical," but that was how Pete felt about the experience. Later he made the mistake of trying to describe it to Donald, who kept asking how much it cost and then acted appalled when Pete told him.

"At least I'm trying something new," Pete said. "At least I'm breaking the pattern."

Not long after that conversation Donald also broke the pattern, by going to live on a farm outside of Paso Robles. The farm was owned by several members of Donald's community, who had bought it and moved there with the idea of forming a family of faith. That was how Donald explained it in the first letter he sent. Every week Pete heard how happy Donald was, how "in the Lord." He told Pete that he was praying for him, he and the rest of Pete's brothers and sisters on the farm.

"I only have one brother," Pete wanted to answer, "and that's enough." But he kept this thought to himself.

In November the letters stopped. Pete didn't worry about this at first, but when   10 he called Donald at Thanksgiving Donald was grim. He tried to sound upbeat but he didn't try hard enough to make it convincing. "Now listen," Pete said, "you don't have to stay in that place if you don't want to."

"I'll be all right," Donald answered.

"That's not the point. Being all right is not the point. If you don't like what's going on up there, then get out."

"I'm all right," Donald said again, more firmly. "I'm doing fine."

But he called Pete a week later and said that he was quitting the farm. When Pete asked him where he intended to go, Donald admitted that he had no plan. His car had been repossessed just before he left the city, and he was flat broke.

"I guess you'll have to stay with us," Pete said.   **15**

Donald put up a show of resistance. Then he gave in. "Just until I get my feet on the ground," he said.

"Right," Pete said. "Check out your options." He told Donald he'd send him money for a bus ticket, but as they were about to hang up Pete changed his mind. He knew that Donald would try hitchhiking to save the fare. Pete didn't want him out on the road all alone where some head case could pick him up, where anything could happen to him.

"Better yet," he said. "I'll come and get you."

"You don't have to do that. I didn't expect you to do that." Donald said. He added, "It's a pretty long drive."

"Just tell me how to get there."   **20**

But Donald wouldn't give him directions. He said that the farm was too depressing, that Pete wouldn't like it. Instead, he insisted on meeting Pete at a service station called Jonathan's Mechanical Emporium.

"You must be kidding," Pete said.

"It's close to the highway," Donald said. "I didn't name it."

"That's one for the collection," Pete said.

The day before he left to bring Donald home, Pete received a letter from a man who   **25**
described himself as "head of household" at the farm where Donald had been living. From this letter Pete learned that Donald had not quit the farm, but had been asked to leave. The letter was written on the back of a mimeographed survey form asking people to record their response to a ceremony of some kind. The last question said:

> What did you feel during the liturgy?
> a)   Being
> b)   Becoming
> c)   Being and Becoming
> d)   None of the Above
> e)   All of the Above

Pete tried to forget the letter. But of course he couldn't. Each time he thought of it he felt crowded and breathless, a feeling that came over him again when he drove into the service station and saw Donald sitting against a wall with his head on his knees. It was late afternoon. A paper cup tumbled slowly past Donald's feet, pushed by the damp wind.

Pete honked and Donald raised his head. He smiled at Pete, then stood and stretched. His arms were long and thin and white. He wore a red bandanna across his forehead, a T-shirt with a couple of words on the front. Pete couldn't read them because the letters were inverted.

"Grow up," Pete yelled. "Get a Mercedes."

Donald came up to the window. He bent down and said, "Thanks for coming. You must be totally whipped."

"I'll make it." Pete pointed at Donald's T-shirt. "What's that supposed to say?"   **30**

Donald looked down at his shirt front. "Try God. I guess I put it on backwards. Pete, could I borrow a couple of dollars? I owe these people for coffee and sand- wiches."

Pete took five twenties from his wallet and held them out the window.

Donald stepped back as if horrified. "I don't need that much."

"I can't keep track of all these nickels and dimes," Pete said. "Just pay me back when your ship comes in." He waved the bills impatiently. "Go on—take it."

"Only for now." Donald took the money and went into the service station office.   **35** He came out carrying two orange sodas, one of which he gave to Pete as he got into the car. "My treat," he said.

"No bags?"

"Wow, thanks for reminding me," Donald said. He balanced his drink on the dashboard, but the slight rocking of the car as he got out tipped it onto the passen- ger's seat, where half its contents foamed over before Pete could snatch it up again. Donald looked on while Pete held the bottle out the window, soda running down his fingers.

"Wipe it up," Pete told him. "Quick!"

"With what?"

Pete stared at Donald. "That shirt. Use the shirt."   **40**

Donald pulled a long face but did as he was told, his pale skin puckering against the wind.

"Great, just great," Pete said. "We haven't even left the gas station yet."

Afterwards, on the highway, Donald said, "This is a new car, isn't it?"

"Yes. This is a new car."

"Is that why you're so upset about the seat?"   **45**

"Forget it, okay? Let's just forget about it."

"I said I was sorry."

Pete said, "I just wish you'd be more careful. These seats are made of leather. That stain won't come out, not to mention the smell. I don't see why I can't have leather seats that smell like leather instead of orange pop."

"What was wrong with the other car?"

Pete glanced over at Donald. Donald had raised the hood of the blue sweatshirt   **50** he'd put on. The peaked hood above his gaunt, watchful face gave him the look of an <u>inquisitor</u>.

"There wasn't anything wrong with it," Pete said. "I just happened to like this one better."

Donald nodded.

There was a long silence between them as Pete drove on and the day darkened toward evening. On either side of the road lay stubble-covered fields. A line of low hills ran along the horizon, topped here and there with trees black against the gray sky. In the approaching line of cars a driver turned on his headlights. Pete did the same.

"So what happened?" he asked. "Farm life not your bag?"

Donald took some time to answer, and at last he said, simply, "It was my fault."   **55**

"What was your fault?"

"The whole thing. Don't play dumb, Pete. I know they wrote to you." Donald looked at Pete, then stared out the windshield again.

"I'm not playing dumb."

Donald shrugged.

"All I really know is they asked you to leave," Pete went on. "I don't know any of the particulars." **60**

"I blew it," Donald said. "Believe me, you don't want to hear the gory details."

"Sure I do," Pete said. He added, "Everybody likes the gory details."

"You mean everybody likes to hear how someone else messed up."

"Right," Pete said. "That's the way it is here on Spaceship Earth."

Donald bent one knee onto the front seat and leaned against the door so that he was facing Pete instead of the windshield. Pete was aware of Donald's <u>scrutiny</u>. He waited. Night was coming on in a rush now, filling the hollows of the land. Donald's long cheeks and deep-set eyes were dark with shadow. His brow was white. "Do you ever dream about me?" Donald asked. **65**

"Do I ever dream about you? What kind of a question is that? Of course I don't dream about you," Pete said, untruthfully.

"What do you dream about?"

"Sex and money. Mostly money. A nightmare is when I dream I don't have any."

"You're just making that up," Donald said.

Pete smiled. **70**

"Sometimes I wake up at night," Donald went on, "and I can tell you're dreaming about me."

"We were talking about the farm," Pete said. "Let's finish that conversation and then we can talk about our various out-of-body experiences and the interesting things we did during previous incarnations."

For a moment Donald looked like a grinning skull; then he turned serious again. "There's not that much to tell," he said. "I just didn't do anything right."

"That's a little vague," Pete said.

"Well, like the groceries. Whenever it was my turn to get the groceries I'd blow it somehow. I'd bring the groceries home and half of them would be missing, or I'd have all the wrong things, the wrong kind of flour or the wrong kind of chocolate or whatever. One time I gave them away. It's not funny, Pete." **75**

Pete said, "Who did you give the groceries to?"

"Just some people I picked up on the way home. Some fieldworkers. They had about eight kids with them and they didn't even speak English—just nodded their heads. Still, I shouldn't have given away the groceries. Not all of them, anyway. I really learned my lesson about that. You have to be practical. You have to be fair to yourself." Donald leaned forward, and Pete could sense his excitement. "There's nothing actually wrong with being in business," he said. "As long as you're fair to other people you can still be fair to yourself. I'm thinking of going into business, Pete."

"We'll talk about it," Pete said. "So, that's the story? There isn't any more to it than that?"

"What did they tell you?" Donald asked.

"Nothing."

"They must have told you something."

Pete shook his head.

"They didn't tell you about the fire?" When Pete shook his head again Donald regarded him for a time, then said, "I don't know. It was stupid. I just completely lost it." He folded his arms across his chest and slumped back into the corner. "Everybody had to take turns cooking dinner. I usually did tuna casserole or spaghetti with garlic bread. But this one night I thought I'd do something different, something really interesting." Donald looked sharply at Pete. "It's all a big laugh to you, isn't it?"

"I'm sorry," Pete said.

"You don't know when to quit. You just keep hitting away."

"Tell me about the fire, Donald."

Donald kept watching him. "You have this compulsion to make me look foolish."

"Come off it, Donald. Don't make a big thing out of this."

"I know why you do it. It's because you don't have any purpose in life. You're afraid to relate to people who do, so you make fun of them."

"Relate," Pete said softly.

"You're basically a very frightened individual," Donald said. "Very threatened. You've always been like that. Do you remember when you used to try to kill me?"

"I don't have any compulsion to make you look foolish, Donald—You do it yourself. You're doing it right now."

They ate dinner at a Denny's on the other side of King City. As Pete was paying the check he heard a man behind him say, "Excuse me, but I wonder if I might ask which way you're going?" and Donald answered, "Santa Cruz."

"Perfect," the man said.

Pete could see him in the fish-eye mirror above the cash register: a red blazer with some kind of crest on the pocket, little black mustache, glossy black hair combed down on his forehead like a Roman emperor's. A rug, Pete thought. Definitely a rug.

Pete got his change and turned. "Why is that perfect?" he asked.

The man looked at Pete. He had a soft ruddy face that was doing its best to express pleasant surprise, as if this new wrinkle were all he could have wished for, but the eyes behind the aviator glasses showed signs of regret. His lips were moist and shiny. "I take it you're together," he said.

"You got it," Pete told him.

"All the better, then," the man went on. "It so happens I'm going to Santa Cruz myself. Had a spot of car trouble down the road. The old Caddy let me down."

"What kind of trouble?" Pete asked.   100

"Engine trouble," the man said. "I'm afraid it's a bit urgent. My daughter is sick. Urgently sick. I've got a telegram here." He patted the breast pocket of his blazer.

Pete grinned. Amazing, he thought, the old sick daughter ploy, but before he could say anything Donald got into the act again. "No problem," Donald said. "We've got tons of room."

"Not that much room," Pete said.

Donald nodded. "I'll put my things in the trunk."

"The trunk's full," Pete told him.   105

"It so happens I'm traveling light," the man said. "This leg of the trip anyway. In fact I don't have any luggage at this particular time."

Pete said, "Left it in the old Caddy, did you?"

"Exactly," the man said.

"No problem," Donald repeated. He walked outside and the man went with him. Together they strolled across the parking lot, Pete following at a distance. When they reached Pete's car Donald raised his face to the sky, and the man did the same. They stood there looking up. "Dark night," Donald said.

"Stygian," the man said.   110

Pete still had it in mind to brush him off, but he didn't do that. Instead he unlocked the door for him. He wanted to see what would happen. It was an adventure, but not a dangerous adventure. The man might steal Pete's ashtrays but he wouldn't kill him. If Pete got killed on the road it would be by some spiritual person in a sweatsuit, someone with his eyes on the far horizon and a wet Try God T-shirt in his duffel bag.

As soon as they left the parking lot the man lit a cigar. He blew a cloud of smoke over Pete's shoulder and sighed with pleasure. "Put it out," Pete told him.

"Of course," the man said. Pete looked into the rear-view mirror and saw the man take another long puff before dropping the cigar out the window. "Forgive me," he said. "I should have asked. Name's Webster, by the way."

Donald turned and looked back at him. "First name or last?"

The man hesitated. "Last," he said finally.   115

"I know a Webster," Donald said. "Mick Webster."

"There are many of us," Webster said.

"Big fellow, wooden leg," Pete said.

Donald gave Pete a look.

Webster shook his head. "Doesn't ring a bell. Still, I wouldn't deny the connec-   120
tion. Might be one of the cousinry."

"What's your daughter got?" Pete asked.

"That isn't clear," Webster answered. "It appears to be a female complaint of some nature. Then again it may be tropical." He was quiet for a moment, and then added: "If indeed it *is* tropical, I will have to assume some of the blame myself. It was my own vaulting ambition that first led us to the tropics and kept us in the tropics all those many years, exposed to every evil. Truly I have much to answer for. I left my wife there."

Donald said quietly, "You mean she died?"

"I buried her with these hands. The earth will be repaid, gold for gold."

"Which tropics?" Pete asked.   **125**

"The tropics of Peru."

"What part of Peru are they in?"

"The lowlands," Webster said.

Pete nodded. "What's it like down there?"

"Another world," Webster said. His tone was <u>sepulchral</u>. "A world better imag-   **130**
ined than described."

"Far out," Pete said.

The three men rode in silence for a time. A line of trucks went past in the other
direction, trailers festooned with running lights, engines roaring.

"Yes," Webster said at last, "I have much to answer for."

Pete smiled at Donald, but Donald had turned in his seat again and was gazing
at Webster. "I'm sorry about your wife," Donald said.

"What did she die of?" Pete asked.   **135**

"A wasting illness," Webster said. "The doctors have no name for it, but I do." He
leaned forward and said, fiercely, "*Greed.*" Then he slumped back against his seat.
"My greed, not hers. She wanted no part of it."

Pete bit his lip. Webster was a find and Pete didn't want to scare him off by hoot-
ing at him. In a voice low and innocent of knowingness, he asked, "What took you
there?"

"It's difficult for me to talk about."

"Try," Pete told him.

"A cigar would make it easier."   **140**

Donald turned to Pete and said, "It's okay with me."

"All right," Pete said. "Go ahead. Just keep the window rolled down."

"Much obliged." A match flared. There were eager sucking sounds.

"Let's hear it," Pete said.

"I am by training an engineer," Webster began. "My work has exposed me to all   **145**
but one of the continents, to desert and alp and forest, to every terrain and season
of the earth. Some years ago I was hired by the Peruvian government to search for
tungsten in the tropics. My wife and daughter accompanied me. We were the only
white people for a thousand miles in any direction, and we had no choice but to live
as the Indians lived—to share their food and drink and even their culture."

Pete said, "You knew the lingo, did you?"

"We picked it up." The ember of the cigar bobbed up and down. "We were used
to learning as necessity decreed. At any rate, it became evident after a couple of years
that there was no tungsten to be found. My wife had fallen ill and was pleading to be
taken home. But I was deaf to her pleas, because by then I was on the trail of another
metal—a metal far more valuable than tungsten."

"Let me guess," Pete said, "Gold?"

Donald looked at Pete, then back at Webster.

"Gold," Webster said. "A vein of gold greater than the Mother Lode itself. After **150** I found the first traces of it nothing could tear me away from my search—not the sickness of my wife nor anything else. I was determined to uncover the vein, and so I did—but not before I laid my wife to rest. As I say, the earth will be repaid."

Webster was quiet. Then he said, "But life must go on. In the years since my wife's death I have been making the arrangements necessary to open the mine. I could have done it immediately, of course, enriching myself beyond measure, but I knew what that would mean—the exploitation of our beloved Indians, the brutal destruction of their environment. I felt I had too much to atone for already." Webster paused, and when he spoke again his voice was dull and rushed, as if he had used up all the interest he had in his own words. "Instead I drew up a program for returning the bulk of the wealth to the Indians themselves. A kind of trust fund. The interest alone will allow them to secure their ancient lands and rights in <u>perpetuity</u>. At the same time, our investors will be rewarded a thousandfold. Two-thousandfold. Everyone will prosper together."

"That's great," Donald said. "That's the way it ought to be."

Pete said, "I'm willing to bet that you just happen to have a few shares left. Am I right?"

Webster made no reply.

"Well?" Pete knew that Webster was on to him now, but he didn't care. The story **155** had bored him. He'd expected something different, something original, and Webster had let him down. He hadn't even tried. Pete felt sour and stale. His eyes burned from cigar smoke and the high beams of road-hogging truckers. "Douse the stogie," he said to Webster. "I told you to keep the window down."

"Got a little nippy back there."

Donald said, "Hey, Pete. Lighten up."

"Douse it!"

Webster sighed. He got rid of the cigar.

"I'm a wreck," Pete said to Donald. "You want to drive for a while?"   **160**

Donald nodded.

Pete pulled over and they changed places.

Webster kept his counsel in the back seat. Donald hummed while he drove, until Pete told him to stop. Then everything was quiet.

Donald was humming again when Pete woke up. Pete stared sullenly at the road, at the white lines sliding past the car. After a few moments of this he turned and said, "How long have I been out?"

Donald glanced at him. "Twenty, twenty-five minutes."   **165**

Pete looked behind him and saw that Webster was gone. "Where's our friend?"

"You just missed him. He got out in Soledad.* He told me to say thanks and good-bye."

---

* Soledad is a city in California where a state prison is located.

"Soledad? What about his sick daughter? How did he explain her away?" Pete leaned over the seat. Both ashtrays were still in place. Floor mats. Door handles.

"He has a brother living there," He's going to borrow a car from him and drive the rest of the way in the morning.

"I'll bet his brother's living there," Pete said. "Doing fifty concurrent life sen- 170 tences. His brother and his sister and his mom and his dad."

"I kind of liked him," Donald said.

"I'm sure you did," Pete said wearily.

"He was interesting. He'd been places."

"His cigars had been places, I'll give you that."

"Come on, Pete."   175

"Come on yourself. What a phony."

"You don't know that."

"Sure I do."

"How? How do you know?"

Pete stretched. "Brother, there are some things you're just born knowing. 180 What's the gas situation?"

"We're a little low."

"Then why didn't you get some more?"

"I wish you wouldn't snap at me like that," Donald said.

"Then why don't you use your head? What if we run out?"

"We'll make it," Donald said. "I'm pretty sure we've got enough to make it. You 185 didn't have to be so rude to him." Donald added.

Pete took a deep breath. "I don't feel like running out of gas tonight, okay?"

Donald pulled in at the next station they came to and filled the tank while Pete went to the men's room. When Pete came back, Donald was sitting in the passenger's seat. The attendant came up to the driver's window as Pete got in behind the wheel. He bent down and said, "Twenty-two fifty-five."

"You heard the man," Pete said to Donald.

Donald looked straight ahead. He didn't move.

"Cough up," Pete said. "This trip's on you."   190

Donald said, softly, "I can't."

"Sure you can. Break out that wad."

Donald glanced up at the attendant, then at Pete. "Please," he said. "Pete, I don't have it anymore."

Pete took this in. He nodded, and paid the attendant.

Donald began to speak when they left the station but Pete cut him off. He said, 195 "I don't want to hear from you right now. You just keep quiet or I swear to God I won't be responsible."

They left the fields and entered a tunnel of tall trees. The trees went on and on. "Let me get this straight," Pete said at last. "You don't have the money I gave you."

"You treated him like a bug or something," Donald said.

"You don't have the money," Pete said again.

Donald shook his head.

"Since I bought dinner, and since we didn't stop anywhere in between, I assume   200
you gave it to Webster. Is that right? Is that what you did with it?"

"Yes."

Pete looked at Donald. His face was dark under the hood but he still managed
to convey a sense of remove, as if none of this had anything to do with him.

"Why?" Pete asked. "Why did you give it to him?" When Donald didn't answer,
Pete said, "A hundred dollars. Gone. Just like that. I *worked* for that money, Donald."

"I know, I know," Donald said.

"You don't know! How could you? You get money by holding out your hand."   205

"I work too," Donald said.

"You work too. Don't kid yourself, brother."

Donald leaned toward Pete, about to say something, but Pete cut him off again.

"You're not the only one on the payroll, Donald. I don't think you understand
that. I have a family."

"Pete, I'll pay you back."   210

"Like hell you will. A hundred dollars!" Pete hit the steering wheel with the palm
of his hand. "Just because you think I hurt some goofball's feelings. Jesus, Donald."

"That's not the reason," Donald said. "And I didn't just *give* him the money."

"What do you call it, then? What do you call what you did?"

"I *invested* it. I wanted a share, Pete." When Pete looked over at him Donald nodded and said again, "I wanted a share."

Pete said, "I take it you're referring to the gold mine in Peru."   215

"Yes," Donald said.

"You believe that such a gold mine exists?"

Donald looked at Pete, and Pete could see him just beginning to catch on. "You'll
believe anything," Pete said. "Won't you? You really will believe anything at all."

"I'm sorry," Donald said, and turned away.

Pete drove on between the trees and considered the truth of what he had just   220
said—that Donald would believe anything at all. And it came to him that it would be
just like this unfair life for Donald to come out ahead in the end, by believing in
some outrageous promise that would turn out to be true and that he, Pete, would
reject out of hand because he was too wised up to listen to anybody's pitch anymore
except for laughs. What a joke. What a joke if there really was a blessing to be had,
and the blessing didn't come to the one who deserved it, the one who did all the
work, but to the other.

And as if this had already happened Pete felt a shadow move upon him, dark-
ening his thoughts. After a time he said, "I can see where all this is going, Donald."

"I'll pay you back," Donald said.

"No," Pete said. "You won't pay me back. You can't. You don't know how. All
you've ever done is take. All your life."

Donald shook his head.

"I see exactly where this is going," Pete went on. "You can't work, you can't take   225
care of yourself, you believe anything anyone tells you. I'm stuck with you, aren't I?"
He looked over at Donald. "I've got you on my hands for good."

Donald pressed his fingers against the dashboard as if to brace himself. "I'll get out," he said.

Pete kept driving.

"Let me out," Donald said. "I mean it, Pete."

"Do you?"

Donald hesitated. "Yes," he said.   230

"Be sure," Pete told him. "This is it. This is for keeps."

"I mean it."

"All right. You made the choice." Pete braked the car sharply and swung it to the shoulder of the road. He turned off the engine and got out. Trees loomed on both sides, shutting out the sky. The air was cold and musty. Pete took Donald's duffel bag from the back seat and set it down behind the car. He stood there, facing Donald in the red glow of the taillights. "It's better this way," Pete said.

Donald just looked at him.

"Better for you," Pete said.   235

Donald hugged himself. He was shaking. "You don't have to say all that," he told Pete. "I don't blame you."

"Blame me? What the hell are you talking about? Blame me for what?"

"For anything," Donald said.

"I want to know what you mean by blame me."

"Nothing. Nothing, Pete. You'd better get going. God bless you."   240

"That's it," Pete said. He dropped to one knee, searching the packed dirt with his hands. He didn't know what he was looking for; his hands would know when they found it.

Donald touched Pete's shoulder. "You'd better go," he said.

Somewhere in the trees Pete heard a branch snap. He stood up. He looked at Donald, then went back to the car and drove away. He drove fast, hunched over the wheel, conscious of the way he was hunched and the shallowness of his breathing, refusing to look at the mirror above his head until there was nothing behind him but darkness.

Then he said, "A hundred dollars," as if there were someone to hear.

The trees gave way to fields. Metal fences ran beside the road, plastered with 245 windblown scraps of paper. Tule fog hung above the ditches, spilling into the road, dimming the ghostly halogen lights that burned in the yards of the farms Pete passed. The fog left beads of water rolling up the windshield.

Pete rummaged among his cassettes. He found Pachelbel's Canon and pushed it into the tape deck. When the violins began to play he leaned back and assumed an attentive expression as if he were really listening to them. He smiled to himself like a man at liberty to enjoy music, a man who has finished his work and settled his debts, done all things meet and due.

And in this way, smiling, nodding to the music, he went another mile or so and pretended that he was not already slowing down, that he was not going to turn back, that he would be able to drive on like this, alone, and have the right answer when his wife stood before him in the doorway of his home and asked, Where is he? Where is your brother?

approximately 5100 words

Questions for Writing and Discussion

1. In what ways are Pete and Donald alike? How are they different from each other?

2. Which of the two brothers did you find more admirable? Why?

3. What is the story's *theme?* How does the value system of each brother help develop the theme?

4. How realistically is the relationship of the two brothers portrayed? How does it compare to your own relationship with siblings? With acquaintances or close friends?

5. The story's ending is indefinite, allowing the reader to reach his or her own conclusion. Rewrite the ending. Decide whether Pete actually does go back and get Donald, or if he drives on, severing his ties with Donald completely.

*J*OURNAL ENTRY

All of us live with some degree of stress. Sometimes, as indicated in the essay "Control Freaks," we create our own stresses. The textbook selection "Personality, Stress, and Health" presents ways to handle stress. In "The Rich Brother," Pete experiences obvious stress in trying to "take care of" his brother. Write a journal entry discussing how you react to stressful situations and describing the coping strategies that work best for you.

6

Refining Reading Style
and Improving Rate

This chapter will help you
* Assess your current reading rate.
* Dispel some of the myths about the reading process and reading rate.
* Learn strategies for becoming a faster, more dynamic reader.

Before reading, think about these questions.
* Do you want to become a faster reader?
* What are some of your present reading habits that prevent you from reading more rapidly?
* What steps could you take to increase your reading rate?

Jot down your thoughts about reading as you consider improving your rate.

_____

_____

_____

✑ Facts and Myths

Fast and Slow Readers

In Chapter 1, we emphasized the vast amount of printed material that our Information Age is producing at speeds seemingly impossible for the average reader to handle. To cope with the mounting paper blitz, speed-reading classes are popular on many college campuses. These can be very valuable, time permitting, but the major thrust of these courses is getting students to practice, practice, and practice. We can reduce their philosophy to a reading rate improvement formula:

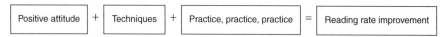

Slow readers usually dislike reading because for them it is so time-consuming. Therefore, they read very little and consequently never practice enough to improve. This, in turn, compounds the problem because they also fail to improve their vocabulary. An enriched vocabulary helps in reading faster because the printed page contains a much broader vocabulary than the spoken words heard and used. On the other hand, better readers usually read a great deal, enjoy reading, and are constantly improving both their vocabulary and reading skills. As a result, those who are good readers get better, while those who aren't, don't.

So you need to begin this chapter by wanting to read faster and trust that you can do it. You have already engaged in strategies, such as previewing and predicting ideas, that assist you in reading more quickly. Now, developing a positive attitude and learning some simple techniques will markedly improve your rate while you maintain good comprehension.

Reading Rate Evaluation

Read the article on pages 313–14 at your normal reading speed. Record your reading time (in minutes and seconds) in the space provided at the end of the article. Then, without referring back to the article, answer the questions that follow it. After you answer the questions, use the chart provided to convert your time into a reading rate of words per minute. To find out your comprehension, check your answers with those at the end of this chapter. By knowing both your present reading rate and your comprehension at that rate, you can best use the information in this chapter.

The author of the following article has written more than forty books and is a well-known philosopher. In this article, he outlines his secrets of success.

Success Means Never Feeling Tired

Mortimer J. Adler

Failure is probably the most fatiguing experience 1
a person ever has. There is nothing more enervating than not succeeding—being blocked, not
moving ahead. It is a vicious circle. Failure breeds
fatigue, and the fatigue makes it harder to get to
work, which compounds the failure.

We experience this tiredness in two main 2
ways: as start-up fatigue and performance fatigue.
In the former case, we keep putting off a task that
we are under some compulsion to discharge.
Either because it is too tedious or too difficult, we
shirk it. And the longer we postpone it, the more
tired we feel.

Such start-up fatigue is very real, even if not 3
actually physical, not something in our muscles
and bones. The remedy is obvious, though perhaps not easy to apply: an exertion of willpower.
The moment I find myself turning away from a
job, or putting it under a pile of other things I
have to do, I clear my desk of everything else and
attack the objectionable item first. To prevent
start-up fatigue, always tackle the most difficult job
first.

Years ago, when editing *Great Books of the* 4
Western World, I undertook to write 102 essays, one
on each of the great ideas discussed by the authors
of those books. The writing took me two and one-
half years, working at it—among my other tasks—
seven days a week. I would never have finished if I
had allowed myself to write first about the ideas I
found easiest to expound. Applying my own rule,
I determined to write the essays in strict alphabetical order, from ANGEL to WORLD, never letting
myself skip a tough idea. And I always started the
day's work with the difficult task of essay-writing.
Experience proved, once again, that the rule
works.

Performance fatigue is more difficult to han- 5
dle. Here we are not reluctant to get started, but
we cannot seem to do the job right. Its difficulties
appear insurmountable and, however hard we
work, we fail again and again. That mounting
experience of failure carries with it an ever-
increasing burden of mental fatigue. In such a situation, I work as hard as I can—then let the
unconscious take over.

When I was planning the 15th edition of 6
Encyclopaedia Britannica, I had to create a topical
table of contents for its alphabetically arranged
articles. Nothing like this had ever been done
before, and day after day I kept coming up with
solutions that fell short. My fatigue became almost
overpowering.

One day, mentally exhausted, I put down on 7
paper all the reasons why this problem could *not*
be solved. I tried to convince myself that what
appeared insoluble really *was* insoluble, that the
trouble was with the problem, not me. Having
gained some relief, I sat back in an easy chair and
went to sleep.

An hour or so later, I woke up suddenly with 8
the solution clearly in mind. In the weeks that followed, the correctness of the solution summoned
up by my unconscious mind was confirmed at
every step. Though I worked every bit as hard, if
not harder, than before, my work was not
attended by any weariness or fatigue. Success was
now as exhilarating as failure had been depressing. I was experiencing the joy of what psychologists today call "flow." Life offers few pleasures
more invigorating than the successful exercise of
our faculties. It unleashes energies for additional
work.

Sometimes the snare is not in the problem 9
itself, but in the social situation—or so it appears.
Other people somehow seem to prevent us from
succeeding. But, as Shakespeare wrote, "The fault,
dear Brutus, is not in our stars but in ourselves."

Why blame other people and shrug off our own responsibility for misunderstandings? Doing a job successfully means doing whatever is necessary—and that *includes* winning the cooperation of others.

10 More often, the snare that blocks us is purely personal. Subject to human distractions, we let personal problems weigh on us, producing a fatigue-failure that blocks our productivity in every sphere.

11 A friend of mine went into a decline over a family problem that she had let slide. Her daughter had secretly married a man she thought her father would disapprove of. The daughter told her mother but made her promise to keep silent. Worrying about the problem, and carrying a burden of guilt over the secrecy, exhausted the mother. Her fatigue spilled over into her job and turned her usual successes there into failures. She was saved from serious depression only when other people intervened and told the father—who didn't display any of the anticipated negative reaction. It seems incredible that a person can allow his or her life to get snarled up in this fashion, but that is how problems can fester if they aren't solved as they come along.

12 So, our first step should be to use inexplicable fatigue that has no physical base as a radar—an early-warning system—and trace the fatigue to its source; to find the defeat we are papering over and not admitting. Then we must diagnose the cause of this failure. In rare cases, it may be that the task really is too difficult for us, that we are in over our head. If so, we can acknowledge the fact and bow out. Or the block may simply be in refusing to confront the problem. In most cases, it can be solved by patient attention to the task at hand—with all the skill and resolution we can muster. That, plus the inspired help of the unconscious.

13 I have already given an example of one way of achieving a breakthrough. First, put down all the reasons why the problem is insoluble. Try to box yourself in, like Houdini, so no escape appears possible. Only then, like Houdini, can you break out. Having tied yourself up in knots, stop thinking consciously about the problem for a while. Let your unconscious work on untying the knots. Nine times out of ten, it will come up with a solution.

14 The worst mistake we can make is to regard mental fatigue as if it were physical fatigue. We can recuperate from the latter by giving our bodies a chance to rest. But mental fatigue that results from failure cannot be removed by giving in to it and taking a rest. That just makes matters worse. Whatever the specific stumbling block is, it must be cleared up, and fast, before the fatigue of failure swamps us.

15 Human beings, I believe, *must* try to succeed. This necessity is built into our biological background. Without trying to define success, it's enough to say that it is related to continuous peak performance, to doing tasks and solving problems as they come along. It is experiencing the exuberance, the joy, the "flow" that goes with the unimpeded exercise of one's human capabilities.

Success, then, means never feeling tired.

approximately 1100 words

Reading Time: _____ min. _____ sec.

Answer the comprehension questions that follow, and refer to the reading rate chart on page 317 to find your words per minute.

COMPREHENSION CHECK

Write the letter that indicates the best possible answer in the space provided.

_____ 1. The main idea of this article is that

    a. mental fatigue is a normal experience.
    b. success cannot be defined or explained.
    c. failure is the result of mental and physical fatigue.
    d. positive attitudes about tasks foster success and help lessen fatigue.

_____ 2. Start-up fatigue is caused by

    a. putting off a task that must be done.
    b. getting tired quickly.
    c. feeling pressure as soon as a task is started.
    d. being bored.

_____ 3. Performance fatigue results from

    a. not having all needed supplies handy.
    b. fear of what others will say.
    c. a seeming inability to do the job right.
    d. a lack of cooperation.

_____ 4. The amount of time it took Adler to complete writing 102 essays for the _Great Books_ series was

    a. one year.
    b. two and a half years.
    c. five and a half years.
    d. ten years.

_____ 5. Adler indicates that in problem solving

    a. the unconscious plays an important role.
    b. the unconscious plays a minor role.
    c. we need the cooperation of family and friends.
    d. mental and physical fatigue are inevitable.

_____ 6. The author believes that

    a. success exhilarates us.
    b. success makes us feel more energetic.
    c. success creates blocks in problem solving.
    d. both a and b.

_____ 7. Fatigue-failure can result from
        a. productivity.
        b. reasoning.
        c. willingness.
        d. personal problems.

Answer the next three questions in complete sentences.

8. Explain how the title of the article is related to the main idea. _____

_____

_____

9. Why does Adler think we blunder greatly if we treat mental fatigue as if it were physical fatigue?

_____

_____

10. Why does Adler state in the first line of paragraph 15 that "human beings . . . must try to succeed"?

_____

_____

Check your responses at the end of this chapter.

"THE BOOK YOU TOOK OUT ON SPEED READING IS 12 MONTHS OVERDUE."

Reading Time (min. & sec.)	Rate (words per minute)	Reading Time (min. & sec.)	Rate (words per minute)
1:00	1100	5:30	200
1:15	880	5:45	191
1:30	733	6:00	183
1:45	639	6:15	176
2:00	550	6:30	169
2:15	489	6:45	163
2:30	440	7:00	157
2:45	400	7:15	152
3:00	367	7:30	147
3:15	338	7:45	142
3:30	314	8:00	138
3:45	293	8:15	133
4:00	275	8:30	129
4:15	259	8:45	126
4:30	244	9:00	122
4:45	232	9:15	119
5:00	220	9:30	116
5:15	210	9:45	113

Convert your reading time (minutes and seconds) to your reading rate (words per minute) by checking the rate chart above. Fill in your words per minute. _____

Now you have a base reading rate to measure against as you work to improve it.

Myths and Misconceptions

How many of the following myths about reading have influenced your reading rate?

Myth 1: Concentrating on Each Word in Print Aids Comprehension and Memory

If you concentrate on each separate word while reading, you create comprehension problems for yourself. In addition, often you may find that after you read a passage you cannot recall much of it. Research shows that in just one second, the brain can sort out 100 million separate messages, distinguishing between the important and the unimportant. The inefficient reader sends to the brain such "weak signals"—seemingly unrelated chunks of information—that the brain loses its focus on reading and gets distracted or bored. The eyes look at the print but the brain wanders: thinking, planning, daydreaming about unrelated topics. If you are unable to concentrate while reading or become easily bored or restless, you are probably reading too slowly to engage your mind in the reading material.

You do not speak in a faltering, robotlike fashion or pause after each word when you talk. You usually speak in groups of words. Since you think in similar fashion, why not read the same way—in idea clusters? It is the natural way to read. Your comprehension will improve if you learn to read for meaning and concentrate on ideas, not words. Recall that in Chapter 4 you noted how long, difficult sentences are more easily understood if you "chunk" the information into meaningful phrases. This practice, extended to all your reading, can help you read more rapidly.

Myth 2: The Only Way to Read Anything Is Slowly and Carefully

Many students read everything at the same habitual rate—slowly—whether it's the TV guide, the evening newspaper, a textbook, or a novel. However, in Chapter 1, we emphasized that efficient readers learn that there is more than just one way to read. They are flexible; that is, they read different kinds of material in different ways. They vary their rate, depending on two main factors: the difficulty of the material and their purpose in reading.

While reading, do you silently say the words or need to hear each word? Then you are limiting yourself to a speed at which average people speak—fewer than 200 words a minute. You may either be vocalizing—moving your lips and saying the words in a whisper—or subvocalizing—hearing them in your head. While you cannot eliminate mentally hearing all words when you read, too much subvocalization reduces your reading rate by as much as 50 percent. Good readers tend to concentrate only on *key words,* those words that give important meaning to the passage. For example, read these two versions of the same sentence. Notice that the first sentence containing only key words can be understood as readily as the sentence in its entirety.

Important part of rocket probe—window through pictures and measurements taken

One of the most important parts of this rocket probe was the window through which many pictures and measurements would be taken.

Can you mark the key terms in the next sentence? "The window had to be extremely strong, and diamond was the only thing in the world that could do the job."*

Myth 3: Going Back Over Just-Read Material Improves Understanding

If you have the habit of "regression," constantly and needlessly going back and rereading parts of the sentences, not only will you be reading slowly but you may also have trouble understanding what you are reading. Here's what your reading may actually be like.

If you have the . . . If you have the habit of "regression," "regression," the habit of "regression," constantly and needlessly going back and "regression," constantly and needlessly going . . .

_____
* window extremely strong, diamond could do job

The smooth, logical flow of thought is broken if you continually regress while reading. Additionally, you more than double your reading time to get through a passage.

Many people regress because they have developed this habit and lack the confidence to believe they can understand what they read the first time. At times, rereading is necessary to understand difficult material and to remember additional details. But the regression discussed here is an unnecessary, unconscious *habit*.

Myth 4: Comprehension Decreases as Rate Increases

Often students say with great pride that they read slowly because they want to be sure to get the full meaning and remember every single word. Actually, by trying to digest every word, these students read so slowly they **hamper** their comprehension and often find themselves confused and disinterested.

Readers who absorb 80 percent of what they read have very good comprehension. Striving for 100 percent all the time makes you read much more slowly than is necessary. If you try to remember everything, you can wind up remembering very little and become frustrated because of the tremendous task you have imposed on yourself. The faster, more efficient reader usually has far better comprehension than the very slow reader because the efficient reader focuses on *ideas* while reading.

Myth 5: It Is Physically Impossible to Read Rapidly Because Your Eyes Cannot Move That Quickly

Eye movement studies disprove this notion. The average first-year college student reads around 200 to 250 words per minute, but these studies indicate that it is physically possible for the eyes to see and transmit printed information to the brain at rates as high as 900 to 1000 words per minute. Beyond this rate students engage in subskills of reading: scanning (searching for a fact or item), skimming, and skipping (getting an overview). People who use the three S's are not engaged in thorough reading, but they are often using reading skills in a highly efficient way.

Our eyes do not really "read"; we read with our minds. Reading takes place when the eyes and mind work together: the eyes do 5 to 10 percent of the work, and the brain does the remaining 90 or 95 percent. The brain scans, sorts, selects, samples, and finally **assimilates** information. So the main limitations in rapid reading are our own physically imposed slow eye movements and a lack of belief that we can read faster.

Myth 6: Faster Reading Takes the Pleasure Out of Reading

It is wrong to assume that fast readers move so rapidly through print they never stop to reflect and "drink in" a favorite passage or a difficult one. Efficient readers

---

hamper (ham′ per) hinder
assimilates (ə sim′ ə lāts) absorbs, takes in, and makes part of

have learned how to speed up or slow down at will, while slow readers are prisoners to slowness.

Slow readers rarely have the experience of reading a novel or a short story at one sitting. Have you ever watched a favorite movie, one you had seen in the theater, on TV? Aren't the intensity of the mood, the flow of the dialogue, the interaction of the characters, and the action of the plot rudely disturbed by all those commercials? The same can be true when a novel is read too slowly—if you always need to put it down after reading a small portion of the story. When reading more rapidly becomes automatic, you derive more pleasure from reading.

Reading Style Flexibility

Carefully study the mode and strategy chart that follows on page 321. It is an extension of the chart in Chapter 1 that pointed out how reading purpose is related to rate. In this chart, note the different strategies to use in reading, depending on your purpose and mode.

⤳ Practical Strategies to Help Refine Your Reading Efficiency

Step 1: Raise Your Reading Consciousness

After reviewing the myths and misconceptions about reading discussed above, describe how you might change your previously held ideas about reading, and indicate your goals for improvement.

To refine my reading style and improve my reading rate, I should

1. _____

   _____

2. _____

   _____

As we have noted, the key to success is positive thinking. Believe in yourself and your ability to improve. Think: "I *can* read faster and better," "I *will* improve my reading rate and comprehension," "I *am* a good reader." From now on, every time you engage in the reading process, make a conscious effort to read faster and understand more. Each time you make that effort, you will push against your current reading barrier. Learn to compete with yourself rather than against your classmates.

Mode and Strategy for Reading Different Materials

Mode	Material/Purpose	Strategy
Analytical reading	Complex essays, technical reports, legal contracts.	Previewing; read to identify inference, make conclusions, and evaluate logic and the writer's craft. Reading and marginal notations, underlining.
Study reading	Textbooks, problem-solving material; information to be recalled for testing; literature.	Previewing; reading and outlining; note making; mapping.
General reading	Any nontechnical material read for enjoyment or good understanding of content.	Read actively with an inquiring mind, recognizing main idea and important details.
Skimming	Any printed material: a. When minimal comprehension is satisfactory for general information in newspapers, magazine articles, "junk mail," correspondence. b. For a preliminary familiarity with format and organization of lengthy or difficult material in textbook chapters, novels, instructional manuals. c. To get the gist or main idea of essays, editorials, reports.	Read titles and subtitles. Then read introductory paragraphs, opening sentences of all other paragraphs, and concluding paragraphs or summary.
Scanning	Any printed materials when looking for specific information or pertinent facts like names, dates, quantities, places. Also used for information from reference guides: Table of contents Index Appendix Dictionary Telephone directory TV schedule Want ads	Examine organization of information first—alphabetical, chronological, conceptual. Look for key ideas or words that guide rapid location of information. When looking up dates or quantity, visualize numbers. When looking for names or particular places, think of capital letters.

Step 2: Make Eye Movements Work for You

As you read, your eyes move along the lines of print in quick, jerking movements; that is, they move and then stop, move and then stop. Your eyes must stop in order to read. They cannot see the print when they are moving. The movement is so rapid, and the "stops," or "fixations," each taking a fraction of a second, are so brief, that the average person is totally unaware of this **sporadic** movement. The bullets (•) in the following three passages represent the fixations for slow (passage 1), average (passage 2), and good (passage 3) readers. Read each passage aloud to become aware of how the number of fixations affects comprehension. Into which category of reader would you place yourself?

Passage 1: Slow Reader

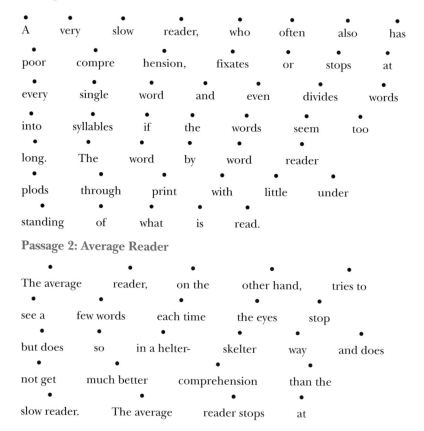

Passage 2: Average Reader

---

sporadic (spō rad′ ik) appearing or happening at irregular intervals

•   •   •   •
every few   words and   tries to   get meaning

•   •
from   them.

Passage 3: Good Reader

•   •   •
The efficient reader   usually fixates   in the middle

•   •
of a group of words   and reads thought units

•   •   •
during each fixation.   Better readers   do not read

•   •   •
single words.   They do not look   at the printed material

•   •   •
in a helter-skelter way.   They have trained   their eyes to work

•   •   •
in such a way   as to perceive ideas   in chunks or groups.

•   •
These are   smooth, rhythmical readers.

•   •
They read in clusters,   connecting ideas naturally.

The fewer fixations you make, the more rapidly you read. To become an efficient reader, you need to look for meaningful groups of words and train your eyes and brain to fixate within the groups rather than to stop at every word or two. Take in as large a meaningful chunk of information as you can with each fixation. As you begin to practice idea clustering, you should be aware that many phrases, such as "for this reason" and "on the other hand," are often repeated and can be perceived by the mind as a single unit. Try reading this: "Inthepast whenIreadslowly I didnotsee groupsofwords." As you can see, it is possible to grasp meaning even when words are clustered together.

Practice more rapid idea clustering below and then in the passage from "The Miracle of Reading" that follows by separating the phrases into meaningful groups.

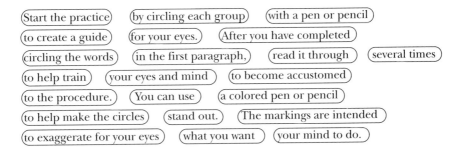

The Miracle of Reading

As you effortlessly scan this paragraph, you are doing something absolutely remarkable: you're reading.

In an instant your eyes and mind are playing hunches, cutting corners, filling gaps, and dealing with an information processing task that would challenge the most ingenious computer.

For example, the eye doesn't register single letters. It takes in several at once, automatically selecting shorter or longer groupings depending on the complexity of the reading matter. A glance may cover a letter or two, or it can take in as many as 20. The average is about 7 letters at a time, with each stop taking less than a quarter of a second. For an accomplished reader to handle 350 words a minute, the eyes can linger no more than an average of four one-hundredths of a second on each letter.

When reading the circled word groups has become somewhat automatic for you, modify your practice by drawing slash marks between groups of words, trying to take in longer meaningful phrases.

Within a short while/ you should be able/ to read/ in groups of words/ without having to draw/ either the circles/ or slash marks./ Try using/ the slash mark method/ on these paragraphs/ from the article "The Miracle of Reading."

Scientists are intrigued by the eye's ability to speedily process unexpected information. "On the basis of computer models, we would predict that the eye can't read," says Caltech research scientist Dr. Raymond Briggs. But a computer, he points out, cannot cope with uncertainties, whereas the eye and the human brain can.

One reason, according to Briggs, is that the eye's job is done by a team: two parts of the eye communicating with two parts of the brain. The fovea, a small, specialized section of the retina, scrutinizes words for meaning and sends signals directly to the conscious, "thinking," part of the brain. But the fovea receives only a small part of the light entering the eye—usually no more than seven letters' worth at a time.

approximately 260 words

These practice exercises were intended to get you started in reading more than a word or two at a time. You should practice idea clustering daily on your own, until reading groups of words in longer thought units becomes an automatic procedure.

Step 3: Pace Yourself Through Print

To pace yourself through print, use a guide or marker when reading. Pacing can be done by using your finger, your entire hand, a pen or pencil, or an index card. It is an excellent way to break the habit of regression.

As you read, the eyes move from left to right to the end of one line to the beginning of the next. This movement from the end of one line to the beginning of the next is called "return sweep."

Eye movements are very much like the operation of a typewriter as the machine carriage returns to the left-hand margin. Some people do not complete the return sweep successfully. Instead, they repeatedly and continuously return to the same line.

Rereading is sometimes necessary to clarify ideas or remember information. But if you have developed the habit of regression, use your finger or hand to guide you through the lines of print. You can use an index card as a pacing device. Place your hand on the card as shown, and slide it down the column of a page of print as you read, covering the just-read material.

Why is the use of a pacer important? First, it forces you to attend to the reading instead of letting your mind wander. Second, it helps you to comprehend better after you become accustomed to it, because you are both physically and mentally involved. Again, improving rate is not something you do automatically because you have read that it is a good idea. Improving rate means practice, practice, and more practice.

How to Pace

Initially, use your whole hand. Sit in a relaxed position, moving your hand from left to right under each line as you read. What you are trying to do is get your eyes to move as rapidly as your hand. Again, you will be uncomfortable at first until you can pace rhythmically and smoothly.

Move your hand under each line and try to read that line faster than you ever have before. Practice for one minute. Now stop for a minute and try to mentally recall something of what you have read. At first you may not be able to recall much of anything because you are so involved with the mechanics of moving your hand! Each time you drill for a minute (increase it gradually to three minutes), begin reading the same information but try to take in an extra half page or more.

Always stop after each practice and try to recall what you read. Initially, this practice makes you aware of the tremendous potential you have to read faster than you do and accustoms you to the hand movements used in pacing. Gradually increase your practice time for longer periods. Also, set time goals for yourself and try to "beat the clock."

Newspapers and magazines like *Reader's Digest* are excellent to use for practice purposes. The columns are narrow and therefore the return sweep of the eye is shorter. The *Reader's Digest* has approximately 450 to 500 words on a full page, with each column having between 225 and 250 words. When practicing, you can determine your words per minute with ease. For example, if you read one column in one minute, you read at approximately 225 to 250 words per minute. When reading longer selections, divide the total words read by the number of minutes used to determine your reading rate.

ACTIVITY 6.1   Pacing Practice

Practice pacing with the passage that follows. Experiment by trying to use your hand, finger, pen, pencil, or a pacing card to discover which guide best suits your own individual style. Then, answer the questions that follow the passage.

Looks Count, Says Study on Earning Power: Attractive People Are Rewarded with Higher Pay

Jonathan Marshall

1 Ten years ago, former TV news anchor Christine Craft sued a Kansas City station that demoted her for being "too ugly," a highly publicized and ultimately unsuccessful case that added "lookism" to the growing list of prejudices condemned by social critics.

2 Now the first full-blown study on the subject by economists shows that lookism carries a big price for its victims—and handsome economic rewards for those blessed with good looks.

3 The earnings gap between attractive and unattractive people, who otherwise share the same education, experience and other characteristics, rivals that between black and white or male and female workers, reported Daniel Hamermesh and Jeff Biddle, economists at the University of Texas and Michigan State University.

4 In a surprising departure from conventional wisdom, their research suggests that men earn even greater rewards for good looks and pay even greater penalties for ugliness than do women in our beauty-conscious society.

5 "The biggest effects are on the bad-looking, not the good-looking," said Hamermesh. "And the effects are if anything bigger for men than women, a result that's startling to me."

6 Attractive people tend to earn about 5 percent more per hour than those with average looks. Homely workers pull in about 7 percent less than average, other things being equal, the researchers found. Men with below-average looks earned 9 percent less, compared with 5 percent for women.

7 The researchers also found that women considered to be unattractive are less likely to work than other women and tend to marry men with lower levels of education.

8 These earnings gaps could be explained by a variety of factors: employers showing simple favoritism toward attractive job applicants, a tendency by consumers or fellow employees to

favor good-looking workers (thus making them more valuable to bosses) or the possibility that attractive workers have higher self-esteem and actually produce more.

Psychologists' Findings

Psychologists have found that attractive people 9 are widely regarded as being more intelligent, friendly, honest and confident than others—all traits that could influence employers and customers to discriminate in favor of them.

And attractive children are often rewarded 10 with more praise from parents and teachers, shaping their personality in ways that may boost their confidence and poise, both valued in the marketplace.

The economists found some evidence that 11 the earnings gap is caused by certain occupations catering to attractive employees more than others. But favoritism toward good looks

and prejudice against homeliness is pervasive in most jobs, they determined.

"It's not just a matter of good-looking 12 people going to work in Hollywood and bad-looking people digging ditches," Hamermesh said. "Even within any given occupation, good-looking people make more."

The Influence of Cosmetics

. . . People can and do influence their looks by 13 spending on cosmetics, hair styling and fashionable clothes. In this sense "lookism" is more easily combatted than racism or sexism.

"People do intuitively understand these 14 results and invest in how well they look," Hamermesh said. "I fully expect that when these results are published, Revlon or some company will advertise that you can make 10 percent more if you buy their lipstick."

approximately 525 words

Jonathan Marshall, "Looks Count, Says Study on Earning Power," *San Francisco Chronicle*

Write *yes* or *no* in the space provided.

_____ 1. The TV news anchor who sued the station that demoted her won her case.

_____ 2. People with good looks earn more money than those who are unattractive.

_____ 3. Women pay greater penalties for ugliness than men.

_____ 4. Generally, good looks are not important or rewarding within most fields of employment.

_____ 5. It is just as difficult to combat the prejudice of "lookism" as it is to fight racism or sexism.

Check your answers at the end of the chapter.

Step 4: Stretch Your Eye Span and Expand Your Focus

An easy way to practice stretching your "eye span" and taking in longer thought units is with newspaper or magazine articles that have narrow columns of print, say five to six words on a line. Don't choose scientific or technical articles, the material should be easy so you can focus on the mechanics of reading without comprehension diffi-culties. Practice for about ten to fifteen minutes daily for at least a week.

Select a practice article, draw a line down the center of the column like the line drawn through "The Swelling Is Telling." Then, take a 3-by-5-inch card and draw a large arrow at the center from top to bottom, as shown below.

Slide the card down the column of print from top to bottom, covering the pre-viously read material and matching the arrow with the line you have drawn. You should be able to see all the words on each line and none of the white space outside the print.

This is also an excellent technique for eliminating regression. Your purpose is to force your eyes to focus on the center, yet see the entire line. At first, you may attain only limited comprehension, but within a few practice sessions, you should be understanding nearly all of what you read. Within a few weeks, you will have trained your eyes and mind to simply focus in the center and read the print at either side.

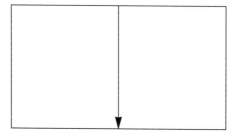

The Swelling Is Telling

It seems that success can lead not only to a swollen head, but to a swollen signature as well. Students' sig-natures are found to be smaller after failure on a task, while after success they balloon.

As reported recently in *Psychology Today,* 28 Rhode Island college students signed their names and then had one minute to unscramble either five easy anagrams like "ohseu" (all succeeded) or five difficult ones like "crlufoneesec" (none got it right). The students then signed again. The successful stu-dents' signatures were now bigger by 45.21 square millimeters (multiplying length by height) while the John Hancocks of those who failed shrunk by 37.57 square millimeters.

And by the way, "ohseu" unscrambled is "house," and "crlufoneesec" is really "fluorescence." O.K., now sign in please.

To further stretch your eye span, that is, to engage your peripheral vision, try a technique called the Z pattern. Try it now, using a pen, pencil, or your finger to follow the Z lines drawn on the next passage. Notice that the position of the lines forces you to begin reading about one-half inch in from each line and to make the return sweep the same way. This helps you avoid the white space, the area on either side of a page where no printed words appear.

When people are good-looking, we assume many other good things about them. Because attractive people are treated as if they have more to offer, they live up to our positive expectations. Sadly, those less pleasing to look at live down to our negative expectations.

In studies looking at the relationship between attractiveness and personality, good-looking people turn out to have higher self-esteem and to be happier, less neurotic, and more resistant to peer pressure than those who are less attractive. Those blessed with good looks also have more influence on others, get higher salaries, receive more lenient decisions in court, are thought by their students to be superior teachers, and are more valued as friends, colleagues, and lovers. The general pattern is true of both men and women.

Beauty in our culture is clearly more than a superficial matter.

Excerpt from David Popenoe, *Sociology*

Step 5: Visualize Ideas While Reading Whenever Possible

To overcome two chronic barriers to efficient reading—vocalization (saying the words) and subvocalization (mentally hearing all the words)—try to channel your mind to think in pictures instead of words. Practice turning the printed words into images in your mind as you read, creating a mental television set for yourself. To see how this can be done, read the following excerpt.

Joe Mondragón was thirty-six years old and for a long time he had held no steady job. He had a wife, Nancy, and three children, and his own house, which he had built with his own hands, a small tight adobe that required mudding every two or three autumns.

Joe was always hard up, always hustling to make a buck. Over the years he had learned how to do almost any job. He knew everything about building houses, he knew how to mix mud and straw just right to make strong adobes that would not crumble. Though unlicensed, he could steal and lay his own plumbing, do all the electric fixtures in a house, and hire five peons at slave wages to install a septic tank that would not over-flow until the day after Joe died or left town. Given half the necessary equipment, he could dig a well, and he understood everything there was to understand about pumps. He could tear down a useless tractor and piece it together again so niftily it would plow like balls of fire for at least a week before blowing up and maiming its driver; and he could disk and seed a field well and irrigate it properly.

The Mondragón house was surrounded by junk, by old engines, by parts of motors, by automobile guts, refrigerator wiring, tractor innards. One shed was filled with wringer washing machines, and when Joe had the time he puttered over them until they were "running" again; then he tried—and often managed—to sell them . . . with pumps that went on the fritz (or wringer gears that neatly stripped themselves) ten minutes after Joe's three-month warranty (in writing) expired.

approximately 265 words

John Nichols, *The Milagro Beanfield War*

As you read the above paragraph, images such as those illustrated below could come to mind, helping you concentrate on ideas rather than words.

Yuk Hing Shum, sketch (De Anza College, June 1995.) Reprinted by permission of the artist.

Put your visualization abilities to work as you read the paragraph on the next page from Hernando Tellez's short story "Just Lather, That's All," by trying to see images as if you were watching a movie. Tellez describes the thoughts of a barber who is shaving a longtime enemy.

I could cut this throat just so, zip zip! I wouldn't give him time to complain and since he has his eyes closed he wouldn't see the glistening knife blade or my glistening eyes. But I'm trembling like a real murderer. Out of his neck a gush of blood would spout onto the sheet, on the chair, on my hands, on the floor. I would have to close the door. And the blood would keep inching along the floor, warm, **ineradicable,** uncontainable, until it reached the street, like a little scarlet stream. I'm sure that one solid stroke, one deep incision, would prevent any pain. He wouldn't suffer. But what would I do with the body? Where would I hide it?

Hernando Tellez, "Just Lather, That's All" from Américas

Were you able to picture the man being shaved and what would happen if the barber did cut his throat?

Step 6: Use Signal Words as Clues to Flexibility

Signal words are frequently guides to a passage's content—the writer's train of thought—as you discovered in Chapter 5. The good reader also uses these signposts to help determine how fast or how slowly to move through print. Recognizing these signals can help you become a more flexible and efficient reader.

The Fast Lane

1. *Go Words:* These words say to the reader, "More of what you just read is being continued." Therefore, you can sp—e—e—d up.

additionally, in addition	besides
again	correspondingly
also	further, furthermore
and, and so	likewise
another, other	more, moreover
as well	

2. *Examples Ahead:* These words tell you, "One or more examples will support, explain, or clarify what is being discussed." If more than one example is given, you can speed through the rest since examples usually are repetitive.

an illustration of, to illustrate	for this reason
as an example	specifically
for instance	such as

---

ineradicable (in i rad′ ə kə bəl) unable to be rooted out or got rid of

The Middle Lane—Yield Signs

With these words the author says, "Now I'm going to emphasize something important." The strategy here is to read carefully but be ready to pick up speed if conditions warrant it. While you can't race at your highest speed when you see these signals, you can venture a stop-and-go kind of action.

"Stay Alert" Signals

a central issue, concern, factor	primarily
chiefly	the principal reason/cause
more important/significant	the basic fact, in fact
most of all	unquestionably, without question
particularly, pay particular attention	

WARNING!

The Slow Lane

1. *Caution Signals:* These signals mean, "There's a detour ahead; I'm going to change my mind, reverse my ideas, or say the opposite of what I just said." As the direction of the ideas change, you must slow down so as not to miss the shift in thought.

although, even though	on the contrary
but	otherwise
conversely	rather
despite, in spite of	unless
however, if	whether, whether or not
in contrast	while
nevertheless	

2. *Mile Markers:* Explanations may be listed in order. If this is the case, then the writer may use any of these signals.

first; second; third	first of all
last	in the first place
some of the advantages, causes	next

End-of-the-Road Signals—Stop

These signals warn the reader to slow down: "I've come to the end of explaining this idea and am going to summarize it for you or tell you what I think is most important." You should be anticipating important information at this point. The most important ideas are about to be presented in brief form or restated.

accordingly	last of all
basically	to summarize
consequently	therefore
finally	the effect
hence	the implication
in conclusion	the most important
in retrospect	thus
in summary	to recapitulate

Of what use is the equipment pictured in the cartoon of the Nordic Trak Reading Machine?

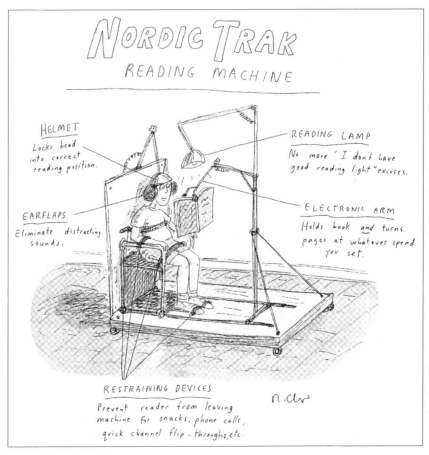

Helmet: _____

Earflaps: _____

Reading Lamp: _____

Electronic Arm: _____

Restraining Devices: _____

Summary

Through practice and the development of a positive attitude, you can become a better, faster reader. A good reader is one who is flexible, reads in idea clusters, and tries to avoid excessive vocalization, subvocalization, and regression, since these habits all hinder reading efficiency. At the same time, a good reader is always an active participant and is involved in what is being read.

Reading comprehension can actually improve as rate increases, and at the same time, reading can become more pleasurable.

We have suggested the following main techniques to improve reading rate:

1. Become aware of your reading habits and work to improve them.
2. Increase your eye span and read in idea clusters, grouping ideas.
3. Pace yourself through print.
4. Stretch your eye span and expand your focus.
5. Visualize ideas while reading whenever possible.
6. Use signal words as clues to improve rate, and practice, practice, practice!

ACTIVITY 6.2   Practice Improving Your Rate with Extended Readings

Elvis Presley

Begin to practice improving your reading rate with the selections that follow. Try the different techniques suggested in this chapter to see which ones best suit your reading style. *Remember to begin each practice by previewing.* After reading a selection, write down the time it took you in minutes and seconds. Then, answer the questions that follow the selection. Refer to the reading rate chart to find your rate in words per minute. Check your answers on page 346 to determine your comprehension at this reading rate.

Elvis Presley died almost a quarter of a century ago; every year, more than 700,000 people visit the Presley estate, now worth more than

$250 million. There have been at least 50 books published about him in the past ten years. In addition, there are 500 fan clubs and 300 college courses focusing on Presley. After reading the following article, decide whether or not Elvis Presley was a "real" celebrity.

Elvis: Another Victim of Myth-Understanding

Richard Cohen

Elvis Presley, it seems, was a junkie. He was allegedly cruel. He was supposedly dim-witted and not ambitious and spent money obscenely. He was sometimes violent and allegedly took unto himself as sexual toys a covey of near-adolescents whom he watched undress from behind a two-way mirror. I won't even tell you about the monkey. 1

But Albert Goldman will. Goldman is the author of a new biography of Presley called *Elvis*. It is one of the few examples of a book that really tells you more than you want to know. Presley, Goldman says, had the emotional maturity of a 12-year-old and the appetite of a garbage disposal. He was a filthy man—literally. He hated to bathe. 2

What emerges from this book is a whole new Presley, or if not that, at least a whole new Presley myth. It can take its place alongside the myth created by Elvis' long-time manager, Col. Tom Parker. That was the Elvis who was sweet to women, said sir and ma'am, loved his country and was in every way normal. With the book, the story of Presley comes full cycle—or almost full cycle. What comes next, of course, is the rehabilitation or, at least, an attempt to deal with the man as an entertainer. After all, he unquestionably had something. 3

For the moment, though, Elvis is just a cog in the myth machine. He follows a pattern. First comes the making of the myth and then, sooner or later, comes the debunking of the myth. This happened to Joan Crawford, Tyrone Power, Judy Garland, John Kennedy and even Bing 4

Crosby. They were all posthumously debunked. In the Soviet Union, people merely get dropped from the official encyclopedia.

The constant repetition of the process makes you wonder what we expected in the first place. Did we think the values of these celebrities were unaffected by their (sudden) stupendous wealth and (sudden) fame? Did we think that all the money, all the adulation and all the power did not exaggerate what was worst in them? When it comes to Elvis, did we think that a man who dressed in rhinestones was in all other ways a diamond? 5

The answer is yes. In fact, it is the answer that explains why we always fall for the myth. What we are doing is projecting, saying that if we were the ones who suddenly got rich and famous we would be unaffected. We would still keep the same old friends, and the same old values. We might get a pair of lizard cowboy boots and a Jacuzzi, but we would not throw out our morality with our old clothes. In this way, we can dream of fame but never pay its price. 6

But we have no idea if this is true. We are not faced with the option of vast amounts of drugs or adoration—of more and more and more. Reality puts a limit on us. In a sense, we have the morality we can afford. The right combination of talent, timing and a marketing whiz like Col. Parker removed all the restrictions from Elvis' life. He was not prepared to deal with this and only he could have told us if it was worth it. 7

In the marketing of celebrities, everything about them gets sold. The celebrity becomes a 8 product and is changed in the process. Everything is affected. Not just their talent, but their families and their background and their private lives get fed into the myth machine. A package is created and people buy in. They promote, they publicize, they manage, they invest the money, they secure the lovers or the limousines or the drugs.

A star becomes something of an industry, a 9 cottage industry to the hangers-on, but something bigger to record studios, publishers, ball clubs, movie studios or television networks. They make money when the celebrity is on the way up, or on the way down. It is ironic, for instance, that the same movie industry that told you Joan Crawford was such a star is now telling you what a bitch she was. Some people may now hate Crawford. Nobody, though, holds a grudge against the movie industry for lying one way or the other.

So here we have it happening to Elvis 10 Presley. He was an industry while he was alive and popular and he will continue to be one dead and infamous. In buying his records and his myth, we helped make him the person he was. Our money and our adoration took away the limitation. First we created the monster. Now we're paying to see it.

approximately 825 words

Reading Time:_____ min._____ sec.

Richard Cohen, "Elvis: Another Victim of Myth-Understanding," *Washington Post.* Copyright © 1980 by The Washington Post Company. Reprinted by permission.

Answer the comprehension questions that follow, and refer to the reading rate chart to find your words per minute.

COMPREHENSION CHECK

Write the letter that best completes each of the following ideas in the space provided. Remember: Do not look back; answer the questions as soon as you have finished reading.

_____ 1. The main topic of the article is

    a. revealing Elvis as he was.
    b. how myths about celebrities are made.
    c. a final tribute to Elvis.
    d. the magical life of celebrities.

_____ 2. The author's thesis is that

    a. it is difficult to create myths about celebrities.
    b. myths about celebrities replace their reality.
    c. Elvis Presley and Colonel Parker always had numerous disagreements.
    d. the public is also responsible for the myths that "make and break" celebrities.

_____ 3. The author claims that

    a. Elvis thought that fame and fortune were worth what he went through.
    b. Elvis did not believe that fame and fortune were worth what he went through.
    c. we will never know what Elvis thought about his fame and fortune.
    d. Colonel Parker stated that Elvis was satisfied with what fame and fortune had brought to him.

_____ 4. Which name was not mentioned as one who was affected by the myth machine?

    a. Joan Crawford
    b. Bing Crosby
    c. John Kennedy
    d. Joan Collins

_____ 5. The statement "In the marketing of celebrities, everything about them gets sold" means

    a. a sale of their belongings takes place after their death.
    b. they are treated as a product and everything about them, including their private lives, gets sold.
    c. people buy the myth for their own selfish reasons.
    d. packaging and marketing go together.

_____ 6. The author's attitude is that sudden wealth and fame

    a. brings out the best in celebrities.
    b. can bring out the worst in celebrities.
    c. is not a factor to consider.
    d. does not affect celebrities who are already wealthy.

_____ 7. A statement such as "Elvis is just a cog in the myth machine" means that Elvis

    a. turns the myth machine.
    b. first fed the myth machine.
    c. created the myth machine.
    d. is just a tiny part of the myth machine.

_____ 8. We always fall for the myth about celebrities because

    a. the hype about them is contagious.
    b. celebrities are viewed as winners.
    c. we project ourselves as being "perfect" celebrities.
    d. celebrities make our lives more interesting.

_____ 9. The author finds it ironic that celebrities

    a. make money for the media whether they are being admired or criticized.
    b. don't always live up to their image.
    c. prefer solitude to fame.
    d. are unaware of their admirers and detractors.

_____ 10. Elvis continues to be "an industry" because

    a. his daughter married and later divorced Michael Jackson.
    b. his ex-wife, Priscilla, has had many acting roles.
    c. the myth of Elvis is still being exploited.
    d. Graceland is visited by millions of Elvis fans.

Check your answers with those at the end of the chapter.

Reading Time (min. & sec.)	Rate (words per minute)	Reading Time (min. & sec.)	Rate (words per minute)
1:00	825	4:45	174
1:15	660	5:00	165
1:30	550	5:15	157
1:45	471	5:30	150
2:00	412	5:45	143
2:15	367	6:00	138
2:30	330	6:15	132
2:45	300	6:30	127
3:00	275	6:45	122
3:15	254	7:00	118
3:30	235	7:15	114
3:45	220	7:30	110
4:00	206	7:45	106
4:15	194	8:00	103
4:30	183		

Convert your reading time (minutes and seconds) to your reading rate (words per minute) by checking the rate chart above. Fill in your words per minute. _____

Read the following essay to learn about the "myths" related to your health and the products we once thought harmful.

Not Everything You Like Is Bad for You

Dr. Isadore Rosenfeld

Patients often ask me, "Why is everything I [1] enjoy bad for me?" Well, that's not actually true, although it often seems that way. For example, you may eat all the chocolate you like, as long as your weight can stand the extra calories. Unlike other fats, the kind in chocolate (stearic acid) won't clog up your arteries as we used to think it would.

Like eggs? Be my guest. If your cholesterol [2] level is normal, you may have three, four or even five eggs a week, yolks and all. People react differently to cholesterol in the diet. In some, it raises the blood levels; in others, it does not. The real villain in forming the plaques that obstruct blood-flow and kill is saturated animal fat. That's because saturated fat stimulates the liver to make more cholesterol, and it's this internally formed cholesterol that stays in the bloodstream and forms plaques. So, if you love eggs—which contain only small amounts of fat—eat some. Just don't go overboard, and make sure you avoid fatty meats and full-fat dairy products.

Have you been avoiding the shrimp and [3] lobster you love because you were told that they're rich in cholesterol? We were wrong there too. These shellfish contain a forerunner of cholesterol, which doesn't convert to the real thing in substantial amounts. So, again, be my guest. . . .

Were you told after your heart attack to be [4] careful about exercising and having sex? We were wrong again. No more confinement for weeks and weeks in the hospital followed by retirement and a quiet, celibate life. No, sir—out of the hospital in just a few days and into a physical-rehabilitation program. And as far as sex is concerned, the latest research has found that the more you have, the longer you'll live.

Remember when doctors told everybody [5] with high blood pressure to avoid salt? Reprieve! Only a minority of people, mostly African-Americans, have salt-sensitive hypertension. If you are salt-deprived and long for a little more flavor in your food, discuss it with your doctor.

Alcohol, always the bad boy on the health [6] block, is the medical profession's latest hero. That's because of the repeated observations that people who don't touch the stuff—ever—have more heart attacks than those who do.

The latest report on the subject, by the [7] American Cancer Society, was published in *The New England Journal of Medicine.* . . . In this study—the largest ever undertaken on lifestyle and cancer—the drinking habits, diseases and death rates among almost half a million men and women aged 30 to 104 were analyzed over a 15-year period. It was found that one drink a day was associated with a 40% reduction in the incidence of heart attacks in persons over 50 and outweighed the risk of death from other causes, such as cancer, liver disease and car accidents.

The liquor industry has naturally made the [8] most of this favorable report. There is now a popularity contest among the various alcohol producers.

Red-wine makers insist that it's only (or [9] mostly) red wine that protects against heart attacks. As proof, they point to the lower cardiac death rate in France—despite all the fat and foie gras consumed there—and conclude that it's because of the red wine. What's special in red wine? Presumably, the skin of the grape (which is removed in making white wine).

This claim didn't sit well with the white-wine, hard-liquor and beer producers, all of whom came up with their own studies asserting that there's nothing special about red wine and that any alcohol is protective. **10**

The controversy rages on. Most of my patients who drink have taken sides. As far as they're concerned, the most protective drink for the heart is the one they like best. The fact is, *how much* you drink is the key to whatever protection you get. . . . **11**

Do these new data warrant giving alcohol a clean bill of health? I don't believe so. The data are sobering (pun intended). **12**

The downside of alcohol is obvious. It is calorically dense and nutritionally sparse. It puts weight on you with few health benefits. Many people don't know when they've had enough. Drinking for years hurts the liver and the brain. It is the No. 1 cause of automobile accidents, broken homes and domestic violence. All drinkers are at greater risk for cirrhosis of the liver and cancers of the mouth, esophagus, pharynx, larynx and liver. **13**

The only reason deaths from all these causes don't statistically overwhelm the cardiac benefits of drinking is because heart disease is much more common, so the numbers are bigger. **14**

In this latest study, the major benefit from alcohol came from *one* drink daily, and no **15**

more. But in the real world, only a minority of Americans who drink limit themselves to a single drink. And when you smoke along with your alcohol, you lose all the benefits from the booze—and then some. Tobacco is much more hazardous to your health than alcohol is protective.

Also in the study: Women who drank had fewer heart attacks—but those who consumed at least one drink a day had 30% more breast cancer. **16**

So what's the bottom line? The middle-aged and elderly, especially those who already have heart trouble, benefit most from a daily drink. Someone 50 or older can receive the maximum benefits for his or her heart by drinking one shot of hard liquor or a 12-ounce bottle of beer or a 6-ounce glass of wine. **17**

However, there are other ways to obtain alcohol's cardiac benefits without any of the risks. **18**

Take cholesterol. It's composed of several parts: Some are good (like HDL); others are bad (LDL). Alcohol protects the heart by raising the level of the good cholesterol, but you can also do this by eating the right diet, exercising and, if necessary, taking a cholesterol-lowering pill. Alcohol also protects the heart by reducing the tendency of the blood to form clots. But so does aspirin. **19**

If you drink moderately and enjoy it, there's probably no reason to stop. But don't drink for therapy. And if you've never had a drink, don't start now. **20**

approximately 1000 words

Reading Time:_____ min ._____ sec.

Dr. Isadore Rosenfeld, "Not Everything You Like Is Bad for You," *Parade* 22 Mar. 1998: 10–12

Answer the comprehension questions that follow, and refer to the reading rate chart to find your words per minute.

COMPREHENSION CHECK

Write the letter that best completes each of the following ideas in the space provided. Remember: Do not look back; answer the questions as soon as you have finished reading.

_____ 1. The topic of the selection is
    a. nutrition and diet.
    b. the cholesterol content of food.
    c. myths about diet.
    d. the pros and cons of alcohol's benefits.

_____ 2. Dr. Rosenfeld says alcohol has become the media's "latest hero" because
    a. alcohol is more effective than exercise in lowering cholesterol.
    b. nondrinkers have more heart attacks than drinkers.
    c. it costs less to buy alcohol than medicine.
    d. it is easy for the body to burn up the calories in alcohol.

_____ 3. Which food was not specifically mentioned by the writer to avoid eating?
    a. eggs
    b. chocolate
    c. ice cream
    d. shrimp

_____ 4. The writer says that advice to avoid exercise and sex after a heart attack is
    a. reasonable.
    b. exaggerated.
    c. wrong.
    d. right.

_____ 5. Which group has the most sensitivity to salt as it relates to high blood pressure?
    a. women over 60.
    b. men over 60.
    c. Anglo Americans.
    d. African Americans.

_____ 6. The type of alcohol that most protects against heart attack is
    a. red wine.
    b. white wine.
    c. beer.
    d. not definitely known.

_____ 7. One fact _not_ stated for giving alcohol a "clean bill of health" is that it
    a. is damaging to important body organs.
    b. does not provide good nutrition.
    c. causes people to gain weight.
    d. causes people to become thieves.

_____ 8. The number of Americans who limit their drinking to a single drink is

   a. a small percentage.
   b. a large majority.
   c. a moderate number.
   d. dependent on their age.

_____ 9. The percentage of women who develop breast cancer having had at least one drink a day is estimated at

   a. 50%.
   b. 30%.
   c. 60%.
   d. 80%.

_____ 10. Which age group is said to benefit most from one daily drink?

   a. 20–24.
   b. 25–35.
   c. 36–49.
   d. 50+.

Check your answers with those at the end of the chapter.

Reading Time (min. & sec.)	Rate (words per minute)	Reading Time (min. & sec.)	Rate (words per minute)
1:00	1000	5:30	182
1:15	800	5:45	174
1:30	667	6:00	167
1:45	571	6:15	160
2:00	500	6:30	154
2:15	444	6:45	148
2:30	400	7:00	143
2:45	364	7:15	138
3:00	333	7:30	133
3:15	308	7:45	129
3:30	286	8:00	125
3:45	267	8:15	121
4:00	250	8:30	118
4:15	235	8:45	114
4:30	222	9:00	111
4:45	211	9:15	108
5:00	200	9:30	105
5:15	190	9:45	103

Convert your reading time (minutes and seconds) to your reading rate (words per minute) by checking the rate chart above. Fill in your words per minute. _____

Read the following textbook excerpt to decide the extent to which media may influence the general public's fear of crime.

Media Impact on the Public's Fear of Crime

Frank Schmalleger

Turn on nightly television in the United States 1 on a typical day and you will see killing after killing, frequent acts of gruesome violence, and murder and mayhem as typical prime-time fare. The same is true whether you choose to view one of the major networks, a pay-per-view channel, or a premium service such as Home Box Office, Cinemax, or Showtime. Only a few specialized forms of programming, such as the Home Shopping Network, the Disney Channel, and Public Broadcasting, are relatively violence free.

Many argue that the networks and cable 2 companies are simply giving viewers what they want. Violence (often tinged with sexuality or combined with explicit sexual behavior), because it is exciting, attracts audiences. And, of course, large audiences attract advertisers whose fees support the networks.

Not to be outdone by their highly visual 3 counterparts, newspapers and newsmagazines depict real-life episodes of violent crime in every issue. For a year following the highly publicized murders of Nicole Brown Simpson and Ronald Goldman, for example, it was almost impossible to find a newspaper in the country which wasn't running a daily story about some aspect of the case, especially when O. J. Simpson, charged in the murders, went to trial. Even computer-based services, among them CompuServe and America Online, set up special O. J. Simpson sections to attract subscribers.

Unfortunately, what some have called the 4 overemphasis on crime and violence, now so characteristic of the media in this country, makes it extremely difficult to separate crime fiction from crime fact. If media emphasis is any guide, it would appear that the United States is awash in crime, especially violent personal crime. The impression given is that crime is likely to strike almost anyone when they least expect it—devastating their lives (should they survive) irreparably. In fact, while there are many victims of violent crime in this country, the media's preoccupation with crime and violence is much overdone. Worse still, such preoccupation had led to an enormous fear of crime among the American public, which, for at least a substantial segment of the population, is probably misplaced.

As one social commentator points out, 5 "Anxiety about crime grips the land but, looking at federal statistics, you have to wonder why. The FBI reports crime is merely crawling upward. Victim surveys show crime actually falling. Yet for many people, an evening stroll, an unlocked car, or going alone to the mall hint at lunacy. After tucking in their children, many parents bolt the doors, check the alarms, and pat the guns under their beds goodnight." According to William Chambliss, past president of the American Society of Criminology, "[t]he best scientific evidence we have clearly shows there is no increase in crime or violent crime in the last 20 years. . . . The fact is, even if the crime rate was going up, the victims who were the victims remain the victims."

Realistically, crime—especially violent per- 6 sonal crime—while it may be on the rise, appears concentrated in certain poverty-stricken population-dense regions of the nation. That is not to say that crime does not make an appearance in affluent neighborhoods and rural areas. It certainly does, but the nature and extent of criminal activity in such areas is a far cry from the inner-city areas where the daily threat of crime is a hard reality for most residents.

Yet, when surveys reporting the fear of 7 crime are examined, Americans everywhere appear to be on guard. Fear of crime festers in people's minds like a specter haunting the land, and frightened residents routinely report taking self-protective steps. Statistics from the most recent *U.S. News/CNN* poll on neighborhood crime, for example, show 37% of Americans own a gun for protection and 45% think it's unsafe to let children play unsupervised where they live. Thirty-one percent of respondents also report that there are areas within a mile of their home in which they would be afraid to walk alone at night. Other surveys, however, have found that those most afraid of crime spend more time watching television than those who are less fearful—lending support to the notion that media portrayals of criminal activity lead to a heightened fear of victimization.

Efforts are currently underway to reduce 8 the degree of crime fear induced by the mass media. A recent U.S. Senate hearing, for example, stressed the need for television producers and network executives to assume a socially responsible role by lowering the amount of violence in aired programming. Unfortunately, no one knows for sure whether television merely broadcasts what viewers most want to see, or whether it presages and helps to determine what we, as a nation, are becoming.

approximately 765 words

Reading Time: _____ min. _____ sec.

Frank Schmalleger, "Media Impact on the Public's Fear of Crime," *Criminal Justice Today* 58. Copyright © by Prentice Hall, 1997.

Answer the comprehension questions that follow and refer to the reading rate chart to find your words per minute.

COMPREHENSION CHECK

Write the letter that best completes each of the following ideas in the space provided. Remember to answer the questions as soon as you have finished reading.

_____ 1. Which of the following television delivery systems does not focus much on violence?

    a. Cinemax
    b. CBS
    c. Cable TV
    d. Public Broadcasting

_____ 2. The reason given for television to air shows depicting violence is

    a. newspapers give wide coverage to stories about violence.
    b. movie studios produce movies with the theme of violence.
    c. audiences find violence exciting.
    d. violence is an accepted part of our culture.

_____ 3. According to the author, crime fiction and crime fact

    a. are very different from each other.
    b. cannot be separated easily.
    c. are terms that need to be defined.
    d. are the basis for most TV stories.

_____ 4. Fear of crime among the American public has been caused by

    a. rising crime rates.
    b. the media's preoccupation with it.
    c. the constant publishing of real-life criminal activities in newsmagazines.
    d. both b and c.

_____ 5. The author suggests that victim surveys show crimes committed to be

    a. falling.
    b. escalating.
    c. limited to assault and murder.
    d. none of the above.

_____ 6. The people who seem to be most affected by violent crimes live in

    a. affluent areas.
    b. the suburbs.
    c. rural areas.
    d. the inner city.

_____ 7. According to one survey, the percentage of people who think it unsafe to let children play unsupervised is

    a. 37%.
    b. 45%.
    c. 31%.
    d. 49%.

_____ 8. What was not mentioned as something people do because of their fear of crime?

    a. Bolt their doors
    b. Check their security alarms
    c. Put iron bars on windows
    d. Keep a gun in the house

_____ 9. The author concludes that media's impact on crime

    a. has caused crime statistics to soar.
    b. is not fully known.
    c. has made crime an accepted way of life.
    d. has been to make no one feel safe in America.

_____ 10. The way to reduce the fear of crime that may be the mass media's fault is to

    a. stop showing violence on TV.
    b. force newspapers and magazines to restrict their coverage of stories dealing with violence.
    c. have the networks and media assume a socially responsible role.
    d. produce more sitcoms and stories promoting family values.

Check your answers at the end of the chapter.

Reading Time (min. & sec.)	Rate (words per minute)	Reading Time (min. & sec.)	Rate (words per minute)
1:00	765	4:45	161
1:15	612	5:00	153
1:30	510	5:15	146
1:45	437	5:30	139
2:00	383	5:45	133
2:15	340	6:00	128
2:30	306	6:15	122
2:45	278	6:30	118
3:00	255	6:45	113
3:15	235	7:00	109
3:30	219	7:15	106
3:45	204	7:30	102
4:00	191	7:45	99
4:15	180	8:00	96
4:30	170		

Convert your reading time (minutes and seconds) to your reading rate (words per minute) by checking the rate chart above. Fill in your words per minute. _____

Answers for Chapter 6

Reading Rate Evaluation

"Success Means Never Feeling Tired," pp. 315–16

1. d **2.** a. **3.** c **4.** b **5.** a **6.** d. **7.** d

8. When we succeed at a task, we become more energetic so that we do not feel tired. The opposite occurs when we put off a task or are unsuccessful.

9. With physical fatigue, we can eliminate the problem by resting our bodies, but with mental fatigue, giving in makes it worse.

10. When we fail to succeed, it sets up a cycle of frustration that leads to a lack of energy and a sense of being tired.

Activity 6.1, p. 327

1. No **2.** Yes **3.** No **4.** No **5.** No

Activity 6.2

"Elvis: Another Victim of Myth-Understanding," pp. 336–38

1. b. **2.** d. **3.** c **4.** d **5.** b **6.** b **7.** d **8.** c **9.** a **10.** c

"Not Everything You Like Is Bad for You," pp. 341–42

1. c   **2.** b   **3.** c   **4.** c   **5.** d   **6.** d   **7.** d   **8.** a   **9.** b   **10.** d

"Media Impact on the Public's Fear of Crime," pp. 344–45

1. d   **2.** c   **3.** b   **4.** d   **5.** a   **6.** d   **7.** b   **8.** c.   **9.** b   **10.** c

JOURNAL ENTRY

You have just completed practicing techniques that will help you to improve your present reading rate. Which of your present reading habits will you need to change in order to become a faster, more effective reader? Describe your feelings about reading faster, and write about how you plan to adopt some of the newly learned techniques to improve your reading rate.

7

Making Inferences and Drawing Conclusions

This chapter will help you

* Distinguish between a fact and an opinion.
* Understand the difference between valid and invalid inferences.
* Develop strategies for making logical inferences and drawing sound conclusions.
* Learn how a judgment and an **assumption** differ.

Before reading, think about these questions.

* What criteria do you use when judging controversial issues?
* Why is it important to question your own conclusions about what you read?
* Why should you look beyond the literal meaning of what is written?

Jot down your thoughts about how critically you evaluate what you read.

_____

_____

_____

_____

---

assumption (ə sump′ shən) supposition; statement accepted as truth without proof

ᔡ Making Inferences: Daily Detective Work

One important aspect of critical comprehension involves making inferences while you read. *Making an inference means forming your own conclusion by reasoning on the basis of what has been suggested by a writer but not stated directly.* You practiced making inferences in earlier chapters by putting pieces of information together to draw reasonable conclusions. As a reader, you

Deduce word meanings from context.

Find unstated main ideas.

Determine a writer's implied thesis.

Recognize organizational patterns.

Inference, as it applies to reading, may be new to you, but we all make inferences daily using our intuition and feelings. We draw inferences from a person's facial expressions, tone of voice, or body language. For instance, if your boss scowls at you when you arrive late for work, you can infer that she is unhappy with your tardiness. You infer from dark, gray, puffy clouds overhead that it may not be the best day for a picnic. In each case, you make an "educated," reasonable guess based on limited information, weighing known facts in light of your background knowledge and past experience. Making inferences is reasoning about what you see or what you read.

To be a critical reader, you need to make connections between what the writer says *and* what the writer wants you to understand. When you are trying to interpret a writer's views on a subject, especially if the topic is political, economic, or social, your own cultural background and assumptions play a major role as you reason, make inferences, and draw conclusions.

Logical Reasoning Leads to Valid Inferences and Sound Conclusions

A *valid* inference is a conclusion or generalization based on clear evidence and logical reasoning about that evidence. An ***invalid*** inference is an assumption that is supported by inadequate evidence or arrived at through faulty logic. For example,

> Most Americans get their political information from television and most say they believe information obtained from television more than that in newspapers.
>
> Michael G. Roskin et al., *Political Science*

Possible valid inferences from this statement might be

1. Television is shaping America's political views more than newspapers.
2. Most Americans place less value on newspaper reporting than on television news.

3. The outcome of the next presidential election will be influenced by television reporting.

Each of these inferences could be made from the statement. An inference, then, is not a statement that appears in print on the page but rather is formed through reasoning with what is given but not stated directly. In the example, the author suggests the popularity of television news over the newspaper, but none of the inferential statements are specifically expressed; they result from logically interpreting the textbook statement.

The following inferential statements would both be *invalid:*

1. It would be cheaper for Americans to buy a daily newspaper than a television set for getting the news.
2. The American public is illiterate and relies on television for information.

There is nothing in the textbook statement about cost or literacy. Usually, an invalid inference results either when a reader's thinking goes beyond what the writer has implied or when the reader's conclusion comes from his or her *own* preconceived ideas. We make sense of our world by thinking, and inferential thinking is actually reasoning and drawing conclusions from what is indirectly stated. In effect, inferential thinking is "detective thinking."

Critical readers try to uncover "hidden," or indirectly stated meanings, when they exist in much the way a detective looks for clues and evidence. When a writer suggests an idea indirectly, it is called an *implication.* The reader's inferences are attempts to understand a writer's implications. A reader *infers;* a writer *implies.* Some people refer to inference as "reading between the lines."

Reading Between the Lines

Why do writers sometimes "hide" their ideas and imply them rather than express them directly? They do so for a variety of reasons.

1. To avoid stating the obvious and to make the reading more interesting and stimulating.
2. To encourage readers to do their own thinking and draw their own conclusions.
3. To create or intensify emotions in a more artistic, literary way.
4. To conceal an unpopular notion, a biased opinion, or a persuasive appeal.
5. To manipulate the unsuspecting reader, as in cases of advertising in which an association is made between a product and a desirable quality.

⤳ Strategies for Making Valid Inferences

Many of the reading skills you have already acquired can be helpful as you use the following strategies to make valid inferences and draw sound conclusions.

Strategy 1:   Separate the facts from the opinions.
Strategy 2:   Evaluate the main ideas and supporting details.
Strategy 3:   Test the logic of your inferences.

Let's begin looking at the first strategy.

Strategy 1: Separating the Facts from the Opinions

Much of what you read is designed to influence your thinking. The critical reader judges which statements to accept and which to question further by first distinguishing facts from opinions. It is not always easy to recognize whether a statement is a fact, an opinion, or a combination of both. Writers are influenced by their own opinions as they write and interpret information. Moreover, as they try to persuade you to their way of thinking, they sometimes word their opinions to appear as facts.

Additionally, your own opinions can influence you when you are evaluating persuasive writing. You may tend to respond positively to ideas that confirm your own beliefs or deny ideas contrary to your belief system. In fairness to the writer, you need to be open-minded while weighing the merits of arguments; at the same time, you must always examine ideas carefully so you do not accept everything in print as truthful. When evaluating what you read, ask yourself:

- Is the author right about this?
- Are there enough facts and valid arguments, or are the statements simply opinions?
- Can the author's idea be supported or proven?

Before learning how to distinguish facts and opinions, see Figure 7.1 on page 352 and study this chart that summarizes their major differences.

Facts

What exactly is a fact, and how can a fact be distinguished from an opinion? *A statement of fact is one that can definitely be verified or proven or tested by experiment.* Facts can be verified, for example, in official documents, reference books, and legal records. They contain information based on some kind of direct evidence, experience, or observation. They often give us information about people, places, and

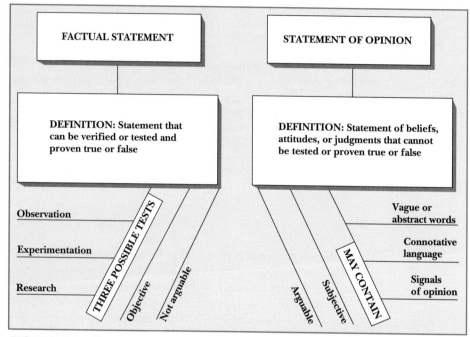

FIGURE 7.1   The Difference Between Statements of Fact and Statements of Opinion

events but do not tell us about a writer's personal perspective or feelings. Facts are not only used to support main ideas and concepts but often are used to support *other facts.*

The following statements are examples of facts, and each can be verified.

Light is essential to photosynthesis.

In 1996, men earned an average $32,144 annually, while women earned $23,710 for the same amount of hours worked, according to a report published by the National Committee on Pay Equity.

Denver Business Journal 10–16 Apr. 1998

A quart is two pints, or 4 cups, or 32 ounces. The term is derived from an Old English word for fourth. It is a fourth of a gallon.

College Mathematics for Technology

As a critical reader, you should evaluate statements of fact to determine whether they are current, **relevant,** and representative. A statement of fact may be true or false, since facts about the world change as scientists and scholars discover more

---

relevant (rel′ ə vent) relating to the matter under consideration

information and gain new insights, particularly in the fields of science, medicine, and history. In Chapter 6, the essay by Dr. Rosenfeld, "Not Everything You Like Is Bad for You" on pages 339–340, gives numerous examples that dispute previously held "facts" about health, such as new understanding about the elevating effects of foods like eggs and shrimp on cholesterol levels. Thus, as more precise knowledge is arrived at, the facts on which theories are based can change. The following article, "Chemicals in Your Food," illustrates this as the writer tries to **debunk** the theory that chemical additives are harmful. Read it to decide whether the theory is true or false.

Chemicals In Your Food

Butylated hydroxytoluene (BHT), aluminum sulfate, ammonium chloride, benzoic acid—they sound like something you'd find in a garage. Try your kitchen pantry. Aluminum sulfate is used to make pickles; ammonium chloride, to condition dough; and benzoic acid helps prevent fungus in packaged food. Without BHT, a bag of potato chips can turn dangerously rancid. Without calcium propionate to stave off mold and mono- and diglycerides to emulsify ingredients, keeping them blended together, a loaf of bread would turn into discolored cardboard after a couple of days.

For years now, we've been told natural is better. From the supermarket shelf, as well as the health-food store, more and more labels scream out: NO ADDITIVES, NO CHEMICALS, NO ARTIFICIAL PRESERVATIVES.

But is natural always better? . . .

Not only can chemical additives prevent deadly strains of bacteria from developing in food, but many of the nation's leading food scientists and researchers agree that adding a little bit of EDTA, IMP, and MSG is OK for most people.

For example, the chelating agent known as EDTA binds metal impurities so that they don't act on their own to discolor or spoil a product. . . .

And as for the much-maligned food additive monosodium glutamate (MSG), it occurs naturally in many foods, including mushrooms, tomatoes, and Parmesan cheese. After reviewing hundreds of studies, the U.S. Food and Drug Administration and the World Health Organization concluded that it's one of the safest additives around. In addition, the American College of Allergy, Asthma and Immunology has decided that MSG is not an allergen. It's unclear exactly what causes "Chinese restaurant syndrome," but Bruhn says it may be chemical histamines found in fish products.

"When you go the natural route, you can't possibly compete with normal, conventional production," says retired University of Massachusetts food chemist Jack Francis, Ph.D., who has written several books on food safety. "Therefore, you need a **niche,** and the niche is: 'Don't eat those dang chemicals.' That's hogwash! There's nothing in the U.S. food supply that's poisonous. If so, the FDA would pull it off the market today."

"We have to **demystify** that which is not understood," says Manfred Kroger, Ph.D., professor of food science at Pennsylvania State University. The scare over chemical additives was born out of ignorance and is overblown, he says. "It is exaggerated by antitech-

---

debunk (dē bunk´) to expose false or exaggerated claims
niche (nich) a particularly suitable place or position, such as a position in the food cycle
demystify (de mis´ tò fī) to remove the mystery from; to clarify

nologists, chemophobes, and others who don't really understand the rationale for their use and are afraid of the unpronounceable names they see on a package."

approximately 375 words

Leonard Novarro, "Chemicals in Your Food," *Modern Maturity* March–April 1998: 68.

✓ Put a check mark next to each of the listed chemical additives that the writer says is not harmful to your health.

_____ aluminum sulfate

_____ ammonium chloride

_____ benzoic acid

_____ calcium propionate

_____ MSG

As you can see from the items you marked, according to the writer not *all* chemicals in food are bad and some even are necessary to preserve certain food.

Opinions

A statement of opinion cannot be proven true or false. It may not necessarily be incorrect; it just has not been proven and cannot be objectively verified. In other words, it cannot be checked in a book or record anywhere. Statements of opinion usually express personal beliefs, feelings, attitudes, values, interpretations, or judgments that someone has about a subject or topic. Opinions are often based on inferences, hunches, guesses, or conclusions. They are the writer's viewpoint on a topic and are generally arrived at on the basis of a person's personal experience or background.

All of the following statements are opinions.

Christian Dior was the most outstanding dress designer of the last century.
(*Most* outstanding? What about Coco Chanel? Liz Claiborne? Donna Karan?)
Premarital sex is the norm today.
(For whom? Everyone?)
In many areas, Nixon's record did look bad.
(Did it look good to others? Bad for whom?)

Although opinions cannot be checked for accuracy or proven true or false, writers need to support or back their opinions with evidence, facts, and reasons before they can convince readers. Therefore, you need to evaluate whether stated opinions are reasonable, based on available information.

Examine the following paragraphs to see whether the authors, both former U.S. Senators, and presently co-chairs of the National Commission on Civic

Renewal, give you any conclusive facts or reasons in their discussion of how Americans feel and think.

> On the eve of the 21st century, America is prosperous, secure, free—and worried. Americans are troubled about their civic and moral culture. And with good reason. For the last 20 years, trends have not been good. A lot of bad things have coursed upward, a lot of good things downward.
>
> These trends are not the work of impersonal forces. Much of what is wrong with America we have done and are still doing to ourselves.
>
> Too many of us have become passive and disengaged. Too many of us lack confidence in our capacity to make basic moral and civic judgments, to join with our neighbors to do the work of community, to make a difference.
>
> Compared with previous generations, Americans today place less value on what we owe others as a matter of common citizenship; less value on personal sacrifice as a moral good; less value on the social importance of respectability; less value on restraint in matters of pleasure and sexuality; and greater value on self expression, self realization, and personal choice.
>
> William J. Bennett and Sam Nunn, "Get Re-Involved with America," *San Jose Mercury News* 8 July 1998: B7.

1. The authors make ten statements. Are any of them supported?

_____

2. What does this say about much of what we read?

_____

An Informed Opinion

To strengthen an opinion, a writer may base it on facts, in which case it is considered an *informed opinion*. The reader must determine whether the thesis is presented honestly or has been slanted. If it is slanted, only favorable or unfavorable points will be presented in order to distort the truth of the situation. In an article about nuclear power plants, for example, the author may discuss only the unfavorable points to sway your thinking: "Nuclear power plants are bad because of their damaging effect on all aspects of the environment."

Providing factual support enables the writer to argue an opinion intelligently. But the reader needs to ask

> Are the facts relevant or unrelated to the main point? Are they current or outdated?
>
> If statistics or studies have been quoted, are the *sources* for the information given? Are actual names specified?
>
> Could there be other points of view or ways of thinking about this?

Finally, you must realize that most writing contains statements that combine or blend both facts and opinions. A good reader knows where fact ends and opinion begins in any given statement.

Word Watch

The critical reader notices words that signal opinions rather than facts.

I believe	I suggest	She alleged	It apparently/presumably is
I conclude	I surmise	He appeared to	It seems that
I feel/think	I hold that	They usually	It probably will

The critical reader is also aware of words that indicate the writer is making a judgment based on his or her own concept of worth or value, such as those listed.

bad	beautiful	best	doubtful
favorable	good	great	inconsequential
meaningful	significant	unsatisfactory	worse

A note of caution: Do not be misled into accepting statements as facts simply because they have been prefaced with any of the following expressions.

As a matter of fact	The fact of the matter is
In fact	The point is
It is a fact that	The truth is

Many times, these words or phrases are followed by an opinion, as in the following statement: "The point is that not everyone should learn a foreign language." There is no fact in the statement, and whether everyone *should* learn a foreign language or not is one person's opinion.

ACTIVITY 7.1

Indicate whether the following statements are facts (F), opinions (O), or a mixture of both (F/O). If a statement is a direct quotation, do not consider it a fact simply because someone has said it. The person making the statement may be merely expressing his or her opinion. If a statement contains an opinion, state whether you can accept what is said because it reveals an informed, not a personal, opinion.

Circle the words that help you decide whether the statement is a fact, and underline the ones that signal an opinion.

_____ 1. The valuable contribution early childhood programs can make by fostering mental health has been emphasized in a recent report by the Joint Commission on the Mental Health of Children.

The Whole Child: Trends in Early Education

_____

_____ 2. The researchers found that joint custody was actually worse for children than sole custody.

Psychology Today

_____

_____ 3. Healthy marriages are the single strongest **antidote** to many social ills—from poor school performance to teen pregnancy to poverty and crime.

"The Marriage Makeover," *San Jose Mercury News*

_____

_____ 4. Justice Oliver Wendell Holmes once remarked, "My freedom to swing my arm stops where the other man's nose begins."

Political Science

_____

_____ 5. The fact is most individuals limit their goals by limiting their knowledge, and they pursue the same humdrum path every day without ever knowing their lives could have been enriched by seeking to learn something about everything.

A Practical Guide to Better Concentration

_____

_____ 6. It is generally now agreed by scientists and philosophers of science that theories may have considerable evidence supporting them, but no theory can be said to be true.

Anthropology

_____

_____ 7. In spite of the reams that have been written on the subject, it may come as a surprise to learn that contraceptive techniques are age-old.

The Family, Society, and the Individual

_____

_____

antidote (an´ ti dōt) anything that relieves or counteracts an injurious effect

_____ 8. Overall, families in the twenty-first century will continue to have more choices than they did in the past.

Marriage and Families

Making Inferences from Facts and Opinions

You will be faced with quite a challenging task when reading critically and making inferences from passages and essays rather than from simple sentences or short paragraphs.

ACTIVITY 7.2

PASSAGE 1

In a startling recent study by the National Violence Against Women Survey, researchers found that one in four stalking targets are men. After you have read the article, underline any *informed opinions* based on actual facts given in order to help you decide what inferences can be drawn from the study's conclusions.

Men Stalking Men: Stalkers Often Gravitate Toward Positions of Power

Richard Willing

The stalker's techniques were familiar. His target's gender was not.   1

Jonathan Norman's letters, verbal threats and unwanted visits were not aimed at a   2 former wife or girlfriend, nor even a woman he wanted to date. Instead, the 31-year-old bodybuilder and would-be screenwriter spent two months stalking another man: film producer and director Steven Spielberg. . . .

In a surprising finding, a study by the National Violence Against Women Survey esti-   3 mated that, like Spielberg, more than one in four of the nation's 1.4 million annual stalking victims are men. And despite the impression left by the movie *Fatal Attraction,* few male victims are pursued by jealous, bunny-boiling females who have been spurned: 90% are stalked by other men.

Experts say the motive can be romantic jealousy; gay men are the most likely victims   4 of male-on-male stalking. But man-stalking often is linked to the high-profile positions that the targets hold in society.

Professors are stalked by students. Attractive celebrities are pursued by lonely men   5 looking for famous buddies. Business and political leaders can become objects of hate when consumer complaints turn ugly. . . .

"He who gets the power gets the stalkers," says Park Dietz, a Newport Beach, Calif., **6** psychiatrist and a longtime student of stalking behavior.

Despite the survey, which is the first of its kind, male-stalking remains a relatively **7** unstudied phenomenon. Experts say that men are more reluctant than women to report being stalked, and can have trouble getting police to take them seriously. Public services for stalking victims are still oriented to the most frequent targets—women. . . .

"Stalking isn't just for women," says Rhonda Saunders, a deputy district attorney in **8** Los Angeles who specializes in stalker cases. "Anybody can be a victim and anybody can be a stalker."

For purposes of the study, its authors, Patricia Tjaden and Nancy Thoennes, defined **9** stalking as more than one occasion of close following, unwelcome conversation or verbal or written threats that would "cause a reasonable person fear." . . .

Fewer than half of stalking victims are **overtly** threatened, and only a fraction are **10** attacked. The far more common case is a female, aged 18 to 39, harassed by a former spouse or boyfriend. Typical stalker behavior includes following the victim, making threatening phone calls and shadowing new male companions. Almost 60% of women listed their pursuer as a current or former husband or live-in partner.

"Men more persistently pursue those they would have romance with as a matter of **11** culture and biology," Dietz says. "Men more aggressively pursue all things."

In contrast, man-on-man stalking is rarely publicized, in part, prosecutors say, **12** because the facts often seem **mundane.**

A typical case involved a bachelor law professor in Los Angeles who began a **platonic** **13** friendship with a younger neighbor. As time went on, the younger man used a ladder to peer into the professor's apartment, kidnapped his cat and stole his list of students. Working from the class list, the younger man called each of the students and said school had been canceled, leaving the professor to face an empty classroom.

The professor, whose name authorities did not disclose, was so traumatized that he **14** quit his job and left town.

"The damage may appear to be minimal, more on the order of a prank," says **15** Saunders, the deputy district attorney who prosecuted the professor's tormentor. "But the psychological toll was immense. . . . It was an act of psychological terrorism, just like all stalking." . . .

Such male-stalking can have an angry edge. . . . **16**

Researchers say men stalk other men for the same reasons they stalk women: a com- **17** plex mix of mental and personality disorders that can include schizophrenia, drug dependency, **narcissism** and anti-social behavior.

California psychologist J. Reed Meloy, who studied stalkers imprisoned in Missouri, **18** says many lost a parent or other important guardian before age 5. Many stalkers also suffered a major setback on the job or in a relationship in the months before their stalking began, Meloy found.

---

overtly (o vurt′ lē) openly and publicly; observably

mundane (mun′ dān) commonplace; ordinary; everyday

platonic (plò tän′ ik) a relationship or love between two people that is purely spiritual or intellectual, without sexual activity

narcissism (när′ sò siz òm) self-love

"Their rage is coupled with a sense of entitlement," says Meloy, editor of *The* **19** *Psychology of Stalking,* a recently published text. "Instead of feeling sad and hurt (by rejection) and then moving on, their anger turns toward the object of rejection."

Research on males stalking males continues. Tjaden and Thoennes, authors of the **20** federal survey, plan a further study of workplace violence. The U.S. Secret Service is interviewing citizens who have harassed public figures in an attempt to predict why stalkers turn violent.

approximately 875 words

Richard Willing, "Men Stalking Men," *USA Today* 17 June 1998: A1–2.

1. List three statements of fact given in the essay.

   _____

   _____

   _____

2. Are the statements in paragraph 5 facts, opinions, or informed opinions? Explain the reason for your choice.

   _____

   _____

3. Why do you suppose "male-stalking remains a relatively unstudied phenomenon" (para. 7) and "is rarely publicized" (para. 12)?

   _____

   _____

   _____

4. Is the definition of stalking (paras. 9–11) clear-cut? Why, or why not?

   _____

   _____

5. Explain which of the steps listed in the chart, "Self-protection Measures," on page 361 seem reasonable for a stalking victim to undertake? Is there anything you would add to the chart as a self-protective measure?

   _____

   _____

   _____

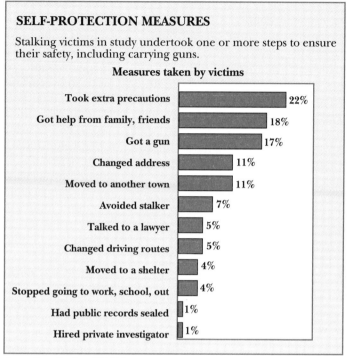

SELF-PROTECTION MEASURES

Stalking victims in study undertook one or more steps to ensure their safety, including carrying guns.

Measures taken by victims

- Took extra precautions — 22%
- Got help from family, friends — 18%
- Got a gun — 17%
- Changed address — 11%
- Moved to another town — 11%
- Avoided stalker — 7%
- Talked to a lawyer — 5%
- Changed driving routes — 5%
- Moved to a shelter — 4%
- Stopped going to work, school, out — 4%
- Had public records sealed — 1%
- Hired private investigator — 1%

Source: Grant Jerding, *USA Today*

PASSAGE 2

The author makes some interesting observations about what he labels as today's "trash." Note the italicized words as you read. They should help you decide which statements are fact and which are opinion before you answer the questions that follow the selection. Remember to *preview* before you begin to examine the article closely.

We Love Trash

Neal Gabler

This, at least, conservatives and liberals seem 1 to agree on: American culture is in a perilous state. Assaulted by rap music and heavy metal, made soft-headed by the novels of Robert James Waller and Danielle Steele, stimulated by violent films, narcotized by mindless TV programs

and obsessed with O.J. Simpson, we slide ever closer to a cultural **abyss** filled with trash and nothing but trash.

Long before O.J. Simpson, however, 2 Americans craved trash. The scandalous penny press, which sprang into existence in the 1830s

---

abyss (ə bis′) a bottomless pit; hell

as a vehicle for the working class, subsisted on juicy tales of criminal conduct. The case of Helen Jewitt, a young prostitute *allegedly* murdered by a rich client named Richard Robinson, held New York City rapt for months as newspapers screamed the **lurid** details and ordinary citizens debated the evidence.

It didn't take long for other **accoutrements** of trash culture to surface. In short order, **3** violence was joined by pornography, scandal, exploitation and the mindless celebration of fame for fame's sake. By the 1870s, the **protagonists** of real-life crime and moral transgression were appearing on the vaudeville stage as similar protagonists today appear on tabloid TV shows: human commodities of trash.

Many conservatives concluded that democracy itself was at fault. Give people what they **4** want, and you will get trash. As a remedy, these cultural custodians promoted **genteel** literature—stories of domesticity or aristocracy or chaste romance illustrating good and decent values. They felt the masses would learn from these as we are supposed to learn from William Bennett's* "Book of Virtues." We would uplift ourselves.

To read trash, to flaunt trash, to prefer trash to "better" literature was a not-so-**subtle** **5** way of asserting one's independence against one's social superiors. *It was a way of saying* that we are masters of our own culture. *It was a way of saying* that we are Americans.

It still is. From crime pamphlets to dime **6** novels to the "yellow press" to the movies to the tabloids to the trash of today, one theme keeps emerging. In a world culturally divided between the genteel and everything else, Americans opt for trash over art that is supposed to be good for them as much because they resent being told what they should like as because they like trash. *Seen this way,* trash is not an escape from life, as some would have it; it is an escape from seriousness, which is *no doubt why* trash in the form of our movies, TV shows, music and popular literature has become one of our chief exports. You don't have to be American to want to play hooky from high culture, though *Americans may be* prouder of it than anyone else.

To its defenders, trash has the virtue of honesty—of not **purporting** to be anything other than what it is, which is, well, trash. . . . **7**

Today's American culture, from exploi- **8** talk programs to tabloid TV to Howard Stern, is perceived as more honest and democratic than the **turgid,** domesticated arts and amusements that cultural conservatives believe *we should like*—and *would like*—if we weren't being shovel-fed trash.

Trash is subversive that way. It exists to **9** taunt.

No doubt that is why cultural conserva- **10** tives . . . hate it so. It is not because they want to save us from **perdition** that they rail against junk. *I suspect* it is because they want to reassert their dominance over a culture that long ago

---

lurid (loor′ id) causing shock or horror
accoutrements (ə koo′ trə mənts) furnishings; clothes or equipment
protagonists (prō tag′ ə nists) leading characters
genteel (jen tēl′) refined in manner; polite
subtle (sut′ l) not immediately obvious; difficult to detect
purporting (pər pôrt′ ing) claiming to be or do something
turgid (tur′ jid) overornate in style or language; using big words
perdition (pər dish′ ən) eternal damnation; complete ruin
* William Bennett headed the "War on Drugs" and is a leading national conservative.

slipped out of their control even as conservatives have come to dominate politics.

Damning trash and pretending that it is 11 being **foisted** upon us by media conspirators is a clever technique—and a very old one.

Most Americans, however, *know better.* Trash is 12 how we distinguish ourselves from all the things others want us to be. Trash may not be good for us, but this we know: It is ours.

approximately 675 words

Neal Gabler, "We Love Trash," *San Jose Mercury News.* Originally published in the *Los Angeles Times* 6 June 1995: 7B. Copyright © by Neal Gabler. Reprinted by permission of the author.

1. Write whether each of the sentences in paragraph 2 is a statement of fact (F), opinion (O), or combined fact and opinion (F/O).

   Sentence 1: _____ Sentence 2: _____ Sentence 3: _____

2. a. Why does the author include information about "trash" from the 1800s?
   b. What inference can you make from this information?

   _____

   _____

3. a. What facts have been included in paragraphs 5 and 6?

   _____

   _____

   b. What inferences does the writer want you to make from these two paragraphs?

   _____

   c. Do you agree with the writer's conclusions?

   _____

   _____

4. Do you "love trash"? Why, or why not?

   _____

   _____

---

foisted (foist′ id) imposed on someone by force or deceit

ACTIVITY 7.3

Having read about Americans' love affair with "trash," examine the cartoon that follows, titled "U.S. Currency Redesign." On the basis of what you see and read, indicate which of the statements below the cartoon are facts (F) and which are opinions (O).

———— 1. Pat Robertson demanded that his name appear on the redesign of the dollar bill.

———— 2. O. J. Simpson's name is signed on the redesigned bill.

———— 3. Cindy Crawford has more appeal than George Washington.

———— 4. You should put a check mark on the bill if you want to donate to Bill Clinton's legal fund.

———— 5. Instead of saying "ONE DOLLAR," the redesign says "ONE BUCK."

Now, let's see how many valid inferences you can draw from examining the cartoon. Write V if the inference given is valid and I if it is invalid. Write the support for the valid inferences in the space provided.

———   6. An extremist group is probably responsible for redesigning the dollar bill.

Support: _____

———   7. The cartoonist is being critical of some American values.

Support: _____

———   8. A dollar bill's value increases when marijuana leaves are printed on it.

Support: _____

———   9. The cartoonist shows disapproval of the study claiming that Americans eat junk food that is far too fattening at movie theaters.

Support: _____

——— 10. What item would you include on the redesigned bill to illustrate some American obsession that you think deserves criticism?

_____

Notice that the ideas we call inferences are not stated anywhere in the picture, but you, the reader, made the inferences on the basis of *factual* evidence gathered. Inferences, then, cannot be proven true or false but are supported by the factual evidence that is directly present or stated. Using facts to make inferences about printed matter is similar to making inferences from photos.

ACTIVITY 7.4

Read the following passages, and then mark the inferences that follow V (valid) or I (invalid). Write the *fact* or *facts* that support your valid inference below each statement in the space provided.

PASSAGE 1

The uppermost **echelon** of women in corporate America have seen their salaries double over the past 10 years, to an average of $187,000, according to a 1993 study. Yet only 69 percent of the female movers and shakers at major U.S. corporations are married, versus 91 percent of males. Sure, getting to the top requires a sacrifice of time that might

_____

echelon (esh′ ə lon) ranking of groups, units, or individuals otherwise be spent cultivating intimate relationships; what's not clear is how much of the marriage gap reflects relationship difficulties high-earning women face just because of their salaries.

Among those who marry, female executives now pull in 66 percent of their household income. But all families increasingly rely on the woman's paycheck to keep the household humming. Layoffs, the high cost of living, medical expenses, falling male wages, the desire for a better lifestyle, and assorted other economic factors have made dual-income families a reality for 59 percent of married couples in the United States.

Working women report that their ability to bring home a paycheck increases feelings of power, improves self-esteem, and gives them fulfillment and independence. But they also sense that society as a whole has yet to embrace female earning power as a positive.

Christy Casamassima, "Love and Work," *Psychology Today* Mar./Apr. 1995: 43.

———— 1. The amount of money earned by women in powerful positions in corporate America has significantly increased over the last ten years.

Support: _____

———— 2. The percentage of men and women who are married and who occupy powerful positions is about equal.

Support: _____

———— 3. There is "marriage anxiety" among women in powerful positions.

Support: _____

———— 4. Divorce occurs more often among married couples with dual incomes.

Support: _____

———— 5. Society approves of high-salaried women in business.

Support: _____

PASSAGE 2

The Misuse of Personal Information

Sources of Personal Data

The issue with the greatest **ethical** overtones is the privacy of personal information. Some people fear that computer-based record-keeping offers too much of an opportunity for

---

ethical (eth′ i kəl) guided by principles of right and wrong governing the conduct of a group

the invasion of an individual's privacy. There is indeed reason for concern. For example, credit-card users unknowingly leave a "trail" of activities and interests that, when examined and evaluated, can provide a surprisingly comprehensive personal profile.

The date and location of all credit-card transactions are recorded. In effect, when you charge lunch, gasoline, or clothing, you are creating a chronological record of where you have been and your spending habits. From this information, a good analyst could compile a very accurate profile of your lifestyle. For example, the analyst could predict how you dress by knowing the type of clothing stores you patronize. On a more personal level, records are kept that detail the duration, time, and numbers of all your telephone calls. With computers, these numbers easily can be matched to people, businesses, institutions, and telephone services. So each time you make a phone call, you also leave a record of whom or what you call. Enormous amounts of personal data are maintained on everyone by the IRS, your college, your employer, your creditors, your hospital, your insurance company, your broker, and on and on.

We hope that information about us is up-to-date and accurate. Unfortunately, much of it is not. Laws permit us to examine our records, but first we must find them. You cannot just write to the federal government and request to see your files. To be completely sure that you examine all your federal records for completeness and accuracy, you would have to write and probably visit more than 5000 agencies that each maintain computer-based files on individuals. The same is true of computer-based personal data maintained in the private sector.

approximately 280 words

Larry Long, *Introduction to Computers and Information Systems*

—— 1. There is potential for abuse within our present credit card system.

   Support: _____

—— 2. Pay cash—do not use credit cards.

   Support: _____

—— 3. It is difficult to find out whether information recorded about you is correct.

   Support: _____

—— 4. Considerable information has been compiled on people without their knowledge.

   Support: _____

—— 5. Congress should investigate the credit card issue.

   Support: _____

PASSAGE 3

One significant difference between traditional downtowns and most new villages and suburban malls is that the latter are private property. People cannot be banned from a traditional downtown, and the right to petition on a public sidewalk is constitutionally protected. People may, however, be banned from private property, and constitutional rights, such as political pamphleteering, may be restricted. In many communities today, malls are the only public gathering places, so if the mall owners are allowed to decide who may speak in them, mall owners can determine the public's access to ideas. Candidates for political office have been banned from busy malls owned by their opponents, and so have labor union organizers.

U.S. law recognizes that private properties can perform functions traditionally associated with government. This is called the *public function doctrine*. The U.S. Supreme Court has ruled that the Constitution does not protect citizens' access to shopping centers against the wishes of the owners. Some states, however, have upheld the right of public access under their state constitutions. Each state has balanced public and private rights differently.

Edward F. Bergman, *Human Geography*

———— 1. Political discussions are limited at shopping malls since their owners' concern is making money.

Support: _____

———— 2. American citizens do not have a constitutional right to campaign for office at a shopping mall.

Support: _____

———— 3. The opinions of the Supreme Court and some states differ on the constitutional rights of citizens to public access.

Support: _____

———— 4. Shopping malls, as gathering places, should permit the exchange of various political views.

Support: _____

———— 5. Banning the right to petition is un-American.

Support: _____

Strategy 2: Evaluating the Main Idea and Supporting Details in Making Inferences

Making inferences from the main ideas and supporting details is somewhat similar to making inferences from facts. You need also, however, to pay particular attention to the sequence of thought in support of the views expressed. To guide yourself in following the sequence, make marginal notations of the most important ideas, such as those you make in locating the main idea, and then evaluate these notations.

In the following passage on our competitive society, marginal notations have been made to assist you in making valid inferences. Also, important qualifying terms have been circled.

In our highly competitive society we compete for grades, athletic honors, jobs, marital partners, and almost everything else we want. (Although) we endorse certain rules for playing the game and may give grudging credit for effort, it is success that gains the rewards. The losing football team does not attract crowds or gain **plaudits** for its performance; the company that fails to gain contracts in competition with other companies is likely to go bankrupt. It is the students with superior records who win the competition for college entrance and later the competition for selection for advanced training. (Nor) does the strain of sustained effort usually cease when the individual leaves school. At (almost) any occupational level a person (may be) under considerable pressure to advance and make the increased income often needed to support a family. In general, most of us are encouraged to be ambitious and "think big." (Yet) not everyone can come in first, and striving to do the impossible invites frustration and self-devaluation.

society stresses competition—only success gets rewards
Ex. of competition:
  sports
  business > stress
  school
  job

pressure to advance
striving   frustration
but not   > self-
winning   devaluation

James C. Coleman and Constance L. Hammen, *Contemporary Psychology and Effective Behavior*

One can infer from the paragraph that Americans are not interested in losers. This is supported by the author's statements that "the losing team does not attract crowds or gain plaudits." A second valid inference, based on the writer's assertion that "striving to do the impossible invites frustration and self-devaluation," is that competition negatively changes our self-perception.

Notice that it becomes easier to make inferences once you understand the stated ideas and have examined the particular supporting details that develop these ideas.

---

plaudits (plô′ dits) rounds of applause; praise

ACTIVITY 7.5

Read the following essay, separating the facts from the opinions as you make marginal notes. On the basis of your notations, decide which of the inferences that appear after the essay are valid. Then, write out one inference of your own.

Drug Peace

*Joseph D. McNamara**

It was clear that the police chiefs were fed up with the drug war. "How," the chief asked, "can we get out of the drug war without evoking such a vivid symbol of surrender and defeat?"

He was speaking the thoughts of many of the 50 law enforcement leaders participating in a two-day conference on drug policy held . . . at the Hoover Institution at Stanford University. . . . The group concluded that studying a medical and public health approach to drug control does not mean putting rock cocaine on store shelves next to soda pop. An evaluation of the drug war and a study of alternative methods of drug control is the way to an honorable peace.

The suggestion sends a powerful message to the politicians trying to outdo each other in being tough on drugs. Ninety percent of the chiefs do not support the federal war against drugs. And the few who do support the war, nevertheless, were part of a **unanimous** vote saying that treatment, education and prevention are more useful than arrests and prison sentences.

The law enforcement leaders were also unanimous in calling for a blue ribbon commission to evaluate the drug war and to study alternative methods of controlling drugs. The message to the politicians is that your political opponent cannot accuse you of being soft on drugs if you are following the recommendations of the majority of America's cops.

Ethan Nadelmann, formerly a Princeton professor, opened the conference with an overview of the drug war's failure to reduce drug use and a challenge to the participants to put aside their moral views on drug use and to consider ways to minimize the harm being done to drug users and society.

Nadelmann was followed by professor Jerome Skolnick of UC-Berkeley, who described studies showing that successful prosecutions of drug rings led to increased homicides and that successful seizures of drugs by the government sometimes led drug users to experiment with even more dangerous drugs.

Former Secretary of State George Shultz reminded the group that powerful economic forces are at work in the illegal drug market and that it is essential to find a way to reduce the demand that leads to such **exorbitant** profits for drug dealers.

Baltimore Mayor Kurt Schmoke was the show stopper. He described how his **constituents,** most of whom are African-Americans,

---

unanimous (yo͞o nan′ ə məs) sharing the same opinions or views; in complete agreement

exorbitant (eg zor′ bə tənt) excessive; extravagant

constituents (kən stich′ o͞o ənts) voters; serving as part of a whole

* Joseph D. McNamara served with the New York City Police Department and as police chief in Kansas City, Mo., and San Jose. He is now a research fellow at the Hoover Institution, studying the effectiveness of government programs against crime and violence.

re-elected him after he had called for the "medicalization" of anti-drug efforts—treating users as people needing help instead of merely jailing them as criminals. . . . Schmoke also described a school visit during which children told him that most of the youngsters dropping out of school did so not because they were hooked on drugs—they were hooked on easy drug money. Schmoke, because of his closeness to African-American neighborhoods, was able to counter Congressman Charles Rangel's charges that it is genocide to consider medicalization approaches to drug control. Schmoke said the drug war itself has a negative effect on African-Americans.

. . . Two federal judges, Vaughn Walker 9 and Robert Sweet, spoke of the inappropriateness of relying upon criminal law enforcement to control the personal behavior of drug use and the cruelty of imposing 10-year mandatory sentences on first-time drug offenders who had committed no other crime.

[Former] San Francisco Mayor Frank 10 Jordon told how his program of sterile needle exchange had lessened the danger of AIDS not only for intravenous drug users but also for the public and police officers. Professor Alfred Blumstein of Carnegie-Mellon University provided a **somber** description of how the illegal drug market had caused the juvenile homicide rate to explode. Easy availability of guns and dope money resulted in the juvenile murder rate by firearms more than doubling nationally since 1985. Blumstein also reported that drug enforcement and punishment fell disproportionately on non-whites.

I pointed out that truth is another casualty 11 in the drug war. During my 18 years as a police chief and more than 35 years in law enforcement, we often celebrated "victories," yet almost everyone in law enforcement believes the drug problem is worse now. Furthermore, it does not make sense to have peace officers in a war.

Gen. Colin Powell once said a soldier's duty 12 is to kill the enemy. The first duty of the police is to protect human lives, including the lives of people unfortunate enough to be addicted to drugs. In addition, every week somewhere across the country there is another police scandal related to the drug war—corruption, brutality and even armed robberies by cops in uniform, as well as consistent violations of civil rights by officers who feel that anything goes in a war.

It is not surprising that when law enforce- 13 ment leaders spend two days analyzing the drug problem, they conclude that the drug war is **futile.** If the president and Congress take the time to reflect on drugs the way the top cops did, they too, would support a study of how to find peace, and an honorable end to the war on drugs.

approximately 825 words

somber (som′ bər) dismal; gloomy
futile (fyoo′ təl) useless; ineffective

Write V (valid) or I (invalid) for each of the following inferences based on "Drug Peace." Space is provided after each statement for your support.

_____ 1. Law enforcement leaders disagree as to whether education and treatment of drug users is more beneficial than arrest and imprisonment of drug sellers.

Support: _____

_____

_____ 2. The author has failed to support his main ideas and thesis.

Support: _____

_____

_____ 3. The "war on drugs" will be won only if the government's present methods continue.

Support: _____

_____

_____ 4. Needle exchange among drug users in one city appears to be working.

Support: _____

_____

_____ 5. The American people agree with and support the approach of drug enforcement leaders in controlling drugs.

Support: _____

_____

_____ 6. Your inference: _____

_____

Support: _____

_____

Be Aware of Signal Words That Qualify the Meaning of the Main Idea

As you recall from your study of fact and opinion, you need to be aware of words that qualify meanings. The chart on page 373 groups the major signal words into four categories according to how they qualify a statement or what they imply about the author's attitude toward his or her statements.

Signal Words That Qualify Meaning

Signal Words of Inference
The following words may signal an implication by the writer. Recall that the writer implies, and the reader infers.

assumption	it is assumed; one can assume; the assumption is
implication	this implies; it may be implied; the result implies
inference	one can infer; this may infer; the inference is
suggestion	this may suggest; it could be suggested; the suggestion here is

Absolute Signal Words
These words should make the reader reject a statement unless there is strong support.

always	definitely	irrefutably
assuredly	indisputably	undeniably
certainly	invariably	without question

Probability Signal Words
These words suggest that the information may be accurate but that other possibilities may exist.

almost	probably
presumably	there is little question

Possibility Signal Words
These words suggest that the ideas are subject to debate and that there is doubt as to their complete validity.

apparently	may/maybe	possibly	somewhat
could be	might	seems	
likely	perhaps	seemingly	

ACTIVITY 7.6

Underline the qualifying word(s) in each sentence. In the space provided, explain what the term implies, and write why you do or do not agree with what is stated.

1. The telephone as we know it today will probably disappear and be replaced by a multifunctional communication workstation.

Business

Qualifying term implies: _____

2. Becoming the largest group of oppressed people is always frightening for those above you, those under you, and those who have been at your side.

Felix Jiminez, "Dangerous Liaisons," *Hispanic*

Qualifying term implies: _____

3. Even though English is generally considered the international language of business, it is nevertheless a mistake to assume that every foreign businessperson either knows English or can understand American usage.

Contemporary Business Communication

Qualifying term implies: _____

4. Perhaps, the single greatest factor affecting family life in the twenty-first century will be the spread of HIV and AIDS.

Marriage and Families

Qualifying term implies: _____

5. While a victim of sexual assault may come out of the ordeal without a scrape, the psychological scars are inescapable.

"A Conspiracy of Silent Abuse . . . ," *USA Today*

Qualifying term implies: _____

ACTIVITY 7.7   Finding the Significance of Signal Words in Textbook Passages

Read the following textbook selection about ancient civilizations. Underline each of the qualifying terms, which will help you determine both how valid are the writers' implications and how sound the conclusions. Then answer the questions that follow.

Archeological Inferences About Civilization

The most ancient civilizations have been studied by archeologists rather than historians because those civilizations evolved before the advent of writing. How do archeologists infer that a particular people in the preliterate past had social classes, cities, or centralized government?

As we have noted, it appears that the earliest Neolithic societies were *egalitarian:* people did not differ much in wealth, prestige, or power. Some later societies show signs of social inequality. One kind of evidence of inequality in an ancient society is provided by burial finds. Archeologists generally assume that inequality in death reflects inequality in life, at least in status and perhaps also in wealth and power. Thus, we can be fairly sure that a society had differences in status if only some people were buried with special objects, such as jewelry or pots filled with food. And we can be fairly sure that high status was assigned at birth rather than achieved in later life if we find noticeable differences in children's tombs. For example, some (but not all) child burials from as early as 5500 to 5000 B.C. at Tell es-Sawwan in Iraq, and from about 800 B.C. at La Venta in Mexico, are filled with statues and ornaments suggesting that some children had high status from birth. But burials indicating differences in status do not necessarily mean a society had significant differences in wealth. It is only when archeologists find other substantial differences, as in house size and furnishings, that we can be sure the society had different socioeconomic classes of people.

approximately 250 words

Carol R. Ember and Melvin Ember, *Anthropology*

1. State at least one conclusion that archeologists have reached about people who lived in the period before writing was invented.

    _____

    _____

2. Is the archeologists' assumption that "inequality in death reflects inequality in life" a valid one? Why, or why not?

    _____

    _____

3. What inferences can you make from the second paragraph, in which the authors use the qualifying term "fairly sure" about conclusions you should reach?

    _____

    _____

    _____

Strategy 3: Assessing the Logic of Your Inferences and Sound Conclusions

You can assess the logic of your inferences by making a check mark in the margin by the evidence that supports it. If you can find no evidence, the inference is probably unreliable. The more support presented for the inference, the more likely it is to be valid.

Use two key questions to help you judge the logic of your inferences.

1. What support validates my inference?
    *   *Ask:* Is this what has been suggested? Can this inference be justified?
2. Is my inference a valid one?
    *   *Ask:* Does it make sense? Is it reasonable based on the facts? Is the development of ideas logical?

Use these same key questions when drawing conclusions from inferences you have made, substituting the word *conclusion*.

- What support has the author provided for the conclusion I have drawn?
- Is my conclusion valid?

ACTIVITY 7.8   **Practice Using All the Strategies to Make Valid Inferences and to Draw Sound Conclusions**

Read each of the following passages, making marginal notations and circling words that may qualify the writer's assertions and implications. Place check marks by phrases that may lead to conclusions.

a. For each statement, circle the letter that makes it a valid inference.
b. Answer the questions that help in assessing whether your reasoning is logical.

PASSAGE 1

Does the threat of the death penalty deter people from murderous behavior more than the threat of imprisonment for life? We do not yet know with anything even approaching certainty whether the death penalty does or does not deter. The question is clearly **empirical,** and it is likely that sophisticated statistical techniques will eventually permit us an answer.

Professor Isaac Ehrlich and his colleagues, utilizing his statistical techniques, argue that there can be little doubt about the ability of the death penalty to deter. Ehrlich concludes that each additional execution prevents about seven or eight people from committing murder. All statistical arguments on the death penalty are, however, excruciatingly complex. Some critics, for example, have argued that increased likelihood of execution leads juries to convict fewer people, thereby offsetting the deterrent effect. If anything, the empirical evidence is that the death penalty *does* deter. But this is inevitably open to dispute. As a result, firm conclusions that the death penalty either does or does not deter are unwarranted and usually determined by one's psychological and moral leanings.

Steven Goldberg, "So What if the Death Penalty Deters," *National Review* 30 June 1989

1. The author implies that the death penalty
    a. definitely deters crime.
    b. probably deters crime.
    c. may possibly deter crime.
    d. allegedly deters crime.

    Support: _____

    _____

    _____

    empirical (em pir′ i kəl) relying or based on experiment or experience

_____ 1. The authors imply that theories about early societies
              a. provide an excellent basis for film and television scripts.
              b. cannot be proven conclusively.
              c. are buried with our ancestors.
              d. inspire admiration and wonder.

_____ 2. You can conclude from the qualifying terms used in the arguments given
              by the researcher, Tellefsen, that his theories are
              a. probably correct.
              b. possibly correct.
              c. unquestionably correct.
              d. absolutely inaccurate.

3. a. How logical is the conclusion stated in the last sentence of the second
       paragraph?

       _____

    b. Discuss another possible explanation of why pyramids may have been built,
       besides the one provided by Tellefsen.

       _____

       _____

PASSAGE 5

Read to decide if there are any actual proven facts about the relationship of weather
to our health and mental conditions.

When Forecast Calls for Pain

. . . A California librarian, far from the nearest window, says she falls asleep every time
it rains. A Michigan man believes his terrible headaches are linked to winter weather.
    Is there a link between your inside and your outside?
    Despite almost a century of research, the subject remains a mystery. Yet many beliefs
have become deeply engrained in our cultural **mythology:**

- Rain makes arthritics ache, especially in an El Niño year. . . .
- Murder rates peak during a full moon.
- Suicides skyrocket over the Christmas holidays. . . .

"Sometimes we find that, yes, there are funny things going on. But the whole subject
is so polluted with 'old wives tales,' longtime beliefs that have taken on lives of their own,
that it makes it very hard to ferret out the truth," said Dr. Dennis M. Driscoll of Texas
A&M University, a climatologist with the International Society of Biometeorology.

_____

mythology (mi thăl′ ò jē) a telling of tales or legends

Most research contradicts the folk beliefs. An elevator ride up the 1,707 feet to the top of the Sears Tower in Chicago causes greater air pressure change than a passing rainstorm. Murder rates are highest in the steamy summer, regardless of the phase of the moon. Suicides peak in the spring, not winter. . . .

The intuitive belief that weather can influence our health has been held throughout human history. In the fourth century B.C., the Greek physician Hippocrates reported physical and psychological reactions to hot and cold winds. In old France the **mistral** wind was once thought to so impair judgment that people who murdered while it was blowing were spared the guillotine.

Ever since, scientists have searched for seasonal trends in human health and mood.

In his definitive study of daily deaths in 10 U.S. cities between 1962 and 1965, Driscoll found that mortality rates jumped during episodes of extreme heat, cold, and air pollution—but also were influenced by more subtle factors such as daily fluctuations in temperature, dewpoint and air pressure.

Since then, dozens of smaller studies have attempted to find correlations between weather and human health. For instance: . . .

- Drug overdoses are a warm-weather phenomenon, with women most likely to succumb in late May and men in early August, according to a 1987 Chicago-based analysis by Dr. Ralph Morris of the University of Illinois. Overdoses in both men and women were most common on Fridays at 6:20 p.m.
- Both the manic and depressive episodes of a mood ailment called bipolar disorder are most common in the spring, according to dozens of studies. . . .

    Modern science finds little support for the ancient belief in moon-induced lunacy. Because of the moon's distance from Earth, and the minuscule tidal effect it could have on an individual, scientists have found no cause-and-effect relationship.
- Suicide, contrary to prevailing wisdom, is a springtime and not a winter holiday phenomenon. In fact, December records fewer suicides than any other month, according to national statistics.

British researchers found that women are more likely to try to kill themselves on cloudy days that are warm and wet and windless. Men also pick warm rainy weather, but seem to prefer wind. For both genders, suicide attempts were most common during spring thunderstorms, researchers reported in the 1994 British *Journal of Psychiatry*. . . .

An eight-year study of murder and weather in Baltimore, published in the 1995 *Journal of Quantitative Criminology*, found that murder rates climbed during long stretches of hot weather. The British *Journal of Criminology* also found high temperatures to be linked to not just murder, but assault, burglary, domestic violence, and rape.

San Franciscans are most likely to die of all causes in January, then December, February and March, according to an analysis of 17,925 deaths reported between 1994–95. . . .

---

mistral (mi sträl′) a cold, dry north wind that blows over the Mediterranean coast of France and nearby regions

These findings, while controversial, suggest that humans are not too far removed from our animal roots. We evolved in a solar and lunar environment that changes drastically but predictably every 24 hours, 30 days, and 365.25 days.

The daily and seasonal rhythms of biological activity, driven by an internal clock buried deep in the brain, are detectable at all levels of life. For instance, the ovary of an Indian catfish weighs an astounding 16 grams during monsoon season; the rest of the year, it weighs merely 1 gram. This pattern persists during years and years of darkness—when the fish swims in an aquarium, far from her river habitat.

These genetically transmitted rhythms are maintained through the generations because they aid in survival, biologists say. An organism has an advantage if it can anticipate a daily or seasonal change in the environment, not just respond to it. Metabolically and reproductively, it can prepare to shift gears. . . .

Through evolution, these internal rhythms have become tightly **synchronized** with external rhythms. . . .

But sudden shifts in weather—whether by El Niño rains, heat waves, a temperature plunge or fast-moving weather fronts—can cause biological **cacophony,** some speculate. Also upsetting are conflicts between internal biology and external social factors, such as when a lonely person sees lovers strolling hand-in-hand on a spring day.

"Many of us live at very different latitudes than where our ancestors came from, so our biology may not fit our circumstances. . . . Our problems may be failures in adaptation," said UC–San Diego's Kripke.

Documentation of human seasonality is tough: Any population large enough to offer reliable statistics is, almost by definition, exposed to very different types of weather. . . .

approximately 850 words

Lisa M. Krieger, Medical writer, "When Forecast Calls for Pain," *San Francisco Examiner* 7 Apr. 1998: A1+.

_____ 1. The writer implies that believing that weather can influence our health is often based on

a. facts.   c. intuition.

b. research.   d. media stories.

_____ 2. You can conclude that correlations between weather and health found in scientific studies are

a. probably accurate.   c. always accurate.

b. never accurate.   d. somewhat accurate.

3. According to the research, what effect do long stretches of hot weather have on people's moods and behavior?

_____

_____

_____

synchronized (sin′ krò nīzd′) to move or occur at the same time or rate

cacophony (kò käf′ ò nē) harsh, jarring sound; dissonance

4. Do you agree with the writer's suggestion that humans are not too far from their animal roots? Why, or why not?

   _____

   _____

5. Describe your reaction to the following statement, made by biometeorologist Dennis M. Driscoll, as it relates to the selection:

   It takes on the air of the **occult**. It's in the same league as astrology. You can't prove there is an effect—but you can't prove there isn't. All I can say is, if you think you're sick, you probably are.

   _____

   _____

ACTIVITY 7.9

In addition to making inferences and drawing conclusions from written text, you can draw inferences from poetry. What inference can be made from the following poem by Maya Angelou?

. . . Mirror twins are different
although their features jibe,
and lovers think quite different
thoughts
while lying side by side.

We love and lose in China,
we weep on England's moors,
and laugh and moan in Guinea,
and thrive on Spanish shores.

We seek success in Finland,
are born and die in Maine.
In minor ways we differ,
in major we're the same.

---

occult (ô kult′) beyond human understanding; hidden; mysterious

I note the obvious differences
between each sort and type,
but we are more alike, my friends,
than we are unalike.

We are more alike, my friends,
than we are unalike.
We are more alike, my friends,
than we are unalike.

Maya Angelou, untitled poem from *Wouldn't Take Nothing for My Journey Now* 124–25.
Copyright © 1993 by Maya Angelou. Reprinted with the permission of
Random House, Inc.

1. What does the writer suggest about human beings and their differences?

    _____

2. State one conclusion you can reach from the poem.

    _____

Inferences can also be made from cartoons dealing with social and political
issues.

3. What can you infer from this cartoon?

    _____

    _____

Hitch, *San Francisco Examiner and Chronicle* (June 18, 1995.) Reprinted by permission.

4. What can you infer from this cartoon?

_____

_____

Willis, *San Jose Mercury News* (May 16, 1991.) Reprinted with the permission of Scott Willis.

5. What can you infer from this cartoon?

_____

_____

Quality Time   by Gail Machlis

6.   What can you infer from this cartoon?

_____

_____

ACTIVITY 7.10   Drawing Inferences from an Essay

The same strategies you have learned for drawing inferences and conclusions in short passages can be applied to longer ones. Read the following essay on date rape to discover the writer's position and conclusions. To help you gather evidence, marginal notes are included and qualifying terms are circled. Study the notations after reading each paragraph.

Crisis on Campus

Avery Corman

A couple of years ago I decided to write a novel **1** about a campus date rape. Little did I know that by the time *Prized Possessions* was published, the subject would be a burning issue at colleges and in the media—and that some critics would say that even by using the label "date rape" I was lessening the crime and blaming the victim. "Rape is rape," the staunch feminists insist. They make no distinction between **pathological** criminals leaping from behind bushes and college students who find themselves in situations where sex goes wrong on a date. Demonstrations are being waged on campuses large and small to "take back the night" from fellow students who are defined as "rapists." On one campus activists besieged men walking alone and slapped "Gotcha" stickers on them—to show what it's like to be a potential victim.

critics say the term "date rape" lessens the crime & blames the victim

extremists make little distinction between a criminal and when sex goes wrong

Date rape is a dreadful, disturbing crime. But **2** if we place the solution in the hands of extremists with a rigid political agenda tailored to blame men as the historic victimizers of women, we could end up souring the relationships between a whole generation of our young people.

extremists have a political agenda (author's opinion)

Before we go any further here, what exactly is **3** going on? Did an epidemic of date rape suddenly break out across the country? (Some) social observers (say) date rapes have always been underreported and we're finally hearing the bad news. (Others,) the writer Stephanie Guttman chief among them, (say) the only epidemic is of media coverage—that date-rape surveys are seriously flawed and that rape is being redefined to include behavior that isn't rape at all. (Logic tells us) that more young women are now willing to come

2 views:
  a. previously underreported
  b. media hype plus cases that are not true rape

author says—more women are "coming forward"

---

pathological (pá thə lăj′ i kəl) relating to any abnormal condition

forward and say they were raped, and that date rape, a relatively new designation, catches in its net behavior that was never so identified in years past.

In my novel a character says, "One rape is too **4** many." That's pretty much (how I feel) about debating the numbers. The real issue is how to eliminate the crimes.

(I think) one reason young men persist when **5** they don't have consent is that in these sexually liberated times some simply refuse to hear the word "no." They say to themselves: "What's the big deal? She's not a virgin anyway." And some have been so indulged in their lives that they're not accustomed to hearing *any* kind of "no."

But what of young **6** women? Don't they bear any responsibility? One important survey indicated that in nearly half the (alleged) campus date rapes, the woman had been drinking. If you raise that issue, however, many activists regard it as blaming the victim. Yet, the **iconoclastic** author and professor Camille Paglia has written: "Every woman must be prudent and cautious about where she goes and with whom. The (only) solution to date rape is female self-awareness and self-control. A woman's number one line of defense against rape is herself."

Well, (I think) you should include men in that **7** line of defense. To involve women *and* men, colleges need to do what they are in business to do: educate. You need a true dialogue between the sexes on campus. You need discussion of the nature of consent. You need to raise the question of drinking and self-control. You need to do this with *all* students.

I don't see how you can succeed with that **8** educational process if you begin with the view that "rape is rape," pure and simple—that men are historic victimizers and women always their victims. (It) (seems to me) the goal should be change, not

---

iconoclastic (ī kăn′ ə klas′ tik) attacking established ideas

Margin notes:

author says young men today not accustomed to hearing "no"

survey
1/2 of alleged date rapes—women had been drinking
Paglia says women have responsibility

needed—
  education
  dialogue
  discussion
  all students

need for change

blame. How are you going to get any young man to change his thinking, to raise his consciousness, if your starting point is to equate him with a stranger wielding a knife? Inevitably, the result will be resentment and anger on both sides, and this coming at a very impressionable time in the lives of young men and women.

accusations lead to anger & frustration

Many college students today (seem) bewildered by their sexual freedom. Back in pre-sexual-revolution days when I was first dating, men were eager and women were virgins, more or less. Turning back the clock is no solution, but neither is a political war between the sexes. Open, constructive dialogue might do it. It has to. One rape is too many.

9

cannot turn back the clock

approximately 800 words

Avery Corman, "Crisis on Campus," *Family Circle* 13 Aug. 1991: 132. Copyright © 1991 by Avery Corman. Reprinted by permission of the author.

1. a. How many actual facts does the writer give you to prove his belief that reports of the recent upsurge in date rapes are exaggerated?

    _____

    _____

    _____

   b. Is there actually an "epidemic" of date rape or has current media coverage—as opposed to underreporting in the past—caused the statistics to soar?

    _____

    _____

    _____

2. What inference can you draw from the statement in paragraph 6 that a recent survey "indicated that in nearly half the alleged campus date rapes, the woman had been drinking." Note the qualifying word *nearly,* the absence of the name of the survey, and the statement "the woman had been drinking," not "drunk."

    _____

    _____

    _____

3. Why did the writer choose to quote Stephanie Guttman and Camille Paglia?

    _____

    _____

    _____

4. The writer concludes the essay by stating that constructive dialogue is the key to solving the problem of date rape. Is this too simplistic a solution? Explain your answer.

    _____

    _____

    _____

⤳ Fallacies in Reasoning

A sound argument is one in which a conclusion or inference is *logical*. If the argument made is based on false beliefs or mistaken ideas, it is called a *fallacy*. Fallacious arguments are incorrect but can seem quite persuasive, and can "sound right," particularly when they affirm your own opinions.

These are some of the most common types of fallacious reasoning used by speakers and writers in their attempt to disguise the truth.

1. Appeal to Authority

This fallacy is not always easy to pinpoint. Writers may attempt to prove or disprove an argument by referring to well-known personalities who are not authorities on the subject being argued. They use someone's character or authority to try to convince you of an idea instead of using actual evidence or support. Sometimes, the reader does not realize how unqualified these famous people are to discuss such subjects. For example, a so-called expert from Harvard who knew nothing about teaching young children and had never taught them wrote a widely publicized book about how it should be done.

An appeal to authority is also made when celebrities endorse products or political candidates to persuade you to do the same. For example, "Noted psychologist Dr. Frasier Crane recommends that you buy a Dux bed if you have lower back pain problems." As you may know, "Frasier Crane" is a make-believe character from a television sitcom.

2. Appeal Based on Statistics

The old saying "Figures don't lie, but liars figure" applies to the use of statistics. Often, statistics presented to support an argument are insufficient, or they may be "weighted" by leaving out important information. Additionally, some statistics are almost impossible to verify. Consider the following.

> You may have read such startling statements as "Fifteen million whiteflies are being hatched every day." Can such a figure be verified? How does anyone count the number of whiteflies?

3. Bandwagon—Everybody Does It, Everybody Agrees with It

The use of statements such as "Everyone agrees that we must eliminate welfare" is merely an attempt to avoid discussing the issue. The purpose in bandwagon is to make readers feel they are the only ones out of step with current thinking if their ideas on an issue differ. The writer tries to get you to "follow the crowd," that is, "jump" on the bandwagon.

4. Begging the Question

Circular reasoning is another way of saying someone has "begged a question." Begging the question does not mean necessarily that there is an actual question. Rather, the writer attempts to distract you from the real issue or supports an argument by simply repeating in different words what he or she is trying to prove. The statement says the same thing in two ways. For example, if tutors teaching you to speed-read were to say, "The main reason you read so slowly is that you *spend too much time on each word;* to read faster, you should practice *spending less time on each word*—that's all there is to speed-reading," they have given you the cause of slow reading twice and have offered no real solution.

5. Card Stacking

With card stacking, writers ignore conflicting facts that contradict their position. Most people naturally emphasize certain facts over others, but "stacking the cards" occurs when someone deliberately fails to include crucial facts that may weaken an argument. For example, in trying to sell a house, a real estate agent may fail to inform a prospective buyer that a shopping center or a superhighway is to be built directly opposite the intended home, which will lessen the home's value.

6. Either-Or Position

The fallacy of *false dilemma,* also known as "either-or," occurs when we are asked to choose between two extremes without being able to consider additional options. If you are given only two choices, both of which are unpleasant or unsatisfactory, you have a true dilemma. For example, if a jury decides a convicted murderer should *either* be sent to the gas chamber *or* be put to death by lethal injection, no choice has been given to continue life.

7. Hasty Generalization

Many generalizations are made on the basis of either one or only a few examples. The size of the sample is too small to support a conclusion. When writers make a generalization, it must be based on both a sufficient number of instances and a representative sample. For instance, if someone says, "The Senate investigation proves all politicians are untrustworthy and self-serving," you must question whether all members of the Senate can be labeled "untrustworthy" on the basis of this single incident. A hasty generalization, therefore, draws a conclusion on insufficient evidence. One form of hasty generalization is stereotyping.

8. Questionable Cause

Also described as *post hoc,* this fallacy occurs when the writer blames one event on another that came before it. For example, if you have an auto accident a few minutes after a black cat crossed your path, you may come to the illogical conclusion that the cat caused your car crash. In suggesting that one thing is the cause of another, a person fails to consider other reasons. Think, for example, about the controversy over the increase in pregnancy among unmarried teenagers and the cause given as a "lack of responsibility on their part." This is not likely to be the only reason, but it is much easier to blame teenagers than to admit that our entire social system may need to be examined. What about lack of parental supervision? Family breakups? The influence of films and videos?

9. Red Herring

The term *red herring* originated with the practice of drawing a herring (a smoked fish) across a trace in hunting to distract the hounds from following the trail. It is, therefore, a technique for diverting attention from the main issue by introducing an irrelevant or unrelated point. The purpose, of course, is to distract the reader from the real concern or issue. For example, if a large corporation is accused of trying to put smaller ones out of business, the corporation's CEO may argue that her corporation pays its employees more and offers extensive health care benefits. These benefits divert attention from the fact that the corporation is trying to become a monopoly.

10. Slippery Slope

The slippery slope is based on an appeal to fear. It claims that a course of action, a single act, should be avoided because it will lead to undesirable consequences, even though there is no evidence to support this assertion. In other words, to show a proposition is unacceptable, a sequence of increasingly alarming events is shown to follow. For example, in the summer of 1989, U. S. Customs officials were informed a shipment of grapes from Chile was poisoned; upon examining all the incoming shipments, they found two damaged grapes injected with enough cyanide to sicken a person. As a result of this single instance of finding two damaged grapes, all South American grapes were banned.

11. Ad Hominem: "To the Man"

This fallacy occurs when attention is directed to the *person* making an argument rather than to the *issue*. Often, a person's character is attacked to mislead you from the real point, or his or her affiliation with a group is used to bias your opinion. For example, if a state official proposes cutting certain programs because of budgetary problems, he could be attacked as being insensitive and uncaring, or the official's own personal wealth could be cited in an argument against the proposal. Opponents would not even mention the fact that no money is available or that the state is on the verge of bankruptcy.

12. Ad Populum: "To the People"

A writer may evade the real issue by appealing to people's emotions. The writer may use positive words or phrases, such as "the American way," "our flag," or "peace-keepers," to show love of country or may resort to negative words or phrases, such as "villains," "fools," or "flag-burning nerds," to show opposition.

⤳ Using Unbiased Judgments

When you make a statement such as "Good looks are important to career goals," it is an assumption—that is, opinion you believe to be true. In contrast, when you make a judgment, you evaluate whether a statement deserves support or has merit in a particular situation. For example, are good looks important in becoming a qualified pilot, doctor, or accountant? Certainly for a model, a movie star, and a TV personality, physical appearance is important. Therefore, judgments are *reasoned* evaluations of particular ideas, concepts, and situations.

As you read, engage in a dialogue with the author, questioning whether the author is correct about his or her beliefs. At the same time, be open-minded to new ideas that may challenge those you hold. Remember that your own experience and what you know about a topic may sometimes be limited, and you may have to reevaluate some of your previously held ideas.

The chart on page 395 lists steps in arriving at valid inferences, sound conclusions, and unbiased judgments. After you have studied it, complete the final activities in this chapter.

Making Valid Inferences, Drawing Sound Conclusions, and Forming Unbiased Judgments	
UNDERSTAND THE ISSUE AND PROBLEM.	Identify the thesis, main idea, and supporting evidence.
SEPARATE THE FACTS FROM OPINIONS.	Verify the facts. Note whether the opinions are informed or simply the author's assumptions.
BEWARE OF BIAS.	Identify the author's bias or biases. Identify your own bias or biases.
USE YOUR EXPERIENCE.	Look to your own experience, but evaluate how limited it might be in regard to the issue.
REASON AND THINK ABOUT THE ISSUE.	Identify fallacies in the writer's arguments. Identify fallacies in your *own* reasoning.
BECOME A CRITICAL READER.	Make valid inferences. Draw sound conclusions. Form unbiased judgments.

ACTIVITY 7.11   "Fighting" Fallacies

Read the following arguments made by a young man who is having trouble with his girlfriend about how much time he spends watching football. Each argument contains faulty logic. Underline the part of each argument that is illogical. Then, in the blank beside each statement, write the name of the fallacy it contains.

_____ 1. Just because my girlfriend can't throw a pass to save her life, or run 100 yards without fainting, or understand the rules of anything more complicated than Go Fish, this shouldn't mean no one else gets to enjoy the game.

_____ 2. She objects to me harmlessly watching the game, not bothering anyone, just relaxing in front of the TV, yet it's perfectly all right for her own beer-guzzling father to jump up and down and scream profanities at the screen every time the opposing team scores a touchdown.

_____ 3. My girlfriend doesn't understand why I have to spend hours watching football every weekend. I spend hours watching football because that's how long it takes to watch a game.

_____ 4. If I can't kick back with the guys and watch sports, it will be her fault when I turn into some middle-aged, wimpy couch potato with no friends and no social life.

_____ 5.   Last week, she made me go out shopping with her, and I missed the big game. My team lost, and now I'm out the fifty bucks I bet on that game with the guys at work, all because of her.

ACTIVITY 7.12

Read the following statements, all of which are assumptions by their author. Judge whether the author's statement has any fallacies. State whether you agree or disagree with the assumption, and why. Use the space provided.

1. Physical attractiveness, of course, is a powerful stimulus, especially for men. Women look for attractiveness, too, but they are also drawn by status, preferring a leader over a follower, or a slightly older man over a slightly younger one, or a man with more education, or a better job.

   Kathleen Stassen Berger, The Developing Person Through the Life Span

   _____

   _____

   _____

2. It has been suggested that all young Americans be required to perform a year of national service: helping the young, the old, the homeless, the environment . . . they owe something for the freedom they enjoy—and surely nothing would spark an appreciation of personal liberty as much as a term of involuntary **servitude.**

   Peter Tauber, "A Free Country," Family Circle

   _____

   _____

   _____

3. "I hope to break even today," said one gambler to another.
   "Why is that?"
   "I really need the money."

   Saul Kassin, Psychology

   _____

   _____

   _____

_____

servitude (sûr′ və to͞od) bondage; acting like a slave

4. Opponents of abortion worry that once abortion is permissible immediately after conception, no argument will restrict it at any later time in the pregnancy. Then, they fear, one day it will be permissible to murder a fetus that is **unambiguously** a human being. Both pro-choice and pro-lifers (at least some of them) are pushed towards absolutist positions by parallel fears of the slippery slope.

Stuart James Kolner, MD., Pharos

_____

_____

_____

5. AIDS is like a modern form of leprosy. Persons with AIDS are rejected by the community, not only for their life-style (since the disease is one that first hit homosexual men), but also because the disease is incurable. . . . AIDS is often perceived as a threat to the health, well-being, and economic viability of our modern society.

David C. Thomasma and Thomas K. McElkinney, "Ethical Concerns About AIDS."
Copyright by ALPHA OMEGA ALPHA HONOR MEDICAL SOCIETY.

_____

_____

_____

6. The good Joe is friendly and easy; he fits in and likes people . . . with Europeans, he sometimes seems to have a kind of inferiority complex—foreigners tell him he is an "ugly American," "go home Yankee," and he may say conscientiously, "You are probably right," or "Everyone's opinion is worth listening to."

Orrin E. Klapp, Heroes, Villains, and Fools: The Changing American Character

_____

_____

_____

7. Denouncing paramilitary groups as terrorists—or hailing them as patriots—ignores the often-subtle interplay of forces that have led to their rebirth some two centuries after Lexington and Concord. The psychological and cultural dynamics

_____

unambiguously (ən am big′ yoo əs le) absolutely clear

behind this resurrection can't be reduced to a catchy sound bite. But either we understand them—or we risk more Oklahoma **conflagrations.**

Peter Doshock, "The Mind of the Militias," *Psychology Today*

_____

_____

_____

8. Clearly, the U.N. is a complaint desk where many customers leave dissatis-fied. . . . It is a favorite target of nationalistic conservatives. . . . The American people seem to know better. A Times-Mirror poll showed that even though the ranks of the critics have increased, more Americans still view the U.N. favorably than approve of the work of Congress or the Courts.

David Broder, "Evaluated Over 50 Years, the UN Is Extraordinary"

_____

_____

_____

9. If I make an exception for you, then I'll have to make an exception for everyone.

_____

_____

_____

10. America: Love it or leave it!

_____

_____

_____

_____

conflagrations (kon flə grā′ shənz) large and destructive fires

⌒ Summary

Drawing conclusions based on valid inferences is an important aspect of critical reading because much of what we read consists simply of assumptions made by writers. We need to engage in a dialogue with authors, questioning whether they are correct in their beliefs. At the same time, we need to be open-minded to new ideas that challenge those we hold.

You make inferences by reasoning, forming your own conclusions or opinions based on what has been suggested but not stated directly by the writer. Inferences can be valid, based on clear evidence and logical reasoning. On the other hand, inferences can be invalid, merely assumptions resulting from inadequate evidence or arrived at through faulty logic.

Three strategies can assist you in making valid inferences and therefore in drawing sound conclusions.

1. Separate the facts from the opinions.
2. Evaluate the main idea and supporting evidence.
3. Test the logic of your inferences and conclusion.

Critical readers who form unbiased judgments

1. Understand the issue and recognize the facts.
2. Become aware of the author's fallacies and their own biases.
3. Reason through their experiences and the use of logic.

Chapter 7
Vocabulary Review
Introduction to Word Analogy

College entrance exams and qualifying tests for some occupations and professions frequently contain vocabulary test items that require inferential thinking. These tests make use of the relationship of words through *analogy*. An analogy is an implied or unstated relationship between pairs of words. Many relationships can exist between words: a pair of words may be synonyms, antonyms, or homonyms, or they may be related through cause-effect, degree, characteristics, parts of speech, and so on. In analogy, you try to associate one paired item with another. Vocabulary analogies use the colon (:) as a type of shorthand. For example, if pairs of words use the relationship of synonyms, they appear as follows:

adversary:enemy::confidant: _____
(*Friend* is a word that could complete the analogy.)

This can be read in either of the following ways:

1. An *adversary* is to an *enemy* in the same way that a *confidant* is to a *friend*.
2. An *adversary* has the same relationship to an *enemy* as a *confidant* has to a *friend*.

Within each pair, the words are synonyms.

Steps in Solving Analogies

1. Consider the preceding example as A:B::C:?
2. Identify the items in the first part of the analogy (A and B).
3. Determine how these items are related.
4. Consider the items in the second part (C:?) in terms of this relationship.
5. Determine the missing item in the second part (?) to complete the analogy.

A. Complete each set of analogies by filling in an appropriate *synonym;* the words you will use have all appeared in Chapter 7. The first one has been done for you.

1. theory:hypothesis::supposition: *assumption* _____

2. discord:jangle::noise: _____

3. virtuous:honorable::moral: _____

4. compartment:nook::corner: _____

5. refined:polished::cultivated: _____

B. The following practice exercise uses the relationship of synonyms. The first set contains words from previous chapters or words you may know. You are to complete the second pair with a word from Chapter 7; select it from the list of bold-faced words. You will not use all the words listed.

somber   unanimous   constituents   futile   lurid   perdition   plaudits

1. hate:anathema::ruin: _____

2. disillusion:disenchant::useless: _____

3. awards:accolades::praise: _____

4. sepulchral:gloomy::grim: _____

5. willing:amenable::agreement: _____

C. Choose the correct word, and write it in the space provided.

1. Is an **exorbitant** price expensive or inexpensive? _____

2. Are **subtle** remarks easy or difficult to understand? _____

3. Is an **egomaniac** proud or modest? _____

4. In business, is it better to be at the top of the **echelon** or in the center?

    _____

5. Are **relevant** details important or unimportant? _____

Selection 13: **ARTICLE**

 Preparation for Reading

Marriage counselors today suggest that some couples should consider a prenuptial agreement, especially since many marriages end in divorce. Couples do not have to be wealthy to obtain a prenuptial agreement. The following article, "The Prenuptial Agreement," discusses why contracting for such an agreement before marriage creates a dilemma for many couples considering it.

The following boldfaced words are underlined in the article.

the **prerogative**	right or privilege
a **facet**	aspect or phase
primogeniture in England	the first-born has a right to inherit money and property
and not **unconscionable**	not guided or restrained by conscience
equitable distribution	fair; just
disillusioning day	disappointing
the **proverbial** ostrich	expressing a well-known truth or fact (in this case, that the ostrich is a "stupid" bird)
a **bulwark** of open-minded fairness	strong defense

Preview, then read the article.

The Prenuptial Agreement

Elaine Louie

The prenuptial agreement isn't just the prerog-   1 ative of the very rich. It's also becoming a facet of middle-class marriages, even those made in the rosy bloom of youth. It is a tradition that is as old as primogeniture in England. There, it was the parents who decided the terms, and seldom the young couple. The French also have a law that distinguishes between separate and marital property. In the United States, it was usually the wealthy who signed these agreements, either to protect inheritances or, on their second and later marriages, to protect the family interests and money for their children.

What Is a Prenuptial Agreement?

Prenuptial agreements are legal, signed con-   2 tracts of the partners' rights to all sorts of items in the event of a divorce: pets, paintings, property, alimony or maintenance, children (whether or not to have them and after a divorce, who gets them), jewelry, silverware, and business interests. One lawyer had a client who negotiated the pick of the litter. In New York State, you cannot contract to divorce a spouse. Neither can you contract to commit adultery nor dissolve a marriage which would make the other a public charge, the responsibility of the state. Agreements can be short or long, but as matrimonial lawyer Eleanor Alter says, "In New York, terms must be fair when made and not <u>unconscionable</u>." She cites an example. "If when a couple first got married, he made $20,000 and she was to receive $5,000 a year in support, but when they divorce 20 years later, he is making $400,000, that $5,000 support has become unconscionable, and can be disputed in court."

Why Do People Sign Them?

One rather romantic reason people sign these 3 agreements, says attorney Morton Geller, "is that it's an opportunity to control your own destiny." Put another way, in the light of women's consciousness, matrimonial lawyer Rona Shays says, "Young women are beginning to believe the equality of their relationship. For a young couple starting out, economics are not the real thrust of the antenuptial agreement. They sign agreements for personal reasons. They want to define the roles of their relationships rather than economics. They do not want to talk about maintenance if they break up. They ask questions like what if his next stage is a step up on the corporate ladder but her next promotion might mean a move to California." Shays wonders why these young people need a lawyer to talk through ideas on career moves. "Shouldn't they be able to discuss with each other their expectations? Are they unable to communicate directly?" Still, for the young, the prenuptial agreement is precisely that—the vehicle for communication and a quest for independence within the structure of a marriage.

The prenuptial agreement can have a 4 stigma of distrust that is just now beginning to be erased. The San Francisco criminal lawyer Melvin Belli says that some people want their fiancés to sign them because "they're stingy, selfish, and mean." And many people are afraid that to disclose expectations and sign a contract will turn a romantic relationship into a business one. . . . A prenuptial agreement can be a test of insecurity as well as security. What motivates people into signing these contracts is as complex as the people themselves. However, prenuptial agreements come attached with symbolism as well as advantages and disadvantages.

Prenuptial agreements reveal an eye- 5 opening on the part of the women. Previously, many women who have been divorced have been shocked to discover that they were victims of their husbands, and perhaps the courts, and that they were not recipients of anything remotely resembling <u>equitable</u> distribution. Prenuptial agreements are preventive medicine against a <u>disillusioning</u> day in court. For a woman to ask a man to disclose his finances at the onset of a marriage, and vice versa, is a sign of greater, not lesser, communication. It also indicates a smarter woman. Attorney Alter deals with 200 divorces a year. . . .

"There are still a lot of women who say they 6 don't want to know about money, that they can say to the man, 'I trust you.' But at the time of divorce, for every woman who says that the man wouldn't explain his finances to her, there were an equal number of women who didn't want to hear about it." To not know the spouse's income is to function like the <u>proverbial</u> ostrich. If ignorance is bliss on the wedding day, why not have bliss at the divorce court?

For the young couple, Shays does not rec- 7 ommend writing custodial clauses for children that have not yet been born. "Custody depends on the nurturing quality of the parent, and to advise on cultural stereotypes—of who has traditionally been the stereotypical nurturer—is terribly wrong." She points out the obvious facts that people change in five years and that men can be as good nurturers of children as women. To decide who is the better nurturer for a child who is unborn and who may be born a boy, a girl, handsome or ugly, brilliant or retarded, is to make a premature, ignorant decision based entirely on the unknown. . . .

The Second Marriages: A Little Less Romance?

Traditionally, the wealthy man who was burned by his wife at the dissolution of his first marriage is the first to ask the second wife to sign a prenuptial agreement. It is assumed that he has been mortally wounded, taken financially to the cleaners, and that he needs the second wife's signature on the contract as proof that she loves him for himself, and not for his money. . . . 8

The problem then is not that these agreements exist, but whether one or the other is humiliated by it, in the event of a divorce. All the lawyers echo the same advice to anyone, man or woman, young or old, who is asked to sign a prenuptial agreement: Find an independent lawyer who will advise you of your rights. 9

Just because a wealthy person—insecure about whether that person loves him or whether the marriage will endure—has the less monied fiancé sign an agreement does not mean that this agreement has to stay as it is, proof of someone's insecurity. Attorney Belli says, "Sign agreements for three or four years, then get it reviewed. Relationships last such a short time, or they change." People sometimes get more generous with each other, as the marriage goes on. That is the usual hope of the woman whose fiancé says, "Sign this agreement 10

or I won't marry you." He is interpreted to be either extremely insecure, scared, or dominating and controlling. She signs, hoping that he will relax, once married.

While lawyers have seen the most cynical and the most romantic couples sign these agreements, they do not, as a rule, like to negotiate the prenuptial contracts. "I prefer to negotiate separation agreements," says attorney Alter. . . . For young people, too, it's hard to talk about divorce and maintenance when they haven't even been married." 11

Rona Shays says, "The psychology of dealing with people going into their first marriage and asking them to talk about business is against the American ideal of marriage, that it's for better or worse. It's tricky emotionally. People are either not trained or don't want to consider their finances in event of a divorce." 12

Women as Instigators of Agreements

Traditionally, more men than women have asked the future spouse to sign the agreements. This is because men had the larger fortunes. There are widows with inheritances from their own families or a previous spouse who sometimes ask new husbands to sign prenuptial agreements. "But you don't find too many women saying to the man, 'If you don't sign this, I won't marry you,'" says Shays. "Women still feel dependent. You don't cure this emotional dependency with sex-neutral statutes." 13

Prenuptial agreements can be rendered null and void during an ongoing marriage. They can also be held up in a divorce court as a legal document. Still, judges who preside over divorces have their own biases, and some prenuptial agreements can be contested. Courts do not like to rewrite contracts, but if one party says the prenuptial agreement is now unconscionable, the judge will look carefully at the contract. Attorney Alter says, "Professional 14 women are signing prenuptial agreements, and as a matter of principle they say that they don't want alimony. They don't know that the principle may fall by the wayside." A woman might get sick. Her job may disappear. Nothing, not even legal contracts, are certain. But a prenuptial agreement can be a <u>bulwark</u> of open-minded fairness against an eventual, bitter day in divorce court. It can be a covenant of romance and commitment. It can be a weapon of dominance. It is whatever you make it to be.

approximately 1575 words

From Elaine Louie "The Prenuptial Agreement," *House & Garden* June 1981: 16–20. Copyright © 1981 by The Condé Nast Publications Inc. Reprinted by permission of the author.

COMPREHENSION CHECK

Part I
General Comprehension Questions: Literal and Interpretive

Write the correct letter in the space provided.

———— 1. Shays does not recommend that children be included in prenuptial agreements because

    a. women are better at bringing up children.
    b. men should have custody of their sons.
    c. people change and the unborn child is an unknown.
    d. prenuptial agreements should focus on money matters.

———— 2. You can characterize prenuptial agreements as legal documents that protect a spouse's

    a. career change.
    b. job.
    c. diverse items.
    d. character.

———— 3. The main idea of this article is that

    a. although prenuptial agreements are soaring in numbers, they are ineffective.
    b. these agreements cause more problems than solutions.
    c. lawyers dislike handling prenuptial agreements and do a poor job.
    d. these agreements are a form of self-protection and deserve consideration, especially by women.

——— 4. The author concludes that

a. women should protect their economic situation.
b. partners should be able to get out of a relationship.
c. you should be wary about asking about your partner's income.
d. high income will lead to high alimony.

——— 5. The writer implies that prenuptial agreements in New York

a. are superior to those of other states.
b. are unnecessary because laws already exist.
c. require that a sense of ethics and fair play be taken into consideration.
d. are always open to renegotiation.

——— 6. The implication to draw from the comparison of one who does not know what a spouse earns and the "proverbial ostrich" is that

a. animals would have better sense in handling money matters.
b. a spouse's income is a personal matter.
c. ignorance about money matters is absurd.
d. prenuptial agreements sour romantic love.

——— 7. From the statement "[prenuptial agreements are] tricky emotionally. People are either not trained or don't want to consider their finances in case of divorce," you can infer that

a. people don't have time to arrange agreements.
b. people cannot afford legal counsel.
c. people still feel romantic about marriage.
d. people don't listen to a marriage counselor.

8. Write F for fact, O for opinion, or C for a combination of fact and opinion in the space provided. Write your support.

——— a.   "Relationships last such a short time, or they change."

Support: _____

——— b.   "All the lawyers echo the same advice to anyone . . . who is asked to sign a prenuptial agreement: Find an independent lawyer who will advise you of your rights."

Support: _____

9. What inferences can you make from the statement "[prenuptial agreements are] becoming a facet of middle-class marriages"?

_____

_____

10. Contrast reasons for the prenuptial agreements of earlier times and societies to reasons given today in the United States.

_____

_____

Part II
Application Questions for Writing and Discussion

11. The reading says, "For a woman to ask a man to disclose his finances at the onset of marriage . . . is a sign of greater, not lesser, communication. It also indicates a smarter woman." Do you agree? Explain.

_____

_____

_____

_____

12. What conclusions have you drawn about a prenuptial agreement? What would you want to see included in one? Do you plan to have one, or have you ever had one? Why, or why not?

_____

_____

_____

_____

Part III
Extend Your Vocabulary

Circle the correct letter, using the context to determine the meaning of the bold-faced words. The sentences have been taken from the selection.

1. "The prenuptial agreement can have a **stigma** of distrust that is just now beginning to be erased."

   (a) finance   (b) lawyer fee   (c) a sign of disgrace   (d) settlement

2. "Shays does not recommend writing **custodial** clauses for children that have not yet been born."

   (a) monied   (b) price   (c) separate   (d) caring, keeping safe

3. "Men can be as good **nurturers** of children as women."

   (a) mothers   (b) at storytelling   (c) loving providers   (d) at fashions

4. "**Traditionally,** the wealthy man who was burned by his [first] wife . . . is the first to ask the second wife to sign a prenuptial agreement."

   (a) according to established custom   (b) at the present time
   (c) only once in a while   (d) in spite of

5. "There are widows with inheritances from their own families or a previous **spouse** who sometimes ask new husbands to sign prenuptial agreements."

   (a) husband   (b) friend   (c) brother   (d) lover

Selection 14: **TEXTBOOK**

 Preparation for Reading

The following textbook chapter excerpt discusses love, marriage, spousal abuse, and divorce. With the changing customs and values of today's society, marriage patterns have also changed, making the very concept of *marriage* more complex. The definition of the *family* includes such nontraditional arrangements as single parents, couples living with a "significant" other, and same-sex marriages. As you read, decide whether these changes offer partners a better, more fulfilling, relationship.

As with most textbooks, the author provides definitions for many key concepts directly, including **cohabitation, homogamy, heterogamy,** and **marital equity.** The boldfaced words defined below are underlined in the essay.

confound any clear link	confuse, bewilder
ostentatious expenses	showing off; attracting attention in a flashy way
such as **cohort,** religion	companions or associates
amicable, ex-partners, find	friendly

Preview, then read the chapter.

Intimacy: The Development of Love and Marriage

Kathleen Stassen Berger

Although having close friends is one important way to satisfy one's need for affilia- 1
tion, for most adults, having a close relationship with a mate is an even more important goal. Humans try to find one partner, one "significant other," one person with whom to bond throughout life.

Living Together

cohabitation
Literally, "cohabitation" means living together. It is used primarily to refer to unrelated adults of the opposite sex who share the same house or apartment, presumably sharing the same bed as well.

Whereas traditional signs of anticipated partnership involved engagement 2
announcements and wedding bells, in contemporary times, many couples take their first steps toward commitment with an informal sharing of domestic life. They might first deepen their intimacy by spending occasional nights and weekends together—learning what it is like to be in each other's company in a domestic setting around the clock. If the partners enjoy the experience but are not prepared—financially, legally, or emotionally—to marry, this intimacy often leads to their living together, or **cohabitation.** . . .

Official statistics indicate that 40 percent of all young adult North Americans 3
acknowledge cohabiting before their first marriage; the actual numbers are

undoubtedly higher.* One large survey found that half of all cohabiting couples have definite plans to marry their current partner, a third are thinking about it, and only one out of five plans not to marry their current roommate, mostly because they plan never to marry anyone (Bumpass et al., 1991). Not only do many couples consider cohabitation a first step toward marriage, they also believe that cohabitation improves the chances of marital success. . . .

Despite such youthful hopes, cohabitation does not appear to strengthen mar- **4** riage. In fact, the opposite seems true. In many studies in North America as well as in Western Europe, marriages that are preceded by cohabitation typically are less happy and less durable (Nock, 1995). Of course, correlation does not prove causation, and many factors <u>confound</u> any clear link between cohabitation and marital outcome. For instance, couples who decide to cohabit are already at higher risk of divorce than couples who do not, since they tend to be less conventional, [and] less religious, . . . than couples who do not live together without benefit of marriage (DeMaris & Rao, 1992). . . . One indication of this is the fact that wives who cohabited before marriage are three times as likely to have an extramarital affair as are those who did not live with their husbands before the wedding (Forste & Tanfer, 1996).

Although relatively little research has been done on the outcome of cohabita- **5** tion among gays and lesbians, it is clear that long-term homosexual relationships, once rare, or at least more hidden, are now more common and open. An estimated 2 to 5 percent of all American adults spend some part of their lives in gay or lesbian partnerships (Laumann et al., 1994), choosing such commitments either exclusively or in a sequence that includes heterosexual relationships (Kurdek, 1992).

Whatever one's sexual orientation, establishing a committed relationship of sex- **6** ual bonding and intimacy is a highly complex undertaking. Now let us look specifically at marriage.

Marriage

In much of the world, marriage is not what it once was—that is, a legal, and usually **7** religious, arrangement sought at the onset of adulthood as the sole avenue for sexual expression, as the only legitimate context for childbearing, and as a lifelong source of intimacy and support. Among the statistics that make this point are the following: in the United States today, the proportion of adults who are unmarried is higher than at any other time in this century; only 10 percent of brides are virgins; 30 percent of all births are to unmarried mothers; at least another 10 percent of first births are conceived before marriage; the divorce rate is 49 percent of the marriage rate; and the rate of first marriages in young adulthood is the lowest in fifty years (U.S. Bureau of the Census, 1996).

Indeed, between ages 20 and 30, the majority of Americans are unmarried, with **8** 60 percent of the men in this age group and 46 percent of the women never having wed and an additional 3 percent of men and 5 percent of women already divorced

---

* Census Bureau statistics in March 1997 indicated there were 4.13 million unwed couples in the United States.

and not yet remarried. Including the roughly 15 percent who have not yet married by age 40, most American adults now spend, on average, about half of their twenty years between ages 20 and 40 single (U.S. Bureau of the Census, 1996). . . .

Nevertheless, marriage remains the most enduring evidence of couple commit- **9** ment, celebrated in every culture of the world by the wedding—complete with special words, clothes, blessings, food, and drink, and, usually, many guests and <u>ostentatious</u> expense. The hoped-for outcome, of course, is a love that deepens over the years, cemented by events such as bearing and raising children, weathering economic and emotional ups and downs, surviving serious illnesses or other setbacks, and sharing a social life and financial commitments. . . .

Given the high rate at which these expectations are dashed, however, many **10** experts and lay people have tried to figure out what makes a marriage work. One important developmental factor is clear: the age and maturity of the partners. In general, the younger marriage partners are when they first wed, the less likely their marriage is to succeed (Greenstein, 1995).

One explanation for the failure rate of marriages between younger people is **11** that, as Erikson points out, intimacy is hard to establish until identity is secure. Because many older adolescents and young adults are still figuring out their values and roles, a young couple might initially see themselves as compatible only to find their values and roles diverging as they become more mature. . . .

Another factor influencing marital success is the degree to which a couple is **12** homogamous or heterogamous. When studying various cultures around the world, anthropologists draw a distinction between the custom of **homogamy,** that is, marriage within the same tribe or ethnic group, and **heterogamy,** or marriage outside the group. In industrialized nations, homogamy and heterogamy are more a matter of the degree to which the partners are similar in interests, attitudes, and goals, as well as in background variables such as <u>cohort</u>, religion, ethnicity, and local origin. In general, the more homogamous a marriage is, the more likely it is to succeed, partly because the couple's being "on the same page" in many dimensions reduces the potential for tension and disagreement.

One study of 168 young couples found that **social homogamy,** defined as simi- **13** larity in leisure interests and role preferences, is particularly important to marital success (Houts et al., 1996). For instance, if both spouses had a similar level of interest in, say, picnicking, dancing, swimming, going to the movies, listening to music, eating out, and entertaining friends, the partners tended to be more "in love" and more committed to the relationship. . . .

However, the authors of this study criticize those who promote the idea that **14** "finding a mate compatible on many dimensions is an achievable goal." In reality, the authors say, "individuals who are seeking a compatible mate must make many compromises if they are to marry at all," because a high level of marital homogamy is extremely rare. Indeed, according to their research, the odds of finding someone who shares a similar interest in at least three of one's favorite leisure activities and holds a similar view regarding at least three of one's most important role preferences is less than 1 percent. Most successful couples share a few

homogamy As used by developmentalists, the term refers to marriage between individuals who tend to be similar with respect to such variables as attitudes, interests, goals, religion, ethnic background, and local origin.

heterogamy As used by developmentalists, the term refers to marriage between individuals who tend to be dissimilar with respect to such variables as attitudes, interests, goals, religion, ethnic background, and local origin.

social homogamy The similarity with which a couple regard leisure interests and role preferences.

crucial values or interests and otherwise learn to compromise, adjust, or agree to disagree.

marital equity
Refers to the marriage partners' perception of the relative equality of their respective contributions to the marriage.

A third factor affecting the fate of a marriage is **marital equity,** the extent to 15 which the two partners perceive a rough equality in the partnership. According to one theory, called **exchange theory,** marriage is an arrangement in which each person contributes something useful to the other, something the other would find difficult to attain alone. The marriage becomes a stable and happy one when both partners consider the exchange fair. Historically, the two sexes traded quite gender-specific commodities: men provided social status and financial security, while women provided homemaking, sex, and children.

exchange theory
The theory that marriage is an arrangement in which each person contributes something useful to the other, something the other would find difficult to attain alone.

In many modern marriages, however, the equity that is sought involves shared 16 contributions of a similar kind: instead of husbands earning all the money and wives doing all the domestic work, both are now expected to do both. Similarly, both partners expect sensitivity to their needs and equity regarding dependence, sexual desire, shared confidences, and so on. Obviously, this combination is not easy to achieve, as divorce statistics reveal.

Divorce

. . . The ending of a marriage does not occur in a social vacuum but, rather, is influ- 17 enced by factors in the overall social context as well as in the immediate family context, affecting the lives of many people for years to come.

One indication of the impact that the social context has on divorce is the wide 18 variation in divorce rates from nation to nation. The United States has the highest rate of any major country: almost one out of every two marriages ends in divorce. Many other industrialized countries (including Canada, Sweden, Great Britain, and Australia) have a divorce rate of about one in three, while others (including Japan, Italy, Israel, and Spain) have markedly lower rates, with less than one in five marriages ending in divorce (U.S. Bureau of the Census, 1996).

The Role of Expectations

Many developmentalists believe that an underlying explanation for the increasing 19 divorce rate is a cognitive shift that has led most spouses today to expect a great deal more from each other than spouses in the past did. In earlier decades marital equity was judged on the basis of firm gender roles. As long as both partners did their jobs, the marriage usually survived. As one woman, married in 1909, advised newlyweds on her seventy-first wedding anniversary:

> Don't stop on the little things. Be satisfied whatever happens. Ben didn't commit adultery, he's not a gambler, not a liar . . . So what's there to complain about? (Elevenstar, 1980)

Husbands and wives in the past usually did not expect to really understand each 20 other: they generally assumed that masculinity and femininity are opposites and that the sexes therefore are naturally a mystery to each other. Today, marriage partners have a much more flexible view of marriage roles and responsibilities and are likely to expect each other to be a friend, lover, and confidant as well as a wage-earner and caregiver.

Ironically, while couples expect more from a relationship than couples once **21** did, they may at the same time devote less of themselves to a marriage.

Uncoupling

What impact does divorce have on development, in the short term and over time? **22** Initially, the consequences of divorce are usually worse than either partner anticipated in almost every dimension—health, happiness, self-esteem, financial stability, social interaction, and child-rearing (Kitson & Morgan, 1990). The longer a couple has been together, the more intimate they once were, and the more commitments they shared—such as joint property, mutual friends, and, most important, children—the more stress a breakup brings.

There are two reasons for the unanticipated problems. First, before the **23** breakup, unhappy partners are often so focused on what is missing in their relationship that they are "hardly aware of needs currently being well served" (Glenn, 1991). Thus when they do separate, they find that they have suddenly lost benefits they had not noticed they had. Second, even in troubled relationships, emotional dependence almost inevitably deepens over time, so feuding as well as friendly ex-partners are often surprised by the currents of emotion that remain after the breakup. Hostile ex-partners often have to face rejection that is now unrestrained, while <u>amicable</u> ex-partners find that their attempts to start a new life are undermined by feelings of regret and doubt.

Of course, sometimes relationships are so destructive that a breakup—the more **24** radical the better—is a welcome relief. (See A Closer Look, [which follows], on the topic of spouse abuse.) And it is also true that sometimes every aspect of love—passion, intimacy, and commitment—dies long before a formal breakup occurs, minimizing the pain at separation. Nonetheless, ending a long-term marital relationship is almost always difficult.

A Closer Look

Spouse Abuse

Violence in intimate relationships is very common. Surveys in the United States and **25** Canada find that each year about 12 percent of all spouses push, grab, shove, or slap the other, and that between 1 and 3 percent use more extreme measures, hitting, kicking, beating up, or making threats with a knife or a gun (Dutton, 1992). Abuse is also common among unmarried couples living together, whether heterosexual, gay, or lesbian.

What leads to such harmful behavior between people who supposedly love each **26** other? Many contributing factors have been identified, including social pressures that create stress, cultural values that condone violence, personality pathologies (such as poor impulse control), and drug and alcohol addiction. From a developmental perspective, one critical factor is a history of child maltreatment. The child who is physically punished, often and harshly, who is sexually abused, or who witnesses regular spousal assault is at increased risk of becoming an abuser or a victim (Straus & Yodanis, 1996).

common couple violence A form of abuse in which one or both partners of a couple engage in outbursts of verbal and physical attack.

A more detailed examination of spouse abuse reveals that it occurs in two forms. 27 The first form of spouse abuse is called **common couple violence.** This form of abuse entails outbursts of yelling, insulting, and physical attack, but it is not part of a systematic campaign of dominance. The perpetrators in common couple violence are as likely to be women as men, with both partners sometimes becoming involved in a violent argument. Indeed, in many cultural groups, some interspousal violence is acceptable, with 25 percent of all Americans agreeing that it is sometimes "okay" to slap a spouse.

patriarchal terrorism The form of spouse abuse in which the husband uses violent methods of accelerating intensity to isolate, degrade, and punish the wife.

There is almost no hope . . . when couples are locked in the second type of 28 spousal abuse: patriarchal terrorism. **Patriarchal terrorism** occurs when one partner, almost always the man, uses a range of methods to isolate, degrade, and punish the other. Patriarchal terrorism leads to the *battered-wife syndrome,* which includes the woman's being not only periodically beaten but also psychologically and socially broken, living in perpetual fear and self-loathing, without friends or family to turn to, increasingly vulnerable to permanent injury and death. In nearly all cases, patriarchal terrorism becomes more extreme the longer the relationship endures, because the cycle of violence and submission feeds on itself. Each act that renders the wife helpless adds to the man's feeling of control and the woman's feeling that she cannot, must not, fight back.

Many people find it difficult to understand why a woman would stay in such a rela- 29 tionship. There are two prime reasons: she has been conditioned, step-by-step, to accept the abuse, and she has been systematically isolated from those who might encourage her to leave. In addition, if the couple have children, the husband typically uses them as hostages by threatening to kill them if the woman leaves. In many cases, such threats eventually backfire, as mothers who endure abuse themselves finally become brave enough to leave when the damage to the children is glaringly obvious.

Since a battered wife, by definition, cannot break the cycle of abuse on her own, 30 her escape from it requires outside assistance. Such intervention has become increasingly available over the past twenty years, although the woman must still reach out for help. Recognition of patriarchal terrorism in the United States has led to a much tougher approach by law-enforcement agencies, with police more likely to arrest perpetrators of domestic violence and judges more likely to issue and enforce orders of protection. It also has led to a network of shelters for battered women and their children.

approximately 2400 words

Kathleen Stassen Berger, "Intimacy: The Development of Love and Marriage" in *The Developing Person Through the Life Span,* 4th ed. 516–25. Copyright © 1998 by Worth Publishers, Inc. Reprinted by permission of the publisher.

COMPREHENSION CHECK

Part I
General Comprehension Questions: Literal and Interpretive

Write the correct letter in the space provided.

_____ 1. The number of couples living together who make plans to get married is

    a. less than 25%.
    b. about 30%.
    c. around 50%.
    d. between 10% and 15%.

_____ 2. According to the author, cohabitation does not appear to strengthen a marriage because such couples are

    a. generally unconventional
    b. less religious.
    c. sometimes unfaithful.
    d. all of the above.

_____ 3. What evidence is given that the institution of marriage is changing?

    a. Only 10% of brides are virgins.
    b. More than 10% of adults are gay or lesbian.
    c. Unwed mothers account for 30% of all births.
    d. Both a and c.

_____ 4. What factors were stated as significant in making a marriage work?

    a. financial security and social status
    b. good looks and sex appeal
    c. age and maturity
    d. religious beliefs and ethnicity

_____ 5. Of those mentioned, which country has the lowest divorce rate?

    a. Japan
    b. China
    c. Canada
    d. Australia

_____ 6. What inference can you draw from the fact that one in two marriages in the United States end in divorce?

    a. American men are fickle.
    b. American women like to flirt.
    c. Most people don't want to be tied down.
    d. Many couples do not realize they are not compatible because they have yet to mature sufficiently.

7. **Fact/Opinion/Combination:** For each statement from the text, write F, O, or F/O in the space provided, and then write support for your answer.

_____ a. "Despite such youthful hopes, cohabitation does not appear to strengthen marriage."

Support: _____

_____ b. "In fact, the opposite seems true."

Support: _____

_____ c. "In general, the younger marriage partners are when they first wed, the less likely their marriage is to succeed."

Support: _____

8. *Valid/Invalid Inferences:* Write V (valid) or I (invalid) for each of the following inferences, based on the section "Spouse Abuse," and give your support in the space provided.

_____ a. Violence is common in many close relationships.

Support: _____

_____ b. Television and other media are responsible for encouraging abusive behavior.

Support: _____

_____ c. The mistreatment of children can often affect them emotionally and psychologically.

Support: _____

_____ d. *Battered-wife syndrome* results in men becoming more controlling and women being more submissive.

Support: _____

Part II
Application Questions for Writing and Discussion

9. a. Is cohabitation, a couple living together, a positive or negative influence on marriage? Explain your answer.

_____

b. Do you think couples should live together before getting married? Why, or why not?

_____

_____

10. Study the graph below, which shows that nearly one of every two marriages currently ends in divorce. What, if anything, can be done to reverse the statistics to the levels of the 1940s and 1950s? (Refer to pages 593–94 if you need assistance in interpreting line graphs.)

_____

_____

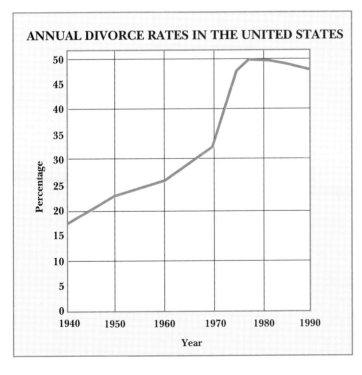

ANNUAL DIVORCE RATES IN THE UNITED STATES

Percentage

50
45
40
35
30
25
20
15
10
5
0

1940 1950 1960 1970 1980 1990

Year

FIGURE 7.3 That the divorce rate has leveled off in recent years in the United States can be seen as an encouraging sign—except for the fact that the leveling-off has occurred at about one divorce for every two marriages, a rate that is higher than that of any other nation in the world.

Part III
Extend Your Vocabulary

A. Note the boldfaced word in the first sentence or excerpt of each set, quoted directly from the chapter. In the second sentence, fill in a different suffixed form of that word to complete the sentence. The first word is completed for you.

1.   " . . . Marriages that are **preceded** by cohabitation typically are less happy and less durable."

They set a _precedent_ by remaining pure before taking their wedding vows.

2.   "One important **developmental** factor is clear: the age and maturity of the partners."

In _____ their plans, the couple decided to adopt a child.

3.   " . . . **Similarity** in leisure interest and role preferences . . . is particularly important to marital success."

The bridesmaids were all dressed _____.

4.   " . . . An underlying explanation for the increasing divorce rate is a **cognitive** shift. . . ."

Her _____ of the situation confirmed she had made a good choice.

5.   "Of course, sometimes relationships are so **destructive** that a breakup . . . is a welcome relief."

Because of the fire's _____, the home had to be completely rebuilt.

B. Match the short definition in column II with the appropriate term in column I.

Column I	Column II
_____ 1. homogamy	a. living together
_____ 2. cohabitation	b. violent husband
_____ 3. patriarchal terrorism	c. similar interests
_____ 4. marital equity	d. different interests
_____ 5. heterogamy	e. equal contributions

Selection 15: **LITERATURE**

 Preparation for Reading

Amy Tan had a meteoric rise to fame as a result of her first book, *The Joy Luck Club,* from which the selection that follows has been excerpted. For that work, she won the National Book Award in 1989.

She was born in Oakland, California, and grew up in the San Francisco Bay Area. Her work has been translated into twenty languages. In 1995, she was awarded the prestigious English literature prize for female authors, the Orange Prize for Fiction. She has written a number of other novels, including *The Kitchen God's Wife, The Hundred Secret Senses,* and *The Chinese Siamese Cat.*

Amy Tan

In this excerpt from *The Joy Luck Club,* Waverly Jong, a thirtyish Chinese-American lawyer, is in a quandary over how to inform her traditionally minded Chinese parents that she plans to marry Rich, a red-haired, freckle-faced Caucasian with whom she works. Read the selection to see what develops, as Waverly introduces Rich to her parents.

From The Joy Luck Club

Amy Tan

"You know, I really don't understand you," said Marlene when I called her the night 1 after I had shown my mother the mink jacket. "You can tell the IRS to piss up a rope, but you can't stand up to your own mother."

"I always intend to and then she says these little sneaky things, smoke bombs and little barbs, and . . ."

"Why don't you tell her to stop torturing you," said Marlene. "Tell her to stop ruining your life. Tell her to shut up."

"That's hilarious," I said with a half-laugh. "You want me to tell my mother to shut up?"

"Sure, why not?"   5

"Well, I don't know if it's explicitly stated in the law, but you can't *ever* tell a Chinese mother to shut up. You could be charged as an accessory to your own murder."

I wasn't so much afraid of my mother as I was afraid for Rich. I already knew what she would do, how she would attack him, how she would criticize him. She would be quiet at first. Then she would say a word about something small, something she had noticed, and then another word, and another, each one flung out like a little piece of sand, one from this direction, another from behind, more and more, until his looks, his character, his soul would have eroded away. And even if I recognized her strategy, her sneak attack, I was afraid that some unseen speck of truth would fly into my eye, blur what I was seeing and transform him from the divine man I thought he was into someone quite mundane, mortally wounded with tiresome habits and irritating imperfections.

This happened to my first marriage, to Marvin Chen, with whom I had eloped when I was eighteen and he was nineteen. When I was in love with Marvin, he was nearly perfect. He graduated third in his class at Lowell and got a full scholarship to Stanford. He played tennis. He had bulging calf muscles and one hundred forty-six straight black hairs on his chest. He made everyone laugh and his own laugh was deep, sonorous, masculinely sexy. He prided himself on having favorite love positions for different days and hours of the week; all he had to whisper was "Wednesday afternoon" and I'd shiver.

But by the time my mother had had her say about him, I saw his brain had shrunk from laziness, so that now it was good only for thinking up excuses. He chased golf and tennis balls to run away from family responsibilities. His eye wandered up and down other girls' legs, so he didn't know how to drive straight home anymore. He liked to tell big jokes to make other people feel little. He made a loud show of leaving ten-dollar tips to strangers but was stingy with presents to family. He thought waxing his red sports car all afternoon was more important than taking his wife somewhere in it.

My feelings for Marvin never reached the level of hate. No, it was worse in a way. **10** It went from disappointment to contempt to apathetic boredom. It wasn't until after we separated, on nights when Shoshana was asleep and I was lonely, that I wondered if perhaps my mother had poisoned my marriage.

Thank God, her poison didn't affect my daughter, Shoshana. I almost aborted her, though. When I found out I was pregnant, I was furious. I secretly referred to my pregnancy as my "growing resentment," and I dragged Marvin down to the clinic so he would have to suffer through this too. It turned out we went to the wrong kind of clinic. They made us watch a film, a terrible bit of puritanical brainwash. I saw those little things, babies they called them even at seven weeks, and they had tiny, tiny fingers. And the film said the baby's translucent fingers could *move,* that we should imagine them clinging for life, grasping for a chance, this miracle of life. If they had shown *anything else* except tiny fingers—so thank God they did. Because Shoshana really was a miracle. She was perfect. I found every detail about her to be remarkable, especially the way she flexed and curled her fingers. From the very moment she flung her fist away from her mouth to cry, I knew my feelings for her were inviolable.

But I worried for Rich. Because I knew my feelings for him were vulnerable to being felled by my mother's suspicions, passing remarks, and innuendos. And I was afraid of what I would then lose, because Rich Schields adored me in the same way I adored Shoshana. His love was unequivocal. Nothing could change it. He expected nothing from me; my mere existence was enough. And at the same time, he said that he had changed—for the *better*—because of me. He was embarrassingly romantic; he insisted he never was until he met me. And this confession made his romantic gestures all the more ennobling. At work, for example, when he would staple "FYI—For Your Information" notes to legal briefs and corporate returns that I had to review, he signed them at the bottom: "FYI—Forever You & I." The firm didn't know about our relationship, and so that kind of reckless behavior on his part thrilled me.

The sexual chemistry was what really surprised me, though. I thought he'd be one of those quiet types who was awkwardly gentle and clumsy, the kind of mild-mannered guy who says, "Am I hurting you?" when I can't feel a thing. But he was so attuned to my every movement I was sure he was reading my mind. He had no inhibitions, and whatever ones he discovered I had he'd pry away from me like little treasures. He saw all those private aspects of me—and I mean not just sexual private parts, but my darker side, my meanness, my pettiness, my self-loathing—all the things I kept hidden. So that with him I was completely naked, and when I was, when I was feeling the most vulnerable—when the wrong word would have sent me flying out the door forever—he always said exactly the right thing at the right moment. He didn't allow me to cover myself up. He would grab my hands, look me straight in the eye and tell me something new about why he loved me.

I'd never known love so pure, and I was afraid that it would become sullied by my mother. So I tried to store every one of these endearments about Rich in my memory, and I planned to call upon them again when the time was necessary.

After much thought, I came up with a brilliant plan. I concocted a way for Rich **15** to meet my mother and win her over. In fact, I arranged it so my mother would want to cook a meal especially for him. I had some help from Auntie Suyuan. Auntie Su was my mother's friend from way back. They were very close, which meant they were ceaselessly tormenting each other with boasts and secrets. And I gave Auntie Su a secret to boast about.

After walking through North Beach one Sunday, I suggested to Rich that we stop by for a surprise visit to my Auntie Su and Uncle Canning. They lived on Leavenworth, just a few blocks west of my mother's apartment. It was late afternoon, just in time to catch Auntie Su preparing Sunday dinner.

"Stay! Stay!" she had insisted.

"No, no. It's just that we were walking by," I said.

"Already cooked enough for you. See? One soup, four dishes. You don't eat it, only have to throw it away. Wasted!"

How could we refuse? Three days later, Auntie Suyuan had a thank-you letter **20** from Rich and me. "Rich said it was the best Chinese food he has ever tasted," I wrote.

And the next day, my mother called me, to invite me to a belated birthday dinner for my father. My brother Vincent was bringing his girlfriend, Lisa Lum. I could bring a friend, too.

I knew she would do this, because cooking was how my mother expressed her love, her pride, her power, her proof that she knew more than Auntie Su. "Just be sure to tell her later that her cooking was the best you ever tasted, that it was far better than Auntie Su's," I told Rich. "Believe me."

The night of the dinner, I sat in the kitchen watching her cook, waiting for the right moment to tell her about our marriage plans, that we had decided to get married next July, about seven months away. She was chopping eggplant into wedges, chattering at the same time about Auntie Suyuan: "She can only cook looking at a recipe. My instructions are in my fingers. I know what secret ingredients to put in just by using my nose!" And she was slicing with such a ferocity, seemingly inattentive to her sharp cleaver, that I was afraid her fingertips would become one of the ingredients of the red-cooked eggplant and shredded pork dish.

I was hoping she would say something first about Rich. I had seen her expression when she opened the door, her forced smile as she scrutinized him from head to toe, checking her appraisal of him against that already given to her by Auntie Suyuan. I tried to anticipate what criticisms she would have.

Rich was not only *not* Chinese, he was a few years younger than I was. And unfortunately, he looked much younger with his curly red hair, smooth pale skin, and the splash of orange freckles across his nose. He was a bit on the short side, compactly built. In his dark business suits, he looked nice but easily forgettable, like somebody's nephew at a funeral. Which was why I didn't notice him the first year we worked together at the firm. But my mother noticed everything. **25**

"So what do you think of Rich?" I finally asked, holding my breath.

She tossed the eggplant in the hot oil and it made a loud, angry hissing sound. "So many spots on his face," she said.

I could feel the pinpricks on my back. "They're freckles. Freckles are good luck, you know," I said a bit too heatedly in trying to raise my voice above the din of the kitchen.

"Oh?" she said innocently.

"Yes, the more spots the better. Everybody knows that." **30**

She considered this a moment and then smiled and spoke in Chinese: "Maybe this is true. When you were young, you got the chicken pox. So many spots, you had to stay home for ten days. So lucky, you thought."

I couldn't save Rich in the kitchen. And I couldn't save him later at the dinner table.

He had brought a bottle of French wine, something he did not know my parents could not appreciate. My parents did not even own wineglasses. And then he also made the mistake of drinking not one but two frosted glasses full, while everybody else had a half-inch "just for taste."

When I offered Rich a fork, he insisted on using the slippery ivory chopsticks. He held them splayed like the knock-kneed legs of an ostrich while picking up a large chunk of sauce-coated eggplant. Halfway between his plate and his open mouth, the chunk fell on his crisp white shirt and then slid into his crotch. It took several minutes to get Shoshana to stop shrieking with laughter.

And then he had helped himself to big portions of the shrimp and snow peas, **35** not realizing he should have taken only a polite spoonful, until everybody had had a morsel.

He had declined the sautéed new greens, the tender and expensive leaves of bean plants plucked before the sprouts turn into beans. And Shoshana refused to eat them also, pointing to Rich: "He didn't eat them! He didn't eat them!"

He thought he was being polite by refusing seconds, when he should have followed my father's example, who made a big show of taking small portions of seconds, thirds, and even fourths, always saying he could not resist another bite of something or other, and then groaning that he was so full he thought he would burst.

But the worst was when Rich criticized my mother's cooking, and he didn't even know what he had done. As is the Chinese cook's custom, my mother always made disparaging remarks about her own cooking. That night she chose to direct it toward her famous steamed pork and preserved vegetable dish, which she always served with special pride.

"Ai! This dish not salty enough, no flavor," she complained, after tasting a small bite. "It is too bad to eat."

This was our family's cue to eat some and proclaim it the best she had ever **40** made. But before we could do so, Rich said, "You know, all it needs is a little soy sauce." And he proceeded to pour a riverful of the salty black stuff on the platter, right before my mother's horrified eyes.

And even though I was hoping throughout the dinner that my mother would somehow see Rich's kindness, his sense of humor and boyish charm, I knew he had failed miserably in her eyes.

Rich obviously had had a different opinion on how the evening had gone. When we got home that night, after we put Shoshana to bed, he said modestly, "Well. I think we hit it off *A-o-kay*." He had the look of a dalmatian, panting, loyal, waiting to be petted.

"Uh-hmm," I said, I was putting on an old nightgown, a hint that I was not feeling amorous. I was still shuddering, remembering how Rich had firmly shaken both my parents' hands with that same easy familiarity he used with nervous new clients. "Linda, Tim," he said, "we'll see you again soon, I'm sure." My parents' names are Lindo and Tin Jong, and nobody, except a few older family friends, ever calls them by their first names.

"So what did she say when you told her?" And I knew he was referring to our getting married. I had told Rich earlier that I would tell my mother first and let her break the news to my father.

"I never had a chance," I said, which was true. How could I have told my mother **45** I was getting married, when at every possible moment we were alone, she seemed to remark on how much expensive wine Rich liked to drink, or how pale and ill he looked, or how sad Shoshana seemed to be.

Rich was smiling. "How long does it take to say, Mom, Dad, I'm getting married?"

"You don't understand. You don't understand my mother."

Rich shook his head. "Whew! You can say that again. Her English was *so* bad. You know, when she was talking about that dead guy showing up on *Dynasty*,

I thought she was talking about something that happened in China a long time ago."

approximately 2200 words

Amy Tan, from "Four Directions," *The Joy Luck Club* 173–79. Copyright © 1989 by Amy Tan. Reprinted by permission of The Putnam Publishing Group.

Questions for Writing and Discussion

1. What are some of the previous assumptions held by Waverly's mother that complicate the present situation?
2. What conclusion can you draw about Rich's personality based on Waverly's description of him: "He had the look of a dalmatian, panting, loyal, waiting to be petted"? How does Rich's personality complicate his relationship with Waverly?
3. If you were Waverly's friend, what advice would you have given her prior to the introduction of Rich to her parents? What advice might you have also offered Rich?
4. Why does the writer include the episode with Waverly's aunt?

Working with the WORLD WIDE WEB

 If you would like to know more about Amy Tan, here is one Web site address with information about her works:

http://www.luminarium.org/contemporary/amytan/

 JOURNAL ENTRY

The three selections you read—the article "The Prenuptial Agreement," the textbook selection "Intimacy: The Development of Love and Marriage," and the literature selection from *The Joy Luck Club*—all deal with difficulties involved in lasting relationships. Discuss how the status of marriage might be viewed in the next decade. What important changes do you see in the future? What kind of marriage would you want to have, and why?

8

Understanding the Power of Persuasive Language

This chapter will help you

* Learn to differentiate between denotative and connotative language.
* Understand the persuasive power of words.
* Become aware of figurative and euphemistic language.

Before reading, think about these questions.

* What are some ways writers of essays and articles slant what they write?
* How many of your daily decisions are influenced by commercial advertising in newspapers, magazines, and on television or the Internet?
* Do the media and governments sometimes abuse the power of persuasive language?

Jot down your thoughts about how critically you evaluate what you read.

_____

_____

_____

⤳ The Two Dimensions of Word Meanings: Denotation and Connotation

During your college years, you will add many new words to your vocabulary. As you have learned, a strong vocabulary is essential in adult and college reading. But it is not enough to know the dictionary definition of words; you must also understand their *suggested* meaning to avoid being manipulated by writers with a particular bias or attitude.

Word choice is often an indication of the writer's attitude toward the subject and should provide you with yet another clue for making valid inferences and drawing reasonable conclusions. Indeed, you can often infer a writer's *unspoken* attitude by the words used. Be aware, too, that the writer's choice of words is often meant to influence you to feel or think the way he or she wants you to. Thus, when you are reading, it is important to recognize both the denotative and connotative language the writer has chosen to express ideas and opinions.

Denotation

Denotation refers to a word's literal meaning, its accepted dictionary definition. *Denotation is the meaning of a word independent of any emotional association.* It is impersonal and neutral.

Textbook writers generally use denotative language, words that are impersonal, factual, objective, or neutral, as in the following example:

> The world's two most populous countries, India and China, will heavily influence future prospects for global overpopulation. These two countries, together encompassing more than one-third of the world's population, have adopted different policies to control population growth. In the absence of strong family-planning programs, India adds about 4 million more people each year than China. At current rates of natural increase, India will surpass China as the world's most populous country by the middle of the twenty-first century.
>
> William H. Renwick and James M. Rubenstein, *Introduction to Geography*

Connotation

When the meaning of a word goes beyond its accepted, agreed-upon dictionary definition, it becomes the *connotation* of the word. *The connotation of a word includes all the ideas, associations, and implications suggested above and beyond the dictionary definition.* Connotations may be either positive or negative. Depending on how they are used, many words can **evoke** an emotional response in the reader, stir up the reader's feelings, or create a visual image. Some words, however, are stronger in connotation than others. For example, the word *relax* generally suggests taking time off to rest. The word *loaf,* on the other hand, also refers to taking time off, but the connotative

---

evoke (i vōk′) to call forth; to produce or elicit a reaction, emotion, or response

meaning implies that the time off is spent idly or wastefully. A clear example of how the connotation of words can be shifted in emphasis is found in the famous remark Bertrand Russell, the philosopher and author, once made: "I am *firm;* you are *stubborn;* he is *pig-headed.*" While all three terms have a similar denotative meaning, their connotations are obviously quite different.

ACTIVITY 8.1 **Practice Distinguishing Denotative and Connotative Language**

To develop your awareness of the two dimensions of words, complete the following activity. First, note the denotative or dictionary meaning of the words in the first column. Then, for each of these words, read the two additional words opposite them, both with connotative meanings. While the denotations of all three words are often quite similar, the words clearly connote different things. Indicate whether you believe the connotations are positive (P) or negative (N). The first one is done for you.

Term	Denotation	Connotation	
1. home	the place where one lives	mansion __P__	shack __N__
2. prison	a place where persons are confined	jail _____	correctional facility _____
3. intoxicated	without control	inebriated _____	drunk _____
4. pornography	indecent writing	erotica _____	smut _____
5. war	armed conflict	freedom fighting _____	massacre _____
6. fear	anxiety caused by danger	reverence _____	dread _____
7. talk	exchange ideas by spoken words	discussion _____	gossip _____
8. love	a deep and tender feeling	infatuation _____	devotion _____
9. frugal	not wasteful; living simply	thrifty _____	cheap _____
10. inquisitive	seeking information	curious _____	prying _____

The Persuasive Power of Words

While denotative language is commonly used in informational writing such as textbooks, connotative language is frequently used in the persuasive writing of editorials, book and film reviews, advertisements, and political speeches. These written forms rely on words with strong connotations, on those words with the power to sway emotions and influence the reader and what the reader may infer.

Depending on their purpose, writers select words that create either pleasant or unpleasant responses. Someone writing an ad for a breakfast cereal, for example, would most likely compose phrases such as "the cereal that fits your light, active lifestyle," "wholesome crunchy taste of sunny corn," and "goodness in every bite," using positive and pleasing words that encourage you to purchase the product.

ACTIVITY 8.2 Practice Finding Connotative Words in Ads

Study the Smith Corona ad and circle the descriptive words used to try to convince you how their products can enhance learning.

Courtesy Smith Corona Corporation

You should have circled phrases such as "do a job right," "no tools more perfect," "Fear of technology is replaced by freedom to think," "writing becomes easier," "Work becomes more enjoyable," "turn on your mind," and "exceedingly simple."

What does the ad imply that Smith Corona products can do?

_____

_____

Circle the descriptive words and phrases in the Data Broadcasting ad used to try to convince you that its product can change your world in 15 minutes!

If you don't think your world can change in 15 minutes, try holding your breath that long.

With DBC's QuoTrek,® you've got your whole financial world right in the palm of your hand.

To make money, you need the right information, right now. The newspaper is yesterday's news, and quotes delayed 15 minutes are ancient history. QuoTrek is the only portable way to stay in touch with the market in real time, so you can buy and sell smarter with real-time quotes for 100,000 stocks, futures, funds, bonds, foreign exchanges, and Dow Jones headlines. Watch your

portfolio throughout the day, and be visually or audibly alerted to changes and money-making opportunities. More investors turn to DBC for real-time information and independent analysis, so they don't miss opportunities to make money. And that's what QuoTrek delivers, right when you need it, where you need it.

Get a hold on your portfolio. Call today.
1-800-779-8717ext.2114
or at http://www.dbc.com

 DATA BROADCASTING CORPORATION

Real real time is <u>real</u> real money.℠

QuoTrek is a registered trademark of Data Broadcasting Corporation.
©1996 Data Broadcasting Corporation

Smart Money (March 1997). Reprinted by permission of Data Broadcasting Corporation.

1. Did you circle phrases such as "right information" and "buy and sell smarter"?

    _____

    _____

    _____

2. What other words or phrases did you circle?

    _____

    _____

    _____

3. Would you purchase this device, based on what this ad promises it can do? Why, or why not?

    _____

    _____

    _____

Like writers of advertisements, essayists imply approval of their ideas by using words with positive connotations, words that flatter or even exaggerate, such as *excellent, superb,* and *outstanding*. While these words imply approval, negative words that **disparage** or criticize—*foolish, awkward,* and *ignorant*—imply disapproval.

Ask this key question to evaluate writers' attempts to influence your thinking by the selection or slant of their words.

Are the descriptive words used primarily positive or negative, favorable or unfavorable, pleasant or unpleasant?

⤳ Connotative Language

After you have identified the connotative language used, you can more accurately understand an author's attitude toward a subject, even if you disagree with that opin-

---

disparage (dis par′ ij) discredit; belittle

ion. In order to distinguish positive or negative connotations and the writer's slant, we can map the connotative terms. By the end of the reading, we have a visual record of the essential words chosen, and we can more readily infer how the writer feels about the topic.

Examine the connotative words about the movie *Titanic* in Letter A, which follows.

LETTER A

I have seen "Titanic" six times, and I am still not tired of it ("Our Titanic Love Affair," The Arts, Feb. 23). It reminds me of how movies used to be made: grand spectacles with dramatic love stories and characters we wish we could be. When every other movie is either a tired action adventure or an edgy independent film, "Titanic" is a fresh dose of old-fashioned drama.

Tanya Chirayil
Ringwood, N.J.
Newsweek

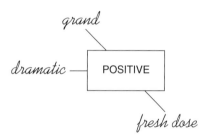

These positive words indicate that the letter writer found the movie exciting, so you can infer that watching it may be worthwhile.

To see how the slant of the message can be reversed, add connotative words to the map following Letter B.

LETTER B

"Titanic" is a brilliant two hours of soppy romance for girls followed by an hour of adventure for boys. James Cameron appeals to mall rats of all ages by tickling their teenage vanity. In his movie the hero and heroine run around the ship giggling, sneaking kisses, spitting over the side, flipping the finger, having sex in the back seat of a car and whining that life is unfair. If "Titanic" does win the Oscar for best picture, it will be for the same reason it's earned more than $1 billion worldwide—not because it's good but because it's just the right kind of lousy.

Jim Lane
Sacramento, Calif.

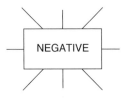

What can you infer is the attitude of the writer of Letter B toward the movie *Titanic?*

_____

_____

ACTIVITY 8.3   Practice Finding Connotative Terms in Passages

PASSAGE 1

Read the following excerpt from the book *The Fashion Conspiracy,* by the British reporter Nicholas Coleridge, to learn about one aspect of the fashion industry and discover his attitude toward it. Circle the descriptive words and phrases, and write them around the mapping boxes. Are these connotative words chiefly negative or positive? Place a check mark in the appropriate box.

It is normal in the fashion industry to have exactly the same conversation in Milan as in London, and in Tokyo as in New York. Because the fashion circus is constantly on the move—not just the designers, but the photographers, store buyers, fashion editors and models—it creates its own homogeneous society, at once international and profoundly **xenophobic.** A buyer for a New York store will fly 200,000 miles a year from fashion capital to fashion capital, inspecting collections, but she will eat at the same few fashion restaurants and discuss the same tiny cast of characters. . . .

The private language of fashion embraces the five capitals. In his essay on "Linguistics and Anthropology" in *Structural Anthropology,* Claude Lévi-Strauss defines the relationship between language and culture. "Among us [western developed man]," he writes, "language is used in a rather reckless way—we talk all the time, we ask questions about many things. This is not at all a universal situation. There are cultures—and I am inclined to say most of the cultures of the world—which are rather thrifty in relation to language. They don't believe that language should be used indiscriminately. . . .

---

xenophobic (zen ə fō bik) *fearing or hating strangers or foreigners*

The fashion industry is the **antithesis** of Lévi-Strauss's thrifty culture. It uses language so indiscriminately that it has actually created a parallel vocabulary, in which everyday words take on specific fashion connotations, entirely misleading to the outsider. Basic (as in "your basic wardrobe," "your best basic") and essential ("the essential black leather skirt") are straightforward antitheses when hijacked by fashion writers. A black leather skirt is clearly not an "essential" garment, any more than a fuchsia wool-and-cashmere Gianfranco Ferre shawl, costing $1,595, can reasonably be described as "basic." But language of fashion is not restricted to magazine copywriting. Because people in the fashion industry tend to be more visually than verbally literate, their conversation takes on an exaggerated cartoon quality. Places are described as "fabulous" or "a nightmare"; collections are "brilliant" or "hideous"; particular restaurants are "to die for" or to be avoided.

approximately 340 words

Nicholas Coleridge, "The Emperor's New Clothes" from *The Fashion Conspiracy*

1. a. Give two examples of specific connotative words used in the world of fashion.

    _____

    _____

    b. What does the writer suggest is the influence of language, particularly its connotations, on the designer industry?

    _____

    _____

2. How much influence do the words clothing advertisers use have on your choice of what to buy and wear? Explain your answer.

    _____

    _____

---

antithesis (an thith′ ò sis) contrast or opposition of thoughts

PASSAGE 2

Read the passage, and circle the connotative words. Are the words chiefly positive or negative? Check the appropriate box, and then answer the question below.

Strength of a Single Syllable

When you speak and write, no law says you have to use big words. Short words are as good as long ones, and short, old words like *sun* and *grass* and *home* are best of all. A lot of small words, more than you might think, can meet your needs with a strength, grace and charm that large words lack.

Big words can make the way dark for those who hear what you say and read what you write. They add fat to your prose. Small words are the ones we seem to have known from birth. They are like the hearth fire that warms the home, and they cast a clear light on big things: night and day, love and hate, war and peace, life and death.

Short words are bright, like sparks that glow in the night; sharp like the blade of a knife; hot like salt tears that scald the cheek; quick like moths that flit from flame to flame; and terse like the dart and sting of a bee.

If a long word says just what you want, do not fear to use it. But know that our tongue is rich in crisp, brisk, swift, short words. Make them the spine and the heart of what you speak and write. Like fast friends, they will not let you down.

Richard Lederer, "Strength of a Single Syllable" from *The Miracle of Language,* in *Reader's Digest*

What do the descriptive words suggest?

_____

_____

_____

PASSAGE 3

Analyze the language in the paragraphs that follow, circling positive and negative words and phrases. These words should help you infer the young writer's attitude toward who is to blame for teenagers' use of drugs.

Teens Take Drugs Because There's Nothing Else to Do

The only way to get teens to stop using drugs is to make reality more appealing.

It is natural for everyone to experiment when they are young, but as a 19-year-old, I can tell you that people I know use drugs mainly because they're *bored*. And I don't blame them.

The measures that have been adopted to control the "problem"—closing beaches at night, curfews, closing clubs to those under 21, persecution of youth-oriented businesses and police patrols harassing youths in public areas—may make supplying drugs more difficult. But they only end up *increasing* demand and inspiring fear and contempt among teens of senseless authoritarian law enforcement that jumps down their throats every time they try to have a little fun.

If as much effort and money were spent on things for young people to *do* at night as has been wasted on jailing users and **draconian** efforts to stop the supply of drugs, nobody would *want* to use drugs because there would be so many other, more fun, alternatives.

It would probably have the added benefit of cutting down on teen pregnancy and sexually transmitted disease, sex being the other big time-killer among bored teens.

Society will never be able to protect us from the supposed evils of drug use through fear and restricted freedoms. It's about time we addressed the problem of *why* everyone is so desperate to get high.

Brad Hill, "Teens Take Drugs Because There's Nothing Else to Do," *San Jose Mercury News*, 23 July 1995. Copyright © 1995. Reprinted by permission.

1. What do the connotative words you circled suggest about the author's feelings for "authoritarian law enforcement"?

   _____

   _____

2. Do you agree with the writer that teens turn to drugs out of boredom?

   _____

_____

draconian (dra kō′ nē ən) of a law or code that is extremely severe or harsh

PASSAGE 4

Is an Obsession with Health a Sign of Sickness?

Day after day this spring, the gyms, pools and Nautilus machines of the city pulse with the thud, splash and grunt of innumerable Americans who claim fervently that they live more healthily than ever.

But the same cannot be said for the society that surrounds them. When it comes to the elusive goal of perfect physical condition, the United States is deluded, uptight and confused, jogging and lifting and power-walking on a joyless quest for an unavailable immortality.

The prospect of 40 million "serious" joggers is bad enough. But what's worse is the creation of a religion of running, a philosophy of fitness that leaves its adherents without the deeper consolations of a true philosophy that reconciles them to their mortal selves.

True, Americans have emerged as among the healthiest people of all time. The average child born in 1984 can expect to live to the age of 74.7. In 1900, the life expectancy was only 47.3 years.

Yet, even so, all this fitness appears not to have bought even short-term happiness. People spend $6 billion a year on running shoes, yet worry constantly about heart fibrillations. They pump iron on the $738 million worth of exercise machines they bought last year, yet read electrocardiograms like horoscopes.

Indeed, so anxious and preoccupied have we become with being healthy that we appear incapable of even enjoying the benefits of good health. No wonder that after 15 years of intense health mania, during which life expectancy increased a staggering 3.8 years, polls show that the numbers of those satisfied with their health have actually dropped.

approximately 375 words

Mark Muro, "Is an Obsession with Health a Sign of Sickness?" *Boston Globe SM*

1. What does the author's choice of words such as thud, splash, and grunt imply about his attitude toward exercise?

    _____

    _____

2. Why does the author think the United States is "deluded, uptight and confused" about the status of its physical well-being?

_____

_____

3. Is the author's conclusion that jogging is a "religion" justified?

_____

_____

4. Is the author's conclusion that there is "an intense health mania" valid or invalid? Defend your opinion.

_____

_____

ACTIVITY 8.4   Practice Finding Connotative Language in Essays

Practice finding the connotative terms in the selections that follow. Analyze the language, and circle positive and negative words. Then, infer the author's attitude toward society and answer the questions.

The first essay concerns the idea that we are becoming less like humans; in other words, we are being *dehumanized*.

PASSAGE 1

Dehumanization Happens

Listen closely to this story. A drunk on the subway wants desperately to impress a woman. He wants to impress her so desperately that he takes it upon himself to open the doors of the train while mumbling some **incoherent** advances, and through a combination of unfortunate mishaps and drunken stupidity, he ends up on the tracks and is **decapitated.**

No one—certainly not the woman—is impressed. She is hysterical.

Can you find any humor whatsoever in this true-life story? If you responded, "No. I see absolutely nothing funny about that story. It's sickening and tragic, what you'd expect to see sensationalized on the evening news," you flunked the test by the standards of modern society.

---

incoherent (in′ kō hir′ ənt) unable to express one's thoughts in an orderly manner
decapitated (dē kap′ ə tāt′ əd) beheaded

However, you may still be one of the few thinking human beings left in America. You have not yet passed over to the dark side—where countless others have gone quite willingly.

I heard the account of the decapitated subway rider on morning talk radio, where taste is clearly not a criterion for success and where vulgarity is a **prerequisite** for popularity among the "shock jocks."

The rhinoceros in the radio studio tried to extract every possible ounce of sick humor from the story. He and his colleagues **guffawed** and cackled and made indecent quips. It made me momentarily wonder whether I perhaps was too prudish. You see, your sense of good taste gets jaded very easily in our culture, and you begin to ignore things that clearly would have sickened you in another decade.

Whether it involves the **misogyny** or violence of gangsta rap, the vulgarity of drive-time radio, or any of the other curious manifestations that make modern America look like Fellini's "Satyricon" or "A Clockwork Orange," we can only shrug over the indignities. They have become so commonplace we are beyond the point of outrage. That's the first sign you are changing.

approximately 315 words

Joe Pisani, "Dehumanization Happens," *San Jose Mercury News*

1. What do the circled words imply about the author's attitude?

    _____

    _____

2. What do you dislike most about particular news stories on television?

    _____

    _____

Read the following essay to learn how segments of society distinguish "good" and "bad" taste. Circle the connotative words and phrases, and then answer the questions that follow.

PASSAGE 2

Cultural Snobbery Is Alive and Well in Britain

One of the ironies of life under a government committed to equal opportunities and social inclusion is how acceptable it now is to sneer at poorer families for their "bad taste."

----

prerequisite (prē rek′ wi zit) requirement
guffawed (gə fod′) hearty or coarse burst of laughter
misogyny (mi sôj′ ə nē) hatred of women

A Matter of Taste   People who would put a souvenir poster of Princess Diana on their wall or buy a cheap Diana doll are held in contempt by those who consider such memorabilia "tacky and inappropriate."

Words like "tacky" and "tasteless" have become routine, uttered alike by media, government and royal family; apparently, what everyone in modern Britain wants is good taste, style and design. Women are central in this attack because, by and large, they define the domestic space. What, one wonders, have they done to deserve such scorn?

This has all been at the forefront in the question of Diana **memorabilia.** The trustees of Diana's charity . . . decided to pursue the Franklin Mint through court for producing a series of Diana dolls with different outfits. "How can you do this?" wailed one of the charity's trustees. "Diana is not a plaything, a toy." It would have been different, apparently, if the doll had been a "collector's item, an **heirloom.**" . . .

Tony Blair condemned as "tacky and inappropriate" plans to sell Diana mugs and T-shirts. Others are even harsher, using words like cheap, distasteful and sentimental, recalling the "excesses" of Diana's funeral. . . .

---

memorabilia (mem ò rò bil′ ē ò) things worth remembering
heirloom (er′ lōōm) any treasured possession handed down from generation to generation

But whatever the real agenda, there is horrendous snobbery at work, a contempt for the sort of people—invariably women—who would buy a decorated mug, give their daughter a cheap Diana doll or put a souvenir poster on their wall. . . .

Words like "good taste" and "style" appear to transcend immediate fashions, but the non-tacky, good taste home is ultimately nothing but the uniform of a particular class. Good taste is merely a way of displaying possessions that is learned from images of ideal homes. It expresses membership of a class that has material and cultural wealth, and shows you don't belong to That Class.

Yet for women of That Class, the domestic space is for living in rather than being seen in, probably the only spaces under their control, the one place to make and display their own meanings. That's what souvenirs are all about. The meanings that attach themselves to objects and pictures are private, arising from their memories and experiences.

Perhaps the manipulable Diana doll offers the possibility of adapting it to memories and associations, which the stiff distance of an "heirloom doll" cannot express. Such mementos will always be tacky because they don't belong to the public world of taste and style. Their world is internal, personal and specific. I know plenty of homes where every available shelf space is crammed with photos—of degree ceremonies, holidays, christenings. . . .

You have to overcome a middle-class education before realizing that when such families bury their dead with wreaths in the shape of MUM or a teddy bear, it isn't bad taste. It's about using objects to express what you felt about that person or what that person liked. Unlike in middle-class families, it isn't considered weak to express feelings of loss or grief, or to use mass-produced images to do so. . . .

People don't often use the terms "high" and "low" culture now, but the whole Diana memorabilia debate simply repackages an old theme in British culture: What we have is good taste, what they have is tackiness. Only this time the object of such disdain is poorer women, the keepers of the mementos and the bearers of the emotions.

There may be an issue about persuading commercial producers of Diana memorabilia to make donations to charity. Most of the purchasers of such goods would want that. But, beyond this, isn't what people choose to buy and their reasons for doing so their own affair?

approximately 540 words

Ros Coward (*The Guardian*), "Cultural snobbery is alive and well in Britain," *San Francisco Examiner* 23 May 1998: C3.

1. According to the selection, how do the British distinguish "good" taste from "bad" taste?

   _____

   _____

2. What are the connotative associations you make with each of the following terms?

   a. tacky _____

   b. collector's item _____

     c.   "good taste"/"style" _____

     d.   That Class _____

3.   What place do souvenirs and memorabilia have in your life? Do you collect and cherish posters, autographs, photos, mementos? Why, or why not?

_____

_____

PASSAGE 3

Read the following article, "Civil Liberties Watch." The author takes a firm stand on what she believes is an **erosion** of our civil liberties and attacks many of our institutions. Circle all the connotative words and phrases, and then answer the questions that follow the essay.

Civil Liberties Watch

Barbara Dority

. . . As the lengthening **tentacles** of censorship crept down alleys and under back doors, civil libertarians did not sleep well. We became increasingly alarmed by the relentless erosion of our intellectual and personal freedoms. . . .

Many of us tried to sound an alarm. "Wake up!" we cried. "We're losing our liberties bit by bit. Look there! The monster is creeping upon us, shrouded in the fog. Can't you see it?"

Most people thought we were alarmists—until recently. Feeding on its many "small" successes, the **insidious** monster has grown bold and confident, revealing itself for all to see.

No medium is safe. Individuals and groups seeking to restrict the flow of information, images, and ideas are targeting public libraries, school classrooms, and resource centers. Motion pictures and television programs are policed by such groups as the American Family Association. Librarians, educators, school boards, publishers, bookstores, theaters, video stores, artists, musicians, and the electronic media are under persistent and organized attack. Under threats of legal action and boycott, many are capitulating to pressure tactics. America's marketplace of ideas is shrinking on a daily basis.

Artists, previously unconcerned, have been rudely awakened. They no longer believe that censorship only happens to other people. With the visual and performing arts under fire, the National Endowment for the Arts has been forced to implement funding restrictions on "offensive" works. Musicians and music distributors have been arrested and charged with violation of **obscenity** laws. Record companies have been pressured into censorship and

_____

erosion (i rō′ zhən) a wearing away
tentacles (ten′ tə kəlz) grasping fingers or arms like those of an octopus
insidious (in sid′ ē əs) sly; crafty
obscenity (äb sen′ ə tē) disgusting words or actions

labeling. The government restricts foreign educational films and speakers. The Supreme Court expands the definition of libel. The Freedom of Information Act slowly continues to erode.

Sexually explicit publications and information about sexuality are subject to severe restrictions. Magazines such as *Playboy* and *Penthouse* have been pulled from many retail shelves. Public school health and sex education books are being challenged and, all too often, banned. In many school districts, opponents of sex education have succeeded in implementing programs based solely upon abstinence—programs which contain no information on prevention of pregnancy or sexually transmitted diseases.

In short, our public schools are under **siege** and held hostage by those who would impose a narrow view of life on all our children. Orchestrated censorship campaigns by highly organized and well-funded conservative groups are successful in over one-third of reported cases.

As a result of this hysterical climate, many are engaging in self-censorship. Librarians don't order "possibly controversial" books, school administrators censor student publications, and textbook publishers remove "controversial" materials from reading and science texts.

Liberty is like good health: we take it for granted until we lose it. During the past year, scores of "ordinary Americans" have seen the face of the monster. . . . They know that we can't sit around the kitchen table agreeing that censorship is wrong and waiting for someone else to do something about it. We can no longer afford to say we support freedom of expression while maintaining serious reservations about the Larry Flynts and the neo-Nazi skinheads.

It is our responsibility to organize and instruct these newly activated individuals. What we do not understand, we cannot effectively combat. Thus, it is essential that we possess and pass on an understanding of the pro-censorship mindset.

The pro-censorship mindset has remained the same throughout the history of civilization. The censors always aim at protecting us from the **perceived** harmful effects of what we read, see, and hear.

approximately 600 words

Barbara Dority, "Civil Liberties Watch," *The Humanist* 51. 1 (Jan–Feb. 1991): 43. Reprinted with permission of the publisher.

1. List the institutions and areas of our society the writer states are under attack.

_____

_____

_____

---

siege (sēj) a long, distressing period
perceived (pər sēvd′) recognized

2. Do you agree with the author? Has her choice of words influenced your opinion about our "loss of civil liberties"?

_____

_____

_____

3. Can you think of a serious instance where violations of civil liberties occurred in your state or country? Are there instances occurring today that you would consider violations of someone's civil liberties?

_____

_____

_____

Figurative Language

You learned in Chapter 2 (pp. 76–79) that _figures of speech are expressions that mean something other than what is actually stated._ They are not meant to be interpreted literally but rather carry implied meanings. The writer goes beyond the direct literal meaning of words and makes imaginative comparisons to express his or her feelings and judgments. Thus, figurative language requires you to use logic to draw inferences about comparisons that are not literally true or factual. They demand that you stretch your mind to understand things compared often in unusual, dramatic, or startling ways. In both nonfiction and fiction writing, three figures of speech used frequently are _simile, metaphor,_ and _personification._

Figuring Out Figures of Speech

Similes and Metaphors

Many figures of speech use comparison, which may be stated in the form of a simile or a metaphor. _A simile is a comparison between two unlike objects and signaled by words such as_ like _or_ as. We can say of a quiet person, "Marc is _as_ quiet _as_ a fading sunset"; of an angry person, "He burst out the door _like_ an explosion"; or of a contented person, "She acts *like* a cat with her soft purring words." Although the comparison is directly stated in the simile, there is also an implied meaning that changes the way you feel about the subject. For example, Marc is quiet but in a gentle way; "bursting out the door like an explosion" suggests a loud, sudden noise; and "purring words" have the effect of soothing and comforting tones.

Do not assume that whenever you see *like* or *as* in a sentence, it is a simile. To be a simile, a sentence must state a comparison between unlike things. For example, there is no simile present in "My house is like your house."

A metaphor is a comparison of unlike objects with some point in common <u>without</u> using the signal words like or as. The metaphor says one thing is *equal* to another thing. For example, to say, "The salesperson is a sly fox" is to imply the person is crafty or clever like a fox. To describe *rage* one might say, "The anger of the man was a consuming fire." Carl Sandburg used a metaphor to describe slang: "Slang is language that rolls up its sleeves, spits on its hands, and gets down to business."

Study the examples that follow to see how statements made about the same topic, "impeachment," differ when made literally and figuratively:

> **Literal:** An impeachment is like an indictment in a criminal trial, a set of charges against someone.
>
> Even though the word "like" was used, this is a directly stated comparison between things that are similar rather than different.
>
> **Simile:** An impeachment trial can be like a runaway train heading toward a cliff.
>
> Here, the writer implies that the trial can be out of control and lead to a disaster.
>
> **Metaphor:** Impeachment should be a shield for its country's citizens, not a sword, aimed at decapitating a person.
>
> Here, the writer equates impeachment to a shield, a protection, as opposed to a sword which can cause destruction.

Personification

Personification is another type of figurative language. *In personification the writer gives an inanimate, nonhuman object human qualities, emotions, or characteristics.* Examples include saying that "the ocean *roared*," "thoughts *raced* through her mind," or "the factory *looked* forlorn."

Four key questions can help the reader understand the implied meanings usually found in figurative language.

1. What qualities are being compared?
2. What is implied in the comparison?
3. Why is the writer making the comparison?
4. Does the writer create a positive or negative image?

ACTIVITY 8.5 Making Comparisons Using Figurative Language

Explain what is meant by each of the following statements.

1. Kindness is a language the deaf can hear and the blind can read.

    Mark Twain

    Kindness is compared to _____ in two ways:

    a. _____

    b. _____

    _____ c. The figure of speech used is

    A. simile.   B. metaphor.   C. personification.

2. There is a difference between climbing the ladder of success and machete-ing a path to the top.

    Ellen Goodman

    a. Explain, in literal words, the different means of attaining success.

    _____

    _____ b. The figure of speech used is

    A. simile.   B. metaphor.   C. personification.

3. Her ideas dried up like a raisin in the sun.

    a. What is meant by an idea drying up?

    _____

    _____ b. The figure of speech used is

    A. simile.   B. metaphor.   C. personification.

4. Internet sales are racing ahead, Wall Street analysts are huffing and puffing to keep track, but the federal government has barely left the starting gate in providing data on the hottest new sales arena since the Home Shopping Network.

Reuters News Service

Copy two of the phrases that use personification and explain what each of them is saying literally about Internet sales.

a. _____

b. _____

5. I saw my life before me, finished, *closed, like a bag,* and yet what was inside was not finished. For a moment I tried to appraise it . . . But it couldn't be appraised. It was only an outline. I had spent my time *writing checks on eternity,* and had understood nothing.

Jean-Paul Satre, "The Wall"

Explain what the narrator, who is about to be executed, is implying in any one of the italicized phrases.

_____

_____

ACTIVITY 8.6 Making Comparisons with Figurative Language in Short Selections

Consider the ideas suggested by the use of figurative language in the following passages. Then answer the questions that follow. The first one has been done for you as an example.

PASSAGE 1

The following passage is a partial transcript of the speech John F. Kennedy gave when he was sworn in as president and voiced his interest in creating the Peace Corps.

In your hands, my fellow citizens, more than in mine, will rest the final success or failure of our course. Since this country was founded, each generation has been summoned to give testimony to its national loyalty. The graves of young Americans who answered that call encircle the globe. Now the trumpet summons us again—not as a call to bear arms, though arms we need—not as a call to battle, though embattled we are—but a call to bear the burden of a long twilight struggle, year in and year out, "rejoicing in hope, patient in tribulation"—a struggle against the common enemies of man: tyranny, poverty, disease and war itself. Can we forge against these enemies a grand and global alliance, north and south, east and west, that can assure a more fruitful life for all mankind? Will you join in that historic effort? In the long history of the world, only a few generations have been granted the role of defending freedom in its hour of maximum danger. I do not shrink from this responsibility—I welcome it. I do not believe that any of us would exchange places with any other people or any other generation. The energy, the faith, and the devotion which we bring to this endeavor will light our country and all who serve it—and the glow from that fire can truly light the world. And so, my fellow Americans: Ask not what your country can do for you—ask what you can do for your country. My fellow citizens of the world: Ask not what America will do for you, but what together we can do for the freedom of man.

John F. Kennedy, Inaugural Address, 20 Jan. 1961

_____ 1.   "And the glow from that fire can truly light the world" is an example of

      a.   simile.   b.   metaphor.   c.   personification.

      Answer: b. "That fire" refers back in the sentence to our patriotism, our devotion. While they are unlike objects, he compares the glow of a fire to the spirit one's enthusiasm can generate.

2.   What is the literal meaning of "Now the trumpet summons us again"?

      _____

      Answer: It means we are called (summoned) to again serve our country.

3.   Is the use of the word _light_ in the sentence "The energy, the faith, and the devotion which we bring to this endeavor will light our country and all who serve it" a good choice? Why, or why not?

      _____

      Answer: Yes, because it suggests warmth and hope.

PASSAGE 2

Genetic engineering, the upstart young science that dares to tinker with the building **1** blocks of life, is suddenly out of its diapers and into a business suit.

Ready or not, it is knocking at the door, carrying a sample case full of wonders both **2** exciting and disturbing:

Soon we will be able to know if our babies will be healthy—before pregnancy.   **3**

We will be treated or cured of diseases once considered hopeless. We will even know **4** how likely we are to get certain illnesses during our lifetimes.

We will shop in supermarkets where the pork is as lean as chicken, the tomatoes are **5** perfect and the produce is free of viruses and pesticides.

Along with its bright promises, genetic engineering is lugging around some heavier **6** baggage: the legacy of Nazi **eugenics** atrocities, fears of runaway mutant microbes, suspicions that a powerful technology will fall into the hands of crackpots and tyrants.

---

eugenics (yoo jen′ iks) movement to improve the human condition by controlling heredity

As it has matured over the past decade, genetic engineering has put some of these 7
fears to rest by showing it can work within regulatory limits and without unpleasant
surprises.

For genetics researchers, whose crowning achievement formerly was a Nobel Prize, 8
the marriage of laboratory discoveries with **entrepreneurship** means they can become
rich by discovering a new gene that can be used to make a valuable product.

Ronald Kotulak and Peter Gomer, "The Gene Is Out of the Bottle," Chicago Tribune

_____ 1. In the first paragraph, the metaphor describing genetic engineering implies
that
   a. genetic engineers are now businesspeople.
   b. the baby boomers have become genetic engineers.
   c. genetic engineering has matured and is making some medical
      advances.
   d. genetic engineering is useful for infertile couples.

Support: _____

_____ 2. The phrase "it is knocking at the door" in paragraph 2 is an example of
   a. simile.
   b. metaphor.
   c. personification.

Support: _____

_____ 3. What is the literal meaning of "the marriage of laboratory discoveries with
entrepreneurship means they can become rich by discovering a new gene
that can be used to make a valuable product" (para. 8)?

_____

_____

PASSAGE 3

[1] . . . enthusiasm for the death penalty seems based less on facts than on superstition.
[2] By some kind of ritual magic, the killing of murderers is supposed to ward off burglars, thieves, muggers, rapists and armed robbers who prey on the innocent citizen
minding his own business. [3] Our Supreme Court Justices, like cynical witch doctors in
some primitive society, seem to agree among themselves that this magic may not be much
good, but it vents frustration and makes people feel that the Government is doing its job.
[4] What it's doing is **condoning** murder as an appropriate response to a terrible grievance, instead of correcting the problems in our society, our courts and our criminal-
justice system.

Playboy

_____

entrepreneurship (ăn trə prə nur′ ship) organizing a business undertaking
condoning (kon dōn′ ing) forgiving or overlooking an offense

_____ 1. The figure of speech used in the third sentence, "Our Supreme Court Justices, like cynical witch doctors in some primitive society," is an example of

   a.   simile.   b.   metaphor.   c.   personification.

2. What does the use of this and other figurative language imply about the writer's attitude toward capital punishment?

_____

_____

ACTIVITY 8.7   Figurative Language in Literature

Read the following excerpts, the first from Eudora Welty's story "Losing Battles" and the second from Julia Sorel's novel *Rocky*. After reading them, go back and underline the figures of speech. Then, answer the questions that follow.

PASSAGE 1

When the rooster crowed, the moon had still not left the world but was going down on flushed cheek, one day short of the full. A long thin cloud crossed it slowly, drawing itself out like a name being called. The air changed, as if a mile or so away a wooden door had swung open, and a smell, more of warmth than wet, from a river at low stage, moved upward into the clay hills that stood in darkness.

Then a house appeared on its ridge, like an old man's silver watch pulled once more out of its pocket. A dog leaped up from where he'd lain like a stone and began barking for today as if he meant never to stop.

Then a baby bolted naked out of the house. She monkey-climbed down the steps and ran open-armed into the yard, knocking at the walls of flowers still colorless as faces, tagging in turn the four big trees that marked off the corners of the yard, tagging the gatepost, the well-piece, the bird-house, the bell post, a log seat, a rope swing, and then, rounding the house, she used all her strength to push over a crate that let a stream of white Plymouth Rocks loose on the world. The chickens rushed ahead of the baby, running frantic, and behind the baby came a girl in a petticoat. A wide circle of curl-papers, paler than the streak of dawn, bounced around her head, but she ran on confident tip-toe as though she believed no eye could see her. She caught the baby and carried her back inside, the baby with her little legs still running like a windmill.

Eudora Welty, "Losing Battles"

PASSAGE 2

Read about a brutal boxing match.

Insanely, Rocky got to his feet and tensed with renewed energy. He was a wounded, wild animal. The tide had suddenly turned and washed Rocky up on Apollo Creed. Rocky dropped low and caught Apollo with a pair of terrific body punches that seemed to drive Apollo's diaphragm up to his throat. A loud crack was heard. A glaze of pain covered Apollo's eyes with the jellied aspic of cruel reality. It was only by a supreme effort that the champion stayed upright. He was so badly hurt that he began to bend in the middle, like store-away furniture: Pretty soon, if he didn't rally, there'd be no room for him, and he'd be put away. Rocky kept coming; he imagined that Apollo was a frozen side of beef just waiting for Rocky to tenderize its dark flesh. But Apollo defrosted like a flash, flicked dread jabs into Rocky's eyes. Still, Rocky waded in with punches that seemed to bulge out Apollo's back. Creed took the punishment like a stoic. He had picked the Italian Stallion, and now that the horse was running wild, stampeding all over him, it was up to him to tame the wild beast or kill it in the name of sport. Blood, like dampened flame, or the soft tongue of the sanguinary soul, ran from Apollo's mouth. He didn't like losing it—blood was personal, his Universal O automotive fuel. In the clinch he leaned over Rocky, and it dripped down the Italian's neck and shoulders like a mantle. Apollo shielded his wound from the ringside judges and continued to fight.

Julia Sorel, *Rocky*

1. Both writers use many figurative expressions. Select two from each passage that you felt were very effective and explain their literal meanings.

   From "Losing Battles"

   a. _____

   b. _____

   From *Rocky*

   a. _____

   b. _____

2. Which of the two passages affected you more emotionally? Why?

   _____

   _____

PASSAGE 3

Read about the feelings one may experience while looking at a volcano.

Kilauea

The volcano is on Hawaii, the largest island of the group. You land at Hilo and drive up, first through fields of rice and sugar-cane and then, climbing all the time, through a forest of great tree-ferns. They are weird and strange like the imaginations of some

draughtsman of the horrible. All manner of climbing plants wind around the trees in an impenetrable tangle. Gradually the vegetation stops and you come to the lava field, grey, dead, silent; here no plants grow and no birds sing; you see the smoke rising, here and there thickly, in other places ascending thin and straight like the smoke from a cottage chimney. You get out and walk. The lava crunches under your feet. Now and then you step over narrow fissures from which the **sulphurous** smoke rises, making you cough. You come to the jagged edge of the crater. Nothing has prepared you for the sight. It is stupendous and alarming. You look down upon a vast sea of lava. It is black and heavy. It is in perpetual movement. The lava is only a thin crust and it is broken at irregular intervals by gashes of red fire, and here and there again are geysers of flame rising into the air, thirty, or forty or fifty feet. They spurt up, white hot, like artificial fountains. The two most impressive things are the roar: it is like the roar of surf on a gloomy day, as unceasing, or like the roar of a **cataract,** as **formidable;** and secondly the movement: the lava moves on, on, all the time, with a stealthy movement in which you may almost see the purpose of a living thing. There is something strangely determined about its quiet progress, it has a **malign** tenacity; and yet it transcends anything living, it has the inevitableness of fate and the ruthlessness of time. The lava is like some huge formless creature born of **primeval** slime crawling slowly in pursuit of some loathsome prey. The lava moves forward steadily towards a fiery gap and then seems to fall into a bottomless cavern of flame. You see vast holes of fire, great caves of flame. A man standing near said: "Gosh, it's like hell," but a priest beside him turned and said: "No, it is like the face of God."

approximately 350 words

W. Somerset Maugham, *A Writer's Notebook*

1. The author wishes to create a certain mood or effect with phrases such as "here no plants grow and no birds sing" and "it is like the roar of surf on a gloomy day, as unceasing, or like the roar of a cataract, as formidable." What feeling does the author try to convey? Why?

    _____

    _____

2. Figurative language is found throughout this selection. For example, smoke from the fissures is compared to smoke from a cottage chimney. List three other figures of speech you found especially descriptive.

    a. _____

    b. _____

    c. _____

_____

draughtsman (drats′ man) British term for a draftsman
sulphurous (sul′ fə rəs) a variant spelling for *sulfurous,* a pale yellow nonmetallic substance
cataract (kat′ ə rakt) a great waterfall
formidable (fôr′ mə də bəl) arousing fear and dread
malign (mə līn′) to speak evil or slander
primeval (pri′ mē vəl) belonging to the earliest ages; original

3. Rewrite two sentences of the selection, using denotative language to make them as objective as possible.

_____

_____

ACTIVITY 8.8 Examining Figurative *and* Connotative Language in an Essay

Read the following excerpted essay to decide whether the Catholic Church is manipulating language to help Catholic couples who end their marriage and later want to marry another person. In the past, Catholic couples who divorced and later remarried were not allowed to keep practicing their religion.

Unmaking of a Marriage

1 . . . Annulment, the Roman Catholic Church's term for dissolving a marriage, has become one of the most **contentious** issues within the faith today. With an annulment, a divorced Catholic can heal from a failed union, remarry in the church and participate in the sacraments.

2 Once granted sparingly—only 338 in 1968—the U.S. church now approves upward of 50,000 annulments every year.

3 Marriage is still forever, church officials say, when it is a true union; annulment is a compassionate way of recognizing those that aren't.

4 But the very apparatus that keeps thousands of divorced Catholics within the flock is also driving away countless others who view annulments as a **hypocritical** farce. They consider annulment a galling attempt by the church to grapple with the divorce rate and allow Catholics to shirk responsibility for failed marriages.

5 "I think God is laughing at us up there," says Father Barry Brunsman, a . . . priest and author of "New Hope for Divorced Catholics," who has processed more than 100 annulments.

6 "Annulment is becoming preposterous. It is being done without discernment."

7 The controversy was brought into focus nationally . . . with the publication of a book by Sheila Rauch Kennedy, who . . . appeal[ed] the annulment of her 12-year marriage to Rep. Joseph P. Kennedy II, D-Mass. In "Shattered Faith," she **lambastes** annulment as a moral corruption.

8 "Unlike a divorce, an annulment does not say something has either broken down or ended," Kennedy writes. "It says the marriage never truly existed in the first place. This distinction . . . was at the root of my rage."

Desire to Remarry

9 Henry VIII wanted an annulment to remarry; when Rome refused, he launched his own church.

---

contentious (kòn ten′ shòs) marked by controversy, dispute, quarrel
hypocritical (hip ò krit′ i kòl) act of pretending to be what one is not, such as pious
lambastes (lam bāstz′) scolds severely

Today, more than four centuries later, most 10 who seek annulment also want to remarry with the church's **sanction**. . . .

In the U.S. church—dubbed the "Las 11 Vegas" of annulments—90 percent are granted. . . .

U.S. churches grant 75 percent of all 12 Catholic annulments, a statistic disturbing to Pope John Paul II, who has termed the American way of annulment too lenient, "easy and hurried."

Such criticism rankles well-intended 13 church officials.

They say annulments are more common 14 here because the churches, unlike those in other countries, financially support the tribunals that handle annulment requests. The U.S. church spends $20 million a year on tribunal operations, says the Canon Law Society. . . .

Additionally, church officials say, annul- 15 ments occur more often here because the U.S. church delves into psychological factors to prove a marriage invalid.

Where once annulments were granted 16 because of force or deception or refusal to have children, today the church tries to diagnose a couple's state of mind at the start of the marriage. The upshot: Most U.S. annulments are now granted because of "psychic immaturity." . . .

Some Rules of Annulment

No power on Earth can convince Jim Greco he 17 was not truly married. So [he] . . . won't seek an annulment for his church marriage that lasted 13 years.

"Nobody put a gun to my head," says Greco, 18 62, a retired manufacturing sales manager. "I married because I thought I was in love. The church is saying all these marriages were a lie. To me an annulment is to deny what I did."

He, like many other divorced Catholics 19 who remarry outside the church, partakes in the sacraments though technically not eligible. He relies on a loophole called "the good conscience solution," for Catholics who cannot or will not get an annulment. . . .

Annulment hinges on what happens at 20 the start of a marriage, not necessarily what occurs *during* the marriage. If a marriage begins as a sacramental one, the church says, later events, such as infidelity or desertion, cannot erase it.

Annulment establishes a "defect," a lack of 21 mutual understanding of the rights and obligations of the union, says the Rev. Randolph Calvo, judicial vicar of the tribunal in San Francisco. It does not **nullify** a civil marriage; it says the union does not exist in God's eyes. . . .

"This is not necessarily about blame but 22 about incapacity," says the Rev. Stephen Meriwether, who serves on the San Francisco tribunal. "You don't blame a paraplegic for not playing basketball. If there is incapacity, there is not blame to be assigned."

Demands for Reform

Lay Catholic groups, led by Catholics Speak 23 Out, are increasingly demanding reform.

They say that if they remarry but refuse to 24 seek an annulment, they are officially considered adulterers by the church and treated as second-class citizens.

From their own outrage, an Indiana cou- 25 ple—sociologists who wed after their first marriages were annulled against their wishes—has launched a national study on the impact of annulments.

Richard Jenks, a professor at Indiana 26 University, fought the annulment of his 16-year marriage, but he believes he wasn't given a fair chance to contest it.

---

sanction (sangk′ shòn) allow or permit
nullify (nul′ ò fī) make legally void; cancel out

"I had a marriage, a valid one," he says. "We 27 didn't go into it blindly. For the church to say to a lot of people that theirs wasn't a valid marriage is a real stab in the back. The Catholic Church will have to start defending annulments more and more—the process itself and the numbers that are granted."

Jenks' wife, Cynthia Woolever, found her 28 own first marriage being annulled. She is Protestant, and married in a Protestant church, but her husband wanted to remarry a Catholic and the 11-year marriage was annulled in 1990.

"It was a very serious commitment on both 29 our parts," Woolever says. "For an institution as powerful as the Catholic Church to say in an arrogant way this wasn't a valid marriage is a very hurtful thing. The church basically invalidates your life. It felt like a drive-by shooting."

approximately 950 words

Elizabeth Fernandez, "Unmaking of a Marriage," *San Francisco Examiner* 18 May 1997: A1+.

1. Reread paragraph 8. Do you think Sheila Rauch Kennedy is justified in being outraged at the distinction the Catholic Church makes between the terms "annulment" and "divorce"? Why, or why not?

_____

_____

2. Explain what "psychic immaturity" means (para. 16) and state whether you think it is or is not a valid reason for granting an annulment and why.

_____

_____

3. Name the figure of speech used in each of the following statements, and explain the literal meaning:

a. "In the U.S. church—dubbed the "Las Vegas" of annulments— . . . "(para. 11).

_____

b. "For the Church to say to a lot of people that theirs wasn't a valid marriage is a real stab in the back." (para. 27)

_____

c. "The Church basically invalidates your life. It felt like a drive-by shooting." (para. 29)

_____

4. a. Look at the sketch printed below, the headline of yet another essay about annulments, and substitute a denotative word for "Erasing."

Sam Ward, "Erasing a Marriage" Illustration, for *USA Today* (May 7, 1997). Copyright © 1997 by *USA Today.* Reprinted by permission of the publishers.

b. How does the concept of annulment change with the denotative word you selected? Does it help you decide whether the Catholic Church's stand on annulment is a manipulation of language or a logical solution to the church's problem? Explain your answer.

Euphemisms

Euphemisms are still another form of figurative language used when writers want to describe an unpleasant subject or situation. They use indirect, less objectionable, more pleasant-sounding words to tell it "like it isn't" rather than "like it is"! Thus, by definition, *a euphemism is a softer, less negative or offensive word or phrase used to replace one that is unpleasant, stronger or harsher.* Its original meaning, from the Greek, is "to use words of good **omen.**"

Euphemistic terms abound in our everyday speaking and writing. We often refer to "old people" as "senior citizens" and to their time of life as the "golden years." Instead of saying someone has been fired, we say that someone's been "offered a career-change opportunity," or we say that a company is "downsizing" or "rightsizing" or "dehiring." Euphemisms are frequently used in job descriptions to elevate a seemingly inferior position: a dogcatcher becomes an "animal control officer," a secretary becomes an "administrative assistant," a garbage collector a "sanitation engineer," and a housewife a "domestic engineer"!

The critical reader checks to see whether the writer has used euphemisms to disguise feelings or develop implications since euphemisms are frequently used to deceive and manipulate thinking. They can hide distasteful or unpleasant information, or they are used to trick the unwary reader into misinterpreting information. When you encounter euphemistic writing, try mentally to substitute direct language to learn what the writer is truly saying. In his classic essay "Politics and the English Language," George Orwell wrote, "Political language has to consist largely of euphemism, question-begging and sheer cloudy vagueness."

The use of euphemisms is sometimes referred to as "doublespeak," a term coined by William Lutz, who says it is language used to mislead while pretending to tell the truth.

ACTIVITY 8.9 Recognizing Euphemistic Expressions

A. Match the euphemistic expression in the first column with its corresponding intended meaning in the second.

Expression	Intended Meaning
_____ 1. folically deprived	a. lie
_____ 2. adjusted the truth	b. have a facelift
_____ 3. rejuvenate one's appearance with cosmetic manipulations	c. vending machine
	d. bald
_____ 4. previously owned vehicle	e. poor
_____ 5. misappropriate the company's funds	f. salesperson
_____ 6. politically correct	g. inoffensive
_____ 7. economically nonaffluent	h. steal
_____ 8. habitual offender	i. criminal
_____ 9. customer service representative	j. used car
_____10. electronic merchandise device	k. suicide

---

omen (ō′ men) something supposed to tell a future happening

B. Printed below is a list of travel expressions compiled by a public relations worker for the travel industry. Examine the expressions and their translations.

"All the amenities": free shower cap
"Gentle breezes": gale-force winds
"Picturesque": theme park or mystery house nearby
"Carefree natives": terrible service
"Bustling metropolis": thousands of hostile locals
"Airy": no air-conditioning
"Brisk": freezing
"Open bar": all the ice cubes you want
"Plush": top and bottom sheets
"Spacious quarters": sparsely furnished room
"Convenient": bring bus fare
"Motor coach": bus
"Deluxe motor coach": bus with clean windows
"Unique": no one else would do it like this

Mim Swartz, " 'Travelese' and All That Really Means," Scripps Howard News Service, *San Francisco Examiner* 17 May 1998: T2.

Here are some additional euphemistic "travelese" expressions. Write your interpretation of each in the space provided.

Expression	Your Interpretation
1. "Quaint"	_____
2. "Off the beaten track"	_____
3. "Tropical"	_____
4. "Majestic setting"	_____
5. "Options galore"	_____

ACTIVITY 8.10

As you read the next essay, underline the euphemisms (doublespeak) used by the Pentagon. When you have finished reading the selection, complete the matching exercise. Before you begin reading, think about what the following cartoon implies about euphemisms.

*Repressive Celibate and the Seven Politically
Correct Height-Challenged.*

No Ordinary Nut

William Lutz

. . . Doublespeak—whether jargon, euphemisms or bureaucratese—is not a slip of the tongue but a conscious use of language as both a tool and a weapon. It is language that conceals or manipulates thought. It makes the bad seem good, the negative appear positive, the unpleasant appear attractive or at least tolerable.

There is doublespeak in everyday life ("nondairy creamer"), business ("nonperforming assets") and government (the Internal Revenue Service). But when it comes to doublespeak, the military has a way with words that is unmatched. Only the military could call a tent a "frame-supported tension structure"; a parachute an "aerodynamic personnel decelerator"; and a zipper an "interlocking slide fastener."

Others may call it a bomb, but to the Army it's a "vertically deployed anti-personnel device."

No More War

Military doublespeak starts at the top. From the founding of our republic, there has been a Department of War. Until 1947, that is, when the military pulled off the doublespeak **coup** of the century. On July 27 President Harry S. Truman signed the National Security Act of 1947, an act that completely reorganized the armed forces. Section 202 establishes the post of Secretary of Defense, while Section 205(a) eliminates the Department of War. Thus, war became "defense."

At first glance this change might not seem all that significant, but examine the implications.

---

coup (kōō) a brilliant action; clever move

Now members of Congress campaign to spend more on "defense." Candidates for public office charge their opponents with wanting to cut the $300 billion defense budget, not the $300 billion war budget.

Doublespeak also is useful when the Pentagon wants expensive items to sound very complicated and worth their high price. It's not an ordinary steel nut; it's a "hexiform rotatable surface compression unit," which is why it cost $2,043 for just one of them. This little piece of doublespeak also allows the military to say that the equipment "suffered dramatically degraded useful operational life owing to the fact that a $2,000 hexiform rotatable surface compression unit underwent catastrophic stress-related shaft detachment," which sounds a lot more impressive than saying it won't work because a 13-cent nut broke.

Some penny-pinchers may think that $31,672 is a lot to pay for a couch, a love seat and 20 dining room chairs (or almost $1,500 for each piece of furniture), but not if you think of it the way the Navy does. All that money was spent on "habitability improvements" for the destroyer USS *Kidd*.

Nothing is ever simple with the Pentagon. Even a newly designed bayonet becomes a "weapons system," while the smoke used in smoke bombs becomes a "universal obscurant." Even that favorite of the GI, field rations or C-rations, has now become MRE or "meal, ready to eat," though changing the name won't make it taste any better.

Then there is the "survivable enduring shelter," or SES, designed by Goodyear Aerospace to be placed on an existing truck chassis. Equipped with a 5,000-pound-plus payload, armor-plated shielding capable of stopping .30 caliber "projectiles" (Pentagon doublespeak for bullets) and an "intrusion detection system" (meaning a burglar alarm), the SES is designed "to meet the most stringent technical requirements for survival during a nuclear event," meaning it's supposed to be able to survive a nuclear bomb attack. . . .

In Other Words, It Blew Up

With doublespeak, weapons never fail. The Pentagon can explain that the cruise missile didn't fly out of control and crash in three pieces during a test flight in Canada. According to the Air Force, the missile merely "impacted with the ground prematurely." Not to be outdone by their U.S. counterparts, an official of the Canadian forces said the test flight was simply "terminated five minutes earlier than planned." When an unarmed Minuteman III intercontinental ballistic missile developed problems after launch and had to be destroyed by commands radioed from the ground, the U.S. Air Force announced, "An **anomaly** occurred during the flight which caused the early termination." Although the Bigeye aerial nerve-gas bomb has been on the drawing boards for more than 20 years, it still doesn't work and, during one test drop in 1982, the bomb malfunctioned, producing what the Pentagon called "a forcible ejection of the internal bomb components." In other words, the bomb blew up.

With doublespeak, the missile can miss the target but the test can still be a success. "We did acquire the target, but we did not hit it. . . . We achieved our objectives," said Jim Kittinger, an official in the air-to-surface guided weapons office at Elgin Air Force Base. . . .

approximately 600 words

---

anomaly (ə nomʹ ə lē) abnormal event

1. Pentagon doublespeak: Match the euphemism with the actual meaning.

   _____ 1. bullets   a. weapon impacted with the ground prematurely

   _____ 2. bayonet   b. vertically deployed anti-personnel device

   _____ 3. weapon failure   c. habitability improvements

   _____ 4. bomb   d. weapons system

   _____ 5. exorbitant money   e. projectiles
            for furnishings

2. Is the Pentagon justified in using euphemisms and doublespeak? Why, or why

   not? _____

   _____

3. What is the author's chief complaint about the military?

   _____

4. What does the cartoon on page 458 say about political correctness? Have we gone too far with its usage?

   _____

   _____

Summary

The critical reader must be aware of the writer's use of denotative and connotative language because writers frequently choose the latter, which carries implied meanings. Denotative language can be taken literally since the words mean exactly what they say, while connotative language uses words that carry suggested meanings and are designed to arouse or allay certain emotions. Recognizing whether words have implied meanings helps the reader comprehend the writer's message and therefore reach sound conclusions and form unbiased judgments about issues.

Figures of speech are one way of using connotative language. Examples of figurative language include simile, metaphor, and personification.

1. A *simile* is a comparison of two unlike objects that have one point or trait in common, signaled with words such as *like* or *as*.
2. A *metaphor* equates two unlike objects that have one point or trait in common.

3. *Personification* expresses a comparison in which an inanimate object is given life-like qualities.

Euphemisms, sometimes referred to as doublespeak, may also be used when a writer wants to say one thing but mean another. In euphemistic writing, a softer or less offensive word or phrase replaces one that is unpleasant, stronger, or harsher.

Chapter 8
Vocabulary Review
Word Analogy

At the end of Chapter 7, you were introduced to the concept of word analogies and learned that analogies are a kind of problem-solving activity because you have to figure out a particular relationship of one word or phrase when three others are given. You practiced in Chapter 7 with synonyms, relationships in which words have similarity in meaning. Another relationship involving analogies is with *antonyms,* words related through differences in meaning.

The following practice exercises use the relationship of antonyms. They are a good means of assuring that you have mastered many of the basic vocabulary for this chapter.

A. In the group that follows, two of the four words share the relationship of being antonyms; that is, two of the words have meanings *opposite* to each other. Underline the two antonyms in each line.

Example: dynamic   <u>incoherent</u>   calamitous   <u>clear</u>
　　　　　　 ("incoherent" means the *opposite* of "clear")

1. antithesis   facilitate   similarity   unique

2. abysmal   besiege   draconian   gentle

3. honest   divisive   insidious   travesty

4. mobility   unaware   perceiving   topical

5. prerequisite   hamper   needlessness   unprecedented

B. In this practice exercise with antonyms, the first set of words may contain a review word from previous chapters or, familiar words. You are to complete the second pair with a word from Chapter 8; select it from the list of boldfaced words below. You will not use all the words. Look at the example before beginning the exercise.

> **Example:** ordinary:bizarre::normal: _____
>
> (*Anomalous* is a word that could complete the analogy.)

draconian   condone   anomaly   obscenity   incoherent   formidable

1. accolade:insult::unalarming: _____

2. clarifying:confusing::clear: _____

3. admonish:praise::condemn: _____

4. conformity:deviance::propriety: _____

5. modest:iconoclastic::regular: _____

C.   Answer *true* (T) or *false* (F) for each of the following statements.

_____ 1. If someone has been **decapitated,** they have lost their capital investment.

_____ 2. When you have **guffawed** at a joke, you've laughed loudly.

_____ 3. To **malign** someone is to show them courtesy while waiting in line.

_____ 4. A **misogynous** person does not like women.

_____ 5. **Xenophobic** people have no fears.

Selection 16: **ESSAY**

 Preparation for Reading

The following essay discusses the effects of a consumer-driven society on the environment. The author makes suggestions for change that are not the ordinary ones we read about in newspapers or hear on television. While reading the essay, decide whether you agree with his conclusions. The following words are underlined in the essay.

so **acquisitive**	eager to acquire money and things; grasping
and **profligate**	recklessly wasteful
the **biosphere** can sustain	earth
the **avarice** of mankind	greed for wealth
is **insatiable**	never satisfied
and **insidiously**	working or spreading harmfully
such as **integrity**	honesty; sincerity

Preview, then read the essay.

How Much Is Enough?

Alan Durning

1 Early in the post–World War II age of affluence, a U.S. retailing analyst named Victor Lebow proclaimed, "Our enormously productive economy . . . demands that we make consumption our way of life, that we convert the buying and use of goods into rituals, that we seek our spiritual satisfaction, our ego satisfaction, in consumption. . . . We need things consumed, burned up, worn out, replaced, and discarded at an ever increasing rate." Americans have risen to Mr. Lebow's call, and much of the world has followed.

2 Since 1950, American consumption has soared. Per capita, energy use climbed 60 percent, car travel more than doubled, plastics use multiplied 20-fold, and air travel jumped 25-fold.

3 We are wealthy beyond the wildest dreams of our ancestors; the average human living today is four-and-a-half times richer than his or her great-grandparents, and the factor is larger still among the world's consuming class. American children under the age of 13 have more spending money—$230 a year—than the 300 million poorest people in the world.*

4 The richest billion people in the world have created a form of civilization so <u>acquisitive</u> and <u>profligate</u> that the planet is in danger. The lifestyle of this top echelon—the car drivers, beef eaters, soda drinkers, and throwaway consumers—constitutes an ecological threat unmatched in severity by anything but perhaps population growth. The wealthiest fifth of humankind pumps out more than half of the greenhouse gases that threaten the earth's climate and almost 90 percent of the chlorofluorocarbons

*In fact, a recent report shows that *one billion* people, from Mongolia to India, live on *less than a dollar a day!* (Ed. note)

that are destroying the earth's protective ozone layer.

Ironically, abundance has not even made people terribly happy. In the United States, repeated opinion polls of people's sense of well-being show that no more Americans are satisfied with their lot now than they were in 1957. Despite phenomenal growth in consumption, the list of wants has grown faster still. 5

Of course, the other extreme from overconsumption—poverty—is no solution to environmental or human problems: it is infinitely worse for people and equally bad for the environment. Dispossessed peasants slash-and-burn their way into the rain forests of Latin America, and hungry nomads turn their herds out onto fragile African range land, reducing it to desert. If environmental decline results when people have either too little or too much, we must ask ourselves: How much is enough? What level of consumption can the earth support? When does consumption cease to add appreciably to human satisfaction? 6

Answering these questions definitively is impossible, but for each of us in the world's consuming class, seeking answers may be a prerequisite to transforming our civilization into one the biosphere can sustain. 7

The Compulsion to Consume

"The avarice of mankind is insatiable," declared Aristotle 23 centuries ago, setting off a debate that has raged ever since among human hearts. But whatever share of our acquisitiveness is part of our nature, the compulsion to have more has never been so actively promoted, nor so easily acted upon, as it is today. 8

We are encouraged to consume at every turn by the advertising industry, which annually spends nearly $500 per U.S. citizen, by the commercialization of everything from sporting events to public spaces, and, insidiously, by the spread of the mass market into realms once dominated by family members and local enterprises. Cooking from scratch is replaced by heating prepared foods in the microwave; the neighborhood baker and greengrocer are driven out by the 24-hour supermarket at the mall. As our day-to-day interactions with the economy lose the face-to-face character that prevails in surviving communities, buying things becomes a substitute source of self-worth. 9

Traditional measures of success, such as integrity, honesty, skill and hard work, are gradually supplanted by a simple, universally recognizable indicator of achievement—money. One Wall Street banker put it bluntly to the *New York Times:* "net worth equals self-worth." Under this definition, there is no such thing as enough. Consumption becomes a treadmill with everyone judging their status by who's ahead of them and who's behind. 10

Ethics for Sustainability

The basic value of a sustainable society, the ecological equivalent of the Golden Rule, is simple: Each generation should meet its needs without jeopardizing the prospects of future generations. What is lacking is the practical knowledge—at each level of society—of what living by that principle means. 11

In a fragile biosphere, the ultimate fate of humanity may depend on whether we can cultivate a deeper sense of self-restraint, founded on a widespread ethic of limiting consumption and finding nonmaterial enrichment. 12

Those who seek to rise to this environmental challenge may find encouragement in the body of human wisdom passed down from antiquity. To seek out sufficiency is to follow the path of voluntary simplicity preached by all the sages from Buddha to Mohammed. Typical of these pronouncements is this passage from the Bible: "What shall it profit a man if he shall gain the whole world and lose his own soul?" 13

Living by this credo is not easy. As historian David Shi of Davidson College in North Carolina chronicles, the call for a simpler life is perennial through the history of the North American continent: the Puritans of Massachusetts Bay, the 14

Quakers of Philadelphia, the Amish, the Shakers, the experimental utopian communities of the 1830s, the hippies of the 1960s, and the back-to-the-land movement of the 1970s.

None of these movements ever gained more than a slim minority of adherents. Elsewhere in the world, entire nations have dedicated themselves to rebuilding human character—sometimes through brutal techniques—in a less self-centered mold, and nowhere have they succeeded with more than a token few of their citizens. **15**

It would be hopelessly naive to believe that entire populations will suddenly experience a moral awakening, renouncing greed, envy, and avarice. The best that can be hoped for is a gradual widening of the circle of those practicing voluntary simplicity. The goal of creating a sustainable culture, that is, a culture of permanence, is best thought of as a challenge that will last several generations. **16**

Voluntary simplicity, or personal restraint, will do little good, however, if it is not wedded to bold political steps that confront the forces advocating consumption. Beyond the oft-repeated agenda of environmental and social reforms necessary to achieve sustainability, such as overhauling energy systems, stabilizing population, and ending poverty, action is needed to restrain the excesses of advertising, to curb the shopping culture, and to revitalize household and community economies as human-scale alternatives to the high-consumption lifestyle. **17**

For example, if fairly distributed between the sexes, cooking from scratch can be dignified and use fewer resources than the frozen instant meal. Just so, communities that turn main streets into walking zones where local artisans and farmers display their products while artists, musicians, and theater troupes perform can provide a richness of human interaction that shopping malls will never match. **18**

There could be many more people ready to begin saying "enough" than prevailing opinion suggests. After all, much of what we consume is wasted or unwanted in the first place. How much of the packaging that wraps products we consume each year—462 pounds per capita in the United States—would we rather never see? How many of the distant farms turned to suburban housing developments could have been left in crops if we insisted on well-planned land use inside city limits? **19**

How many of the unsolicited sales pitches each American receives each day in the mail—37 percent of all mail—are nothing but bothersome junk? How much of the advertising in our morning newspaper—covering 65 percent of the newsprint in American papers—would we not gladly see left out? **20**

How many of the miles we drive—almost 6,000 a year apiece in the United States—would we not happily give up if livable neighborhoods were closer to work, a variety of local merchants closer to home, streets safe to walk and bicycle, and public transit easier and faster? How much of the fossil energy we use is wasted because utility companies fail to put money into efficient renewable energy systems before building new coal plants? **21**

In the final analysis, accepting and living by sufficiency rather than excess offers a return to what is, culturally speaking, the human home: the ancient order of family, community, good work and good life; to a reverence for excellence of craftsmanship; to a true materialism that does not just care *about* things but cares *for* them; to communities worth spending a lifetime in. **22**

Maybe Henry David Thoreau had it right when he scribbled in his notebook beside Walden Pond, "A man is rich in proportion to the things he can afford to let alone." **23**

approximately 1500 words

COMPREHENSION CHECK

Part I
General Comprehension Questions: Literal and Interpretive

A. Write the correct letter in the space provided.

_____ 1. Which of the following statements best expresses the author's thesis?

    a. Governments must dictate a simpler lifestyle for their citizens.
    b. A simpler lifestyle would eliminate car drivers, beef eaters, and throwaway consumers.
    c. We need to return to the biblical ways of the Puritans and Quakers.
    d. A simpler lifestyle based on sufficiency, not excess, is needed to save our biosphere.

_____ 2. The statement by Aristotle, "The avarice of mankind is insatiable," strengthens Durning's thesis because it means

    a. people live by greed.
    b. human greed can never be satisfied.
    c. people should have no part of greed.
    d. human greed is natural.

_____ 3. The author believes the real culprits in this difficult situation are

    a. the advertising industry and mass marketing.
    b. consumers.
    c. poor nations.
    d. all of the above.

_____ 4. In terms of success, Durning concludes we are measured

    a. by the position we hold.
    b. by the clothes we wear.
    c. by the amount of money we have.
    d. by our lifestyle.

B. Answer in the spaces provided.

5. ***Fact, Opinion, or Combination:*** Write F, O, or F/O in the space provided. Write your support.

    a. "American children under the age of 13 have more spending money—$230 a year—than the 300 million poorest people in the world." (para. 3)

    _____

    Support: _____

b. "The richest billion people in the world have created a form of civilization so acquisitive and profligate that the planet is in danger." (para. 4)

_____

Support: _____

c. "None of these movements [that called for a simpler life] ever gained more than a slim minority of adherents." (para. 15)

_____

Support: _____

6. **Connotative/Denotative Language:** Determine whether the following statements contain connotative language. Write _yes_ or _no_ in the space provided. Underline the connotative phrase.

a. "The lifestyle of this top echelon—the car drivers, beef eaters, soda drinkers, and throwaway consumers—constitutes an ecological threat unmatched in severity. . . . " (para. 4)

_____

b. "We are encouraged to consume at every turn by the advertising industry . . . and, insidiously, by the spread of the mass market. . . . " (para. 9)

_____

c. "In a fragile biosphere, the ultimate fate of humanity may depend on whether we can cultivate a deeper sense of self-restraint. . . . " (para. 12)

_____

7. **Figurative Language:** In the space provided, indicate what is being compared, what type of figurative language is being used, and what the author actually means.

a. "Consumption becomes a treadmill with everyone judging their status by who's ahead of them and who's behind." (para. 10)

_____

b. "Voluntary simplicity, or personal restraint, will do little good, however, if it is not wedded to bold political steps. . . . " (para. 17)

_____

_____

8. Judge the merits of these statements, the first by the author, the second a quote from Thoreau. Are they valid or invalid? Write a V or I in the space provided.

   a. " . . . Buying things becomes a substitute for self-worth." _____

      _____

      Reason: _____

   b. "A man is rich in proportion to the things he can afford to let alone."

      _____

      Reason: _____

9. Explain how paragraph 1, with a quote by Victor Lebow, strengthens Durning's thesis statement.

   _____

   _____

10. The author states, "Elsewhere in the world, entire nations have dedicated them-selves to rebuilding human character—sometimes through brutal techniques—in a less self-centered mold, and nowhere have they succeeded with more than a token few of their citizens." What nations could he have been referring to? Are there any such nations today?

   _____

   _____

Part II
Application Questions for Writing and Discussion

11. The author states that "action is needed to restrain the excesses of advertisers, to curb the shopping culture, and to revitalize household and community economies. . . . " How realistic are his suggestions?

   _____

   _____

   _____

12. What steps would you consider taking to eliminate some of the excesses of materialism in our society?

_____

_____

Part III
Extend Your Vocabulary

Match these terms. Write the correct letter in the space provided.

_____ 1. profligate   a. working or spreading harmfully

_____ 2. insatiable   b. never satisfied

_____ 3. insidiously   c. recklessly wasteful

_____ 4. echelon   d. eager to acquire money and things

_____ 5. acquisitive   e. level of responsibility in an organization

Preparation for Reading

The senior policy analyst at the Office of National Drug Control, Ross Deck, said recently, "We are not fighting a drug war anymore. To have a war, we must have enemies. In this situation, we are our own enemy. And we cannot declare war simply because we killed ourselves."* Read to learn how we are "killing" ourselves, how the definition of the term *drug* has been evolving, and what constitutes a drinking problem and drug addiction. As you read, consider some of the staggering costs to society as a whole that are the direct result of substance abuse. The boldfaced words are underlined in the text.

stereotype of the drug user	a fixed concept of a person, group, or idea
to be continuing **unabated**	without being stopped
to **ferret** out substance abuse	to search for or to discover
euphoric appearance	high-spirited feeling
deterioration of work habits	lowering of quality

Preview, then read the selection.

The Wrong Way to Manage Distress: Substance Abuse

Michael W. Drafke and Stan Kossen

Substance abuse has emerged in recent decades as a major concern both on and off 1
the job. Although reasons vary, substance abuse can be a way that some people try to manage or reduce distress. Here, a general overview of the nature and extent of the problems of alcohol and drug abuse are presented.

What Constitutes a Drinking Problem?

We should be clear about what is generally meant by a drinking problem. In all cases 2
related to alcohol abuse, a common factor is the unfavorable effect alcohol has on the health or well-being of the drinker and his or her associates. Common signs and symptoms that frequently indicate a drinking problem are listed in Table 8.1. In general:

- Alcoholics are absent from work two to four times more often than non-alcoholics.
- On-the-job accidents for alcoholics are two to four times more frequent than for nonalcoholics. Off-the-job accidents are four to six times more numerous.

*Frank Schmalleger, *Criminal Justice Today* 568.

TABLE 8.1
Common Signs and Symptoms of Alcohol Dependency

Early morning drinking

Drinking to calm nerves, forget worries, or reduce depression

Getting drunk often (more than three or five times during a year)

Going to work intoxicated

Drinking alone with increased frequency

Injuring oneself, or someone else, while intoxicated

Gulping drinks and drinking too fast

Loss of interest in food

Driving a motorized vehicle while intoxicated

Regularly acting irritable, resentful, or unreasonable when not drinking

Doing something under the influence of alcohol that one avows would never occur without alcohol

Absenteeism, especially on Monday mornings and after holidays

Hand tremors

Occasional complaints from customers of the company

Decline in work performance

- Sickness and accident benefits paid out for alcoholics are three times greater than for the average nonalcoholic.
- Alcoholics file four times more grievances than nonalcoholics.

Easy to Cover Up?

Alcoholic employees can sometimes go undetected for years. Coworkers cover up   3
for those unable to perform their jobs because of drunkenness. Even managers may
be adept at concealing their alcohol abuse problems. Their secretaries or loyal associates may cover up for them. Alcoholics can be clever at inventing "credible"
excuses when detected. "I must have a drink or two when I'm entertaining customers, of course."

Drug Abuse

Drug abuse, or drug addiction, exists when the taking of drugs, whether prescribed   4
or nonprescribed, legal or illegal, causes difficulties in any area of an individual's
life. Years ago, the stereotype of the drug user was either of a glazed-eyed musician
frantically beating his sticks on the tight skin of a drum or of a person who dwelled
in a ghetto. Mass publicity on drug abuse has long since caused that stereotype to
fade from view.

Complicating the ongoing war on drugs are changes in public attitudes and 5 drug-use patterns. It sometimes seems that no sooner is progress made in combatting one illegal drug than a different kind of substance abuse comes into vogue. Ethyl alcohol was the social drug during Prohibition, marijuana became the social drug of the 1960s and 1970s, and some observers believe that crack cocaine and possibly ecstasy—another so-called upper—have become the social drugs of the 1980s and 1990s. The drugs of choice and people's attitudes toward them may constantly change, but the problem of drug abuse appears to be continuing <u>unabated</u>.

Recognizing Alcohol and Drug Abuse in the Workplace

Pinpointing the specific symptoms of alcohol and drug abuse problems is not a sim- 6 ple task. A supervisor's main responsibility, therefore, should not necessarily be uncovering evidence of dependency on alcohol and drugs but instead be observant for declining job performance. Yet there are certain behavioral patterns that some excessive users of alcohol and drugs display. These patterns can sometimes be spotted through simple observation. Increasingly, however, employers are taking more aggressive steps to <u>ferret</u> out substance abuse among their workforces. A growing number of companies, especially large ones with more than 5,000 people and those in businesses with the potential to affect public health or safety (e.g., transportation companies, utilities, hazardous-materials handlers), are adopting drug-testing programs.

Signs of Alcohol Dependency

The signs of alcohol dependency, unfortunately, do not always become manifest 7 until the middle or late stages of the problem. The earlier treatment begins, naturally, the easier it will be. A person could experience some isolated incidents of such drinking problems without necessarily being an alcoholic. However, alcohol abuse usually results in declining job performance.

Signs of Drug Dependency

Drug dependency also produces observable changes in work performance. The 8 signs of drug dependency, however, are not always obvious. Some managers have mistaken an employee's <u>euphoric</u> appearance for the "look of love." Some of the symptoms associated with alcoholism could also be related to drug dependency. Some of the principal warning signs related to drug use are listed in Table 8.2.

No one person would necessarily have all or any of the symptoms cited in Table 9 8.2, and a supervisor should guard against assuming that the presence of one or more symptoms is conclusive proof of alcohol or drug abuse. Symptoms will likewise vary with the stage of alcoholism or the type of drug used as well as with the experience of the drug user. Urine samples have indicated the taking of certain drugs in quantities that would kill less experienced users; yet the users went undetected until examined medically.

TABLE 8.2
Possible Warning Signs Related to Drug Abuse

Anxiety reactions and states of panic

Accidents due to impaired judgment and distorted perceptions of space or time

Attitudes of paranoia or excessive suspicion of others

Mental confusion, loss of contact with reality, and lapses of memory

Indifferent, apathetic, and sometimes compulsive behavior

Dilated pupils, a flushed face, and a feeling of being chilly

Chronic sniffles

Occasional convulsions

A deterioration of values

Falling asleep on the job, drowsiness

Abscesses, needle marks, and "tracks" (discolorations along the course of veins in the arms and legs)

The regular wearing of dark sunglasses indoors (to protect dilated pupils)

An unhealthy appearance because of poor diet and personal neglect

Drugs and the Workplace

The owner of a small family-run business in the Midwest took a walk through his 10
plant one day. He didn't know what to do with the suspicious looking packet of white powder he found on his way through the building, so he called in the local police to take a look. An investigation revealed a ring of cocaine dealers operating out of the company's facilities. They were moving the drug inside the stuffed animals manufactured there.

This is a true story, and its meaning is plain: drugs can be present in any work- 11
place—anywhere, anytime. In recent years, there have been numerous documented cases of work-related accidents due to drug abuse, such events as train and plane crashes. Even managees at some nuclear plants were reported as having been high on drugs while working with highly dangerous radioactive materials.

Organizational Approaches to Alcohol and Drug Abuse

Until relatively recently, most managers seemed not to want to recognize that alco- 12
hol and drug abuse were organizational behavior problems in need of their attention. When cases did become known, they were often covered up until the managee could no longer function effectively on the job and had to be dismissed, which did little to correct the individual's problem. At long last, however, most authorities recognize that alcoholism and drug addiction are treatable diseases and therefore require medical attention or therapy, as do other diseases.

An increasing number of organizations, private and public, have taken an active 13
interest in attempting to reduce the prevalence of these two costly afflictions by
developing employee assistance programs that offer help for alcoholism, drug
abuse, and other behavioral problems and chronic illness. Many corporations have
established in-house employee assistance programs. Many executives believe that
their businesses have actually saved money as a result of investing in such programs.

The Nature of Company Programs

Organizations with established programs have attempted to steer clear of the tradi- 14
tional solutions of either firing the person with a drinking or drug problem, giving
sermons on the evils of excessive consumption of alcohol, or calling in the police.
Instead, modern organizations have concentrated on counseling people to seek
treatment, generally with an outside agency while keeping them on the job.
Although sympathetic understanding of the problem is conveyed, the employee is
told that <u>deterioration</u> of work habits, absenteeism, or other troubles created by
alcohol or drug abuse will not be tolerated indefinitely. Typical programs, therefore,
deal with three principal stages: detection, treatment, and rehabilitation.

The Stigma of Alcoholism and Drug Programs

The words *alcoholic* and *drug addict* have disagreeable and frightening connotations 15
to most people. Company managers involved with the establishment of Employee
Assistance Programs (EAPs) need to be concerned with semantics when determining what to call their plans. A key problem, therefore, is how to eliminate the stigma
of such programs.

As we've already mentioned, the programs shouldn't be considered as some- 16
thing separate and apart from other medical and counseling services. Some
employee relations directors believe that calling something an alcohol program
gives it the kiss of death. Some organizations use broad titles such as "Employee
Counseling Service" or "Employee Assistance Program," preferring not to
stress solely the problems of alcohol and drug dependency. These programs frequently include assistance in a variety of other areas such as self-identity, health, marriage, and financial difficulties. Some firms even prefer to avoid any stigma that
might be associated with the words *counseling* or *therapy*. To make it easier for
employees to get advice on drug programs, some companies, such as Xerox, have
established toll-free numbers that workers and their families can call to get advice
on drug problems. These services guarantee privacy to employees. The hotline
counselors attempt to encourage employees to seek help through EAPs or local clinical programs.

approximately 1480 words

Michael W. Drafke and Stan Kossen, "The Wrong Way to Manage Distress: Substance
Abuse," *The Human Side of Organizations,* 7th ed. 422–26. Copyright © 1998 by
Addison Wesley Longman, Inc. Reprinted by permission of the publishers.

COMPREHENSION CHECK

Part I
General Comprehension Questions: Literal and Interpretive

Write the correct letter in the space provided.

_____ 1. One sign of a drinking problem not listed in Table 8.1 is
    a. early morning drinking.
    b. hand tremors.
    c. hiding liquor in closets.
    d. drinking too fast.

_____ 2. According to the author, the problem of drug abuse appears to be
    a. lessening.
    b. curbed.
    c. restricted.
    d. unstoppable.

_____ 3. Possible warning signs related to drug abuse include
    a. excessive suspicion of others.
    b. stealing money.
    c. lapses of memory.
    d. both a and c.

_____ 4. Today, the method of handling employees with substance abuse problems for most employers is to
    a. fire them.
    b. offer guidance programs.
    c. lecture them.
    d. cover up for them.

_____ 5. On the job, alcoholics are often found to
    a. be high-paid workers.
    b. act happy-go-lucky.
    c. be less creative.
    d. file more grievances than nonalcoholics.

6. ***Denotative/Connotative and Persuasive Language:*** Underline the figurative expression in this sentence and explain its literal meaning: "Some managers have mistaken an employee's euphoric appearance for the 'look of love.' "

_____

7. Why do the terms "alcoholic" and "drug addiction" have frightening connotations for many?

_____

_____

_____

8. What conclusion can you draw from the fact that, according to the author, there is a stigma attached to certain words chosen to label drug rehabilitation programs?

_____

_____

_____

_____

_____

Part II
Application Questions for Writing and Discussion

9. Given the staggering cost to society of dealing with alcoholism, who should bear the financial cost: the alcoholic, the taxpayers, businesses, or the government? Should cases be resolved in the courts or by the medical profession?

_____

_____

_____

_____

_____

10. Complete the checklist on page 477, which was included in the chapter you just read an excerpt of, and then answer the question that follows here.

Discuss how valid you think the questions are to help determine whether someone has a drinking problem. Would you exclude some of the questions, or include others not mentioned, if you were to compile such a list?

_____

_____

_____

_____

_____

Don't Say Yes

Anyone concerned about alcohol abuse should ask himself or herself the following questions (any *yes* answers could be an indication of a current or potential alcohol problem):

Yes   No

1. Do you drink to feel better about yourself?
2. Do you turn to alcohol when you have troubles?
3. Do you make excuses for the reasons you drink?
4. Do you feel guilty after drinking?
5. Do you drink to help you sleep?
6. Do you often have diarrhea, indigestion, or nausea due to drinking?
7. Have you had other health problems related to drinking?
8. Have you ever fallen down or burned yourself while drinking?
9. Do you feel worried, anxious, or depressed most of the time?
10. Do you find yourself not realizing you are repeating things while drinking?
11. Have you ever put yourself or others in danger by driving after drinking?
12. Have you ever missed work or put off work because of drinking?
13. Have you had financial or legal problems in which drinking was involved?
14. Do you drink alone?
15. Do you drink less with others?
16. Do you feel isolated and alone?
17. Do you often feel the need to telephone people when you are drinking?
18. Have you changed friends to be around people who drink like you do?
19. Do you hide your drinking from your spouse or children?
20. Have others told you that they think you drink too much?
21. Is your parent or spouse a heavy drinker?
22. Do you think you drink too much?
23. Do you plan activities around being able to drink?
24. Do you find yourself thinking of drinking in-between times?
25. Have you failed in promises to yourself to cut down on your drinking?
26. Are there times when you don't drink because you're afraid you'll lose control of yourself?
27. Do you drink and use other drugs?

Part III
Extend Your Vocabulary

Use the context to determine the meaning of each of the boldfaced words in the following sentences, quoted from the text. Write the correct letter in the space provided.

_____ 1. "Alcoholics can be clever at inventing "**credible**" excuses when detected." (para. 3)

     a. many   b. unreal   c. believable   d. questionable

_____ 2. " . . . Employers are taking more **aggressive** steps to ferret out substance abuse among their workforces." (para. 6)

     a. annoying   b. obvious   c. painful   d. resourceful

_____ 3. "The signs of alcohol dependency, unfortunately, do not always become **manifest** until the middle or late stages. . . . " (para. 7)

     a. unmanageable   b. obvious   c. complex   d. addictive

_____ 4. "Company managers . . . need to be concerned with **semantics** when determining what to call their plans." (para. 15)

     a. syntax   b. diversity   c. political correctness   d. word meaning

_____ 5. "A key problem, therefore, is how to eliminate the **stigma** of such programs." (para. 15)

     a. requirement   b. burden   c. disgrace   d. attitude

Selection 18: **LITERATURE**

 Preparation for Reading

José Vasconcelos, author of "The Boar Hunt," was an educator, a journalist, a prolific writer of essays, a politician, and a longtime public figure in Mexico. At one time, he was a presidential candidate. Although born at a time when such ideas were unpopular in his country (he died in 1959), he declared that

Latin America needed to do something about its soaring birthrate.
People of all races should be treated fairly and should have equal opportunity rights.
Every individual is obligated to contribute his or her talents to the betterment of society.

In a manner of speaking, we can say that the short story that follows, "The Boar Hunt," is actually an essay on human behavior. Four hunters engage in what they believe will be an exhilarating experience. They are to explore territory that they have always dreamed about, and they believe their dreams are about to come true. Read to find out if their dreams actually do become a reality or if there is irony in the adventure.

Note the meaning of the boldfaced words before reading. They are underlined in the text.

assured ourselves **reciprocally**	performing or having an experience by both sides
lethargy of the jungle	lazy stupor; sluggish indifference
prevent the **methodical** killing	done in a systematic or regular order
infamy of the hunter	evil fame or reputation

The Boar Hunt

José Vasconcelos

We were four companions, and we went by the names of our respective nationalities: 1
the Columbian, the Peruvian, the Mexican; the fourth, a native of Ecuador, was
called Quito for short. Unforeseen chance had joined us together a few years ago on
a large sugar plantation on the Peruvian coast. We worked at different occupations
during the day and met during the evening in our off time. Not being Englishmen,
we did not play cards. Instead, our constant discussions led to disputes. These didn't
stop us from wanting to see each other the next night, however, to continue the
interrupted debates and support them with new arguments. Nor did the rough sentences of the preceding wrangles indicate a lessening of our affection, of which we
assured ourselves <u>reciprocally</u> with the clasping of hands and a look. On Sundays we
used to go on hunting parties. We roamed the fertile glens, stalking, generally with

poor results, the game of the warm region around the coast, or we entertained ourselves killing birds that flew in the sunlight during the siesta hour.

We came to be tireless wanderers and excellent marksmen. Whenever we **2** climbed a hill and gazed at the imposing range of mountains in the interior, its attractiveness stirred us and we wanted to climb it. What attracted us more was the trans-Andean region: fertile plateaus extending on the other side of the range in the direction of the Atlantic toward the immense land of Brazil. It was as if primitive nature called us to her breast. The vigor of the fertile, untouched jungles promised to rejuvenate our minds, the same vigor which rejuvenates the strength and the thickness of the trees each year. At times we devised crazy plans. As with all things that are given a lot of thought, these schemes generally materialized. Ultimately nature and events are largely what our imaginations make them out to be. And so we went ahead planning and acting. At the end of the year, with arranged vacations, accumulated money, good rifles, abundant munitions, stone- and mud-proof boots, four hammocks, and a half dozen faithful Indians, our caravan descended the Andean slopes, leading to the endless green ocean.

At last we came upon a village at the edge of the Marañón River. Here we **3** changed our safari. The region we were going to penetrate had no roads. It was unexplored underbrush into which we could enter only by going down the river in a canoe. In time we came to the area where we proposed to carry out the purpose of our journey, the hunting of wild boars.

We had been informed that boars travel in herds of several thousands, occupy- **4** ing a region, eating grass and staying together, exploiting the grazing areas, organized just like an army. They are very easy to kill if one attacks them when they are scattered out satisfying their appetites—an army given over to the delights of victory. When they march about hungry, on the other hand, they are usually vicious. In our search we glided down river between imposing jungles with our provisions and the company of three faithful Indian oarsmen.

One morning we stopped at some huts near the river. Thanks to the information **5** gathered there, we decided to disembark a little farther on in order to spend the night on land and continue the hunt for the boars in the thicket the following day.

Sheltered in a backwater, we came ashore, and after a short exploration found **6** a clearing in which to make camp. We unloaded the provisions and the rifles, tied the boat securely, then with the help of the Indians set up our camp one-half kilometer from the riverbank. In marking the path to the landing, we were careful not to lose ourselves in the thicket. The Indians withdrew toward their huts, promising to return two days later. At dawn we would set out in search of the prey.

Though night had scarcely come and the heat was great, we gathered at the fire **7** to see each other's faces, to look instinctively for protection. We talked a little, confessed to being tired, and decided to go to bed. Each hammock had been tied by one end to a single tree, firm though not very thick in the trunk. Stretching out from this axis in different directions, the hammocks were supported by the other end on other trunks. Each of us carried his rifle, cartridges, and some provisions which couldn't remain exposed on the ground. The sight of the weapons made us consider the place where we were, surrounded by the unknown. A slight feeling of terror made us laugh, cough, and talk. But fatigue overcame us, that heavy fatigue which compels the soldier to scorn danger, to put down his rifle, and to fall asleep though the most persistent enemy pursues him. We scarcely noticed the supreme grandeur of that remote tropical night.

8 I don't know whether it was the light of the magnificent dawn or the strange noises which awakened me and made me sit up in my hammock and look carefully at my surroundings. I saw nothing but the awakening of that life which at night falls into the <u>lethargy</u> of the jungle. I called my sleeping companions and, alert and seated in our hanging beds, we dressed ourselves. We were preparing to jump to the ground when we clearly heard a somewhat distant, sudden sound of rustling branches. Since it did not continue, however, we descended confidently, washed our faces with water from our canteens, and slowly prepared and served breakfast. By about 11:00 in the morning we were armed and bold and preparing to make our way through the jungle.

9 But then the sound again. Its persistence and proximity in the thicket made us change our minds. An instinct made us take refuge in our hammocks. We cautiously moved our cartridges and rifles into them again, and without consulting each other we agreed on the idea of putting our firearms safely away. We passed them up into the hammocks, and we ourselves finally climbed in. Stretched out face down, comfortably suspended with rifles in hand, we did not have to wait long. Black, agile boars quickly appeared from all directions. We welcomed them with shouts of joy and well-aimed shots. Some fell immediately, giving comical snorts, but many more came out of the jungle. We shot again, spending all the cartridges in the magazine. Then we stopped to reload. Finding ourselves safe in the height of our hammocks, we continued after a pause.

10 We counted dozens of them. At a glance we made rapid calculations of the magnitude of the destruction, while the boars continued to come out of the jungle in uncountable numbers. Instead of going on their way or fleeing, they seemed confused. All of them emerged from the jungle where it was easy for us to shoot them. Occasionally we had to stop firing because the frequent shooting heated the barrels of our rifles. While they were cooling we were able to joke, celebrating our good fortune. The impotent anger of the boars amazed us. They raised their tusks in our direction, uselessly threatening us. We laughed at their snorts, quietly aimed at those who were near, and Bang! a dead boar. We carefully studied the angle of the shoulder blade so that the bullet would cross the heart. The slaughter lasted for hours.

11 At 4:00 P.M. we noticed an alarming shortage of our ammunition. We had been well supplied and had shot at will. Though the slaughter was gratifying, the boars must have numbered, as we had been informed previously, several thousands, because their hordes didn't diminish. On the contrary, they gathered directly beneath our hammocks in increasing groups. They slashed furiously at the trunk of the tree which held the four points of the hammocks. The marks of the tusks remained on the hard bark. Not without a certain fear we watched them gather compactly, tenaciously, in tight masses against the resisting trunk. We wondered

what would happen to a man who fell within their reach. Our shots were now spo-radic, well aimed, carefully husbanded. They did not drive away the aggressive beasts, but only redoubled their fury. One of us ironically noted that from being the attackers we had gone on the defensive. We did not laugh very long at the joke. Now we hardly shot at all. We needed to save our cartridges.

The afternoon waned and evening came upon us. After consulting each other, **12** we decided to eat in our hammocks. We applauded ourselves for taking the food up—meat, bread, and bottles of water. Stretching ourselves on our hammocks, we passed things to each other, sharing what we needed. The boars deafened us with their angry snorts.

After eating, we began to feel calm. We lit cigars. Surely the boars would go. **13** Their numbers were great, but they would finally leave peacefully. As we said so, how-ever, we looked with greedy eyes at the few unused cartridges that remained. Our enemies, like enormous angry ants, stirred beneath us, encouraged by the ceasing of our fire. From time to time we carefully aimed and killed one or two of them, dri-ving off the huge group of uselessly enraged boars at the base of the trunk which served as a prop for our hammocks.

Night enveloped us almost without our noticing the change from twilight. **14** Anxiety also overtook us. When would the cursed boars leave? Already there were enough dead to serve as trophies to several dozen hunters. Our feat would be talked about; we had to show ourselves worthy of such fame. Since there was nothing else to do, it was necessary to sleep. Even if we had had enough bullets it would have been impossible to continue the fight in the darkness. It occurred to us to start a fire to drive the herd off with flames, but apart from the fact that we couldn't leave the place in which we were suspended, there were no dry branches in the lush forest. Finally, we slept.

We woke up a little after midnight. The darkness was profound, but the well- **15** known noise made us aware that our enemies were still there. We imagined they must be the last ones which were leaving, however. If a good army needs several hours to break camp and march off, what can be expected of a vile army of boars but disorder and delay? The following morning we would fire upon the stragglers, but this painful thought bothered us: they were in large and apparently active numbers. What were they up to? Why didn't they leave? We thus spent long hours of worry. Dawn finally came, splendid in the sky but noisy in the jungle still enveloped inwardly in shadows. We eagerly waited for the sun to penetrate the foliage in order to survey the appearance of the field of battle of the day before.

What we finally saw made us gasp. It terrified us. The boars were painstakingly **16** continuing the work which they had engaged in throughout the entire night. Guided by some extraordinary instinct, with their tusks they were digging out the ground underneath the tree from which our hammocks hung; they gnawed the roots and continued to undermine them like large, industrious rats. Presently the tree was bound to fall and we with it, among the beasts. From that moment we neither thought nor talked. In desperation we used up our last shots, killing more ferocious beasts. Still, the rest renewed their activity. They seemed to be endowed with intelligence. However much we concentrated our fire against them, they did not stop their attack against the tree.

Soon our shots stopped. We emptied our pistols, and then silently listened to the **17** tusks gnawing beneath the soft, wet, pleasant-smelling earth. From time to time the boars pressed against the tree, pushing it and making it creak, eager to smash it quickly. We looked on, hypnotized by their devilish activity. It was impossible to flee because the black monsters covered every inch in sight. It seemed to us that, by a sudden inspiration, they were preparing to take revenge on us for the ruthless nature of man, the unpunished destroyer of animals since the beginning of time. Our imagination, distorted by fear, showed us our fate as an atonement for the unpardonable crimes implicit in the struggle of biological selection. Before my eyes passed the vision of sacred India, where the believer refuses to eat meat in order to prevent the <u>methodical</u> killing of beasts and in order to atone for man's evil, bloody, treacherous slaughter, such as ours, for mere vicious pleasure. I felt that the multitude of boars was raising its accusing voice against me. I now understood the <u>infamy</u> of the hunter, but what was repentance worth if I was going to die with my companions, hopelessly devoured by that horde of brutes with demonlike eyes?

Stirred by terror and without realizing what I was doing, I hung from the upper **18** end of my hammock, I balanced myself in the air, I swung in a long leap, I grasped a branch of a tree facing the one on which the boars were digging. From there I leaped to other branches and to others, reviving in myself habits which the species had forgotten.

The next moment a terrifying sound and unforgettable cries told me of the fall **19** of the tree and the end of my companions. I clung to a trunk, trembling and listening to the chattering of my jaws. Later, the desire to flee gave me back my strength. Leaning out over the foliage, I looked for a path, and I saw boars in the distance, marching in compressed ranks and holding their insolent snouts in the air. I knew that they were now withdrawing, and I got down from the tree. Horror overwhelmed me as I approached the site of our encampment, but some idea of duty made me return there. Perhaps one of my friends had managed to save himself. I approached hesitantly. Each dead boar made me tremble with fear.

But what I saw next was so frightful that I could not fix it clearly in my mind: **20** remains of clothing—and footwear. There was no doubt; the boars had devoured them. Then I ran toward the river, following the tracks we had made two days before. I fled with great haste, limbs stiff from panic.

Running with long strides, I came upon the boat. With a great effort, I managed **21** to row to the huts. There I went to bed with a high fever which lasted many days.

I will participate in no more hunts. I will contribute, if I have to, to the exter- **22** mination of harmful beasts. But I will not kill for pleasure. I will not amuse myself with the ignoble pleasure of the hunt.

approximately 2500 words

José Vasconcelos, "The Boar Hunt," translated by Paul Waldorf from *The Muse in Mexico: A Mid-Century Miscellany,* Supplement to the *Texas Quarterly* 11. 1 (Spring 1959). 64–69. Copyright © 1959 by The University of Texas Press. Reprinted by permission of the publisher.

Questions for Writing and Discussion

1. What were some important facts the hunters failed to consider that might have prevented the final outcome of the hunt?

2. Contrast the difference in the narrator's attitude toward the hunt at the beginning of the story, in the middle, and at the end.

3. The author uses the word *slaughter* several times in detailing his adventure. How is this choice related to the author's message and conclusion?

 *JOURNAL ENTRY*

In the essay "How Much Is Enough?" the textbook selection "The Wrong Way to Manage Distress: Substance Abuse," and the literature selection "The Boar Hunt," the subject of "excess" in our society is a common theme. Which selection affected you the most? Write a journal entry and describe whether these reading experiences have changed any of your views concerning your role and responsibility both in society and to the environment. You might also want to write about other excesses not described in these selections about which you feel strongly.

9

Recognizing Tone, Purpose, and Point of View: Aids to Critical Thinking

This chapter will help you

❋ Understand the relationship between tone, purpose, and style.

❋ Learn key terms and descriptive words useful in identifying tone.

❋ Recognize different points of view.

❋ Develop the ability to evaluate a writer's credibility.

❋ Evaluate the reliability of Internet information.

Before reading, think about these questions.

❋ What purpose might a writer have besides informing or entertaining the reader?

❋ How does tone of voice differ from tone in writing?

❋ Why is it important to examine an author's credentials and background?

❋ Is the Internet a reliable source for researching controversial topics?

Jot down how you go about deciding what to believe when you read.

_____

_____

⤳ Tuning in to Tone

When people speak, we generally recognize their attitude, feelings, or point of view by their tone of voice and physical gestures. Tone of voice can include loudness, pitch, inflection, choice of words, and speed of delivery. Physical gestures refer to body language: the smile on a face, a raised eyebrow, a wink, a frown, the speaker's stance. Whether the speaker is pleased, angry, serious, or sad is indicated by voice and gestures.

In writing, the tone is chiefly controlled by the words the writer chooses, words that color ideas, evoke desired emotions, and imply judgments. Recognizing a writer's tone is a valuable clue to determining purpose (*why* the writer says something) and point of view (*how* the writer looks at a topic), both important in critical reading.

Tone reflects the writer's atttitude toward a topic. It is the emotional message behind the writer's words. As you learned in Chapter 8, the writer's intent when choosing emotional words is to influence the reader's thinking. "An important function of language," says Richard Altick in *Preface to Critical Reading*, "is to mold the reader's attitude toward the subject discussed. Tone determines just what that attitude should be."

In literary writing, such as short stories, novels, and plays, the tone is referred to as the *atmosphere* or *mood*. The emotional atmosphere can be created by a writer's description or the choice of words used by the characters. The mood in stories, for example, can make the setting exciting, romantic, frightening, or gloomy and is based on the writer's purpose in developing the story's plot.

Depending on the purpose, an author's tone will vary. For example, if the purpose is to entertain, a humorous tone might be used. If the purpose is to voice disapproval, a sarcastic, bitter tone is displayed. When writing seriously, an author may use a **sentimental** tone to express nostalgic feelings. In technical, scientific, and general textbook writing, the tone is usually objective, impartial, or neutral. Often, more than one tone is used in a passage, essay, or story.

To determine the author's tone, a critical reader can ask these three key questions.

1. *How does the writer use words?*

   The writer's choice of words and the manner in which they are used helps to signal the writer's tone. Note that emotional words not only help you recognize the writer's true feelings but can be used to express anger or show positive support of an issue.

---

sentimental (sen′ tə men′ təl) showing tender feelings

2. *What is the writer's attitude?*

   To a large extent, tone is based on attitude, the way an author feels about the topic because of his or her background and experience. For example, given the topic "Living in a Big City," one writer may use humor to describe amusing experiences he or she had while living there, another may wish to be sentimental because of a romance while living there, and a third may be sarcastic because of personal unpleasant experiences associated with a stay there.

3. *How do I feel after reading this passage or selection?*

   Determine your overall feeling or reaction to what you've read. Were you angry, happy, unconcerned, upset, and so on? Your own emotional reaction to your reading can help you pinpoint the writer's tone.

Some people use the words *tone* and *style* interchangably. However, their meanings are not the same. *Style is the manner in which people say what they want to communicate.* What may make a particular writer unique is known as that author's writing *style*. It is an overall effect and consists in a writer's choice of words, arrangements of ideas through sentence formation, and level of language as well as in point of view, purpose, and tone. In other words, the "voice" or personality of the writer is found in his or her style. Writers have a manner of expressing themselves that's quite easy to recognize once you become familiar with their writings.

Writers generally have to vary their style to suit their intended audience just as people shift their style in speaking. For example, parents speak differently to their children than they do to co-workers, to family members, and to friends. So, too, with writers: For newspaper and magazine articles, for example, writers select an informal style to appeal to the general public. For textbook writing, the style is often more scholarly or learned. If the writer wants to target a particular group (religious or political, for instance) or profession (medical or legal), the style will change. Being aware of the writer's style helps the critical reader focus on the intended purpose as well as recognize the writer's tone.

⤳ Major Tones in Writing

Writers often use these eight tones.

1. *Serious or neutral tone:* This tone is used in writing that focuses on important topics and is presented in a straightforward manner without hidden meaning. It is typically found in textbooks and often in newspaper and magazine articles. The term *neutral* is sometimes used to indicate that the author is being objective in presenting both sides of an issue.

2. *Solemn tone:* The writer is extremely serious and uses formal language. His or her attitude is dignified or grave. When the writer's tone is solemn, there are usually

no humorous or informal expressions. Generally, funeral orations or **eulogies,** a governor's state address, or a presidential message on a very serious matter are expressed solemnly.

3. *Critical tone:* The writer expresses judgments on what is good or bad about something. When criticizing, the writer may directly state approval or disapproval. For example, if a writer states, "*Scarlett* (the sequel to *Gone with the Wind*) is a spellbinding and powerful novel that I highly recommend," the criticism is positive and shows approval. But if the writer says, "*Scarlett* is highly overrated and not worth a reader's time," the critic shows a negative reaction and disapproval. Sometimes authors color a critical tone with sarcasm and even cynicism.

4. *Cynical tone:* The writer is not only negatively critical but also expresses doubt about the goodness of human actions or motives or even the essential worth of a subject. Words used are often angry and **pessimistic.** The author's attitude is that humankind is selfish and corrupt and always acts out of self-interest.

5. *Sarcastic tone:* Like cynicism, sarcasm too is negatively critical and, here, words used are often harsh and bitter. While cynicism tries to show that people are selfish, sarcasm tries to show that people are foolish. The writer's attitude is cruel, brutal, and sometimes downright nasty. The purpose is to hurt and **belittle** rather than simply to state disagreement or disapproval. While a sarcastic remark may appear to be funny on the surface, it generally expresses anger, spite, or contempt.

6. *Ironic tone:* With irony, the writer's true feelings are not obvious. The author generally says the opposite of what he or she feels, thinks, or means, and the attitude is implied or stated indirectly. The writer hopes you will see this and realize that the words are not to be taken literally. For example, if the writer says, "We wore a gas mask for most of the day to enjoy the gorgeous weather," the writer wants the reader to understand the air was polluted and that the weather was terrible! In addition to irony in language, irony can also be situational. An essay written about how a fire station burned down might be extremely ironic. Often, in fiction, the irony lies in a twist of fate, a somewhat surprising and, generally, painful reversal of the expected outcome. For instance, in O. Henry's classic short story "The Gift of the Magi," a poor but loving husband sells his treasured watch to buy some combs for his wife's exquisite long hair, only to find she has cut her hair and sold it to buy a fob (a watch chain that fits into a trouser pocket) for his watch!

7. *Humorous and witty tone:* A humorous tone is intended to create laughter and to entertain or amuse. Sometimes, humor can point out the foolishness or stupidity of humankind in a gentle way. When humor is used with irony or sarcasm, however, its intention usually is to ridicule. Writing that expresses humor that is

---

eulogies (yoo′ lə jez) speeches or written tributes praising one who is recently deceased; high tributes

pessimistic (pes′ ə mis′ tik) always expecting the worst

belittle (bi lit′ l) to speak of as being unimportant

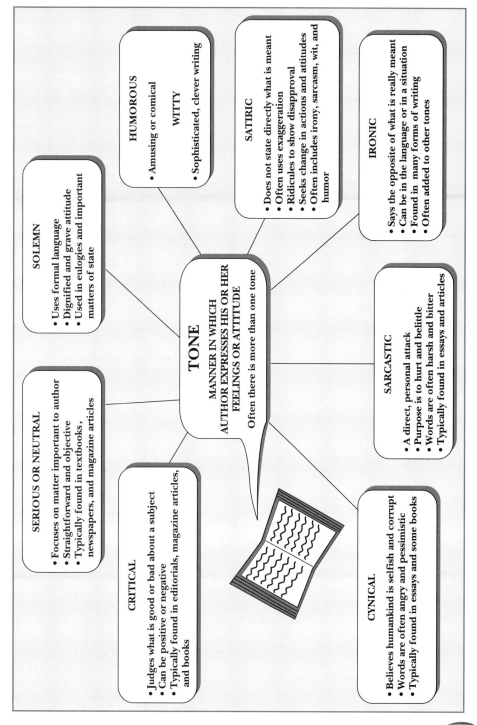

TONE

MANNER IN WHICH AUTHOR EXPRESSES HIS OR HER FEELINGS OR ATTITUDE

Often there is more than one tone

HUMOROUS
- Amusing or comical

WITTY
- Sophisticated, clever writing

SATIRIC
- Does not state directly what is meant
- Often uses exaggeration
- Ridicules to show disapproval
- Seeks change in actions and attitudes
- Often includes irony, sarcasm, wit, and humor

IRONIC
- Says the opposite of what is really meant
- Can be in the language or in a situation
- Found in many forms of writing
- Often added to other tones

SOLEMN
- Uses formal language
- Dignified and grave attitude
- Used in eulogies and important matters of state

SERIOUS OR NEUTRAL
- Focuses on matter important to author
- Straightforward and objective
- Typically found in textbooks, newspapers, and magazine articles

CRITICAL
- Judges what is good or bad about a subject
- Can be positive or negative
- Typically found in editorials, magazine articles, and books

SARCASTIC
- A direct, personal attack
- Purpose is to hurt and belittle
- Words are often harsh and bitter
- Typically found in essays and articles

CYNICAL
- Believes humankind is selfish and corrupt
- Words are often angry and pessimistic
- Typically found in essays and some books

sophisticated is said to be witty. For example, when author Dorothy Parker was informed that President Coolidge, an extremely quiet and reserved man, had died, she remarked, "How can they tell?" A witty tone is often clever and thought-provoking, while a humorous tone is simply enjoyable.

8. *Satiric tone:* For satire, the tone is often a blend of sarcasm, irony, wit, or humor. As with irony, a writer's true feelings are not obvious; the writer does not mean exactly what is stated. Sometimes, the writer *appears* to be joking but, if you read between the lines, you realize the writer is voicing some kind of displeasure. When authors use satire, they are often being critical, but their intention is not only to show disapproval but also to look for a remedy to a situation. They may use gross exaggeration, expressing disapproval of something in hopes of its being changed for the better. The **satirist** may direct comments at one individual, at a class in society, or at people with a specific ideology or belief system.

Words Used to Describe Tone

Although the previous eight categories describe the most widely used tones, countless other words may also be used to express it. As you can see from the list below,

Words That Express Tone			
accusing	depressing	honest	outraged
amused	detached	hopeful	outspoken
angry	dignified	hostile	passionate
arrogant	distressed	impassioned	pathetic
astonished	earnest	incredulous	pessimistic
authoritative	enthusiastic	indignant	playful
bitter	evasive	insulting	positive
caustic	excited	intense	proud
cheerful	fair	irreverent	righteous
comical	fearful	joking	romantic
compassionate	fervent	joyful	scornful
condescending	foolish	mocking	sentimental
contradictory	funny	morbid	sympathetic
cruel	gentle	nostalgic	uneasy
delightful	grim	optimistic	unrealistic

---

sophisticated (sə fis′ tə kāt əd) worldly wise; knowledgeable
satirist (sat′ ə rist) someone who writes satire

most of these words are adjectives that identify a person's emotions, attitude, or feelings.

Add four descriptive words not included in the list that can indicate a person's feelings or attitude.

_____ _____ _____ _____

Examples of Various Tones

You have read many examples of serious, neutral, and even critical tone in this textbook. Now, let's analyze these as well as some of the additional types.

ACTIVITY 9.1

PASSAGE 1

Read passage 1, a commentary on the welfare system. Decide whether the language is positive or negative in demonstrating how the writer feels about the social welfare system. Circle any descriptive words that indicate the writer's feelings or attitude.

> The social welfare system is a runaway **juggernaut.** It has devoured more than $5 trillion in hundreds of programs since 1965. . . . But the staggering cost is only part of the story. If all this treasure had given us happy, healthy families in our low-income neighborhoods, millions of hard-working Americans would have judged the sacrifice in taxes a badge of honor. The tragedy is that the reverse is the case. The welfare system has deterred parents from marrying. It has **consigned** untold children to lives of bitterness and failure; dismaying numbers of them have sought revenge on the society that intended to help.
>
> The sentiment for stopping the juggernaut is overwhelming. Over two-thirds of all Americans are skeptical about the needs of most welfare recipients. They are appalled to be subsidizing out-of-wedlock childbearing, and they resent the abuse of their goodwill.
>
> Today, most women on welfare have not been married but go on receiving benefits for years. The system has become a holding pen for the poor, not a helping hand for the dependent to become independent. It has been transformed from a remedy for poverty into a cause of it, from a stimulus to social **cohesion** into a destroyer of it. These malign consequences arise because welfare **frays** the fabric of a family and undermines the role of a father.
>
> Mortimer B. Zuckerman, "Fixing the Welfare Mess," *U.S. News & World Report*

_____

juggernaut (jug′ ər nôt) a frightening force that destroys everything it encounters
consigned (kən sīnd′) given over to the care of another
cohesion (kō hē′ zhən) force that holds things together
frays (frāz) wears away; unravels

By comparing the welfare system to a juggernaut, the writer reveals his disapproval of today's program. He could simply have said, "I think the welfare system needs improvement," but with this comparison and the figurative language in phrases such as "holding pen for the poor" and "frays the fabric of a family," he has made a far stronger criticism. Essentially, the writer's tone is serious and critical; he finds faults and complains. It is also sarcastic; remember, there can be more than one tone.

With these comments in mind, answer the following questions.

1. What words or phrases does the writer use in paragraph 2 that reveal his negative attitude?

_____

_____

2. In the last paragraph, "The system has become a holding pen for the poor, not a helping hand for the dependent to become independent" is an ironic statement. What does the writer mean by this?

_____

_____

PASSAGE 2

Read the following selection to discover how the Pulitzer Prize–winning columnist Ellen Goodman incorporates several tones to develop her thesis. Pay particular attention to the title of the essay, the italicized words, and the marginal notations. Her attitude toward this subject will be quite evident!

Defining Lite, Ultra-Lite and Truth

Ellen Goodman

Sarcastic
Ironic

The story began like a typical American breakfast, with a bracing dose of orange juice. Back in April, the Food and Drug Administration seized a batch of o.j. saying that it carried a false label. Citrus Hill Fresh Choice wasn't "fresh," dear Breakfast Clubbers and Wordsmiths, it was concentrated. Having gotten the *business folk to swallow that,* the regulators went after cooking oil next. In May they told three manufacturers they couldn't put *those cute little hearts* and no-cholesterol signs on bottles of high-fat vegetable oil. The labels weren't exactly false, but they were misleading. *They suggested that you could fry a path to good health.*

These two moves sent a message that the regulators are back in the business of

linguists (lin´ gwists) specialists in the study of language

Sarcastic

regulating. And that it isn't only **linguists** who are interested in the labels. Soon, *we may be unraveling the mysteries of Low-fat, Low-salt, and Lite confusion that reign in the marketplace.*

But there is still a missing entree in the regulatory menu. Every day 50 million Americans put something into their mouths that is exempt from the safety, health or truth-in-labeling laws that affect virtually every other product: Tobacco.

Critical

Tobacco remains the glaring renegade. *It is the absolute outlaw on the American market.* Consider, for example, NEXT cigarettes which are **brazenly** promoted for

Sarcastic

their "de-nicotined" tobacco. *De-Nic has that nice de-caf ring about its name. It promises all the flavor with none of the evil buzz.*

But NEXT has nicotine, .1 milligrams a smoke, about the same amount as the older cigarettes, Carlton and NOW. In short, the makers of low-tar and low-nicotine

Critical

cigarettes do precisely what the vegetable-oil folk did. They make an implied health claim in their ads. *But they get away with it. . . .*

Tobacco, the love child of politics, has been exempt from every federal health and safety act since the surgeon general's first report on the dangers of smoking. By now, we just assume everyone knows what the tobacco companies deny: that smoking is addictive and **lethal.** *There is an almost casually judgmental attitude toward people who are dumb or dependent enough to keep smoking.* On the other side, those who want to regulate cigarettes and cigarette advertising are often regarded as closet **prohibitionists. . . .**

Serious

If the government can define what's Lite, then it can define what's Ultra-Lite. If ads for cholesterol-free make false safety claims, what about the ads for Merit Free? And how about the ads that associate Virginia with slimness, and Camels with cartoons aimed at kids?

Ironic

At the moment, there is one cigarette manufacturer who tells it like it is in smoking country. From California, we have a brand bearing its dire message in a neat black pack with a skull and crossbones. It's called "Death." Now that's truth in advertising.

approximately 440 words

1. How does the writer's use of several tones help to strengthen her criticism of product advertising?

   _____

2. Specifically, what does she want the government to do?

   _____

---

brazenly (brā′ zən lē) shamelessly and boldly
lethal (lē′ thəl) causing death; fatal
prohibitionists (prō′ ə bish′ ən ists) those who wish to forbid by law

Working with the WORLD WIDE WEB

If you enjoyed Ellen Goodman's writing style, you can access her daily editorial commentaries written for the *Boston Globe* at:

> http://www.boston.com/globe/columns/goodman/

Many other newspaper writers, including Art Buchwald (a sample of whose writing appears in the next selection), can be accessed on the Web through this address:

> http://usnewspapers.miningco.com/

The next passage is a satire that demonstrates how a writer can use humor, exaggeration, and sarcasm in combination. This is how satire is created. The writer, Art Buchwald, has been a columnist for the *Washington Post* for several decades and is a world-renowned political and social satirist. Although the essay is funny, underlying the humor are criticism and exaggeration, which make it satiric. As you read, think about what Art Buchwald is *really* saying. To help you recognize satire, we have included short questions in the margins for you to think about as you analyze Buchwald's style.

PASSAGE 3

Acid Indigestion

Serious?

Why these words?

Sarcastic? →

Is this true? → Inference?

Real people? →

Art Buchwald

America is an abundant land that seems to have more of everything than anybody else. And if one were to ask what we have the most of the answer would be acid indigestion.

No country can touch us when it comes to heartburn and upset stomachs. This nation, under God, with liberty and justice for all, neutralizes more stomach acid in one day than the Soviet Union does in a year. We give more relief from discomfort of the intestinal tract than China and Japan combined.

They can say what they will about us, but we Americans know what to do with our excess gas.

It is no accident that the United States became the largest producer of acid indigestion in the world. When the first settlers came to the New World they found their lives fraught with danger. First they had to worry about Indians, then they had to worry about their crops. Afterward they had to worry about witches. This played hell with everyone's stomach and the early settlers realized if they ever hoped to survive they would have to come up with a cure for acid indigestion.

Providence was on their side, because amongst the early settlers were two brothers, Alka and Bromo Seltzer. They were both chemists who had experimented with various potions that had been given to them by the Indians.

Is he serious? Kidding?

One potion was a white powder that the Indians used for athlete's foot. Why, asked the Seltzer brothers, couldn't the same powder be used for upset stomachs. Al was neater than Bromo and rolled his powder into a tablet which he then dropped into a mug of water where it immediately fizzed. Bromo said it was too expensive to make tablets, and it was much easier just to dump the powder into the water, which would produce the same effect.

Familiar to you?

The brothers split in anger, and Al put out his product under the name <u>Alka-Seltzer,</u> while Bromo put his out as <u>Bromo-Seltzer</u>. Fortunately for the country, both methods worked, and as soon as the cure for acid indigestion had been concocted the New World could be settled once and for all.

Critical of what here?

You would think that after we killed all the Indians and won the West and became a large industrial nation, Americans would have stopped having queasy stomachs. But the truth is we suffer more from the blaahhs now than we ever did before. Some of it still comes from fear, some of it comes from ambition, and some of it comes from <u>eating the whole thing</u>.

What does he mean?

Literal meaning?

As a people who strive for the best we must accept the fact that it <u>takes a cup of acid for every step we take up the ladder of success</u>. It is no accident that the men and women who run our corporations and our advertising agencies and our networks and our government are the same people who keep the Maalox, Pepto-Bismol, Bisodol, Tums, and Rolaid companies alive.

Got an ulcer?

Show me a man who has to <u>drink milk instead of wine</u> with his meals and I'll show you a **titan** of American industry.

Critical?

For years other nations have tried to catch up with us when it came to sour stomachs and heartburn. But they never had the drive to produce a good case of acid indigestion. They never understood what it takes to keep up with the Joneses or outdo the Smiths. They don't realize that in order to live in the best of all possible worlds you have to have a certain amount of stomach discomfort to go with it.

Kidding again?

Acid indigestion is as American as <u>Mom's apple pie (which is one of the reasons we get it)</u> and as long as there is enough heartburn to go around, we, as a great nation, will survive.

approximately 600 words

Art Buchwald, "Acid Indigestion," *Esquire* Dec. 1974. Reprinted by permission of *Esquire.*

What is Buchwald really making fun of? What does he want us to change?

_____

_____

_____

———————

titan (tī tan) giant

ACTIVITY 9.2 Practice Recognizing Tone

As you read the following selections, you may want to refer back to the tone chart on page 489. Remember that more than one tone may be used in a passage, but look first for the dominant tone.

These two passages discuss the topic of peace. Read the selections to determine which employs a serious tone and which uses a solemn tone.

PASSAGE 1

With malice toward none, with charity for all, with firmness in the right as God gives us to see the right, let us strive on to finish the work we are in, to bind up the nation's wounds, to care for him who shall have borne the battle and for his widow and his orphan, to do all which may achieve and cherish a just and lasting peace among ourselves and with all nations.

Abraham Lincoln, Second Inaugural Address

1. The tone of this passage is _____.

PASSAGE 2

For in the final analysis, our most basic common link is that we all live on this small planet. We all breathe the same air. We all cherish our children's future. And we are a mortal. . . . And is not peace . . . basically a matter of human rights—rights to live out our lives without fear of devastation—the right to breathe air as nature provided—the right of future generations to a healthy existence.

John F. Kennedy, Commencement Address at American University, 1963

2. The tone of this passage is_____.

Having just read quotations from two former presidents, now examine how a cartoonist employs tone to specify a message.

3. Select one word from the list of words on page 490 that best illustrates the cartoonist's feelings.

    _____

4. Is the cartoonist mainly sarcastic, serious, or ironic about presidential hopefuls?

    _____

    Support your answer: _____

5. If you were undecided as to whether the first cartoonist was being ironic, examine the following cartoon. Here, a cartoonist illustrates the meaning of the word *irony,* using Ross Perot, a Texas billionaire who was unsuccessful by a large margin in his bid to become president because many people consider him **eccentric.** Is Ross Perot the best person to be making the remarks in the cartoon about an opposing presidential candidate?

    _____

---

eccentric (òk sen′ trik) odd or unconventional

Monitor your emotional reactions while reading the next two passages.

PASSAGE 3

Read to understand how Mark Twain felt about humankind.

> Cats are loose in their morals, but not consciously so. Man, in his descent from the cat, has brought the cat's looseness with him but has left the unconsciousness behind—the saving grace which excuses the cat. The cat is innocent, man is not.
>
> The higher animals engage in individual fights, but never in organized masses. Man is the only animal that deals in that atrocity of atrocities, WAR. He is the only one that gathers his brethren about him and goes forth in cold blood and with calm pulse to exterminate his kind. He is the only animal that for **sordid** wages will march out and help to slaughter strangers of his own species who have done him no harm and with whom he has no quarrel.
>
> Man is the only animal that robs his helpless fellow of his country—takes possession of it and drives him out of it or destroys him. Man has done this in all the ages. There is not an acre of ground on the globe that is in possession of its rightful owner, or that has not been taken away from owner after owner, cycle after cycle, by force and bloodshed.
>
> Mark Twain, *Letters from the Earth*

1. What tone does Mark Twain use? Explain the reason for your choice.

   _____

   _____

2. Does Mark Twain say anything redeeming about people? Support your answer.

   _____

   _____

PASSAGE 4

Read to learn whether the narrator in this excerpt from a tale by the Russian storyteller Anton Chekhov is as negative about humankind as Mark Twain.

> Only the dimming lights of the receding harbor were visible in an ink-black sky. We could feel the heavy storm clouds overhead about to burst into rain, and it was suffocating, in spite of the wind and cold.
>
> Crowded together in the crew's quarters we, the sailors, were casting lots. Loud, drunken laughter filled the air. One of our comrades was playfully crowing like a cock. slight shiver ran through me from the back of my neck to my heels, as if cold small shot were pouring down my naked body from a hole in the back of my head. I was shivering both from the cold and certain other causes, which I wish to describe.
>
> In my opinion, man is, as a rule, foul; and the sailor can sometimes be the foulest of all the creatures of the earth—fouler than the lowest beast, which has, at least, the excuse

---

sordid (sôr′ did) dirty, filthy

of obeying his instincts. It is possible that I may be mistaken, since I do not know life, but it appears to me that a sailor has more occasion than anyone else to despise and curse himself. A man who at any moment may fall headlong from a mast to be forever hidden beneath a wave, a man who may drown, God alone knows when, has need of nothing, and one on dry land feels pity for him. We sailors drink a lot of vodka and are **dissolute** because we do not know what one needs virtue for at sea. However, I shall continue.

Anton Chekhov, "At Sea: A Sailor's Story," translated by Ann Dunnigan

1. Is the tone used by Chehkov in passage 4 the same as Mark Twain's in passage 3? Explain your answer.

   _____

2. Do you think the narrator is mistaken, as he says he might be, in thinking that "the sailor can sometimes be the foulest of all the creatures of the earth . . . "? Why, or why not?

   _____

   _____

3. Find a word from the list on page 490 to describe your emotional reaction to each of these selections.

   Passage 3: _____

   Passage 4: _____

Passage 5 was written in 1966; passage 6, in 1998. Read to discover whether both writers use the same tone and have the same attitude about the world in which we live.

PASSAGE 5

Read to analyze what John Steinbeck, one of America's best story writers, said about Americans in general more than thirty years ago.

One of the generalities most often noted about Americans is that we are a restless, a dissatisfied, a searching people. We spend our time searching for security, and hate it when we get it. For the most part we are an **intemperate** people: We eat too much when we can, drink too much, indulge our senses too much. Even in our so-called virtues we are intemperate: A teetotaler is not content not to drink—he must stop all the drinking in the world; a vegetarian among us would outlaw the eating of meat. We work too hard, and many die under the strain; and then to make up for that we play with a violence just as suicidal. The result is that we seem to be in a state of turmoil all the time, both physically and mentally. We are able to believe that our Government is weak, stupid, overbearing,

---

dissolute (dis′ ō lōot) immoral
intemperate (in tem′ pər it) lacking in self-control; not moderate

dishonest, and inefficient, and at the same time we are deeply convinced that it is the best Government in the world, and we would like to impose it upon everyone else.

Americans overindulge their children and do not like them; the children in turn are overly dependent and full of hate for their parents. Americans are remarkably kind and hospitable and open with both guests and strangers; and yet they will make a wide circle around a man dying on the pavement rather than become involved. Fortunes are spent getting cats out of trees and dogs out of sewer pipes; but a girl screaming for help in the street draws only slammed doors, closed windows and silence.

Americans seem to live and breathe and function by paradox; but in nothing are we so paradoxical as in our passionate belief in our own myths. We truly believe ourselves to be natural-born mechanics and do-it-yourselfers. We spend our lives in motorcars, yet most of us—a great many of us at least—do not know enough about a car to check the gas tank when the motor fails. Our believed myths are everywhere: We shout that we are a nation of laws, not men—and then proceed to break every law we can if we can get away with it. From **puberty** we are preoccupied with sex; but our courts, our counselors, and our psychiatrists are dealing constantly with cases of sexual failure or charges of frigidity or impotence, which amounts to the same thing.

approximately 370 words

John Steinbeck, *America and Americans* (Viking Press, 1966)

1. Is Steinbeck's tone sarcastic, critical, or ironic? _____

2. Give two examples of the paradoxes—that is, contradictions—that Steinbeck cites about the behavior of Americans in general.

_____

_____

3. With which of Steinbeck's statements about Americans do you disagree?

_____

Keep this question in mind as you read the next passage: Was the behavior of Americans at the end of the twentieth century different from that described by Steinbeck in the 1960s?

PASSAGE 6

Growing up in the 50s was a time of innocence and fun. I can look back and see that I have 1 enjoyed a period blessed, if you will, with blandness. In fact, most of 20th century America is remarkable for the positive things it produced—the Industrial Revolution, television, computers and enormous advancements in medicine and information access. . . .

———————
puberty (pyōo bər tē) age of becoming first able to produce offspring; the physical beginning of manhood or womanhood

But now, knowing as we do that the only thing constant in life is change, I am begin- **2** ning to understand that moving from the Renaissance to the Victorian era was predictable. So, too, is the swell of political and social change I feel engulfing our world today, and I am beginning to be worried for my children and grandchildren. Like our relationships or our golf game, the minute we begin to feel really comfortable with them is the very moment the downturn begins. It's built into the system and I believe it's a microcosm of how our universe works. . . .

In a culture that seems to be moving away from me faster than I can run, I am wor- **3** ried particularly about our increasing willingness to allow our government and lawyers to legislate morality and equality. With so many laws telling us how we should feel, what we can say and who we can say it to, and deciding for us what we can and can't do, we're on track to literally breed the "conscience" gene right out of our DNA strain. . . .

Civil liberties are supposed to guarantee fundamental rights, such as freedom of **4** speech and freedom to exercise our rights without unwarranted government interference. I consider it unwarranted government interference when the courts allow every citizen the right to blame all their problems on someone else. And when I heard that Little League baseball had disallowed the batting box because of the fear of being sued by a parent whose child might be hit by an accidentally flung bat, I was speechless. Now the airlines can't serve peanuts for fear of being sued by a peanut-allergic passenger. It seem to me the legal system is working very methodically to legislate common sense, morality and, God forbid, fun! While the arms race continues at a maddening pace around the world, we can't even let our children have sparklers on the 4th of July. What kind of free dom is this? . . .

Too much government and too many laws do not create a healthy society. I want the **5** government and the lawyers to leave my children's lives alone. Let me be allowed to teach them to listen to their own conscience, to develop their own moral fiber, to know right from wrong and to follow their heart. Too many laws stifle productivity and dilute the very essence of humanity.

If we can all hang from the pendulum while it's at its mid-point, perhaps we can slow **6** down its inevitable movement. Maybe we can even tip it back a little to a less complicated world where you can interact with real people on the telephone, where, if you call your broker or your bank, you don't end up somewhere in Ohio, where children are allowed to dress up on Halloween without it being viewed as offensive to some minority group, where landowners have rights, where self-confessed killers are not set free because somebody forgot to read them their rights, where convincing evidence of a crime is not disallowed for some legal technicality, where if you smoke yourself to death you can't blame it on the manufacturer, where golf caddies have not all but disappeared because of the cost of liability insurance, where you can stop at the scene of an accident to help a victim without fear of being sued, where our tolerance level for violence is dramatically lessened, where some of America's finest feel free to run for political office, and where integrity, morality, manners, decency and un-financially motivated acts of kindness are integral to our **ethos.**

approximately 625 words

Elsie Floriani, "A Special Time, A Special Place," *Gentry* Dec.–Jan. 1998–9

---

ethos (ē thäs) the distinguishing habits, beliefs, attitudes of a people or group

1. Which word, from the list describing tone on page 490, describes the writing style in the following paragraphs?

   Paragraph 1: _____

   Paragraph 3: _____

   Paragraph 5: _____

   Paragraph 6: _____

2. How does the criticism of society in passage 6 differ from that of passage 5?

   _____

   _____

3. Based on the tone and style of writing, which passage did you find most convincing? Explain your answer.

   _____

   _____

Each of the writers of the next two passages *appears* to be making jokes. Read to decide if either, or both, writers uses a dominant tone other than humor

PASSAGE 7

Read the following selection on *procrastinators,* people who put things off or delay doing them, and decide whether you should take the writer seriously.

And Tomorrow and Tomorrow

Procrastinators are simply less intimidated by time . . . people like Les Waas, president of the Procrastinators Club of America. (Motto: "We're behind you all the way.") Founded in 1956, the club numbers a half million, though Waas says only 12,000 have signed up. It even boasts two members who have missed planes that crashed. . . . Waas loathes people who lay out their next day's clothes before bed, who dream of 21,000-mile car tuneups at 20,000 miles, and who fancy themselves (more often than not) "morning people." Waas calls them "Anticrastinators." He avoids them as he would oven-cleaning.

"These are nervous and uptight folks," he says. "They're too high-strung and usually leave the world earlier than the rest of us. Then they're referred to as 'the late so and so.' "

"It's the ultimate irony."

. . . We gather each year at the Post Office, near midnight, on April 15, Tax Day. Our expressions mingle the harried relief and quiet satisfaction that is our badge of honor.

We'll reunite (in spirit if not body) at the auto registry the day our licenses expire, or at the airport terminal seconds before take-off. And our endgame **regimen** will work for us. No late fines accrued (if we're lucky). No planes missed (usually). No sweat (well, maybe a little).

. . . I live with a procrastinator. (You should see our bathroom!) I'm even marrying her this summer. We were engaged three years before we set a wedding date, which should tell you all you need to know about our procrastinating compatibility. Call us a Match Delayed in Heaven.

Nuptials are a procrastinator's bounty. Take, for instance, the rule that sanctions a year's leeway for wedding gifts. It supports the philosophy embraced by procrastinators and Chicago Cubs fans alike: "Wait Till Next Year."

Except I usually take a decade. I've attended 10 weddings in the last four years, which puts me eight gifts behind the curve today (thanks to two early divorces). But here's the upside: Now that I'm getting married, I tell the couples I'm indebted to to forget my gift and we'll call it even. It spares me the guilt.

And the thank-you notes.

approximately 370 words

Mark Leibovich, "And Tomorrow and Tomorrow," *San Jose Mercury News* 15 Mar: 1994: 7. Copyright © 1994 by San Jose Mercury News. Reprinted by permission.

1. Is the writing basically an example of irony or humor? _____

2. Give two examples from the selection to support your analysis of the tone.

   _____

   _____

3. Discuss one situation that often causes you to procrastinate.

   _____

   _____

PASSAGE 8

In passage 7, the writer was not very serious about his subject. See whether this is also true in passage 8. Think about the tone of the title before you begin reading. What kind of person is a "spineless whiner"?

Don't Worry, Be Happy, You Spineless Whiner

As though worrying about love handles and pot bellies isn't causing enough misery, **1**
Fitness magazine provides **fodder** for darker **angst:** "There's incredible pleasure

---

regimen (rej′ i mən) set of habits or rules; systematic procedure
fodder (fäd′ ər) coarse food for cattle, horses, sheep, etc.
angst (ängst) a gloomy, often neurotic feeling of anxiety and depression

potential buried deep in your soul," says the magazine. "Happiness is the norm for most people."

But what if you, like me, aren't sure that you're "most people"? What if we're not 2 normal enough? What if we're not happy enough? If we were truly happy, would there be any reason to read *Fitness* magazine?

Darn, drat, dammit. It's not only that we fall short as workers; as lovers; as sex objects 3 as friends; as parents; as money-managers, PTA members, home-owners and masters of low-fat cuisine. We may be falling short in the happiness department, too.

Happily (see, I'm trying to look on the bright side), *Fitness* offers 10 tips for achiev- 4 ing that pleasure potential. . . .

Tip No. 1 is "Keep track of the good stuff," says *Fitness,* and amen, say I. In the year 5 between the time I was 11 and 12 years old, I misplaced my wristwatch, and in those days—before battery-powered $2.99 wristwatches were invented—one's wristwatch was really one's best stuff. My failure to remember where I'd put it for safekeeping before a family vacation explains my failure to concentrate on geometry and the ensuing middle school crisis. . . .

Tip No. 2 is "Look for the humor in everything," one direction I take seriously as I 6 glance at today's headlines: "Pedestrian fatalities on train tracks are mostly avoidable"; and "Eleven nations seal deal for shared currency." . . .

No. 3: "Make friends and keep them. Try to hang around with happy people." It's 7 hard to think of anything more depressing than hanging around with someone habitually happier than you are, a person who applauds her every move and basks in every triumph. . . .

Long experience teaches that the way to bond with a friend is to share your real 8 weaknesses and worries, and to listen sympathetically to his. . . .

No. 4 is "Be yourself," a tip that's hard to take seriously in a magazine crammed with 9 directions for becoming someone better than you are. "We waste so much energy hating our looks," says Samahria Lyte Kaufman, founder of the Option Institute, a New England thought-processing center that "claims to be the only place on the planet that teaches happiness full time."

Of course, there are other options—crack houses and opium dens—but most of us 10 don't want to do anything illegal or travel to Massachusetts. . . .

Tip No. 5 is "Fall in love," which according to Dr. Dean Ornish, is the "root of hap- 11 piness." Ornish, who became famous espousing healthy eating habits, has now turned to "Love & Survival: The Scientific Basis for the Healing Power of Intimacy," which is the name of his latest book.

In the years he was making a living by boosting broccoli and dissing Doritos, Ornish 12 visited the Clintons to offer personal advice on low-fat meals in the White House. His new field of expertise may qualify him for another trip to Washington.

Tip No. 6, "Choose time over money," has been adopted involuntarily by millions of 13 Americans, many dwelling on downtown sidewalks. To this observer, they don't look all that elated. Perhaps they ought to read *Fitness,* which says that "87 percent of workers who voluntarily cut back on work hours are happy with their decision. Among the top bene- fits: less stress and more family time."

"Wake up your senses," says Tip No. 7. One practical exercise is to "look at some- 14 thing yellow, then visualize the color and repeat to yourself: 'It's safe to move to the rhythm of life.' " . . .

Tip No. 8 is "Take care of your body," including the recommendation, "Drink seven **15** or more glasses of water a day," which happens to come from the Brita Products Company, manufacturer of water filters. Those who drink a lot of water are actual pier than those who don't, says the magazine, thereby explaining in one fell swoop why a freshwater fish looks grumpy but the countenance of a camel can convey sporadic joy. (The former, in case you were wondering, don't drink anything; a camel can drink 30 gallons in an hour.)

"Turn off that TV," says Tip No. 9, which claims that if you use "no-brainer activities" **16** to fill the hours, "the quality of your life will suffer." Alas, this warning seems in direct contradiction with Tip No. 5, the logical result of which is the best no-brainer activity of all.

Finally, "Make happiness your No. 1 priority," says *Fitness,* even going so far as to **17** "write down those things in life that make you truly happy."

I'd do it, of course, but I'm out of ink. **18**

approximately 625 words

Leah Garchik, "Don't Worry, Be Happy, You Spineless Whiner," *San Francisco Chronicle* 24 May 1998: 2

1. a. The author used a wide variety of tones. For example, name the tone in each of the following paragraphs:

    Paragraph 1 _____

    Paragraph 2 _____

    Paragraph 5 _____

    Paragraph 11 _____

    Paragraph 13 _____

   b. When combined, do the various tones you've listed justify calling the selection *satire?* Explain your answer.

    _____

    _____

2. In addition to being critical of *Fitness* magazine's statement that "happiness is the norm for most people," what other issues is the writer criticizing?

    _____

    _____

3. What is the purpose of the last sentence of the passage?

    _____

    _____

Before reading the next two passages, consider these statistics, revealed in a telephone survey of 600 teenagers between the ages of 13 and 17.*

Only 41% can name the three branches of government but 59% can name the Three Stooges.

Fully 74% can name the city where cartoon character Bart Simpson lives (Springfield) but only 12% know that Abraham Lincoln lived in Springfield, Illinois.

Less than 2% recognize James Madison as the father of the Constitution but 58% know Bill Gates as the "father" of Microsoft.

Nearly 95% could name the actor who played the Fresh Prince of Bel Air (Will Smith) on television but only 2% knew the name of the chief justice of the United States (William Rehnquist).

The next passage is slanted toward courses some university professors offer to college students. Analyze the writer's remarks to learn how she feels about these "enlightened" course offerings, reflected by her choice of tone. Note the title of the passage.

PASSAGE 9

Finally, Educators Figure Out What's Interesting

Madonna

I used to worry about the hole in the ozone. Not any more. I don't worry about the greenhouse effect, lead in the air, nuclea waste or the loss of biodiversity. The energy problem? No problem. I know our future is in good hands because our college students are finally studying the right stuff: Madonna.

We don't need to administer national tests to our schoolchildren. We don't need to throw more money into the endless drain of our school districts. We don't need to pay teachers higher salaries. We need more videos.

Professor Jesse Nash is teaching a course in Madonna at Loyola University, where tuition is $10,000 per year. If you get you pay for, it must be a good school. And if it is a good school it must know what it is doing when it offers courses in Madonna.

Those who have plowed through Western Civilization as college freshmen may think it is a joke, but I am not making this up. Professor Cathy Schwictenberg at the University of Massachusetts says it is significant to study Madonna because she's part of our culture.

A graduate student at the University of Florida is doing his master's thesis on her. He says that you can learn the same things by studying the Material Girl that you can by perusing Aristotle, Plato and Socrates. Who needs physics and philosophy? They're so boring.

Since Madonna's musical masturbatory expressionism, so un-Like a Virgin, is the new university equivalent of Plato's *Theaetetus*, surely there are other, more interesting substitutions for such dull courses as history, math and biology. High school dropouts

* Associated Press, 3 Sept. 1998.

would flock to higher education if we offered credit in finite mathematics in exchange for viewing a Marilyn Monroe retrospective. I guess that would show those study-mad Japanese a thing or two!

Wouldn't you be reassured to know your cardiologist studied M.C. Hammer and Vanilla Ice as an undergraduate? When assessing heart function, the doctor who studied Tina Turner wouldn't be tempted to wonder what love's got to do with it. If I needed bypass surgery I'd want the steady hands that must inevitably emerge from years of immersion in dependable iambic rap. It must at least be the equivalent of a semester of anatomy.

Since Madonna is equivalent to the Greek philosophers, surely Judy Garland films could replace Constitutional law. We could throw in a few Busby Berkeley extravaganzas for the intellectually hungry, and judging from the decisions handed down by the current Supreme Court, a refresher course on Ginger Rogers musicals couldn't hurt.

But law and medicine are not the only areas that could be improved by enlightened course offerings. Think of the kinds of weapons Silicon Valley engineers could turn out by studying Madonna. We could admit women to combat positions, dress them in pointed aluminum bras and let them hurl themselves at the enemy.

Besides achieving educational excellence and eliminating dropouts, we could reduce the budgets for elementary and high schools and eliminate the hassle of a national test. After all, you don't need to read or write to watch videos.

By integrating the educational trends of our universities into primary and secondary schools we will produce a generation of students qualified for admission to those universities. I guess that ought to prove to the rest of the world we're still Number One!

approximately 570 words

1. What words in the first paragraph help you to realize the writer is being satiric rather than serious?

_____

2. Does the writer actually believe we need more videos rather than providing more money for education?

_____

3. Is the remark in the third paragraph, "If you get what you pay for, it must be a good school," sarcastic? Why, or why not?

_____

_____

4. List three examples of exaggeration the writer uses to help the reader understand that she is ridiculing the course offering at Loyola.

_____

5. The writer never states her thesis directly but implies it throughout the essay, particularly in the last paragraph. What is the thesis?

PASSAGE 10

Elvis 101 Is Now in Session

Not long before Elvis Presley died in 1977, he bought a machine that allowed him to view microfilm.

His longtime friend Janelle McComb saw the device at his home, Graceland, and told him, "You know, one day you're going to be a part of history. . . . One day, kids ar going to be studying about you."

"And now," says McComb, "it's true."

The official name of the course being taught at the University of Mississippi is "In Search of Elvis: Music, Race, Religion, Art, Performance."

The text is pure Presley.

No grades are being given at the International Conference on Elvis Presley, which is expected to be an annual event. The course lasts only six days. And at least one-third of the 150 participants are members of the media. The other two-thirds include an odd assortment of scholars, fans and men in spangled jumpsuits who fervently believe Elvis is still the King.

Many of the scholars at the conference believe the study of Presley and his impact on popular culture is here to stay.

Already, there's a course at Ole Miss, taught during the regular semester, that compares Presley's Hawaiian movies to author Herman Melville's books set in Polynesia.

Other Elvis courses are being taught or planned at such institutions of higher learning as Emory University in Atlanta; Mercer University in Macon, Ga.; Alcorn State University in Lorman, Miss.; and Birmingham (Ala.) Southern College.

William Ferris, director of the Center for the Study of Southern Culture, a sponsor of the conference, makes no apologies for scholarly study of the singer.

"He's the most popular entertainer of the 20th century," says Ferris. "This is a world-class opportunity to talk about someone that everyone is interested in."

Some lecturers at the conference believe Presley is worthy of study because of his role in race relations. They say his music, which relied heavily on blues music of the Mississippi Delta, opened opportunities for black artists.

approximately 310 words

Clifford Pugh, "Elvis 101 Is Now in Session," *San Francisco Examiner* 10 Aug. 1995: C13. Copyright © 1991. Reprinted by permission.

1. How does the tone in this article differ from the tone in passage 8 on Madonna?

---

2. Based on the tone, which passage, 8 or 9, did you find more interesting to read? Why?

---

3. Do you think celebrities should be used as the basis for college course offerings? Why, or why not?

_____

_____

Understanding the Author's Purpose

Tone and purpose are closely related, so when we examine an author's tone, we also look at his or her purpose. In the passage you just read on education, the purpose is to ridicule course offerings on topics like Madonna in order to *persuade* both administrators and interested citizens to do something about such courses. The language relies on the connotative meanings of emotional statements such as "show those study-mad Japanese a thing or two!" The writer's purpose becomes apparent once you examine the words and determine their tone.

At times, writers want to influence your beliefs, emotions, or actions: *to persuade you*. Often, they write to help you learn: *to inform you*. Or, they may try to amuse you: *to entertain you*. But they can also combine their purposes. Entertaining writing can be used to persuade, for example. Even in textbooks, in which the main purpose is to provide information, the writer can shift from facts (to inform you) to a personal anecdote (to amuse you). A writer's purpose or reason for writing an essay, article, or literary piece will vary, as can be seen in the chart that follows.

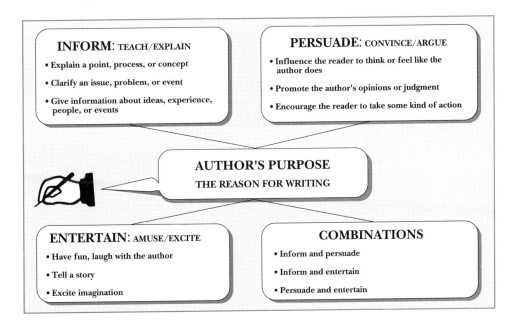

INFORM: TEACH/EXPLAIN
- Explain a point, process, or concept
- Clarify an issue, problem, or event
- Give information about ideas, experience, people, or events

PERSUADE: CONVINCE/ARGUE
- Influence the reader to think or feel like the author does
- Promote the author's opinions or judgment
- Encourage the reader to take some kind of action

AUTHOR'S PURPOSE
THE REASON FOR WRITING

ENTERTAIN: AMUSE/EXCITE
- Have fun, laugh with the author
- Tell a story
- Excite imagination

COMBINATIONS
- Inform and persuade
- Inform and entertain
- Persuade and entertain

Since a writer does not usually say, "In this article, I intend to amuse you or prove to you or argue that . . . ," it is up to the reader to discover or infer the purpose. The reader must look at the language and decide whether the author intends to inform, persuade, entertain, or combine purposes.

To find the writer's purpose, the critical reader asks these key questions:

1. What is the writer's reason for making these statements?
2. Why does the writer use these particular words?
3. What is the author's attitude about the topic?
4. What is the writer trying to convince me of or prove to me?

ACTIVITY 9.3 **Finding the Purpose and Its Relationship to Tone**

Use the terms *inform, persuade,* and *entertain* as you select the author's purpose in the following selections. The commentary preceding each selection will assist you in determining purpose and its connection to the tone.

PASSAGE 1

Read the following passage, which compares the attitudes of men and women toward each other, to see whether the writer is being critical or informati

Mr. Fix-It and the Home-Improvement Committee

The most frequently expressed complaint women have about men is that men don't listen. Either a man completely ignores her when she speaks to him, or he listens for a few beats, assesses what is bothering her, and then proudly puts on his Mr. Fix-It cap and offers her a solution to make her feel better. He is confused when she doesn't appreciate this gesture of love. No matter how many times she tells him that he's not listening, he doesn't get it and keeps doing the same thing. She wants empathy, but he thinks she wants solutions.

The most frequently expressed complaint men have about women is that women are always trying to change them. When a woman loves a man she feels responsible to assist him in growing and tries to help him improve the way he does things. She forms a home-improvement committee, and he becomes her primary focus. No matter how much he resists her help, she persists—waiting for any opportunity to help him or tell him what to do. She thinks she's nurturing him, while he feels he's being controlled. Instead, he wants her acceptance.

These two problems can finally be solved by first understanding why men offer solutions and why women seek to improve. . . .

John Gray, *Men Are from Mars, Women Are from Venus* 15

1. What are the author's tone and purpose?

    _____

2. What language helped you arrive at this conclusion?

    _____

3. Do you agree with the author's basic premise about the attitudes of women and men? Why, or why not?

    _____

    _____

4. a. How do the tone and purpose of the cartoon that follows differ from that of the excerpt you just read?

    _____

    _____ b. What type of figurative language is used for the title of the group?

    A. hyperbole   B. euphemism   C. metaphor

PASSAGE 2

How do you feel about gun control? Read to learn the writer's reaction to Charlton Heston's statement about guns and the writer's attitude toward bearing arms.

What's Going On with Charlton Heston?

Donald Kaul

Has someone dropped Charlton Heston on his head recently or is he going senile? He's not making sense. As, for example, when he told a group of mostly journalists that of all the rights guaranteed by the Constitution—freedom of religion, speech, press—the right to bear arms was the most important.

"It alone offers the absolute capacity to live without fear," he said of the Second Amendment. "The right to keep and bear arms is the one right that allows rights to exist at all."

That's weird; batty, actually. Oh, I know Heston is first vice president of the National Rifle Association, but I've always considered him one of the more rational gun nuts. Certainly, he is not a stupid man. He's a graduate of Northwestern, for crying out loud. The least we should be able to expect from him is a view of life more sophisticated than a John Wayne movie.

The fact is that guns are vastly overrated as instruments of self-defense. They have some use in shooting intruders—especially if the intruder is the guy down the block who gets drunk and wanders into the wrong house late at night—but Heston is talking about a whole different thing. He seems to think that personal guns, handguns and such, can be used by an alert citizenry to fight government oppression. That's nonsense.

If the government, good or bad, really wants to oppress you, it will. That is the lesson of Waco and Ruby Ridge; one of them, anyway. The citizens in both of those cases were heavily armed and willing to fight for their rights. Dead is what they got. Had they chosen to surrender peaceably and exercise the less **bellicose** rights guaranteed by the Constitution—like trial by a jury of their peers—things would probably have turned out all right for them.

Name me one country where the gun rules and justice prevails. There is no such animal.

If one wants further proof of the dysfunctionality of guns, consider the case of those so-called bounty hunters who burst into a house in Phoenix and killed two people. The man in the house opened fire on the armed, masked intruders, surely his Constitutional right. He was defending his castle. So what? He's dead. He was outgunned.

And so it must always be. The bad guys will outgun the good guys nine times out of ten.

Heston would do well to rent a copy of his most famous film, "The Ten Commandments." There's a commandment right there at the beginning that mig him sort things out.

approximately 410 words

Donald Kaul, "What's Going On with Charlton Heston?" *San Jose Mercury News* 21 Sept. 1997: P3. Donald Kaul is a syndicated columnist. You can e-mail him at <otcoffee@aol.com> .

1. a.   Circle any three of the connotative words that help to reveal the writer's attitude toward his topic.

    b.   What is the topic? _____

---

bellicose (bel′ i kōs) of a quarrelsome or hostile nature; eager to fight

  c. What is the tone? _____

  d. What is the writer's purpose? _____

2. Do you agree with Charlton Heston that the right to bear arms is the most impor-
    tant freedom guaranteed by the Constitution? If so, why? If not, which constitu-
    tional right do you regard as the most important?

    _____

    _____

3. a. In the last paragraph, the author is referring to the Commandment that states:

        _____

    b. What conclusion can you draw from the last paragraph regarding the author's
        stand on gun control, and do you agree, or disagree, with him? Explain your
        response.

        _____

        _____

PASSAGE 3

One of the purposes of the essay "Crisis on Campus" (see p. 388-90) is to persuade
the reader that date rape reports are exaggerated and, therefore, its tone is critical.
Compare its tone and purpose to the following textbook excerpt on the same topic.

Date Rape: Exposing Dangerous Myths

   . . . Even today, in most incidences of sexual attack, a victim makes no report to police,
and no offender is arrested. The reason for such inaction is that many people have a misguided understanding of rape. Three false notions about rape are so common in the
United States that they might be called "rape myths."
   A first myth is that rape involves strangers. A sexual attack brings to mind young men
lurking in the shadows who suddenly spring on their unsuspecting victims. But this pattern is the exception rather than the rule: Four out of five rapes are committed by offenders known to their victims. . . .
   A second myth about rape holds that women provoke their attackers. Surely, many
people think, a woman claiming to have been raped must have done *something* to encourage the man, to lead him on, to make him think that she really wanted to have sex. . . .
   A third myth is the notion that rape is simply sex. If there is no knife held to a
woman's throat, or if she is not bound and gagged, then how can sex be a crime? Th
answer is simply that *forcing a woman to have sex without her consent is a violent crime.* To
accept the idea that rape is sex one would also have to see no difference between brutal
combat and playful wrestling. "Having sex" implies intimacy, caring, communication,

and, most important of all, consent—none of which is present in cases of rape. Beyond the brutality of being physically violated, date rape also undermines a victim's sense of trust. This psychological burden is especially serious among rape victims under eighteen—half of the total—about one-fourth of whom are attacked by their own fathers.

The more people believe these myths about rape, the more women will fall victim to sexual violence. The ancient Babylonians stoned married women who became victims of rape, convinced that the women had committed adultery. Ideas about rape have changed little over thousands of years, which helps to explain why, even today, only about one in twenty rapes results in an offender being sent to jail.

Nowhere has the issue of date rape been more widely discussed than on the college campus. The collegiate environment promotes easy friendships and a sense of trust. At the same time, many students have a great deal to learn about relationships and about themselves. So while college life encourages communication, it also invites sexual violence.

approximately 450 words

John J. Macionis, *Sociology* (Prentice Hall, 1997) 218–19.

1. Are the tone and purpose of "Crisis on Campus" and "Date Rape: Exposing Dangerous Myths" similar or different? Explain your answer.

   _____

   _____

2. Why have attitudes and ideas about rape changed so little "over thousands of years"?

   _____

   _____

PASSAGE 4

"Mea culpa," the title of the following passage, is a Latin expression meaning "It's my fault." You have read several passages dealing with women and minority rights. Now look at the issue of "rights" from a white man's perspective, as you closely examine his tone to arrive at his reason for writing this essay.

Mea Culpa

In the first meeting of my Harvard class on African American writers, an argument erupted over whether the reading list was sexist.

"Why are there no *women* writers on this syllabus?" asked one student, a white man.

The professor said that the major black authors of the period happened to be men.

Big mistake. For the next half hour or so, I learned that maybe we just weren't *aware* of black women writers in the mid-twentieth century. If they were considered unimportant, it was because white men determined what was thought significant about black culture and, deep down, white men want black women only for clandestine mistresses.

I sat quietly through the hubbub. Anything I said would have been automatically discounted. And that's not because I'm a conservative, you understand. On a quick checklist of liberal credentials, I have a pretty high rating. I'm pro-choice, pro-affirmative action, pro-gay rights, and pro-social spending, and I've never voted Republican in my life (except for William Weld). But none of that counts, because for reasons beyond my control I'm the **archetype** of political incorrectness. I grew up in Fairfield, Connecticut, where the country clubs have no black members because the town has no black citizens. My ancestors didn't come over on the Mayflower, but close enough. I attended prep school (Groton) and an Ivy League college (Yale). I'm not differently abled. I was born with a politically incorrect sexual orientation. What right do I have to complain?

Some of this isn't just well-deserved psychological **retribution** for all my previous advantages. Female and minority applicants get into graduate school over a white male with equal or better qualifications. "Sometimes minority applicants are almost dragged in kicking and screaming and told that this will be a great experience for them," says one admissions officer. I did get in, but because I'm a white male it's harder to stay here. Harvard gives full financial aid to all minority graduate students regardless of need. I pay about $8,000 a year, not including living expenses. This breeds cynicism, even among those who benefit from it. . . .

If I weren't a white male, I'd have little difficulty getting a teaching job when I finish my dissertation. Female and minority Ph.D.s are so much in demand, they're courted like baseball's free agents. My female and minority peers will be snapped up as soon as they enter the job market. Merit is moot. This hiring is based on the idea that one can teach only what one is. That knocks me out of the ring: white men have nothing of value to impart.

But a lot to atone for. As a straight white man, I've probably committed date rape, seeing as it's now defined so loosely as to include a peck on the cheek that's not explicitly demanded. My whiteness has contributed to the oppression of non-whites since the beginning of history. I crushed the proletariat, shackled the slaves, exterminated the Indi—Native Americans, I mean. . . .

In this environment, keeping one's liberal convictions takes work. I have to remind myself that I *believe* in affirmative action, I support opening up the literary canon. I know I've had a privileged life. But that isn't enough for my correcter colleagues. Their idea of diversity is a chorus of voices all saying the same thing.

But maybe I shouldn't say that.

approximately 450 words

Richard Blow, "Mea Culpa," *The New Republic* 18 Feb. 1991: 32. Copyright © 1991 by The New Republic. Reprinted with the permission of *The New Republic*.

1. Select one word from the list of words on page 490 that best illustrates how you think the *writer* feels.

_____

---

archetype (är kə tīp) an original pattern or model
retribution (ret′ rə byoo′ shən) deserved punishment

2. Choose one word that expresses how you felt after reading the selection.

_____

3. State the thesis and explain how the writer's tone strengthens the thesis and supports his purpose.

_____

_____

The following satire was written several days before Christmas when Congress was debating whether to impeach William Jefferson Clinton. As you read it, note the many allusions (references to things beyond the literal text meaning) the writer, Arthur Hoppe, makes to a real-life situation through the mythological Santa Claus.

The Impeachment of Santa Claus

Arthur Hoppe

After a four-year, $40 million investigation, Congress today voted to impeach Santa Claus. The charges were perjury, abuse of power and obstruction of chimneys.

Democrats contended that the obstruction of chimneys, while perhaps a high crime, was certainly no misdemeanor and thus not an impeachable offense. "Overly stuffing his sack is a personal matter and not subject to harassment and humiliation," said Democratic Congressman Richard Gephardt.

"This is not about sacks," countered Republican Henry Hyde. "This is about lying to the American person."

The American person Claus is accused of lying to is Little Timmy Tucker, age 8, of Virginia City, Calif. Timmy testified that Claus had clearly told him he would receive an AK-47 assault rifle for Christmas and all he got was "a lousy Super Soaker."

At an emotional protest meeting in his home town, Little Timmy dramatically told the assembled citizens: "Yes, Virginia City, there is a Santa Claus—and he's a fink."

The abuse of power charge stems from Claus's admission that he was keeping a list and checking it twice and that he knew without doubt who'd been naughty and who'd been nice.

"This is a clear case of using the power of his office as Chief Christmas Enforcer to collect milk and cookies from innocent children," Hyde said. "And why does he keep this extortion list twice? We can only assume the second copy is for the Tooth Fairy."

Hyde said that impeaching Claus was "an agonizing decision," but telling the truth must be upheld at all costs. He held up an e-mail signed "Little Samantha Bosnik." It read: "I am only 3 years old but I'm moved to write you in order to solve my mind-plaguing **conundrum:** If Santa Claus can lie, why can't I?"

Speaking for the Democrats, Congressman Gephardt said impeaching Claus would have "a disastrous effect on faith, hope and retail sales." On *Meet the Press* he shouted at Hyde: "It's the economy, stupid," and he staunchly defended Claus, saying that instead of being impeached, he should only be censured for being "a fat, dumb, lying, mostly unemployed slob."

This spirited defense was enthusiastically accepted by the public and Toys 'R' Us. The definitive Alfred E. Barber Poll showed that 63 percent of the people were against impeachment, 62 percent were for censure and 71 percent were for getting the whole damn thing off TV so they could watch "As the World Churns."

Hyde said Republicans would certainly not **cravenly** give in to public opinion. He said his conservative constituents who favored impeachment would be furious with him if he did.

"This historic moment is too momentous for crass partisanship," he said. "I am confident that each and every congressperson will simply vote his or her conscience."

And he proved to be absolutely right. The final tally was 218 Republican consciences to 214 Democratic consciences.

Most pleased was little Timmy Tucker. "It just shows you that our politicians follow their consciences," he said, "and their consciences follow the party line."

approximately 460 words

Arthur Hoppe, "The Impeachment of Santa Claus," *San Francisco Chronicle* 21 Dec. 1998: A29

1. What is Arthur Hoppe's purpose for writing this selection: to amuse or to criticize? Defend your choice.

_____

_____

2. a. Does Hoppe approve of the impeachment proceedings?

_____

   b. Do you agree or disagree with Hoppe's attitude about impeachment? Why, or why not?

_____

_____

---

conundrum (kò nun′ dròm) any puzzling question or problem
cravenly (kra′ vòn lē) cowardly

◌ Assessing the Author's Reliability

In addition to determining an author's tone and purpose, the critical reader questions the writer's reliability—his or her credentials and background as they relate to the information presented. It is important to determine whether the writer is an expert in the field, has had professional training or experience, and has quoted reliable sources in developing the thesis of an essay or textbook passage. Sometimes, facts about the writer are given at the bottom of the page or at the end of the essay or may be included in the introduction of the textbook. If no information is provided about the author, you must be especially careful when reading critically; the information presented should be based on facts and reasoned opinions, and it should be backed by evidence from authoritative sources.

Be on guard for vague references such as "reliable sources said," "reports point out," and "a survey shows" if no actual name is given for the source. Ask, "Who is the reliable source?" "Which specific report or survey is cited?" Do not accept information as factual when the identification of the source is missing.

If a writer presents both sides of an issue fairly, the writing is considered *objective* or *neutral* since it provides information readers can use to form their own opinions on the subject. It excludes any personal references or bias; the writer simply presents the information. But if the writing includes many personal opinions or slanted information to favor one side, we say it is *subjective* with the writer trying to influence the reader's thinking.

In order to determine how reliable the information is, the critical reader asks several key questions.

1. What is the author's background? Is he or she qualified to discuss the topic?
2. How much evidence is provided to support the point of view?
3. Are all aspects of the subject treated fairly?
4. Are reliable sources quoted?
5. Does the author ask for the reader's agreement?
6. Are all relevant arguments considered, or has the author omitted certain aspects of the topic?

The mind map that follows on page 519 details the main differences between objective and subjective writing.

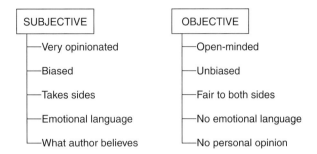

The paragraphs that follow are the conclusion to a selection on student **passivity** in college. Determine whether the information presented is objective and neutral or subjective and biased.

> [Social scientists] Karp and Yoels systematically observed classes and conducted a survey of students at a coeducational university. They included various disciplines in their research, and studied both small (under forty students) and large (over forty students) classes. Although the small classes were characterized by slightly more student participation, in no case were more than a few students active. In small classes, only four or five students typically made more than one comment during a class period, and these few students were responsible for three-fourths of all interaction in the class. In larger classes, only two or three students were active participants; their discussion accounted for more than half of all class interaction. These results contradict the familiar argument that smaller classes encourage extensive student participation. In classes of *all* sizes, the vast majority of students are passive.
>
> Karp and Yoels also found that students themselves became irritated when one of their number was especially active in a class discussion. More than 60 percent of both male and female students reported that they were annoyed by students who "talked too much."
>
> John J. Macionis, *Sociology*

The excerpt is objective since the writer does not attempt to influence the reader to believe that student passivity is either good or bad. The writer quotes a source and presents information without using emotional language or stating opinions. The reader is free to draw his or her own conclusions about student passivity in the classroom. Therefore, this passage is objective and neutral.

ACTIVITY 9.4   Practice Assessing the Author's Reliability

Read the following article, which first appeared in the *New York Times*, and then determine the author's reliability and degree of objectivity about brief, early marriages. Decide whether the information is backed by statistics, quotations, and people who are experts in assessing the success or failure of marriages.

---

passivity (pas iv′ ə tē) inactivity; submissive stance

"Starter" Marriages Often End

Deborah Schupack

Tim Barnard married when he was 25, fresh out of graduate school. His wife was a 21-year-old college student. "At that age," recalled Barnard, now 36, "I didn't comprehend what it took to stay in a long-lasting relationship. It seemed that if you're in a serious relationship and you're committed to another person, the next logical step is to get married."

Four years later, they were divorced. He got the credit-card debt and she got the washer and dryer.

Barnard's marriage was typical of the many brief, early marriages that end in divorce by age 30, with no children and little more joint property than wedding gifts and a stereo. While couples in these marriages do not wed with the intention of divorcing, their temporary stay in marriage is much like the starter home of a generation ago, shed as the family outgrew it.

"The idea of a starter marriage is a fascinating one," said Dr. Constance Ahrons, professor of sociology at the University of Southern California in Los Angeles and associate director of its marriage and family therapy doctoral program. "These marriages are very common, but they are not given much credibility. . . . "

Barometer of Society

Marriage and family experts—psychologists, sociologists, lawyers and clergy—are beginning to look at these brief young unions, seeing in their implications a barometer of society's attitudes about marriage and divorce.

Some say starter marriages signal the need for more premarital counseling. Others have begun to rethink the whole notion of early, pre-children marriages, suggesting that it may be time to lessen the legal and social burdens of divorce for couples at this stage.

No statistics are kept on such marriages, but according to the Census Bureau, in 1992 there were 1.3 million divorces among people age 25 to 29, up from 253,000 in 1962—a five-fold increase—while the population for that age group did not even double in that time period.

Psychotherapists say brief, early marriages have been around as long as divorce has, although they often are overlooked in studies. "There may be no children, no property, and the marriage doesn't make headlines," said Ahrons, [who wrote] "The Good Divorce." . . . "But people still enter marriage with expectations, with dreams, with fantasies of the house we're going to buy, the children we're going to have." . . .

There is debate about how much people should pay in brief marriages without children. Margaret Mead recommended in the 1960s that such unions be codified as "trial marriages." Believing that it is the presence of children that should render a marriage lifelong, Mead described an alternative relationship that would last for a finite period, whereupon the couple would decide whether to have children and enter what she viewed as the more permanent stage of matrimony—or not. . . .

More Cohabitation

Mead's views on trial marriages came before the **proliferation** of **cohabitation.** In 1990, 2.9 million unmarried couples were living together, up 80 percent from 1980 and up 454 percent from 1970, according to the Census Bureau. Some of those couples may be replacing couples who could find themselves in a starter marriage, but cohabitation has not reduced the divorce rate.

Society has a vested interest in making the breakup of a marriage difficult, said Michael Albano, president of the American Academy of Matrimonial Lawyers. . . .

Religious beliefs, too, tend to hold marriage as a **linchpin** of community, and many churches and synagogues offer marital counseling. In the Roman Catholic Church, for instance, couples undergo pre-wedding counseling on the specifics of married life, such as raising children and handling finances, said the Rev. Francis Muller, a judge with the Marriage Tribunal of the Archdiocese of New York. . . .

All marriages go through stages of evaluation, typically in the first year or two after marriage and again after seven years or so, said Dr. Anna Beth Benningfield, president of the American Association for Marriage and Family Therapy, a professional organization of therapists. At these junctures, the challenges of one's 20s—living independently for the first time, beginning a career—can strain a marriage to the breaking point. . . .

Those who have been through young marriages point to the divorce—not the wedding—as the real rite of passage of their 20s. "Marriage is very easy; divorce is very hard," said Pachett. . . .

Albano, the lawyer, . . . speaks to high school classes about the need to communicate in a marriage, about changing gender roles of spouses and parents, and about weathering the inevitable bad times.

"They really don't know that there are going to be days when he's obnoxious or she's so tired she can't deal with him, or the fact that she may make more money than he does" he said. "The Church tells them marriages are made in heaven, but so are thunder and lightning."

approximately 700 words

1.   What is the author's purpose?

_____

---

proliferation (prō lif′ ə rā′ shən) rapid spread or increase

cohabitation (kō hab′ i tā shən) living together in a sexual relationship when not legally married

linchpin (linch′ pin) pin that holds a wheel to its axle; any person, thing, or place that holds together the elements of a group

2. How reliable are the sources quoted to support the writer's thesis? Give some specific examples to support your answer.

    _____

    _____

3. Is the information presented objectively or subjectively? Explain your answer.

    _____

    _____

⬰ Evaluating Reliability of Internet Information

The Internet is a worldwide network of computers containing anywhere from 20 to 50 million pages of data created from a variety of sources—individuals, businesses, schools, special interest groups, and so on. More and more, students are turning to the Internet for needed information. Bear in mind that the Internet is not just a network but a *network of networks* that grows and changes constantly. Not all Internet sources are reliable, nor is all the information accurate, unbiased, scientifically valid, or up-to-date. Unlike most publications, such as newspapers, magazines, or scholarly journals, there is no editorial supervision for most Internet information. For instance, a typical essay or textbook may be evaluated by an editor or expert in a field, whereas anyone can write on the Web or create a Web site. There are no rules regarding what can or cannot be published, and no analysis that anyone makes of what is written. If you have had little experience with doing computerized research, begin by seeking assistance from a reference or resource librarian. Many college libraries now have their own database to assist you or you can turn to a *virtual* library, a directory that contains collections of resources that librarians and information specialists have compiled. Two of the best known are the *Internet Public Library* <http://www.ipl.org> and the *Librarians' Index to the Internet* <http://sunsite.berkeley.edu/internetindex>.

The first thing to do when using Internet sources for school assignments is to determine which resources to use. We recommend that you use *several* search tools rather than just looking at one source since there is no guarantee that any one search tool will supply you with a complete resource list. One way to do this is through a meta-search tool, one that allows you to search several search engines simultaneously, such as *savvysearch* whose address is <http://www.savvysearch.com>.

Other commercial search directories include:

Yahoo: http://www.yahoo.com (the most comprehensive to date)
Excite: http://www.excite.com
Magellan: http://www.magellan.mckinley.com
Infoseek: http://guide.infoseek.com

Explore links that are related to your topic, looking for ones that have a large collection of links. Be specific when you key in your subject or topic.

Many of the suggestions we have made for analyzing the reliability of printed information also apply to searches on the Internet. Here is what you must check:

1. *Source of information:* You can quickly determine the source of the information by looking at the URL, that is, the Internet site address. Check to see the "domain" (the local or host area) of the source. This can be done by looking at the end part of any Web site address. Domain names are grouped into categories, such as:

.edu	educational institutions, like colleges and universities
.com	commercial organizations, including newspapers, businesses
.gov	government, including the Bureau of Statistics
.org	nonprofit organizations
.net	networking organizations
.mil	military

    An address such as <http://www.stanford.edu> gives you the name of an institution (Stanford University) and the "edu" at the end of the address tells you it is an educational institution. An educational institution is probably a good resource for reliable information.

2. *Author:* Just as you must assess the author's credentials for printed information, you need to find out if the writer on the Internet is an expert or a novice on the topic. Check whether the Internet gives you the author's institutional affiliation, position, or experience. If none is given, determine whether the person in question has an e-mail address where you can obtain some background or affiliation information.

3. *Accuracy:* Try to determine how accurate the information is and whether the article or report is researched or is simply someone's personal opinion. Apply all the critical reading and thinking skills you have been learning in your *Effective Reading* textbook.

4. *Timeliness:* Determine how up-to-date the information is by looking for a publication date.

5. *Verification:* Determine whether the information can be verified and if it is well-researched. As with all other research, it is generally not sufficient to simply check one source. Try to find several related pieces of information and assess how worthwhile the material is.

Some Internet users join a *newsgroup,* another resource when you are seeking information on a subject. *Usenet newsgroups* are a number of people with similar interests from around the world who share information. Currently, there are over 20,000 newsgroups; approximately 200 to 300 are added weekly. Usenet groups are organized by subject and divided into major categories, such as

comp.	computer-related topics
rec.	recreational activities/hobbies
sci.	scientific research and associated issues
soc.	social issues and world cultures
talk.	discussions and debates on controversial social issues

Anyone can form a newsgroup. Therefore, much of the information is based on opinion and may or may not be correct. If you use a newsgroup for a class assignment, be sure to evaluate it as you would all other opinionated writing.

⮑ Looking at the Author's Point of View

Writers' beliefs often influence the point of view they take in each piece of writing. In **colloquial** terms, point of view tells the reader "where the author is coming from." It is, in effect, the writer's *bias,* the particular angle from which he or she views things, the position or stance the writer takes. Point of view or bias is not necessarily bad or wrong. The writer's point of view toward a subject is an attitude that helps the writer decide what is important to include and/or exclude as well as how much emphasis to place on certain information. Don't assume that *all* objective writing is good and that *all* biased material is bad.

It is only natural that a person's background would influence his or her views or opinions on a particular topic. For example, would not an article written on alcoholism have a different degree of credibility if written by a member of Alcoholics Anonymous? A doctor? A priest? You should therefore examine the writer's point of view in order to recognize what bias or prejudice the writer expresses. Also, bear in mind that both readers *and* writers have biases, preconceived ideas, or judgments that come into play.

The critical reader asks these key questions:

1. Is the writer's position for or against an issue? What does this imply about the writer?

2. How do the biases and beliefs of the author affect the presentation of ideas?

3. Do I share the same views as the writer? If not, can I read with an open mind so as to evaluate ideas different from my own without being narrow or close-minded?

---

colloquial (kə lō′ kwē əl) characteristic of informal speech

When the subject matter presented is controversial in nature, the critical reader must determine which side the writer favors. If the writer presents only one side of an issue, the writing is generally *subjective* or can be opinionated and often biased. If all sides of an issue are presented, the writing may be neutral, *objective,* and impartial.

The ability to search out and understand differing perspectives is the cornerstone of critical thinking and reading. As a critical reader, you need to understand the point of view of others, questioning the facts, opinions, and ideas expressed. Critical readers are those who think and then ask themselves whether the author changed their mind or at least exposed them to new or different positions.

As indicated earlier, authors do not always state their stance or position directly. The reader may have to carefully combine what authors say outright with the clues they provide—through word choices, for example—and then infer the points of view or positions. In making such analyses, the critical reader raises even more questions:

1. Is the support one-sided or objective?
2. Are the sources quoted and references cited sufficient and reliable?
3. Does the writer have the necessary background to write on the subject?
4. Are the word choices objectively descriptive?

Read the following differing points of view of particular people when asked their opinion of the Constitution of the United States. Note the descriptions of the authors at the time they made the statements, and then answer the question that follows.

1. **Antonia Hernandez, president, Mexican American Legal Defense and Educational Fund**

    Not having been born in the United States, I had to go through the process of becoming a citizen. I didn't think that the ceremony would have such an impact on me. But it really gave me the feeling that the Constitution was a part of me and I was a part of it.

2. **Roger Wilkins, African-American political commentator**

    I was very young when I learned that although white people wrote rules that were grossly unfair, there were some limits that were imposed on them by the Constitution. What I appreciate most about the document is the 13th Amendment (abolishing slavery). If you have to go back to basics, that's it. The fact is that the 13th Amendment is the single most significant thing about the document to me and the thing that has the most meaning in my daily life.

3. **Gordon Hirabayashi, jailed during World War II for challenging the internment of his fellow Japanese Americans**

    My objection has been not so much with the Constitution but with the people administering it, who either manipulated the Constitution or had a different view of it than I have. The Constitution is just a scrap of paper unless people care enough to make it work.

How do the three views differ? What are the particular biases of each?

_____

_____

ACTIVITY 9.5   Looking at Point of View Visually

1. Examine what the cartoonist is saying about one's point of view.

Modern Maturity (Mar.-Apr. 1995) 56. Copyright © 1995 by American Association of Retired Persons. Reprinted with permission of *Modern Maturity*.

"It's all according to your point of view: To me, you're a monster."

Explain what the cartoonist implies about one's point of view.

_____

_____

2. Examine the three drawings and three photographs of the same scene that follow. Each photograph was taken by a different person; the drawings were also done by three different individuals. How do the points of view, of either the photographers or artists, differ?

_____

_____

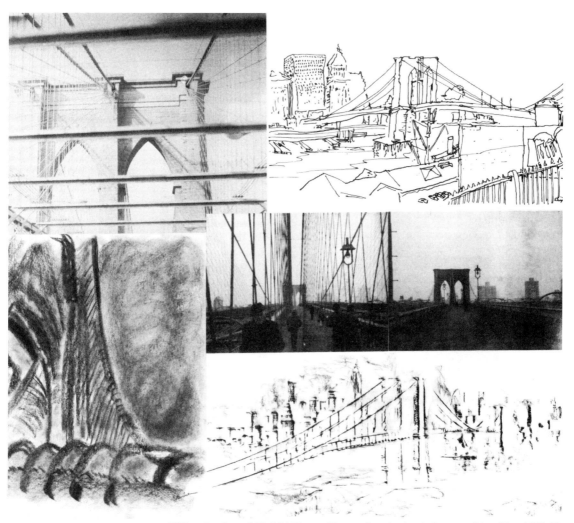

William Sparke and Clark McKowen, *Montage: Investigations in Language* (Macmillan, 1970) 98.

ACTIVITY 9.6   Assessing Author's Bias

Identify the author's particular bias in the following selections.

PASSAGE 1

The New Prohibitionism

The oddest thing about the current national crusade against tobacco is not its frenzy—our culture lives from one frenzy to the next—but its selectivity. Of course tobacco is a great national killer. It deserves all the pummeling it gets. But alcohol is a great national killer too, and it has enjoyed an amazingly free ride amid the fury of the New Prohibitionism. **1**

Joe Camel has been banished forever, but those beloved Budweiser frogs—succeeded by even cuter Budweiser lizards—keep marching along, right into the consciousness of every TV-watching kid in the country. **2**

For 26 years television has been free of cigarette ads. Why? Because TV persuades as nothing else, and we don't want young people—**inveterate** TV watchers—persuaded. Yet television is bursting with **exhortations** to drink. TV sports in particular, a staple of adolescents, is one long hymn to the glories of beer. **3**

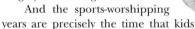

And the sports-worshipping years are precisely the time that kids learn to drink. The median age at which they start drinking is just over 13. A 1990 survey found that 56% of students in Grades 5 through 12 say alcohol advertising encourages them to drink. Surprise! **4**

. . . Alcohol is still a cause of staggering devastation. It kills 100,000 Americans a year—not only from disease but also from accidents. . . . Why, then, do the Bud frogs get to play the Super Bowl while Joe Camel goes the way of the Marlboro Man? **5**

The most plausible answer is that tobacco is worse because it kills more people. Indeed it does. But 100,000 people a year is still a fair carnage. Moreover, the really compelling comparison is this: alcohol is far more deadly than tobacco *to innocent bystanders*. In a free society, should we not consider behavior that injures others more worthy of regulation than behavior that merely injures oneself? The primary motive for gun control, after all, is concern about homicide, not suicide. **6**

The antitobacco folk, aware of this bedrock belief, try to play up the harm smokers cause others. Thus the attorneys general seeking billions of dollars in damages from the tobacco companies are claiming that taxpayers have been unfairly made to pay for the treatment of smoking-related illnesses. **7**

---

inveterate (in vet′ ər it) settled in a habit or practice; habitual
exhortations (eg zôr tā′ shòns) pleas; urging earnestly

A clever ploy. But the hardheaded truth is that premature death from smoking, **8** which generally affects people in their late-middle and early retirement years, is an economic boon to society. The money saved on pensions and on the truly expensive health care that comes with old age—something these smokers never achieve—surely balances, if it does not exceed, the cost of treating tobacco-related diseases.

Unlike secondhand smoke, secondhand booze is a world-class killer. Drunk driving **9** alone kills 17,000 people a year. And alcohol's influence extends far beyond driving: it contributes to everything from bar fights to domestic violence. One study found that 44% of assailants in cases of marital abuse had been drinking. Another study found that 60% of wife batterers had been under the influence. Whatever claims you make against tobacco, you'd have quite a time looking for cases of the nicotine-crazed turning on their wives with a butcher knife.

Moreover, look at the *kinds* of people alcohol kills. Drunk drivers kill toddlers. They **10** kill teens. They kill whole families. Tobacco does not kill toddlers and teens. Tobacco strikes late. It kills, but at a very long remove in time. Its victims generally have already had their chance at life. Tobacco merely shortens life; alcohol can deprive people of it.

Still undecided which of the two poisons is more deserving of social **disapprobation?** **11** Here's the ultimate test. Ask yourself this: If you knew your child was going to become addicted to either alcohol or tobacco, which would you choose?

approximately 550 words

Charles Krauthammer, "The New Prohibitionism," *Time* 6 Oct. 1997: 112

1. What is the writer's bias?

   _____

2. What is the writer's purpose?

   _____

3. How is the tone, particularly in paragraphs 2, 3, and 7, related to the writer's purpose and bias?

   _____

4. Examine your own bias about the problems of tobacco and alcohol. Write a short paragraph in answer to the question posed in the last sentence of paragraph 11.

   _____

   _____

   _____

---

disapprobation (dis′ ap rò bā shòn) disapproval

PASSAGE 2

What's Behind the Attack on Public Education?

The crisis afflicting America's system of free public education is apparent to all, but particularly to parents whose children must attend the public schools and the teachers who work in them. **1**

This crisis in public education is marked by the spread of crime and violence, drug selling and drug abuse, racism, anarchy and other problems that seem to run rampant in schools and schoolyards across the country. **2**

Some of these problems are worse in the inner cities, where the poor and most oppressed elements of the working class are herded like so many cattle—worse, that is, than in the suburbs that surround the cities. . . . **3**

. . . The quality of education itself is in decline, and that decline has nothing whatever to do with the capacities of teachers to teach or of children to learn. **4**

Teachers today are as skilled and devoted to their trade as workers are in any other industry, but their skills and motivation are being subverted in much the same way that the skills and motivation of workers in other industries are being undermined. The same is true of the children, who start to school as bright and eager as children ever did. There is something else at work—something that eats at and destroys the natural human spirit of wanting to share and absorb knowledge. **5**

Socialists believe that the common link is the capitalist system. Antisocialists trace it to other sources—to bureaucracy, to an erosion of "traditional values" or the breakdown of the traditional family, to "bad elements" or to a decline in religious faith. . . . **6**

The crisis in America's public schools reflects the crisis of capitalist society. In fact, "public education" institutions, whether on the local, county, state or federal level, are integral parts of the capitalist state. **7**

. . . The fundamental purpose of education under capitalism is to train the younger generation of workers to take their places on the labor market. **8**

One might think this would provide the capitalist class with a powerful motivation to exert great pressure on the state to preserve and improve on the quality of public education and to keep the meddlers out. Indeed, a great racket has been raised about how new technology is revolutionizing industry at all levels, and of the need for a new generation of workers trained and disciplined to operate them. What better motivation do the corporate owners of the country's industries need to exert that pressure than their demand for workers capable of being employed and exploited? **9**

Actions speak louder than words, however, and despite the talk it is obvious that the school system is falling apart. Instead of a new generation of highly skilled working men and women, we hear of students graduating from high schools and colleges who are "functionally illiterate" and incapable of solving the simplest of mathematical problems. **10**

To understand the apparent contradiction it is only necessary to remember that "new technology" and "labor-displacing technology" are two names for the same thing. Capitalists need a new generation of workers to exploit, but not necessarily an entire generation. Automation means that fewer workers will be needed to operate the new industries. . . . **11**

Rather than get drawn into this or that movement for educational reform, workers should unite in defense of their class interests based on the understanding that educa- **12** tion under capitalism exists to create another generation of workers to sell their labor to the capitalist owners of industry—*but only as they are needed.* Only under socialism, where the means of production are owned and operated collectively by workers, will education be free of the fetters of a decaying social order.

approximately 600 words

"What's Behind the Attack on Public Education?" A Socialist Labor Party Statement, 1998

1. List two words from either the second or third paragraph that give you a clue to the writer's bias?

   _____

2. Against whom or what specifically is the writer biased?

   _____

3. Do you agree with the writer that "new technology" and "labor-displacing technology" are words used to cover up the exploitation of the working class? Why, or why not?

   _____

   _____

4. Is socialism, as the writer suggests, the solution to the crisis in American education? Defend your answer.

   _____

   _____

ACTIVITY 9.7 Distinguishing Differing Points of View

Before reading the first two passages, jot down your feelings about e-mail.

_____

_____

Now, think about the following remarks, proclaimed in a recent magazine editorial about the topic of e-mail.

E-mail is forever. Everything else about the so-called information superhighway may be transient or faddish or dumb, but e-mail is going to survive as long as telephone poles are functioning. It's too easy; it's too useful. It's too much fun. . . . E-mail is the blood that flows through the veins of international commerce; it brings the oxygen of information to the best brains in the world. . . . It is more precise than a telephone conversation, more flexible, more permanent. It is your friend and your enemy; it is a tool and an addiction.*

As you read each of the two passages that follow, make marginal notes to help you determine which writer considers e-mail a friend and/or tool and which thinks of it as an enemy or an addiction.

PASSAGE 1

E-mail is a writer's medium. . . . Hunched over our computers, we're no longer working in isolation. We can defer a response until we've crafted the perfect phrase, hit on the right tone. But on the other end, there's always the expectation of an answer; our readership is waiting, hands poised to applaud or to pound on their own keyboards in furious response. E-mail is performing without a net.

It's the perfect medium, too, for those of us who have never warmed up to the telephone as a device for witty banter or long, soul-searching conversations. Some of us—cautious, shy, uncertain—want to think before we talk. E-mail serves us well. It has the immediacy of a phone call, without the obligation to respond in real time. It offers the luxury of letter-writing, allowing you to think, to choose your words carefully, to get past the anger, annoyance or astonishment of your first off-the-wall response. It's my preferred mode, by far, of machine-assisted communication.

You can answer your e-mail, or choose not to, at any hour of the day or night. . . . Women friends who've struck up cyber-relationships talk about "sweet morning e-mail," the unmatchable bliss of logging in to find a pre-dawn message from their beloved—and the gut-wrenching desolation when the system coldly announces "No new mail." . . .

It's not uncommon, once you sink into the virtual life, to find a dozen or more messages waiting whenever you check in. . . . Meandering through your mail **queue,** you find junk mail intercut with impassioned confessions, business letters mixed with juicy interoffice gossip, passive-aggressive whining, jokes-of-the-day, gems of casual correspondence that practically leap off the screen in their brilliance. E-mail flattens hierarchies; there's no telling who you'll hear from. . . .

Let's not overlook the miracle of being able to send the equivalent of an overstuffed FedEx envelope, or to chat with your cousin in Paris or your colleague in Taiwan, without paying postage or long-distance charges. Many electronic mail programs make it easy to send files—executive reports, recipes, digital snapshots—through e-mail, just like clipping them to a letter. I'm charmed by the thought of legions of elders zapping photos of their grandkids back and forth through the ether. Stand back: Granny's got a scanner, and she knows how to use it!

The e-mail resisters strike me as cranky and inconsiderate; at this stage, it's like not having an answering machine. E-mail keeps me sane, grounded, in touch with the world. Whether I'm writing, reading, or staring blankly out the window, my e-mail autopilot knows to go online and check for new mail every fifteen or twenty minutes. Social crea-

---

queue (kyōō) a stored arrangement of computer data, waiting to be processed in the order submitted; in Britain, a line of persons, vehicles, etc., waiting as to be served

* *San Francisco Focus* Nov. 1996: 59.

ture though I am at heart, I'm content in my solitary dominion, knowing that several times an hour the cherished little message will pop up, drawing me back to what really matters: "You Have Mail!"

approximately 450 words

Reva Basch, "I Love It," *San Francisco Focus* Nov. 1996: 60

PASSAGE 2

A year ago, I left my job at a daily newspaper to become an editor at the Web magazine *Salon*. Although I was a complete **neophyte,** I looked forward with the zeal of the newly converted to the joys of my brave new electronic workplace.

And chief among that world's anticipated pleasures was e-mail. Any hack could bang away on a keyboard, but only the Digital Elect had e-mail. E-mail! The very name held a mysterious, almost sinister allure. . . .

Of course, the bridge to the twenty-first century cannot be crossed without doing battle with certain trolls. But after a traumatic initial encounter with the angeldust-abusing thug who controls access to the e-mail universe. . . . I found myself in proud possession of my very own electronic mailbox, complete with password and a binary menagerie consisting of one **Chaucerian** rooster (who announced "You have new mail" with a happy flourish). . . .

I was as pleased as Punch when I received and responded to my first bona fide business communication. With an imperious stroke of my finger . . . I fired off an executive mandate. Now this, I told myself, was electronic livin'! No more fumbling for stamps! No more cutting your tongue on badly gummed envelopes! No more enduring the insolence of the Postal Service, and risking your life at the hands of its frequently homicidal employees! As I merrily e-mailed hither and yon, I pictured myself as one of those Businessmen of Tomorrow. . . . Buy! Sell! Increase productivity in sector C-3 by 32 percent! The future was mine.

Soon, alas, the dream vanished and disillusionment sunk in. After a year of e-mail, I know from bitter experience that, with rare exceptions, all e-mail messages fall into one of three categories: 1) interminable jokes based on a heavy-handed conceit . . . ; 2) sarcastic comments . . . ; 3) queries from freelancers pitching a six-thousand-word piece about a coming-of-age trip they took with their cousin Larry across southern Minnesota in 1987.

None of these makes pleasurable reading, and two of them are teeth-gnashing impositions that I would not have had to deal with in the days when envelopes sailed unchallenged across the skies. E-mail may have improved productivity by 32 percent in Sector C-3, but its real effect is far more significant: it has exposed the country's workforce to more bad jokes than ever.

Endless lists of **execrable** puns on foreign words, ridiculous satires penned by shameless, cackling shut-ins—American minds are increasingly filled with this **dreck.**

---

neophyte (nē o fīt) a new convert; one just beginning a new kind of work
Chaucerian (chô′ si rē′ n) referring to Geoffrey Chaucer, a fourteenth-century English poet
execrable (ek′ si krò bòl) very inferior; of poorest quality; detestable
dreck (drek) slang for trash; rubbish

True, e-mail may have made interoffice communication easier than ever before, but this has simply made it easier for co-workers to point out each other's shortcomings in cold, lucid prose.

Of course, e-mail does make my job easier. Meaningless pieces of data now pile up inside a machine instead of in great archaeological piles on a desk: thanks to American know-how, we have elevated the six-year-old's technique of shoving the mess under the bed to undreamed-of heights. Actually, I'm more likely to answer an e-mail query than a letter, at least for now. An East Coast editor told me, "In six months, I probably won't even look at my e-mail, but right now, it's a writer's secret weapon." Because you can't readily identify the content of an e-mail from its header, you're more likely to read it. But once the volume reaches critical mass, and the novelty wears off, this too will fade.

approximately 480 words

Gary Kamiya, "I Hate It," *San Francisco Focus* Nov. 1996: 61

1. Contrast the point of view of e-mail expressed in passage 1 with that in passage 2.

    _____

    _____

2. Which writer gives the more convincing argument? Explain why.

    _____

    _____

3. Based on what you wrote at the beginning of this activity, has reading either selection changed your own viewpoint? Why, or why not?

    _____

    _____

Before reading passage 3, write about where you stand on the abortion issue—are you pro-choice or pro-life? Should women be allowed legally to abort an unborn fetus?

_____

_____

PASSAGE 3

Roe v. *Wade*

When the U.S. Supreme Court made abortion legal by striking down a Texas antiabortion law on January 22, 1973, women on both sides of the issue predicted that the decision, known thereafter as *Roe* v. *Wade,* would transform American society.

Since then *Roe* has indeed had a tremendous impact—but not in the ways either side imagined. Viewed 25 years later, their predictions mostly reveal how little anyone grasped the complex realities of sex and social change that, then and now, lurk beneath the neatly **dichotomized** surface of the abortion debate.

Opponents of abortion warned that if women weren't restrained by strict social controls, "abortion mills" would soon spring up in every neighborhood. Commentators in the conservative magazine *National Review* foresaw "an orgy of permissive abortion," with "tax-supported public clinics and hospitals . . . performing abortions on a mass basis."

Two-and-a-half decades later, far from being some sort of impulse buy, abortion remains a costly and hard-to-obtain option for many women:

- Abortion providers are available in only 16 percent of U.S. counties.
- The current pro-life majority in Congress has not only barred the use of federal funds for abortions for poor women, but it has also forbidden abortion coverage in health insurance for federal employees, blocked military women overseas from getting abortions in military hospitals and thrown up other barriers to abortion access.
- Although a first-trimester abortion is, in medical terms, usually a simple office procedure, the cost averages almost $300 and can be well over $1,500.

The pro-choice crystal ball was no more accurate. Abortion-rights advocates believed that *Roe*—coming on the heels of a 1965 Supreme Court decision to overturn state laws that had made contraception illegal—would usher in a new era of rational reproduction. They expected the need for abortion to lessen as birth-control options expanded. "We thought that having a full range of options to avoid unwanted pregnancy would have an impact, especially on teenagers," recalls Sarah Weddington, who as a young lawyer argued *Roe* before the Supreme Court.

That isn't how things look 25 years later:

- Adolescent pregnancy rates rose steadily throughout the 1970s and have remained high ever since, while sex education programs of all kinds continue to face intense opposition.
- Instead of sparking development of new contraceptive options, abortion has given pro-lifers a rationale for attacking Planned Parenthood and similar organizations and blocking advances in contraceptive technology, such as RU 486.

---

dichotomized (dī kat′ ŏ mized) divided into two parts or groups that are sharply opposed to each other

- The rate of unplanned pregnancy has remained shockingly high—3.5 million per year. And consequently, so has the need for abortion: 1.5 million are performed each year.

The assumption about the future that turned out to be most **deluded,** however, was one both sides shared: that the national debate over abortion would be resolved within a few years. Cynthia Gorney, author of the new book *Articles of Faith,* which chronicles abortion politics since the sixties, reports that pro-choice advocates didn't expect the pro-life movement, then small and fragmented, to gain momentum, while abortion foes believed that public opinion would quickly force a reversal of a court decision they regarded as outrageously misguided. Says Gorney: "Neither side ever dreamed they'd still be fighting this battle 25 years later."

Nor could either side have imagined the depth of **ambivalence** about abortion that would linger in our society a quarter century later. Consider: While voters are willing to see abortion access restricted for someone else (women on welfare, women overseas), the majority has consistently opposed efforts to make abortion illegal again—that is, to restrict access for themselves.

Abortion is a subject about which it's easy to have mixed feelings. In the abstract, weighing a woman's rights against those of an unborn child is a tough balancing act. In the abstract, some women's reasons for abortion may seem irresponsible.

But real women's lives are no abstraction—one reason that everyone's expectations in 1973 proved so wrong. And abortion is certainly not abstract; it's a physical invasion, submitted to by real women making real choices that are sometimes agonizing, but always individual and not theoretical at all. *Roe* v. *Wade* recognized that this decision is so deeply personal that it must rest with the woman herself, not with politicians, pastors or police. If we want to safeguard that principle of choice for ourselves, we can no longer be ambivalent about defending choice—and real access to choice—for other women.

Whatever we may think about abortion in the abstract, whatever individual decisions about abortion each of us may make, the right to make that choice for ourselves remains as vital to the well-being of women and their families in 1998 as it was in 1973.

approximately 760 words

"Roe v. *Wade," Teen People* Mar. 1998: 87

1. What are the writer's tone and purpose?

_____

2. Is the writer pro-life or pro-choice? Defend your answer.

_____

3. State two arguments given by each side of the abortion issue.

_____

_____

_____

deluded (di lo͞od′ id) deceived; misled; fooled
ambivalence (am biv′ ə ləns) simultaneous conflicting feelings toward a person or thing

4. Has reading this selection changed your point of view about abortion in any way? Why, or why not?

_____

_____

In 1997, a Scottish scientist fused a single cell from the udder of a six-year-old ewe (a female sheep) with a single egg from another sheep in order to create a clone named Dolly. This astonishing event has led to a flurry of debate over the potential for benefit as well as harm in cloning and the ethics involved in this phenomenon. Having just read about the controversy of abortion, how do you react now to arguments about cloning? Do you believe cloning research should be continued or stopped?

_____

_____

As you read the following selection, make marginal notations to help you think about the arguments about the cloning of humans.

PASSAGE 4

Scientists Argue Pros-Cons of the Cloning of Humans

To those terrified by Frankenstein and Jurassic Park and other cautionary tales, the breakthrough in cloning research . . . must have been a letdown. Far from a frightening monster, the sensational experiment brought forth . . . a little lamb.

But despite appearances, Dolly was anything but ordinary. Her arrival signaled the rewriting of the rules of reproduction. For the first time, an adult mammal had produced offspring without an egg being fertilized by a sperm.

Ultimately, the hoopla was not about an endearing ewe, but Dolly's potentially chilling implications. Could Dolly lead to the cloning of a human being? And if so, was it morally permissible?

There is deep disagreement over the ethics of human cloning. . . .

Ian Wilmut, the English scientist who led Scotland's Roslin Institute to its historic achievement with Dolly, is among those who want human cloning research banned. Critics argue that cloning will offer few if any benefits to science while requiring unacceptable ethical and medical risks.

Opponents also say that cloning would undermine our fundamental concept of humanness. What, for example, would become of individuality in a world where a person could be copied not once but an infinite number of times? And what would happen

Dolly the cloned sheep is sheared by Geordie Bayne in Scotland to help raise money for a charity.

to the fundamental assumption that children are created by the union of a man and a woman, by two parents?

"The bottom line is, cloning a person would change the definition of what it means to be human," said George Annas, a professor of health law at Boston University's School of Public Health. "Who has the right to do that for the rest of us?"

Surveys show that the American public solidly opposes cloning, human or otherwise. According to a Time/CNN poll taken just days after Wilmut's announcement, 93 percent of U.S. citizens said cloning a human was a bad idea, and 66 percent also opposed cloning animals.

Other scientists warn, though, against moving too quickly to stop human cloning research. Such work should be encouraged, they say, because it could provide invaluable insight into how cells work, opening the door to treating cancer and other diseases. . . .

The debate over cloning has been marked by hyperbole. News stories often seem to refer to armies of Hitlers (or Mozarts) to illustrate the potential dangers or benefits of cloning. . . .

While the dangers of human cloning may be exaggerated, supporters of cloning research do not argue that it will bring immediate, untold benefits to humanity. Instead, they say, human cloning research would probably only produce modest societal gains, at least at first.

Human cloning research also might help combat certain diseases. Scientists know that an adult cell **deactivates** all of its genes, except those needed to maintain itself and to fulfill its special function in the body.

Cloning research might also allow scientists to **replicate** certain tissues—even organs—for transplantation. If the genetic material used in the cloning came from the

---

deactivates (dē ak′ tō vāts) makes inactive or inoperative
replicate (rep′ li kāt) to repeat or duplicate

patient, the chance that the body would reject the new organ or other tissue would be greatly reduced, if not eliminated.

Others say that humans have no business **perverting** God's method of creation. "The human body is God's property, not man's laboratory," wrote Munawar Ahmad Anees, an Islamic scholar and author.

approximately 500 words

David Masci, "Scientists Argue Pros-Cons of the Cloning of Humans," *Congressional Quarterly* (From *San Francisco Examiner* 29 May 1997)

1. Are the arguments presented in the selection about cloning based mainly on fact or on opinion?

   _____

2. List one argument given for continuing the research on cloning and one argument against it.

   _____

   _____

3. How do you react to the viewpoint expressed in this statement from the last paragraph: "The human body is God's property, not man's laboratory." Do you agree or disagree with it? Explain why.

   _____

   _____

4. Would you like to have a clone of yourself? Why, or why not?

   _____

   _____

ACTIVITY 9.8 Thinking Critically While You Read

A final assessment to determine whether you have learned to read and think critically is to analyze opposing arguments in fairly long essays. To do so, you must

- identify the issue or opinion of the writer;
- find the author's support for or reason for believing that his or her opinion should be shared by others;

---

perverting (pòr vurt′ ing) changing or corrupting; misusing

- evaluate the merits and shortcomings of the support;
- determine the soundness of the arguments;
- reach a conclusion as to whether you should accept or reject the writer's arguments;
- decide whether you should alter your own point of view or bias, based on the writer's arguments.

After you read contrasting viewpoints on the following issue, in the columns provided on page 545, list the most significant points presented by each author. Then, based on your critical analysis, act as a judge, writing down your "verdict" of the issue. In so doing, consider the following:

Which writer's position is based chiefly on facts, sounder logic, and reasoning?
What is each author's purpose? How reliable are the author and the publication?
What are the biases of each author and publication?

Also consider these questions:

Can inferences be drawn from some of their statements?
Is the choice of language chiefly objective or subjective? Denotative or connotative?
Does either author omit or suppress any information that would help you reach a valid conclusion?

The Environment versus the Lumber Industry

Concern for the environment becomes especially heated when it affects our own national forests, as many people consider them a nonrenewable national treasure. Others, however, claim that we depend on wood products and that these products produce jobs and bolster our economy. Laws to limit cutting of the giant trees are entangled in court proceedings. Environmental groups attack the lumber industry as greedy and insensitive, while the lumber industry attacks the environmental groups as zealots who know little about forestry and logging. Again, this is a complex issue, and it is necessary to be a critical reader to judge it fairly.

The first article, in support of the preservation of our national forests, was written by Harry Lonsdale. At the time the article was written, Mr. Lonsdale was chairman of Bend (Oregon) Research, Inc., and former chairman of the Native Forest Council. He also was a candidate for the U.S. Senate in 1990. The article appeared in *USA Today*.

Can We Save Our National Forests?

Harry Lonsdale

If we don't act soon, the last of our native forests **1** will be destroyed. The trouble is, most Americans don't even know that their forests are being cut down. We tend to think of our woodlands as national parks, as preserves where the deer and the antelope play, birds sing, and clear water flows. In fact, they long ago were declared to be areas of "multiple use," where logging as well as recreational and other values supposedly could be sustained indefinitely. However, at the current rate of timber extraction, the last of the most valuable trees—the "old growth"—will be gone in a couple of decades. In even less time, those forests may be fragmented beyond the point of no return.

. . . John Muir at the beginning of this cen- **2** tury introduced the concept that, simply left alone, the natural world and especially the wilderness areas had a priceless and irreplaceable ecological value that science has yet to comprehend. In his words, "In wildness is the preservation of the world."

However, that same wildness also harbors **3** vast wealth. Because of the fine, clear grain of the wood in the ancient trees, those forests are extremely valuable when reduced to lumber. The remaining woodlands of the Pacific Northwest contain a preponderance of trees with 100 feet or more of branchless trunks, which yield some of the most highly valued lumber in the world. An acre of such old growth can have a value in excess of $100,000 to the timber industry. Thus, the millions of acres of ancient, publicly owned forests in Oregon and Washington alone are worth hundreds of billions of dollars in the open marketplace.

What those trees are worth if left standing **4** is a much harder figure to arrive at, and almost any reasonable method of calculation comes up far short of the purely utilitarian value. Thomas Power, an economist at the University of Montana, and a team at Colorado State University headed by Richard Walsh have attempted to put a value on forests. One of the preferred methods of evaluation is to ask campers and hikers what they would pay to spend a day in the woods, or how much they expended as a part of their annual vacation costs to get to and enjoy the forests. Others, like Randall O'Toole of Cascade Holistic Economic Consultants, Corvallis, Ore., would have us pay the true costs of a forest experience with a fairly high annual user fee. Whatever the logic or method, it quickly becomes abundantly clear that there's much more money in lumber than in forests.

So, do we chop them all down and grow **5** trees on farms as they do in Europe? The Forest Service is planning just that. Its "tree of the future" will grow in rows and be cut down, or "harvested," when it reaches a diameter of 17 inches. If all we want is trees, that will give us enough forever, or at least until the soil is so depleted of nutrients that it won't support them any more. Chris Maser, a forest ecologist who for many years was on the staff of the Bureau of Land Management, believes that only about three such "crops" can be grown on a patch of land before the soil is depleted irreparably.

It well may be that all of this ecology vs. **6** economy talk soon will have become irrelevant. There's a new thinking loose in the world that says we must preserve and restore this planet before it's too late. Such thoughts may turn out to be irrepressible. As more Americans become aware of the fact that, somewhere on Earth, an acre of ancient forests is being destroyed every second, around the clock, the pressure to preserve what's left will mount irresistibly.

Before we throw up our hands, let's recognize that there is plenty of timber to go around, at least for our own country's needs. Over 72% of the nation's supply is privately owned and, while it's true that most of the country's native forests now are gone, we still have the capacity to grow more trees for all the 2x4s, newsprint, and toilet paper we'll ever need, if we manage those woodlands wisely. In 1976, Congress passed the National Forest Management Act (NFMA '76). That law provides, in part, that the national forests shall be managed so as to supply us with a minimum amount of timber "in perpetuity." That sounds reassuring, but NFMA '76 has been interpreted by the Forest Service to mean that they will produce at least a minimum amount of wood fiber per year, without regard to what the forests look like. Thus, because we've been overcutting for decades and because younger trees add more fiber per year than older ones, in order to meet the requirements of NFMA '76, we're heading for those tree farms—unless we change the law. 7

We Can't Supply the World

While we have plenty of timber for our own needs, we don't have enough to supply the world. Other countries, notably Japan, see our timber as grossly underpriced and are buying our logs as fast as we can cut them down. The world price of raw logs is greatly in excess of our domestic price. Thus, industry giants like Weyerhauser sell logs off their own lands to Japan while, at the same time, supplying logs to their U.S. mills from trees cut in our forests. The direct export of most logs cut in our national forests is illegal, but there's a huge 8

loophole that allows this substitution that circumvents the spirit of the law.

Every time we export raw logs, we export the jobs that their processing would have produced. With a dwindling supply of ancient trees and with more improvements in automation, employment in the timber industry actually is contracting, just as production and corporate profits are at all-time highs. The industry, in a major national public relations campaign, unfairly is blaming the loss of jobs on the environmentalists who want to save the ancient forests. The timber industry is after short-term profits, and it wants to continue to earn them by continuing what it has been doing quite legally for years—chopping down our national forests. When the present trees in our national forests are gone, it plans to grow its own or cut those grown on national forest tree farms. It's been the tradition in that industry to "cut and move on," but we have reached the point where there's no place left to move on *to*. 9

If we'd stop the exports, we would have plenty of timber for our domestic use. After all, we now export more raw logs and other barely processed wood products from Northwest ports than we cut on all the national forests in Oregon and Washington. If we'd get smart and start exporting value-added wood products, we could create enough new jobs to more than replace those that might be lost due to a decrease in timber production that is inevitable at our present pace of overcutting. Only by stretching out the cutting of those forests can we produce wood products and the jobs that go with them indefinitely. The Swiss sell a cuckoo clock for more than we Americans sell a five-ton log! The wood products companies of the future in the Pacific Northwest will be those that manufacture furniture, doors and windows, and modular homes for domestic and foreign markets. 10

How can we bring about this change in a powerful, entrenched, and politically astute industry which is so strong that not one Congressperson from Idaho, Oregon, or Washington dares to antagonize it by suggesting that we manage our national forests on a truly sustainable basis? By virtue of their wealth, the timber barons are represented on every major corporate and charitable foundation board in the Northwest. . . .

Our ancient forests provide us with pure water, clean air, wildlife habitat, and, most importantly, a tranquil sanctuary. We can't let the search for profit lead us into the equivalent of the last buffalo hunt.

approximately 1370 words

Harry Lonsdale, "Can We Save Our National Forest?" *USA Today* Mar. 1991: 22–24. Copyright © 1991 by the Society for the Advancement of Education. Reprinted by permission of *USA Today*.

The second article, in defense of the lumber industry, appeared in *Newsweek* magazine. At the time she wrote this article, Leila Kysar was the business manager of a tree-farm-management business in Washington state.

A Logger's Lament

Leila L. Kysar

My father was a logger. My husband is a logger. My sons will not be loggers. Loggers are an endangered species, but the environmental groups, which so righteously protect endangered species in the animal kingdom, have no concern for their fellow human beings under siege. Loggers are a much misunderstood people, pictured as brutal rapists of our planet, out to denude it of trees and, as a result, of wildlife.

It is time to set the record straight. Loggers take great pride in the old-growth trees, the dinosaurs of the forests, and would be sorry to see them all cut. There are in the national forests in Washington and Oregon (not to mention other states) approximately 8.5 million acres of forested land, mostly old growth set aside, never to be used for timber production. In order to see it all, a man would have to spend every weekend and holiday for 60 years looking at timber at a rate of more than 1,000 acres per day. This does not include acreage to be set aside for spotted-owl protection.

In addition to this huge amount of forested land never to be logged, the State of Washington Forest Practices Act, established in 1973, specifies that all land that is clear-cut of trees must be replanted unless converted to some other use. As a tree farmer generally plants more trees per acre than he removes, more trees are being planted than are being cut. In the last 20 years in Clark County, Wash., alone, the Department of Natural Resources has overseen the planting of at least 15,000 acres of previously unforested private lands.

The term logger applies to the person harvesting trees. A tree farmer is the one who owns the land and determines what is to be done with it. To a tree farmer, clear-cutting is no more than the final harvest of that generation of trees. The next spring, he reforests the land. To the public, clear-cutting is a bad word. Does the public cry shame when a wheat farmer harvests his crop and leaves a field of stubble in place of the beautiful wheat?

In the Pacific Northwest, in five years, the newly planted trees will grow taller than the farmer's head; in 10 years, more than 15 feet tall; and in 20 to 30 years, the trees will be ready for the first commercial harvest. The farmer then thins the trees to make room for better growth. In 40 to 50 years, he will be ready to clear-cut his farm and replant again. Contrary to public opinion, it does *not* take 300 to 400 years to grow a Douglas fir tree to harvestable age.

Tree farming keeps us in wood products. We build with wood, write on paper and even use the unmentionable in the bathroom. But in order to keep this flow of wood products available, we need to keep it economically feasible to grow trees. If we restrict the tree-farming practices because we do not like clear-cuts or because some animal might (and probably might not) become extinct, or we restrict markets for the timber by banning log exports or overtax the farmer, we are creating a situation where the farmer will no longer grow trees. If he cannot make money, he will not tree-farm. He will sell his tree farm so that it can grow houses. The *land* that grows trees is the natural resource; the *trees* are just a crop.

Legislation is constantly being introduced to take away the private-property rights of tree farmers. They are beleaguered by the public, who believe that any forest belongs to the public. Who, after all, buys the land and pays the taxes? Who invests money in property that will yield them an income only once every 20 to 30 years? Would John Q. Public picnic in a farmer's wheat field?

The tree farmer must have a diversified market. When there is a building slump in this country, it is vital to the industry to have an export market. Earlier recessions were devastating to tree farmers until markets were developed overseas. Some trees have little market value in the United States. The logs China and Korea bought in the late '80s could not be sold here to cover the cost of delivery.

As to the wildlife becoming extinct, that is a joke that is not very funny. Animals thrive in clear-cuts better than in old-growth timber. Look at the Mount St. Helens blast area. Nature created an immense clearing and now deer, elk and other wildlife are returning in numbers. Why? Because there is more food growing in an open area than under the tall trees. And as for the spotted owl, surely the 8.5 million acres set aside is enough to maintain quite a respectable owl population. Numerous recent observations show that the owl lives in second-growth timber as well as in old growth. In the Wenatchie National Forest there are more than 250 examples of spotted owls living in other than old-growth timber. The owl is a tool of the environmentalist groups to get what they want: the complete eradication of the species *Logger.*

Beautiful New Trees

Consider the scenic value of a preserved old-growth forest versus a managed stand of timber. In Glacier National Park, Mont., for example, which is totally untouched, one sees the old trees, the dead and dying trees, the windfalls crisscrossing the forest. In a managed forest, one sees the older stands with the forest floor cleared of the dead windfalls, leaving a more parklike setting. In the younger stands, one sees the beautiful new trees with their brilliant greens thrusting their tops to the sky and, in the clear-cuts, before the new trees obscure the view, one sees the huckleberry bushes with their luscious-tasting berries, the bright pink of fireweed and deer and elk feeding. True environmentalists husband the land; they do not let the crops stagnate and rot. Tree farming regenerates the trees *and* utilizes the product.

A tree farmer from Sweden (where they are fined if they do *not* tree-farm their forests) asked me recently why we do not just explain these facts to the environmental groups so that they will work *with* us instead of against us. Well, do you know the difference between a terrorist and an environmentalist? It is easier to reason with the terrorist.

approximately 1040 words

Leila L. Kysar, "A Logger's Lament," *Newsweek* 22 Oct. 1990: 10

List the most significant points made in each of the two essays. Remember to consider the author's thesis, purpose, objectivity, reliability, and language.

Significant Points *For* Prohibiting the Cutting of Our National Forests	Significant Points *Against* Prohibiting the Cutting of Our National Forests

Arguments not included:

1. What is your verdict on the pros and cons of legalizing the cutting of lumber in our national forests?

   _____

   _____

2. What are your reasons for your decision?

   _____

   _____

ᕆ Summary

A writer's tone, purpose, reliability, point of view, and bias are factors to consider when reading critically. While many tones are used by writers, eight major tones predominate:

1. Serious or neutral (straightforward and objective)
2. Solemn (dignified and grave)
3. Critical (good or bad features considered)
4. Sarcastic (harsh, bitter words that hurt and belittle)
5. Ironic (opposite of what is really intended)
6. Satiric (exaggeration and ridicule to bring about change)
7. Cynical (pessimistic and doubtful about humankind)
8. Humorous (amusing and comical writing; a witty tone has sophisticated, clever writing)

An author may use more than one tone, and the tone or tones are related to the author's purpose in writing. Writers do not state their purpose; the reader infers or discovers it. These purposes consist primarily of entertaining, informing, or persuading the reader, but as with tone, writers may have more than one purpose for writing. For example, entertaining writing also can be meant to persuade.

Critical readers also question the writer's reliability, his or her credentials and background, as they analyze the issue or information presented. The personal beliefs and background of an author influence his or her point of view. Critical readers note whether only one side of an argument is presented and whether the writing is subjective—and therefore probably biased—or whether the writer presents both sides of an issue and lets the reader determine the merits of each.

With the increasing use of research on the Internet, it is equally important to verify the reliability of given information. You must check especially the source of information and determine its accuracy and timeliness.

Chapter 9
Vocabulary Review
Word Analogies

You have learned in previous chapters that word analogies can show a relationship of words with similar meanings (synonyms) as well as those with opposite meanings (antonyms). Word analogies can also be related through the process of *cause and effect*. For example:

sorrow:tears::happiness:smiles

The analogy suggests that sorrow can *cause* tears just as happiness can *cause* smiles.

A. In the practice that follows, the first set contains a review word from previous chapters. Complete the second pair by writing in the blank space the appropriate word from Chapter 9 from the three choices listed below the analogy. The first one has been done for you.

    1. arsenic:demise::cyanide: ___lethal_____

       (poison, lethal, cults)

    2. misunderstanding:calamity::dispute: _____

       (error, bellicosity, complaint)

    3. great talent:icon::great wealth: _____

       (sovereign, affluent, titan)

    4. perversion:deviant::immorality: _____

       (wrong, denial, dissolute)

    5. rivalry:antagonism::resentment: _____

       (jealousy, confusion, angst)

B. For this final practice with analogies, you are to decide whether the paired words are related by similarities (*synonyms*) or differences (*antonyms*). The first set contains a review word from previous chapters or a familiar word. Complete the second pair with a word from Chapter 9. Select it from the list of boldfaced words on page 548. You will not use all the words listed. In completing the practice, indicate the relationship of the pairs of words in the space provided, determining whether they are synonyms or antonyms as shown in the example.

discredit:disparage::run down: _____

(*Belittle* is a word that could complete the analogy.)

Relationship: *synonyms* _____

intemperance   proliferation   passive   lethal   frays   sordid   archetype

1. self-denial:hedonist::self-control: _____

    Relationship: _____

2. inactive:dynamic::lively: _____

    Relationship: _____

3. sensational:lurid::contemptible: _____

    Relationship: _____

4. destroy:decimate::deadly: _____

    Relationship: _____

5. increase:diminish::reduction: _____

    Relationship: _____

C. For this last review practice, use the *context clues* to determine which of the words listed is appropriate in each sentence. You will not use all the words.

   regimen   cohabitation   pessimistic   colloquial   satirist   titan

1. Their parents disapproved of the young, unmarried couple's _____.

2. Using _____ language and slang in formal essays is generally considered inappropriate.

3. Voters were _____ and doubted that the proposed state tax decrease would appear on the ballot.

4. Bill Gates, the billionaire entrepreneur and _____ of the computer industry, has influenced business operations in the United States and abroad.

5. Essays by Art Buchwald, a well-known _____ and critic of politics, appear weekly in newspapers nationwide.

Selection 19: **ESSAY**

 ## Preparation for Reading

Ward Connerly

Ward Connerly, the University of California regent who is a vocal opponent of affirmative action, recently said: "I scratch my head over it and I scratch my head over it, and I just don't know. Why is it that the black middle class—which is arguably the most obvious beneficiary of affirmative action—the group that's falling furthest behind?" Before you begin to read to learn the answer to Connerly's question, think for a moment about your own viewpoint about the merits of affirmative action. Are you in favor of or opposed to the policy of affirmative action? Complete the following sentence now.

I think that affirmative action _____

_____.

These boldfaced words are underlined in the essay.

most **blatant** discrimination	glaringly conspicuous
disparities occurred	inequalities or differences
revealed its **precariousness**	uncertainty; insecurity
marginality	closeness to the limit or boundary, especially a lower limit
fragility	easily damaged or destroyed
impoverished members	made poor

Preview, then read the essay.

Culture Plays Key Role

Annie Nakao

To Ward Connerly, the nation's leading opponent of affirmative action, the black middle class had its start years before the civil rights movement of the 1960s. **1**

Its creators, Connerly says, were the "victims of the most blatant discrimination, who overcame and went out and attacked the wall. They're the ones who got the black middle class growing." **2**

It is with deep pride that Connerly and many other blacks cite the African American **3** struggle against great odds—to go to college, to enter the professional ranks and to raise families as members of the nation's middle class.

Now, with studies showing that middle-class **4** blacks lag behind whites and Asians of the same class by all traditional measures of academic achievement—from standardized tests to grades to college graduation rates—Connerly, 58, blames affirmative action.

That drive to overcome has been diluted by **5** affirmative action, says Connerly.

Yet his theory is contradicted by studies 6 showing that the middle-class academic achievement gap is not recent.

These differences were apparent in the first 7 national study of academic performance of American students conducted by the late University of Chicago sociologist James Coleman in the mid-1960s, before the effects of affirmative action could be measured.

A Matter of Wealth

Studies show that the academic performance 8 difference may have more to do with the fact that African Americans are not experiencing the same middle-class culture as whites.

It's a matter of wealth, not income, says 9 University of Florida sociologist Joe Feagin.

"They [African Americans] have far less 10 wealth—a house, stocks, bonds, cash—and the wealth is shallow in terms of generations," Feagin said.

The same findings were reported in a 1995 11 book, "Black Wealth/White Wealth," co-written by sociologists Melvin L. Oliver of UCLA and Thomas M. Shapiro of Northeastern University in Boston.

In 1989, blacks on average earned 60 per- 12 cent of the income of whites, but the average white family had 12 times as much median net worth—$43,800 for whites vs. $3,700 for blacks, the book said.

In starker contrast, the average white 13 household controlled $6,999 in net financial assets, while the average black household had no nest egg.

Blacks also work harder to be middle class, 14 the authors reported.

Among married couples, it took two full- 15 time workers in 60 percent of black homes to earn between $25,000 and $50,000; the same was true for only 37 percent of white homes.

Put another way, one full-time breadwinner 16 supported 57 percent of white households but only 42 percent of black households.

The size of the gaps has either remained 17 unchanged or increased in the past nine years, Shapiro said.

Blacks Missed Suburban Land Rush

These disparities occurred because blacks 18 never participated in what Shapiro and Oliver called "one of the greatest mass-based opportunities for wealth accumulation in American history": government-subsidized suburbanization in the 1950s.

Blocked from low-interest loans by discrim- 19 inatory federal housing practices, blacks had no homes to pass on to their children.

" . . . an accurate and realistic appraisal of 20 the economic footing of the black middle class reveals its precariousness, marginality and fragility," wrote Oliver and Shapiro.

Just as accumulated wealth can cushion 21 economic hard times, it can also facilitate academic success.

"It determines what neighborhood you can 22 live in, what school your kids go to . . . ," said UC-Berkeley sociologist Claude Fischer.

For middle-class blacks, neighborhood 23 choice is often limited by segregation.

"There is very clear evidence that middle- 24 class blacks and to a lesser extent, middle-class Latinos, end up living near low-income, impoverished members of their same race to a degree that can't be explained by income," Fischer said. "So even an affluent black family runs a much greater risk of having their kids in a lousy school or social environment."

Accumulated Education Gap

Another way middle-class experiences might 25 differ dramatically between groups is the amount of human capital, or formal education, acquired by families over generations.

Some effects of human capital are concrete—educational achievement that translates into high-paying jobs and professions. 26

Others may be subtle: how much time parents spend with their children in education-related activities, parenting styles, even what magazines or books are in the home. 27

"Black parents and grandparents, on average, have less adequate education than white parents and grandparents," Feagin said, "Even though they may possess the same degree. You can get a high school degree from a ghetto school in the urban inner city and it's not worth as much as a degree from a suburban school where the educational environment is much more challenging and supportive." 28

That is generally true, though not always, said San Francisco schools Superintendent Bill Rojas. 29

"It isn't true 100 percent," he said. "You will find schools like Lowell or Wallenberg here in San Francisco, or Stuyvesant on the East Coast, that are public schools in an urban setting. Yet they provide more rigorous and challenging courses than you'd find in any suburban school." 30

Still, one stunning finding of adult literacy studies is that many of today's blacks with college degrees may have skill levels closer to that of white high school graduates, according to a 1995 book, "An American Imperative: Accelerating Minority Educational Advancement," by L. Scott Miller. 31

"Credential for credential, they don't have as much human capital," said Miller, who directs the College Board's National Task Force on Minority High Achievement. . . . 32

Parenting Makes a Difference

Differences in the amount of education families accumulate over generations can affect parenting styles. 33

Studies suggest black middle-class families tend to have authoritarian, blue-collar parenting styles, while white middle-class parents tend toward more flexible styles that encourage problem-solving. 34

Such differences may stem from historically harsh social conditions for blacks in the United States. Black parents felt it necessary to exercise strong control over their children to protect them. 35

These differences can affect testing behavior and results. 36

In a 1988 study of black children adopted by white and black parents, researcher Elsie Moore noted different styles of parenting during IQ tests given to the children with their mothers present. 37

The white mothers smiled, joked, offered hints and encouraged their children by telling them it was all right to be wrong. 38

The black mothers were more likely to scowl, offer negative evaluations of how the children were doing and give very specific instructions about what to do. 39

Moore's study, reported in the *Journal of Negro Education* in 1987 and *Developmental Psychology* in 1988, suggests the different styles probably had an impact: The children with white parents scored an average of 13 points higher than those in black homes. 40

Differences in the middle-class experience play out in other subtle ways, noted Edmund W. Gordon, emeritus professor of psychology at Yale University and co-chair of the College Board's minority achievement task force. 41

"In carrying on discussions, for example, middle-class kids learn to listen to the direction 42 the debate is going," said Gordon, who is black. "Lower-class kids don't have to listen as much because there is just less debate . . . it's more authoritarian. Now a middle-class black family will have more discussion, but less than a middle-class white family.

"So being a middle-class black person 43 doesn't necessarily mean one shares the same cultural experience of a middle-class white person."

approximately 1120 words

Annie Nakao, "Culture Plays Key Role," *San Francisco Examiner* 8 June 1998: A12

COMPREHENSION CHECK

Part I
General Comprehension Questions: Literal and Interpretive

A.   Write the correct letter in the space provided.

_____ 1.   Ward Connerly thinks the black middle class began

a. in the last decade.
b. because of the civil rights movement.
c. before the 1960s.
d. none of the above.

_____ 2.   The percentage of income earned by blacks in comparison to whites in 1989 was

a. one-half less.
b. roughly equal.
c. about three-quarters less.
d. almost one-third less.

_____ 3.   Sociologists Oliver and Shapiro believe the difference in wealth between blacks and whites is due to the fact that in the past

a. fewer blacks had college degrees.
b. blacks could not afford to buy homes subsidized by the government.
c. blacks were migrants.
d. most blacks had low-paying jobs.

_____ 4.   "Human capital" in the selection is defined as

a. stocks and bonds.
b. owning a business.
c. money in the bank.
d. a formal education.

_____ 5.   According to the essay, culture plays a key role in one's

a. ambition.
b. intellectual growth.
c. social class.
d. self-sufficiency.

6. a. Why does Connerly think that affirmative action is responsible for causing blacks to lag behind whites and Asians in their scholastic achievement?

_____

_____

   b. Do you agree with Connerly? Why, or why not?

_____

_____

B. _Inferences/Conclusions:_

7. a. What can you conclude about the effect of wealth on culture?

_____

_____

   b. What does the writer imply is responsible for different parenting styles among races?

_____

_____

   c. State one conclusion you can reach from the statistics given below.

	Income	Net worth
White	$25,000–$50,000	$44,069
College degree	$38,700	$74,922
White collar	$33,765	$56,487
Black	$25,000–$50,000	$15,250
College degree	$29,440	$17,437
White collar	$23,799	$ 8,299

Source: *Black Wealth/White Wealth*

_____

_____

8. Is the language in the essay primarily denotative or connotative? Why do you think so?

_____

_____

9. What is the overall tone of the essay?

_____

_____

10. Is the author's purpose directly related to the tone? Explain.

_____

_____

_____

11. Is the author objective or subjective about her topic, that is, does she reveal any personal bias?

_____

_____

_____

12. Does the author provide sufficient evidence to convince you of her thesis? Explain whether the author has cited any reliable sources.

_____

_____

_____

13. Explain the contradiction between the information given in paragraphs 21 and 24.

_____

_____

_____

Part II
Application Questions for Writing and Discussion

14. a.   The writer describes two distinctive parenting styles, authoritative versus flexible (paragraph 36). Which parenting style have you experienced? Is it in line with the writer's explanation of racial differences?

_____

_____

   b.   Which parenting style would you choose for raising your own children?

_____

_____

15.   What is your definition of culture, and how important is culture in your life?

_____

_____

Part III
Extend Your Vocabulary

You have read these words and sentences in the context of the essay. Determine the meaning of the boldfaced word, and select the best definition from the choices given. Circle the correct letter.

1.   "That drive to overcome has been **diluted** by affirmative action. . . . "

   (a) defined   (b) weakened   (c) described   (d) maintained

2.   " . . . and the wealth is **shallow** in terms of generations. . . . "

   (a) not deep   (b) not sufficient   (c) not attractive   (d) not important

3.   " . . . while the average black household had no **nest egg**."

   (a) savings   (b) security   (c) power   (d) food

4.   "Just as accumulated wealth can cushion economic hard times, it can also **facilitate** academic success."

   (a) make harder   (b) make softer   (c) make easier   (d) make quicker

5.   "The black mothers were more likely to **scowl,** offer negative evaluations of how the children were doing. . . . "

   (a) remark   (b) criticize   (c) show displeasure   (d) show pleasure

Selection 20: **TEXTBOOK**

 Preparation for Reading

The previous essay, "Culture Plays a Key Role," (Selection 19) focused on the role of culture relative to one's social status. The following textbook selection also deals with social class in the United States but from a much broader perspective. Despite the fact that we are considered a democracy with equal opportunity for all, the actual distribution of wealth and opportunity for educational and social advancement among the classes is far from equal.

Read to see where you can place yourself in the suggested class hierarchy. At the same time, note the range in social prestige in our country, as defined by different occupations.

The following boldfaced words are underlined in the text.

social **stratification**	arrangement in layers
aristocracy	a ruling class of wealthy nobles
individual **autonomy** and achievement	independence

Preview, then read the selection.

Social Class in the United States

John J. Macionis

Nigeria Collins died one month and one day **1** after she was born. She now lies in a corner of Evergreen Cemetery in Camden, New Jersey, a small city across the river from Philadelphia. She is not the only infant buried beneath this patch of scrub grass littered with trash and broken glass. Hundreds of other babies lie here in a place that should guard the remains of people who grew up, grew old, and eventually died.

A half-century ago, Camden was one of the **2** busiest industrial cities in the United States. Its shipyard built battleships, its factories turned out record players and other consumer goods, and its processing plants canned soup for a hungry nation.

But today Camden is among the most **3** down-and-out cities in the country. The downward slide started in the 1950s, as people with the initiative and the cash escaped to the leafy green of the surrounding suburbs, leaving behind those with less schooling and fewer skills. Today, two-thirds of the city's households are poor, and block upon block of housing is falling down, burned out, or boarded up. Camden also bears other familiar marks of cities in crisis: While some two hundred stores sell liquor, there is not a single movie theater; Camden has a flourishing drug trade but no safe park; street violence erupts everywhere, often, and without warning.

This urban tragedy is all the more wrench- **4** ing because Camden is a city of children: About half of its people (who now number barely 100,000) are under the age of twenty-one. These youngsters cope in a world twisted by poverty, in which drug dealing or prostitution is a way of life; some like Nigeria Collins succumb before they are even old enough to know what did them in (Fedarko, 1992).

The story of Camden stands as stark evidence of the pervasive power of social stratification to shape the lives of people throughout the United States. Whether individuals achieve great success or collapse with broken spirits is not simply a matter of their individual talents and personal ambitions. Our fate also reflects the distribution of wealth, power, and opportunity in our society.

Dimensions of Social Inequality

The United States is distinguished from most countries of the world because we never had a titled aristocracy. With the significant exception of our racial history, this nation has never known a caste system that rigidly ranks categories of people.

Even so, U.S. society is highly stratified. Not only do the rich control most of the money, they also benefit from the most schooling, they enjoy the best health, and they consume the greatest share of almost all goods and services. Such privileges contrast sharply with the poverty of millions of women and men who struggle from day to day simply to secure food and keep a roof over their heads.

People tend to think of the United States as a "middle-class society." Indeed, it is easy to underestimate the extent of stratification in our society for four reasons:

1. **We support equal standing under the law.** Because our legal system accords equal rights to everyone, we tend to think that all people have basically the same social standing.

2. **Our culture celebrates individual autonomy and achievement.** Our belief that people forge their own destinies through talent and hard work leads us to downplay the significance of birth on social position.

3. **We tend to interact with people like ourselves.** Throughout the United States, primary groups—including family, neighbors, and friends—typically are composed of people with similar social standing. While we may speak of "how the other half lives," generally we have only brief and impersonal encounters with people very different from ourselves.

4. **The United States is an affluent society. . . .** The overall standard of living in the United States is the highest in the world. Such affluence lulls us into believing that everyone in our society is relatively well off.

When people do acknowledge their differences, they often speak of a "ladder of social class" as if inequality were a matter of a single factor such as money. More accurately, however, social class in the United States has several, more subtle, dimensions. *Socioeconomic status (SES),* . . . amounts to a composite measure of social position that encompasses not just money but power, occupational prestige, and schooling.

Income

One important dimension of inequality involves **income,** *occupational wages or salaries and earnings from investments.* The Bureau of the Census reports that the average (mean) U.S. family income in 1994 was $38,808. The first part of Figure 9.1 [on page 558] illustrates the distribution of income among all families[1] in

---

[1] Some Census Bureau reports use means, others provide median data. For 1994, median family income was $36,782; this figure is lower than the mean because high-income families pull the mean upward. Reported for households rather than families, income statistics are somewhat lower: $32,385 (mean) and $31,241 (median). Most of this difference is due to size: Families averaged 3.20 persons, households 2.67. The Census Bureau defines a household as two or more persons sharing a living unit; they define a family as two or more persons related by blood, marriage, or adoption.

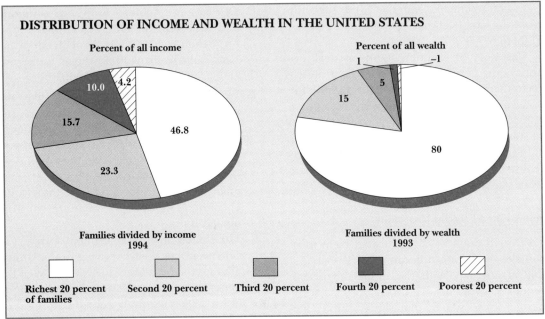

FIGURE 9.1 Distribution of Income and Wealth in the United States

Sources: Income data from U.S. Bureau of the Census (1996); wealth data are author estimates based on the Joint Economic Committee (1986) and Kennickell & Shack-Marquez (1992).

the country. The richest 20 percent of families (earning at least $70,000 annually) with a mean of about $115,000) received 46.8 percent of all income, while the bottom 20 percent (earning less than $18,000, with a mean of about $10,000) received only about 4.2 percent.

Table 9.1 provides a closer look at income distribution. The highest-paid 5 percent of U.S. families, who earn six-figure incomes (with a mean of $198,336) secured 20.1 percent of all income, surpassing in earnings the lowest-paid 40 percent. At the very top of the pyramid, the richest half of 1 percent earn at least $1 million annually. In short, the bulk of the nation's income is earned by a small proportion of families, while the rest of the population makes do with far less.

. . . Income disparity in the United States increased during the 1980s as a result of changes in the economy, new tax policies, more two-earner couples, and cuts in social programs

11

12

TABLE 9.1
U.S. Family Income, 1994

Highest paid . . .	Annually earns at least . . .
0.5%	$1,000,000
1	200,000
5	105,000
10	85,000
20	70,000
30	55,000
40	47,500
50	39,000
60	31,000
70	25,000
80	18,000
90	10,000

Source: U.S. Bureau of the Census (1996) and author calculations.

that assist low-income people (Levy, 1987; Reich, 1989; Cutler & Katz, 1992). Since 1990, however, income disparity has eased downward, a trend accelerated in 1993 by higher income tax rates on the top-earning 5 percent.

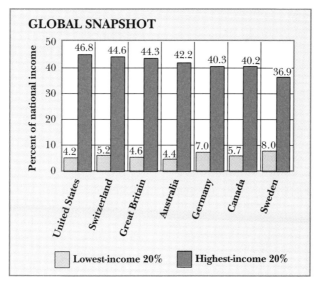

FIGURE 9.2   Income Disparities for Selected Industrial Countries

Source: The World Bank (1995).

. . . Social inequality declines as industrialization proceeds. . . . Thus, the United States has far less income inequality than, say, Venezuela (in South America), Kenya (Africa), or Sri Lanka (Asia). However, as Figure 9.2 . . . [above] indicates, U. S. society does permit more income inequality than is found in many other industrial societies. 13

Wealth

Income is but one component of a person's or family's **wealth,** *the total value of money and other assets, minus outstanding debts.* The second part of Figure 9.1 [on page 558] shows that wealth—in the form of stocks, bonds, real estate, and other privately owned property—is distributed even less equally than income. 14

In 1993, the richest 20 percent of U.S. families owned approximately 80 percent of the country's entire wealth. High up in this privileged category are the wealthiest 5 percent of families—the "very rich"—who control more than half the nation's property. With wealth into 15 the tens of millions of dollars, the "super-rich" comprise the 1 percent of U.S. households that possess one-third of our nation's privately held resources. And capping the wealth pyramid, the one dozen richest U.S. families have a combined net worth approaching $150 billion, which equals the total wealth of 1 million average families, including enough people to fill the cities of Alexandria, Virginia; Akron, Ohio; Anchorage, Alaska; and Albuquerque, New Mexico (Rogers, 1993; Weicher, 1995).

Recent government calculations place the wealth of the average U.S. household at $37,587, about equal to an average family's annual income. This reflects the value of homes, cars, investments, insurance policies, retirement pensions, furniture, clothing, and all other personal property, minus the home mortgage and other debts (Weicher, 1995). While "ordinary" wealth usually centers on a home and a car or two—that is, property that generates no income—the great wealth of the rich is mostly in the form of stocks and other income-producing investments. 16

When financial liabilities are balanced against assets, the least affluent 40 percent of U.S. families have virtually no wealth at all. The negative percentage shown in Figure 9.1 for the poorest 20 percent of the population means that these people actually live in debt.

Power

In the United States, as elsewhere, wealth stands as an important source of power. Major owners of corporate stock, for example, make decisions that create jobs for ordinary people or scale back operations, throwing men and women out of work.

More broadly, the "super-rich" families who own most of the nation's wealth have a great deal of say about the national political agenda. Thomas Jefferson (1953; orig. 1785), the third U.S. president and a wealthy man himself, cautioned that the vitality of a democratic system depends on "subdividing property" so that the many, not just the few, have a strong voice in political affairs. . . .

Occupational Prestige

Occupation, too, is an important element of social standing, since one's job affects all the factors noted thus far: income, wealth, and power. In addition, occupation serves as a key source of social prestige since we commonly evaluate each other according to the kind of work we do, holding some in high esteem while looking down on others.

For more than half a century, sociologists have assessed the social prestige of various occupations (Counts, 1925; Hodge, Treiman & Rossi, 1966; NORC, 1994). Table 9.2 presents the results of a recent survey involving a random sample of U. S. adults. In general, people attach high prestige to occupations—such as medicine, law, and engineering —that also generate high income.

Prestige reflects more than just pay, however, since favored occupations typically require considerable ability and demand exten-

sive education and training. By contrast, less prestigious work—as a waitress or janitor, for example—not only pays less but usually requires less ability and schooling.

In global perspective, occupational prestige rankings are much the same in all industrial societies. . . . Almost everywhere, white-collar work that involves mental activity free from extensive supervision confers greater prestige than blue-collar occupations that require supervised, manual labor. There are exceptions to this pattern, however. In the United States, for example, a blue-collar police officer enjoys greater social prestige than a white-collar bank teller.

In any society, high-prestige occupations go to privileged categories of people. Reading down from the beginning of Table 9.2 [on page 561], one passes a dozen occupations before reaching "registered nurse," an occupation in which *most* workers are women. Moreover, women are concentrated in so-called pink-collar occupations—service and clerical positions, such as secretaries, waitresses, and beauticians—that yield little income and fall near the bottom of the prestige hierarchy. Similarly, reading the table in reverse order shows that many jobs that provide the least amount of prestige and income are commonly performed by people of color. The important point here is that social stratification typically spans various dimensions of inequality (based on income and prestige as well as sex and race) *that are superimposed on each other,* forming a complex, deeply ingrained, and often steep, hierarchy.

Schooling

In industrial societies, schooling is necessary for adults to perform their work; thus, primary, secondary, and some college education is available at public expense. Like other dimensions of inequality, however, schooling is a resource enjoyed in abundance by some and very little by others.

TABLE 9.2

The Relative Social Prestige of Selected Occupations in the United States

White-collar Occupations	Prestige Score	Blue-collar Occupations	White-collar Occupations	Prestige Score	Blue-collar Occupations
Physician	86		Funeral director	49	
Lawyer	75		Realtor	49	
College/university professor	74		Bookkeeper	47	
Architect	73			47	Machinist
Chemist	73			47	Mail carrier
Physicist/astronomer	73		Musician/ composer	47	
Aerospace engineer	72			46	Secretary
Dentist	72		Photographer	45	
Member of clergy	69		Bank teller	43	
Psychologist	69			42	Tailor
Pharmacist	68			42	Welder
Optometrist	67			40	Farmer
Registered nurse	66			40	Telephone operator
Secondary-school teacher	66			39	Carpenter
Accountant	65			36	Brick/stone mason
Athlete	65		File clerk	36	Child-care worker
Electrical engineer	64			36	
Elementary-school teacher	64			36	Hairdresser
Economist	63			35	Baker
Veterinarian	62			34	Bulldozer operator
Airplane pilot	61			31	Auto body repairperson
Computer programmer	61		Retail apparel salesperson	30	
Sociologist	61			30	Truck driver
Editor/reporter	60		Cashier	29	
	60	Police officer		28	Elevator operator
Actor	58			28	Garbage collector
Radio/TV announcer	55			28	Taxi driver
Librarian	54			28	Waiter/waitress
	53	Aircraft mechanic		27	Bellhop
	53	Firefighter		25	Bartender
Dental hygienist	52			23	Farm laborer
Painter/sculptor	52			23	Household laborer
Social worker	52			22	Door-to-door salesperson
	51	Electrician		22	Janitor
Computer operator	50			09	Shoe shiner

Source: Adapted from *General Social Surveys 1972-1994: Cumulative Codebook* (Chicago: National Opinion Research Center, 1994) 881–89.

TABLE 9.3
Schooling of U.S. Adults, 1991 (aged 25 and over)

	Women	Men
Not a high-school graduate	**20.0%**	**19.5%**
8 years or less	9.2	9.4
9–11 years	10.8	10.1
High-school graduate	**80.0**	**80.5**
High school only	37.4	33.2
1–3 years college	23.4	22.6
College graduate or more	19.2	24.7

Source: U.S. Bureau of the Census, 1992.

Table 9.3 [above] indicates the level of formal education reached by U.S. men and women. According to the table, more than three-fourths of adults had completed high school, although just over 20 percent are college graduates. 26

Here, again, we see how dimensions of inequality are linked. Schooling affects both occupation and income, since most (but not all) of the better paying, white-collar jobs shown in Table 9.2 [on page 561] require a college degree or other advanced study. On the other hand, most blue-collar occupations that offer less income and social prestige demand less schooling. 27

Ascription and Social Stratification

To a considerable degree, the class system in the United States rewards individual talent and effort. But, our class system also retains distinct elements of caste. Ascription—who we are at birth—greatly influences what we become later in life. 28

Ancestry

Nothing affects social standing in the United States as much as our birth into a particular family, an event over which we have no control. Ancestry determines our point of entry into the 29 system of social inequality. Some families in the United States, including the duPonts, Rockefellers, Roosevelts, and Kennedys, are renowned around the world. And almost every city and town contain families who have amassed wealth and power on a more modest scale.

Being born to privilege or poverty sets the stage for our future schooling, occupation, and income. Research reveals that at least half of the richest individuals—those with hundreds of millions of dollars in wealth—derived their fortunes primarily from inheritance. By the same token, the "inheritance" of poverty and the lack of opportunity that inevitably goes with it just as surely shape the future of those in need. The operation of the family, which serves to transmit property, power, and possibilities from one generation to the next, accounts, more than any other single factor, for the persistence of social stratification. 30

Race and Ethnicity

Race has a strong connection to social position in the United States. Overall, white people have higher occupational standing than African Americans and also receive more schooling, especially at the college level and beyond. These differences are evident in median income: for African Americans, families earned $21,548 in 1994, which was about 55 percent of the $39,308 earned by white families (U.S. Bureau of the Census, 1995). 31

Another reason for this disparity involves family patterns: African-American families with children are three times more likely than their white counterparts to have only one parent in the home. Single parenthood, in turn, is a strong predictor of low family income. If we compare only families headed by married couples, the racial disparity shrinks dramatically, with African Americans earning 81 percent of what whites do. 32

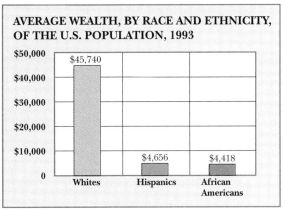

FIGURE 9.3   Average Wealth, by Race
and Ethnicity, of the U.S. Population, 1993

Source: U.S. Bureau of the Census (1995).

Over time, any income differential builds 33
into a considerable "wealth gap." Figure 9.3
shows that, while the typical white household
has a net worth exceeding $45,000, the
comparable figure for Hispanics and African
Americans is roughly one-tenth as much. . . .

Ethnicity, as well as race, shapes social strat- 34
ification in the United States. Throughout our
nation's history, people of English ancestry controlled the most wealth and wielded the
greatest power. The rapidly growing Latino
population in the United States, by contrast,
has long been relatively disadvantaged. In 1993,
median family income among all Hispanics was
$23,654, 60 percent of the comparable figure
for all white families. . . .

Gender

People of both sexes are born into families at 35
every social level. Yet, on average, women earn
lower income, accumulate less wealth, enjoy
lower occupational prestige, and rank lower in
some aspects of educational achievement than
men do.

Perhaps the most dramatic difference, how- 36
ever, is that households headed by women are
ten times more likely to be poor than those
headed by men. . . .

Religion

Religion, too, has a bearing on social stand- 37
ing in the United States. Among Protestant
denominations, with which almost two-thirds of
individuals   identify,   Episcopalians   and
Presbyterians have significantly higher social
standing, on average, than Lutherans and
Baptists. Jews, too, have high social standing,
while Roman Catholics hold a more modest
position (Roof, 1979; Davidson, Pyle, & Reyes,
1995).

Even John Fitzgerald Kennedy—a member 38
of one of this country's wealthiest and most
powerful   families—was   elected   our   first
Catholic president in 1960 only by overcoming
considerable opposition directed against him
because of his religion. Understandably, then,
throughout our history many upwardly mobile
people have converted to a higher-ranking
religion.

approximately 2350 words

John J. Macionis, *Sociology*, 6th ed. Copyright © 1997 by Prentice Hall, Inc.
Reprinted by permission of publisher.

COMPREHENSION CHECK

Part I
General Comprehension Questions: Literal and Interpretive

Write the correct letter in the space provided.

_____ 1. Which of the following is *not* stated by the author as a reason for most people's failure to perceive the full range of social inequality?

    a. We think that all are equal under the law.
    b. We interact with people of a similar social position.
    c. The United States is wealthy, and by world standards everyone seems reasonably well off.
    d. Most people do not read critically about issues related to social inequality.

_____ 2. Social class, and therefore social position, in the United States encompasses

    a. money and power.
    b. occupational prestige.
    c. schooling.
    d. all of the above.

_____ 3. According to the government, statistics on economic power in the United States indicate that

    a. the richest 20 percent of families receive one-third of all the income.
    b. the poorest 20 percent receive about one-fourth of the total income.
    c. the richest 5 percent of the population controls more than one-half of the nation's wealth.
    d. the richest people do not pay their share of taxes.

_____ 4. Most industrial societies

    a. cannot measure social prestige because changes have occurred.
    b. generally disagree on which occupations have prestige.
    c. generally agree on which occupations have prestige.
    d. rely on statistics on prestige from the United Nations.

_____ 5. Which statement about the United States is correct?

    a. Half of the population has a college education.
    b. Less than one-fourth of the population has a college education.
    c. Only 10 percent of the population has a college degree.
    d. Two-year college degree programs are increasing.

6. **Inference/Conclusion:** What inference/conclusion can you draw from the fact that the disparity in the way wealth is distributed in the United States is far greater than the disparity in income?

_____

_____

_____

7. **Denotative/Connotative Language:** What does the author mean literally with the statement " . . . people with the initiative and the cash escaped to the leafy green of the surrounding suburbs . . . "?

_____

_____

_____

8. **Figurative Language:** Explain the meaning of the following phrases.

"ladder of social class"

_____

_____

"pink-collar jobs"

_____

_____

9. *Judgment:* What change needs to be made so that one's forebears do not play such an important role in determining the future wealth of individuals in our society?

_____

_____

_____

10. ***Author's Tone and Purpose:***

a.   How would you describe the tone and purpose of this selection?

_____

_____

_____

b.   If you were writing an essay on this subject, what tone would you have selected, and why?

_____

_____

_____

Part II
Application Questions for Writing and Discussion

11. Thomas Jefferson said that a democracy depends on "subdividing property" among people. Do you agree with this statement, made more than 200 years ago?

_____

_____

_____

_____

_____

12. Which do you believe affords the greater social prestige in our country today—economic wealth or one's occupation? What kind of "prestige" is your goal for the future?

_____

_____

_____

_____

Part III
Extend Your Vocabulary

Note the boldfaced word in the first sentence of each set, quoted directly from the chapter. In the second sentence, fill in a different suffixed form of that word to complete the sentence.

1. "The United States is distinguished from most countries of the world because we never had a titled **aristocracy**."

   Although he assumed an _____ manner, he came from a very humble background.

2. "Our culture celebrates individual **autonomy** and achievement."

   Many countries today are struggling to become _____.

3. "Since 1990 . . . income **disparity** has eased downward. . . . "

   A _____ amount of work was allotted to various employees.

4. " . . . the 'inheritance' of poverty and the lack of opportunity that **inevitably** goes with it just as surely shape the future of those in need."

   We all believed it was _____ that he would regret selling the stock at this time.

5. "The United States is an **affluent** society."

   Because of her _____, she enjoyed great political power and prestige in the community.

Selection 21: **LITERATURE**

 Preparation for Reading

John Grisham

John Grisham is one of America's most prolific and successful contemporary novelists. He is best known for his legal thrillers. He said in a 1995 interview in *West,* a newsmagazine, that he had never planned to be a writer. He was practicing law in Mississippi when he was influenced to write *A Time to Kill* by a legal case he had heard about in the 1980s. Soon after its publication, he wrote *The Firm,* the first chapter of which is printed here. Grisham has also written *The Pelican Brief, The Client, The Rainmaker, The Street Lawyer,* and *The Testament. The Client* became the basis for a television series in 1995.

The first chapter of *The Firm* gives us yet another view of social class in America and the materialism that motivates the decisions of many people.

Note the meaning of the boldfaced words before reading. These are underlined in the text.

that was **mandatory**	required or obligatory
studied a **dossier**	a collection of papers about a person; a file
was **glib** and engaging	performing with ease and informality
braced for another **reprimand**	severe scolding; admonishment
She **deflected** this	turned aside; changed direction
treated him like a **leper**	a person afflicted with leprosy, a disfiguring disease

From The Firm

John Grisham

The senior partner studied the résumé for the hundredth time and again found   1
nothing he disliked about Mitchell Y. McDeere, at least not on paper. He had the
brains, the ambition, the good looks. And he was hungry; with his background, he
had to be. He was married, and that was <u>mandatory</u>. The firm had never hired an
unmarried lawyer, and it frowned heavily on divorce, as well as womanizing and
drinking. Drug testing was in the contract. He had a degree in accounting, passed
the CPA exam the first time he took it and wanted to be a tax lawyer, which of course
was a requirement with a tax firm. He was white, and the firm had never hired a
black. They managed this by being secretive and clubbish and never soliciting job
applications. Other firms solicited, and hired blacks. This firm recruited, and
remained lily white. Plus, the firm was in Memphis, of all places, and the top blacks
wanted New York or Washington or Chicago. McDeere was a male, and there were

Selection 21: **LITERATURE**

☞ Preparation for Reading

John Grisham

John Grisham is one of America's most prolific and successful contemporary novelists. He is best known for his legal thrillers. He said in a 1995 interview in *West,* a newsmagazine, that he had never planned to be a writer. He was practicing law in Mississippi when he was influenced to write *A Time to Kill* by a legal case he had heard about in the 1980s. Soon after its publication, he wrote *The Firm,* the first chapter of which is printed here. Grisham has also written *The Pelican Brief, The Client, The Rainmaker, The Street Lawyer,* and *The Testament. The Client* became the basis for a television series in 1995.

The first chapter of *The Firm* gives us yet another view of social class in America and the materialism that motivates the decisions of many people.

Note the meaning of the boldfaced words before reading. These are underlined in the text.

that was **mandatory**	required or obligatory
studied a **dossier**	a collection of papers about a person; a file
was **glib** and engaging	performing with ease and informality
braced for another **reprimand**	severe scolding; admonishment
She **deflected** this	turned aside; changed direction
treated him like a **leper**	a person afflicted with leprosy, a disfiguring disease

From The Firm

John Grisham

The senior partner studied the résumé for the hundredth time and again found 1 nothing he disliked about Mitchell Y. McDeere, at least not on paper. He had the brains, the ambition, the good looks. And he was hungry; with his background, he had to be. He was married, and that was <u>mandatory</u>. The firm had never hired an unmarried lawyer, and it frowned heavily on divorce, as well as womanizing and drinking. Drug testing was in the contract. He had a degree in accounting, passed the CPA exam the first time he took it and wanted to be a tax lawyer, which of course was a requirement with a tax firm. He was white, and the firm had never hired a black. They managed this by being secretive and clubbish and never soliciting job applications. Other firms solicited, and hired blacks. This firm recruited, and remained lily white. Plus, the firm was in Memphis, of all places, and the top blacks wanted New York or Washington or Chicago. McDeere was a male, and there were

12. Which do you believe affords the greater social prestige in our country today—economic wealth or one's occupation? What kind of "prestige" is your goal for the future?

_____

_____

_____

_____

Part III
Extend Your Vocabulary

Note the boldfaced word in the first sentence of each set, quoted directly from the chapter. In the second sentence, fill in a different suffixed form of that word to complete the sentence.

1. "The United States is distinguished from most countries of the world because we never had a titled **aristocracy**."

   Although he assumed an _____ manner, he came from a very humble background.

2. "Our culture celebrates individual **autonomy** and achievement."

   Many countries today are struggling to become _____.

3. "Since 1990 . . . income **disparity** has eased downward. . . . "

   A _____ amount of work was allotted to various employees.

4. " . . . the 'inheritance' of poverty and the lack of opportunity that **inevitably** goes with it just as surely shape the future of those in need."

   We all believed it was _____ that he would regret selling the stock at this time.

5. "The United States is an **affluent** society."

   Because of her _____, she enjoyed great political power and prestige in the community.

no women in the firm. That mistake had been made in the mid-seventies when they recruited the number one grad from Harvard, who happened to be a she and a wizard at taxation. She lasted four turbulent years and was killed in a car wreck.

He looked good, on paper. He was their top choice. In fact, for this year there were no other prospects. The list was very short. It was McDeere or no one.

The managing partner, Royce McKnight, studied a <u>dossier</u> labeled "Mitchell Y. McDeere—Harvard." An inch thick with small print and a few photographs, it had been prepared by some ex-CIA agents in a private intelligence outfit in Bethesda. They were clients of the firm and each year did the investigating for no fee. It was easy work, they said, checking out unsuspecting law students. They learned, for instance, that he preferred to leave the Northeast, that he was holding three job offers, two in New York and one in Chicago, and that the highest offer was $76,000 and the lowest was $68,000. He was in demand. He had been given the opportunity to cheat on a securities exam during his second year. He declined, and made the highest grade in the class. Two months ago he had been offered cocaine at a law school party. He said no and left when everyone began snorting. He drank an occasional beer, but drinking was expensive and he had no money. He owed close to $23,000 in student loans. He was hungry.

Royce McKnight flipped through the dossier and smiled. McDeere was their man.

Lamar Quin was thirty-two and not yet a partner. He had been brought along to   5
look young and act young and project a youthful image for Bendini, Lambert & Locke, which in fact was a young firm, since most of the partners retired in their late forties or early fifties with money to burn. He would make partner in this firm. With a six-figure income guaranteed for the rest of his life, Lamar could enjoy the twelve-hundred-dollar tailored suits that hung so comfortably from his tall, athletic frame. He strolled nonchalantly across the thousand-dollar-a-day suite and poured another cup of decaf. He checked his watch. He glanced at the two partners sitting at the small conference table near the windows.

Precisely at two-thirty someone knocked on the door. Lamar looked at the partners, who slid the résumé and dossier into an open briefcase. All three reached for their jackets. Lamar buttoned his top button and opened the door.

"Mitchell McDeere?" he asked with a huge smile and a hand thrust forward.

"Yes." They shook hands violently.

"Nice to meet you, Mitchell. I'm Lamar Quin."

"My pleasure. Please call me Mitch." He stepped inside and quickly surveyed the   10
spacious room.

"Sure, Mitch." Lamar grabbed his shoulder and led him across the suite, where the partners introduced themselves. They were exceedingly warm and cordial. They offered him coffee, then water. They sat around a shiny mahogany conference table and exchanged pleasantries. McDeere unbuttoned his coat and crossed his legs. He was now a seasoned veteran in the search of employment, and he knew they wanted him. He relaxed. With three job offers from three of the most prestigious firms in the country, he did not need this interview, this firm. He could afford to be a little overconfident now. He was there out of curiosity. And he longed for warmer weather.

Oliver Lambert, the senior partner, leaned forward on his elbows and took control of the preliminary chitchat. He was <u>glib</u> and engaging with a mellow, almost professional baritone. At sixty-one, he was the grandfather of the firm and spent most of his time administering and balancing the enormous egos of some of the richest lawyers in the country. He was the counselor, the one the younger associates went to with their troubles. Mr. Lambert also handled the recruiting, and it was his mission to sign Mitchell Y. McDeere.

"Are you tired of interviewing?" asked Oliver Lambert.

"Not really. It's part of it."

Yes, yes, they all agreed. Seemed like yesterday they were interviewing and sub- **15** mitting résumés and scared to death they wouldn't find a job and three years of sweat and torture would be down the drain. They knew what he was going through, all right.

"May I ask a question?" Mitch asked.

"Certainly."

"Sure."

"Anything."

"Why are we interviewing in this hotel room? The other firms interview on cam- **20** pus through the placement office."

"Good question." They all nodded and looked at each other and agreed it was a good question.

"Perhaps I can answer that, Mitch," said Royce McKnight, the managing partner. "You must understand our firm. We are different, and we take pride in that. We have forty-one lawyers, so we are small compared with other firms. We don't hire too many people; about one every other year. We offer the highest salary and fringes in the country, and I'm not exaggerating. So we are very selective. We selected you. The letter you received last month was sent after we screened over two thousand third-year law students at the best schools. Only one letter was sent. We don't advertise openings and we don't solicit applications. We keep a low profile, and we do things differently. That's our explanation."

"Fair enough. What kind of firm is it?"

"Tax. Some securities, real estate and banking, but eighty percent is tax work. That's why we wanted to meet you, Mitch. You have an incredibly strong tax background."

"Why'd you go to Western Kentucky?" asked Oliver Lambert. **25**

"Simple. They offered me a full scholarship to play football. Had it not been for that, college would've been impossible."

"Tell us about your family."

"Why is that important?"

"It's very important to us, Mitch," Royce McKnight said warmly.

They all say that, thought McDeere. "Okay, my father was killed in the **30** coal mines when I was seven years old. My mother remarried and lives in Florida. I had two brothers. Rusty was killed in Vietnam. I have a brother named Ray McDeere."

"Where is he?"

"I'm afraid that's none of your business." He stared at Royce McKnight and exposed a mammoth chip on his shoulder. The dossier said little about Ray.

"I'm sorry," the managing partner said softly.

"Mitch, our firm is in Memphis," Lamar said. "Does that bother you?"

"Not at all. I'm not fond of cold weather."   **35**

"Have you ever been to Memphis?"

"No."

"We'll have you down soon. You'll love it."

Mitch smiled and nodded and played along. Were these guys serious? How could he consider such a small firm in such a small town when Wall Street was waiting?

"How are you ranked in your class?" Mr. Lambert asked.   **40**

"Top five." Not top five percent, but top five. That was enough of an answer for all of them. Top five out of three hundred. He could have said number three, a fraction away from number two, and within striking distance of number one. But he didn't. They came from inferior schools—Chicago, Columbia and Vanderbilt, as he recalled from a cursory examination of Martindale-Hubbell's Legal Directory. He knew they would not dwell on academics.

"Why did you select Harvard?"

"Actually, Harvard selected me. I applied at several schools and was accepted everywhere. Harvard offered more financial assistance. I thought it was the best school. Still do."

"You've done quite well here, Mitch," Mr. Lambert said, admiring the résumé. The dossier was in the briefcase, under the table.

"Thank you. I've worked hard."   **45**

"You made extremely high grades in your tax and securities courses."

"That's where my interest lies."

"We've reviewed your writing sample, and it's quite impressive."

"Thank you. I enjoy research."

They nodded and acknowledged this obvious lie. It was part of the ritual. No law **50** student or lawyer in his right mind enjoyed research, yet, without fail, every prospective associate professed a deep love for the library.

"Tell us about your wife," Royce McKnight said, almost meekly. They braced for another <u>reprimand</u>. But it was a standard, nonsacred area explored by every firm.

"Her name is Abby. She has a degree in elementary education from Western Kentucky. We graduated one week and got married the next. For the past three years she's taught at a private kindergarten near Boston College."

"And is the marriage—"

"We're very happy. We've known each other since high school."

"What position did you play?" asked Lamar, in the direction of less sensitive **55** matters.

"Quarterback. I was heavily recruited until I messed up a knee in my last high school game. Everyone disappeared except Western Kentucky. I played off and on for four years, even started some as a junior, but the knee would never hold up."

"How'd you make straight A's and play football?"

"I put the books first."

"I don't imagine Western Kentucky is much of an academic school," Lamar blurted with a stupid grin, and immediately wished he could take it back. Lambert and McKnight frowned and acknowledged the mistake.

"Sort of like Kansas State," Mitch replied. They froze, all of them froze, and for   60 a few seconds stared incredulously at each other. This guy McDeere knew Lamar Quin went to Kansas State. He had never met Lamar Quin and had no idea who would appear on behalf of the firm and conduct the interview. Yet, he knew. He had gone to Martindale-Hubbell's and checked them out. He had read the biographical sketches of all of the forty-one lawyers in the firm, and in a split second he had recalled that Lamar Quin, just one of the forty-one, had gone to Kansas State. Damn, they were impressed.

"I guess that came out wrong," Lamar apologized.

"No problem." Mitch smiled warmly. It was forgotten.

Oliver Lambert cleared his throat and decided to get personal again. "Mitch, our firm frowns on drinking and chasing women. We're not a bunch of Holy Rollers, but we put business ahead of everything. We keep low profiles and we work very hard. And we make plenty of money."

"I can live with all that."

"We reserve the right to test any member of the firm for drug use."   65

"I don't use drugs."

"Good. What's your religious affiliation?"

"Methodist."

"Good. You'll find a wide variety in our firm. Catholics, Baptists, Episcopalians. It's really none of our business, but we like to know. We want stable families. Happy lawyers are productive lawyers. That's why we ask these questions."

Mitch smiled and nodded. He'd heard this before.   70

The three looked at each other, then at Mitch. This meant they had reached the point in the interview where the interviewee was supposed to ask one or two intelligent questions. Mitch recrossed his legs. Money, that was the big question, particularly how it compared to his other offers. If it isn't enough, thought Mitch, then it was nice to meet you fellas. If the pay is attractive, *then* we can discuss families and marriages and football and churches. But, he knew, like all the other firms they had to shadowbox around the issue until things got awkward and it was apparent they had discussed everything in the world but money. So, hit them with a soft question first.

"What type of work will I do initially?"

They nodded and approved of the question. Lambert and McKnight looked at Lamar. This answer was his.

"Quarterback. I was heavily recruited until I messed up a knee in my last high school game. Everyone disappeared except Western Kentucky. I played off and on for four years, even started some as a junior, but the knee would never hold up."

"How'd you make straight A's and play football?"

"I put the books first."

"I don't imagine Western Kentucky is much of an academic school," Lamar blurted with a stupid grin, and immediately wished he could take it back. Lambert and McKnight frowned and acknowledged the mistake.

"Sort of like Kansas State," Mitch replied. They froze, all of them froze, and for   **60** a few seconds stared incredulously at each other. This guy McDeere knew Lamar Quin went to Kansas State. He had never met Lamar Quin and had no idea who would appear on behalf of the firm and conduct the interview. Yet, he knew. He had gone to Martindale-Hubbell's and checked them out. He had read the biographical sketches of all of the forty-one lawyers in the firm, and in a split second he had recalled that Lamar Quin, just one of the forty-one, had gone to Kansas State. Damn, they were impressed.

"I guess that came out wrong," Lamar apologized.

"No problem." Mitch smiled warmly. It was forgotten.

Oliver Lambert cleared his throat and decided to get personal again. "Mitch, our firm frowns on drinking and chasing women. We're not a bunch of Holy Rollers, but we put business ahead of everything. We keep low profiles and we work very hard. And we make plenty of money."

"I can live with all that."

"We reserve the right to test any member of the firm for drug use."   **65**

"I don't use drugs."

"Good. What's your religious affiliation?"

"Methodist."

"Good. You'll find a wide variety in our firm. Catholics, Baptists, Episcopalians. It's really none of our business, but we like to know. We want stable families. Happy lawyers are productive lawyers. That's why we ask these questions."

Mitch smiled and nodded. He'd heard this before.   **70**

The three looked at each other, then at Mitch. This meant they had reached the point in the interview where the interviewee was supposed to ask one or two intelligent questions. Mitch recrossed his legs. Money, that was the big question, particularly how it compared to his other offers. If it isn't enough, thought Mitch, then it was nice to meet you fellas. If the pay is attractive, *then* we can discuss families and marriages and football and churches. But, he knew, like all the other firms they had to shadowbox around the issue until things got awkward and it was apparent they had discussed everything in the world but money. So, hit them with a soft question first.

"What type of work will I do initially?"

They nodded and approved of the question. Lambert and McKnight looked at Lamar. This answer was his.

had two brothers. Rusty was killed in Vietnam. I have a brother named Ray McDeere."

"Where is he?"

"I'm afraid that's none of your business." He stared at Royce McKnight and exposed a mammoth chip on his shoulder. The dossier said little about Ray.

"I'm sorry," the managing partner said softly.

"Mitch, our firm is in Memphis," Lamar said. "Does that bother you?"

"Not at all. I'm not fond of cold weather."   35

"Have you ever been to Memphis?"

"No."

"We'll have you down soon. You'll love it."

Mitch smiled and nodded and played along. Were these guys serious? How could he consider such a small firm in such a small town when Wall Street was waiting?

"How are you ranked in your class?" Mr. Lambert asked.   40

"Top five." Not top five percent, but top five. That was enough of an answer for all of them. Top five out of three hundred. He could have said number three, a fraction away from number two, and within striking distance of number one. But he didn't. They came from inferior schools—Chicago, Columbia and Vanderbilt, as he recalled from a cursory examination of Martindale-Hubbell's Legal Directory. He knew they would not dwell on academics.

"Why did you select Harvard?"

"Actually, Harvard selected me. I applied at several schools and was accepted everywhere. Harvard offered more financial assistance. I thought it was the best school. Still do."

"You've done quite well here, Mitch," Mr. Lambert said, admiring the résumé. The dossier was in the briefcase, under the table.

"Thank you. I've worked hard."   45

"You made extremely high grades in your tax and securities courses."

"That's where my interest lies."

"We've reviewed your writing sample, and it's quite impressive."

"Thank you. I enjoy research."

They nodded and acknowledged this obvious lie. It was part of the ritual. No law 50
student or lawyer in his right mind enjoyed research, yet, without fail, every prospective associate professed a deep love for the library.

"Tell us about your wife," Royce McKnight said, almost meekly. They braced for another <u>reprimand</u>. But it was a standard, nonsacred area explored by every firm.

"Her name is Abby. She has a degree in elementary education from Western Kentucky. We graduated one week and got married the next. For the past three years she's taught at a private kindergarten near Boston College."

"And is the marriage—"

"We're very happy. We've known each other since high school."

"What position did you play?" asked Lamar, in the direction of less sensitive   55
matters.

"We have something similar to a two-year apprenticeship, although we don't call it that. We'll send you all over the country to tax seminars. Your education is far from over. You'll spend two weeks next winter in Washington at the American Tax Institute. We take great pride in our technical expertise, and the training is continual, for all of us. If you want to pursue a master's in taxation, we'll pay for it. As far as practicing law, it won't be very exciting for the first two years. You'll do a lot of research and generally boring stuff. But you'll be paid handsomely."

"How much?"   75

Lamar looked at Royce McKnight, who eyed Mitch and said, "We'll discuss the compensation and other benefits when you come to Memphis."

"I want a ballpark figure or I may not come to Memphis." He smiled, arrogant but cordial. He spoke like a man with three job offers.

The partners smiled at each other, and Mr. Lambert spoke first. "Okay. A base salary of eighty thousand the first year, plus bonuses. Eighty-five the second year, plus bonuses. A low-interest mortgage so you can buy a home. Two country club memberships. And a new BMW. You pick the color, of course."

They focused on his lips, and waited for the wrinkles to form on his cheeks and the teeth to break through. He tried to conceal a smile, but it was impossible. He chuckled.

"That's incredible," he mumbled. Eighty thousand in Memphis equaled a hun-   80
dred and twenty thousand in New York. Did the man say BMW! His Mazda hatchback had a million miles on it and for the moment had to be jump-started while he saved for a rebuilt starter.

"Plus a few more fringes we'll be glad to discuss in Memphis."

Suddenly he had a strong desire to visit Memphis. Wasn't it by the river?

The smile vanished and he regained his composure. He looked sternly, importantly at Oliver Lambert and said, as if he'd forgotten about the money and the home and the BMW, "Tell me about your firm."

"Forty-one lawyers. Last year we earned more per lawyer than any firm our size or larger. That includes every big firm in the country. We take only rich clients—corporations, banks and wealthy people who pay our healthy fees and never complain. We've developed a specialty in international taxation, and it's both exciting and very profitable. We deal only with people who can pay."

"How long does it take to make partner?"   85

"On the average, ten years, and it's a hard ten years. It's not unusual for our partners to earn half a million a year, and most retire before they're fifty. You've got to pay your dues, put in eighty-hour weeks, but it's worth it when you make partner."

Lamar leaned forward. "You don't have to be a partner to earn six figures. I've been with the firm seven years, and went over a hundred thousand four years ago."

Mitch thought about this for a second and figured by the time he was thirty he could be well over a hundred thousand, maybe close to two hundred thousand. At the age of thirty!

They watched him carefully and knew exactly what he was calculating.

"What's an international tax firm doing in Memphis?" he asked.   90

That brought smiles. Mr. Lambert removed his reading glasses and twirled them. "Now that's a good question. Mr. Bendini founded the firm in 1944. He had been a tax lawyer in Philadelphia and had picked up some wealthy clients in the South. He got a wild idea and landed in Memphis. For twenty-five years he hired nothing but tax lawyers, and the firm prospered nicely down there. None of us are from Memphis, but we have grown to love it. It's a very pleasant old Southern town. By the way, Mr. Bendini died in 1970."

"How many partners in the firm?"

"Twenty, active. We try to keep a ratio of one partner for each associate. That's high for the industry, but we like it. Again, we do things differently."

"All of our partners are multimillionaires by the age of forty-five," Royce McKnight said.

"All of them?"   95

"Yes, sir. We don't guarantee it, but if you join our firm, put in ten hard years, make partner and put in ten more years, and you're not a millionaire at the age of forty-five, you'll be the first in twenty years."

"That's an impressive statistic."

"It's an impressive firm, Mitch," Oliver Lambert said, "and we're very proud of it. We're a close-knit fraternity. We're small and we take care of each other. We don't have the cutthroat competition the big firms are famous for. We're very careful whom we hire, and our goal is for each new associate to become a partner as soon as possible. Toward that end we invest an enormous amount of time and money in ourselves, especially our new people. It is a rare, extremely rare occasion when a lawyer leaves our firm. It is simply unheard of. We go the extra mile to keep careers on track. We want our people happy. We think it is the most profitable way to operate."

"I have another impressive statistic," Mr. McKnight added. "Last year, for firms our size or larger, the average turnover rate among associates was twenty-eight percent. At Bendini, Lambert & Locke, it was zero. Year before, zero. It's been a long time since a lawyer left our firm."

They watched him carefully to make sure all of this sank in. Each term and each   100
condition of the employment was important, but the permanence, the finality of his acceptance overshadowed all other items on the checklist. They explained as best they could, for now. Further explanation would come later.

Of course, they knew much more than they could talk about. For instance, his mother lived in a cheap trailer park in Panama City Beach, remarried to a retired truck driver with a violent drinking problem. They knew she had received $41,000 from the mine explosion, squandered most of it, then went crazy after her oldest son was killed in Vietnam. They knew he had been neglected, raised in poverty by his brother Ray (whom they could not find) and some sympathetic relatives. The poverty hurt, and they assumed, correctly, it had bred the intense desire to succeed. He had worked thirty hours a week at an all-night convenience store while playing football and making perfect grades. They knew he seldom slept. They knew he was hungry. He was their man.

"Would you like to come visit us?" asked Oliver Lambert.

"When?" asked Mitch, dreaming of a black 318i with a sunroof.

The ancient Mazda hatchback with three hubcaps and a badly cracked windshield hung in the gutter with its front wheels sideways, aiming at the curb, preventing a roll down the hill. Abby grabbed the door handle on the inside, yanked twice and opened the door. She inserted the key, pressed the clutch and turned the wheel. The Mazda began a slow roll. As it gained speed, she held her breath, released the clutch and bit her lip until the unmuffled rotary engine began whining.

With three job offers on the table, a new car was four months away. She could   105 last. For three years they had endured poverty in a two-room student apartment on a campus covered with Porsches and little Mercedes convertibles. For the most part they had ignored the snubs from the classmates and co-workers in this bastion of East Coast snobbery. They were hillbillies from Kentucky, with few friends. But they had endured and succeeded quite nicely all to themselves.

She preferred Chicago to New York, even for a lower salary, largely because it was farther from Boston and closer to Kentucky. But Mitch remained noncommittal, characteristically weighing it all carefully and keeping most of it to himself. She had not been invited to visit New York and Chicago with her husband. And she was tired of guessing. She wanted an answer.

She parked illegally on the hill nearest the apartment and walked two blocks. Their unit was one of thirty in a two-story red-brick rectangle. Abby stood outside her door and fumbled through the purse looking for keys. Suddenly, the door jerked open. He grabbed her, yanked her inside the tiny apartment, threw her on the sofa and attacked her neck with his lips. She yelled and giggled as arms and legs thrashed about. They kissed, one of those long, wet, ten-minute embraces with groping and fondling and moaning, the kind they had enjoyed as teenagers when kissing was fun and mysterious and the ultimate.

"My goodness," she said when they finished. "What's the occasion?"

"Do you smell anything?" Mitch asked.

She looked away and sniffed. "Well, yes. What is it?"   110

"Chicken chow mein and egg foo yung. From Wong Boys."

"Okay, what's the occasion?"

"Plus an expensive bottle of Chablis. It's even got a cork."

"What have you done, Mitch?"

"Follow me." On the small, painted kitchen table, among the legal pads and   115 casebooks, sat a large bottle of wine and a sack of Chinese food. They shoved the law school paraphernalia aside and spread the food. Mitch opened the wine and filled two plastic wineglasses.

"I had a great interview today," he said.

"Who?"

"Remember that firm in Memphis I received a letter from last month?"

"Yes. You weren't too impressed."

"That's the one. I'm very impressed. It's all tax work and the money looks good."   120

"How good?"

He ceremoniously dipped chow mein from the container onto both plates, then ripped open the tiny packages of soy sauce. She waited for an answer. He opened another container and began dividing the egg foo yung. He sipped his wine and smacked his lips.

"How much?" she repeated.

"More than Chicago. More than Wall Street."

She took a long, deliberate drink of wine and eyed him suspiciously. Her brown   125 eyes narrowed and glowed. The eyebrows lowered and the forehead wrinkled. She waited.

"How much?"

"Eighty thousand, first year, plus bonuses. Eighty-five, second year, plus bonuses." He said this nonchalantly while studying the celery bits in the chow mein.

"Eighty thousand," she repeated.

"Eighty thousand, babe. Eighty thousand bucks in Memphis, Tennessee, is about the same as a hundred and twenty thousand bucks in New York."

"Who wants New York?" she asked.   130

"Plus a low-interest mortgage loan."

That word—mortgage—had not been uttered in the apartment in a long time. In fact, she could not, at the moment, recall the last discussion about a home or anything related to one. For months now it had been accepted that they would *rent* some place until some distant, unimaginable point in the future when they achieved affluence and would then qualify for a large mortgage.

She sat her glass of wine on the table and said matter-of-factly, "I didn't hear that."

"A low-interest mortgage loan. The firm loans enough money to buy a house. It's very important to these guys that their associates look prosperous, so they give us the money at a much lower rate."

"You mean as in a *home,* with grass around it and shrubs?"   135

"Yep. Not some overpriced apartment in Manhattan, but a three-bedroom house in the suburbs with a driveway and a two-car garage where we can park the BMW."

The reaction was delayed by a second or two, but she finally said, "BMW? Whose BMW?"

"Ours, babe. Our BMW. The firm leases a new one and gives us the keys. It's sort of like a signing bonus for a first-round draft pick. It's worth another five thousand a year. We pick the color, of course. I think black would be nice. What do you think?"

"No more clunkers. No more leftovers. No more hand-me-downs," she said as she slowly shook her head.

He crunched on a mouthful of noodles and smiled at her. She was dreaming, he   140 could tell, probably of furniture, and wallpaper, and perhaps a pool before too long.

And babies, little dark-eyed children with light brown hair.

"And there are some other benefits to be discussed later."

"I don't understand, Mitch. Why are they so generous?"

"I asked that question. They're very selective, and they take a lot of pride in paying top dollar. They go for the best and don't mind shelling out the bucks. Their turnover rate is zero. Plus, I think it costs more to entice the top people to Memphis."

"It would be closer to home," she said without looking at him.

"I don't have a home. It would be closer to your parents, and that worries me."   **145**

She <u>deflected</u> this, as she did most of his comments about her family. "You'd be closer to Ray."

He nodded, bit into an egg roll and imagined her parents' first visit, that sweet moment when they pulled into the driveway in their well-used Cadillac and stared in shock at the new French colonial with two new cars in the garage. They would burn with envy and wonder how the poor kid with no family and no status could afford all this at twenty-five and fresh out of law school. They would force painful smiles and comment on how nice everything was, and before long Mr. Sutherland would break down and ask how much the house cost and Mitch would tell him to mind his own business, and it would drive the old man crazy. They'd leave after a short visit and return to Kentucky, where all their friends would hear how great the daughter and the son-in-law were doing down in Memphis. Abby would be sorry they couldn't get along but wouldn't say much. From the start they had treated him like a <u>leper</u>. He was so unworthy they had boycotted the small wedding.

"Have you ever been to Memphis?" he asked.

"Once when I was a little girl. Some kind of convention for the church. All I remember is the river."

"They want us to visit."   **150**

"Us! You mean I'm invited?"

"Yes. They insist on you coming."

"When?"

"Couple of weeks. They'll fly us down Thursday afternoon for the weekend."

"I like this firm already."   **155**

approximately 3775 words

Working with the WORLD WIDE WEB

If you would like to learn more about John Grisham's writings or obtain reviews of his works, you can access endless information about him at:

http://www/celebsite.com/people/johngrisham.content/sites.html

From this address, you can reach his Web site, which gives you access to all his book titles, with jacket covers as well as print and audio excerpts.

Questions for Writing and Discussion

1. a. What is the tone of the story during the interview between Mitch and the members of the firm?

    b. How does the tone change when Mitch arrives home and discusses his interview with his wife, Abby?

2. What does the author mean when he says the characters must "shadowbox" through the issues in the interview (paragraph 71)?

3. Why do you think the firm was seeking a man who was "hungry," and how did they know that Mitch was "their man"?

4. Why was money such a big issue for Mitch in selecting the firm? Is there anything he failed to realize about the price he was going to pay to achieve the status he desired?

5. What can you infer about a firm that is described as "lily white" and condones no drugs, drinking, or womanizing (paragraph 1)? Would you be willing to work for such a firm if offered a salary and benefits similar to those offered to Mitch? Why, or why not?

JOURNAL ENTRY

What influence did the previous three selections have on your recognition of the disparities that exist in America because of both the class and caste systems? Which selection provided the most ideas for your consideration? Explain why.

Also, write about your current social class standing; is it lower, middle, or upper class? Would you like to change your social ranking in the future? Discuss why, or why not. What would you need to do to change your social rank?

10

Reading Visual Information

This chapter will help you

❋ Understand how to read graphs, charts, tables, and diagrams.
❋ Learn the major purpose of graphic information.
❋ Learn how to integrate graphic information with the text.
❋ Appreciate the special use of graphics in the sciences and business.
❋ Evaluate visual information critically.

Before reading, think about these questions.

❋ How well do you read and analyze graphs, charts, and diagrams?
❋ What questions do you ask as you study graphic information?
❋ What may be the major purpose of graphic information?

Jot down your own method of reading graphic information.

_____

_____

⤳ The Value of Visual Aids

In the first chapter, we pointed out that we are living in an Information Age, in which a vast array of new knowledge and information bombards us every day. As an effective reader of this information, you have learned to think critically and judge issues on their merits and not on presupposed assumptions that you may have held. In this final chapter, we examine how to become more effective readers of visual information, which is increasing in volume, in large measure because of computer technology. Reading, then, includes not only thinking critically about words but evaluating information from all forms of visual or graphic material: graphs, charts, diagrams, maps, tables, pictograms, and photographs.

Visual literacy is important because much information can be compacted into a small amount of space. Moreover, visuals can dramatically show and summarize information. Business advertisements, for example, commonly make comparisons and use easy-to-read visuals to highlight the major selling points of a particular product. The media frequently use visuals, such as weather maps and tables, for comparison purposes. Political analysts use visuals to highlight information such as voting trends. Each visual requires a particular method of interpretation.

Perhaps most important for you at this time as a student, when effectively reading your college textbooks often means integrating a substantial amount of visual information with printed information, visual literacy is critical. Tables, charts, diagrams, and graphs are included in textbooks to give you important information in condensed form. The illustrations often try to help you understand difficult concepts presented in the text in a simpler format. If you overlook "reading" visual aids, you are ignoring a valuable source of information.

Graphics are expensive to reproduce and are included in your textbook for several important reasons. They

- clarify concepts that are difficult to understand;
- consolidate detailed, often lengthy, pages of information into a single design;
- take the place of text in illustrating ideas or information;
- add information to the text.

To read graphics critically, you should consider the source of the data and whether the information is current or not. Usually, the source is included at the bottom of the graphic or in a footnote. *Read* the graphic as you would information in a passage, looking for the main idea or key point and the *relationship* of the supporting statements. Then, compare the graphic to the information printed in the textbook.

Although reading visual information is not the same as reading prose, similar strategies can be used. Looking over a graph initially to get an overall idea is comparable to previewing written text; examining facts and putting them together can be compared to getting the main idea; and noting trends, patterns, and relationships can be compared to making inferences and drawing conclusions. It is also possible to apply the information, where appropriate, to yourself and your lifestyle.

How to Interpret Visual Information

The following general guidelines will help you read graphic information effectively:

1. First, carefully read the title and subtitles when given. Often, the title is a brief summary of the graph's content and purpose, which tells you what you can expect to learn from it and why it is important. Turn the title into a question. Ask how, what, or why. Also, be aware how recent the information is by noting all dates. Generally, trends and conditions are temporary and change rapidly.

2. Next, read the legend (or captions or column headings) to learn how to interpret the details presented. Sometimes, the legend is at the bottom of the graph and explains any symbols used or what particular colors, lines, or shapes represent. For example, the legend may help to clarify whether the numbers are in thousands, millions, or billions.

3. Check for other explanatory notes. These might include an explanation of abbreviations, information on how the data was collected, or whether the information is incomplete. Such information usually appears in a footnote, printed at the bottom of the graphic.

4. Then, determine the organization of the graphic. Skim the data up and down the vertical column ($\updownarrow$) as well as the data across the horizontal column ($\leftrightarrow$) for bar and line graphs. You will sometimes have to approximate the numbers; the bars or lines of many graphs fall between the numbers given. Find out what units of measurement have been used.

5. Finally, determine the relationship of the information shown in the horizontal and vertical columns. Understanding this relationship is the key to reading not only graphs but tables, charts, and some diagrams. Mark the graphic, making marginal notations of trends and patterns.

6. Write a sentence, answering any question you posed in step 1.

7. Ask yourself some key questions to interpret and critically analyze the graphic.

   a. What general information is presented, and for what purpose?
   b. What relationship has been plotted?
   c. What inferences and conclusions can be made?

In making your inferences and drawing conclusions, ask yourself these questions:

Is the source of the data reliable?
How were the data gathered?
Is there any bias in how the data are presented?

You may be unable to apply all these steps to every form of graphic presentation since there is a great variety to the multiple forms visuals can take. Let's apply as many of the guidelines as possible now to Table 10.1.

1. *Table number* ───▶ **TABLE 10.1**
 and Table title ───▶ **Industries with the Highest Rate of Job Growth: 1991–1996***

2. *Column headings* ───▶

	Total Jobs in 1996 (first quarter)	Average Annual Growth Rate	Average Annual Earnings in 1993
Business services	7,009 (in thousands)	6.7%	$22,499
Leisure	1,505	6.2	21,018
Nonbanking financial institutions	496	5.7	n.a.
Social services	2,370	5.6	15,320
Brokerage	531	4.9	96,497
Local transit	439	4.7	20,496
Transportation services	430	4.4	31,617
Motion pictures	516	4.4	31,692
Agricultural services	599	4.2	n.a.
Museum and zoos	83	4.0	19,514
Auto repair and parking	1,059	3.6	20,430
Furniture stores	950	3.4	21,208
Building materials stores	883	3.3	22,914
Health services	9,463	3.3	34,200
Trucking and warehousing	1,879	3.2	27,289
Engineering and management	2,849	3.1	33,709
Special trade contractors	3,334	3.1	26,443
Education	1,982	3.0	20,088
Eating and drinking places	7,419	2.8	11,920
Misc. services	44	2.5	n.a.
Auto dealers and service stations	2,234	2.2	25,433
Rubber and plastics	962	2.2	33,103
Air transportation	828	2.2	43,093
Lumber products	754	2.1	27,713
State and local government	16,584	1.5	28,859

3. *Source note* ───▶ *Source: U.S. Bureau of Labor Statistics, 1997.*
 and footnote ───▶ * This table is printed in Ronald J. Ebert and Ricky W. Griffin, *Business Essentials* (Prentice Hall, 1998) 485.

1. Read the title (and subtitle when given) carefully and turn it into a question.

    Title: _____

    Your question: _____

2. Read the legend or captions (or column headings) to see how details are presented, and then note whether the figures are listed in hundreds, thousands, or millions for the total jobs.

    Figures are presented in _____.

3. Check to see if there is a source or footnote given for the data and whether the source is reliable.

    Source: _____

    Date published: _____

    How reliable? _____

4. Determine the organization of the data to find out what is being described.

    The four columns of information describe:

    a. _____

    b. _____

    c. _____

    d. _____

5. Determine the relationship(s) shown, with the aid of your own marginal notes as needed. Then, examine the trends in job growth and verify which industries have the highest and lowest earnings and fill-in the answers.

    The industry earning the highest amount is _____ compared

    with _____, which earned the lowest amount in 1993.

6. Answer the question you posed in step 1.

    _____

7. State one conclusion you can draw from the data.

    _____

∽ Integrating Text with Visual Information

When reading textbooks, especially in the sciences, economics, or business, you need to integrate the information in graphics with the printed text. Sometimes, what you read is clarified or explained in a graphic, but in many cases, the graphic simply adds more information to the text. You will need to go back and forth, analyzing and integrating both sets of information. Some instructors refer to this as "two-finger" reading; that is, you hold your place in the text while reading the graphic, moving back and forth through a chapter.

Do not ignore a textbook author's instruction, such as "See Figure 10.1" or "Examine Table 10.2." When such directions are given, the author expects you to stop reading the printed material and use the visual illustration for further enlightenment or clarification.

In reading math and science textbooks, since the information often builds on what has preceded it, you must read very carefully, not skipping anything. Science information is dense and requires very slow and deliberate concentration, with several rereadings and much note taking. This is true even for those readers who may have some familiarity with the subject.

Atmospheric pressure is more easily understood by integrating the text and the diagram in Figure 10.1.

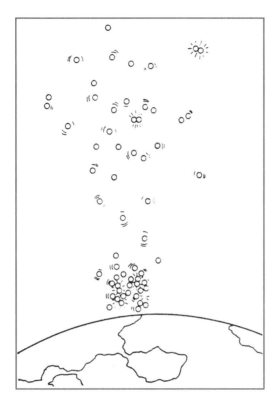

FIGURE 10.1
In the upper atmosphere, gaseous molecules are far apart and collide infrequently, which produces relatively low pressure. In lower layers, the molecules are closer together, and there are many more collisions, which produces higher pressure.

Source: Tom L. McKnight, "Atmospheric Pressure and Wind," *Essentials of Physical Geography,* 73. Copyright © 1992 by Prentice Hall, Inc. Reprinted by permission of the publisher.

The atmosphere is held to the Earth by the force of gravity, which prevents the gaseous molecules from escaping into space. At lower levels in the atmosphere, the molecules are packed more densely together because of the weight of the overlying air. Hence there are more molecular collisions and, therefore, higher pressure at lower levels. At higher elevations, the air is less dense, and there is a corresponding decrease in pressure. At any level in the atmosphere, then, the pressure is equivalent to the "weight" of the air directly above; thus the lower the elevation, the greater the pressure.

Why is atmospheric pressure greater at the earth's surface?

_____

_____

_____

✎ Types of Visual Information

Textbooks, newspapers, and magazines all use many types of graphics to enhance printed information. The message writers want to stress and their basic writing purpose help them choose one type of presentation over another. Additionally, a different kind of relationship can be conveyed with each type of graphic. For example, a circle graph represents a whole-part relationship, whereas a flowchart demonstrates a particular process or procedure.

✎ Graphs

Most often, graphs present statistics or quantities that are compared to one another by the use of bars, lines, or circles. In looking at the graph, the reader has to analyze the comparisons given. On the basis of these comparisons, the reader then makes inferences and draws conclusions. There are three types of graphs: bar, line, and circle or pie graphs.

Bar and Line Graphs

Bar and line graphs have the same underlying structure, as shown in Figure 10.2.

1. Both types of graphs have two lines drawn at right angles.
2. Each of these lines is referred to as an *axis*.
3. Each axis shows a measure of something.

FIGURE 10.2   The Two Axes of a Graph Show Measures

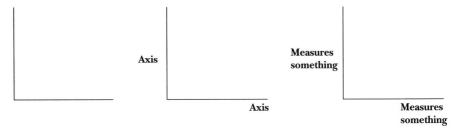

Bar Graphs

The purpose of a bar graph is to show the relationship between two measures (shown as rectangles rather than single lines) and, sometimes, to indicate change over time. The length of each bar represents an amount or number. Dots or stripes, or even color, can add to their impact. Bars can be placed either *vertically* (arranged from top to bottom) or *horizontally* (arranged from side to side).

   Let's first look at a *single vertical bar graph* (Figure 10.3) to learn how many children under 18 years of age were being raised by a single parent, their mother, in 1996 compared to 1960.

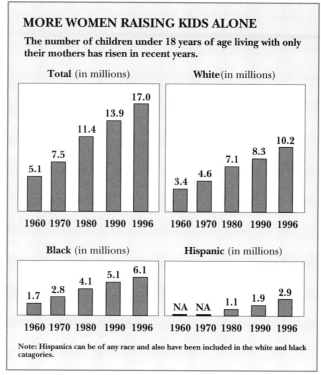

FIGURE 10.3

Source: From *USA Today* (June 19, 1998): 3-A. Data from U.S. Census Bureau.
Copyright © 1998 by *USA Today*. Reprinted with the permission of the publishers.

Which population group—among those identified here as White, Black, or Hispanic—has experienced the greatest increase of children living with single parents between 1960 and 1996? After writing your answer, state one conclusion you can reach from examining this graph.

a. Group with greatest increase of single parents is _____ .

b. I can conclude that _____ .

Examine now an example of a *single horizontal bar graph* (Figure 10.4) and the excerpted accompanying text to help you decide which airline you might choose and which you might avoid when making travel plans.

U.S. AIRLINES FLY HIGHER

Marianne Constantinou

Performance by the nation's top 10 airlines is up.

Complaints from airline passengers are up.

The amount of lost baggage is down. So is the number of airport fatalities.

Promptness, up. Bumped passengers, down.

The dizzying statistics go on and on. . . .

This one, Airline Quality Rating 1998, was conducted by two academicians using U.S. Department of Transportation data. . . .

Since only numerical, calculable criteria were used—including average age of fleet, number of accidents, frequent flier programs and the **ubiquitous** "other"—the survey is heralded as objective, and is viewed with some seriousness within the airline industry.

In the Best Of category, the survey rated Southwest Airlines No. 1 for the third consecutive year. It had "the best annual average on-time arrival percentage . . . the second highest denied boardings rate and the fewest number of complaints per passenger flown." . . .

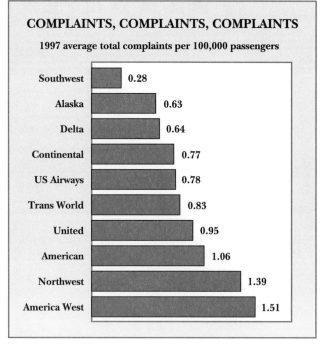

FIGURE 10.4

Source: Air Travel Consumer Report, U.S. Department of Transportation, Office of Aviation Enforcement and Proceedings.

---

ubiquitous (yoo bik′ wò tòs) seeming to be present, everywhere at the same time

In 10th and last place was US Airways. . . . [Passengers] gave the survey a big "hohum"—especially after learning that the survey didn't measure the airlines by the criteria they viewed as most important: cheapest fares, best leg room, best food and best in-flight movies.

"Price is number one," said Jane Elizabeth, 26. . . .

"On a long flight, you've got to have a good movie," said Louise Taylor. . . .

"It was cramped," complained Lisa Cuevas, 18, coming home with her family from Las Vegas aboard America West. "The tray was practically in my face. You didn't have to pick up your drink. All you had to do was lean forward and slurp it."

But these things are opinions, and the professors, Brent Bowen of the Aviation Institute at the University of Nebraska at Omaha, and Dean Headley of Wichita State University in Kansas, dealt only with hard-core numbers in their survey.

"You can't measure personal taste," said Joseph Kleinsasser, spokesman at Wichita State. . . .

But to some consumer advocates, the Airline Quality Rating has holes wide enough for a 747 to fly through. . . .

At the airport, passengers said they are most loyal to airlines with the lowest fares. If they've had a good experience with an airline in the past, they tend to go with it again—all fares being equal.

But sometimes a cheap rate isn't enough. John George, 53, who flies about two dozen times a year, travels via US Air when he can go for free using his frequent flier miles. But when he has to pay cash, he heads for Southwest Airlines—reluctantly.

Southwest often has the cheapest fares. . . . But cheap fares have other costs.

Southwest has no reserved seating, . . . which requires getting to the airport early to avoid a seat in the john.

"That's really Spartan, when you go Southwest," said George. "You almost have to bring your own chair. They don't even serve peanuts on some flights. And forget about a Coke."

approximately 375 words

Marianne Costantinou, "U.S. Airlines Fly Higher," *San Francisco Examiner* 21 Apr. 1998: A1+.

1. The airline ranked with the lowest average total passenger complaints in 1997 is

    _____ ; the airline listed as having the highest num-

    ber in 1997 is _____ .

2. What information given in the printed text accompanying the graph might influence you to think twice before concluding that Southwest Airline is the best carrier to choose?

    _____

3. What criteria do you consider the most important when selecting air transportation? The least important? Explain your answers.

    Most important criteria: _____

    Least important criteria: _____

Below is an example of a *vertical bar graph with more than one bar*. In this graph, different colors or shades of color are used to show the percentage of male and female Internet users from 1994 to 1998. Examine it now to see the kinds of changes that have taken place during this time span.

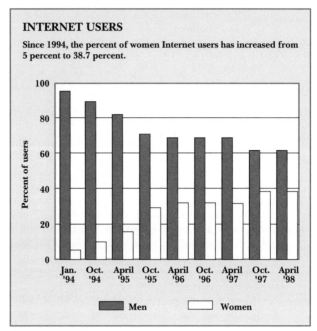

FIGURE 10.5

Source: Georgia Tech University.

1. What is the purpose of this graph?

   _____

2. a. Did the percentage of male Internet users increase or decrease from April 1997 to October 1997?

   _____

   b. What is the approximate percentage increase for female Internet users from October 1994 to October 1997?

   _____

3. a. Why do you think the percentage of female Internet users has increased so dramatically?

   _____

b. Read the following excerpted text that accompanied the bar graph to see if your inference is confirmed or contradicted by the reporter's statements:

. . . In the last year, a range of studies has made it clear that women are rapidly joining the global network. But analysts say the numbers reflect changes much broader than gender.

"What it says is that the Internet is becoming more mainstream, rather than saying anything about women in particular or men in particular," said Sorcha Ni hEildhe, Internet survey editor for Nua Ltd., an Irish group that tracks Internet trends.

. . . Jupiter Communications, a New York research company, predicted . . . that women will make up more than half the entire country's Internet users by 2002.

There are reflections of the trend worldwide. Nearly two-thirds of the people who stopped by Internet search tool AltaVista's Asian site (http://altavista.skali.com.my) in January were women, as were 85 percent of April's visitors to Russia's largest Internet publisher, Infoart (www.infoart.ru), according to Nua. . . .

Since its inception as a military and then academic network back in the '60s and '70s, the Internet, and its topics, widened gradually—and then explosively in the mid-'90s after the development of the World Wide Web.

Experts don't know whether the new content attracted more women or whether the influx of women spurred new content. Either way, "more women being on-line is definitely changing the face and the energy and the content of what's there," said Aliza Sherman, who should know. She's responsible for some of the change.

Sherman runs Cybergrrl (www.cybergrrl.com), a New York–based business that aims to link women to the Web, both for their own benefit and for the benefit of marketers. It started three years ago with six women in a cafe. Now it has established 100 chapters of "webgrrls" networking groups, published a book listing women's Web sites, gotten the traditional media's attention and made Sherman a conference-circuit persona.

But Cybergrrl is still an outsider compared to mainstream women's Internet sites like New York–based iVillage (www.iVillage.com) and San Mateo–based Women.com (www.women.com). Women.com logs 2.3 million different visitors every month and has a permanent spot in America Online's women's area, according to Women.com founder Ellen Pack. iVillage garners 3 million individual hits per month.

approximately 300 words

Jennifer Peltz "On-line Equality," Medill News Service. *San Francisco Examiner* 1 Nov. 1998: B5

According to the writer, why has female Internet usage increased?

_____

_____

_____

Stacked Bar Graphs

Rather than being arranged side by side, some bars are placed one on top of the other, thus creating what is known as a *stacked bar graph*. It is an effective means of demonstrating a whole-to-part relationship, graphically showing the various parts that make up a total amount. Since stacked bar graphs consolidate even more information than regular bar graphs, they demand more of the reader. The best strategy for reading such illustrations is to read carefully and understand the *key*, that is, the guide to what each shaded or colored bar represents.

Stacked bar graphs can be composed either vertically or horizontally, as Figures 10.6A and B demonstrate. Examine each of them now to understand the relationship of three regions of the United State and how by specific measures they have changed over time. Reading the textual footnote *first* will help illuminate the graphic information.

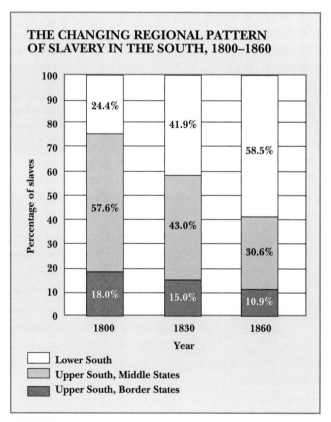

FIGURE 10.6A

As the nineteenth century progressed, slavery increasingly became identified with the cotton-growing Lower South.

Source: The Times Atlas of World History. Copyright © 1978. Reprinted with permission of Times Books, HarperCollins Publishers, Ltd.

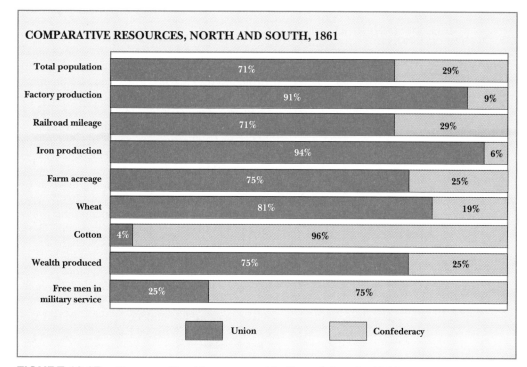

COMPARATIVE RESOURCES, NORTH AND SOUTH, 1861

	Union	Confederacy
Total population	71%	29%
Factory production	91%	9%
Railroad mileage	71%	29%
Iron production	94%	6%
Farm acreage	75%	25%
Wheat	81%	19%
Cotton	4%	96%
Wealth produced	75%	25%
Free men in military service	25%	75%

FIGURE 10.6B   Comparative Resources, North and South, 1861

By 1865, the North's overwhelming advantage in population, industrial strength, railroad mileage, agriculture, and wealth was decisive in the final victory. But initially these strengths made little difference in a struggle that began as a traditional war of maneuver in which the South held the defensive advantage. Only slowly did the Civil War become a modern war in which all of the resources of society, including the property and lives of civilians, were mobilized for battle.

Source: The Times Atlas of World History. Copyright © 1978. Reprinted with permission of Times Books, HarperCollins Publishers, Ltd.

Line Graphs

Line graphs are used to show trends over a period of time. In examining them, readers need to focus their attention on whether the trends are moving upward or downward. With a line graph, the relationship between two or more items is shown by a line (or several lines) plotted between the numbers or measures on the horizontal and vertical axes. The points drawn along these axes are connected to form a continuous line. The reader must determine how the information along the horizontal scale is related to that along the vertical one. If there is a great difference in the data being illustrated, the lines change direction and become quite jagged. Note how Figure 10.7 on page 594 dramatizes the upward trend in the amount of temporary workers in the United States within a decade by the use of just one line, and how the author has **accentuated** this fact with the inserted arrows and text explanation.

---

accentuated (ak sen′ choͤo̅ ā tid) emphasized; heightened the effect

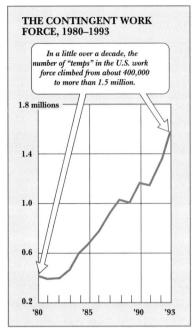

THE CONTINGENT WORK FORCE, 1980–1993

In a little over a decade, the number of "temps" in the U.S. work force climbed from about 400,000 to more than 1.5 million.

1.8 millions

1.4

1.0

0.6

0.2

'80   '85   '90   '93

FIGURE 10.7

By most accounts, the number of contingent workers is on the rise. Figure 10.7, for example, shows the increase in daily temporary workers, from just over 400,000 in 1980 to 2.25 million in 1994. That number is projected to rise to 3.6 million by 2005. According to a poll conducted by the research firm of Clark Martire & Bartolomeo, 44 percent of Fortune 500 CEOs said that they use more temps than they did 5 years ago; only 13 percent said they used fewer. Moreover, 44 percent indicated that they would be using more in the future. In the nearly 2 decades since 1983, 20 percent of the 20 million jobs created in the United States have been temporary or part-time. Some analysts predict that by the year 2000, half of all U.S. workers will be among the contingency workers supplied by agencies like Manpower. "Any worker still expecting to hold one job from cradle to grave," says Sara Lee CEO John Bryan, "will need to adjust his thinking."   *Source:* Ronald J. Ebert and Ricky W. Griffin, *Business Essentials,* 2nd ed. (Prentice Hall, 1998) 245.

Based on the graphic and textual information, do you think the projected figure for the year 2005 is logical? Why, or why not?

_____

_____

Circle or Pie Graphs

Circle graphs, which are also sometimes called "pie charts," divide a quantity of something into its parts, in wedge-shaped sections, like a pie. When the parts are measured in percentages, the entire circle graph represents 100 percent of a given item or quantity, and each wedge is a portion of the whole. When fractions are used, the whole equals 1. Each wedge, then, represents a percentage or fraction of the graph. It is the reader's task to discover the relationship of the whole represented in the graph to its parts.

The graph in Figure 10.8 on page 595 allows a reader to see quickly which type of lottery game garners the most revenue and which segment of society reaps the largest benefits.

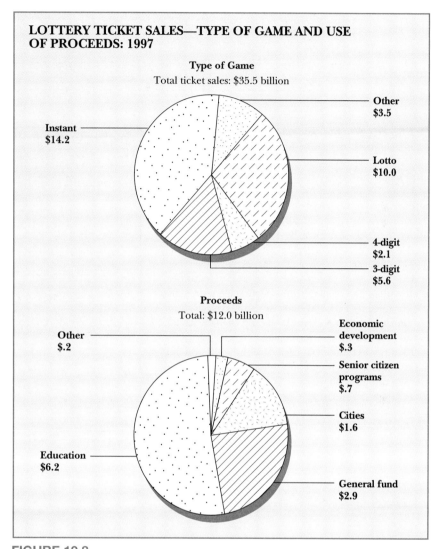

FIGURE 10.8

Source: Chart prepared by U.S. Bureau of the Census. *U.S. Census Bureau, The Official Statistics™. Statistical Abstract of the United States:* 1998, 306.

Not only do the four circle graphs in Figure 10.9 on page 596 condense the accompanying textual information, they show vividly the vast **discrepancy** in the number of women convicted of killing their spouses compared with males. Before

_____

discrepancy (di skrep' òn sē) inconsistency

examining this graphic, jot down why you think far fewer women than men are con-victed of spousal murders.

_____

_____

. . . Only 2 percent of husbands charged with killing their wives are acquitted at trial, a Justice Department study finds. . . .

One major finding of the . . . study was that wives charged with killing their husbands were convicted less often than husbands facing spouse murder charges—largely because women successfully argued that they were defending themselves from a husband who had abused them. . . .

The Justice study sampled spousal murder cases concluded in 1988 in the nation's 75 largest counties, where more than half of all murders occur each year. "This is the best and most comprehensive study ever done of spouse murder," said Marvin Wolfgang, University of Pennsylvania professor of criminology and law.

The study said that the cases of 318 husbands and 222 wives accused of killing their spouses had been concluded in those 75 counties that year.

Of the male defendants, 46 percent pleaded guilty, 41 percent were convicted at trial, 11 percent were not pros-ecuted, and 2 percent were acquitted at trial. Of the guilty, 81 percent were sent to prison, for an average of 16.5 years.

Of the female defendants, 39 percent pleaded guilty, 31 percent were convicted at trial, 16 percent were not prosecuted, and 14 percent were acquitted at trial. Of the guilty, 57 percent were sent to prison, for an average of 6 years.

Patrick A. Langan, senior Justice statistician and co-author of the study, said self-defense by women clearly accounted for their 10 percent conviction difference. Of the female defendants, 44 percent had been threatened with a weapon or physically assaulted by their mate at or near the time of the killing, compared with only 10 percent of the male defendants.

"In cases where there was no provocation, husbands and wives had an identical conviction rate," Langan said.

approximately 275 words

Michael J. Sniffen, "Acquittals Rare in Wife-Killing Trials, Study Says," *San Francisco Examiner* 5 Oct. 1995

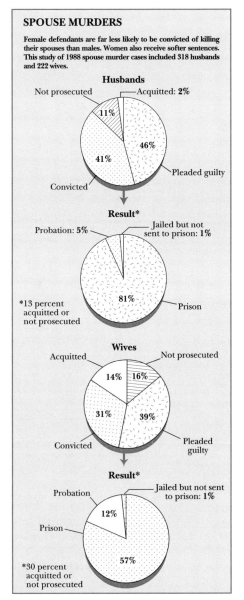

SPOUSE MURDERS

Female defendants are far less likely to be convicted of killing their spouses than males. Women also receive softer sentences. This study of 1988 spouse murder cases included 318 husbands and 222 wives.

Husbands

Not prosecuted — Acquitted: 2%
11%
46%
41%
Convicted — Pleaded guilty

Result*

Probation: 5% — Jailed but not sent to prison: 1%
*13 percent acquitted or not prosecuted
81% — Prison

Wives

Acquitted — Not prosecuted
14% 16%
31% 39%
Convicted — Pleaded guilty

Result*

Probation — Jailed but not sent to prison: 1%
Prison
12%
*30 percent acquitted or not prosecuted
57%

FIGURE 10.9

Source: U.S. Department of Justice.

on the relationship between rising unemployment and the new influx of foreigners. The American Federation of Labor proposed stopping all immigration for two years. Sensational press coverage of organized crime figures, many of them Italian or Jewish, also played a part.

In 1921 Congress passed the Immigration Act setting a maximum of 357,000 new immigrants each year. Quotas limited annual immigration from any European country to 3 percent of the number of its natives counted in the 1910 U.S. census. But restrictionists complained that the new law still allowed too many southern and eastern Europeans in, especially since the northern and western Europeans did not fill their quotas. The Johnson-Reed Immigration Act of 1924 revised the quotas to 2 percent of the number of foreign-born counted for each nationality in the census for 1890, when far fewer southern or eastern Europeans were present in the United States.

approximately 500 words

John Mack Faragher et al., *Out of Many: A History of the American People,* 2nd ed. (Prentice Hall, 1997) 739–40.

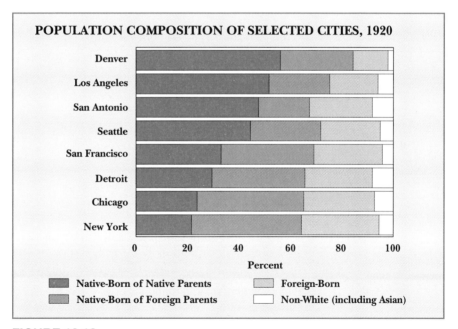

FIGURE 10.12

By 1920 the demographic impact of several decades of heavy immigration was especially evident in the nation's cities. The combined population of the foreign-born and those born of foreign parents frequently surpassed that of the native-born of native parents.

3. a. How does the stacked bar graph help to highlight the main point of the text?

_____

_____

b. Which city had the largest percentage of native-born people of native parents in 1920?

_____

_____

c. Which group composed the smallest population in the 1920s?

_____

_____

d. State one conclusion you can draw from the information given on the graph.

_____

_____

e. Write one inference you can make from the textual information.

_____

_____

You have just examined immigration trends in 1920 with the aid of a stacked bar graph. Now look at more information about 1920 immigration but displayed with a line graph and a circle graph in Figure 10.13 on page 603.

4. a. What kind of different information is provided in the line graph compared with the circle graph?

_____

b. Which years had the highest numbers of immigrants? _____

The lowest? _____

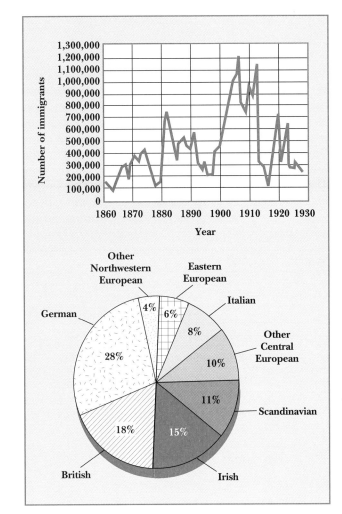

FIGURE 10.13

Immigration to the United States, 1860–1929

The peak years of immigration in the last half of the nineteenth century were 1872, 1882, and 1892, each also marking the beginning of an economic recession. Immigration slowed when jobs were scarce, especially following the financial Panics of 1873 and 1893, and picked up again during periods of recovery.

Source: Statistical Abstract of the United States, 1921 and 1930.

c. Which ethnic group comprised the largest number of immigrants between 1860 and 1929? _____The second largest? _____

d. Examine the information given in the text excerpt, see pages 600–601, for question 3 above and, with that knowledge, state one conclusion you can reach from the line graph.

_____

◈ Tables

Tables, too, are often used to show comparisons or provide statistics. They are a systematic arrangement of data, from numbers to steps to descriptions, in list form. The information is generally given in rows (horizontally) and columns (vertically) with headings that explain what the numbers or listed items mean. The reader has to look at the two different directions of the displayed information and think about the comparisons being made in order to draw conclusions. Usually, you are trying to find out whether any of the numbers are significantly larger or smaller than others and to decide what trends or conclusions they suggest. Thinking carefully about the title of the table should help you understand its main point. The following table has been labeled to point out the important parts to examine in order to best understand the information.

Title (purpose of chart) →
Special note →
Headings →
Rows, horizontal: Specific data →

Book Purchasing by Adults: 1991 and 1996

[In percent. Excludes books purchased for or by children under age 13. Based on a survey of 16,000 households conducted over 12 months ending in December of year shown.]

Characteristic	Total		Mass Market[1]		Trade[2]		Hardcover	
	1991	1996	1991	1996	1991	1996	1991	1996
Total	100.0	100.0	100.0	100.0	100.0	100.0	100.0	100.0
Age of purchaser:								
Under 25 years old	4.3	3.9	3.7	3.6	5.2	4.4	4.4	3.6
25 to 34 years old	18.8	15.7	13.9	13.7	25.4	17.9	19.6	14.8
35 to 44 years old	23.7	25.9	22.8	22.1	25.2	29.7	23.7	26.5
45 to 54 years old	22.4	22.3	26.0	21.5	18.5	21.9	20.5	23.7
55 to 64 years old	15.6	15.6	15.8	16.5	13.9	14.1	17.2	16.0
65 years old and over	15.2	16.6	17.8	22.6	11.8	12.0	14.6	15.4
Household income:								
Under $30,000	37.1	32.7	41.7	40.9	32.6	28.3	34.1	27.6
$30,000 to 49,999	27.2	23.8	27.3	22.4	27.7	24.6	26.5	24.6
$50,000 to 59,999	11.0	7.9	9.8	6.9	12.3	8.4	11.5	8.3
$60,000 to 69,999	6.9	9.1	7.0	7.9	7.2	9.9	6.3	9.6
$70,000 and over	17.8	26.5	14.2	21.9	20.2	28.8	21.6	29.9
Household size:								
Singles	20.8	18.7	17.7	20.1	24.1	17.8	22.8	18.1
Families with no children	40.4	43.4	42.3	42.1	38.0	43.2	39.7	45.1
Families with children	38.8	37.9	40.0	37.8	37.9	39.0	37.5	36.8
Age of reader:								
Under 25 years old	7.3	6.9	5.2	5.1	10.1	9.2	7.7	6.3
25 to 34 years old	18.7	16.6	14.1	14.2	24.7	19.2	20.2	16.2
35 to 44 years old	22.9	24.8	22.3	21.6	24.0	28.0	22.7	25.2
45 to 54 years old	20.8	20.2	24.9	20.0	16.5	19.6	18.4	21.6
55 to 64 years old	14.9	14.4	15.9	16.9	12.7	11.8	15.6	14.3
65 years old and over	15.4	17.1	17.6	22.2	12.0	12.2	15.6	16.4

← *Percents based on 100%*
Columns, vertical: Compare 1991–96 in three areas

(*continued*)

Characteristic	Total		Mass Market[1]		Trade[2]		Hardcover	
	1991	**1996**	**1991**	**1996**	**1991**	**1996**	**1991**	**1996**
Category of book:								
Popular fiction	54.9	50.9	93.0	93.6	14.9	14.5	31.8	40.4
General nonfiction	10.3	9.4	3.6	2.7	15.6	12.2	16.5	14.4
Cooking/crafts	10.2	10.2	0.4	0.4	20.6	16.9	18.2	14.3
Other	24.6	29.5	3.0	3.3	48.9	56.4	33.5	30.9
Stores outlet:								
Independent	32.5	18.6	26.5	11.3	44.9	27.6	29.0	17.2
Chain book store	22.0	25.6	17.2	22.0	27.4	27.6	25.2	27.7
Book clubs	16.6	18.0	17.8	18.7	9.5	13.6	22.6	22.0
Other[3]	28.9	37.8	38.5	48.0	18.2	31.2	23.2	33.1

Source
note →

Footnotes →

Source: Book Industry Study Group, Inc., New York, NY, *Consumer Research Study on Book Purchasing,* annual. U.S. Census Bureau, *The Official Statistics™, Statistical Abstract of the United States: 1998.*

[1] "Pocket size" books sold primarily through magazine and news outlets, supermarkets, variety stores, etc.
[2] All paperbound books except mass market.
[3] Includes mail order, price clubs, discount stores, food/drug stores, used book stores, and other outlets.

The table details the percentage of books purchased by adults in 1991 compared with 1996, the age of purchaser and reader household income and size, book type, and place of purchase. The special note lets the reader know that children under 13 were excluded; and the footnotes state among other things that the word "Other" under "Sales outlet" includes mail order, price clubs, and so on. As you can see, a great deal of information has been presented in very compact form. Examining the table, we find that the percentage of books purchased by age group did not change significantly during the given time period, but that the most affected area for household income was for those earning over $70,000, among whom there was a significant increase.

1. In the sales outlet listing, what is the most significant change in the percentage of the total from 1991 to 1996?

2. What conclusion can be drawn from the fact that the age of the purchaser, under 25, does not match the age of the reader?

To reach other conclusions based on this table, you might pose questions, such as those that follow.

1. Is the percentage of people who purchased books of fiction greater or smaller than those who purchased nonfiction?

2. Did any group, by age, purchase more books in 1996 than 1991?

    _____

3. What effect does the size of a household have on the number of books purchased?

    _____

4. Why were Internet sales not included?

    _____

Answer the above questions, and then add and answer one of your own.

5. _____

    _____

ACTIVITY 10.2 Examining the Contents of a Table

Apply the strategies you just learned for understanding a table's contents to the following information that appeared in *Strangers to These Shores* by Vincent N. Parillo.

Occupations of Hispanic Workers Age 16 and Over, 1980 and 1993

	Percentages in Each Occupational Category				
	All Hispanics	Mexicans	Puerto Ricans	Cubans	Other Hispanics*
1980					
White-collar	35.0	31.0	35.3	NA	NA
Service	16.5	16.6	19.3	NA	NA
Agri/Forest	3.4	4.7	1.0	NA	NA
Blue-collar	45.2	47.7	44.5	NA	NA
1993					
White-collar	39.0	34.8	51.2	57.9	40.9
Service	19.9	19.1	19.9	12.9	23.8
Agri/Forest	5.8	8.0	1.2	2.2	2.3
Blue-collar	35.4	38.1	27.7	27.2	32.9

Source: U.S. Bureau of Labor Statistics, *Employment and Earnings,* January issues, 1981, 1994.
* Includes Central and South Americans and others of Hispanic origin.

1. a. Does the table give you the number of Hispanic workers by quantity or

    percentage? _____

b.   Will it make any difference in reaching conclusions whether the figures are given by number of people or percentage? _____

2.   How many occupational areas have been included? _____

3.   Why do you think no data was available (NA) in 1980 for Cubans and "Other Hispanics"?

_____

4.   a.   Which group had the highest percentage of white-collar occupations in 1993?

_____   The lowest percentage? _____

b.   State one inference you can make based on your answers to part a.

_____

⤶ Diagrams

A diagram refers to some form of drawing with distinctive labeled parts. A diagram can be as simple as a line drawing or as complex as a causal analysis in an astronomy or chemistry text. Diagrams can be used in diverse areas, from plotting how a plane flies to the stages an embryo goes through to become a fetus and eventually a new-born baby. They can also take the form of organizational charts or flowcharts in a business management or computer science text or maps in a geography or history book.

Diagrams are generally included to enhance difficult textual information. In reading diagrams, you have to think about what the various parts represent and how they can be tied together. Often, the title or a caption will provide the reader with the main idea, the relationship being illustrated. The reader must identify the main idea, find out its purpose, and understand what is implied within a section or portion of the diagram.

The diagrams (parts a and b of Figure 10.14) illustrate the importance of this kind of visual aid when studying complex theories. As you read the text excerpt below, refer to the diagrams to visualize and conceptualize the structure of atoms and to understand how a helium atom differs from a carbon atom. The diagrams clearly demonstrate how they differ, as you compare their structures.

> The next simplest element after hydrogen is helium. The central nucleus of the most common form of helium is made up of two protons and two neutrons (another kind of elementary particle having a mass slightly larger than that of a proton but carrying no electrical charge). About this nucleus orbit two electrons. As with hydrogen and all other atoms, the "normal" condition for helium is to be electrically neutral, with the negative

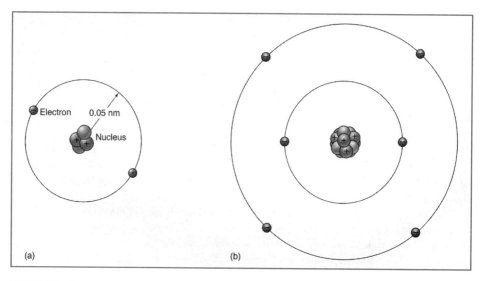

FIGURE 10.14
(a) A helium atom in its ground state. Two electrons occupy the lowest-energy orbital around a nucleus containing two protons and two neutrons. (b) A carbon atom in its ground state. Six electrons orbit a six-proton, six-neutron nucleus; two of the electrons are in an inner orbital, the other four are at a greater distance from the center.

charge of the orbiting electrons exactly canceling the positive charge of the nucleus (Figure 10.14a).

More complex atoms contain more protons (and neutrons) in the nucleus and have correspondingly more orbiting electrons. For example, an atom of carbon (Figure 10.14b) consists of six electrons orbiting a nucleus containing six protons and six neutrons. As we progress to heavier and heavier elements, the number of orbiting electrons increases, and consequently the number of possible electronic transitions rises rapidly. The result is that very complicated spectra can be produced. The complexity of atomic spectra generally reflects the complexity of the source atoms. A good example is the element iron, which contributes several hundred of the Fraunhofer absorption lines seen in the solar spectrum. The many possible transitions of its 26 orbiting electrons yield an extremely rich line spectrum.

Eric Chaisson and Steve McMillan, *Astronomy: A Beginner's Guide to the Universe*, 2nd ed. (Prentice Hall, 1998) 64.

⌒ Maps

Maps graphically represent specific information about places; for example, their *exact* location, features, and characteristics or their *relative* location—that is, where they are in relation to others areas. Such maps are sometimes referred to as *locational maps,* and they generally illustrate a part-to-whole relationship by using distance, direction, size, and shape. Maps are also used to show the relevance of *place* geography: They represent what is happening in a particular place. They can give us spatial patterns or make comparisons related to our physical, cultural, political, or economic environment; these are often referred to as *thematic maps.* Maps are included in textbooks to further your understanding of place facts, concepts, or relationships.

To read a map effectively, first carefully read the *title,* which will give you the map's subject and tell you what is displayed. Then, read the *key* or *legend* to understand what symbols, colors, or other codes represent on a particular map. It is also important to understand the *scale* used. As geographer Edward F. Bergman defines it, "The relationship between length measured on the map and corresponding distance on the ground is called the scale of the map." A reader needs to understand the scale in order to interpret the data. As Figure 10.15 demonstrates, the scale can be presented with words and illustrations (a), purely graphically (b), or fractionally (c).

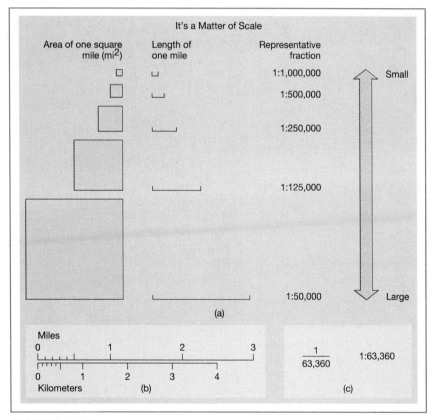

FIGURE 10.15

Drawing (a) shows that a small-scale map can portray a large part of the Earth's surface, whereas a large-scale map can show only a small part of the surface. Drawing (b) is a graphic scale, and (c) shows fractional scales.

Source: Edward F. Bergman, *Human Geography* (Prentice Hall, 1995) 11.

Looking at Figures 10.16A and 10.16B, you can see a significant difference between the information presented in a large and small scale map of Central Africa.

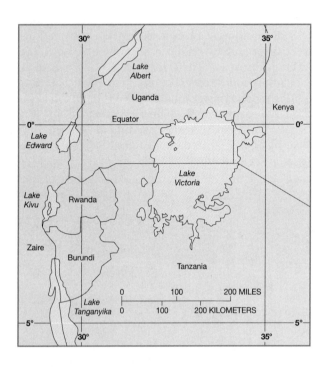

FIGURE 10.16A   Large Scale

Rwanda and Burundi: Political collapse and tribalism in central Africa.

Source: Charles A. Stansfield, Jr., *Building Geographic Literacy* (Prentice Hall, 1998) 186.

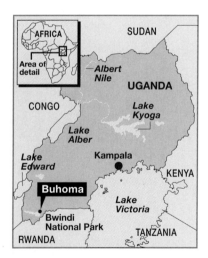

FIGURE 10.16B   Small Scale

Source: "Tourist Slaughter" from *San Francisco Examiner* (March 2, 1999). Copyright © 1999 by *San Francisco Examiner.* Reprinted with permission of the publisher.

Examine the contents of the map in (Figure 10.17), making marginal notations of its purpose, legend, and scale.

FIGURE 10.17   The Distribution of the Major Christian Sects in Europe

Source: Edward F. Bergman, *Human Geography* (Prentice Hall, 1995) 273.

Without the benefit of the textual portion accompanying the map, you can still learn from the map where the major Christian sects are located in Northern and Southern Europe. Let's see what other information you derived from examining the map.

1. What is the amount of distance that has been plotted, according to the legend?

    _____

2. How have the four major Christian sects been coded on the map?

    _____

3. Name three European countries in which Roman Catholicism is dominant:

    _____ Name three

    countries in which Protestant sects are dominant: _____

    _____

4. Are there any countries where Protestant and Roman Catholic sects overlap?

    _____

5. Which religious sect is the most predominant in Europe? _____

    The least predominant? _____

☙ Flowcharts

Flowcharts are yet another type of drawing or diagram. Their purpose is to help the reader understand a sequence of elements or how a process works. Shapes, such as circles, boxes, or squares, are used to enclose key ideas and their supporting details, which "flow" on the page, with lines or arrows linking them. Complicated procedures, such as the one that appears in Figure 10.18, are shown step by step.

In reading a flowchart, first examine the title to learn the procedure or sequence being illustrated; then, find out where the first step begins. The arrows or lines indicate the direction to follow, usually from top to bottom or left to right. If the arrows appear in one direction, the steps are in sequence, but if the arrows point both up and down, it means the procedure can go back and forth.

Look over Figure 10.18 to see how the information is organized and in which direction the arrows have been drawn. Then, read the title, which in this case tells the reader that the flowchart will demonstrate the internal adjustments needed to

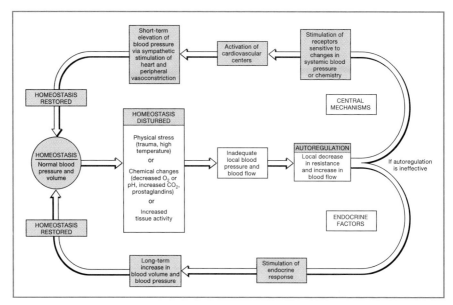

FIGURE 10.18   Homeostatic Adjustments That Maintain Blood Pressure and Blood Flow

Source: Frederic H. Martini et al., *Fundamentals of Anatomy and Physiology* (Prentice Hall, 1998) 728.

maintain blood pressure and blood flow. Start to read the flowchart by looking at the left-center circle where *homeostasis* is defined. Write its meaning here.

Homeostasis means _____.

Follow the arrow that points to the large rectangle, which itemizes possible disturbances to homeostasis, and list two of them.

1. _____

2. _____

Continue to read, following the arrows to the right, to understand the results of these disturbances (inadequate local blood pressure and blood flow) and what happens if autoregulation fails to normalize or return homeostasis. There are two ways homeostasis can be restored. If you follow the upper rim of information, with arrows now pointing from right to left, which mechanisms are activated—the central or endocrine?

_____

As you can see, if you ask questions and make notations as you read graphic information, you can develop an outline or summary of complicated procedures, making the information easier to understand and remember.

⟡ Pictograms

Another type of drawing or diagram is the *pictogram,* which generally combines the concept of a chart with that of a graph. Its most significant feature is its use of sketches or icons (symbols or drawings) to represent numbers. By replacing columns of numbers with picture representations, writers are able to capture your imagination and visually dramatize information they want you to know. Notice the impact of the icons in Figure 10.19, in which sketches of alcohol bottles have been used to send the reader a strong message about the nature of criminal offenses and alcohol abuse.

FIGURE 10.19

Percentage of Inmates Who Had Been Drinking Prior to Crime Commission

Source: Bureau of Justice Statistics, *Report to the Nation on Crime and Justice,* 2nd ed. (Washington, D.C.: U.S. Government Printing Office, 1988) 51. In Frank Schmalleger, *Criminal Justice Today,* 4th ed. (Prentice Hall, 1997) 573.

ACTIVITY 10.3 Summarizing the Contents of a Diagram

The diagram that follows on page 615 combines the concept of a flowchart with pictogram drawings. Use the strategies you have learned for understanding graphic information to read it. Then, write a summary paragraph, in your own words, explaining the DNA fingerprinting process.

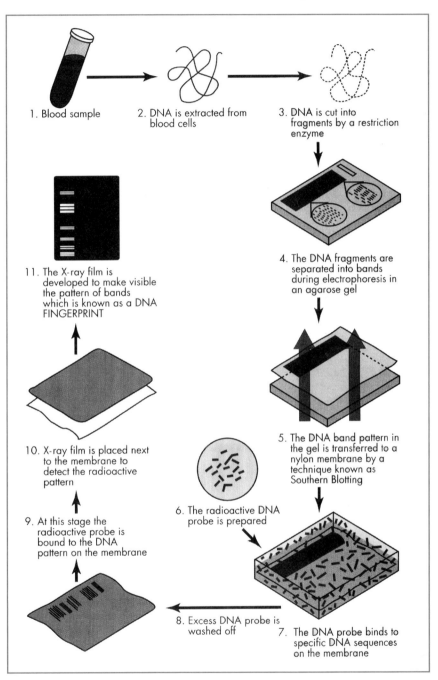

The DNA Fingerprinting Process

Source: Cellmark Diagnostics, Inc., Germantown, Maryland.

ACTIVITY 10.4 Examining Information from Multiple Graphics

1. The following table shows the hazardous waste sites on the National Priority List, by state, for 1990 (which includes both proposed and final sites listed on the National Priorities List for the Superfund program, as authorized by the Comprehensive Environmental Response, Compensation, and Liability Act of 1980 and the Superfund Amendments and Reauthorization Act of 1986). Examine the contents of the table, and then use the information to study the related map on page 617, which illustrates exactly where hazardous waste sites are located in the United States.

State	Total Sites	Rank	Percent Distribution	State	Total Sites	Rank	Percent Distribution
Total	1,207	(x)	(x)	Missouri	24	15	2.0
United States	**1,197**	**(x)**	**100.0**	Montana	10	34	0.8
				Nebraska	6	43	0.5
Alabama	12	27	1.0	Nevada	1	50	0.1
Alaska	6	43	0.5	New Hampshire	16	22	1.3
Arizona	11	29	0.9	New Jersey	109	1	9.1
Arkansas	10	34	0.8	New Mexico	10	34	0.8
California	88	3	7.4	New York	83	4	6.9
Colorado	16	22	1.3	North Carolina	22	17	1.8
Connecticut	15	24	1.3	North Dakota	2	48	0.2
Delaware	20	19	1.7	Ohio	33	12	2.8
District of Columbia	—	(x)	—	Oklahoma	11	29	0.9
Florida	51	6	4.3	Oregon	8	40	0.7
Georgia	13	26	1.1	Pennsylvania	95	2	7.9
Hawaii	7	42	0.6	Rhode Island	11	29	0.9
Idaho	9	38	0.8	South Carolina	23	16	1.9
Illinois	37	10	3.1	South Dakota	3	46	0.3
Indiana	35	11	2.9	Tennessee	14	25	1.2
Iowa	21	18	1.8	Texas	28	13	2.3
Kansas	11	29	0.9	Utah	12	27	1.0
Kentucky	17	21	1.4	Vermont	8	40	0.7
Louisiana	11	29	0.9	Virginia	20	19	1.7
Maine	9	38	0.8	Washington	45	7	3.8
Maryland	10	34	0.8	West Virginia	5	45	0.4
Massachusetts	25	14	2.1	Wisconsin	39	9	3.3
Michigan	78	5	6.5	Wyoming	3	46	0.3
Minnesota	42	8	3.5	Guam	1	(x)	(x)
Mississippi	2	48	0.2	Puerto Rico	9	(x)	(x)

Source: U.S. Environmental Protection Agency, press release, August 1990, *Statistical Abstract of the United States,* 1991.

Note: — Represents zero; (x) Not applicable

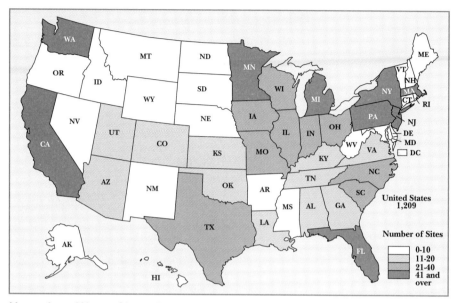

Hazardous Waste Sites: June 1990

Source: Statistical Abstract of the United States, 1991.

a. Which three states have the largest total number of sites?

_____

b. Which three states have the lowest total number of sites?

_____

c. Which three states have the highest concentration of hazardous waste in terms of percentage of the total?

_____

d. Which three states have the lowest concentration of hazardous waste in terms of percentage of the total?

_____

e. Based on the map and the table, what inferences and what conclusions can you draw about hazardous waste sites in the United States?

_____

_____

2. Study the following graphics that present a profile of how the U.S. population changed over a four-year period between 1990 and 1994. Then, answer the questions that follow.

A SHIFTING PROFILE

How the U.S. population has changed in age and other demographics from the 1990 U.S. Census to Census figures for July 1, 1994. Numbers in thousands*

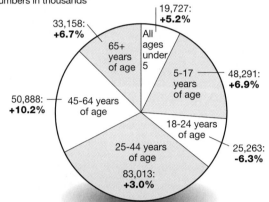

19,727: **+5.2%**

33,158: **+6.7%**

65+ years of age

All ages under 5

5-17 years of age

48,291: **+6.9%**

50,888: **+10.2%**

45-64 years of age

18-24 years of age

25,263: **-6.3%**

25-44 years of age

83,013: **+3.0%**

Median age of all United States: **34.0**
Total Population: **260,341,000, +4.7%**

Oldest, youngest states

States with highest median age of population		States with lowest median age of population	
State	**Age**	**State**	**Age**
Florida	37.1	Utah	26.7
West Virginia	37.0	Alaska	30.9
Pennsylvania	36.3	California	32.2
Maine	35.7	Louisiana	32.4
Connecticut	35.6	New Mexico	32.4

Population growth

by region

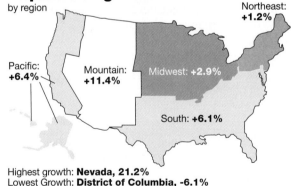

Northeast: **+1.2%**

Pacific: **+6.4%**

Mountain: **+11.4%**

Midwest: **+2.9%**

South: **+6.1%**

Highest growth: **Nevada, 21.2%**
Lowest Growth: **District of Columbia, -6.1%**

*Figures include members of armed forces residing in each state
NOTE: Number may not add up to 100 percent because of rounding

Source: "A Shifting Profile," *San Francisco Examiner* (March 1, 1995) A13. Copyright © 1995 by the *San Francisco Examiner.* Reprinted by permission of the publisher.

a. Which age group has experienced the largest percentage of growth?

_____

_____

b. Which age group has had the smallest percentage of growth?

_____

_____

c. Which state has the population with the highest median age?

_____

d. What is the lowest median age of population reported?

_____

_____

e. What region of the United States has the second-highest growth rate?

_____

_____

f. What region of the United States has the next-to-lowest growth rate?

_____

_____

g. What inferences or conclusions can you reach about U.S. population changes between 1990 and 1994?

_____

_____

ACTIVITY 10.5

Note how a combination of text and several graphic sources about tornadoes can help you understand the major ideas of a section of a physical geography textbook that deals with the weather.

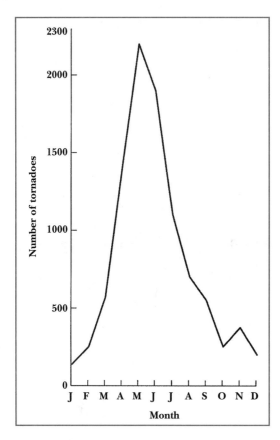

Seasonality of Tornadoes in the United States, 1953–67
Late spring and early summer comprise the prime time.

Source: Tom L. McKnight, "Transient Atmospheric Flows and Disturbances," *Essentials of Physical Geography,* 150–151. Copyright © 1992 by Prentice Hall, Inc. Reprinted by permission of the publisher.

Large parcels of air in the troposphere that have relatively uniform horizontal physical characteristics are referred to as air masses. When air masses move away from their source regions, they cause significant weather changes as they go. When unlike air masses meet, a front is established between them, which is usually a zone of unsettled, sometimes stormy, weather.

Air masses and fronts are prominent components of major migratory pressure systems called extratropical cyclones and anticyclones that dominate midlatitude circulation, particularly in winter. The former are battlegrounds of tropical and polar air with dynamically and dramatically changing weather conditions, whereas the latter represent stable, nonstormy interludes. Other notable storms include tropical cyclones (hurricanes), easterly waves, thunderstorms, and tornadoes.

1. What might be called the typical tornado season?

_____

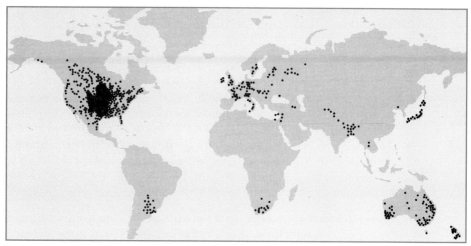

Anticipated distribution of tornadoes over the world in any given half-decade.

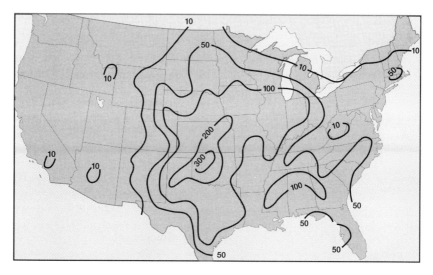

Distribution of tornadoes in the conterminous United States. Isolines refer to average number of observed tornadoes on an annual basis.

2. What country will be subject to the greatest number of tornadoes?

_____

3. What particular areas of that country will have the greatest number of tornadoes?

_____

ᗛ Evaluating Visual Information Critically: Statistics

As you have learned, the purpose of most graphic formats is to condense information into a visually appealing, easy-to-read design. However, as a critical reader you must be cautious, especially with tables, charts, or graphics that summarize numerical data, not to reach any final conclusions until you consider what the figures do and do not "say." Statistics can be misleading, and the evidence given is often not conclusive. Many times, statistics are not reported in their complete context, particularly by the news media. If excerpts are used, a critical reader always considers what may have been excluded. Ask questions like the following to evaluate the merits of statistics.

1. *How many* people or items were surveyed or analyzed? If the sample is too small—or, as is sometimes the case, too large—you may not get an accurate picture.
2. Have *all* significant characteristics been included?
3. Were the questions asked by the researcher objective or biased? Statistics can be slanted on the basis of the type of questions asked or the figures presented.
4. Who compiled the data? How reliable is the source and how up-to-date is the information?

Examine the following first two paragraphs of a newspaper article entitled "Hate-Crime Reports Increase" and the chart and table that accompanied it.

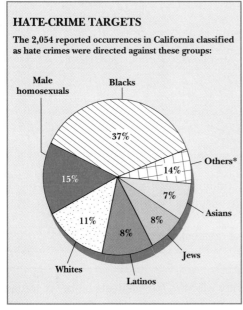

HATE-CRIME TARGETS

The 2,054 reported occurrences in California classified as hate crimes were directed against these groups:

Male homosexuals

Blacks 37%

Others* 14%

Asians 7%

Jews 8%

Latinos 8%

Whites 11%

15%

Source: California Department of Justice.

A survey released Wednesday by California's attorney general suggests that hate crimes climbed 15 percent from 1995 to 1996, the first full years for which they were tracked.

The news stories that such surveys often prompt—"Big jump in hate crime reports," "Hate crimes against Asians rising"—depict a nation increasingly embroiled in racial conflict.

*Other targets

Lesbians	2.2%
Protestants	1.6%
Muslims	0.4%
Homosexuals of either sex	0.3%
Catholics	0.2%
Bisexuals	0.1%
Physically, mentally disabled	0.1%
Heterosexuals	< 0.1%
Multiracial groups	3.4%
Other race or ethnic groups	4.6%
Other or multiple religions	0.7%

1. Based on what you have just read, do you think hate crimes are increasing?

    _____

2. Which is the largest targeted group? _____

3. Has any group been excluded in the chart? _____ In the table? _____

4. What percentage of hate crimes has been reported for the ethnic group of

    which you are a member? _____ For your religious affiliation? _____

Now, read the next three paragraphs of the article.

> But these often-alarmist surveys leave out an important fact. These statistics show an increase in the number of hate crimes *reported,* which could mean a real increase or simply reflect the fact that more people are aware of them.
>
> The actual number of hate crimes in 1995 and 1996 may be as much as five times higher, experts say. But that doesn't mean that racial conflict is growing. Rather, the imprecise statistics highlight the extent to which today's hate-crime tallies are plagued by victims' fears of reporting such crimes over the years, the inadequate training of the officers charged with classifying crimes as "bias-motivated" and the state law itself.
>
> "There is no agency, no group in any city or county or state in this country, that you can go to get an accurate picture," said Fred Persily, executive director of the California Association of Human Relations Organizations.
>
> Ariana E. Cha, "Hate-Crime Reports Increase," *San Jose Mercury News* 18 Jan. 1998: B3

1. How misleading is the headline? Explain your answer on the basis of what you

    read in the last three paragraphs? _____

    _____

2. Based on the statement made by Fred Persily in the last paragraph, what conclusion can you reach about hate crimes?

    _____

3. Why were the chart and table included with the article?

    _____

4. How reliable is the graphic information? Has anything been excluded in the table and/or in the chart? Look at them again now. You might ask questions like these as you evaluate their accuracy and reliability: Is the information that is presented representative of all of the United States or of only one part of the

country? What year was used to compile the statistical data? Who compiled the statistics?

_____

_____

◌ Summary

Graphics have several standard forms; especially common are graphs, charts, diagrams, and tables. They are common because considerable information can be condensed in a small space. Graphics are an important part of articles and textbook chapters, so a reader must integrate them with the text for better comprehension and understanding. Reading graphics demands careful attention and analysis. For college students, graphics are very important in reading in the sciences and in math-related areas such as business and economics.

The major purpose of reading graphics is to note trends and patterns and, after doing so, to draw inferences and conclusions about relationships and issues.

Graphics enhance and dramatize the text, indicate trends and patterns, and, essential for students, clarify the text and aid in the recall of particularly pertinent information. But one must be cautious—especially when analyzing visual information—to evaluate for reliability. Since statistical data can be manipulated, the critical reader must always read with a questioning mind.

Selection 22: **TEXTBOOK**

 # Preparation for Reading

Many people today are interested in the state of our economy and in those factors that contribute to the growth of that economy. Many people are unaware of the major role played by small businesses in the economy of the United States. Read to find out about their importance and about the difficulty in maintaining the profitably of a small business. Perhaps you have thought of starting such a small venture of your own someday.

Note while you are reading how the graphics help to summarize major points. The boldfaced words are underlined in the selection.

innovation, and importance	a new method or device
the **spectrum** of business	a continuous range or entire extent
big business **expatriates**	persons who leave, as from a country or homeland

Preview, then read the selection.

Understanding Entrepreneurship and the Small Business

Ronald J. Ebert and Ricky W. Griffin

What Is a Small Business?

The term *small business* defies easy definition. Clearly, locally owned and operated groceries, video stores, and restaurants are small businesses, while giant corporations like Sony, Caterpillar, and Eastman Kodak are big businesses. Between these two extremes fall thousands of companies that cannot be easily categorized. . . . 1

small business
Independently owned and managed business that does not dominate its market

Because it is difficult to define a small business in numerical terms, we will define a **small business** as one that is independently owned and managed and that does not dominate its market. A small business cannot be part of another business. Operators must be their own bosses, free to run their businesses as they please. In addition, the small business must have relatively little influence in its market. For example, from a single store in 1985, Blockbuster Entertainment now operates over 4,000 video stores and 500 music stores in 16 countries. Although a very small business only a little more than a decade ago, Blockbuster is now the dominant company in the home video-rental market. 2

The Importance of Small Business in the U.S. Economy

As Figure 10.20 shows, most U.S. businesses employ fewer than 100 people, and most U.S. workers are employed by small firms. For example, Figure 10.20(a) shows that approximately 87 percent of all U.S. businesses employ 20 or fewer people; 3

another 11 percent employ between 20 and 99 people. Figure 10.20(b) shows that 27 percent of all U.S. workers are employed by firms with fewer than 20 people; another 29 percent work in firms that employ between 20 and 99 people. The vast majority of these companies are owner-operated.

On the basis of numbers alone, then, small business is a strong presence in the economy. This is true in virtually all the world's mature economies. In Germany, for example, companies with fewer than 500 employees produce two-thirds of the nation's gross national product, train nine out of ten apprentices, and employ four out of every five workers. Small businesses also play major roles in the economies of Italy, France, and Brazil. In a recent five-year period, while large and mid-size European businesses lost 700,000 jobs, small businesses posted a gain of 2 million. In addition, experts agree that small businesses will be important in the emerging economies of countries like Russia and Vietnam.

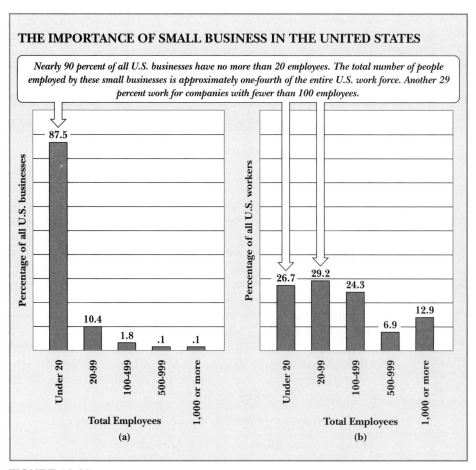

THE IMPORTANCE OF SMALL BUSINESS IN THE UNITED STATES

Nearly 90 percent of all U.S. businesses have no more than 20 employees. The total number of people employed by these small businesses is approximately one-fourth of the entire U.S. work force. Another 29 percent work for companies with fewer than 100 employees.

FIGURE 10.20

The contribution of small business can be measured in terms of its effects on key 5
aspects of an economic system: In the United States, these aspects include *job cre-*
ation, innovation, and *importance to big business*. . . .

Adjusting the Myth: The Big Business Job Machine   While small businesses create many 6
new jobs each year, the importance of big businesses in job creation should not be
overlooked. The large-scale layoffs and cutbacks of the late 1980s and early 1990s
have contributed to an impression that jobs in all big businesses were on the decline.
In reality many large businesses have been creating thousands of new jobs every year.
Figure 10.21, for example, details the increase in jobs at eight large U.S. companies
between 1992 and 1994. As you can see, Wal-Mart alone created 182,000 new jobs
during that period. Moreover, the other firms on the list span the <u>spectrum</u> of business areas from manufacturing to service.

At least one message is clear: business success, more than business size, accounts 7
for most new job creation. In 1993, for example, while struggling retail chains like
Sears and Woolworth eliminated 80,000 jobs, Wal-Mart more than made up the difference by adding 85,000. . . .

"Size isn't the issue," reports M.I.T. economist Frank Levy. "The issue is which 8
firms are adding jobs." Jobs are created by companies of all sizes, all of which hire
workers and all of which lay them off. Admittedly, recent studies by Levy and others
show that, *relative to their total employment,* small firms hire at twice the rate as large
ones. But they also eliminate jobs at a far higher rate. Small firms are the first to hire
in times of economic recovery, large firms the last. Big companies, however, are also
the last to lay off workers during economic downswings.

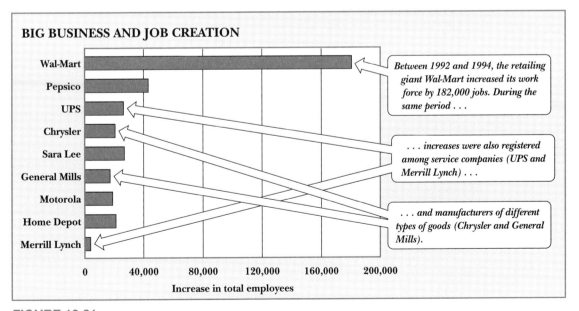

FIGURE 10.21

Innovation   History has shown that major innovations are as likely to come from   **9**
small businesses (or individuals) as from big businesses. For example, small firms
and individuals invented the personal computer and the stainless-steel razor blade,
the transistor radio and the photocopying machine, the jet engine and the self-
developing photograph. They also gave us the helicopter and power steering, automatic transmissions and air conditioning, cellophane, and the $.19 ballpoint pen.

Not surprisingly, history is repeating itself much more rapidly in the age of com-   **10**
puters and high-tech communications. Since it was founded in 1983, for example, a
small firm called Maxim Integrated Products has introduced more than 600 semi-
conductor chips for use in computers, telecommunications, and high-tech instruments. . . .

Popular Forms of Small Business Enterprise

Small businesses are more common in some industries than in others. The four   **11**
major small business industry groups are *services, retailing, wholesaling,* and *manufacturing.* Each group differs in its requirements for employees, money, materials, and
machines. Remember: the more resources an industry requires, the harder it is to
start a business and the less likely the industry is to be dominated by small firms.
Remember, too, that "small" is a relative term. The criteria—number of employees
and total annual sales—differ from industry to industry and are often meaningful
only when compared with businesses that are truly "large."

Finally, remember that, as a general rule, manufacturing businesses are the   **12**
hardest to start and service businesses the easiest. To make sewing machines, for
example, a manufacturer must invest not only in people but also in raw materials
and machines. It must also develop a distribution network and advertise heavily. To
prepare tax forms, however, an entrepreneur need invest only in an education and
a few office supplies and reference books. The business can be run out of a store-
front or a home.

Services   Partly because they require relatively few resources, service businesses   **13**
are the largest—and fastest-growing—segment of small business enterprise. No
other industry group offers a higher return on time invested. Services tend to appeal
to the talent for innovation typified by many small enterprises.

Small business services range from shoeshine parlors to car rental agencies,   **14**
from marriage counseling to computer software, from accounting and management
consulting to professional dog walking. In Cambridge, Massachusetts, Marcia J.
Radosevich started HPR Inc., a health care consultancy firm that assists health maintenance organizations (HMOs) spot medical claims that do not comply with company standards. . . . Business Opportunities Online is an electronic database that
provides listings for basic transactions—buying, selling, and even the criteria used
by about 500 potential investors. It also collects information on about 500 franchis-
ers and 350 professional consultants.

Retailing   A *retail business* sells products manufactured by other firms directly to   **15**
consumers. There are hundreds of different kinds of retailers, ranging from

wig shops and frozen yogurt stands to automobile dealerships and department stores. Usually, however, small businesspeople favor specialty shops—say, big men's clothing or gourmet coffee stores—that let them focus limited resources on narrow market segments. . . .

Wholesaling   As with services and retailing, small businesspeople dominate 16 wholesaling. A *wholesale business* buys products from manufacturers or other producers and then sells them to retailers. Wholesalers usually buy goods in bulk and store them in quantities and places convenient for retailers. For a given volume of business, therefore, they need fewer employees than do manufacturers, retailers, or service providers.

The Distinction between Entrepreneurship and Small Business

entrepreneur
Businessperson who accepts both the risks and the opportunities involved in creating and operating a new business venture

Many small businesspersons like to think of themselves as **entrepreneurs**—individuals who assume the risk of business ownership with the primary goal of growth and expansion. In reality, however, a person may be a small businessperson only, an entrepreneur only, or both. Consider an individual who starts a small pizza parlor with no plans other than to earn enough money from the restaurant to lead a comfortable life style. That individual is clearly a small businessperson. With no plans to grow and expand, however, he is not really an entrepreneur. In contrast, an entrepreneur may start with one pizza parlor and turn it into a national chain to rival Domino's or Little Caesar's. Although this individual may have started with a small business, the growth of the firm resulted from entrepreneurial vision and activity.

Failure and Success in Small Business

For every Henry Ford, Walt Disney, or Bill Gates—people who transformed small 18 businesses into major corporations—there are many small businesspeople and entrepreneurs who fail. Figure 10.22 illustrates recent trends in new business start-ups and failures. As you can see, new business start-ups have exceeded 800,000 a year since 1994. But although failures have declined recently, almost 100,000 firms fail each year. In this section, . . . we examine some of the main reasons for both failure and success in small business undertakings.

Trends in Small Business Start-Ups

Thousands of new businesses are started in the United States every year. Several fac- 19 tors account for this trend. . . .

Crossovers from Big Business   More and more, small businesses are being started 20 by people who have opted to leave large corporations and put their experience and know-how to work for themselves.

For example, Ely Callaway left Burlington Industries Inc. after seventeen years 21 to found Callaway Golf Co. Callaway developed the Big Bertha Metal Wood driver and a set of equally innovative irons that now enjoy the highest dollar sales of any golf clubs in the United States. Callaway credits his years at Burlington for making

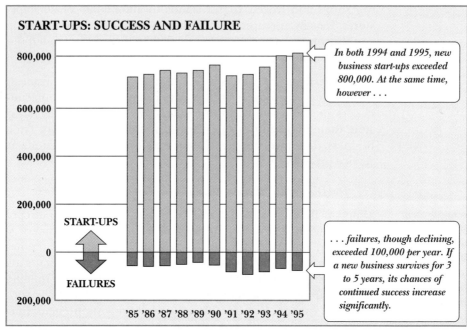

FIGURE 10.22

him the manager he is today. "I'd rather learn how to ride a bike on somebody else's bicycle," he says, "than on my own."

Opportunities for Minorities and Women In addition to big business expatriates, **22** more small businesses are being started by minorities and women. Black-owned businesses, for example, are increasing two and one-half times as fast as all other types of start-ups. T. J. Walker and Carl Jones operate Threads 4 Life, a California-based fashion firm that makes and markets hip, inner-city designs—colorful T-shirts and outsized pants—for young black consumers.

As you can see in Figure 10.23, the number of women entrepreneurs is also **23** growing rapidly. Almost a third of all U.S. firms with fewer than 500 employees— some 6.5 million enterprises—are owned or controlled by women. These companies currently employ 11 million people—more than the total employed by the entire Fortune 500 list. By the year 2000, 40 percent of all U.S. businesses will be owned by women.

The chart in Figure 10.23 also shows rates of increase between 1980 and 1990. **24** Although the greatest gain was in services, the increase in the number of women-owned companies cuts across the business spectrum. In 1978, for example, Brenda French founded a small scarf-making business in a spare bedroom. In 1989, French

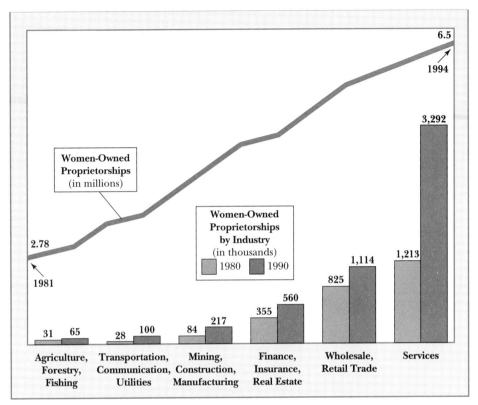

FIGURE 10.23   Women-Owned Businesses in the United States

learned about a new machine that can duplicate hand-knit quality with mass-production speed. . . .

Global Opportunities   Many entrepreneurs today are also finding new opportu- 25
nities in foreign markets. For example, Michael Giles left a well-paying job at IBM to
start a new venture in South Africa. Giles saw that the country's black townships had
few laundromats. One area, for example, had only four laundromats for 4.5 million
people. Using a loan from the U.S. Overseas Private Investment Corp., Giles
launched a chain of 108 coin-operated laundromats throughout the region's black
townships.

Reasons for Failure

Unfortunately, 60 percent of all new businesses do not survive more than five years. 26
Why do some succeed and others fail? Although there is no set pattern, there are some
common causes of both failure and success, as can be summarized in Figure 10.24.

SUCCESS	FAILURE
Hard work, drive, and dedication	Managerial incompetence/ Inexperience
Market demand for products/services	Neglect
Managerial competence	Weak control systems
Luck	Insufficient capital

FIGURE 10.24
A variety of factors contribute to small business success and failure.

Four general factors contribute to small business failure: **27**

1. *Managerial incompetence or inexperience.* If managers do not know how to make basic business decisions, they are unlikely to be successful in the long run.
2. *Neglect.* Starting a small business requires an overwhelming time commitment.
3. *Weak control systems.* If control systems do not signal impending problems, managers may be in serious trouble before more visible difficulties alert them.
4. *Insufficient capital.* Here is a rule of thumb: a new business should have enough capital to operate at least six months without earning a profit.

Reasons for Success

Four basic factors are typically cited to explain small business success: **28**

1. *Hard work, drive, and dedication.* Small business owners must be committed to succeeding and be willing to put in the time and effort to do so.
2. *Market demand for the products or services being provided.* Careful analysis of market conditions can help small businesspeople assess the probable reception of their products in the marketplace.
3. *Managerial competence.* Successful small businesspeople may acquire competence through training, experience, or by using the expertise of others.
4. *Luck.* Luck also plays a role in the success of some firms. For example, after Alan McKim started Clean Harbors, an environmental cleanup firm based in New England, he struggled to keep his business afloat. Then the U.S. government committed $1.6 billion to toxic waste clean-up, McKim's specialty. As a result, he was able to get several large government contracts and put his business on solid financial footing. Had the government fund not been created at just the right time, McKim's business may well have failed.

approximately 2000 words*

Ronald J. Ebert and Ricky W. Griffin, "Understanding Entrepreneurship and the Small Business," *Business Essentials,* 2nd ed. (Prentice Hall, 1998) 178–189.

* The approximate word count does not include words in illustrations or tables.

1. How important is small-business employment to the U.S. economy? In your answer, integrate the graphic information presented.

   _____

   _____

2. Name two business corporations, other than Wal-Mart, that created large numbers of new jobs between 1992 and 1994. Use the graphics to help you answer the question.

   a. _____

   b. _____

3. In speaking about business organizations, the authors say that "'small' is a relative term." Explain what this statement means.

   _____

4. What is the difference between a *wholesaler* and a *retailer?*

   _____

5. Use the text and graphics to answer the following questions.

   a. Did the number of successful start-up small businesses increase or

      decrease between 1994 and 1995? _____

   b. Are failures of start-up small businesses increasing or decreasing?

      _____

   c. How many years are used to estimate whether a new small business will be successful?

      _____

6. Name two areas, other than services, in which women-owned businesses increased significantly between 1980 and 1990.

   a. _____

   b. _____

7. a. If you were to start a small business, which area or field would you choose? Explain the reason for your choice. If you would not consider starting a small business, explain why.

_____

_____

_____

b. If you were to start a small business, which "success factor" would you be most certain of? Which "failure factor" would you be especially careful of, knowing yourself and your business potential?

_____

_____

_____

Selection 23: **TEXTBOOK**

 Preparation for Reading

This selection deals with the body's response to injury and inflammation. As you read the text, note how the diagram (Figure 10.25) and chart (Table 10.2 on page 637) that follow make the process much clearer. You would have to have some familiarity with some of the specialized terms before you could begin to understand this chapter excerpt. Remember that in both math and science, information builds upon what has preceded it, so a careful, deliberate, disciplined reading-study method becomes essential.

You might have to refer to a glossary frequently while reading a science textbook. Glossary terms, written in academic language, must often be "translated" by you into everyday English, as illustrated by the italics in the definitions below.

The following boldfaced terms, which are underlined in the selection, were introduced in previous chapters of the source textbook.

homeostasis	a constant internal environment (*you're healthy*)
bacterium	a single-celled microorganism, which may be pathogenic (*these guys can cause disease*)
mast cells	connective tissue cells that initiate the inflammatory response (*this starts getting rid of the problem*)
histamine and **heparin**	two chemicals released by mast cells to initiate the inflammatory response (*these two are needed to start the process*)
macrophages	cells that engulf foreign or pathogenic materials for removal (*this is the "heavy hitter" in the process*)
phagocytizing	destroying by phagocytic cells (*this is the work*)
lymphocytes	cells of the lymphatic system that participate in the inflammatory response (*these cells also help initially*)

Preview, noting the graphics, and then read the selection.

Homeostasis at the Tissue Level

Frederic Martini

The Inflammatory Response

Life is an adventure, and injuries often occur. 1 The restoration of <u>homeostasis</u>, following an injury involves two related processes. First the area is isolated, while damaged cells, tissue components, and dangerous microorganisms are cleaned up. Second, the damaged tissues are replaced or repaired. These two phases overlap. Isolation establishes a framework that guides the cells responsible for reconstruction,

and repairs begin well before cleanup operations have ended. Unless unusual conditions exist, the repair leaves the tissue almost "good as new." In general, epithelia and connective tissues show the greatest abilities to restore homeostasis after injury.

Whenever tissue damage occurs, it triggers **2** an inflammatory response. Inflammation produces symptoms of swelling, redness, heat, tenderness, and reduced function. The stimulus provoking this response might be a mechanical stress, such as abrasion, chemical irritation, or a temperature extreme (hot or cold). An infection is an inflammation resulting from the presence of some biological invader, such as a bacterium.

The inflammatory response, diagrammed **3** in Figure 10.25 depends on the activities of mast cells in connective tissues. When stimulated by alterations in their environment, these cells release chemicals (histamine and heparin) that affect blood vessels in the immediate area. The vessels enlarge, or dilate, and as blood flow increases, the region becomes reddish in color and warm to the touch. The increased blood supply brings nutrients, oxygen, and cellular defenders into the area, and removes dissolved waste products and toxic chemicals.

These chemicals also make the capillary **4** walls more permeable, and fluid containing dissolved materials enters the injured tissue. The area then becomes swollen, and combined pressure and chemicals released by injured cells stimulate nerve endings that produce the sensation of pain. Some of the proteins introduced from the blood are dissolved molecules of fibrinogen (fī-BRIN-ō-jen; *gennan*, to produce). These proteins can interact to form large, insoluble fibers of fibrin. Fibrin formation at the injury site is slowed by the heparin released by mast cells, but around the edges of the affected area fibrin appears in a meshwork, or clot. Clot formation walls off the inflamed region, slowing the spread of cellular debris or bacteria into surrounding tissues.

FIGURE 10.25   The Inflammatory Response

This diagram summarizes key features in the inflammatory response. The regulatory mechanism provides another example of homeostatic control through negative feedback.

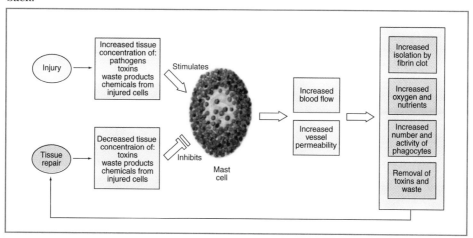

TABLE 10.2
A Summary of the Inflammatory Response

	Event	Primary Effect	Secondary Effect	Functional Significance
Step 1	Injury disrupts homeostasis.	Tissue damage with or without microorganisms.	Chemical change in interstitial fluids.	Triggers inflammatory response.
Step 2	Chemical change in interstitial fluids.	Mast cells release histamine and heparin.	Dilation of vessels, increase in blood flow and vessel permeability.	Area becomes red, swollen, and warm.
Step 3	Increased blood flow and vessel permeability.	Increased oxygen, nutrients; fewer toxins, wastes.	Slower spread of inflammation; abnormal chemicals appear in the bloodstream.	Increases metabolic activity of phagocytic and repair cells.
Step 4a	Increased permeability of vessels.	Leakage of fibrinogen from plasma.	Clot formation.	Encloses area, slows the spread of inflammation or infection.
Step 4b	Abnormal chemicals appear in bloodstream.	Stimulates plasma cells.	Production of antibodies.	Helps destroy or inactivate invading microorganisms or foreign toxins.
		Free macrophages and microphages attracted to area.	Migration of cells into inflammation site.	Removes cell debris, toxins, and microorganisms.
Step 5	Reduction in tissue concentrations of debris, toxins, microorganisms.	Histamine and heparin release by mast cells stops.	Reduction of inflammation.	Return to homeostasis.

Meanwhile, fixed <u>macrophages</u> and free 5 macrophages are <u>phagocytizing</u> the debris and bacteria. Chemicals released by mast cells, active macrophages, and injured cells attract other cellular defenders, and white blood cells squeeze through the capillary walls to join the attack. Some of the <u>lymphocytes</u> within the tissue differentiate into plasma cells that begin producing antibodies. Macrophages and microphages arriving from the blood increase the number of phagocytic cells in the region; the microphages known as neutrophils (NŪ-trō-filz) are most abundant. Actively phagocytic cells are short-lived, most surviving for just a few hours before dying and disintegrating. Pus is the mixture of living and dead cells and tissue debris that develops within an area of inflammation. The inflammatory response has been summarized in Table 10.2.

Tissues heal fastest in young and healthy 6 individuals whose diet contains adequate amino acids, energy sources, and vitamins C, D, E, and K. Repairs are always slowed by poor health, infection, or an inadequate diet. Age is also a factor, for healing takes more time in elderly patients, even healthy ones.

approximately 600 words*

1. Identify the two tissues that usually heal the quickest.

   _____

2. An infection is a particular type of inflammation. What characterizes it?

   _____

3. Complete the outline of the inflammatory response after injury occurs.

   I. Mast cells in the connective tissue release the chemicals _____

      and _____.

   II. These chemicals affect blood vessels in the immediate area.

      A. Blood flow increases and brings in _____.

      B. Blood flow then removes _____.

   III. Chemicals also make the walls of the blood vessel more _____, and fluids can enter the injured tissue.

      A. Within the fluids are molecules of _____.

* The approximate word count does not include words in illustrations or tables.

B. These help in _____
   formation and keep surrounding tissue clear.

IV. Joining the attack on the injured area are _____
     that phagocytize the debris and bacteria.

V.   Production of antibodies is then caused by _____.

VI. Removal of toxins and waste lead to a return to _____.

Selection 24: **TEXTBOOK**

 Preparation for Reading

The first paragraph of the selection describes us as denizens of the atmosphere living at the bottom of the ocean of air much like the fish living at the bottom of the sea. Our atmosphere both nourishes and sustains us, and especially today, it is important for us to understand it.

As you read, integrate the graphic information with the text so you will be better prepared to answer the final question at the conclusion of this text. The boldfaced words are underlined in the selection.

hospitable **milieu** for life — environment, especially a social setting

denizen of the atmosphere — inhabitant of a particular place

inert gaseous element — inactive

inordinately significant — excessive

in **minuscule** quantities — tiny

Preview, then read the selection.

Constituents of the Atmosphere

Tom K. McKnight

The atmosphere interacts significantly with other components of the earthly environment, and it is instrumental in providing a hospitable milieu for life. Whereas we often speak of human beings as creatures of the Earth, it is perhaps more accurate to consider them as creatures of the atmosphere. As surely as a crab crawling on the sea bottom is a resident of the ocean, so a person living at the bottom of the ocean of air is a denizen of the atmosphere.

Constituents of the Atmosphere

The atmosphere is composed of a mixture of discrete gases and an immense number of tiny suspended particles in solid or liquid form. The chemical composition of pure, dry air at lower elevations is simple, uniform, and basically unvarying through time. Certain minor gases and nongaseous particles, however, vary markedly from place to place and from time to time, as does the amount of moisture in the air.

The Gases

Most of the volume of the atmosphere is provided by two chemical elements: *nitrogen* and *oxygen.* Nitrogen comprises more than 78 percent of the total, and oxygen makes up nearly 21 percent. See Table 10.3 and Figure 10.26. Nitrogen is added to the air by the decay and burning of organic matter, by volcanic eruptions, and by the chemical breakdown of certain rocks. It is utilized in the atmosphere by certain biological processes and by being washed away in rain or snow. Overall, the addition and removal of nitrogen gas are balanced, and the quantity remains constant. Oxygen is

TABLE 10.3
Principal Gases of Earth's Atmosphere

Component	Percent of Volume of Dry Air	Concentration in Parts per Million of Air
Uniform gases:		
Nitrogen (N_2)	78.084	
Oxygen (O_2)	20.948	
Argon (A)	0.934	
Neon (Ne)	0.00182	18.2
Helium (He)	0.00052	5.2
Methane (CH_4)	0.00015	1.5
Krypton (Kr)	0.00011	1.1
Hydrogen (H_2)	0.00005	0.5
Important variable gases:		
Water vapor (H_2O)	0–4	
Carbon dioxide (CO_2)	0.0353	353
Carbon monoxide (CO)		< 100
Ozone (O_3)		< 2
Sulfur dioxide (SO_2)		< 1
Nitrogen dioxide (NO_2)		< 0.2

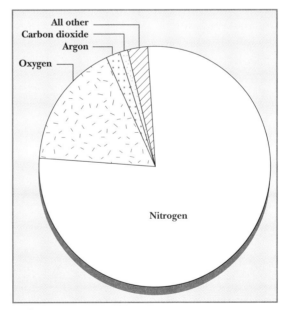

FIGURE 10.26
Proportional volume of the gaseous components
of the atmosphere. Nitrogen and oxygen are the
dominant elements.

produced by vegetation and is removed by a variety of organic and inorganic processes; its total quantity also apparently remains stable. The remaining 1 percent of the atmosphere's volume consists mostly of the <u>inert</u> gaseous element *argon*. These three principal atmospheric elements—nitrogen, oxygen, argon—are of minimal importance in their effect on weather and climate and therefore need no further consideration here.

Several other gases occur in sparse, 4 although highly variable, quantities in the atmosphere, but their influence on weather and climate is prominent. See Figure 10.27. *Water vapor* is the gaseous phase of moisture in the air and represents the humidity of the atmosphere. It is largely absent from the upper atmosphere, but near the surface it is often present in notable proportions. It is most common in those portions of the atmosphere overlying warm, moist surface areas, such as tropical oceans, where it may amount to as much as 4 percent of total volume. Over deserts and in polar regions, the amount of water vapor is but

a tiny fraction of 1 percent. For the atmosphere as a whole, the total component of water vapor remains virtually constant. Water vapor is <u>inordinately</u> significant to weather and climate in that it is the source of all clouds and precipitation and is intimately involved in energy transfer (the storage, movement, and release of heat).

Carbon dioxide is important to life processes 5 because of its role in photosynthesis but it also has a significant influence on climate. This is primarily due to its potent ability to absorb infrared radiant energy, which maintains the warmth of the lower atmosphere. It is distributed fairly uniformly in the lower layers, but its accumulation has been increasing for the last century or so, and the rate of accumulation has been accelerating, presumably because of the increased burning of fossil fuels. The long-range effect of increasing amounts of carbon dioxide in the atmosphere is debatable, but many scientists believe that it will warm up the lower atmosphere sufficiently to produce major, and still unpredictable, global climatic

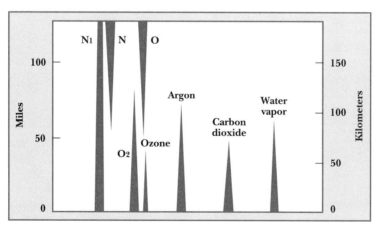

FIGURE 10.27
Vertical distribution of the major gaseous components in the atmosphere. The width of each column shows the relative distribution of that component by altitude. The columns are *not* comparable with one another volumetrically, only proportionally.

changes. The proportion of carbon dioxide in the atmosphere has been increasing at a rate of about 0.0007 percent (7 parts per million) per year, and at present is about 400 parts per million.

Another minor but vital gas in the atmos- **6** phere is ozone. For the most part, ozone is concentrated a few miles above the Earth, particularly between 9 and 30 miles (15 and 48 km) above the Earth. Ozone is an excellent absorber of ultraviolet solar radiation: it filters out enough of these burning rays to protect earthly life from potentially deadly effects.

Several other minor gases exist in the **7** atmosphere in <u>minuscule</u> quantities. Some of them—particularly carbon monoxide, sulfur dioxide, nitrogen oxides, and various hydrocarbons—are increasingly introduced into the atmosphere by emission from machines such as furnaces, factories, and automobiles. All these gaseous pollutants are hazardous to life and at least potentially influential on climate.

approximately 700 words*

Tom L. McKnight, "Introduction to the Atmosphere," *Essentials of Physical Geography* 34–35. © 1992 by Prentice Hall, Inc.

1. What gases are of minimal importance to weather and climate?

   _____

2. Why is water vapor very significant in weather patterns?

   _____

3. CO_2 in the atmosphere can produce problems. Why?

   _____

4. What is the major role of the ozone layer?

   _____

5. What dangers do we encounter from other minor gases in the atmosphere?

   _____

More and more, textbooks such as the physical geography text from which the excerpt above—as well as the selection that follows on page 644—was taken are integrating essays along with graphics to make textbook reading relevant to today's concerns. As we have read and understood the complexity of our atmosphere with its finite gaseous components, we can appreciate the danger at present to our planet from the depletion of the ozone layer.

* The approximate word count does not include words in illustrations or tables.

☞ Reading About Our Changing World

Read this final essay to answer one last very important question in your journal.

People and the Environment: Depletion of the Ozone Layer

Tom L. McKnight

Only within the last two decades has the significance of the ozone layer been understood. Ozone is a form of the oxygen molecule that has three atoms (O_3) rather than the more common two (O_2). It is created in the upper atmosphere by the action of solar radiation on oxygen molecules; sunlight splits apart O_2 molecules, some of which recombine as O_3 molecules.

The concentration of ozone molecules in a definite layer serves as a shield for the Earth, absorbing most of the potentially dangerous ultraviolet radiation found in sunlight. Ultraviolet radiation is biologically destructive in many ways. It causes skin cancer and cataracts, it suppresses the human immune system, it diminishes the yield of many crops, it disrupts the aquatic food chain by killing microorganisms on the ocean surface, and doubtless causes other negative effects still undiscovered.

But the ozone layer is a fragile shield. It is paper-thin at best and has been thinning even more in recent years, apparently because of the release of certain human-produced synthetic chemicals into the air. These chemicals, classed as chlorofluorocarbons, or CFCs, are widely used in refrigeration and air conditioning (Freon), in foam and plastic manufacturing, and in aerosol sprays. They were thought to be exceedingly benign, for they are odorless, nonflammable, noncorrosive, and nontoxic.

Although extremely stable and inert in the lower atmosphere, at high levels CFCs are broken down by ultraviolet radiation, releasing chlorine and bromine. Under certain circumstances a chemical reaction occurs that destroys large quantities of ozone. As many as 100,000 ozone molecules can be removed from the atmosphere for every chlorine molecule released. [See Figure 10.28.]

Not only is the ozone layer thinning, in some places it has disappeared entirely, on a temporary basis. A "hole" in the ozone layer has developed over Antarctica every year since 1979, and the duration of the missing layer has increased every year. [See Figure 10.29.] In 1988 a second ozone hole was found over the Arctic for the first time.

In response to these alarming discoveries, several countries (including the United States) banned the use of CFCs in aerosol sprays in 1978. A major international treaty was promulgated in 1987 that would diminish the production of all ozone-depleting chemicals by 50 percent by 1999. The Du Pont Company, the world's largest producer of CFCs (25 percent of total world output), voluntarily decided in 1988 to phase out all production of chlorofluorocarbons.

Thus serious steps are now under way to control a global pollutant, for the first time. One hopes that it is not too late.

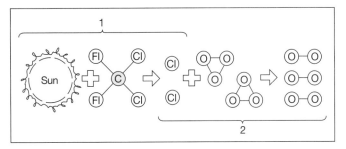

FIGURE 10.28   The Chemical Breakdown of Ozone

1. A typical CFC molecule has one carbon atom (C) bonded to two chlorine atoms (Cl) and two fluorine atoms (Fl). Sunlight breaks the bonds in CFCs, releasing chlorine atoms.
2. Chlorine atoms engage in a complex chemical reaction with ozone, resulting in the breakdown of ozone molecules into oxygen molecules. Chlorine atoms are unchanged by the reaction and can repeat the process. Thus a single chorine atom can destroy tens of thousands of ozone molecules.

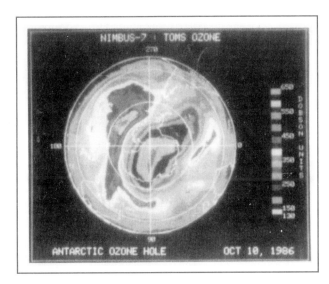

FIGURE 10.29

The Antarctic ozone hole as imaged from the Nimbus 7 satellite in 1986. The "hole" is the gray oval feature covering most of the Antarctic continent. (Courtesy of NASA).

approximately 500 words

Tom L. McKnight, "Introduction to the Atmosphere," *Essentials of Physical Geography* 37. Copyright © 1992 by Prentice Hall, Inc. Reprinted by permission of the publisher.

JOURNAL ENTRY

The last essay in this text explains the dangers to our environment from the depletion of the ozone layer. In this Information Age, does it appear that adequate technology exists to solve the problem? Are American citizens willing to change their behavior in order to reduce the risk of excessive radiation that results from the ozone layer's deterioration? What are our expectations from other countries in regard to this global environmental problem?

As a future citizen of this twenty-first century, how do you view your own responsibilities in this area? What are some positive steps you can take? As an effective reader, how do you plan to stay informed?

Appendix A

Vocabulary Words Defined as Bottom-Line Words

abridged, 32
abstract, 264
abysmal, 141
abyss, 361
accentuated, 593
accoutrements, 362
adversarial, 281
affirmation, 282
affluent, 263
ambivalence, 536
angst, 503
anomaly, 459
antagonistic, 138
antidote, 357
antithesis, 433
antitrust, 242
antonyms, 36
archetype, 515
aspirations, 200
assimilates, 319
assumption, 348

banderillero, 241
belittle, 488
bellicose, 512
benign, 204
besiege, 123
bicameral, 125
brazenly, 493
burgeoning, 32

cacophony, 383
calamitous, 39
cardiac, 116
cartel, 188
cataract, 451

categorized, 234
charisma, 254
Chaucerian, 533
clarify, 41
climax, 201
cohabitation, 521
cohesion, 491
colloquial, 524
components, 234
concisely, 183
concurrence, 244
condoning, 448
conflagrations, 398
conscientious, 35
consecrated, 115
consigned, 491
constituents, 370
contentious, 452
conundrum, 517
coup, 458
cravenly, 517
credo, 129
critical, 185

de facto, 132
deactivates, 538
debunk, 353
decapitated, 437
decimation, 267
deluded, 536
demeans, 267
demise, 125
demonstrable, 378
demystify, 353
denigrated, 138
deprivation, 260
deviant, 243

dialogue, 201
dichotomized, 535
digerati, 65
dilemma, 201
diminishes, 170
disapprobation, 529
discrepancy, 595
disdain, 245
disparage, 430
dissolute, 499
dissuading, 186
divisive, 128
draconian, 435
draughtsman, 451
dreck, 533
dynamic, 5

eccentric, 497
echelon, 365
ecological, 267
egomaniacal, 380
elitist, 115
emanate, 32
empathy, 249
empirical, 376
emulate, 279
entrepreneurial, 275
entrepreneurship, 448
erosion, 441
erudite, 32
espionage, 243
ethical, 366
ethos, 501
eugenics, 447
eulogies, 488
evoke, 426
execrable, 533

exhortations, 528
exorbitant, 370
exotically, 126

facilitate, 67
fodder, 503
foisted, 363
formidable, 451
frays, 491
futile, 371

genres, 168
genteel, 362
glossary, 59
gringos, 126
guffawed, 438
guile, 139

hallmarks, 139
hamper, 319
hedgehog, 255
heighten, 185
heirloom, 439
hierarchy, 195
homogeneous, 281
hypocritical, 552

iconoclastic, 389
icons, 117
ideology, 118
imbue, 254
implied, 127
inalienable, 204
incoherent, 437

Appendix B

Vocabulary Words Defined for End-of-Chapter Reading Selections

Credits